W9-BKR-185

BACH

BACH

❖ ❖ ❖

ESSAYS ON
HIS LIFE
AND
MUSIC

❖

Christoph Wolff

Harvard University Press
Cambridge, Massachusetts
London, England
1991

This book is printed on acid-free paper, and its binding materials
have been chosen for strength and durability.

Library of Congress Cataloging in Publication Data

Wolff, Christoph.
Bach: essays on his life and music / Christoph Wolff.
p.   cm.
Includes bibliographical references and indexes.
ISBN 0–674–05925–5
1. Bach, Johann Sebastian, 1685–1750. 2. Bach, Johann Sebastian.
1685–1750—Criticism and interpretation.   I. Title.
ML410.B1W79 1991   90–5247
780'.92—dc20   CIP
[B]   MN

To my colleagues and students,
past and present,
at the University of Toronto,
Columbia University, and
Harvard University

Contents

Preface

THIS VOLUME may well be understood as a book about a book the author doesn't feel quite ready to write. Writing knowledgeably and responsibly on virtually any aspect of Bach and his music is one of the more arduous and perplexing tasks in the business of musical scholarship. It actually proves even more difficult and challenging for someone who has devoted a good part of his professional activities to the music of Johann Sebastian Bach. So I readily admit my apprehension about undertaking a comprehensive life and works. On the other hand, since there hardly exists a more fascinating and rewarding subject in the history of art than the music of Bach, I became intensely involved in Bach scholarship and have made some headway. While the following pages certainly don't match a monographic account, they nevertheless offer a wide range of fundamental materials and interpretive thoughts toward such an endeavor. This book, then, reflects the humbling task of uncovering the manifold layers and dimensions one must consider if one wants to come close to understanding one of the most powerful artistic minds and creative geniuses of all times and all peoples. This seemingly exaggerated phrase ("of all times and all peoples") can actually be traced back to the later eighteenth century, as the penultimate chapter will show. Holding Bach in awe began early, at least in professional circles; even musicians as unsuspiciously self-confident as Haydn, Mozart, and Beethoven took this attitude.

In these collected essays I try to bring into focus the image of a uniquely gifted, ambitious, self-critical and self-challenging musician whose genius combined outstanding performance virtuosity with supreme creative prowess; whose compositions offer a most remarkable absorption and synthesis of traditional and contemporary technical and stylistic features, and demonstrate a perfect balance of forceful inventiveness and intellectual control—qualities that established new aesthetic standards for later generations. These many and diverse aspects—whether they relate to Bach the human being, to the composer's workshop, to the realizations of his musical ideas, or to his place in history—have always been of great interest to me and, therefore, thoroughly pervade these Bach studies. The chapters in this volume were selected from some five dozen Bach essays written over a twenty-five-year period, between 1963 and 1988, and addressing quite different audiences. The material covers a wide spectrum of topics and inquiries which, I hope, will spark the reader's awareness of the sweeping complexity, richness, and excitement of Bach scholarship and, in the last analysis, of Bach's music and creative genius itself.

The chapters have been organized to give the multifaceted character of the collection a clearer definition, yet the five section headings merely suggest the scope and emphasis within each group of essays. Neither issues of biography, context, and reception history on the one hand nor aspects of source studies, chronology, and style on the other can be reasonably confined to any single section. The discussion of new sources, for instance, is not limited to the second group of essays but figures rather prominently in Chapters 8, 16, 18, and 22 as well. Moreover, biographical details turn up fairly constantly throughout, as do discussions of sources—be they musical, literary, or archival—or considerations of compositional procedures, style, and aesthetic principles. To those familiar with my work, the virtual omnipresence of philology, analysis, criticism, and interpretation in however varying applications and configurations will not come as a surprise. It is indeed my hope that the reader will be able to detect and follow the "red thread" running through all chapters: traces of a deliberately integrated examination whose aims are to uncover historical evidence of various kinds; to refine our understanding of Bach's creative life (from a biographical standpoint inadequately documented) and of his artistic development, work habits, and compositional intentions; as well as, finally, to illuminate the substance of his musical language and the significance of his oeuvre.

The thirty-two essays in this collection, half of them heretofore not available in English, remain for the most part as originally published. Substantial deletions, major textual modifications, and additions of notes are identified as such. Bringing the individual essays into an agreeably coherent sequence, however, required many silent adjustments here and there. Bibliographic citations, annotation style, and other external details have been standardized, cross-references added. Since the original essays—whether reprinted or translated—have basically not been rewritten or changed with respect to content and substance, it seemed appropriate, in some cases mandatory, to provide postscripts with explanatory notes, comments, important corrections of fact, updated information, and references to recent research.

In collecting these essays I had first to overcome the conviction that I should not divert my energies to past projects at the expense of new endeavors. However, the vigorous and persistent efforts of Professor George J. Buelow of Indiana University prevailed. It was he who originated the idea of collecting my Bach essays and who devised a plot enlisting a close mutual friend, Alfred Mann, Professor Emeritus at the Eastman School of Music, to translate for this volume the essays written and available only in German. Now that the project has reached its conclusion I feel obliged to express my profound gratitude above all to the two men who initiated it. The translating of the sixteen German essays was a vital, indeed essential, task, and Alfred did a selfless, admirable, and remarkably expeditious job. Our discussions of linguistic details disclosed again and again his intimate knowledge of the material at hand; they also revealed to me his true identity, namely that of a generous and faithful friend. There is another true friend I cannot leave unmentioned: Hans-Joachim Schulze of the Leipzig Bach-Archiv, my tireless and indispensable companion in matters of Bach scholarship. Although he was not involved in this particular book, our collaboration is evident in it nevertheless.

In addition, I am most grateful to Carolyn Mann, Ethel Rider, and Jenny Shallenberger for their kind assistance in the preparation of the manuscript, to Kate Schmit for her careful and competent copy editing, and to Peter Wollny for preparing the index. My special thanks go to Margaretta Fulton, the resourceful Humanities Editor of Harvard University Press, who for some time has wanted a new book from me but who nevertheless gracefully accepted—and helped to shape—a bundle of what I hope is a little more than just "old stuff."

In all likelihood, this volume would not have come into being had it not happened that my professional career led me from my native country—without having to abandon it—to America. I don't wish to conceal at this point that I am intensely conscious of the fact that numerous German colleagues from an earlier generation—Alfred Mann among them—came to cross the Atlantic under very different, indeed gruesome, auspices. What I count among the most important experiences of my personal and professional life is the privilege of many a close and rewarding encounter with a number of émigré scholars who contributed so much to American intellectual life in general and to musicology in particular. And then there are the many newly gained acquaintances and friends, particularly my colleagues and students from the academic institutions I have been associated with. Their support, encouragement, and expectations as well as many a lively, productive, and sometimes challenging exchange had, without a question, a most profound impact on my searching, thinking, and writing. This if anything is in fact quite well documented by the present volume, whose dedication page only inadequately registers what I perceive as particularly meaningful bonds and a deep sense of affection.

Abbreviations

Bach Compendium	Hans-Joachim Schulze and Christoph Wolff, *Bach Compendium. Analytisch-bibliographisches Repertorium der Werke Johann Sebastian Bachs,* vol. I, parts 1–4 (Leipzig, Frankfurt, London, and New York, 1985–1989), vols. II–III (forthcoming)
Dok I–III	*Bach-Dokumente,* ed. Bach-Archiv Leipzig
	Volume I: *Schriftstücke von der Hand Johann Sebastian Bachs,* ed. Werner Neumann and Hans-Joachim Schulze (Leipzig and Kassel, 1963)
	Volume II: *Fremdschriftliche und gedruckte Dokumente zur Lebensgeschichte Johann Sebastian Bachs 1785–1750,* ed. Werner Neumann and Hans-Joachim Schulze (Leipzig and Kassel, 1969)
	Volume III: *Dokumente zum Nachwirken Johann Sebastian Bachs 1750–1800,* ed. Hans-Joachim Schulze (Leipzig and Kassel, 1972)
Bach Reader	*The Bach Reader. A Life of Johann Sebastian Bach in Letters and Documents,* ed. Hans T. David and Arthur Mendel (New York, 1945; rev. edition, 1966)
BG	*Johann Sebastian Bachs Werke. Gesamtausgabe der Bachgesellschaft* (Leipzig, 1851–1899; rpt., Ann Arbor, 1947)
BJ	*Bach-Jahrbuch,* ed. Arnold Schering (1904–1939); ed. Max Schneider (1940–1952); ed. Alfred Dürr and Werner Neumann (1953–1974); ed. Hans-Joachim Schulze and Christoph Wolff (1975ff.)
BWV	Wolfgang Schmieder, *Thematisch-systematisches Verzeichnis der musikalischen Werke Johann Sebastian Bachs. Bach-Werke-Verzeichnis* (Leipzig, 1950; rev. and expanded edition: Wiesbaden, 1990)
Dadelsen *Chr*	Georg von Dadelsen, *Beiträge zur Chronologie der Werke Johann Sebastian Bachs,* Tübinger Bach-Studien, vols. 4–5 (Trossingen, 1958)
DSB	Deutsche Staatsbibliothek, Berlin*
Dürr *Chr, Chr* 2	Alfred Dürr, "Zur Chronologie der Leipziger Vokalwerke J. S. Bachs," first published in *BJ* 1957, pp. 5–162; rev. and expanded edition: Kassel, 1976

Forkel	Johann Nicolaus Forkel, *Ueber Johann Sebastian Bachs Leben, Kunst und Kunstwerke* (Leipzig, 1802; rpt., Frankfurt, 1950); trans. Augustus C. F. Kollmann [1820], in *Bach Reader*, pp. 295–356
Kinsky	Georg Kinsky, *Die Originalausgaben der Werke Johann Sebastian Bachs* (Vienna, Leipzig, and Zurich, 1937; rpt., Hilversum, 1968)
Kobayashi *Chr*	Yoshitake Kobayashi, "Zur Chronologie der Spätwerke Johann Sebastian Bachs. Kompositions- und Aufführungstätigkeit von 1736 bis 1750," *BJ* 1988, pp. 7–72; partially translated in Gerhard Herz, "Yoshitake Kobayashi's Article, 'On the Last Phase of Bach's Work—Compositions and Performances: 1736 to 1750.' An Analysis with Translated Portions of the Original Text," *Bach. The Journal of the Riemenschneider Bach Institute* 21 (1990), pp. 3–25
Marshall *Bach*	Robert L. Marshall, *The Music of Johann Sebastian Bach. The Sources, the Style, the Significance* (New York, 1989)
NBA	Johann Sebastian Bach, *Neue Ausgabe sämtlicher Werke* (*Neue Bach-Ausgabe*), ed. Johann-Sebastian-Bach-Institut Göttingen and Bach-Archiv Leipzig (Leipzig and Kassel, 1954ff.) [*NBA* I/2 = series I, vol. 2; *Krit. Bericht* = critical commentary]
Spitta I–III	Philipp Spitta, *Joh. Seb. Bach,* 2 vols. (Leipzig, 1873–1880; rpt., Wiesbaden, 1962); *Johann Sebastian Bach: His Work and Influence on the Music of Germany, 1685–1750*, trans. Clara Bell and J. A. Fuller-Maitland, 3 vols. (London, 1884; rpt., New York, 1952) [all references are to the English edition unless otherwise indicated]
SPK	Staatsbibliothek Preußischer Kulturbesitz, Berlin*
Wolff *Stile antico*	Christoph Wolff, *Der stile antico in der Musik Johann Sebastian Bachs. Studien zu Bachs Spätwerk,* Beihefte zum Archiv für Musikwissenschaft, vol. 6 (Wiesbaden, 1968)

*Bach manuscripts originally belonging to the former Preußische Staatsbibliothek Berlin are now divided between DSB and SPK (formerly East and West Berlin, respectively) and carry the designations Mus. ms. Bach P and Mus. ms. Bach St. For practical reasons and following established custom in the scholarly Bach literature, these Berlin call numbers are now and then reduced to P (P[artitur] = score) and St (St[immen] = parts).

❖   ❖   ❖

OUTLINES OF A
MUSICAL PORTRAIT

1

New Perspectives on Bach Biography

THE TRACING of the manifold subtle and often complex interconnection of life and works has always been, and continues to be, the central concern of biography. In the case of a painter, poet, or musician the primary interest focuses, without a doubt, on the works and their aesthetic presence, but a deeper understanding of works of art presupposes also a special awareness of their historical context. Among the particularly relevant aspects we find a whole spectrum of biography-related issues, from the genesis of a work and its artistic conception to its social and aesthetic function, regardless of whether we are dealing with a single work of art or a whole repertory of creative output.

Biographical perspectives are supposed to provide a credible framework for the integration of the creative output in the story of an artist's life and to aim at an interpretation of the complicated and many-layered interrelationship. This should ultimately let us perceive even a single work as a part of a greater whole. But the ideal case of a complete, coherent, and logical presentation of a "life and works" story without gaps can hardly be realized. Biography is bound to be fragmentary. One need only consider how difficult it is to reconstruct faithfully the events of the past if one were to attempt one's own autobiography. All the more intricate is the researching of the often blurred, if not lost, traces of a historical figure. The unavoidable merging of objective facts and subjective interpretation poses additional problems. As far as the matter of objectivity and subjectivity is concerned, artist biography faces very serious questions resulting from the juxtaposition of, on the one hand, the artist's life as a historically self-contained phenomenon and, on the other hand, the continuing presence of a historically fraught but living oeuvre. This dilemma nevertheless implies the chance of putting the works themselves in the very center of the discussion. There lies, after all, our primary interest.

Biography, as a special branch of historiography, is obliged to shed light not only on external circumstances and events but—especially in the case of an artist—on inner, immaterial, intellectual, and creative developments. Data of all kinds need to be compiled, ordered, analyzed, evaluated, and, finally, synthesized toward a truthful and vivid portrait.

I

We are in the very fortunate position of possessing—in the case of Bach—a biographical masterpiece of the first rank. This is Philipp Spitta's magisterial two-volume monograph, *Johann Sebastian Bach* (Leipzig, 1873–80; English edition: London, 1884). It became almost immediately the standard work of Bach scholarship and ideally complemented the complete critical edition of the Bach-Gesellschaft then still in progress. Going well beyond the scope of Otto Jahn's *W. A. Mozart* (Leipzig, 1856–59) and Friedrich Chrysander's *Georg Friedrich Händel* (Leipzig, 1858–67), Spitta conceived his book in the then still young but already significant German tradition of critical-historical biography, which combined extensive source studies with large-scale inquiries into the historical background and general cultural, specifically humanistic ("geistesgeschichtlichen"), context. In so doing, he followed, both in scholarly ambition and methodological goals, biographical standard works which have remained significant models until today, such as Johann Gustav Droysen's *Leben des Grafen York* (Göttingen, 1851–52) or Hermann Grimm's *Leben Michel-Angelos* (Hannover, 1860–63), the prototypes of an entirely new kind of biography.

The enormous weight of Spitta's compilation, analysis, and synthesis of material concerning Bach pushed aside the older Bach biographies of Johann Nicolaus Forkel, *Über Johann Sebastian Bach's Leben, Kunst und Kunstwerke* (Leipzig, 1802; English edition: London, 1820); Carl Ludwig Hilgenfeldt, *Johann Sebastian Bach's Leben, Wirken und Werke: ein Beitrag zur Kunstgeschichte des achtzehnten Jahrhunderts* (Leipzig, 1850); and Carl Hermann Bitter, *Johann Sebastian Bach* (Berlin, 1865; 2nd edition, 1880). Spitta's work surpassed its predecessors to such an extent that they became less and less attractive as sources to rely on, to cite, and to refer to. But Spitta's broader historical perspectives and particularly his enormous ability to synthesize, formulate, and shape a Bach picture implied at the same time the danger of an all too well-rounded, logical, definitive biographical statement. Indeed, as a result, a critical continuation of Spitta's work did not really take place. Without an exception, the later biographies of Schweitzer, *J. S. Bach, le musicien-poéte* (Leipzig, 1905; English edition: London, 1911); Charles Sanford Terry's *Bach: A Biography* (London 1928; here for the first time with some new biographical documents); Rudolf Steglich's *J. S. Bach* (Potsdam, 1935)—as well as Karl Geiringer's *Johann Sebastian Bach: The Culmination of an Era* (New York, 1966) and Malcolm Boyd's *Bach* (London, 1983), both incorporating results of more recent Bach research—are still based on Spitta's premises and methodology, and hence correct or change only minor details of his overall picture. Without a doubt they, legitimately and in their own right, stress aspects of Bach and his music which were disregarded or underemphasized by Spitta, but on the whole they all follow rather closely Spitta's model and method.

In recent years we have observed a new, general interest in biographical writings of artists, poets, political figures, and so on. Also developing is a clear trend toward biography which considers sociological and, particularly, psychological elements much more seriously and competently. This often results in a necessary de-idealization of historical figures as typified by nineteenth-century biography, especially by those classic examples of "heroic" biography.

A case in point is Wolfgang Hildesheimer's *Mozart* (Frankfurt am Main, 1977; English edition: London, 1979) or Maynard Solomon's *Beethoven* (New York, 1977). Beethoven and Mozart, of course, as well as Wagner, Mahler, and many others, represent much better objects for psychobiography than Bach. For example, the wealth of letters from the Mozart family, with their multi-faceted insights into daily life, presents a sharp contrast to the rather narrow and dry nature of the surviving Bach correspondence. Only very rarely do we get a glimpse of truly human elements, such as Anna Magdalena Bach asking her husband in a letter of June 1740 to bring back a singing bird from a trip to Berlin.[1] Letters of the late 1730s showing Johann Sebastian's concern for his son Johann Gottfried Bernhard are similarly touching documents of familial tenderness.[2]

Nevertheless, the Bach correspondence, together with further autograph, apograph, and printed documents, is a largely untapped source of information. The source materials compiled by the Leipzig Bach Archive in three volumes of *Bach-Dokumente* practically double the source repertory known to Spitta. But the results of Bach research in the area of musical source studies, with some rather drastic changes in the chronology of the works, with new insights into the genesis and performance history of individual works, or groups of works, call for substantial biographical revisions. In addition, our knowledge concerning the transmission of sources after 1750 sheds new light on the understanding and traditions of Bach's music in the later eighteenth and early nineteenth centuries, the aspect of reception history ("Rezeptionsgeschichte"). If biography should make sense, we must take this latter aspect more seriously and, therefore, reconsider also the contributions made by the early biographers Forkel, Hilgenfeldt, and Bitter.

This does not mean, however, that we should call for a new standard biography to replace Spitta. It seems much more important and prudent— quite apart from the questionable value of so-called definitive standard works—to investigate on a smaller scale some crucial biographical questions, to examine limited areas more systematically and by using better methods, and to aim for a critical synthesis. In the case of Bach we shall always discover blind spots or find ourselves ending up on dead-end roads. This does not only happen in areas such as local history (for instance, what do we really know about musical life in Weimar, Cöthen, or Leipzig?) or the repertories of Bach's contemporaries (for example, what do we actually know about the vocal works of Kuhnau, Fasch, or Stölzel; we don't even possess an edition of Hasse's opera, *Cleofide*, which Bach is known to have heard in 1731). Furthermore, there are numerous problems in the documentation of Bach's life between 1700 and 1714, which make it extremely difficult to discuss the composer's formative years.

One can safely say that a documentary biography of Bach, along the lines of Otto Erich Deutsch's *Schubert* (London, 1944) is an impossibility. In the case of Bach, only biography which focuses on the many-layered unfolding of his creative work seems to be a realistic as well as desirable project. It is by no means just a coincidence that it was not primarily the discovery of new archival documents, but rather the re-evaluation of the musical sources themselves that made biographical revisions necessary.

II

Among the crucial points of any biographical representation is the question of periodization; that is, the organization of life and works into logical narrative units and chronological periods. When the understanding of personality and creative output is sought, decisions regarding this organization become extremely relevant. Pragmatic aspects generally prevail in the disposition of the monographic biographical account. In this respect Spitta's universally accepted five-part periodization of Bach's life appears to be a case in point and to have had its repercussions until very recent times.

His first main chapter deals with Bach's youth and education, 1685–1707. The Mühlhausen-Weimar decade 1708–1717 is described as the first period of mastership and is followed by a chapter on Cöthen, 1717–1723. The two main chapters of the second volume are exclusively concerned with the Leipzig years, which are divided into two periods: 1723–1734 and 1735–1750. Spitta's concept and goal is obvious: he portrays Bach's life in terms of the evolution of a composer who developed his mastership rather slowly through the stages of organist, capellmeister, and cantor; its culmination is—*cum grano salis*—the Protestant "arch-cantor," that is, the creator of the chorale cantata representing the ideal genre of true Lutheran church music. We quickly recognize the functional aim of Spitta's periodization as well as the stability of its ideological fundament. However, in testing the strength of the underlying documentary base we discover the problems to their full extent.

One of the legitimate premises for Spitta's discussion of Bach's music was the assumption that, according to the circumstances of Bach's time, the positions of the composer determined his output in almost every respect; personal decisions were clearly of secondary value. And indeed, we can observe the act of balancing between the artist and the employee at a number of occasions in Bach's life. But on the whole, he surprisingly behaved a lot more like a free and emancipated person than our basically nineteenth-century image of Bach would permit us to believe. The tenor of Spitta's biography cannot, *a priori,* be considered mistaken, but it can only result in a vicious circle when a chronology of Bach's artistic achievement is pressed into a logical, developmental biographical structure, each supporting the other. Thus, for instance, the famous organ Passacaglia in C Minor could only have been a late Weimar masterpiece, just as the Cöthen period had to culminate in the Brandenburg Concertos.

New chronological findings, which are by no means restricted to the Leipzig cantatas, challenge Spitta's periodization without, however, suggesting a similarly strong alternative. The borderlines of the emerging biographical phases are definitely more blurred than Spitta and traditional Bach biography suggested. Thus, for instance, the years up to 1707 have to be seen in a much more differentiated way—the early works of Bach are not only more numerous than we previously thought, but also quite a bit weightier. We must, furthermore, recognize that Bach's appointment as concertmaster in Weimar in 1714 marks a significant turning point with decisive consequences regarding his creative activities. As yet another example, the new chronology of the Leipzig vocal works allows the first years after 1723 to appear as a relatively closed and coherent unit (primarily dedicated to cantata production) while the following decade (ca. 1728/29 to 1738/39) shows Bach's preoccupation with his Collegium Musicum; this necessarily results in a rather clear-cut division of the Leipzig years into three periods: approximately 1723 to 1728/29; 1729 to 1738/39; and 1739 to 1750. However, biography would benefit from not fixing those time spans as really separate units because any such schematism implies the danger of a falsified picture. This can easily be exemplified on the basis of the two periods which are so readily defined as more or less self-contained chapters: the Cöthen years, 1717–1723, and the early Leipzig years, 1723–1729.

There is, first of all, the question of the change from courtly to municipal and church office. In Bach's letter to his friend Georg Erdmann of October 1730, he referred to this change, in retrospect, as a change for the worse—a step downward on the social ladder. The letter indicates as the principal motivation for the change: first, the declining musical interest of Prince Leopold since his marriage with the "amusa" princess of Bernburg; second, better chances for the education of his adolescent sons in Leipzig. There were, of course, no reasons for Bach to provide detailed explanations concerning his move from Cöthen to Leipzig, because they could not have been of any interest to Erdmann. Therefore, alone, we should not overestimate the informative value of the Erdmann letter. But why indeed did Bach leave Cöthen, where he (as he also put it in the letter of 1730) thought to stay until the end of his life? The story of the unmusical princess appears, under close scrutiny, as somewhat doubtful. Already well before Leopold's marriage, Bach had tried to get away from Cöthen, as his application for the position of organist at St. Jacobi in Hamburg of 1720 demonstrates. His dedication of the score of the so-called Brandenburg Concertos of spring 1721 to the margrave of Brandenburg may similarly signify his interest in a change of position. A principal reason for Bach's desire to get away from Cöthen in 1720–21 seems to have been the gradual reduction of the Cöthen Hof-Capelle after 1718, which had been built up only shortly before 1717 as a remarkably strong band of instrumental virtuosos. We do not know what exactly caused Leopold to do this, but there seems to be some evidence for economic austerity moves resulting from pressure on the Cöthen court to supply Prussia with military support. It would have been most unlikely that Leopold would have informed his capellmeister about financial troubles of the court. Also, the sovereign himself would hardly have blamed his wife for his own alleged "declining interest" in music. It seems, rather, as though Bach himself had tried to find an explanation for the apparently noticeable changes, and he may have found it in the "*amusa*"—a very naive explanation for such a drastic change in the cultural affairs of the court. But it must have become clear to him around 1720–21 (also in consideration of his previous Weimar experience) that a slowly moving, democratic municipal administration would provide a much more stable and safer political-economic situation than any absolutist government that depended on the whim of the sovereign ruler.

Bach's move into the university town and commercial metropolis of Leipzig and his appointment to one of the most respected and influential musical offices of Protestant Germany was definitely not a step downward, and additionally Bach kept the title of capellmeister for the rest of his life. The statement made in conjunction with the deliberations concerning Bach's successor at the Leipzig town council—"We need a cantor and not a capellmeister"—is quite significant here. As we know today, the faction of the Leipzig town council that supported the candidacies of Telemann, Graupner, and Bach were interested in appointing a capellmeister to the St. Thomas cantorate and not a schoolmaster. There was never a real chance for candidates like Tufen, Steindorf, or Rolle since they would not have satisfied the ambitions of the town council. Bach's office as "Cantor and Director Musices," as church and municipal capellmeister, was considerably more flexible than his Cöthen position. And like the previous changes in position (from Arnstadt to Mühlhausen to Weimar to Cöthen), the move to Leipzig must surely have appeared to Bach in 1723 as a change for the better.

The alleged unfavorable contrast between the Cöthen capellmeistership and the Leipzig cantorate disappears immediately if we take a look at Bach's compositional activities in the later Cöthen and earlier Leipzig years. The majority of the so-called capellmeister repertory, namely, courtly chamber music for large and small ensembles, can be dated primarily in the first half of the Cöthen years. Moreover, a considerable amount of chamber music must already have originated in the later Weimar years. Perhaps little more than half of the Brandenburg Concertos stem from the Cöthen years, and what is to be considered the most modern of them—namely, Concerto no. 5 (with obbligato harpsichord—may originate from before 1719. On the other hand, a great number of soloistic compositions stem from the early 1720s, when things became more difficult for the Capelle. Here we have in particular the violin soli (1720), Clavier-Büchlein for Wilhelm Friedemann

Bach (1720); Well-Tempered Clavier, Book I (1722); Clavier-Büchlein for Anna Magdelena Bach (1722); Inventions and Sinfonias (1723). This seems to indicate that Bach favored solo works in those years of austerity and put aside more ambitious orchestral projects.

The Cöthen period then shows at least two distinct phases as visible in two very different kinds of instrumental repertoires, and there are similar aspects in the first Leipzig years. Of course, according to the new chronology of the vocal works, the years immediately after 1723 are dominated by cantata production. However, we have to argue very cautiously in regard to the rhythm of Bach's church music output. The first annual cantata cycle of 1723–24 incorporates a large number of Weimar works. Weekly new composition is true primarily only of the second cycle, 1724–25. Even there he gives up the attractive chorale cantata project prematurely in February 1725. The third cycle develops only over two years, at least, and we can only speculate about the other two "Jahrgänge." In any case, they would not have matched the level of regular activity seen to emerge in 1723–25.

Concerning the greater flexibility of Bach's Leipzig position, his activity as performer in and outside of Leipzig in addition to his church job can be clearly documented. In conjunction with this we also have to see a new emphasis on instrumental composition. There is in 1725 the beginning of the second Clavier-Büchlein for Anna Magdalena and the completion of the set of six sonatas for violin and obbligato harpsichord from about the same time, also the commencement of Bach's activity as publisher, starting with Partita I of 1726. Among the organ works, the trio sonatas as well as some of the large-scale preludes and fugues (for instance, B Minor BWV 544; E Minor BWV 548) seem to belong in the mid 1720s. Our traditional view, which synchronizes the duties of the office and the resulting preoccupations with the scope of Bach's compositional interests, requires some fundamental modifications.

To be fair to Spitta, he had seen things often in a much more differentiated way than most of his successors. Nevertheless, his principal aim consisted in the drawing up of an image of Bach's artistic personality, the logic of which may indeed appear today as a distortion. His exclusive derivation of the dominating form and style elements in Bach's early vocal music from Bach's exposure to and experience with the organ literature represents such a case. Bach was, considering his background, a very broad-minded musician who had an intimate familiarity with nearly all of the compositional genre traditions. He specifically mentions in his Mühlhausen letter of resignation that he had put together "a whole repertory of selected church pieces," a collection of vocal music which, unfortunately, can no longer be reconstructed. But as can be demonstrated, he was clearly influenced in his early vocal writing by the vocal style of the late-seventeenth-century post-Schütz tradition in Thuringia. Even in the area of Bach's early keyboard music, the fundament of biographical integration has been shaken. The repertoires to be found in some of the central early sources for the transmission of Bach's music, especially those of the Andreas Bach Book and the Möller Manuscript,[3] have been totally neglected in assessing the context of Bach's early keyboard composition. The scope of the repertories, which go well beyond the German tradition (Albinoni, Steffani, Dieupart, Lully, Marais, Lebègue, Marchand, among others), plus the high quality of the selection seems representative of the interest and experience of Bach and his circle. Further research in this direction will, without a doubt, force us to modify our view concerning the dominant North German influence on the young Bach (mainly Böhm and Buxtehude).

Also, the biographical fixation on Bach's Lübeck visit to see Buxtehude in 1705/06 requires some reassessment. It seems most unlikely that Bach took formal lessons from Buxtehude during the four-month stay. Rather, as a finished and versatile musician, Bach may have participated in the performances of Buxtehude's "Abendmusiken" cycle, which took place during that very time; this would also have been necessary for the financing of the stay and the fact that he had to pay his Arnstadt substitute out of his own pocket. Beyond such a collegial participation in Buxtehude's "Abendmusiken" he probably benefited in many ways from the Buxtehude connection, also in view of the access to new repertories. His impetus toward learning through studying and copying goes back to the very early days. The obituary of 1750 (published in 1754) reports the story of nightly copying by the small boy. And there are documents for this restless studying through his very last years. This has to be considered a very significant phenomenon, because—compared with other important composers of his generation—he might well have been the best-informed musician regarding the major repertories, and this despite his rather limited geographical horizon. His universal command of all genres and the stylistically many-layered approach of his compositional art can only be understood on the basis of this background.

Bach's musical cosmopolitanism makes it very difficult to balance external data and less concrete "inner" criteria. For instance, Bach's appointment as concertmaster in 1714 was rather decisive concerning his composition duties and schedule. For his compositional development, however, his encounter with the new Italian style, especially Vivaldi's style in 1712–13, is infinitely more important because it resulted in a radical change of Bach's personal style. It affected him at all stylistic levels, from thematic invention, voice leading, rhythmic profile, and harmonic modulatory disposition to small-scale and large-scale structural organization in both instrumental and vocal genres.

The manifold overlappings of similar data and developments in Bach's Leipzig years are among the most problematic issues in Bach biography, beginning with an analysis of Bach's relationship with his principal office as the cantor of St. Thomas. He began energetically to put together a working repertory of cantatas. And his later practice of adding to the older repertory (as in the B Minor Mass, Christmas Oratorio, other oratorios, the St. Matthew Passion) signifies his continuing interest in giving his main business, at least occasionally, new impulses. Nevertheless, the decade after 1729 sees his preoccupation with the Collegium Musicum: a bourgeois-professional organization which performed ordinarily once a week (twice during the Easter and St. Michael's Fair). But it seems a strange fact that after his resignation from the Collegium Musicum around 1740, he did not turn more intensively back to church music. On the contrary, he reduced his official activities to a bare minimum, merely administering the position rather than filling it with life. It is symptomatic of his behavior that he put on performances of Passion compositions by other masters, such as Graun, Telemann, and Handel, but left his own St. John Passion unfinished in its last revision. One gets the impression that Bach in 1740, at the age of approximately fifty-five, entered a kind of self-styled retirement in order to be free for projects that interested him personally, not in his capacity as cantor.

At the beginning of this decade we find between Scheibe and Birnbaum the aesthetic controversy concerning Bach's compositional style. Bach did not get directly involved in the discussion, but he clearly used Magister Birnbaum of the University of Leipzig as his very own spokesman. One can recognize this on the basis of the argumentation regarding Scheibe blaming Bach for the absence of a main voice ("Hauptstimme") in his music. Bach then explained his understanding of harmony and polyphony in terms of historical examples, specifically citing works of Palestrina and others. He clearly attempted to give his compositional convictions historical dimensions and authority. At the same time (the later 1730s), Bach was surrounded by a number of very gifted theory students: Mizler, Kirnberger, Agricola, for example. Thus, it is not at all a surprise that, for the first time, in Clavier-Übung III (1739), Bach included a strong theoretical-historical component introducing a new dimension in his personal style. This is evident in his systematic approach to dealing with the old church modes (aiming at enrichment of the standard major-minor tonality) and in the juxtaposition of retrospective and modernistic styles of *cantus firmus* treatment (compare the two chorales "Aus tiefer Not" and "Vater unser im Himmelreich"). Bach's focus on his own place in history is also evident from the fact that in 1735 he put together a chronicle of his family, in which the short autobiographical note as such is clearly less relevant than its integration in the historical microcosm of the family.

His historical grounding must have provided him with a great sense of security and self-confidence as the necessary precondition for the activities of the 1740s: the period of largely free creative enterprise. He performed his regular duties clearly on the side and concentrated on compositional projects, which he designed for himself and in which the theoretical-historical dimension plays an important role. The spectrum encompasses contemporary popular tunes as we encounter them in the Goldberg Variations or in the Peasant Cantata, Gregorian chant in the B Minor Mass, retrospective *stile antico* in several late vocal and instrumental works, the mannerisms of the Berlin School as we find them in the Musical Offering, and often free-style and canonic counterpoint in close juxtaposition. Bach's late style displays an amazing zest for systematic penetration of compositional problems. This is particularly reflected in the thoughtful planning of the late monothematic instrumental works, which balance musical variety and theoretical-historical speculation by way of Bach's virtuosity as both composer and performer. This is also true of the B Minor Mass, whose completion falls into those years as the only major vocal project, and it seems not to be just a coincidence that Bach turned to composition of a Mass rather than the final revision of the St. John Passion. Composition of the Mass as a genre reflecting centuries of tradition quite naturally implies a historical dimension and complements in a number of ways Bach's simultaneous work on the Art of Fugue, which also preoccupied his time for most of the 1740s.

The general relationship between personal interests and official duties sheds some light on biographical perspectives. From the very beginning, Bach understood how to take the initiative concerning his professional life. Consider, for example, how astonishing it must have been to see the fifteen-year-old, contrary to the family tradition, leave the familiar middle-German territory and move to the remote Lüneburg. In later years he was never afraid of conflicts with courtly, church, or municipal offices. He learned how to take care of his own promotions in a very professional way, considering the negotiations over the concertmaster appointment in 1714 or the application for a Dresden court title in 1733 to strengthen his authority in Leipzig. His changes of position—even, if necessary, putting aside his official duties—prove in every single case that he himself was the prime mover acting in his own best interest.

One of the basic premises of Bach's talent for protecting his relative independence can be found in his many-sided and thoroughly professional musicianship. Having grown up as a member of a traditional musician's family, he understood all the facets of his trade. The broad spectrum of his Leipzig activities appears here as a real culmination point in his career; besides his duties as cantor and Director Musices and his temporary engagement as director of the Collegium Musicum, he advanced his position as a concertizing virtuoso, kept a busy private teaching schedule, functioned frequently as organological consultant (also turned to the development of new instruments such as the Lautenclavier, viola pomposa, fortepiano, as well as, possibly, the oboe da caccia), kept a music shop (stocking, for instance, Johann Gottfried Walther's *Musicalisches Lexicon* of 1732 and Johann David Heinichen's *Der General-Bass in der Composition* of 1728) and a music and instrument rental service, and pursued the publication as well as the distribution of his own works. The life of the "arch-cantor" moved indeed on a very earthly path.

This diversity and breadth of interests stimulated without a doubt Bach's compositional ambitions. His uncompromising attitude is reflected by the degree of elaboration, the technical demands, and the general difficulty of his works. This is demonstrated in an exemplary manner in his Clavier-Übung series, which might be understood as some kind of musical self-portrait: it comprises a well-planned repertory of keyboard music of all genres (suite, concerto, prelude, fugue, *cantus firmus* composition, from two- to six-part scoring, displaying style models and techniques of all sorts) for the main keyboard instruments (one- and two-manual harpsichords, large organ, and positive organ). Bach's versatility and universality appear here in a nutshell and represent the decisive source of his musical language, essentially formed by integrating stylistic and technical pluralism. Striving for new stylistic and unexplored technical horizons and, at the same time, researching and penetrating the accumulated historical traditions of the art of composing became an ever-increasing and most important characteristic of his unique musical goals.

A statement like this goes well beyond the factual, of course, but entering the sphere of interpretation is an essential element of biography. Especially in the case of Bach, we gain very little by merely collecting data and documents. Their messages remain for the most part very meager unless they are intellectually penetrated by critical questions with the aim of detecting inner connections that make historical sense. Analysis of sources and synthesis of ideas complement one another in the conscientious search for a truthful picture of Bach, which—for lack of evidence—will always be far from a psychological character image. A genuine, enlightened, and lively musical portrait is, however, a realistic goal.

2

The Family

"JOHANN SEBASTIAN BACH belongs to a family whose love and aptitude for music seems like a gift accorded by Nature in common to each of its members."[1] So begins the obituary of 1754, the first comprehensive biography of Bach. Bach's firmly rooted place in what was certainly the most important musical family of all time is fundamentally and decisively germane to an understanding of his personality and work. True, he himself could not have realized that his own position in history was that of the dominant figure in that seemingly endless line of musicians; yet he understood, quite unequivocally, that he was a member of that family, so rich in traditions, whose legendary musicality, according to a remark by Johann Nicolaus Bach (no. 27 in the genealogical table; see Fig. 2.1), "perhaps derives from the fact that even the letters B. A. C. H. in sequence form a melody."[2]*

It was Johann Sebastian Bach who, in 1735, was the first to set down detailed observations about his forebears and their descendants, under the title *Ursprung der musicalisch-Bachischen Familie* (Origins of the musical Bach family).[3] He too was responsible for the *Alt-Bachisches Archiv* (Archive of the early Bachs), an anthology of vocal compositions by the older members of the family, beginning with Johann (4). He was able to describe all of his own children as "born musicians" and thus to make clear that within the family musical talent was taken for granted as a wholly natural heritage.

The era of the Bach family of musicians' life and activity lasted from late in the sixteenth century to the early nineteenth throughout Thuringia, with Eisenach, Gotha, Erfurt, Arnstadt, Mühlhausen, and Weimar as its most important centers. On this scene, bitterly split politically but unified denominationally and, despite all the turmoils of war and other vicissitudes of the day, economically vigorous, there blossomed a thriving musical culture in court, town, and church. The rise and decline of the Bach family are very closely bound up with the socio-historical circumstances of this cultivation

---

*In German terminology, B is equivalent to the English B♭, H to the English B.

of music. From the middle of the sixteenth century onward an exemplary upward swing and development in the practice of music was noted there, especially at the pocket-size courts intent on the ambitious display of their magnificence, in cities conscious of their image, and in churches impelled by post-Reformation zeal. Thus rich possibilities of expansion offered themselves to a musical profession organized on guild principles, and the Bachs wielded influence on every level as performers, town musicians (with a fixed hierarchy—apprentice, journeyman, violinist, town piper), court musicians, concertmaster and capellmeister, organists and cantors. When, however, in the course of the development of bourgeois musical culture during the late eighteenth century, the significance of the musically influential institutions (court chapels, town piper bands, and Kantoreien) rapidly decreased, the ground was cut from under the feet of traditional families of musicians like the Bachs.

Musical life in Thuringia manifested its brilliance in a multitude of details; yet it lacked a leading cultural center of the order of, say, the Saxon metropolis Dresden as a magnet for really important musicians. Thus even in the Bach family a robust mediocrity held sway. Only a few of them achieved anything out of the ordinary, largely due to their drifting away from their home environment. The unusual concentration of musical talent within an area so narrowly enclosed (in family as well as geographically), with Johann Sebastian as a culminating point in an ever-increasing and then suddenly ebbing flood of talent, remains a unique phenomenon.

One essential prerequisite to the development of such a family of musicians lay in the widespread emphasis on craftsmanship in practical musical activities, the male members of the family having their professional path designated for them from their earliest childhood. Their training was undertaken largely within the family circle, at the hands of father, uncles, and brothers. Thus it was entirely typical that even Johann Sebastian brought up not only his own sons but six of his nephews: Johann Bernhard (41), Johann Lorenz (38), Johann Heinrich (43), Johann Ernst (34), Johann Elias (39), and Samuel Anton (75). He himself had as a child been taken under the wing of his father and his father's twin brother, Johann Christoph (12), as well as of his famous second cousin, Johann Christoph (13), all court musicians and town musicians in Eisenach, before being taken into the care of his eldest brother, the Ohrdruf organist Johann Christoph (22). Among musical families, external studies and educational journeys were far from customary, although there are rare examples of journeys to Italy by the sons of Caspar (3), by Johann Nicolaus (27), and lastly Johann Christian (50). In the circumstances, however, even Johann Sebastian's stay for several months in Lübeck, studying with Dietrich Buxtehude in 1705–06, counted as unusual.

In the enclosed circle of family life among musicians ruled by professional regulations, marital alliances with other musical families are to be noted. Wilcke, Lämmerhirt, and Hoffmann were the names of the most important Thuringian families apart from the Bachs, and between these, indeed, family

Genealogical table

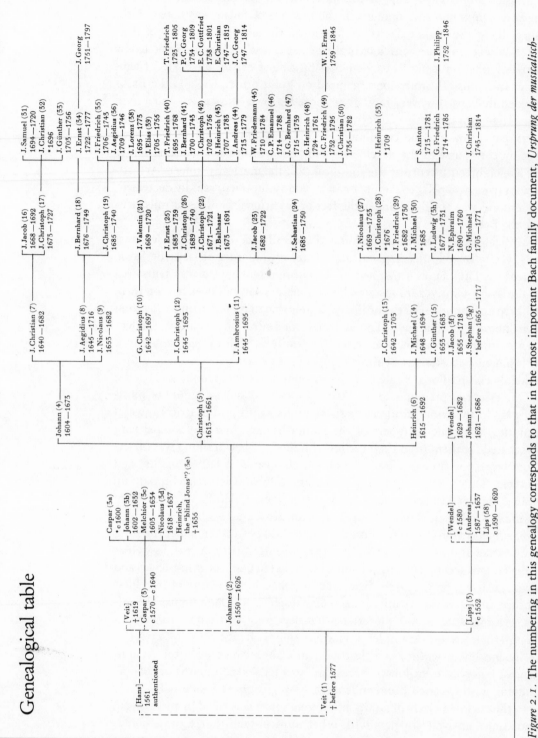

Figure 2.1. The numbering in this genealogy corresponds to that in the most important Bach family document, *Ursprung der musicalisch-Bachischen Familie* ("Origins of the musical Bach family"), which was compiled by J. S. Bach in ca. 1735 and contains short biographies of fifty-three family members. Unproved relationships are indicated by dotted lines.

connections were numerous. Thus Johann (4) had married a Lämmerhirt; his first marriage, like that of his brother Heinrich (6), was to a Hoffmann. The father, Christoph Hoffmann, town piper of Suhl, had had both Bach brothers under his tuition. Here again Johann Sebastian offers a typical example: his mother was a Lämmerhirt; his first wife, Maria Barbara, was a Bach, youngest daughter of Johann Michael (14), and his second wife was a Wilcke, Anna Magdalena, youngest daughter of the court trumpeter of Weissenfels, Johann Caspar Wilcke.

Through common social status—musicians of lower status did not normally enjoy the rights of citizens—as well as professional interests, family unity was very close. Family visiting days (which must have resembled small musical galas) deepened these connections: "Since the company consisted of none but cantors, organists and town musicians, all of whom had to do with the Church . . . first of all, when all were assembled, a chorale was sung. From this devotional opening they proceeded to jesting, often in strong contrast to it. For now they would sing folksongs, the contents of which were partly comic and partly indelicate, all together and extempore, but in such a way that the several improvised parts made up a kind of harmony, although the text was different for each voice. They called this kind of extemporary ensemble a quodlibet and enjoyed a hearty laugh at it."[4] Johann Sebastian's Quodlibet BWV 524 only partly preserved, provides a characteristic example. Cooperation and mutual assistance between members of the family were taken for granted. Thus, during his stay in Lübeck, Johann Sebastian easily found in his cousin Johann Ernst (25) a reliable deputy in his post as organist in Arnstadt. And when a post needed to be filled, a principal concern was that the successor to one Bach should be another. Many positions were passed on in this way through several generations.

THE FAMILY TREE of Johann Sebastian Bach can be traced without a gap to the middle of the sixteenth century, in fact to Veit (Vitus) Bach (1), who, following the counter-Reformation expulsion of Protestants at the time of the Schmalkaldic War, was driven from Moravia. Of Veit the baker, who then settled in Wechmar near Gotha, the family chronicle records that "he found his greatest pleasure in a Cythringen [a small cittern] which he even took with him to the mill and played during the milling. And this, as it were, was the beginning of the musical inclination of his descendants."

Veit's son Johannes (2) was the first representative of the family to receive a basic grounding in music, which he had from Matz Ziesecke, town piper in Gotha, before he took over his father's bakery. From Wechmar, however, he traveled "very frequently to Gotha, Arnstadt, Erfurt, Eisenach, Schmalkalden and Suhl in order to assist the town musicians in those places." He also appears as "minstrel" in the register of death. Not until his sons Johann (4), Christoph (5) and Heinrich (6) do we find an exclusive devotion to music. Their settling down and accepting salaried posts as court, town, and church musicians completed the departure from amateur traditions, the distinction from nonorganized musicians known as Bierfiedler (beer-fiddlers). Music as a profession was from now on designated as the course for successive generations to follow, and the Bachs soon climbed to the top of the professional ladder in every sphere of the musical world. But no sooner had the attainment of higher posts succeeded in raising them to the middle class than new prospects of education were opened up to them. From the second third of the eighteenth century onward practically all the Bachs went to university, and many of them took up nonmusical professions. Previously no choice had been offered them: they had had to be musicians. It was elevation to the middle class, together with the break-up of permanent musical organizations, which deprived musician families of the basis of their existence. In this connection it is interesting to note the short-lived surge of pictorial talent among the Bachs. Some of the descendants of Johann Ludwig (3h) were active, outside their duties as court organists in Meiningen, as "cabinet-painters." And Carl Philipp Emanuel's youngest son, Johann Sebastian, Jr. (1748–1778), became a pupil of Adam Friedrich Oeser at the Leipzig Academy of Art. At his matriculation there it was said that his great gifts would "extend the fame of that name which his grandfather Johann Sebastian had already established here, from the realm of music to that of the pictorial arts."[5] He died untimely young, however, in Rome.

In accordance with their sphere of origin, all the Bachs were first and foremost instrumentalists. The organ and harpsichord took pride of place among the instruments, although well-nigh all the others were also represented. Most members of the family, in good town piper tradition, learned several instruments, though mostly specializing later. Johann Ambrosius (11) especially must have been an outstandingly versatile musician. Shortly after his appointment to the Eisenach post, the town chronicler noted: "In 1672 the new Hausmann [director of town music] made music at Easter with organ, violins, singing voices, and trumpets and kettle-drums, such as never happened before in the history of Eisenach."[6] A series of members of the family was further active in instrument making: Johann Michael (14) as violin maker, Johann Michael (30) as organ builder; Johann Nicolaus (27) invented the so-called Lautenclavier. Johann Sebastian too, over and above his skill in playing various instruments, possessed these technical gifts: he was profoundly expert on the organ, he encouraged the Leipzig violin maker Johann Christian Hoffmann to make the viola pomposa, and he took an expert interest in the instruments made by Gottfried Silbermann, the pianoforte builder. It was inherent in the universal emphasis on instrumental playing that, with the Bachs, composition ordinarily remained in the background. Composing was reserved for those who were trained for it, and from whom musical works were commissioned—the organists, cantors, concertmasters, and capellmeisters among them.

The first composers worthy of the name among the Bachs were the two brothers Johann Christoph (13) and Johann Michael (14), whose numerous motets and vocal works belong to the great achievements of Lutheran church music after Heinrich Schütz. Above all Johann Christoph (to whom his brother was certainly not inferior) was considered in the family "the great and expressive composer," whose works were performed by Johann Sebastian in Leipzig and still later by Carl Philipp Emanuel in Hamburg. Johann Bernhard (18), organist and court musician in Eisenach, was a writer principally of instrumental music of the highest quality. Four of his orchestral suites "in the style of Telemann" were adopted by Johann Sebastian for his Collegium Musicum in Leipzig. Johann Ludwig (3h), court capellmeister in Meiningen, was a productive and sound composer of vocal works. Eighteen of his cantatas were performed in 1726 by Johann Sebastian in Leipzig. Johann Nicolaus (27), organist of the city and college church in Jena, was likewise a profound composer. Johann Sebastian wrote out one of his Masses for his own use, demonstrating once again how much importance he attached to the compositions of various members of the family.

Among the younger generation only Johann Ernst (34), besides Johann Sebastian's sons, can be numbered among the outstanding names. He was obliged, as early as 1758, to give up his post as court capellmeister in Eisenach because of the dissolution of the capelle, but he remained active as a composer. Among his most important works is a great Passion oratorio "O Seele, deren Sehnen" (1764); many of his instrumental pieces were printed during his lifetime. Johann Sebastian's only grandson to achieve a relatively significant musical role was Wilhelm Friedrich Ernst, son of Johann Christoph Friedrich (49). He stayed for some time with his uncle Johann Christian in London, and after concert tours in Holland and France went to Minden as a musical director, then in 1789 to Berlin as court harpsichordist to Queen Luise of Prussia and musical tutor to the Prussian princes. Despite his many cantatas, songs, stage works, and instrumental pieces, he enjoyed little recognition in his lifetime. In 1811 he gave up his posts and thereafter lived in retirement in Berlin.

FOR JOHANN SEBASTIAN BACH, whose posts and titles had elevated him (outwardly only) far above the family average, the strictly ordered frame of musical family life remained decisive at every level of his life and work, even when he had left his Thuringian origins for Cöthen and Leipzig. He is a wholly typical representative of his family—in his way perhaps also the last of his clan for whom the interplay of professional and family life constituted a basic condition of existence.

When he proudly reported to his childhood friend Georg Erdmann in 1730 that he was able "to put on a vocal and instrumental concert with my own family,"[7] this reflected not so much idyllic domestic music as the abundant opportunities in Leipzig at the time for public, semi-public and private music-making. Anna Magdalena had been "singer to the Prince's Court" of Cöthen in her day, and Johann Sebastian made various concert tours from

Leipzig with her, praising her "pure soprano."[8] Even his first wife, Maria Barbara, who died at an early age, was evidently a singer, that "stranger maid"[9] about whose appearances as soloist in the service the Arnstadt church authorities had complained. His children too, as soon as they were old enough, assisted in their father's performances, especially as instrumentalists. Works such as the concertos for two or more harpsichords probably afforded the opportunity primarily for father and sons to appear as soloists together. The family regularly shared in the preparations for performances, especially—apart from the tuning of the harpsichord (Carl Philipp Emanuel's preferred sphere of activity)—in copying orchestral parts from the original score. For example, Anna Magdalena, Wilhelm Friedemann, and Carl Philipp Emanuel were all among the copyists of the choral and orchestral parts of the Kyrie and Gloria of the Missa in B Minor of 1733.

How far the family life was permeated with music is shown by such invaluable records as the two Clavier-Büchlein for Anna Magdalena Bach, of 1722 and 1725. In these presentation albums Johann Sebastian entered lesser or greater works dedicated to his wife (partly first drafts of works printed later), and even the children made attempts at composing little pieces, in which from time to time their father's correcting hand can be seen. He took immense and meticulous pains over his sons' musical education. For his eldest

Figure 2.2. This oil painting has until recently been attributed to Herman van der Myn, but new research suggests that it may be a portrait of J. S. Bach and three of his sons executed in ca. 1733 by Johann Balthasar Denner (1685–1749). See the Postscript to this chapter for more details.

he specially prepared a Clavier-Büchlein for pedagogic purposes. Carl Philipp Emanuel was later able to acknowledge: "In composition and keyboard-playing I have never had any tutor other than my father." [10] Home education was by no means one-sided, for he stressed that he would have suffered from "the lack of foreign travels" had he not "had the great good fortune from my earliest days to hear around me all that was finest in every branch of music, and to make the acquaintance of many masters of the highest rank, and partly to enjoy their friendship . . . for no master of music found it easy to pass through this place [Leipzig] without making my father's acquaintance and letting himself be heard by him. The greatness of my father was far too well known for a musician of any standing to let slip the opportunity, if it were possible, of making the closer acquaintance of this great man." Johann Sebastian followed his sons' professional careers from their inception, drawing up letters of application for them, giving them recommendations of every kind, and paying them visits. He assisted them in procuring printers for their first efforts and concerned himself with their sale, as the following notice in a Leipzig newspaper shows: "We hereby give notice to all harpsichord-lovers that the first sonata of the Dresden Herr [W. F.] Bach is now complete and may be obtained from his father, the court composer Bach, at the Thomas-Schule." [11] The Bach sons, in their turn, rendered their father the same service; thus the latter was able to remark, for example, on the title-page of the so-called Schübler Chorales (BWV 645–650), "Obtainable in Leipzig from Herr Capellmeister Bach, his sons in Berlin and Halle, and the publisher in Zella." [12]

The exemplary collaboration within this family of musicians still applied for a while after Johann Sebastian's death. Thus it went almost without saying that at least one of his sons would compete for his father's post in Leipzig. Carl Philipp Emanuel did so, but lost to Gottlob Harrer, protégé of the prime minister of Saxony, Count Brühl. The sons also concerned themselves with the publication of his uncompleted legacy, the Art of Fugue. A proof comment such as this one by Johann Christoph Friedrich, "My late father ["der seelige Papa"] had had engraved on the plate the legend *Canon per Augment: in Contrapuncto all octava,* but had struck it out again on the proof plate and marked it as above" [13] shows their strenuous endeavors to realize their father's intentions to the best of their ability. But the family, after all, broke up with the death of Johann Sebastian, not least through the sordid wrangling over the estate between Maria Barbara's sons and those of Anna Magdalena. The children increasingly lost contact with one another, and what common interests there remained dwindled. The structure of what was once so close a family of musicians had changed radically, even in respect of the other branches of the family. For a while the memory of their father proved their sole focal point. Wilhelm Friedemann and Carl Philipp Emanuel provided Bach's later biographer Johann Nikolaus Forkel with information about him. His musical legacy had been divided up among the family in 1750, and thereby became subject not only to fragmentation but to loss. Wilhelm Friedemann, for example, found himself obliged by financial difficulties to sell his inheritance, whereas Carl Philipp Emanuel strove valiantly to gain possession of this priceless legacy, even attempting to get back what his brother had let go. But with the sale of Emanuel's estate after 1790 this major collection of Bachiana was dispersed, along with the remnants of Johann Sebastian's works, the *Alt-Bachisches Archiv,* and the family portraits of Johann Sebastian, Johann Ambrosius, Anna Magdalena, and others of the Bach line, since no "natural" heirs were to hand for the preservation and use of the estate.

The musical dynasty as such had ceased to be. When, some decades later, Wilhelm Friedrich Ernst Bach was invited, as Johann Sebastian's last direct descendant, to unveil the Leipzig Bach memorial dedicated by Mendelssohn, this was only a pious gesture. The followers of the Bach movement, with Mendelssohn at their head, were at that time, frankly, more intimate with Bach's work than was his grandson. For Johann Sebastian had, with his works, burst through the bounds of his family, on whose name he had bestowed the highest glory.

3

Decisive Career Steps

BACH'S LIFE moved in far narrower confines than that of any other major figures in the history of music. All the more powerful do Bach's achievements in isolation appear, and the incomparable consequences of his work, right up to our own day and across all frontiers. The geographical framework of his life was set in the Central German territories of Thuringia, Anhalt, and Saxony, beyond whose area he had gone only for a few times for short periods: north to Hamburg, Lübeck, and Berlin; west to Kassel; south to Carlsbad; and Bach apparently never went further east than Dresden. And as regards the professional scope of his work, the obvious career of a court, church, and municipal musician was laid down for him by family tradition and in all spheres he climbed relatively early to the topmost branches of the hierarchy: court capellmeister as well as cantor and municipal director of music.

On comparing, on the one hand, the locales of Bach's life and the external conditions they afforded for his composition, and on the other those of his exact contemporary Handel, his provincialism becomes clear. Handel stands for the cosmopolitan composer who (in some respects like earlier representatives, such as Lasso, Monteverdi, and Schütz) knew how to employ his gifts for organization and creation in the great musical centers of the Europe of that time. Handel was able to celebrate major triumphs, but he also had to suffer severe reverses. Bach's life, though not devoid of either glory or conflict, in essence ran evenly and without extremes of either kind. Precisely for this reason, however, Handel's personality must have held a special fascination for him. In 1719 and 1729 Bach endeavored to meet him. But his attempts (which in retrospect seem almost touching) to make the acquaintance of his great contemporary were frustrated. It was Bach who had taken the initiative to make contact, not Handel. And without question he was more familiar with Handel's works than was Handel with his. Here one of Bach's exceptional characteristics becomes evident: his tremendous will to acquaint himself, despite often adverse circumstances, with everything

Figure 3.1. Principal places in Bach's life and career.

Places Bach lived in

Places Bach visited

Places for reference

within his reach: composers, styles, genres, works. There is no doubt that in the last analysis Bach was superior to Handel in musical erudition and experience. Bach's spiritual horizon and the diversity of his musical nature were anything but provincial.

It was normal, for a musician of the Baroque period, for there to be a close correlation of his sphere of activity and his work as a composer, for the independent, free-lance artist did not yet exist. As a consequence, his artistic development was decisively influenced above all by external factors and circumstances, whereas the respective degree of musical originality depended mainly on the creative power of the individual. General conditions for Bach's artistic development were on the whole exceptionally favorable, even though his career lacked any spectacular features. He was, however, offered opportunities (and for the most part the decision whether or not to take them lay in his own hands) to extend himself in nearly all spheres of current musical practice. Even if opera was the sole important genre missing from his oeuvre, entirely equivalent possibilities for the creation of large-scale vocal and instrumental works presented themselves to Bach in the Passions and secular *drammi per musica*. For an understanding of Bach's life and work it must further be borne in mind that to an exceptional degree he knew how to combine the qualities of a creative and of a performing musician. His regular demands reveal maximum technical challenges, since he approached composition from the viewpoint of a virtuoso.

BECAUSE of his posts as organist, Bach's first years as a young composer were spent entirely in the field of keyboard music. How far this was influenced by his early musical education it is difficult to estimate. Yet he was trained not exclusively as a clavier player but on many instruments, in accordance with the rules of his town-piper father's household. (His first, though only brief, professional engagement, from March to July 1703, was in fact as a court violinist in the private band of Duke Johann Ernst of Saxe-Weimar.) He had spent his childhood entirely in the bosom of his family, which certainly gave him but little security: as a nine-year-old he lost his mother, and a year later his father, upon which he was taken into the house of his eldest brother, who was organist in Ohrdruf. Without doubt he had taken with him formative impressions of his circumstances at Eisenach: there his father, Johann Ambrosius Bach, had held the post of a court trumpeter along with that of head of the town-piper band, and his cousin Johann Christoph was court harpsichordist and organist to the city church of St. George (with the cantor Andreas Christian Dedekind) and as a composer was perhaps the first outstanding talent in the Bach family of musicians. But certainly the Ohrdruf years must have been decisive. There he was a pupil of his brother Johann Christoph, who had studied with Johann Pachelbel in Erfurt, and (according to the 1754 obituary) "under his guidance he laid the foundations of his keyboard playing."[1] That young Johann Sebastian left Ohrdruf in 1700 is explicable much less by family friction (the obituary relates the cruel story of the "book full of clavier pieces by the most famous masters of the day," laboriously copied out by moonlight, which his brother had confiscated) than by the fact that he had to leave the lyceum in Ohrdruf in default of a scholarship on which he, as an orphan, was dependent. Together with his friend Georg Erdmann he went off to Lüneburg, where "because of his uncommonly beautiful soprano voice" he obtained a place as a matins pupil, in the special choir of the choir school of St. Michael's. It says much for Bach's need for emancipation that at so young an age he wished to turn his back, at least for a while, on the restricted circle of Thuringian musical society.

In many respects Lüneburg was a significant station for Bach. For one thing, there for the first time he came into really active contact with the highly developed choir school tradition of a long-famous institution like St. Michael's monastery and was able to get to know the choral repertoire of the sixteenth and seventeenth centuries. For another, he must have had adequate opportunities to perfect his dexterity in organ playing, possibly under the guidance of the famous organist at the Johanniskirche in Lüneburg, Georg Böhm: later, in the 1720s, old Böhm had taken care of the distribution of Bach's first printed Partitas. Third, he utilized the time in excursions to the neighboring musical centers of Hamburg and Celle. The obituary relates: "From Lüneburg he traveled now and again to Hamburg to hear the then famous organist of the Catharinenkirche, Johann Adam Reinken. Here too he had the opportunity, through more frequent hearings of a then famous band maintained by the Duke of Celle, consisting mainly of Frenchmen, to acquire a thorough grounding in French taste, which in those parts was something quite new at the time." Last but not least, in Lüneburg Bach brought his academic schooling, which he had begun at the Eisenach Latin school, to a satisfactory conclusion. The scholarly library Bach left behind him provides eloquent witness to his lively and advanced interests at this time, especially in theological literature.

When in August 1703 Bach obtained the appointment as organist at the New Church in Arnstadt, he was already esteemed as a renowned organist, commanding a good salary (which was reduced again after his departure). And in the ensuing years he had the opportunity of sharpening his profile as an organ virtuoso. In this connection must be seen his prolonged stay in Lübeck in the winter of 1705–06—to the annoyance of the Arnstadt consistory—for study with Dietrich Buxtehude. Beside Böhm's influence, which is discernible particularly in Bach's early chorale variations, now figured Buxtehude's decisive strength, especially in the appearance of large-scale free organ pieces, which require a mature manual and pedal technique. For the citizens of Arnstadt the stormy development of their ambitious organist must have been bewildering. The consistory complained "that he had hitherto made many curious variations in the chorale, and mingled many strange notes in it";[2] furthermore they deplored that Bach took no interest in the figured music for the choir. This last clearly indicates that Bach in fact quite consciously devoted himself to the purely organistic, and certainly more to playing than to composing, since very few compositions have been preserved from those years.

When Bach took over the post of organist to the church of St. Blasius in the free imperial city of Mühlhausen in June 1707, one thing in particular was decisively changed as against Arnstadt: he developed an interest in composing vocal church music; and his discontent that he did not find sufficient support for the organization of a "well-regulated church music"[3] (that is, regular performances of cantatas) led him a year later already to tender his resignation. Among the vocal works originating in Mühlhausen (five have been preserved) was the only cantata printed in Bach's lifetime, that on the council election, "Gott ist mein König" BWV 71. The early vocal works reveal how deeply Bach was rooted in the central German choir school tradition: predominant are the musical forms bound up with the seventeenth century—the motet, concerted vocal work, strophic aria and chorale, textually confined to the words of the Bible and church hymns. For study purposes he had at that time, in his own words, "acquired, not without cost, a good store of the choicest church compositions."[4] Despite this interest in the vocal field, however, even in Mühlhausen keyboard music took pride of place, as emerges not least from the extensive work of reconstruction which he instigated on his organ at Mühlhausen. In the "project for new repairs" he outlined for this he produced his first expert opinion on organs. As a recognized adviser on organ matters he was also, henceforth, increasingly active as a consultant and tester.

IN JULY 1708 Bach took up the attractive post of court organist in Weimar. He did not leave Mühlhausen on bad terms, for he was still asked in the two following years to write cantatas on the change of the council. But the first years in Weimar were otherwise again devoted entirely to the field of keyboard music. As court organist he was at the same time also court harpsichordist, and consequently he was obliged to apply himself whole-heatedly to the harpsichord repertoire. For the first time Bach now also took up teaching: among his first pupils was Johann Tobias Krebs, but soon young Bachs also came to him, like his cousin Johann Lorenz and his nephew Johann Bernhard.

Of great significance for Bach was his encounter with the modern Italian style, to which the Weimar court orchestra began to adapt itself. In particular Vivaldi played a part in this, and Bach's involvement with his work (specifically with his 1712 collection of concertos, L'Estro armonico) was immediately reflected in organ transcriptions. A thoroughly worked out setting for the outer voices with concise and unified thematic material and a clearly articulated plan of modulation, which is typical of Vivaldi, from then on remained an essential element in Bach's style of composition. This adoption was indeed coupled with complex counterpoint, distinct and lively texture of middle voices, and harmonic finesse, and thus it was elevated to a highly characteristic and idiosyncratic level.

The years 1713–14 form a definite turning point in Bach's Weimar period: inclined toward independent activity, he applied to succeed Friedrich Wilhelm Zachow, Handel's teacher, as organist of the Liebfrauenkirche in Halle. He submitted a test (probably the cantata "Ich hatte viel Bekümmernis" BWV 21) and was elected in December 1713. With this entry Bach unquestionably exploited to the full the possibilities of composition of larger concerted works. Already in early 1713, during a guest appearance at the court of Weissenfels, he had performed his Hunting Cantata (BWV 208), in which for the first time he made systematic use in a vocal work of elements of Italian style, particularly recitative. This kind of composing must have been very stimulating to him; so it was understandable that he should accept a counteroffer from the court of Weimar and refuse the post in Halle. In March 1714, that is to say, he obtained the appointment of concertmaster while retaining his position as court organist. With that promotion, along with a considerable increase in salary, went above all the responsibility of "performing new works monthly."[5] By this was meant the regular composition and performance of cantatas, a task to which Bach applied himself in the following years with great zeal. There now arose a series of some thirty cantatas of the modern kind (with free-verse texts as the essential basis for the composition of recitatives and da capo arias, which are entirely lacking in the early cantatas). Moreover, to this period belongs a larger Passion music, which has however not been preserved. Alongside vocal works Bach was also busy with keyboard music. Toward the end of his Weimar period, at all events, the greater part of his organ works was completed, as well as a considerable part of his harpsichord compositions. Certainly Bach also wrote at this time a series of orchestral and chamber music works, though nothing has been preserved of them except in the form of later adaptations (like, perhaps, the first and sixth Brandenburg Concertos). Outstanding among the instrumental works is the Orgel-Büchlein, a collection of organ chorales in novel formats, in which the *cantus firmi,* combined with striking motifs, were woven in elaborate counterpoint into highly expressive settings.

Bach was at the peak of his mastery, and it is therefore not to be wondered at that Johann Mattheson, in the earliest reference in print to Bach, commented: "I have seen things by the famous organist of Weimar, Herr Joh. Sebastian Bach, both for the church [i.e. cantatas] and for the hand [i.e. keyboard music] that are certainly such as must make one esteem the man highly" (*Das Beschützte Orchestre,* Hamburg, 1717).[6] In the year 1717 also occurred the contest in improvisation with the French virtuoso Louis Marchand at the court of Dresden, in which Bach was brilliantly victorious (in fact the competition never took place because Marchand refused to participate). So it is only understandable that Bach must have felt himself neglected in the appointment for the post of court capellmeister in Weimar on the death of Johann Samuel Drese (Drese's son received the appointment). He accepted an equivalent offer from the court of Cöthen and left Weimar in anger, after a month's arrest "for his stubborn forcing of the issue of his discharge."[7]

From mid-December 1717 in Cöthen Bach was completely absorbed in his new sphere of work as capellmeister to the prince's court, under an intelligent ruler who was a musical enthusiast. The emphasis of his work lay in the instrumental field, now principally in the sector of orchestral and chamber music. For this he relied on a hand-picked ensemble largely consisting of Berlin musicians, with which it was possible to play the finest and most difficult pieces. Early in 1719 he procured from Berlin a new large harpsichord, which then was presented at the court in the fifth Brandenburg Concerto. He produced concertos for all kinds of instrumentation, over and above the conventional, but also accompanied and unaccompanied solo works, particularly for violin and violoncello. In addition he composed two major keyboard works, the Inventionen und Sinfonien and the first part of the Well-Tempered Clavier. Vocal music plainly fell behind, although he wrote various occasional works, of which only the texts have been preserved.

What made Bach apply in 1720 for the post of organist at St. Jacobi in Hamburg is difficult to understand, in view of his extremely favorable conditions in Cöthen. Probably what attracted him was the famous four-manual Schnitger organ of 1689–1693 (Bach had hitherto never had a really large and fine instrument at his disposal), and possibly also the prospect of working with the renowned cantata-poet Erdmann Neumeister, who as principal minister of the St. Jacobi church was among the supporters of Bach's application. His petition was unsuccessful, however, despite his enthusiastically received organ concerts, since the application was bound up with a not inconsiderable contribution to the church funds. Another, and perhaps the deciding, reason for moving away from Cöthen may be looked for in the domestic tragedy which befell Bach in the summer of 1720, a few months before his journey to Hamburg. While, with the court ensemble, he was entertaining his prince, who was taking the waters in Carlsbad, his wife Maria Barbara, whom he had married in 1707 and who was the mother of his later-famous sons Wilhelm Friedemann and Carl Philipp Emanuel, died. However, a year later he found a new life-partner in the court singer Anna Magdalena Wilcke. From this marriage, contracted in December 1721, later issued the two other great sons, Johann Christoph Friedrich and Johann Christian.

THE REASONS for Bach's move to Leipzig were that circumstances at the court of Cöthen had changed for him through the prince's marriage to an unmusical princess, and that Bach was concerned about the possibilities of education for his growing children, although he "initially did not consider it at all seemly for a capellmeister to become a cantor."[8] He was selected in

April 1723 as successor to Johann Kuhnau, after Georg Philipp Telemann had declined the post and Christoph Graupner was not released from the court of Darmstadt. Previously, on Quinquagesima Sunday (the Sunday before Lent, also known as Estomihi), he had performed in the St. Thomas's Church his musical test, for which he had written the two cantatas "Du wahrer Gott und Davids Sohn" BWV 23 and "Jesus nahm zu sich die Zwölfe" BWV 22. His Leipzig post made a twofold claim on him: as "Cantor zu St. Thomae" he was responsible for the musical education of the pupils of the school at St. Thomas's (he was later exempted from giving them Latin lessons) and for the musical supervision of the four principal churches of Leipzig; and as "Director musices" he was the senior musician of the city and answerable for the musical organization of official occasions like council elections and homage ceremonies. Bach moved to Leipzig in May, and on the thirtieth of that month, the first Sunday after Trinity, performed in St. Nicholas's Church "his first music here, to great approval" (the cantata "Die Elenden sollen essen" BWV 75).[9] With this Bach began an artistic undertaking on the largest scale: in the ensuing years he wrote a cantata for almost every Sunday and church holiday, until he had altogether five complete yearly runs. There were interruptions in this immense process of creation only when he fell back on other works or compositions by others. Embedded in the great continuity of the annual series of cantatas are also found the two great Passions according to St. John (1724) and St. Matthew (1727). The St. Matthew Passion forms a climax, yet at the same time also the conclusion, of the first Leipzig phase, which was spent entirely in the sphere of choir school music. In the approximately twenty years remaining he could in the main draw on the accumulated fund of vocal music through repeat performances. New works for ecclesiastical use arose only in a relatively limited range, including nevertheless compositions such as the Christmas Oratorio and the Masses.

In March 1729 Bach assumed the direction of the Collegium Musicum in Leipzig, founded in his time by Telemann: it was an association of professional musicians and students which each week (more frequently at the time of the Fair) held public concerts. These Collegia Musica played a significant role in the beginnings of middle-class musical culture and public concert life, and in the trade metropolis of Leipzig Bach, with his distinguished ensemble, was not left out. With only a short interruption from 1737 to 1739, Bach retained his directorship until the early 1740s. Unfortunately we know nothing of the programs of the "ordinary" weekly concerts, which took place in winter on Friday evenings from eight until ten o'clock in the Zimmermann coffee house, and in summer on Wednesday afternoons from four to six in the coffee garden "in front of the Grimmische Tor." [10] But Bach's Collegium Musicum would have chiefly played works by their director, including overtures, sinfonias, concertos, duo sonatas and trio sonatas. Certainly the concertos for one or more harpsichords (remolded from Cöthen works), which Bach played with his sons and pupils as soloists, belong here. About the occasional "extraordinary concerts" we are better informed. There were presented most of the large secular cantatas such as, for example, the homage and birthday pieces for the ruling house of Saxony. Work with his Collegium Musicum must often have been, for Bach, a welcome diversion from the difficulties which loomed up in the church music field and of which neither the school authorities nor the city council showed any real understanding. His position was indeed considerably improved by his nomination as court composer to the king of Poland and the elector of Saxony in 1736 (as a consequence of his dedication of the Kyrie and Gloria of the Missa in B Minor in 1733 to the king in Dresden); yet this removed no problems from his path, as for example the long smouldering dispute about the prefects, in which Bach insisted on his right to appoint the leader of the school choral group himself.

Besides his Leipzig public functions, Bach turned increasingly to private interests. Thus he not infrequently went off on concert tours, which took him several times to Dresden and Berlin, among other places. From 1727 he busied himself above all with the publication of his harpsichord and organ works: this was ultimately due to his wide reputation as a clavier virtuoso. In 1731 he was able to open the series of the Clavier-Übungen with his "opus 1" (six Partitas). A second part followed in 1735 (Italian Concerto, French Overture), and a third in 1739 (Mass and Catechism chorales etc. for organ); then about 1742 the last (Goldberg Variations). These publications were later concluded with the Musical Offering (1747), the canonic work Vom Himmel hoch (1747), the Schübler Chorales (1748) and the unfinished Art of Fugue (which appeared in 1751). Besides these publications there still came into being, around 1740, the second part of the Well-Tempered Clavier. From all this industry it is clear how Bach's very own sphere of keyboard music held him captive. In later years he also took the time to sift, tidy up, copy out, or revise older compositions. The composer's generally more reflective attitude made itself decisively felt in the character of most of the later works. His thoughts constantly revolved round refuge and canon in particular. In so doing he in no way closed his mind to contemporary currents in music. Indeed, with types of movement influenced by folk music as well as the *galant* and expressive ideals of style, in Peasant Cantata, Goldberg Variations, or Musical Offering he provided the best examples that he could definitely keep up with the young generation.

In his last years Bach became very weakened and frail through his eye trouble. Presumably from the summer of 1749 he was no longer active in his post, since in June 1749 the Leipzig council had the tactlessness to approve an "audition for a future Cantor of St. Thomas's, in case the Capellmeister and Cantor Herr Sebastian Bach should die"[11] and to nominate Gottlob Harrer as his successor. Two eye operations, which the English oculist John Taylor performed on Bach early in 1750, went badly. On the evening of 28 July 1750 he died as a result of a stroke. The press contained brief obituary notices on the deceased "famous musician."[12] But at that time those who knew his work had scarcely any notion—let alone appreciation—of his greatness.

4

Employers and Patrons

IT WAS IN ACCORDANCE with the inferior status of musicians in the structure of society in the Baroque period that performing and composing should be understood as forms of service. For the most part court, city, and church, as the powers then supporting public musical life, were the employers of musicians and at the same time those who commissioned musical works. A musician's dependence normally covered the complete field of his practical activities, in which, in senior posts, composition was also understood as a matter of course. For a court capellmeister or concertmaster, municipal director of music, organist, or cantor had in the main himself to supply the "utility music" expected of him. The respective demands on a composer were governed by the well-defined traditions and conventions of the institutions in question, and not infrequently even by the precise ideas of their chief representatives—the princes, town councillors, and consistories. Thus a musician's conditions of service to his superior in authority manifested themselves not only in the nature of the commission assigned to him but also, in part, in the form the composition took. For an understanding of Bach's music the question of the external circumstances of his work is therefore of great importance.

The exercise of influence by employers and patrons could work either as a stimulus or a restraint on the productivity and work of the artist. Yet here the composer was clearly at an advantage compared with the librettist. For while all texts, whether sacred or secular, were subject to censorship, musical ideas did not let themselves be determined literally, at any rate not in detail. Nevertheless there was occasional dictation of taste and pressure on style when, for example, a prince insisted on his court musician following French fashions or a church consistory forbade concerted music as unliturgical. Only if economic and social dependence and artistic independence were balanced as of equal importance did favorable conditions present themselves for the development of creative talents. To bring about this equality of importance was of course largely up to the musician himself and the strength of his personal accomplishment. All his life Bach had managed, despite all obligations and subordinate status, to obtain an astonishing personal latitude. He undertook his employments when he could expect something from them and then used to the full all the possibilities they offered him. But as soon as a post became burdensome to him he managed to give it up or at least to provide for suitable compensation.

IN ALL, Bach spent about fifteen years in court posts. These were very crucial years which provided him with musical experience on the widest basis, instrumental as well as vocal, in both sacred and secular fields. Service at court was not only looked upon as of the highest standing but was at the same time also the most varied: musical duties at court ranged from opera through chamber music to music for the court chapel. And that only opera should be missing from the types of work in Bach's output is simply explained, by the fact that he was active only in courts without a theater.

Because his life was spent in such a narrowly restricted area geographically, a special role in Bach's career was played by the Saxon ruling house of Wettin, with its two main branches—the Ernestine, which owned the greater part of the Thuringian petty princedoms, and the Albertine, which possessed the crown of the electorate of Saxony as well as, for a time, that of Poland. Bach's first post took him in 1703 to the court of Duke Johann Ernst of Saxe-Weimar (1664–1707), co-regent with his brother Wilhelm Ernst, whom Bach was to serve later. Bach was taken in as a "lackey" [1] among those employed in the Red Castle in Weimar, although probably he was mostly active as a violinist in the duke's small private band. He retained this post, however, only for a few months, from which it can be deduced that the work, which involved numerous subservient minor duties, could not have been exactly fascinating.

Five years later Bach returned to the court of Weimar, by now under Wilhelm Ernst of Saxe-Weimar (1662–1728), residing in the Wilhelmsburg. The duke was a man very devoted to the arts, above all poetry, painting, and music. Bach first of all worked for him as chamber musician and court organist, and "the pleasure His Grace took in his playing fired him with the desire to try every possible artistry in his treatment of the organ." [2] Wilhelm Ernst was very open to new styles in music, and by the acquisition of musical works provided his court orchestra of twenty-two musicians with the opportunity of examining the newest Italian literature. Thus Bach had the chance to become familiar with Vivaldi's concerto structure, in particular. The pious duke was principally interested in church affairs and hence accorded a special place to church music. In 1714, on Bach's promotion to concertmaster, he commissioned him to write church cantatas regularly. Here too modernism was cultivated: the new type of cantata with free-verse recitatives and arias allowed Bach to adopt essential elements of Italian instrumental and vocal construction. The texts were mostly supplied to him by the Weimar court poet, librarian, and chief secretary of the consistory, Salomo Franck (1659–1725).

During his activity in Weimar Bach also came into close contact with Prince Johann Ernst (1696–1715), a composition pupil of Johann Gottfried Walther and extremely gifted musically, who died young. The organ concertos in C and G major (BWV 595 and 592) were arrangements of works by the young prince. When his elder brother, Duke Ernst August (1688–1748), who was co-regent from 1709, married Princess Eleonore Wilhelmine of Anhalt-Cöthen in 1716, Bach provided the music for the ceremony. And it was on this occasion that the bride's brother, Prince Leopold (later his employer), came to know and appreciate him.

Bach had already achieved such a reputation as a composer in Weimar that outside engagements and commissions could not be lacking. The first ascertainable guest appearance took him in February 1713 to Weissenfels and established the close connection which lasted for many years with the princely court there. At that period he wrote, for the birthday of Duke Christian of Saxe-Weissenfels (1682–1736), the Hunting Cantata "Was mir behagt, ist nur die muntre Jagd" (BWV 208). He again traveled to a guest appearance in Weissenfels from Leipzig in 1729 on the occasion of receiving the title of capellmeister to the court of Saxe-Weissenfels.

In the year 1717 Bach left Weimar to become capellmeister (a position that had hitherto been denied him) at the court of Anhalt-Cöthen. There he found in Prince Leopold (1694–1728) a "great connoisseur and amateur of music,"[3] an employer who gave him his friendship. Before assuming sovereignty Leopold had made extensive artistic and educational journeys through Holland, England, and Italy and had formed the ambition to surround himself with musicians of the first rank. He himself evidently possessed some instrumental dexterity and had been for a short while a pupil of Johann David Heinichen. Bach now had a free rein. In contrast to Weimar, church music in Cöthen remained very much in the background, certainly because of the Calvinist persuasion of the prince's house. The numerous court festivities gave him instead all the more opportunities to devote himself to secular solo cantatas. Unfortunately only a fraction of the Cöthen vocal repertoire has been preserved. Nevertheless Bach's real sphere of activity at this time was instrumental ensemble composition. For the demanding chamber music works he relied on an efficient, hand-picked ensemble, about whose regular rehearsals a notice of 1722 records that "even the most famous virtuosi rehearse and practice their material together beforehand, of which we have a clear example in the prince's orchestra here, which holds its Exercitium musicum every week."[4] Bach wrote orchestral music, particularly concertos, as well as works for small ensemble, especially duo and trio sonatas.

From Cöthen Bach also came into contact for the first time with the Berlin court; that was on the occasion of the purchase of a new harpsichord for the court orchestra, which he himself fetched from Berlin in the spring of 1719. Two years later he sent to the margrave Christian Ludwig of Brandenburg (1677–1734), for the court orchestra at the Berlin Schloss, six concertos, in the dedication to which he refers to the earlier visit: "As a couple of years ago I had the pleasure of being heard by Your Royal Highness at your command, and as I then noticed that Your Highness took some pleasure in the small talents for music which Heaven has granted me, and as on taking my leave Your Royal Highness deigned to honor me with the command to send you some pieces of my composition, so I have, in accordance with your most gracious orders, taken the liberty of rendering my most humble duty to Your Royal Highness with the present concertos, which I have disposed for several instruments"[5] [original in French].

His happy conditions in Cöthen changed early in 1722 with the marriage of Prince Leopold. Bach later reported in a letter to his childhood friend Erdmann that at that time he had had the impression that "the musical inclinations of the said prince were becoming somewhat lukewarm, particularly as the new princess [Friederica Henrietta of Anhalt-Bernburg] seemed unmusical."[6] This reveals the extent to which the musician depended on his employer's favor. Bach had no alternative but to take the consequences and to look about for a new post. However, he did not sever his connections with Cöthen altogether, but returned several times (1724, 1725, and 1728) for guest performances at the court. As a token of genuine affection, on the birth of the hereditary prince Emanuel Ludwig on 12 September 1726 (Prince Leopold had in 1725 taken as his second wife Charlotte Friederica Wilhelmine of Nassau-Siegen), Bach sent the autograph of his Partita I (BWV 825), subsequently printed, with a small dedicatory poem, in which he said:

> Forgive me if I wake thee from sleep
> while the playing of my page
> does homage to thee.
> It is the first fruit that my strings yield;
> thou art the first prince
> thy Princess has kissed . . .[7]

In 1729 the court of Cöthen called him for the last time "to prepare in Leipzig the funeral music for the prince he had so dearly loved and to perform it in person in Cöthen"[8] (in the words of the obituary).

With his departure from Cöthen Bach finally quitted court employment. Indirectly, it is true, in Leipzig he also came under the authority of the elector of Saxony. He knew how to make skillful use of this situation, though not always with the desired result, when in various disputes with his Leipzig superiors he addressed himself directly to the Dresden court, to whom he had been known since the memorable contest with the French harpsichordist Louis Marchand in 1717. Thus it was also in the first instance a political move when in 1733 Bach presented the elector Friedrich August II (1696–1764) with the Kyrie and Gloria of the Mass in B Minor, with the aim of obtaining the title of a court composer. The choice of this "interdenominational" subject was precisely because of the conversion of the reigning electoral house to Catholicism: by this means Friedrich August I (Augustus the Strong, 1670–1733) had acquired the Polish crown. Bach indeed secured the desired title only in 1736, but in so doing his relations with the court of Dresden became institutionalized, as it were. Whether in fact in this connection there happened to be any concrete commissions for compositions remains unknown. Possibly he supplied the four short Masses (BWV 233–236) for the Protestant service in Dresden (the estates of the realm were not converted!), if they were not intended for the Bohemian Count Franz Anton von Sporck (1662–1738), who between 1724 and 1727 had borrowed the parts of the Sanctus of the B Minor Mass (Bach noted in his own hand in the score of the Sanctus: "the parts are in Bohemia with Count Sporck").[9]

Through his Dresden connections Bach came into contact with the circles of the higher aristocracy. Among the personalities in question Hermann Carl, Count von Keyserlingk (1696–1764), occupies a special place as a patron of Bach's. Through his intervention Bach's nomination was finally effected as court composer to the king of Poland and the elector of Saxony.[10] The count maintained a small private band, in which a pupil of Bach's and of his son Wilhelm Friedemann was engaged as harpsichordist: Johann Gottlieb Goldberg. An anecdote later handed down to tradition links the genesis of the Aria mit verschiedenen Veränderungen (BWV 988) with Keyserlingk and Goldberg: "The count was often sickly, and then had sleepless nights. At these times Goldberg, who lived in the house with him, had to pass the night in an adjoining room to play something to him when he could not sleep. The count once said to Bach that he would like to have some clavier pieces for his Goldberg, which should be of such a soft and somewhat lively character that he might be a little cheered up by them in his sleepless nights. Bach thought he could best fulfil this wish by variations . . . The count thereafter called them nothing but *his* variations. He was never weary of hearing them; and for a long time, when the sleepless nights came, he used to say, 'Dear Goldberg, do play me one of my variations.'"[11]

Count Keyserlingk, from 1746 ambassador to the court of Berlin, was certainly also instrumental in arranging Bach's visit to Frederick the Great (1712–1786) in Potsdam. To this memorable event in 1747 the Musical Offering owes its origin. Bach dedicated to the Prussian king, not as a commissioned work but of his own free will, a printed work "whose noblest part derives from Your Majesty's own august hand"[12] (in the words of Bach's dedication). By this he alludes to the theme which the king had given him and which underlies every movement of the work. Moreover it includes as a principal movement a trio sonata for flute, violin, and continuo as a special homage to the flute-playing Frederick.

Two other Dresden court officials can also be mentioned as direct patrons of commissioned compositions. The minister Johann Christian von Hennicke (1681–1752) ordered from Bach some music for the celebration of his becoming lord of the manor in Wiederau, near Leipzig. Bach wrote the *dramma per musica*, "Angenehmes Wiederau" (BWV 30a). Three years later, for a similar occasion, he performed the so-called Peasant Cantata (BWV 212) in the manor of Klein-Zschocher, near Leipzig, at the behest of Carl

Heinrich von Dieskau (1706–1782), director of music for the royal chapel and chamber in Dresden; with its elements from folk music, this is unusual in Bach's output.

BACH'S LIFELONG ASSOCIATION with court circles should not obscure the fact that he spent the greater part of his professional career under ecclesiastical and municipal employers. The conditions of work here were, compared with those at court, generally more restricted and more regimented, as is reflected in the contrasts of employment and service instructions of the time. The reasons are obvious: music in court circles was seen principally as the natural expression of a luxurious, feudal way of life which set few limits on expenditure, while in the spheres of church and city music was a traditional and functional element of which it was wished to make the greatest possible use with the smallest possible means. Herein are to be seen the main causes for the various conflicts of interests which, if fewer in Arnstadt and Mühlhausen, arose all the more clearly later in Leipzig.

Bach's tenure at Arnstadt got off to a good and promising start with a splendid new organ and a benevolent consistory. But the church authorities' notions of church music soon collided with the young organist's temperament and plans. Certainly Bach had contributed to the discord through diverse gaucheries (such as "going into the wine-cellar during the sermon"),[13] but it was the consistory's interference in his administration that finally made Bach quit his post in 1707. He was expected to perform concerted music. In view of the undisciplined and unqualified choir of pupils, Bach considered this unreasonable. The clergy was disturbed, again, that Bach should present solo vocal pieces with the cooperation of that "stranger maid"[14] (probably Maria Barbara, whom he later married). Moreover, they objected to Bach's manifestly too virtuosic way of playing chorales.

The reasons for Bach's short stay as organist of the church of St. Blasius in Mühlhausen were clearly set out in Bach's request for discharge to the town council, the authority responsible for his employment. According to that, he had not in his position succeeded in achieving "a well-regulated church music"—that is, regular performances of cantatas on Sundays.[15] The cause lay in certain "hindrances" related to the theological dissension then smoldering in Mühlhausen and elsewhere between orthodox Lutherans and Pietists. The Pietists, whose champion was Bach's immediate superior, the superintendent Johann Adolf Frohne (1652–1713), aimed at a drastic reduction of traditional and modern concerted music in favor of simple and elevating congregational singing. It should not be surprising that Bach adopted the opposite side, to which also belonged the pastor of St. Mary's Church, Georg Christian Eilmar (1665–1715). At his commission (and probably also for that church) Bach wrote the cantata "Aus der Tiefen rufe ich" BWV 131, openly noting in his own hand on the title page of the score: "set to music at the request of Herr D. Georg Christian Eilmar."[16] It is probable that Eilmar also compiled the text, which was entirely based on words from the Bible and from a chorale. This cantata belongs—together with the "Actus Tragicus" (BWV 106), a funeral work for an unknown patron, and the festal music ordered by the Mühlhausen city council for the change of the council (BWV 71) and later printed—among Bach's earliest commissioned works. At that time, to be sure, single commissioned compositions appealed to him less than the possibility of a regular and steady production of large concerted works. The opportunity for this first presented itself to him about fifteen years later in Leipzig.

When he assumed the distinguished position, rich in traditions, of cantor at St. Thomas's and Director Musices in Leipzig in 1723, Bach entered an employment whose complexity was matched only by the extent of his field of activity there. Servant of three masters, as it were, he was subordinate to the city council as the supervisory body, then to the rector of the St. Thomas's School and to the church superintendent as his immediate superiors.

The council had unanimously appointed Bach after the submission of a test, but in the final analysis it showed little understanding of Bach's real importance. The council—and not it alone—was never aware that between 1723 and 1750 Bach had created and performed in Leipzig an exceptionally varied musical repertoire of such quality as could have put the musical centers of the world at that time into the shade. When Bach desperately demanded more resources (as in his famous memorandum of 23 August 1730), with the argument that "state of music is quite different from what it was, since our artistry has very much increased, and taste has changed astonishingly: accordingly the former style of music no longer pleases our ears, and considerable help is therefore all the more needed," [17] the council evidently could not understand his plea. It left unchanged the number of town musicians placed under Bach at seven, as had been customary since the seventeenth century and which at that time had sufficed. On this point Bach was reprimanded, since by instrumental instruction he could enlist the desired extra forces free of charge from the pupils themselves, not taking into account that by so doing he would simultaneously be sacrificing his best singers.

Thus to the end of his activity in Leipzig Bach remained dependent on voluntary collaboration, particularly of university students. And it is not surprising if at the appointment of Bach's successor to the post a voice was raised in the council: "We need a cantor, not a capellmeister." [18] The city did not wish to show any musical ambitions; Mercury's aria in Bach's cantata of homage to the municipal council (BWV 216a) alludes to its real main interest:

> My trade, which here
> I firmly plant,
> shall provide you with
> the greatest part of your lustre. [19]

At the school Bach lived through three rectorates in all: 1684–1729, Johann Heinrich Ernesti (1652–1729: for his funeral Bach wrote the motet "Der Geist hilft unser Schwachheit auf" BWV 226); 1730–1734, Johann Matthias Gesner (1691–1761); 1734–1759, Johann August Ernesti (1707–1781). The management of the school had in the first instance to consider the orderly curriculum and the quality of the tuition. Here there easily arose conflicts between the rectors, who as noted scholars also taught at the university and paid great attention to the school's academic level, and the cantor, who on the admission of boarders had to place musical before academic considerations and had constantly to tire the pupils out with rehearsals, performances, music copying, and so on. While, above all, between the younger Ernesti and Bach no good relations prevailed, Bach had a close alliance, even on an intimate basis, with Gesner, who held office only for a short time (and who was appointed as a classical philologist to the newly founded University of Göttingen). From Gesner we also possess the sole detailed contemporary account of Bach as conductor, keyboard player, and organist:

> You would regard this all, Fabius, as totally insignificant if you . . . could see Bach; . . . how with all the fingers of both hands he played our clavier, which in itself contains many citharas in one; or the organ, whose innumerable pipes were brought to life by bellows, hurrying over the keys here with both hands, there with swift feet, producing by himself the most varied but also mutually harmonious sounds: if you could see how, when he is conducting . . . he watches over everything at the same time, and holds to the rhythm and beat 30 or even 40 musicians, this one by a nod of the head, another by tapping his foot, a third by a warning finger, giving the note to one in the upper part, to another in the lower, to a third in the middle register; how all alone, amid the loudest playing by the musicians, although he himself has the most difficult part, he yet immediately notices if anything is wrong anywhere; how he holds everyone together and corrects everywhere, restoring security if there is anywhere a weakness; how he feels the pulse in his every limb, checks all the harmonies with a keen ear, and produces all the voices from his own limited throat. Though an enthusiastic worshipper of antiquity, I believe that friend Bach outshines Orpheus many times and Arion twenty times.[20]

During Bach's whole time in Leipzig Salomon Deyling (1677–1755) held the post of superintendent in Leipzig. The relationship between the two seems to have been one of mutual respect. Within the given liturgical framework Deyling had obviously guaranteed Bach the scope he needed to realize his ideas on church music. On his appointment he had to guarantee "not to make music operatically."[21] Objections in this regard never arose from the side of the consistory. So in this connection he could follow up his own plans and ideals for church music uninfluenced, which he did especially in his first years in Leipzig, with great dedication and the utmost expenditure of his personality. The chief emphasis plainly lay on the so-called Sunday Hauptmusic, the cantata, which for a long time in Leipzig was considered an integral ingredient of the liturgy.[22] The placing of the cantata next to the sermon indicates their comparable functions in regard to the promulgation of the Bible. The external formal structure of the cantata therefore also follows the traditional pattern of the sermon and falls into four sections: (a) introductory text (quotation from the Bible or a hymn); (b) poetic exegesis and (c) guidance in living (respectively in recitative and aria); (d) chorale as closing prayer. Until 1728–29 Bach created with quite unbelievable industry the major part of a repertoire of five annual cantata cycles, on which he could draw in the following two decades. The St. Matthew Passion of 1727 constitutes the great keystone of this most intensive period of sacred production.

In the 1730s a change came into Bach's life and activity which was utterly decisive. His assumption of the direction of the Collegium Musicum in 1729, which he then ran for twelve years under his own management, and his increasing involvement with the printing of his own works make it clear that he more and more wished to make himself independent of his Leipzig employers. The rhythm of his production was now dictated by his own initiatives toward composition, particularly of keyboard music and of larger commissioned works which thronged upon him, above all from the university and from wealthy citizens. Congratulatory cantatas, homage, wedding, and funeral music came into being in great quantities. The more important events, like the homage music of the university on the occasion of the anniversary of the election of the Polish king on 5 October 1734 (Bach's cantata "Preise dein Glücke, gesegnetes Sachsen BWV 215), were even reflected in the annals of the city: "Toward nine o'clock in the evening the students of the university here most humbly offered His Majesty an evening serenade with trumpets and drums which Herr Capellmeister Johann Sebastian Bach, Cantor at St. Thomas's, composed. Whereby 600 students carried pure wax tapers and four counts as marshals led off the music . . . On presenting the libretto the four counts were allowed to kiss hands. Afterwards His Royal Majesty, with his Royal Consort and the Royal Princes, did not leave the window for as long as the music lasted, but most graciously listened, and His Majesty was heartily well pleased."[23] Bach probably did not very often receive approbation of this kind, at least not from his Leipzig masters. This must have driven him to seek contact with appreciative patrons or to follow a direct course to musical "connoisseurs and amateurs" through his own publishing activities (as with the four parts of the Clavier-Übung).[24] Only in this way could a satisfying degree of independence be attained, and therewith a balance between official duty and personal inclination. Toward the end of his life Bach came astonishingly close to the romantic ideal of the freelance artist.

5

Buxtehude, Bach, and Seventeenth-Century
Music in Retrospect

FROM A MODERN PERSPECTIVE, it is no easy task to define the position of Dietrich Buxtehude in the history of music. To be sure, he readily and rightly escaped the fate of being labeled a "Kleinmeister," a minor master, largely on account of his extensive and extraordinarily original output of organ music. Nevertheless, in virtually every aspect of his creative activity he continues to be perceived primarily as forerunner or predecessor. The influence of nineteenth-century music historiography, with its emphasis on single heroic figures, has long hindered the historical and aesthetic evaluation of numerous important composers as artists in their own right. Though certain composers—and Buxtehude figures prominently among them—are frequently and correctly characterized as having been part of the "background" for a later master's achievements, they of course made their contributions without being able to anticipate the subsequent evolution of styles and genres.

No less a musicological authority than Philipp Spitta expressly evoked in his Bach biography[1] the image of Buxtehude as forerunner. He placed clear emphasis on Buxtehude the organist, an image that he subsequently reinforced with the first critical edition of Buxtehude's complete organ works.[2] The relationship between the older master and Bach appeared to him so close that he proceeded in his edition to title Buxtehude's multisectional preludes and toccatas as "prelude and fugue" or "toccata and fugue." This unfortunate distortion, though it served his argument, went contrary both to the evidence of the sources and to the structure of the compositions themselves. The serious consequences of this artificial terminology have been with us ever since, and they have surely played a role in the prevailing inadequate perception of the interrelationship of two very different organ repertoires and their premises.

Spitta developed little if any interest in the vocal output of Dietrich Buxtehude, and therefore he chose not to complement his edition of the organ works with the publication of Buxtehude's vocal music. Furthermore, his knowledge of the vocal repertoire was necessarily quite limited, since the majority of Buxtehude's surviving vocal works were discovered only in the late 1880s in the Düben Collection at Uppsala.[3] Spitta's prejudices against the quality of Buxtehude's vocal music prevailed even after André Pirro's extensive Buxtehude monograph, where much space was devoted to discussion of the vocal works.[4] Not until 1925, nearly fifty years after Spitta's edition of the *Orgelcompositionen* was there a first attempt at a vocal sequel, this time in conjunction with an ambitious project for a complete edition. Unfortunately, the project was several times subjected to lengthy interruptions. Today, more than half a century later, only nine of a projected fourteen or fifteen vocal volumes have been published.[5] Nevertheless, the available volumes, together with a detailed *catalogue raisonné* of Buxtehude's oeuvre,[6] set the quantitative record straight: not only the vocal works but also Buxtehude's chamber works far outnumber his organ compositions. Yet neither the chamber music nor the vocal works have made any significant impact in twentieth-century musical life. A partial exception is the cantata "Alles was ihr tut" (BuxWV 4), yet although the piece has achieved at least some degree of renown, it is a composition utterly unrepresentative of the overall quality and artistic goals of Buxtehude's vocal works. Its fame has not contributed to any truly increased awareness of the hidden riches of Buxtehude's oeuvre; if anything, its isolated popularity has only served to reemphasize the one-sided preference for the organ music and to reaffirm the persistent image of Buxtehude as forerunner.

Hence, modern-day Buxtehude reception will most likely continue to focus first and foremost on Buxtehude as organist. The subtitle of Kerala Snyder's recent monograph[7] typically refers to the "organist in Lübeck" rather than to the "world-renowned, incomparable musician and composer" (Weltberühmte Hr. Diederich Buxtehude, Unvergleichlicher MUSICUS und COMPONISTE), as Buxtehude is addressed on the title page of Johann Caspar Ulich's mourning poem on his death (Lübeck, 1707).[8] To which Buxtehude is Ulich referring? Certainly to the organist of St. Mary's, but Buxtehude considered himself to be more than merely that: "Musicus" stands for the broadly oriented and talented universal musician, "Componiste" for the composer who, in a general sense, is creative, active, and productive in all branches of music. If we wish to understand the notably high esteem accorded to Buxtehude at the time of his death, we need to consider him from the perspective of an early-eighteenth-century observer, who would have placed him within the context of seventeenth-century music. And to determine what contributed to the narrowing of Buxtehude's reputation, we must consider later-eighteenth-century opinions as well.

AMONG THE MOST COMPETENT, knowledgeable, and reliable observers of the German and European music scene of the early eighteenth century was the lexicographer Johann Gottfried Walther. Through his close personal connections with Buxtehude's friend Andreas Werckmeister, he acquired for his collection many manuscript copies of Buxtehude's keyboard music, specifically autograph tablature copies of the organ chorales.[9] Walther's Buxtehude article in the *Musicalisches Lexicon* (Leipzig, 1732)[10] disappoints, however, in virtually every respect. Besides presenting only meager biographical information, it contains an extremely abbreviated worklist, and there is scant reference to the scope of Buxtehude's output or to his general reputation. Though we owe to Walther the preservation of the bulk of Buxtehude's organ chorales,[11] his famous dictionary contributed little to the documentation of Buxtehude's accomplishments.

The first more comprehensive article on Buxtehude appeared in Ernst Ludwig Gerber's *Neues historisch-biographisches Lexikon der Tonkünstler* (Leipzig, 1812).[12] The article reveals surprisingly detailed knowledge, despite Gerber's own complaint regarding the general difficulty of obtaining works by Buxtehude; he specifically mentions that not even the otherwise extensive Breitkopf collection in Leipzig contains Buxtehudiana. Nevertheless, Gerber cites twelve published items (among them librettos of the Abendmusiken) and mentions in particular the "profound" quality of Buxtehude's keyboard pieces. Although Gerber himself owned only two Buxtehude compositions, and those in somewhat flawed manuscript versions, he states that these suffice for recognition of "the lion by its paws," and that in one piece only the mention of the composer's name in the title prevents him from attributing the work to Johann Sebastian Bach.[13]

For Ernst Ludwig Gerber, Bach provides the obvious and appropriate frame of reference for Buxtehude. We must assume that this starting point reflects a tradition based on the experience of his father, Heinrich Nicolaus Gerber, who had studied during the 1720s with Bach in Leipzig. For Johann Sebastian Bach, Dietrich Buxtehude was anything but an empty name. It seems reasonable, therefore, to attempt to consider Buxtehude from a Bachian perspective, at least as far as that is possible. Interestingly enough, it appears that it was with none other than Bach that the disproportionate emphasis on Buxtehude's organ music originated. As the transmission of the sources indicates, neither Buxtehude's vocal works, nor his chamber music, nor even his harpsichord suites or variations were cultivated in the Bach circle. The organ works, however, especially the large-scale pedaliter preludes and toccatas, owe their principal and most reliable, if selective, transmission largely to their importance within the collecting, teaching, and performing activities of Johann Sebastian Bach and his circle.[14] Certain pieces, such as the three ostinato compositions (BuxWV 159–61) or the Prelude in F♯ Minor (BuxWV 146), survived not in North German or Scandinavian tablature sources, but rather in unique copies from the inner Bach circle. It cannot, therefore, be considered a mere coincidence that Spitta saw in Buxtehude the culmination point of organ music before Bach. Bach's contemporaries, as Johann Joachim Quantz testifies, had already taken this position: "The organists and clavier players—among the latter especially Froberger and Pachelbel, and among the former Reinken, Buxtehude, Bruhns and some others—were almost the first to contrive the most tasteful instrumental compositions of their period for their instruments. But particularly the art of organ playing, which had to a great extent been learned from the Netherlanders, was already at this time in a high state of advancement, thanks to the above-mentioned and some other able men. Finally the admirable Johann Sebastian Bach brought it to its greatest perfection in recent times." [15]

To Bach, Dietrich Buxtehude must indeed have appeared as the most impressive representative of an earlier generation, an earlier era, an earlier century. Bach of course encountered other major representatives of the late seventeenth century as well. For instance, he knew Johann Kuhnau from a joint organ examination in Halle in 1716. Later, as Kuhnau's successor in Leipzig, he had to accustom himself to a profoundly traditional office and perspective. Even for the young Bach, connections with the older generation were already manifold. There were distinguished musicians within his own family, especially Johann Christoph Bach of Eisenach. His Ohrdruf brother, Johann Christoph, provided a direct link with Johann Pachelbel. Georg Böhm of Lüneburg and Johann Adam Reinken of Hamburg opened up for him the idiosyncratic North German scene. The influence of all these notables, however, was greatly surpassed by that of Buxtehude, whose artistic impact on the young Bach was far stronger and far more enduring. In addition, the reaction of Bach and his circle to the compositions of the Lübeck master ultimately resulted in the beginning of a Buxtehude reception, one that fundamentally affected later impressions of that composer.

The virtually exclusive emphasis on Buxtehude the organist is not characteristic of the young Bach, but rather of the mature composer, who included Buxtehude's vocal compositions in the category of "the former style of music" that "no longer seems to please our ears." [16] Bach, defending himself in 1706 when reproved for prolonged absence, told the Arnstadt consistory that "he had been to Lübeck [to visit Buxtehude] in order to comprehend one thing and another about his art" (*umb daselbst ein und anderes in seiner Kunst zu begreifen*). [17] This formulation is kept deliberately general and is certainly not limited to keyboard music. What in particular could Bach have learned from Buxtehude's art? To answer this question, we must first attempt to understand what Buxtehude's music represented at the very beginning of the eighteenth century. It was music that reflected a broad spectrum of compositional choices and stylistic possibilities, since Buxtehude was no composer of narrow specialization but rather one who aimed at the ideal type of the universal musician.

The following discussion will examine Buxtehude's music in retrospect and specifically from the vantage point of the young Johann Sebastian Bach, first in more general terms and then on the basis of a close examination of two representative compositions.

IT CANNOT BE mere coincidence that Buxtehude attracted the attention of the two men who were later recognized as the most significant composers of the first half of the eighteenth century. Prior to Bach's Lübeck trip, Handel and his companion Johann Mattheson had paid a short visit to Buxtehude in 1703, from which they returned with powerful impressions.[18] For Bach's stated aim to "comprehend one thing and another about his art," a short visit would not have sufficed; he stayed for more than three months. Why and to what end? Certainly not just to get to know and perhaps copy organ compositions so far unknown to him. Certainly not only to attend, and perhaps participate in, the two *extraordinaire Abend-Musiken* ("Castrum doloris" BuxWV 134 and "Templum honoris" BuxWV 135) in December 1705. Certainly not only to explore the possibilities for employment, if this aspect played a role at all.

For both Handel and Bach, Buxtehude must have represented a kind of "father figure," one who anticipated in many ways the ideal of a later type: the autonomous composer. The bourgeois, commercial, and liberal atmosphere of the free imperial city of Lübeck provided Buxtehude with considerable flexibility in developing and realizing his own various projects. He, of course, held the position of organist at St. Mary's Church, an office with specific duties. Nevertheless, his overall activities were characterized by a display of artistic initiative combined with unusual managerial independence. Courtly service would not have permitted such free conduct. Buxtehude was able to develop his career as a virtuoso, he traveled, and he surrounded himself with pupils. He seized opportunities for composing vocal works of both sacred and secular orientation, and as his own impresario, he organized and financed performances of large-scale Abendmusiken. For this purpose he created a new oratorio type far beyond the scope of the Carissimi model, and he regularly published the librettos for these works as well. In order to broaden the compass of his activities he printed two chamber music collections, the sonatas op. 1 and sonatas op. 2 of 1694 and 1696, respectively. In other words, Buxtehude conducted his organist office very much in the style of a municipal capellmeister, thereby providing a clear role model for Telemann in Hamburg and Bach in Leipzig.

Buxtehude exemplified the ideal type of the universal musician in a number of additional ways. First, he balanced theory and practice. Since the generation of Michael Praetorius or even earlier, scholarly theoretical erudition had belonged among the prerequisites for a preeminent musical office, and Buxtehude was no exception. His theoretical background reflected the Italian tradition of Zarlino (supplied most likely through Matthias Weckmann and Reinken),[19] but in comparison with Christoph Bernhard or Johann Theile, Buxtehude placed more emphasis on practice with a strong theoretical foundation. Rather than writing treatises, he demonstrated his contrapuntal sophistication in diverse practical applications, such as the Missa Brevis (BuxWV 114), the Klag-Lied of 1675 (BuxWV 76), and the canons (BuxWV 123–124).[20] In this regard, Buxtehude proceeded in a manner comparable to that of Bach in the Well-Tempered Clavier, the Art of Fugue, and similar works.

Second, Buxtehude involved himself in organology and the technology of musical instruments. As a widely recognized organ expert, he held close ties with Andreas Werckmeister, seventeenth-century Germany's premier musical scientist and speculative theorist. Buxtehude not only became the most prominent advocate of Werckmeister's new systems of temperament,[21] but also explored in his works the immediate compositional implications of a more flexible and expressive harmonic language (through employment of keys with three and more sharps and flats, as well as through a notable preference for "functional" harmony, with frequent use of double dominants and the like).

Third, Buxtehude's compositional orientation included a broad spectrum of styles and genres:

1. Retrospective as well as modern tendencies complemented each other (as in the music of Monteverdi or Schütz).
2. Dutch and Hanseatic traditions (Sweelinck, Scheidemann, Reinken), English elements (viola da gamba writing), French manners (*style brisé* in keyboard music, Lully-style opera chorus in vocal music), and Italian influence (Frescobaldi, Legrenzi, Carissimi) are discernible, but Buxtehude always aimed at synthesizing them.
3. Practically all new genres of the seventeenth century can be found in his music: concerto, motet, chorale, aria (strophic and free), and recitative in the vocal realm; toccata/prelude, fugue, ciacona/passacaglia, canzona, suite, sonata, dance, and variation in the instrumental realm.

Fourth, around 1678, Buxtehude created the prototype of the large-scale, multisectional German oratorio on the basis of his detailed knowledge of the Hamburg opera convention.[22] Typical is the title of an oratorio presented in 1684: *Himmlische Seelenlust auf Erden über die Menschwerdung und Geburt unsers allerliebsten Heil- und Seligmachers Jesu Christi, in 5 unterschiedlichen Abhandlungen auf der Operen Art mit vielen Arien und Ritornellen . . .* Keiser's and Telemann's oratorios as well as Handel's English oratorios profited from Buxtehude's ideas. Bach's Christmas Oratorio followed the Buxtehude pattern with respect to the presentation of a unified multisectional work over several weeks.

Fifth, Buxtehude redirected two well-established genres of organ music by drawing inspiration from the compositions of his North German predecessors and contemporaries (primarily Scheidemann, Tunder, Weckmann, and Reinken). He established two predominant types: first, the monodic organ chorale for two manuals and pedal with melismatic *cantus firmus* and structured, polyphonic accompaniment, in both large-scale (chorale fantasia) and small-scale formats; and second, the Praeludium pedaliter as an extended unit of five to seven parts, integrating the aesthetic concept of the *stylus phantasticus* and the formal and compositional devices of the ensemble sonata.

Consideration of Buxtehude and his music in light of the major compositional and stylistic tendencies of the seventeenth century reveals that his works virtually never rely on specific, identifiable models. Yet Buxtehude embodies all the distinguishing features of a powerful integrating figure. He combined as well as redirected various style and form tendencies, with compositional results that are as highly original as they are ambitious. Particularly characteristic in this respect are his oratorios (in their curious mixture of opera and traditional church music), the pedaliter organ preludes, and to a certain extent his keyboard suites with their early, perhaps even prototypical movement order (Allemande-Courante-Sarabande-Gigue).[23] There is no seventeenth-century musician who, in comparison with Bach, shows as many clear analogies in virtually all major areas, theoretical and practical.

TWO REPRESENTATIVE EXAMPLES may serve to illustrate Buxtehude's ability to sum up in his vocal and instrumental music the principal achievements of the seventeenth century. These are the "Templum honoris" (BuxWV 135) and the Praeludium in G Minor (BuxWV 149).

"Templum honoris" (BuxWV 135)

This oratorio was performed on 3 December 1705, one day after its companion piece, "Castrum doloris" (BuxWV 134). It seems reasonable to assume that Johann Sebastian Bach, who stayed in Lübeck for approximately four months until early February 1706, would not have missed the performances of these major and unique Abendmusiken. With these two works, respectively, the free imperial city of Lübeck mourned the death of Emperor Leopold I and paid homage to his successor, Joseph I. If Bach was indeed present, he was in all probability not merely a member of the audience, but rather a participant in the very large performing ensemble under Buxtehude's direction. After all, Bach had to finance his extended trip, and offering his services as violinist or keyboard player would have been a logical course of action for the young and ambitious professional musician. The music of "Templum honoris" has not survived, as is the case with virtually all of Buxtehude's oratorios. The printed libretto, however, has come down to us and supplies a number of crucial details that also allow us to infer some of the more important musical features[24] (see Figs. 5.1 and 5.2). Thus it is possible to form a general impression of what the young Bach may have experienced.

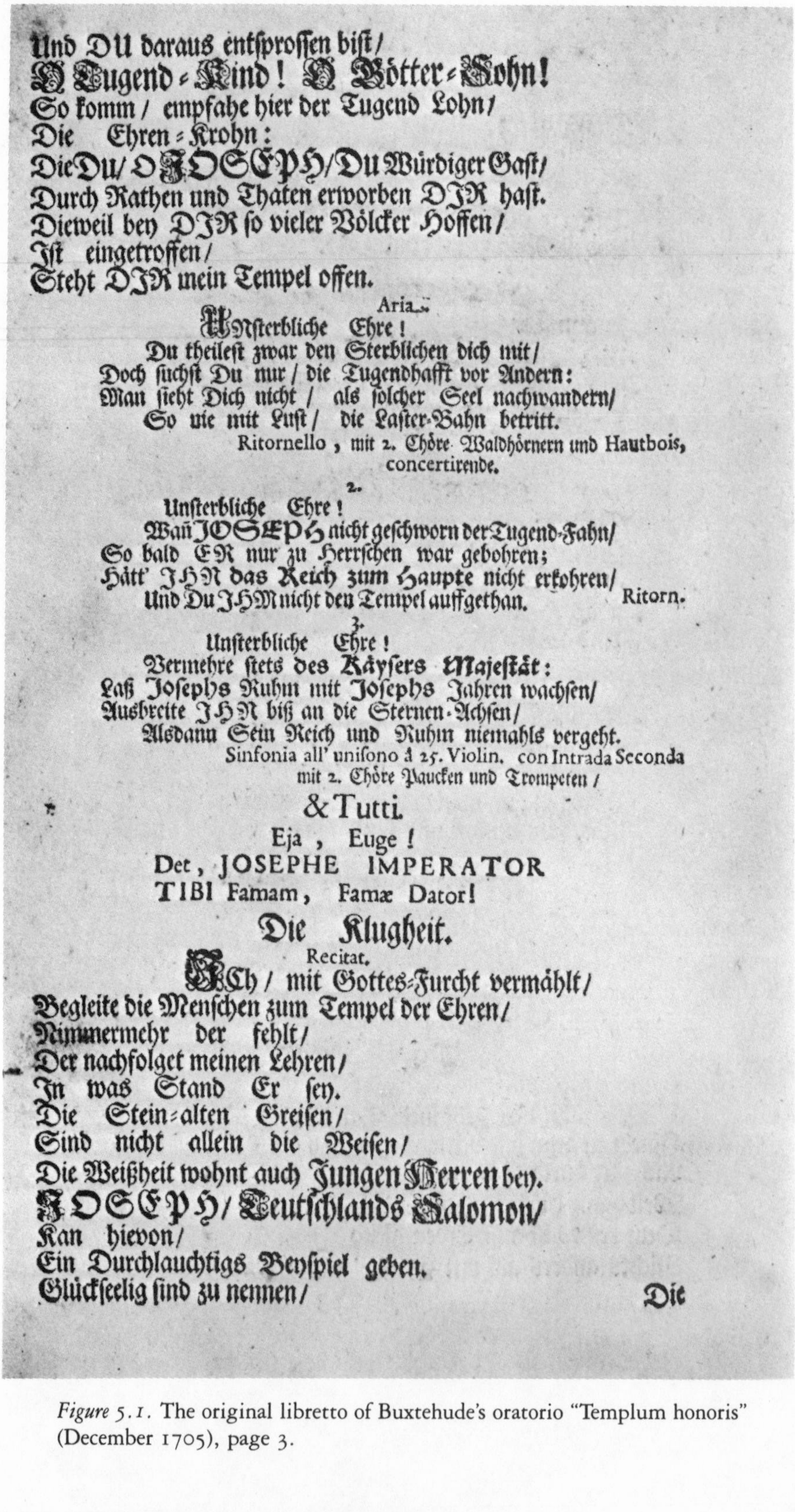

Und DU daraus entsprossen bist/
O Tugend = Kind! O Götter = Sohn!
So komm/ empfahe hier der Tugend Lohn/
Die Ehren = Krohn:
Die Du/ O JOSEPH/ Du Würdiger Gast/
Durch Rathen und Thaten erworben DIR hast.
Dieweil bey DIR so vieler Völcker Hoffen/
Ist eingetroffen/
Steht DIR mein Tempel offen.

Aria.
Unsterbliche Ehre!
Du theilest zwar den Sterblichen dich mit/
Doch suchst Du nur/ die Tugendhafft vor Andern:
Man sieht Dich nicht/ als solcher Seel nachwandern/
So wie mit Lust/ die Laster = Bahn betritt.
Ritornello, mit 2. Chöre Waldhörnern und Hautbois,
concertirende.

2.
Unsterbliche Ehre!
Wañ JOSEPH nicht geschworn der Tugend = Fahn/
So bald ER nur zu Herrschen war gebohren;
Hätt' IHN das Reich zum Haupte nicht erkohren/
Und Du IHM nicht den Tempel auffgethan.
Ritorn.

3.
Unsterbliche Ehre!
Vermehre stets des Käysers Majestät:
Laß Josephs Ruhm mit Josephs Jahren wachsen/
Ausbreite IHN biß an die Sternen = Achsen/
Alsdann Sein Reich und Ruhm niemahls vergeht.
Sinfonia all' unisono à 25. Violin. con Intrada Seconda
mit 2. Chöre Paucken und Trompeten/

& Tutti.
Eja , Euge !
Det, JOSEPHE IMPERATOR
TIBI Famam, Famæ Dator!

Die Klugheit.
Recitat.
ICh/ mit Gottes = Furcht vermählt/
Begleite die Menschen zum Tempel der Ehren/
Nimmermehr der fehlt/
Der nachfolget meinen Lehren/
In was Stand Er sey.
Die Stein = alten Greisen/
Sind nicht allein die Weisen/
Die Weißheit wohnt auch Jungen Herren bey.
JOSEPH/ Teutschlands Salomon/
Kan hievon/
Ein Durchlauchtigs Beyspiel geben.
Glückseelig sind zu nennen/
Die

Figure 5.1. The original libretto of Buxtehude's oratorio "Templum honoris"
(December 1705), page 3.

ER beut den Feinden Trutz/
Durch GOTTES des Mächtigen Schutz/
Auff DEN ER Sich verläßt.
Ich geh mit JOSEPH Aus und Ein/
Er soll Glückselig seyn!
Gesegnet aller Wegen/
Mit himmlisch- und irrdischen Seegen!

Tutti von allen Chören.

Es geh JOSEPH/ dem Hohen Held
Nach Wunsch/ der Hohen in der Welt!

Glückwünschende ARIA.

1.

JOSEPH wachse/ wachse fort/
Wie an einer Quelle!
Seine Krohn an allem Ohrt/
Scheine Sternen-helle.
Rhodes Sonne/ Stambuls Mond
Müssen voller Ehr-bezeigen
Sich vor Diesem Joseph neigen/
Und wo Heyd und Barbar wohnt.
Ritornello.

2.

Seines Vaters Segen komm
Starck auff Josephs Scheittel!
Wer dieß wünscht/ist treu und fromm;
Wers nicht wünscht/ ist Eitel.
Unter Josephs Regiment
Muß man Reiche mit den Städten/
Sehn im Wohlstand einher treten.
Jeder rufft: Glück zu/ Regent!
Ritornello.

3.

Auch DEIN LUBECK schweigt hier nicht/
Höchst-gekröhnter Kåyser!
Wünscht an Heil'ger Statt aus Pflicht
DIR viel Sieges-Reißer.
GOTT erhöre unser Flehn/
Daß/ zu vieler tausend Frommen/
Stein' und Hirten aus DIR kommen:
Daß wir Josephs Saamen sehn!

I. CHOR. Eja, Euge!
DET, JOSEPHE IMPERATOR,
TIBI PROLEM, PROLIS DATOR!

II. CHOR. Eja, Euge!
DET, JOSEPHE IMPERATOR,
TIBI VITAM, VITÆ DATOR!

Tutti.

Es leb' JOSEPH der Kåyser-Held/
Nach Wunsch der Hohen in der Welt!
Worauff zum Schluß:
Una Passagaglia con divers. Instrom. Vivace.

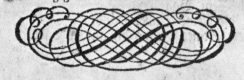

Figure 5.2. Page 4 of the libretto.

The libretto indicates that the performances were occasions of grandiose spectacle in the St. Mary's church, which had been specifically decorated and illuminated for the event. The musical presentations themselves involved several instrumental and vocal choirs, both large organs and, at least at the end of "Castrum doloris," the entire congregation as well.[25]

The text of both oratorios represents a curious mixture of sacred and secular elements chosen to suit the politically oriented occasion.[26] The dialogue format calls for two soloists as allegorical figures—*Gerücht* (Fame) and *Klugheit* (Prudence)—and two choirs. The musical forms include double chorus with *da capo* rounding off, recitative,[27] and strophic aria with instrumental ritornellos. The instrumental requirements of the piece are particularly striking and apparently without precedent or parallel. There are two intradas for two choirs of trumpets and timpani, a ritornello for two concerted choirs of *Waldhörner und Hautbois*, a *Sinfonia all' unisono a 25. Violin*, and at the end a *Passacaglia con divers. Instrom.*[28]

The young Bach had, so far as we know, no opportunity to compose pieces in an oratorio-like format. Elements of Buxtehude-style instrumental splendor seem to be reflected, however, in Bach's two Mühlhausen town council election cantatas, of which one (BWV 71) has been preserved. This piece (published in 1708, well before any vocal work of Handel's or Telemann's was printed) originated one year after Buxtehude's death and only two years after his last two oratorios (BuxWV 134–35). It demonstrates in particular Bach's ambitious and inventive instrumental scoring and may provide, together with the more modestly dimensioned cantatas BWV 150 and BWV 106 from about the same time, the only extant, albeit indirect link to Buxtehude's late vocal music. The oratorio "Wacht! Euch zum Streit gefasset macht" attributed to Buxtehude appears to be less suitable for comparative purposes; it has a much more modest instrumental format and, perhaps more importantly, as a work from the early 1680s it belongs to a very different period.

The reason for the virtually complete disappearance of Buxtehude's large-scale Abendmusiken cannot be attributed to any lack of artistic worth or compositional quality, but rather to the fact that these oratorios were not conceived as repertory pieces. In this sense they are comparable to the operas of the same time, especially the Hamburg operas which have also not survived. Occasional works were without exception designed to fit specific circumstances. Moreover, the style of these oratorios had to be adjusted to the requirements of the day. The situation was by no means fundamentally different for the vocal works of the young Handel and Bach, and their coincidental, fragmentary transmission can be explained similarly. For Bach, a systematic preservation of his early vocal works would have been utterly unrealistic since these works were no longer even remotely fashionable. Under exceptional conditions a new context could save them, as was the case, for example, with the thorough revision of the very early chorale cantata BWV 4 for a Leipzig performance, or with the transfer of the choral passacaglia "Weinen, Klagen, Sorgen, Zagen" (BWV 12/2) of 1714 into the B Minor

Mass of 1748–49. Bach's later self-critical attitude toward his own early vocal oeuvre would in all likelihood not have differed, in principle, from what he must have thought about the slightly older vocal works of Buxtehude and their even more old-fashioned outlook.

Praeludium in G Minor (BuxWV 149)

In later life, Bach appears by the same token to have regarded much of his early instrumental music such as a chorale partita or the ensemble sonata and symphonia as equally passé. There are exceptions, however, most notably involving the genre of pedaliter organ prelude. Again the analogy is quite striking: a substantial number of Buxtehude's preludes and toccatas have survived and so have a goodly number of Bach's compositions from the same category. In fact, the extant Buxtehude repertoire actually outnumbers that of the young Bach, and the explanation for this most likely includes an aesthetic component. Buxtehude's preludes held the rank of *exempla classica* within the Bach circle and throughout virtually the entire eighteenth century. The G minor prelude, in terms of format and length the greatest of Buxtehude's pedaliter works, may serve as a case in point.

The large-scale structure of the piece comprises five parts of differing lengths: passaggio (mm. 1–20 [see Ex. 5.1]); fugue (mm. 21–54 [see Ex.

Example 5.1. Buxtehude, Praeludium in G Minor BuxWV 149, opening passaggio

Example 5.2. Praeludium in G Minor, fugue I

Example 5.3. Praeludium in G Minor, interlude

Example 5.4. Praeludium in G Minor, fugue II

5.2]); interlude (mm. 55–78 [see Ex. 5.3]); fugue (mm. 78–143 [see Ex. 5.4]); and finale (mm. 144–59 [see Ex. 5.5]).

The overall organization is a model of clarity. It demonstrates how Buxtehude created a novel type which, while it synthesized elements of earlier keyboard traditions, actually went far beyond the scope of the compositions of Tunder, Weckmann, Scheidemann, Froberger, Frescobaldi, or Sweelinck. The work also displays two particularly modern and forward-looking elements.

Example 5.5. Praeludium in G Minor, finale

First, the prelude embodies the sophisticated and deliberate application of a harmonic language that approaches or anticipates functional harmony. That this occurs in conjunction with the minor mode, which before 1700 normally carried strong Dorian implications, is all the more remarkable. The repetitive definition of the G minor key happens at the very beginning of the piece. The many surprising harmonic effects, including the prolongation of the dominant of m. 49 in mm. 50–53 through harmonic shifts introducing C and A major (Ex. 5.6), as well as the Neapolitan cadence in m. 125 (Ex. 5.7), always stay within a strong G minor framework.

Second, the work employs a degree of thematic control that results in a multisectional composition of remarkable unity. The passaggio figuration introduces in m. 2 a harmonic pattern that is subsequently spelled out in an ostinato subject. The same subject, slightly modified, is treated in both fugal sections. Moreover, the interlude (mm. 67ff.) as well as the finale (mm. 141ff.) return in their bass parts to the melodic and harmonic fundament of the work.

Example 5.6. Praeludium in G Minor, interlude

Example 5.7. Praeludium in G Minor, fugue II

Buxtehude's expansion of the traditional multisectional prelude/toccata of the *stylus phantasticus* genre into an unprecedented large-scale and thematically controlled format suggests a general path that Bach later pursued as well, although in a different fashion. In his later organ works at least, Bach ordinarily separated the fugal and free structures from one another, adhering to the form scheme *Praeludium et Fuga* preferred in Middle and South Germany. As his Passacaglia (BWV 582) demonstrates, he invoked this separation even in the ostinato genre, and thereby introduced a clear alternative to Buxtehude's solution. Nevertheless, with respect to the extraordinarily expansive tendencies of prelude and fugue as separate entities, Buxtehude's synthesis unquestionably provided the point of departure for Bach.

As BuxWV 149 shows, the seventeenth-century spectrum of compositional forms and types was sufficient for Buxtehude's purposes in designing large-scale structures. What he deemed insufficient was the traditional lack of coherence in genres of composition that originated first and foremost from improvisation. His sense for larger form, corresponding elements, and formal rounding off led to unschematic, highly individual solutions. Bach, on the other hand, accepted and adjusted to the growing tendency toward categorization of instrumental forms (prelude and fugue, sonata, concerto). Nevertheless, the Buxtehudian manner of extreme diversity and individuality was a decisive precedent for Bach.

Handel and Telemann were more open to compromise. Their instrumental concertos and vocal arias, for instance, reveal a much higher degree of standardization and homogenization in terms of musical form and thematic-motivic, rhythmic, and harmonic contents. Bach's compositional solutions, like Buxtehude's, stress the principle of individuality and resist the tendency toward conformity and regularity. All of Handel's oratorios and keyboard suites and all of Telemann's cantatas and concertos actually possess many more elements in common than Bach's Brandenburg Concertos, violin soli, or Passions taken by themselves. Bach, in this sense, preserved the Buxtehudian spirit, just as Buxtehude had in his own right foreshadowed a later ideal.

6

Bach and Johann Adam Reinken:
A Context for the Early Works

MORE THAN A HUNDRED years ago Philipp Spitta endeavored to place the musical beginnings of the young Bach in proper perspective, taking as his point of departure a chronological ordering of compositional repertoire he classified as early works. He succeeded not only in presenting a multitude of fundamental observations on biographical and stylistic matters—perceptions that have remained valid up to the present day—but also in offering an exemplary, discriminating, and, in its basic features, still unsurpassed synopsis of musical currents in Germany in the closing years of the seventeenth century.[1] Since Spitta's day, Bach research, especially in the last three decades, has somewhat filled in the picture of Bach the young composer as sketched by Spitta, expanding new aspects and modifying numerous details in the process.[2]

However, it seems that no other creative period of Bach's life presents so many unsolved problems, and the list has been expanding rather than shrinking as a result of more recent research.[3] The central questions continually revolve around the establishment of an authentic body of works, the chronology of the compositions, and the direct and indirect spheres of musical influence that might have affected the young Bach. These critical questions are so closely intertwined that they cannot be treated separately. Moreover, the acute lack of firm biographical and compositional data makes a broader approach to the matter all the more necessary.

I

Except for his older brother Johann Christoph of Ohrdruf, "under whose guidance"—run the words of the obituary[4]—"he learned the fundamentals of clavier playing," Bach does not appear to have had a real teacher. But certainly the three renowned North German organists, Johann Adam Reinken, Dietrich Buxtehude, and Georg Böhm, must be counted among the decisive mentors of the young Bach—and not simply in the broad general sense. Böhm, organist of St. John's Church in Lüneburg, may well have served in some ways as Bach's instructor, at least in part, in the years after 1700. Although the biographical sources say nothing in this regard, one suspects that Carl Philipp Emanuel Bach had good reason to use the phrase "his Lüneburg teacher Böhm"[5] with regard to his father's training. Emanuel subsequently corrected the passage, neutralizing it to read "the Lüneburg organist Böhm,"[6] perhaps to extol his father further as a self-taught genius. In any event, there were personal bonds between Bach and Böhm. These ties lasted into the Leipzig years and were still strong enough in 1727 that Bach was able to turn to the aging Böhm and enlist him as an agent for the sale of the individual prints of his second and third partitas, BWV 826 and 827.[7]

Bach's personal encounter with Dietrich Buxtehude did not take place until the middle of the Arnstadt period. During the winter of 1705–1706, Bach spent several months in Lübeck in order "to listen to" the master; this stay, as the obituary put it, was "not without profit."[8] The Lübeck trip must have made a very strong impression on Bach, for he himself stated (according to the Arnstadt protocol of 21 February 1706) that the journey had enabled him "to comprehend one thing and another about his art."[9] Since the beginnings of Bach research, the Buxtehude encounter has been taken as one of the decisive biographical and stylistic turning points, especially with regard to the chronology of the organ works—whether for the better or the worse will be discussed shortly.

The third and eldest of this completely congenial North German trio of organists, Johann Adam Reinken, was ranked below his Lüneburg colleagues in terms of significance for Bach by Spitta and, as a rule, by those writing since. The noticeable downplaying of Reinken's role and importance might be explained by the fact that at the time Spitta was writing the first volume of his Bach biography, he was not aware of the direct link between Bach and Reinken's music; not until later was Spitta able to identify the sonata and fugue arrangements from Reinken's "Hortus Musicus" in Bach's keyboard pieces BWV 954, 965, and 966, in a special essay, "Umarbeitungen fremder Originale."[10]

Even though the precise circumstances of the relationship between the aged Reinken, the organist of St. Catherine's in Hamburg, and Bach, who was nearly two generations younger and a student at St. Michael's School in Lüneburg, remain for the most part in the dark, Reinken represents a major, perhaps even *the* major, figure in young Bach's life. It is worth noting that Reinken is the only one of the three great North German organists to be mentioned in two prominent places in the obituary. One may view that as an indication of the weight his name carried in the Bach household. It is certainly no more than a fortunate coincidence that after Bach's early visits from Lüneburg to Reinken in Hamburg still another encounter took place, in 1720, between Bach, now elevated to Cöthen Capellmeister, and the 97-year-old Reinken, on the occasion of Bach's competing for the organist's post at the Jacobikirche in Hamburg.[11] Although that may have been fortuitous happenstance, it underlines an affinity clearly felt on both sides. The reaction of the venerable Reinken to Bach's organ playing ("I thought that this art was dead, but I see that it lives on in you"),[12] passed down in the obituary, can hardly be overrated.[13] For in fact Bach was—and not only from Reinken's perspective—the only organist of rank in his generation who not only preserved the traditions of the seventeenth century but developed them further. For Bach, Reinken's pronouncement must have been more than a simple "compliment." He must have sensed the historical significance of the phrase. Indeed, Bach probably even shaped its precise formulation, since he himself was undoubtedly the primary preserver and disseminator of the Reinken citation and therefore was responsible for its inclusion in the annals of music history. By 1752, when Johann Joachim Quantz was able to write that "the art of organ playing, which had been received from the Netherlanders, was carried quite far . . . by the above named [among them Froberger, Pachelbel, Reinken, Buxtehude, and Bruhns]" and that it "had in recent times been brought to its greatest perfection by the admirable Johann Sebastian Bach,"[14] it appears that Reinken's prophetic words had become historical fact.

While the short reunion of Reinken and Bach in 1720 may be viewed as no more than a noteworthy meeting of a special nature, the earlier encounter, during Bach's Lüneburg period, must be rated as a much more momentous event, one that could not have failed to influence the young musician, thirsty for experience and searching for direction. An attempt to discuss the early Reinken-Bach tie must enter the realm of hypothesis, for documentary sources are lacking. The obituary gives no more than a pithy confirmation: "From Lüneburg he journeyed occasionally to Hamburg in order to hear the then-famous organist of St. Catherine's Church, Johann Adam Reinken."[15] The more anecdotal report in Friedrich Wilhelm Marpurg's *Legenden einiger Musikheiligen* (1786) adds nothing substantial to the account, though Reinken is expressly described as a "solid organist and composer." It also mentions that Bach "traveled frequently" to Hamburg and that the unanticipated discovery of a ducat made possible "a new pilgrimage to Herr Reinken."[16]

It is significant that the obituary, in its generally succinct sketch of Bach's Lüneburg years, singles out Reinken for mention, not Böhm or August Braun, the Cantor of St. Michael's. One cannot exclude the possibility that the allusion of Reinken alone corresponds to his importance within Bach's family and student circle. From Bach's perspective in Ohrdruf, St. Michael's School in Lüneburg probably represented an immediate and realistic goal with economic security—but no more than that. The Hamburg scene, by contrast, may have represented the true ideal and a future goal, one that was being pursued at the same time by Handel. Perhaps Lüneburg, with Böhm, offered Bach an additional bonus. On the one hand, Böhm was an attractive organ teacher *sui generis*.[17] On the other, he could also offer Bach an introduction to the North German organ school and especially to Reinken, whose fame as an organist was equal to Buxtehude's, if not even greater.[18]

That Hamburg and Reinken were targets Bach aimed at, perhaps as early as his Ohrdruf years, seems corroborated by the parallel experience of his cousin and one-time schoolmate at the Ohrdruf Lyceum, Johann Ernst Bach. Johann Ernst remained at the Lyceum until April 1701 and then "visited Hamburg for a half-year at great expense, in order to improve his understanding of the organ." [19] Lüneburg may have offered Johann Sebastian better possibilities for subsistence—with a long-range contact with Hamburg thrown into the bargain—than the more financially taxing route taken by his cousin. Just how long Bach received his modest income as a member of the Mettenchor at St. Michael's is unknown; documentation exists only for the beginning of 1700. [20] Gustav Fock has already established that Bach could hardly have remained in the first class at St. Michael's School beyond Easter 1702. [21] Moreover, his candidacy for the organist's post at the Jacobikirche in Sangerhausen in the summer of 1702 [22] suggests that his ties to Lüneburg were loosening. How these ties may have been viewed after he had lost—in the words of the obituary—"his unusually fine soprano voice," [23] is an open question. But without a doubt numerous opportunities for employment as an instrumentalist were open to him. That he was even considered for the post in Sangerhausen testifies to his qualifications as an organist, a skill he must have developed to a passable level in Lüneburg.

II

A number of reference points and analogies enable us to estimate—at least in broad outline—Bach's musical development between the ages of fifteen and eighteen. The invitation from the Arnstadt Church Council for the eighteen-year-old Bach to test and inaugurate the Wender organ in the New Church [24] can only be taken as a sign of unusually high esteem. The false title given to Bach on the honorarium receipt, "Court Organist to the Prince of Weimar," [25] underlines the reputation of the young virtuoso; and one might assume that his professional abilities in 1703 considerably exceeded the skills he had acquired in Ohrdruf up to the beginning of the year 1700. It also seems that he had long since overcome the original disparity with his elder brother Johann Christoph, whose professional development was similar to Sebastian's. Johann Christoph began his studies at age fifteen with Pachelbel in Erfurt, a tutelage that three years later led to an organist position at St. Thomas's Church in Erfurt. [26] The external chronology is the same, but the differences in circumstances are striking: Johann Sebastian did not spend a journeyman period with a single master, but rather took part in an academic program that permitted him to explore what must have been for its time the most attractive organ scene in Germany. At the conclusion of this independent tutorial period came the assumption of a well-paying organist post with a new instrument. [27] The younger brother must have outstripped the older at a very early point, even though the latter was termed "optimus artifex" (premier artist) in the Ohrdruf funeral register. [28] The description in the obituary of the acceptance of the ten-year-old orphan into his brother's household is significant: "Little Johann Sebastian's love of music was uncommonly great even at this tender age. In a short time he had mastered all the pieces that his brother had voluntarily set before him." [29] His desire to learn was difficult to keep in bounds: the story of the secret copying of the book "full of clavier pieces by the most famous masters of the day, Froberger, Kerll, and Pachelbel,"[50] serves as a striking example.

Corrections are needed in the portrait of the years 1695–1700 as projected by Friedrich Blume, which claims, by way of summary, that the period elapsed "without leaving us the smallest clue about Bach's musical progress."[31] And certainly it is inappropriate to reduce, as Spitta did, the relationship between Johann Sebastian and Johann Christoph Bach to the transmission of "Pachelbel's creations and artistic spirit."[32] On the contrary, as the offspring of a musical family, Johann Sebastian had most certainly achieved musical and instrumental polish even before he was ten years old, else why would the decision to send him on his way toward professional training be made as early as 1695? That decision may have been comparable to the one Bach made in 1720, the tenth year of the life of his own son Wilhelm Friedemann, when Johann Sebastian began writing the Clavier-Büchlein.

Johann Christoph must have wished, above all, to pass on to his brother what had been suggested to him by his own training. The anxiously guarded book copied by Sebastian contained works by Pachelbel, Kerll, and Froberger as repertoire to be emulated, and in a sense it must have represented Johann Christoph's own musical ambitions. The book as well as the copy made by Sebastian "by moonlight" during the course of six months are lost.[33] However, one can get an idea of the type of repertoire involved from the 1692 tablature book of Johann Valentin Eckelt.[34]

Eckelt, born in 1673, was two years younger than Johann Christoph Bach. Both boys studied with Pachelbel in Erfurt, and Eckelt took the occasion to assemble a tablature book[35] whose basic contents are written in Pachelbel's hand.[36] The compositions are principally those of Pachelbel and Froberger (most of the latter were apparently purchased from Pachelbel).[37] In addition, there are pieces by Philipp Heinrich Erlebach, Andreas Nicolaus Vetter, Johann Caspar Kerll, Johann Philipp Krieger, and, mainly toward the end, a large number of anonymous pieces, evidently compositions by Eckelt himself.[38] The "core" of the volume—especially the pieces by Pachelbel and Froberger—is probably roughly the same as the repertoire entrusted to Johann Christoph Bach. It includes the following works published in the *Denkmäler der Tonkunst in Bayern* (DTB)[39] and *Denkmäler der Tonkunst in Österreich* (DTÖ)[40]:

Johann Pachelbel:
    Toccatas, Preludes, Fugues, and Ciacona (DTB IV/1, Part 1: nos. 1, 4,
        5, 7–9, 11, 20, 23, 25, 26, 31, 41, 42)
    Chorale Preludes (DTB IV/1, Part 2: nos. 5, 11, 26, 60)
    Suites (DTB II/1: nos. 16, 33b)

Johann Jacob Froberger:
    Ricercar (DTÖ 21: no. 7)
    Canzonas (DTÖ 13: no. 6; DTÖ 21, no. 4)
    Capriccios (DTÖ 21: nos. 12, 18)

Toccatas (DTÖ 21: nos. 23–25)

Fantasia (DTÖ 21: no. 7)

Capriccio, Prelude, and Fugue (DTÖ 21: Doubtful Works, pp. 125–126)

The repertoire of the Eckelt tablature book was probably somewhat smaller than that assembled by Johann Christoph Bach and differed in some respects. However, it offers welcome insights into the knowledge of contemporary keyboard literature, the level of technical skill, and the rudiments of composition that Johann Sebastian might have possessed by the time he departed for Lüneburg.

The copying and playing of works by recognized masters also signified for Bach, as for other budding musicians of the day, the study of *exempla classica* of composition. Thus, we can assume that toward the end of the Ohrdruf period, at least, he was studying composition through the models available to him. Ever since Spitta, there has been a pronounced tendency to grant no importance whatsoever to this aspect of the Ohrdruf period. For instance, Spitta says of the Fugue in E Minor BWV 945: "Of all the Bach fugues I know, this is the most immature and can hardly have been composed later than the Ohrdruf years."[41] However, this fugue shows none of the characteristics that would be expected of a work written under the influences of the Pachelbel circle. Moreover, it has recently been shown to be an inauthentic piece.[42] Thus one must search for new and more reliable traces of Bach's earliest compositional activity, if they have survived. They probably are to be found in works such as the Canzona in D Minor BWV 588, or the Fantasia in C Major BWV 570, two pieces handed down (perhaps in revised form) in the two large collections assembled shortly after 1700 by Johann Christoph Bach, the so-called Möller Manuscript and the Andreas Bach Book.[43]

In his Lüneburg years, Bach was probably entrusted with an entirely new repertoire of keyboard works, but there is no concrete evidence that he had already been exposed to North German music through his brother. It seems more likely that the handsome assemblage of North German keyboard music, as represented in the Möller Manuscript and the Andreas Bach Book, was placed into the hands of Johann Christoph by his younger brother, and not vice versa. The two collections are, in fact, principal sources for the transmission of music by Reinken, Buxtehude, Bruhns, and Böhm—something that must be credited to the Bach brothers, perhaps especially to the young Sebastian.

Bach's first direct access to North German organ music probably came through Georg Böhm. But it should not be overlooked that Böhm's organ in St. John's Church, like the other instruments in Lüneburg, was then in deplorable condition and did not allow true obbligato pedal playing. An appraisal by Arp Schnitger in 1683 is also relevant for the period 1700–1702:

> The organ in St. John's is in a very bad state of repair. The wind chests are old and completely unserviceable. The keyboards go no higher than a² in the treble and completely lack lower semi-tones. The pedal is coupled to the middle

clavier and has only a Sub-Bass 16', and therefore can provide no real gravity, since it is so dependent on manual stops. . . .[44]

It was not until 1712–1714 that Matthias Dropa added two pedal towers to the organ, from plans drawn up by Böhm.[45] Thus the relatively small number of pedal pieces by Böhm would seem to stem from the time after 1714. In light of this situation, it appears more plausible that Böhm's direct influence on the young Bach was less in the area of the specifically North German manner of pedal playing than in the sphere of French-derived manual repertoire. Böhm's chorale partitas and clavier suites stand out in this regard. It is surely no accident that the works by him preserved in the Möller Manuscript and the Andreas Bach Book are almost exclusively clavier suites. Clavecin music by Lebèbue in the Möller Manuscript points to the French connection. Bach was exposed to it in Lüneburg through Böhm and, in a more general way, through the Braunschweig-Lüneburg court, which was dominated by the "Frantzösischer Geschmack." The obituary speaks not of *trips* by Bach to the relatively faraway Celle, but only of his "hearing several times a then-famous Capelle maintained by the Duke of Zelle."[46] This orchestra could have made music in the Lüneburg town castle,[47] among other places, for that edifice had been chosen to be the dowager's estate of Duchess Eleanore d'Olbreuse after 1700.

If Lüneburg offered Bach only limited opportunities for an intensive encounter with North German organ style, then the trips to Hamburg and Lübeck must be given greater emphasis. Ever since Spitta, Bach's successful trip from Arnstadt to Lübeck around the turn of the year 1705–1706 and his several-months' stay with Dietrich Buxtehude have been assigned the key role in this regard, even though the plausibility of this idea is not obvious. The thesis that the Lübeck trip was of crucial importance for Bach's understanding of Buxtehude's organ style rests on two premises: that Bach's visit was chiefly concerned with Buxtehude's organ music, and that Bach was only vaguely familiar with Buxtehude's organ music before 1705–1706. But even his choice of date for his trip, Advent 1705, suggests that Bach expected to attend concerts of Abendmusik arranged by Buxtehude.[48] Unfortunately, of the two oratorio-like Abendmusik works that were performed in St. Mary's on December 2–3, 1705, "Castrum doloris" Bux WV 134 and "Templum honoris" Bux WV 135, only the printed texts have survived;[49] the precise musical impressions Bach received must remain illusive. Since Buxtehude's Abendmusik ranked as the most significant church music program in Protestant circles of the day, it must have hold a strong attraction for Bach. The wording of the obituary, that Bach traveled to Lübeck in order "to listen" to Buxtehude and stayed "for almost a quarter of a year, not without profit,"[50] is certainly neutral. But it suggests that during the extended stay Bach must also have profited from Buxtehude, the master of organ playing. However, the influence of Buxtehude's vocal writing should not be overlooked in Bach's earliest vocal works, written soon after the Lübeck trip. Buxtehudian qualities stand out most clearly in the "Actus Tragicus" (Cantata 106, "Gottes Zeist ist die allerbeste Zeit"), especially in the section based on chorale melodies (above all in the closing segment, "Durch Jesum Christum, Amen"). One cannot exclude the possibility that for its conception as well as its performance, this unusually elaborate and grandly wrought composition had as its musical model the funeral music for Emperor Leopold, "Castrum doloris." [51]

To say that Bach's reception of Buxtehude's organ music culminated in the middle of the Arnstadt period means that the Lüneburg years are essentially excluded from consideration and that Reinken's role, in particular, is rated very low. Such a viewpoint has serious consequences for the chronology of Bach's early keyboard music. The few surviving original sources for this repertoire (the autographs of the Prelude and Fugue in G Minor BWV 535a; the organ chorale "Wie schön leuchtet der Morgenstern" BWV 739; and the 23-measure fragment of a chorale prelude on the same melody, BWV 764) elude exact chronological placement, but they can be assigned with certainty to the period "before 1707." [52] The autograph of the Prelude and Fugue in G Minor is found in the Möller Manuscript, [53] and that of the organ chorales on "Wie schön leuchtet der Morgenstern" [54] is closely connected to the Möller Manuscript and the Andreas Bach Book in turn. Nothing speaks against placing all three compositions in the years before the Lübeck trip. At the same time, the chorale preludes might claim chronological priority over the Prelude and Fugue. However, all three works breathe a special North German spirit and, therefore, belong to Bach's compositional involvement with corresponding models. But since BWV 739, especially, with its extensive virtuosic echo passages is indebted to a Reinken model rather than to a Buxtehude one (Reinken's only surviving organ chorales, "An Wasserflüssen Babylon" and "Was kann uns kommen an für Not," show numerous stylistic parallels), [55] the organist of St. Catherine's in Hamburg moves into the foreground as a decisive mediator and catalyst for Bach during his formative years.

III

It was certainly to Bach's advantage to attempt to establish ties with Reinken from Lüneburg, for Reinken was the senior and most widely recognized representative of the North German organ school. Spitta acknowledged, with good reason, that Böhm may have bridged the gap between the generations, although the oft-mentioned student-teacher relationship between Böhm and Reinken has eluded verification up to the present day. In any case, before accepting his post in Lüneburg in 1698, Böhm had resided in Hamburg for at least five years, a circumstance that gives a solid basis to his connection with the Hamburg scene. [56] In the organ of St. Catherine's, Reinken possessed the largest, most famous, and most beautiful instrument in North Germany. Buxtehude never had anything comparable at his disposal. [57] In a description of the legendary 32' pedal stops of the St. Catherine's organ,

Johann Friedrich Agricola referred specifically to Bach's admiring appraisal of the instrument.[58] Bach's encompassing knowledge of instruments, the foundation for which must have been laid by the ongoing repairs on the organs in the Eisenach, Ohrdruf, and Lüneburg, could have received a decisive rounding out from the Hamburg experiences.

To a young musician such as Bach, Reinken offered direct access to the main repertoire of North German organ music, its principles, and its manner of performance. Included in the repertoire available through Reinken was the encompassing and certainly most considerable oeuvre of Buxtehude, for the close connection between Buxtehude and Reinken—something not touched upon by Spitta and later Bach biographers—has recently been demonstrated.[59] And thus one can proceed with the assumption that even during his Lüneburg years, Bach could have studied Buxtehude's organ works. The Lübeck trip of 1705–1706 would then be viewed as the culmination, not the beginning, of a long, intensive involvement with matters of organ writing. Because of the paucity of reliable documentation, the details remain unclear. Nevertheless, Bach's involvement with specific North German compositional models (clearly seen in the Toccata in E Major BWV 566, for instance) should be shifted to the early Arnstadt period, if not even earlier.

Without a doubt, Reinken represented a versatile and colorful musical personality of a special sort. He was a virtuoso of high order and an esteemed organ expert. He was a founding member of the Hamburg opera and sat on its directorate, thereby assuming an important role in the musical life of the city. At the same time, he also possessed theoretical interests and clearly had an encompassing professional knowledge of the musical literature.[60] In this respect, Reinken must have appeared incomparably more fascinating to the young Bach than Buxtehude or Böhm. While the relationship between Bach and Reinken escapes a closer description, Bach's arrangements of Reinken's sonata movements, BWV 954, 965, and 966, offer a few confirmable clues, at least. The very fact that Bach did not arrange any works by a North German composer other than Reinken, not even by Buxtehude or Böhm, underlines Reinken's significance for the student at St. Michael's, Lüneburg.

Spitta first identified the Reinken arrangements and linked them with Bach's visit to Hamburg in 1720,[61] a dating that by and large has remained unchallenged. But the provenance of the sources as well as comparison with other fugue arrangements suggest that the compositions spring from Bach's early years. Of course, that does not mean that the arrangements had to originate under Reinken's eye during Bach's Lüneburg period. In truth, it seems more reasonable to suppose that they were written during the period of Bach's general encounter with Reinken and that they should be seen in direct connection with Bach's own course of self-study in counterpoint. This view gains support from Carl Philipp Emanuel Bach. In 1775, he borrowed an appropriate phrase from the obituary to characterize his father's early training: "Through his own study alone he became, even in his youth, a pure and strong fugue writer,"[62] and indeed he advanced principally "through the observation of the most famous and profound composers of the time."[63]

Bach's arrangements from Reinken's *HORTUS MUSICUS recentibus aliquot flosculis SONATEN, ALLEMANDEN, COURANTEN, SAR[A]BANDEN, et GIQUEN Cum 2. Violin, Viola* [da Gamba], *et Basso continuo* . . . (MUSICAL GARDEN of fresh little flowers SONATAS, ALLEMANDES, COURANTES, SARABANDES, and GIGUES for 2 violins, viola [da gamba], and Basso continuo . . ., Hamburg, n.d. [1687]),[64] involve the works listed in Table 6.1.

The individual movements are numbered from 1 to 30 in the original print of "Hortus Musicus," but they are grouped into six tonally closed trio sonatas with suite appendixes. While BWV 965 encompasses an entire sonata with suite, BWV 966 includes the Sonata in C Major and the ensuing Allemande, and BWV 954 is limited to the imitative Allegro section of the Sonata in B♭ Major. To all appearances, this sequence corresponds to the course of Bach's study through arranging: he begins with the transcription of a complete sonata but then concentrates increasingly on the contrapuntal movements. Bach's arrangements of the noncontrapuntal movements consist of richly figured but generally exact clavier transcriptions of Reinken's instrumental originals. The gigues and allegro movements, by contrast, are not simply expanded but are actually newly composed. Bach's own interest extends to the unfolding of the imitative allegro movements in the sense of a formal fugue. Hermann Keller[65] and Ulrich Siegele[66] have analyzed Bach's Reinken transcriptions from various points of view, and they stress the structural similarity and chronological proximity to the fugues of Well-Tempered Clavier I. However, their discussions are based on Spitta's dating of the works in connection with Bach's Hamburg trip of 1720. New discoveries regarding the manuscript sources of the arrangements force one to abandon this dating and think through the style of the pieces once again.

The earliest source for BWV 965 and 966 is in the Deutsche Staatsbibliothek, Berlin, where the arrangements are entered in the hand of Johann Gottfried Walther (probably around 1712 at the latest).[67] BWV 965 and 966, together with BWV 954, are also transmitted in the Staatsbibliothek Preußischer Kulturbesitz, Berlin, along with other early works by Bach written out by Johann Peter Kellner some time after 1725.[68] Since the manuscripts from which Walther and Kellner made their copies (perhaps Bach's autographs?) have not survived, there is no firm evidence for a more

Table 6.1. Synopsis of Bach's arrangements from Reinken's "Hortus Musicus"

BWV 965	BWV 966	BWV 954
Sonata 1ᵐᵃ (in A minor)	Sonata 11ᵐᵃ (in C major)	Sonata 6ᵗᵃ (in B♭ major)
Adagio	Lento	Allegro
Allegro	Allegro	
Solo. Largo-Presto	Solo. Largo-Allegro	
Allemand 2ᵈᵃ Allegro	Allemand 12ᵐᵃ. Allegro	
Courant 3ᵗⁱᵃ		
Saraband 4ᵗᵃ		
Gigue 5ᵗᵃ		

precise dating of the arrangements. They surely stem from before 1710, and probably even earlier. Speaking in favor of this early date is the direct stylistic connection with Bach's fugue compositions after Italian trio sonata models: Fugue in B Minor BWV 579, after Corelli, op. 3, no. 4 (Rome, 1689); Fugues in A Major, B Minor, and C Major BWV 950, 951/951a, and 946, after Albinoni, op. 1, nos. 3, 8, and 12 (Venice, 1694); and Fugue in C Minor BWV 574/574a/574b, after Legrenzi, op. 2, no. 11, "La Mont' Albana" (Venice, 1655).[69]

The similarities of genre (Reinken's sonatas represent a North German variant of the Italian trio sonata, standing between the Legrenzi type and the Corelli and Albinoni models)[70] already point to a distinct link, implying that Bach became occupied with the chamber music of the passing seventeenth century, together with its performance practices, when this repertoire was still current.[71] A bit of chronological evidence for the early dating of Bach's Italian transcriptions can be gleaned from the sources, for the early version of the Legrenzi Fugue BWV 574b is handed down in the Andreas Bach Book.[72] The Andreas Bach Book also contains open scores of the first two Trio Sonatas from Albinoni's op. 1. The sister manuscript, the Möller Manuscript, contains an arrangement of a Reinken fugue[73] made by Peter Heidorn, which completes the chain of circumstances that appears to confirm the North German origin of this sort of keyboard transcription of instrumental sonatas. This situation seems to be an early parallel to the Netherlandish origin of the concerto transcriptions for keyboard instruments.[74] In this case, Reinken would seem to be the logical connecting link.

Thus Bach's arrangements of Reinken's works must be grouped with his arrangements of Italian trio sonatas, especially with regard to the technical, formal, and stylistic evolution of the Bach keyboard fugue as it unfolded before 1710.[75] In this context the following theoretical considerations—in which the musical analysis must necessarily remain cursory—can be set forth:

1. The term *arrangement* for a fugue fashioned by Bach from a trio-sonata movement is misleading and, in truth, inappropriate. Without exception, one is dealing with a new composition, based on given thematic materials, generally thematic combinations with fixed countersubjects. Bach's approach, which results in fully altering the structural and formal proportions of the original, can be sensed even from a simple comparison of the expansiveness of the new compositions with the sonata models: the arrangements of Reinken's music are almost twice as long as the pieces on which they are based (BWV 965 = 85 mm., the Reinken movement = 50 mm.; BWV 966 = 97 mm., the Reinken original = 47 mm.; BWV 954 = 95 mm., the Reinken original = 50 mm.). The arrangement of the Corelli work goes even further and is almost three times the length of its model (BWV 579 = 102 mm., the Corelli movement = 39 mm.).

2. Although the young Bach immersed himself in the composition of

suites in the French manner (including the corresponding models by Böhm and Reinken), when it came to writing contrapuntal movements he relied primarily on Italian style. The basis for this tendency was established with his early schooling in the Pachelbel tradition. This development took a decisive turn, however, as Bach strove to achieve a synthesis of the North German archetype (expansive form) and the Italian ideal (clear thematic profile, closed disposition)—and indeed under the influence of trio-sonata practice. In the process, additional qualities entered into Bach's keyboard fugues that did not stem simply from the tradition of keyboard music. It is precisely in this connection that the influence on Bach of the older Italian sonata and concerto style (especially the elements of ritornello, episode, and sequence techniques) must be reappraised, in order to differentiate it from the influence of the new Italian writing of the Vivaldian stamp, which did not take hold until Weimar.

3. In his keyboard fugues Bach developed principal structural components from the model of the contrapuntal trio-sonata movement. To these components belong especially:

a. Consistent and logical part writing.

b. The production of an independent, closed movement. The concept of the fugue as a movement, not a section, makes possible the form pair later so greatly preferred by Bach, the prelude and fugue.

c. The development of motivically unified contrapuntal fabric. See, for instance, Example 6.1, where the closing figuration of Reinken's theme (m. 4) is refashioned by Bach into an independent imitative motif (m. 24 and elsewhere), or Example 6.2, where the running motion of the theme is, in contrast to Reinken's original, expanded contrapuntally.

d. The differentiation of thematic exposition and episode. Reinken's contrapuntal sonata movements are episode-free, while the Italian counterparts display episodes without exception (although they are sometimes extremely short). Bach appropriates episodic technique for his Reinken fugues and uses it to expand the pieces.

Example 6.1. Reinken, Fugue from Sonata I, "Hortus Musicus," and Bach, Fugue in A Minor BWV 965/2

Example 6.2. Reinken, Fugue from Sonata XI, and Bach,
Fugue in C Major BWV 966/2

Example 6.3. Bach, Fugue in A Minor BWV 965/2

e. The expansion of sequential patterns, especially through the setting of thematic expositions in other keys. Sequential schemes, which also belong to the North German keyboard idiom, are employed in the modulatory manner of the Italian trio sonata (see Ex. 6.3).

4. Bach strove to endow his subjects and countersubjects with a pronounced rhythmic and melodic contour, which finds its clearest precedent in Corelli's works (see Ex. 6.6 below). In Examples 6.4 and 6.5, Reinken's countersubject, which is consistently maintained, is varied by Bach and treated in a nonuniform manner—a sign of an experimental phase reflected throughout BWV 965, 966, and 954.

5. As a critical feature of his fugues modeled after trio-sonata movements, Bach relied on the logical and systematic use of double counterpoint. The procedure of voice exchange found in three-voice movements is thereby extended to four- or five-voice textures. In so doing, Bach avoided the systematic use of permutation technique—employed above all by Reinken (Table

Example 6.4. Reinken, Allegro from Sonata VI, and Bach,
Fugue in B♭ Major BWV 954

Example 6.5. Reinken, Allegro from Sonata VI, and Bach,
Fugue in B♭ Major BWV 954

6.2)—as well as the asymmetrical ordering of entries, often seen, for instance, in Corelli (Exs. 6.6 and 6.7).

6. The permutation and voice-exchange techniques of Reinken furnish the models for Bach's thematic expositions in double counterpoint, which are, however, handled much more flexibly (including modulation to distant keys). The expansion of the fugue through a new harmonic dimension and the extension of the form through strategically placed episodes appear to have been among Bach's early goals. In 1759 Friedrich Wilhelm Marpurg reported a conversation with Bach concerning these techniques:

> Just consider his fugues. How many ingenious transpositions of the principal subject, how many splendidly assorted subsidiary ideas you will find there! I myself once heard him, when during my stay in Leipzig I was discussing with him certain matters concerning the fugue, pronounce the works of an old and hard-working contrapuntist dry and wooden, and certain fugues by a more modern and no less great contrapuntist—that is, in the form in which they are arranged for clavier—pedantic; the first because the composer stuck continuously to his principal subject, without any change; and the second be-

Table 6.2. Permutation structures in Reinken's fugues

Sonata in A Minor, Allegro

Violin 1	a	b			a	b	
Violin 2		a	b			a	b
Continuo			a	b			a
	v	i	v	i	v	i	

This scheme is repeated exactly in the second half of the movement. N.B.: in BWV 965 (Bach's arrangement of the movement) the thematic entries are likewise limited to the tonic (i) and dominant (v). Double counterpoint is not maintained strictly.

Sonata in C Major, Allegro

Violin 1	a	b			a	b	
Violin 2		a	b			a	b
Continuo			a	b			a
	v	i	v	i	v	i	

The segment marked with a bracket is repeated five times. N.B.: BWV 966 (Bach's arrangement of the movement) includes thematic entries in b and c as well at the tonic (i) and dominant (v). Double counterpoint is not maintained strictly.

Sonata in B♭ Major, Allegro

Violin 1	a	b			a	b	
Violin 2		a	b			a	b
Continuo			a	b			a
	v	i	v	i	v	i	

The scheme is repeated in the fashion of the Sonata in C Major. N.B.: BWV 954 (Bach's arrangement of the movement) also includes thematic entries in D minor, G minor, E♭ major, C major, and F major (including a diminution of the theme in inversion). Double counterpoint is not carried out strictly.

cause, at least in the fugues under discussion, he had not shown enough fire to reanimate the theme by interludes.[76]

Permutation technique, used consistently, allows neither episodes nor harmonic digressions—essential elements of Bach's instrumental fugues, but not of his vocal fugues. His involvement with permutation technique in a number of early keyboard works,[77] however, appears to precede his development of the vocal permutation fugue, as it first appears in cantata 71 of 1708.[78] This clearly contradicts the conventional view that Bach's permutation fugue is a specifically vocal phenomenon.[79]

The new dating and briefly sketched reappraisal of the Reinken fugues within the broad and narrow context of Bach's early works raise questions that are not well served by hasty answers. Rather, they lead to the plea that the youthful and first master periods of Bach be thought through once again, in terms of both biography and musical style. The reassignment of compo-

Example 6.6. Corelli, Vivace from Sonata, op. 3, no. 4

Example 6.7. Bach, Fugue in B Minor BWV 579

sitions long dated ca. 1720 to a time nearly half a generation earlier signifies that one must grant the young Bach a greater measure of compositional craft and artistic discipline than has been done in the past.

But above all, Bach's fugues after Reinken, Corelli, Albinoni, Legrenzi, and perhaps other still-to-be identified masters offer a concrete look into that sphere of intense "study" that made Bach, according to the testimony of Carl Philipp Emanuel, "even in his youth a pure and strong fugue writer." At a very early point, there emerge elements of the most characteristic and essential parameters of Bach's compositional art:[80] the probing elaboration, modification, and transformation of a given musical *res facta* originating from himself or another composer, with the aim of improvement and further individualization. Bach's Reinken fugues reflect both of these goals. They are more expansive and represent more perfect realizations of a new idea of fugal genre, yet at the same time they carry a more personal stamp than do their original models.

7

Vivaldi's Compositional Art, Bach, and the Process
of "Musical Thinking"

THE RECEPTION and reputation of Vivaldi's music have benefited as well as suffered from linking the Venetian composer with Johann Sebastian Bach. In the later nineteenth century Bach scholarship contributed a great deal toward rescuing Vivaldi from oblivion. His works, together with those of other Baroque composers, such as Schütz and Buxtehude, were studied and looked upon primarily from the perspective of their influence on Bach. This practice in turn often prevented the reception, evaluation, and estimation of the musical contributions of those so-called forerunners as art of its own kind and in its own right.

In Vivaldi's case, Bach-oriented scholarship and practice can clearly be held responsible for placing emphasis, eventually overemphasis, on the concerto compositions at the expense of other genres and repertoires in which Vivaldi had written extensively as well. Of course, concerto production dominates Vivaldi's output, but if his concerto style is primarily looked upon from the viewpoint of Bach's transcriptions, it will only fix existing misconceptions and result in further misunderstandings of the music of both composers. A more comprehensive style-critical examination of the instrumental and vocal repertoires outside the concerto realm has hardly begun, and the recently published monumental work and source catalogue[1] demonstrates how nearly insurmountable any pertinent large-scale analytical undertaking might be.

Fortunately, there have been a number of insightful analytical studies, beginning with Arnold Schering's path-breaking book,[2] but more recently the writings especially of Rudolf Eller,[3] Walter Kolneder,[4] Michael Talbot,[5] and Peter Ryom,[6] which focused on the manifold and unique qualities of Vivaldi's concerto compositions and resulted in a fairly detailed and remarkably balanced general perception of Vivaldi's historical and artistic merits. Nevertheless, primarily on the level of aesthetic value judgment but also in areas beyond, the Vivaldi-Bach relationship rests on a rather fragile and sensitive commensurability.

It is not my intention here to address this issue of commensurability. I shall again approach Vivaldi's music from a Bach perspective, but from one that differs fundamentally, however, from the customary view, because I call on Bach as an early—and without question the most prominent—analyst of Vivaldi's compositional art. I shall also pay particular attention to the Bach-Vivaldi transcriptions. I propose, however, not to look at them for purposes of comparison, but rather for identifying—through the screen of Bach's transcriptions—the foundations and principles of Vivaldi's compositional art. My point of departure is the famous Vivaldi reference in Johann Nicolaus Forkel's Bach book of 1802,[7] where he discusses how Bach gave himself tuition in musical composition by studying and transcribing the violin concertos of Vivaldi.

There are a number of problems with Forkel's discussion of this matter, as Hans-Joachim Schulze has pointed out in connection with his research on the origin and transmission of Bach's concerto transcriptions.[8] First of all, Forkel's chronological frame is wrong; he puts the Vivaldi transcriptions together with Bach's studying the music of Frescobaldi, Froberger, Kerll, Pachelbel, Buxtehude, and others. That means Forkel is off by at least a decade, for Bach's Vivaldi transcriptions can be dated rather exactly in the years 1713–1714.[9] Second, the question of Bach's concerto transcriptions serving exclusively for study purposes cannot be put aside without recognizing that those transcriptions must have functioned in addition, if not primarily, as practical arrangements and virtuoso commissioned works to satisfy the demand at the Weimar court for this new and fashionable genre. The young duke, Johann Ernst, had encountered it on his trip to Amsterdam, from where he returned in the summer of 1713 with a large collection of new music. Third, Forkel mentions transcriptions only of Vivaldi concertos although Bach definitely arranged also works of other composers—among the Italians most notably Alessandro Marcello (BWV 974), Benedetto Marcello (BWV 981), and Giuseppe Torelli (BWV 979).

The fact that Forkel misdated and oversimplified the pertinent circumstances does not necessarily mean that he was merely conjecturing. There are enough other, analogous cases where he applied the right information to the wrong context. Hence it seems advisable to differentiate between the core of the matter and its biographical attribution. Forkel's key statement says that the Vivaldi transcriptions "taught him [Bach] how to think musically." Forkel could[10] never have invented such a phrase because his limited knowledge of Vivaldi's music could provide him with absolutely no basis for passing this kind of judgment. Thus the information most likely came from his principal biographical sources, namely the two eldest Bach sons, Wilhelm Friedemann and Carl Philipp Emanuel. In the same paragraph, for example, Forkel discusses—as mentioned above—the influence of Frescobaldi, Froberger, Pachelbel, Buxtehude, and other seventeenth-century keyboard masters—and this discussion can be traced directly to its source: a letter written by Carl Philipp Emanuel Bach in the year 1775.[11] The Vivaldi reference appears to have come from a similarly reliable source—namely, ultimately from Johann Sebastian Bach himself, who had passed this kind of information on to his family and students.

The tendency to stress Bach's intensive self-study goes back to Carl Philipp Emanuel Bach's obituary, published in 1754. There, for instance, it is said that Bach became a strong fugue writer at an early age "through his own applied reflection" (*durch angewandtes eigenes Nachsinnen*) on the basis of models provided by Buxtehude, Reinken, and others. Forkel's remark that Vivaldi's works taught Bach "musical thinking" goes in the same direction, although the implications are far more universal. But this makes sense too, because the time of the concerto transcriptions, the years 1713–1714, coincides exactly with the period in which Bach's personal style takes on its most characteristic shape.[13] His confrontation in 1713–1714 with the new concerto style provoked what was certainly the strongest single developmental step toward the formation of a genuinely personal style. And that style's unmistakable identity came about primarily through his coupling of Italianisms with complex counterpoint, marked by busy interweavings of the inner voices as well as harmonic refinement.

The fact that only Vivaldi's name is linked to the concerto transcriptions suggests his preeminent role for Bach, as is evidenced also by the number of Vivaldi transcriptions, most of which (five out of nine) are based on *L'Estro armonico* (Op. 3) of 1711.[14] It is likely, therefore, that Bach himself passed on the impression that it was specifically the Vivaldi experience that taught him how to think musically ("lehrte ihn musikalisch denken").

The phrase *musikalisch denken* (to think musically) means "to be conscious of, and to proceed consciously with, ideas in a way that is related to music,"[15] that is, to think in terms of music about musical subject matter. As a matter of fact, with respect to Bach's Vivaldi transcriptions, Forkel is quite a bit more detailed stating "that 'Ordnung, Zusammenhang und Verhältnis' [not easily rendered by single words: order/organization, connection/continuity, and relation/proportion] must be brought to bear on ideas and that to such an end some kind of guide was necessary."[16] Bach recognized and realized that Vivaldi's concertos reflected a concrete compositional system based on a process of musical thinking in terms of order, continuity, and proportion. This must be considered the most abstract and at the same time the most illuminating definition of Vivaldi's compositional system as primarily exemplified in his concertos, but penetrating his work in other genres as well.

"Thinking musically" in terms of order and organization, continuity and connection, as well as proportion and relation: What does this mean with respect to the process of musical composition? It is important to realize that Bach's statement actually makes no reference to form and genre as objects of learning; concerto transcription represents only the means toward the goal of learning how to think musically. Furthermore, no reference is made to the fundamentals of compositional technique: counterpoint, harmony, melody, meter and rhythm, thoroughbass, voice leading, and so on. Bach describes compositional method in abstract functional terms (as he also, for example, defines harmony for Birnbaum's reply to Scheibe).[17]

This decidedly functional approach is fundamentally novel both as a concept in the history of musical composition and in Bach's own compositional experience. His study of fugue, motet, suite, concerto, sonata, and other genres and compositional techniques moved along the traditional paths, which he tried to expand and successfully so. Vivaldi's concertos, however, confronted him with an entirely new set of problems and possibilities. This is not to say that Vivaldi was the first and only one to develop a new compositional concept, but he certainly was the principal exponent and, more likely than not, the decisive intellectual and practical architect of a new way of musical composition based on genuine "musical thinking" exemplified first and foremost in his concertos (beginning with opus 3) but not limited to this genre.

II

I propose to look upon Vivaldi's concertos less from the point of view of formal design and characteristics of genre but, rather, from a perspective of general compositional procedure. This analytical approach is at best hinted at, here and there, in certain discussions of Vivaldi's concerto form (especially in the writings of Rudolf Eller) but it has not been broadly applied. Michael Talbot, who provided us with the most comprehensive description of Vivaldi's personal style, has identified the various sources that constitute Vivaldi's distinct musical language.[18] Nevertheless, the core of Vivaldi's compositional concept and method—opening up new dimensions of musical composition that influenced through many channels the course of eighteenth-century music—had early on been recognized and defined by Johann Sebastian Bach.

I should like to apply Bach's analytical approach to a concrete example of Vivaldi's compositional art, the Concerto in G Major (op. 3, no. 3), stressing the fact that this exemplary work provided Vivaldi and Bach (in his transcription as Concerto in F Major BWV 978) with the ideal vehicle for exploring and developing specific ways of "musical thinking" and that those ways quickly penetrated other instrumental and vocal genres as well. The concerto as a musical genre or form is indeed secondary, and the same is true of counterpoint, thematic invention, and other technical aspects of musical composition (including word-tone relationships in vocal music). What Bach calls "musical thinking" is, in fact, nothing but the conscious application of generative and formative procedures, the thorough rationalization of the creative act.

The Largo of op. 3, no. 3, presents a case in point irrespective of its being a concerto movement (see Ex. 7.1). The notational form of the examples to be discussed is generally adopted directly from Bach's transcription rather

Example 7.1. Largo from Concerto in F Major BWV 978, Bach's transcription of Vivaldi's Concerto in G Major, op. 3, no. 3

than from Vivaldi's original full score: not for purposes of comparing Bach and Vivaldi, but because the notational image of Bach's keyboard score represents, in effect, a first step toward abstracting musical substance. In other words, it helps us to examine the compositional material as such, apart from its realization in sound.

The inseparable functions of Ordnung, Zusammenhang, and Verhältnis become clear from the very beginning of the movement, which consists of an essentially straightforward elaboration of a basic, not to say primitive, musical idea: a plain D minor triad. It hardly needs to be mentioned that Bach certainly never claimed to have turned to Vivaldi for receiving inspiration regarding the *ars inveniendi* (Vivaldi's themes are often rather bare, rudimentary, and even poor), but for learning how to apply the process of "musical thinking" to developing musical ideas of varying substance. It seems possible to reconstruct this process and to identify its components and logical stages, respectively:

1. The point of departure is the formation of a germinal cell representing in a nutshell the musical substance of the entire movement (see Ex. 7.2). It consists of a triad (a: m. 1) generating both a linear melodic variant (b: mm. 2, 4, 6, etc.) and a coherent sequence of modified chords (c: mm. 1, 3, 5, 7, etc.).

2. The thematic substance contains the potential for developing both related and contrasting motifs: mm. 1–2 (3–4, 5–6, etc.) juxtapose motifs that are related (primarily by means of their common triadic nature) as well as contrasting (primarily by means of their different rhythmic and dynamic gestures).

3. The motifs are differentiated by hierarchical means (m. 1: primary = tutti; m. 2: secondary = solo) with their organizational sequence being irreversible.

4. Both primary and secondary motifs develop variants in order to secure

Example 7.2.

continuity and change (note, for instance, in measures 2, 4, 6, 8, etc., the constantly changing pitch organization of a basically stable figurative pattern).

5. Each measure possesses an unmistakable individuality, yet the successive order of measures constitutes a chain whose members display clearly structured correlations:

mm. 1 + 2 = same harmony; vertical chords vs. linear melody
mm. 1 + 3 = different harmony; similar vertical chords
mm. 2 + 4 = different harmony; varied melodic figuration
mm. 1 + 5 = identical chords
mm. 2 + 6 = same harmony; modified melodic figuration
and so on

6. The gradually unfolding scheme of Ordnung, Zusammenhang, and Verhältnis tends to focus on regular metric periodization: proportion 1 : 1 (mm. 1 + 2, 3 + 4, 5 + 6, etc.); proportion 2 : 1 (mm. 15/16 + 17); proportion 2 : 2 (mm. 18/19 + 20/21). Moreover, it establishes carefully placed sections of greater declamatory density: mm. 12–14 = first three-measure unit and first extended solo; mm. 20–21 = first ascending figurative scale pattern, followed by mm. 26–27 = double descending figurative scale pattern. In the latter instances (mm. 22, 26–27) Bach adds to Vivaldi's score a second figurative line in parallel sixths and tenths [*], apparently in order to emphasize these singular melodic phrases and give them stronger harmonic direction.

"Musical thinking" in this movement means something very different from pursuing conventional compositional techniques such as, for instance, designing a fugal exposition by finding the proper scheme of subject and answer or harmonizing a melody. Vivaldi's novel compositional method means identifying the substance of a musical idea in order to elaborate on it; the process of elaboration then has to observe the closely interrelated categories of Ordnung, and Zusammenhang, and Verhältnis that provide the functional framework for developing, organizing, and unifying a piece.

It seems important to stress the fact that Vivaldi's compositional procedure here is an "abstract" one; in other words, it has nothing to do with the genre of concerto. For example, the tutti-solo indications in this piece that are to be found in Schering's edition are editorial and neither notated in the original manuscript nor actually required as a structural element for keyboard performance. In other words, Bach's transcription represents an analytical approach in that it reduces the complex fabric of the full score to its generic compositional substance.

TURNING NOW to the opening Allegro movement of op. 3, no. 4 (see Ex. 7.3), I should like to focus primarily on the structural design and generative

a.

Vivaldi's
basso continuo,
transposed

b.
7

Example 7.3. Allegro from Concerto in F Major BWV 978

potential of the ritornello (= mm. 1–11). The ritornello is composed of four
sections, each one made up of motifs that function as constituent members
of the whole. The "antecedent" section (a: mm. 1–2) consists of a "motto" or
head motif that gives the entire piece, from the very beginning, its identity
and makes the ritornello distinctly recognizable as the most crucial part of
the formal structure. The two measures establish, particularly in Vivaldi's
original version, a very strong contrast in that m. 1 represents an anticipating linear-melodic projection of the simple triadic sequence (tonic-

Example 7.4.

dominant-tonic = T-D-T) that follows in m. 2 in its plain chordal version (see Ex. 7.4).

Bach's modified version cancels Vivaldi's sharp juxtaposition of the two measures (which in a nutshell also foreshadow the application of the solo-tutti principle in the movement) and thereby loosens the strongly asymmetric rhythmic pulse (♪/m. 1 vs. ♩/m. 2). What Bach's version gains, however, is a new contrapuntal dimension (mm. 1 and 2 are now linked by means of imitation) and rhythmic continuity, which both underscore the material identity of the two measures.

The "consequent" section (b: mm. 3–4) basically presents a spun-out and rhythmically animated, intensified continuation of the material from m. 2, harmonically serving as a double confirmation of the T-D motion. Vivaldi's original provides this section with a steady and regular harmonic underpinning (eighth-note tremolo: twice T-D), whereas Bach's version introduces "perpetuum mobile" (sixteenth-note) motion by introducing complementary rhythm in the bass line for the second half of each measure.

The following section (c: mm. 5–6) establishes a cadence in the dominant key, introducing for the first time conjunct melodic-harmonic progressions, that is, an ascending scale pattern in both treble and bass parts. Bach's version again redefines Vivaldi's original in that it extends, for both rhythmic and contrapuntal purposes, the ascending bass line to a full octave F–f,* beginning in m. 4.

The final section (d: mm. 7–11, actually ending at beginning of m. 12) consists of a modulating sequential motif (spanning one octave and presenting a direct expansion of the scale pattern of the previous section). Bach changes Vivaldi's eighth-note tremolo bass, an effective orchestral continuo figure, to a more idiomatic keyboard bass that matches and regularizes the declamatory gesture of the treble line at the same time.

In what way does this ritornello structure reflect genuine "musical thinking"?

---

* In this book I have followed the convention that represents middle c as a lower-case *c*. The lower octaves are represented by capital letters and numerical subscripts, and the higher octaves by primes added to the lower-case letters. Therefore: C_1, C, [middle] c, c', c'', etc.

1. At the very beginning the composer formulates a germinal cell (= section a) that offers strong potential for multi-faceted elaboration. Almost everything that occurs later in the ritornello as well as in the episodes can be related to the harmonic, melodic, and rhythmic contents of this head motif.

2. The ritornello itself establishes Ordnung: an organizational scheme with the proper order of musical ideas, their organization, their systematic connection as well as their correlation, and finally, their logical succession. Moreover, it introduces a ranking of the individual sections in terms of striking musical character and recognizability (section a outweighs all others), and of the classification of harmonic functions (section a is the only harmonically closed one: T-D-T; section b: D-T; section c: D-DD-D; section d: D-T). Therefore, the order of the four members of the ritornello is not changeable, although the head motif can function independently, as is demonstrated in a modulatory passage later in the movement (mm. 45ff.; see Ex. 7.5).

Particularly effective is the very end where the final statement of the ritornello reverses the order so that section a follows section d (see Ex. 7.6).

3. The ritornello emphasizes and propels the principle of Zusammenhang: the mutual connection of its members and motifs, the continuity of texture and declamation, and the preservation of a multi-layered context. This becomes evident if one observes the connection between m. 1 and m. 2 of section a, between section a and section b, between sections a-b and section c, and so on. These connections are likewise projected in the continuity that exists in the uniform accompanimental style of the bass line (eighth-note tremolo) in Vivaldi's original version, originating in mm. 3–4, continuing in mm. 7–11, and even carried into the solo episode, mm. 12ff. Bach's redefinition of the bass line eliminates the uniformity of the accompanimental underpinning. His version protects, however, the element of continuity on a more complex level; for example, the sixteenth-note arpeggio bass (mm. 7ff.) is transformed into its eighth-note equivalent (mm. 12ff.).

Example 7.5.

Example 7.6.

The question of relationship between tutti ritornello and solo episodes raises the issue of large-scale context, meaning the issue of unity within a movement. Vivaldi carefully observed the principle of compositional Zusammenhang on many levels. For instance, in the first solo episode (mm. 12ff.) he introduced a new, and for the first time uninterrupted, sixteenth-note figuration in the treble; he preserved continuity, however, not only by deriving the figurative pattern from that of ritornello motif b (mm. 3–4) but especially by not changing the bass accompaniment (see Ex. 7.3).

The bass accompaniment serves in general as a stabilizing factor throughout the movement and draws particular attention only when it departs from its mold (for example, mm. 25ff.: changing from diatonic to chromatic steps; mm. 41ff.: changing to quarter notes). The various subtle modifications in accompanimental style result in a symmetric organization of the four solo episodes: solos 1 (mm. 12–15) and 4 (mm. 51b–55a) show identical accompaniment, solos 3 (mm. 22b–29) and 4 (mm. 37b–45a) present two different modifications.

4. The ritornello regulates the interplay of its sections by the principle of Verhältnis—by emphasizing both mutual relation and rational proportion—and projects these relations and proportions onto a larger scale for the entire movement. The periodicity, for example, is governed by proportional organization: section a ($= 1 + 1$), b ($= 1 + 1$), a + b ($= 2 + 2$), a/b + c ($= 4 + 2$), d ($= 1 + 1 + 1 + 1 + 1$), a/b/c + d ($= 6 + 5$). The openly asymmetric 6 : 5 proportion, nevertheless, has its logical foundation in that it modulates from D to T in exactly five steps (these five steps from c to g are actually anticipated in section c, mm. 5–6); in other words, the number 5 is a well-reasoned number, a case in point of "musical thinking." The period structure of the solo episodes depends on the ritornello model as well; compare, for instance, the half-measure harmonic rhythm and whole-measure repeat in mm. 12–13 ($= 2 \times 1$) with that of mm. 3–4 ($= 2 \times 1$).

Verhältnis refers not only to periodicity (with its even and uneven, but rational proportions), but also to tonal and modulatory planning, the changing degrees of harmonic rhythm (compare, for example, mm. 1–4 and mm. 5–6: half-measure vs. quarter-note rhythm), modulatory procedures (compare mm. 1–2 and 45–51), and regulation of overall diastematic activity of the outer voices (particularly crucial in the alternation of ritornello, episodes, and parts thereof). As Forkel reported, Bach "studied the chain of the ideas, their relation [Verhältnis] to each other, the variety of the modulations, and many other particulars."[21] In short, whatever is covered under the Verhältnis principle intimately relates to Ordnung and Zusammenhang as well. All three parameters are both interdependent and interpenetrating.

IF ONE EXAMINES a Vivaldi piece beyond its largely external formal structures—be it a concerto, aria, or other genre—one reaches the essence of this compositional art. The historical significance of Vivaldi's compositional method, which is reflected in the widespread influence his music exercised primarily after the publication of *L'Estro armonico* (1711), has its foundation in an enormously fruitful dialectic of two extremely different aesthetic premises: simplicity (implying a broad spectrum from purity, clarity, and correctness to graceful and natural elegance) and complexity (implying intellectual involvement, sophisticated elaboration, and rational control).

These poles allowed for a wide range of possibilities, which were governed by a multi-faceted yet crystal-clear system that Vivaldi had developed virtually single-handedly. He developed this system on the basis of a synthetic approach toward individual traditional compositional features and elements primarily from the realm of instrumental music and especially from the concerto and sonata genres, and it was none other than Johann Sebastian Bach who identified it as a process of genuine "musical thinking." By this he meant a functional and material interplay of musical ideas (not limited to themes and motifs) that are to be generated and regulated by inner musical criteria beyond the conventional boundaries established for the treatment of themes and motifs, achieved by applying traditional—mainly contrapuntal—compositional rules and techniques.

Vivaldi's ingenious process of "musical thinking" and Bach's understanding and further development of its manifold implications provided one of the more decisive points of departure in the early eighteenth century for a fast-growing tendency in the history of musical composition: the prevailing role and eventual dominance of instrumental music as the principal and most congenial vehicle for the rigorous pursuit of a process of absolute "musical thinking." This process, guided by abstract principles of Ordnung, Zusammenhang and Verhältnis (order/organization, connection/continuity, relation/proportion) introduced at the same time a new yardstick by which compositional competence, artistic individuality, and aesthetic value was to be measured.

8

Bach and the Tradition of the
Palestrina Style

ON SUMMER TRAVELS IN 1827, the eighteen-year-old Felix Mendelssohn Bartholdy encountered the Heidelberg professor of law Anton Friedrich Justus Thibaut, a gifted musical amateur who had established a choral organization devoted, under his ardent guidance, to the older a cappella repertoire. His enthusiasm as one of the founders of the revival of early music was characterized in the report Mendelssohn sent home, as follows:[1]

> . . . he sparked my commitment to the old Italian music, the flame of his fire
> has warmed me. A glow of fervor speaks from him . . . As we took leave just
> now, I spoke to him about Seb. Bach and told him that what mattered most
> was still unknown to him, for in Sebastian all converges and he said: Farewell,
> our friendship shall be founded in Luis de Victoria [the master closest to Palestrina] and Sebastian Bach.

The art of Bach and that of Palestrina: two totally heterogeneous musical phenomena are here joined. Both were to exert, in different ways, the most lasting influence upon the history of music, especially that of the nineteenth century. It was not accidental that in this period of an awakening consciousness of history there arose a Bach movement as well as a Palestrina renaissance, which, despite obvious dissimilarities, must be closely associated in our view. Taking their point of departure from the writings of Wilhelm Heinrich Wackenroder and Ludwig Tieck, the Romantics began to discover the treasures of the musical past. It was the first time that historical concerts were presented; and Mendelssohn's circle took the lead.

That which is rediscovered necessarily represents the lost or the forgotten. It is true that neither the names of the old masters nor some of their works were ever entirely forgotten (Schütz, for instance, knew some of Lasso's compositions, Haydn some of Handel's, and there was also an unbroken eighteenth-century Bach tradition), but their legacy as a whole was hidden, was no longer a living force in the musical world. Palestrina's music forms a certain exception, based not on his works so much as on a style of vocal polyphony inseparably connected with his name since the early seventeenth century. This was a tradition to which composers of all later generations—from 1600 to 1900—responded. Our interest in the present context will be centered upon the reasons, manner, and circumstances of the lasting recognition accorded to the so-called Palestrina style, so that we may gain a larger historical perspective that will afford an insight into Bach's attitude toward it.

I

What is understood by the style of vocal polyphony—for this must be our first concern—can be seen in the beginning of Palestrina's "Missa sine Nomine" (1590); see Example 8.1. The predominant six-voice texture exhibits strict part-writing in which the individual voices unfold on the basis of motet-like imitation. The melodic style is beholden to the single line, vocally conceived, consistently diatonic, avoiding chromaticism, and evenly balanced between thesis and arsis. The rhythmic structure shuns strong accents and contrasts; it is shaped in the manner of prose, the flow of the vocal contours corresponding to unconstrained gestures of speech. In this sense the age of classical vocal polyphony is still linked to the Flemish mensural practice marked by fluent declamation and unencumbered by regular metric accents. The affinity to mensural music is readily seen in the preponderance of large note values (the quarter note is the smallest unit). The performance speed is governed by the natural pulse of the *integer valor notarum,* the un-

Example 8.1. Palestrina, "Missa sine Nomine"

Example 8.2. Monteverdi, "Exulta, filia Sion"

Example 8.3. Monteverdi, *Combattimento di Tancredi e Clorinda*

changeable pace represented principally by half-note motion; it allows occasionally for proportional but never for arbitrary tempo modification. The harmonic nature arises from the vertical sonorities of the polyphonic fabric, it does not function as a primary element of structure, as it does in later periods.

There are many detailed precepts of composition regarding, for instance, the use of dissonance or intervalic progressions. Because of such strict regulations of part-writing, the style of vocal polyphony was unequaled as a didactic model, and even today it serves as a basis of contrapuntal studies aimed at a training in musical logic. The sixteenth century, well aware of other manners of composition (such as those germane to madrigal and chanson writing), saw in this style, with its even, "classical" texture, an *ars perfecta*, the highest achievement of musical art.

By 1600 radical innovations set in. The *nuove musiche,* characteristically represented by monody, opened unknown vistas for the relationship of word and music. The technical means permitted an expression of the verbal text in vocal music that ranged from lyric introspection to passionate ecstasy. Claudio Monteverdi's *stile concitato* renders the expressive and aesthetic departures from the old art with greatest clarity, as for instance in his motet "Exulta, filia Sion" (1629); see Example 8.2. Everything is now subservient to a heightened expressiveness in the interest of which—according to the measure of text interpretation indicated—the rules of part writing were broken. Such a case can be seen in the final cadence of Monteverdi's *Combattimento di Tancredi e Clorinda* (1624), where the syncopated fourth, in disregard of the rule, fails to resolve into the third prior to the final measure (Ex. 8.3).

A sophisticated procedure of composition such as this would have been unthinkable in the sixteenth century. Yet the old style was not devoid of expression, as is demonstrated in Palestrina's music and even more so in the works of Lasso. It merely adhered to means of expression subject to the limitations of contrapuntal clarity—and herein apparently lay its classical quality. Seventeenth-century theorists were given to formulating the resulting dichotomy of styles, with reference to Plato, as follows. "Harmonia orationis domina—Oratio harmoniae domina absolutissima": in older music harmonic euphony rules over the word, whereas in modern music it is the expression of text that rules supreme.

The old art was not entirely abandoned in the seventeenth century, and even Monteverdi, spokesman of *le nuove musiche,* paid obeisance to it; witness his "Missa in illo tempore" (1610). But traditional vocal polyphony was almost entirely bound to liturgical practice, predominantly in works with Latin texts; it became the *stile antico.* And the archaic texture of such works distinguished them clearly from the "affective" literature of the *seconda prattica* representing the *stile moderno.*

The continued cultivation of the style of vocal polyphony even influenced instrumental music. Again, we are dealing primarily with liturgical pieces, such as the Kyrie versets on *cantus firmi* in Girolamo Frescobaldi's *Fiori Musicali* of 1635 (Ex. 8.4.). The stately organ sound here emulates the vocal a cappella ideal, a sonority in which the polyphonic fabric can evolve with optimum clarity and transparency. Frescobaldi's collection, placing side by side the free forms of toccata and canzona and the strict forms of ricercar and verset, discloses a tendency that henceforth was to determine the tradition of the style of vocal polyphony. The constant confrontation of *stile antico* and *stile moderno* produced a trend that, given the preponderance of new idioms, could not fail to reshape the concept of the Palestrina style. The result entailed not only a more colorful harmonic language, departing from the modal system that emerged, but also a more liberal melodic language as well as a certain assimilation of instrumental elements. The dominance of tranquil polyphonic flow was not, however, impaired. A perceptible separation of *stile moderno* and *stile antico* remained, except that the latter no longer embodied classical vocal polyphony but an imitation of it.

The original print of the *Fiori Musicali* (Venice, 1635) introduces a new factor. The notation in four-part score (not in the customary Italian keyboard tablature on two systems) suggests that the work is to serve not only for performance but also for contrapuntal instruction. In the interest of a more readily intelligible exposition of part-writing, each voice is separately rendered, a manner of notation which can be traced through similar works rang-

Example 8.4. Frescobaldi, Kyrie verset from *Fiori Musicali*

ing from Scheidt's *Tabulatura Nova* (Hamburg, 1624) to Bach's Art of Fugue. In manuscript sources of the seventeenth and eighteenth centuries the *Fiori Musicali* are often placed next to Palestrina's Masses, an indication that they were understood as classical models for the study of strict counterpoint. We might thus distinguish two tenets of continuing tradition: (1) the application of vocal polyphony in the liturgical domain and (2) the study of counterpoint.

In Germany the stylistic dichotomy was not as pronounced as in Italy since a conservative motet style remained relatively constant. Protestant church music was especially conservative, even though structural elements of monody and concertato style were soon interspersed. The Palestrinian manner eventually assumed a marginal role, as it did in Italy and in the other European countries. The work of Heinrich Schütz, for instance, is governed by the modern orientation, especially in his younger years. Yet it is indicative of the attitude of the aged master that he asked his student Christoph Bernhard to write a Latin funeral motet for him "in the Palestrinian contrapuntal style." The followers of Schütz, who had categorically turned to the "stylus without basso continuo" in his *Geistliche Chormusik* (Dresden, 1648), were remarkably committed to conservative polyphony, as is evident from the Palestrina examples in Bernhard's *Tractatus Compositionis Augmentatus* and Johann Theile's *Musicalisches Kunstbuch*. Even in Protestant church music the old polyphonic manner appears exclusively with Latin texts, especially in settings of the Mass texts, as for instance in the well-known Missa Brevis ascribed to Buxtehude. To name just two contemporaries of Bach, Georg Philipp Telemann and Gottfried Heinrich Stölzel are also represented with such Masses. Because these Masses, like numerous similar works of the period, have remained unpublished, however, we cannot as yet arrive at a total assessment of the role held by the *stile antico* in the church music of the seventeenth century and, especially, the eighteenth century.

In the High Baroque of the Catholic south the figure of Johann Joseph Fux comes to the fore, the principal Viennese capellmeister who in his *Gradus ad Parnassum* (Vienna, 1725) produced the fundamental manual based on the Palestrina style—the work that has remained the model for almost all textbooks on counterpoint. Masses and motets in *stile antico* represent again a major share of Fux's own oeuvre, even though their number is smaller than that of his operas and chamber music works, as well as that of his other church compositions. The very fact that he, like other masters of his time, did not devote a larger share of his work to the old style favored the acceptance of contemporary elements. His influence applies equally to his didactic work, which by no means observes the principles of Palestrina's style in all details. But it was the presence of Fux, above all, and that of his colleague Antonio Caldara, that made Vienna one of the most important centers for the cultivation of the *stile antico*. Many currents emanated from there, such as Fux's influence upon the music in Dresden through his student Jan Dismas Zelenka, director of church music at the Saxon court. Turning to the music of Italy in the second half of the eighteenth century, we must single out,

Example 8.5. Motet "Quaerite primum regnum" in versions by Padre Martini and the young Mozart

together with the unbroken Roman Palestrina tradition, the figure of Padre Giambattista Martini, who transmitted the study of strict counterpoint to the large circle of students in Bologna and who edited an important anthology of *cantus firmus* compositions in *stile antico,* ranging from the sixteenth century to the eighteenth. During the summer of 1770, the fourteen-year-old Mozart was among those who studied with him. In order to be admitted to the famous Bolognese Accademia Filarmonica, Mozart had to pass an examination under close supervision, consisting of an elaboration of the antiphone "Quaerite primum regnum" in strict counterpoint. The small work (K. 86), which according to the minutes of the examining committee turned out "satisfactory under the given circumstances," is not free of deviations from the accepted norm, whereas the corrected version by Padre Martini shows the writing of a church musician thoroughly familiar with the Palestrina style (see Ex. 8.5).

Thus we encounter once again the style of vocal polyphony as a didactic model, a model that was followed by nearly all major and minor masters of the Classic era (influential Viennese teachers of counterpoint were, above all, Johann Georg Albrechtsberger and, later, Simon Sechter). In addition, however, the style played a certain role in the practice of church music, though often merely in the form of interpolations, such as are found, for example, in Beethoven's Missa Solemnis.

In Beethoven's work there appears a further, totally new aspect of the Palestrina tradition. The third movement of his String Quartet in A Minor (op. 132) contains extensive passages in an archaic manner of part-writing (see Ex. 8.6). What stands out as a novel feature compared with earlier tradition is not so much the transference of the Palestrina style to the medium of the chamber music ensemble but rather Beethoven's added superscription: "a convalescent's devout thank offering to the deity, in the Lydian mode." Thus the style of the composition of 1825 becomes the expression of subjective religious thought founded in secularized piety. That which formerly was the prototype of church music is now drawn into the sphere of personal utterance. The work, designed in a motet-like imitative manner, contains a quasi *cantus firmus* in the upper part. In deference to the Lydian mode, B flat is consistently avoided, producing a rather plain but doubtless intended harmonic idiom. The departure from sacred modal music of the sixteenth century is underlined by the directions for dynamic expression.

This late work of Beethoven's, highly unusual in its stylistic solution, cannot be understood without some reference to the basis of a Romantic orientation, as clearly formulated in E. T. A. Hoffmann's 1814 essay "Alte und neue Kirchenmusik." Hoffmann is emphatic in recommending the study of the repertoire of classical vocal polyphony, which, as true and pure church music, is to serve for a new orientation. Next to the expression of somewhat self-willed views, we find here characterizations of the style of Palestrina's music that offer us deep insight into the Romantic attitude toward music and its transcendental qualities:

> Without any ornament, devoid of melodic sweep, predominantly full consonant chords follow one another, and by their strength and boldness the mind is seized and elevated with unspeakable force . . . the motion of the individual parts reflects that of *canto firmo;* they rarely exceed the ambitus of a sixth, and no interval is ever used that would be difficult to execute. It is to be understood that Palestrina, according to the custom of his time, wrote only for

Example 8.6. Beethoven, String Quartet in A Minor, op. 132

voices, without the accompaniment of any instrument; for the praise of the Almighty, Most Holy, must sound forth through human breath alone, free from the intervention of foreign medium or sonority. The succession of complete, consonant chords, especially in the minor mode, has become so alien to us in the degeneration of our taste that many . . . will take it only for awkwardness of technical structure . . . Palestrina is plain, true, of childlike devotion, yet strong and powerful . . . his composing was worship.[2]

A rather similar train of thought prevails in the 1825 essay, "Über Reinheit der Tonkunst" by Thibaut, whose orientation and restorative program proved to be of great influence. His parting words to Mendelssohn might here be recalled as a veritable guiding star for part of the evolution of nineteenth-century music history. In the course of the century, however, the religious fervor that marked the approach to old music gave way to one more objectively grounded and indebted in no small measure to scholarly labors (such as those of Carl von Winterfeld or Carl Proske) as well as to practical performances (such as those of Mendelssohn). The editions of collected works by various masters were begun and, as a matter of course, a composer like Brahms was among the subscribers for the Bach-Gesellschaft edition. He considered its completion one of the greatest events of his life. Palestrina and Bach became major factors of inspiration for an entire series of musical figures, chief among them perhaps Mendelssohn, Schumann, Brahms, Bruckner, and finally Reger. Doubtless Bach is his universality ("for in Sebastian all converges" is what Mendelssohn said) was the most profitable source for composers seeking a reflective orientation. Part of the reason may be that his music does not possess such a precisely definable stylistic nature as the music of Palestrina, which tends to lend itself to the process of codification. The Palestrinian style model invariably dominated the works devoted to the ideal of vocal polyphony, especially within Catholic church music oriented by the Cecilian movement. Yet here, among compositions that today might be considered epigonic style imitations (such as Liszt's Missa Choralis of 1865, with its pseudo-Gregorian elements), one also finds the indubitable high point in the nineteenth-century tradition of vocal polyphony, namely in the work of Anton Bruckner. He succeeded—by dint of immersion into the art of Palestrina and of simple piety, and by foregoing the Wagnerian achievements (to which he paid such generous homage in his symphonic work)—in incorporating the old choral polyphony in samples of his church music through an ingenious blend of personal and borrowed styles, as for instance in his E Minor Mass (1866), in which the Sanctus composition is a late afterglow of Palestrina's Missa Papae Marcelli, severe yet passionate music (Ex. 8.7). The real tradition of vocal polyphony ends, in fact, with the Bruckner generation. No truly fertile development followed, for the boundaries of the established tonal systems were exceeded by 1900, thus eliminating the foundation of strict contrapuntal part-writing in the Palestrinian manner. It could not be regained even in the more modern, eclectic a capella music. A "total change" had become irrevocable.

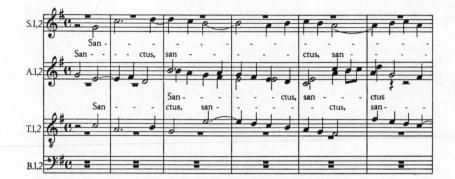

Example 8.7. Palestrina, Sanctus from Missa Papae Marcelli

II

This review of music history has been conducted at an accelerated pace, without regard for some essential and often highly interesting details. Yet the perspective it opens allows for a deeper understanding of Bach's position within the tradition of vocal polyphony. Singling out the figure of Bach is not meant to signify a special role or a high point in this tradition. We are merely concerned with placing Bach vis-à-vis the musical phenomenon of the old vocal-polyphonic style, a question that has not been sufficiently investigated.

We must first identify which of Bach's works clearly evince a connection to the Palestrina style. Considering his immense output, we are dealing with a very small number of compositions (see Table 8.1). It may seem strange that such works as the five-part C♯ Minor Fugue from the Well-Tempered Clavier I, the cantata movement "Es ist der alte Bund" ("Actus Tragicus"), the six-part ricercar from Musical Offering, or similar ones are not included. But despite affinity to the ones listed above these works show in general a different stylistic derivation and texture. They, too, exhibit archaic tendencies here and there. Nevertheless, these *alla breve* compositions represent a mixture of old and new styles—a fusion of homophonic cantabile elements with polyphonic traits, as we know it for instance from the motets by Johann Christoph Bach or fugues by Johann Caspar Ferdinand Fischer. It is necessary to draw a distinction between such *alla breves* (to use a contemporary term) and pieces conceived in the sense of the Palestrina style, the distinguishing factors being those of degree rather than principle.

The works enumerated above have two properties in common. First, the choral movements belong without exception to the figural music written for the Latin service; the keyboard works are essentially liturgical organ music. And second, they were all written during the last twelve years of Bach's Leipzig tenure (the second Kyrie from the 1733 Missa in B Minor forming an exception; thus they derive from the St. Thomas cantor's late period, beginning about the time of Clavier-Übung III (published in 1739).

Where now are the premises for Bach's fascination with classical vocal polyphony? Why did he compose in this style? We might quite generally point to the musical-liturgical tradition of St. Thomas's in Leipzig that Bach embraced in his position as cantor and music director. His office called upon him not only to write church music but also to adhere to the older choral repertory of the worship service. We know that the holdings of the St. Thomas School library, no longer extant, were especially rich in literature of vocal polyphony from the fifteenth, sixteenth, and seventeenth centuries. How Bach managed to use these holdings for his purposes is shown, for instance, in his arrangement of the Sanctus, there preserved, from the Missa Superba by Johann Caspar Kerll (BWV 241).

More significant are direct source references by which Bach's familiarity with theoretical and practical works associated with the style of vocal polyphony can be documented. Particularly valuable in this respect is Bach's personal copy, bearing his autograph signature, of the original Latin edition of Fux's *Gradus ad Parnassum* (now in the Staats- und Universitätsbibliothek, Hamburg). Thus he was informed about the eighteenth-century study of the Palestrina style through its principal source. It is equally notable that its first German translation appeared in Leipzig, edited, with commentary, by Bach's student Lorenz Christoph Mizler, founder of the Leipzig Correspon-

Table 8.1. Works in *stile antico* by J. S. Bach

BWV 232^{I}	Kyrie II	
BWV 232^{II}	Credo in unum Deum	B Minor Mass
	Confiteor unum baptisma	
BWV 552	Fugue in E♭ Major, section 1	
BWV 669	Kyrie, Gott Vater	
BWV 670	Christe, aller Welt Trost	Clavier-Übung III
BWV 671	Kyrie, Gott Heiliger Geist	
BWV 686	Aus tiefer Not	
BWV 878/2	Fugue in E Major	Well-Tempered Clavier II

dierende Societät der musicalischen Wissenschaften. In other words, the edition emanated directly from Bach's circle, and it must be assumed that Bach was among its immediate initiators. The book contains a large number of model examples for the Palestrina style.

The question of Bach's familiarity with compositions by other composers is given detailed answer in a letter by C. P. E. Bach addressed to the Bach biographer Forkel, which says: "In his last years he esteemed highly: Fux, Caldara, Handel, Keiser, Hasse, both Grauns, Telemann, Zelenka, Benda, and in general everything that was worthy of esteem in Berlin and Dresden. Except for the first four, he knew the rest personally."[3] Of special interest in the context of vocal polyphony is the fact that three of those named—Fux, Caldara, and Zelenka—are among the principal exponents of the contemporary conception of the *stile antico.* Yet this is merely a citation of names. What works of other masters were included in Bach's private library?

A considerable portion of this collection has been lost, not even counting the manuscripts of Bach's own compositions. Nevertheless, careful investigation has attested to a holding of approximately thirty masses, individual Mass sections, Magnificats, and other works by different masters (now located predominantly in the collections of the former Prussian State Library, Berlin). This number encompasses only the library segment that is of particular importance for the *stile antico,* namely figural music on Latin texts. It is a much larger segment than identified in the catalogues based on Spitta's and Rust's studies, and this also throws new light upon Bach's own Latin works and their use. There is no doubt that these copies were created for the Leipzig service in the first place. What other reason could there be for Bach's copying, or having copies made of, numerous works by others for his own use, which he was composing new works for other purposes? We must not exclude the possibility that his own works were at times performed in other circumstances, such as the Protestant court service in Dresden—a matter that requires new thought especially in view of the fact that this service was transferred in 1738 to St. Sophia's Church, where Wilhelm Friedemann Bach was organist until 1746; thus there is a direct personal connection.

Among the copies of works by other composers there is only a limited number of direct interest in connection with the *stile antico.* The showpiece, so to speak, is a copy of Palestrina's six-part "Missa sine nomine" (see Ex. 8.1 and Fig. 8.1). Bach provided an instrumentation for the piece, involving two cornetti and four trombones, in order to assure an archaic sound. The copy of Frescobaldi's *Fiori Musicali* from Bach's library unfortunately is lost, but preserved is a collection including two Chorale Masses by Schütz's student Christoph Bernhard and a six-part (fragmentary) Missa of Bernhard's student Johann Christoph Schmidt—an important proof for Bach's connection with the Schütz tradition. Movements in the *stile antico* are also incorporated in an anonymous Magnificat (BWV Anh. 30) and Pergolesi's "Stabat Mater." A copy of the latter is not extant, but we do have the score and parts of Bach's parody of the work on the text "Tilge, Höchster, meine Sünden."

Figure 8.1. Palestrina, "Missa sine Nomine": the organ part in Bach's hand.

Georg von Dadelsen discovered a copy of Giovanni Battista Bassani's *Acroama Missale* from Bach's library. Illuminating are Bach's intervening touches for the beginning of the Credo movements for all six Masses. In the fifth Mass we even find an autograph choral intonation, an interpolated original composition by Bach (see Ex. 8.8 and Figure 8.2). It is a setting in *stile antico,* as can be gathered at first glance from the telling large note values, the arrangement in extended measures of breves, and the frequency of consonant or dissonant syncopations. Unusual is the continuo part, a basso ostinato, heard eight times, in quarter-note motion. The continuo, however, assumes no dominant role against the linear motion of the upper parts. The small piece shows direct parallels with the Credo of the B Minor Mass, as is evident from the visual appearance of part-writing. This movement, too, places a group of upper voices in strict vocal polyphony against a continuo in steady quarter-note motion, yet the connections go beyond this: the first exposition of vocal parts unfolds over an ostinato of eight measures, heard twice and leading into a third repeat. It is no small surprise to recognize in the brief Credo setting for Bassani's Mass collection a study for the large movement from the B Minor Mass. The use of ostinato technique (which recurs in the large Credo setting of Clavier-Übung III) has a deeper reason. In the musical-rhetorical doctrine of figures there is the figure of "anaphora," which, according to the explanation in J. G. Walther's *Musicalisches Lexicon* (1732), takes the form of an ostinato bass, especially "when a passage, or even a single word, for the sake of particular emphasis, is often repeated in a work." In both compositions it is the article of creed, "Credo in unum Deum," the central thought that is consistently repeated and acquires "particular emphasis" through music. It becomes clear why Bach combines the *stile antico* with the *contrapunctus ostinatus:* the lasting validity of the ancient Christian formula of creed and the confessional reliance on belief are to be given symbolic musical expression.

No less interesting is a further unknown Bach composition, belonging to the copy of a Magnificat in C Major by Antonio Caldara, its middle movement, "Suscepit Israel," being written in *stile antico*. Bach research long over-

Example 8.8. Bach, Credo intonation BWV 1081

Figure 8.2. Bach, "Credo in unum Deum" BWV 1081: an interpolation in Bassani's Missa in F Major.

Figure 8.3. "Suscepit Israel" BWV 1082: a six-part arrangement by Bach of the four-part original setting by Caldara.

looked a single leaf in Bach's handwriting, which, due to a bookbinder's error at the beginning of the nineteenth century, was inserted at an almost concealed place in the large volume that in its opening pages contained the Magnificat copy belonging to Bach. The single leaf (Figure 8.3) represents the composing score for the mentioned *stile antico* setting in which Bach added to Caldara's four-part texture two obbligato violin parts. Bach did not superimpose instrumental parts in the concertato style—as might be expected—but adapted his style totally to Caldara's model.[4] While the polyphony of the setting (Ex. 8.9) truly assumes the hue of Bach's writing, two components of different derivation merge, on the basis of the *stile antico,* into an admirable entity. There is only one counterpart in Bach's work: again the Credo from the B Minor Mass. Here, too, Bach does not treat the violin parts as a typically instrumental element—as he does in the similar scoring of "Et incarnatus est"—but as agents of the vocal fabric that do not deprive the composition of its a cappella character.

The most general feature of the style of vocal polyphony is the archaic semblance of the score with its large note values. The criteria for the musical substance itself can be gleaned from the compositional principles of the Palestrina style, as described above. The fundamental component is a vocally conceived melodic texture that is derived from individual linear writing patterned upon the modal *cantus firmus.* Baroque figuration is eschewed in favor of certain contained contrapuntal formulae. The free-flowing rhythm, asymmetric in its prose-like manner, is based upon a mensural conception of meter, not upon a metric-periodic system subject to grouped successions of measures. Its fixed unit is the *integer valor* of the half note governing a *tempo ordinario.* The harmonic formation remains subordinate to the polyphonic structure. Contrapuntal writing in a chordal sense is avoided, a linear orientation rules throughout. Harmonic expressiveness is replaced by polyphonic transparency. The structural shape is free of any schematic patterns. Its aim is restraint of the musical material, density of texture (often by means of special contrapuntal techniques), and avoidance of episodic formations. The

Example 8.9. Caldara-Bach, "Suscepit Israel" BWV 1082

homogeneous texture is reflected in a homogeneous sonority, the pure choral sound and the static sound of the keyboard instrument, respectively. What is involved is an unchanging evenness of sound (*stylus a cappella sive pleni chori*) without change of tonal color, stressing the clarity of polyphonic nature.

Bach fully embraces this tradition of vocal polyphony in his *stile antico* works. Like most of the composers discussed, he is not concerned with an inflexible, scholastic style imitation but rather with creative work carried out in the spirit of the old style. Thus there are rather individual traits to be found within Bach's *stile antico,* such as a striking rhythmic diversification or a penchant for a full sound that (in distinction, for instance, to Lotti's or Fux's works) forgoes the use of passages written for a limited number of parts. Yet such individuality always subordinates the personal style and its degree of originality to the compositional manner of the *stile antico.* It is this manner that determines the original conception; the means of classical vocal polyphony invariably remain regulating elements.

The process of style-critical analysis called for might be briefly outlined with the use of two examples drawn from rhythmic-melodic practice that are particular constituents of the style of vocal polyphony.

The thematic-motivic idea as point of departure for the *ars inveniendi* of the composer is a determining element of the unified course of the Baroque work, an element that governs the whole piece. If we compare two of Bach's themes as representing, on the one hand, the *stile moderno* and, on the other, the *stile antico,* essential style differences become immediately apparent. Bach derived the theme of the G minor organ fugue (see Ex. 8.10) from a Netherlandish folk tune. He transforms its rhythmical structure by the hammering motoric pulsation of contrasting sixteenth-and eighth-note motion and transforms its melodic structure into a correlative play of small and large—in part chordal—intervals. At the same time he creates a harmonic scheme leading to the dominant in the second measure, to the relative major in the third, and the tonic in the fourth. The theme is an example entirely characteristic of Bach's complementary melodic particles by which, within a series of rhythmic-melodic groupings, certain formulations are related to one another. Its poignant profile arises from the organic interaction of small units (a, b) and large units (x = aa, y = ba). The chorale theme of the organ Kyrie BWV 669 (Ex. 8.10) suggests an entirely different musical orienta-

Example 8.10.

Example 8.11.

tion. It also follows a melodic model though it adheres much more closely to it. The ambitus of the modal fourth is maintained without being harmonically reinterpreted or defined in more detail. Bach's changes are rather of rhythmic nature, yet he consciously avoids a grouping of corresponding units or metric accents. Thus he obtains an innately vocal, flowing soggetto, which in growing tension reaches its melodic high point on the upper fourth in order to revert in gradual descent to the tonic.

In rounding out these style-critical observations concerning rhythm and melody, we turn briefly to questions of contrapuntal structure, using two examples that at first glance seem to share many characteristics (see Ex. 8.11). The chorale setting of the cantata "Aus tiefer Not" BWV 38 and the six-part organ chorale bearing the same title reveal, upon closer examination, fundamental differences. The cantata movement shows a clear tendency toward the *contrapunctus simplex,* that is note-against-note writing, whereas the organ work, with its densely entwined polyphony, is a model of the *contrapunctus floridus.* The former moves in steady half-note progressions with occasional passing quarter notes and gentle syncopation, whereas the contrapuntal texture of the latter is enlivened by consistent and detailed rhythmic elaboration, lending to each part a considerable measure of individuality. The distinctiveness of parts is heightened in the organ setting through a transparent polyphonic fabric typical of the Palestrina style. By contrast, the cantata movement—which we should list among the mentioned *alla breve* settings—has an unmistakably homophonic bearing that runs counter to the principles of the *stile antico.*

The style characteristics of the works in *stile antico* might be further analyzed in this manner. Such style criticism should by no means be understood as a dry scientific process; on the contrary, it will often yield results that might prove of direct use, for instance in the sense of performance practice. The styles of composition and performance are firmly related to one another. With this in mind—to cite a specific example—the first Kyrie of the B Minor Mass, with its accent-laden and driving modulatory theme, should be declaimed in a manner quite different from that to be applied to the second Kyrie, more dynamically and expressively. The second Kyrie knows no periodic accents of meter but moves, evenly flowing, from thesis to arsis in ever suspended mensural manner. Such stylistic-musical contrast must not remain without consequence in rendering the masterwork, if one is not to misrepresent the composer's intentions.

What are, finally, the aims of the composer in turning to classic vocal polyphony? What do our stylistic findings convey to us regarding the spirit and essence of Bach's music? We might see in the choice of stylistic texture above all an expression of genre emerging from among the manifold partial styles at the disposal of the Baroque master. Bach's attitude toward the Baroque doctrine of styles is surprisingly unexplored. We do not have, for instance, an inquiry into his commitment to the *stile francese,* a commitment that can be traced from his early works through the Art of Fugue.

As a partial style, the *stile antico* served several goals. For one thing, we find it in such collections as the Well-Tempered Clavier and Clavier-Übung III which, in accordance with their didactic nature, display a variety of compositional styles. Among the chorale settings in Clavier-Übung III there are verset-like preambles, fugues and fughettas, trios, embellished organ chorales, as well as ricercar-like or motet-like *cantus firmus* settings in *stile antico.* Next to this more varying use of stylistic and compositional techniques, partial styles occur in cyclic works, specifically for the purpose of architectonic design. In some measure this use of partial styles applies to the nine arrangements of the German Mass appearing as an entity in Clavier-Übung III. There is a grouping of three-times-three settings, the large Kyries in *stile antico,* three smaller Kyrie versets, and three three-part settings (in F, G, and A major) of the German Gloria. This arrangement in three groups, each in turn comprised of three settings, as it appears in the original print (which does not need to be understood in the sense of prescribing an order of performance), can ostensibly be interpreted as a symbol of the Trinity. It indeed corresponds to the contemporaneous conception of these liturgical pieces, as is shown in the title for the hymnal by Vopelius (Leipzig, 1682) that Bach used: "Missa, or: The Kyrie Eleison, together with additions traditionally made by the Church in praise of Holy Trinity."

We encounter architectonic design on a larger scale in the Symbolum Nicenum of the B Minor Mass, which has an opening and closing pair of choruses. In each pair, a *stile antico* movement, with liturgical *cantus firmus,* is followed by a concertato tutti movement. Within this larger frame stands a smaller one, formed by the solo settings of arias. The clearly marked center is formed by three choruses, whose texts, in turn, mark the Christological center of the Nicene dogma (see Table 8.2). In this chiastic-symmetrical form, as described and interpreted especially by Friedrich Smend for other Bach works as well, the *stile antico* emerges as a palpable architectonic unit.

The artistic significance of the style of classical vocal polyphony is in no way exhausted with its use as a means of formal structure; it represents a definite means of expression, for the different styles were to be applied to composition "as demanded by the *expressiones*" (Johann Gottfried Walther). *Majestas* and *gravitas,* grandeur and seriousness, were designations in the doctrine of affections for the expressive quality of the style of classic vocal

Table 8.2. The architectonic design of the Symbolum Nicenum

$$
\left[
\begin{array}{l}
\left\{
\begin{array}{l}
\text{Credo (plenum-chorus setting in \textit{stile antico})} \\
\text{Patrem (tutti movement in \textit{stile moderno})}
\end{array}
\right. \\
\quad
\left[
\begin{array}{l}
\text{Et in unum Deum} \\
\quad
\left\{
\begin{array}{l}
\text{Et in carnatus est} \\
\text{Crucifixus} \\
\text{Et resurrexit}
\end{array}
\right. \\
\text{Et in Spiritum Sanctum}
\end{array}
\right. \\
\left\{
\begin{array}{l}
\text{Confiteor (plenum-chorus setting in \textit{stile antico})} \\
\text{Et expecto (tutti movement in \textit{stile moderno})}
\end{array}
\right.
\end{array}
\right.
$$

polyphony. It is here that the decisive distance from other affections favored in Baroque music is shown, affections related to passion and other conditions of the soul, such as *amor, tristitia,* and *odium.* The *stile antico* is intended to preclude such allurements of affective practice, and it is indicative that the style is not associated with texts inviting madrigalisms (as in the Passion settings) but is reserved for liturgical texts far removed from the sphere of subjectivity. Bach's choice of style for these liturgical works bears out a dogmatic abstract character linked to the *stylus ecclesiasticus* as music of "gravitas, devotio et affectuum spiritualium expressio." The same expressive attitude is imparted to the instrumental works in *stile antico,* music not bound to the verbal text and, like the fugues in E and E♭ major, reflecting the spirit of the *fuga grave.* Thus Walther's dictionary designates the "grave fugue, marked by long note values and a slow meter."

We have tried to gain a picture of the appearances and meanings of the style of classical vocal polyphony in Bach's works. In conclusion, we should look at the position of the *stile antico* within Bach's total oeuvre. This is not the place to deal with specific problems of chronology. I mentioned initially the close connection with Bach's last works. Source study affords us rather clear boundary lines of about 1737 to 1745 for Bach's involvement with the *stile antico.* Also relevant is the period 1737–1739, when Bach was relieved of his official duty to direct the Collegium Musicum; to these years we owe, in addition to Clavier-Übung III and the major part of Well-Tempered Clavier II, his studies in classical vocal polyphony. A direct connection may also be seen with the publication date of Mizler's translation of Fux (Leipzig, 1742).

We begin to envisage how the aging Bach reviews in those years the foundations of his polyphonic art by re-examining the music of the old masters. At the conclusion of the life's work, genius turns student once more, deriving new inspiration from the school of the strict style. Our thoughts are directed to comparable aspects offered by the last creations of Schütz, Mozart, and Beethoven. Autonomous artistry recedes, and—as if "sub specie aeternitatis"—personal creativity is placed within the traditions of music. It is part of the image of the aging Bach that he sought to preserve the bequest that inspired the essence of the last contrapuntal-speculative works such as the Art of Fugue, the Musical Offering, and the canonic variations on Vom Himmel hoch. Even where the *stile antico* is not prevalent, we can recognize its originating force, which lends a glow to all of the last works. In its inherent orderliness and regularity, less aimed at *movere* or *delectare* than *docere,* the *stile antico* heralds the tenets of the last works. In this sense the immersion in the style of classical vocal polyphony, through which the foundations of musical composition are tangibly represented, forms part of the spiritual basis of Bach's last period. In the announcement for his edition of the *Gradus ad Parnassum* (subtitled "Manual for the Regulated Musical Composition"), Mizler provides a classical formulation—for which his teacher Bach may have stood godfather—when he speaks of the foundations exemplified in the style of classical vocal polyphony as "being rooted in the unchangeable rules of harmony that have always existed, are existing, and will be so, as long as the edifice and the principles on which it rests do not change, may music as a phenomenon change as it will."[5]

❖   ❖   ❖

NEW SOURCES:
BROADENED PERSPECTIVES

9

The Neumeister Collection of Chorale Preludes
from the Bach Circle

THE JOHN HERRICK JACKSON MUSIC LIBRARY at Yale University
has long been known as one of America's major repositories of seventeenth-
and eighteenth-century musical sources, in manuscript or print. Much
scholarly work has already been done on these materials, but the actual research potential is far from being exhausted. This is true of the Bach manuscripts despite the fact that they belong among the sources which have been
studied the most. In Gerhard Herz's meticulously annotated catalogue, *Bach
Sources in America,*[1] which contains a summary account of the Bach materials
at Yale, he mentioned that he had been unable to deal with all the Bach
sources there and that a considerable amount of work remains to be done.
Two early-eighteenth-century manuscripts from the Rinck Library in the
Lowell Mason Collection[2] have for a long time received insufficient attention:
LM 4982 and 4983 (the latter known as the "Johann Günther Bach Book").[3]
These large anthologies of keyboard music, compiled by Johann Christoph
Bach,[4] contain important material related to Johann Sebastian and other
members of the Bach family (most notably a large number of compositions
by Johann Christoph himself),[5] and also works of Pachelbel, Buxtehude, and
other late-seventeenth-century musicians. Both sources deserve further scrutiny, especially with respect to music of the Bach circle. As for other manuscripts to be examined more closely, it might suffice to single out the famous "Codex E. B. 1688," a late-seventeenth-century manuscript with an
eighteenth-century appendix containing BWV 548,[6] and some nineteenth-
century manuscript copies by Christian Heinrich Rinck, such as LM 4839b
and LM 4843,[7] which comprise works that are attributed to Johann Sebastian Bach but whose authenticity needs to be determined.

Another manuscript from the Lowell Mason Collection, LM 4708 (call
number Ma. 21. Y 11. A 30), had heretofore completely escaped the attention of Bach scholars. It came to light very recently in the course of a comprehensive examination of source materials in preparation for a newly conceived and systematically organized scholarly reference manual on the works
of Johann Sebastian Bach, coauthored by Hans-Joachim Schulze and myself.[8]

LM 4708, bearing the rather misleading identifying title "Choräle ohne Texte" [chorales without texts], had obviously been underestimated by Henry C. Fall.[9] Hence its full content, comprising an important organ repertoire of eighty-two chorale preludes, was never adequately described. Nevertheless, Cutler's reference to this manuscript led to an examination of the four chorale preludes by Friedrich Wilhelm Zachow [Zachau], the teacher of George Frideric Handel, contained in LM 4708.[10] Two of the Zachow pieces are transmitted uniquely in this late-eighteenth-century manuscript source. This fact alone should have roused scholarly interest in it, since Zachow belongs among the seminal figures of the generation before Bach and Handel. However, the Zachow chorale preludes are not the only important repertory in this rather inconspicuous volume. The manuscript's true value reveals itself primarily through the music of three of the most prominent members of the Bach family, the brothers Johann Christoph and Johann Michael Bach, and the latter's son-in-law, Johann Sebastian.

The Manuscript and Its Compiler: Johann Gottfried Neumeister

The physical makeup of the volume can be described as follows: eighty-three folios (one flyleaf, twenty binio gatherings plus one bifolio), measuring 23 × 33.5 centimeters, in their original binding (cardboard with leather spine and edges). Title on flyleaf (lead pencil, unidentified hand): "Yale University. Lowell Mason Library of Music (4708) / *Choräle ohne Texte* / (L. M. entry)." Folios 1–75 r, = pages 1–149 (original pagination): music; folio 75 v ruled with staff lines. There follow stubs of sixteen folios (= four gatherings), which were cut out, and seven intact folios: two blank pages, eight pages of index (first lines of chorale texts), three blank pages. The paper, of sturdy quality throughout (greyish white, last gatherings bluish white) and uniformly showing the watermark "IGF LANG" (= leaf a) / Hollandia figure "PRO PATRIA" (= leaf b), stems from the paper mill of Ober-Eschbach/ Hesse (owner since 1764: *Johann Gottfried Lang*).[11] (See Figs. 9.1 and 9.2.)

The inscription on the inside cover (brown ink, hand of Christian Heinrich Rinck) reads: "*Diese Samlung von Chorälen habe ich zum Andenken von Hl.* [abbr. "Herrn"] *Conrector u. Organisten* [last two words added] *Neumeister / in Homburg vor der Höhe erhalten. Dieser war ein Schüler von Sorge in Lobenstein.* [I have received this collection of chorales as a token of remembrance from Herr conrector and organist Neumeister of Homburg vor der Höhe. He was a student of Sorge's at Lobenstein.] *C. H. Rinck.*" This note refers to the fact that the Darmstadt court organist Rinck (1770–1846)[12] had received this volume from Johann Gottfried Neumeister, who, from 1807 to 1831, was conrector and organist in Homburg,[13] near Frankfurt am Main. Rinck's extensive collection of music manuscripts and prints was acquired by Lowell Mason in 1852 and bequeathed to Yale University in 1873.[14]

Little is known about Neumeister, who was born in 1757 at Ebersdorf (Vogtland), in the southeastern part of Thuringia. In 1790 he moved to

Figure 9.1. Watermark "IGF" in manuscript LM 4708, leaf a (beta-radiograph).

Figure 9.2. Watermark "LANG" in manuscript LM 4708, leaf a (beta-radiograph).

Hesse in order to take up a post as first German teacher at the Latin School, as well as sexton, bell-ringer, and second organist of the Stadtkirche, in the then free imperial city of Friedberg.[15] His elder brother, the Frankfurt miniature painter Karl David Neumeister,[16] who had some personal connections with an influential member of the Friedberg town council, appears to have been responsible for bringing him to this part of Germany. In a letter dated 21 March 1790 to the Friedberg lay assessor [Schöffe], Wilhelm Ludwig Schmid,[17] he proposed Johann Gottfried for the vacant school position in Friedberg and introduced him as a very experienced schoolmaster, who had begun his career some sixteen years earlier (that is, around 1774) as a teacher in Friesen (Vogtland), near his birthplace, and later accepted a post as school-teacher at the Herrnhutter (Moravian Brethren) Congregation in Copenhagen.[18] Since nothing specific is mentioned in the letter about his musical activities, it seems safe to assume that music did not play a predominant role in Neumeister's professional life. His functions as organist in Friedberg and later in Homburg seem to have remained a secondary activity.[19] The contract for his Friedberg position, dated 17 July 1790,[20] specifies his duties as second organist: playing the organ at Friday afternoon services and assisting and substituting for the first organist at Sunday and feastday services at the Stadtkirche and the Burgkirche.

According to Rinck's entry in LM 4708, Neumeister had received his musical training in Lobenstein, near Ebersdorf, from the organist, composer, and noted theorist Georg Andreas Sorge (1703–1778),[21] who—like Bach—was a member of Lorenz Christoph Mizler's Leipzig-based Correspondierende Societät der musicalischen Wissenschaften. Sorge's reputation suggests that Neumeister's musical studies reached beyond the merely elementary level. At any rate, Neumeister apparently remained a practicing organist for most of his life. He must have compiled the manuscript LM 4708 for his repertoire needs, particularly during his Friedberg years. Since the paper of the volume originates from that region in Hesse, the manuscript could not have been put together before 1790. Moreover, because the owner's initials in the watermark of the Lang paper mill changed by 1801 (at the very latest) to "JHG LANG,"[22] LM 4708 most likely dates from the last decade of the eighteenth century. In all probability, Neumeister prepared the volume after his arrival in Friedberg in the early 1790s. The handwriting style is so consistent throughout the manuscript that the chorale repertoire seems not to have been entered over an extended period. Although no samples of Neumeister's music hand are extant, it would appear logical that he was not only the compiler but also the copyist. The contents of LM 4708 seem to reflect both Neumeister's technical limitations as organist (most of the preludes are playable either manualiter or with limited use of the pedal) and his repertoire needs for special worship services (there is less emphasis on *de tempore* chorales than on hymns with specific theological themes, such as Catechism, Christian Life and Conduct, or Death and Dying).[23]

The exact date of his passing the volume on to Rinck is not known. It must have occurred after his appointment on 1 October 1807 as "Conrector" of the school at Homburg vor der Höhe and before his promotion to "Titular-Schulrat." Neumeister, who also served as organist of the Homburg Stadtkirche, retired from active school service in 1831 and died at the age of eighty-three in Homburg. The nature and extent of Neumeister's music library is not known. LM 4708 seems to be the only item that ended in Rinck's large collection, which is particularly rich in keyboard music from the Bach circle and its context. Rinck (1770–1846) had studied in Erfurt in 1786–1789 with one of Johann Sebastian Bach's last pupils, Johann Christian Kittel (1732–1809), and belongs—together with Michael Gotthard Fischer (1773–1829), Friedrich Conrad Griepenkerl (1782–1849), the somewhat younger Gotthilf Wilhelm Körner (1809–1865), and August Gottfried Ritter (1811–1885)—among the most significant nineteenth-century representatives of an unbroken Bach keyboard tradition.[24] Their interests in collecting, compiling, cataloguing, copying, editing, and publishing—besides performing and teaching—played a major role in the preservation, transmission, and dissemination of the organ music of Johann Sebastian Bach and his wider circle.[25] Rinck, whose knowledge of Bach's organ repertoire was probably unmatched at the time, must have immediately realized both the significance and uniqueness of the music in Neumeister's volume, and Neumeister in turn must have thought Rinck its most worthy recipient.[26]

The Repertoire and Its Provenance

LM 4708 represents a carefully selected Herrnhutter-choice anthology of chorale preludes with a clear preference for both the classic Lutheran chorale repertoire and the conservative musical style of the inner Bach circle from around the year 1700. The compilation of the material clearly shows two layers, namely that of the principal repertoire and that of a supplementary repertoire. The latter consists of pieces taken from a published collection of chorale preludes by Neumeister's teacher, Sorge.

The principal repertoire in LM 4708 consists of seventy-seven chorale preludes representing two different but rather equally balanced musical strata: thirty-eight compositions by Johann Sebastian Bach and thirty-nine works by composers of the immediately preceding generation. The latter group again divides into two parts, with the twenty-five compositions by Johann Michael Bach forming a dominating unit in its own right. The fact that music from the Bach family makes up the bulk of the collection suggests that a close link must have existed between LM 4708 and one or more sources originating from the Bach family circle. Since over half of the repertoire contained in LM 4708 is transmitted in no other source, the provenance of the material cannot be indisputably established, but it seems logical that the entire repertoire (with the exception of Sorge's music) stems from a single Vorlage or source model. Certain elements in LM 4708 permit us to draw some conclusions about that Vorlage:

1. The design of the collection and the uniformity of the entries suggest that everything but the Sorge chorales was copied from a single manuscript source rather than from several different sources. The manuscript model seems to have been a chorale anthology, the first part of which was organized largely according to the *de tempore* of the liturgical year (Advent to Trinity Sunday: nos. 1–28), and the second part, in less stringent order, according to major categories of the traditional Lutheran hymnbooks, such as Catechism, Confession, Penitence and Justification, Christian Life and Conduct, Word of God and Christian Church, and Death and Dying (with occasional illogical departures from the standard groupings). It seems either that the source was incomplete with respect to the coverage of the *de tempore* (the repertoire from Advent to Trinity Sunday is extremely sketchy) or, more likely, that the compiler of LM 4708 copied rather selectively in order to suit his own purposes and functions (in this case those of a second organist). If the copyist proceeded selectively, he demonstrated a clear preference for Jo-

hann Sebastian and, to a slightly lesser degree, for Johann Michael Bach. One may well assume that the source contained a more representative collection of the works of Johann Christoph Bach, Zachow, and Pachelbel.

2. The scribe of LM 4708 modernized the notation during the copying process, but not consistently, so that some old-fashioned notational features such as the use of sharps (instead of naturals) to cancel flats and vice versa are preserved here and there (for example, p. 38, m. 23). This permits, first of all, dating the source in the very early part of the eighteenth century (Johann Sebastian Bach, for one, gave up this notational practice circa 1715) and, second, determining that the source was written primarily in staff notation[27] (as seems to have been the prevailing practice in the Bach circle), with perhaps occasional use of tablature (as, for instance, in the autograph of Bach's Orgel-Büchlein). The numerous copying errors in LM 4708 point both to legibility problems in the model copy and to the copyist's lack of experience.[28]

3. The manuscript Vorlage, which has not survived, may have been comparable in structure and size to one of the most typical Lutheran service collections, the so-called Plauen Organ Book of 1708, with it 325 chorale preludes.[29] The provenance of Neumeister's repertoire is unknown, but it must have been related to the inner Bach family circle, if it did not originate directly in it. In fact, it may well point to a lost anthology of chorale preludes that must have complemented the major anthologies of free organ works represented in the famous Andreas Bach Book[30] and Möller Manuscript,[31] copied by Johann Sebastian Bach's elder brother, Johann Christoph. It is characteristic of these manuscripts, as well as of the model for LM 4708, that they emphasize, within a largely conservative repertoire, the works of the young genius, Johann Sebastian.[32] It is also hardly a coincidence that the most modern compositions, namely those of the young Johann Sebastian Bach, appear in all three collections at the end—presumably a later appendix (in LM 4708 nos. 77–78 = the Orgel-Büchlein chorales). There is no evidence that Neumeister could have had direct access to an anthology originating in the Bach family circle. He more likely compiled LM 4708 from an intermediary source, perhaps made available to him through his former association with Sorge or through connections with his native Thuringia that he encountered only in Friedberg. The latter possibility seems more likely, since Neumeister apparently compiled the collection only after his arrival at the Friedberg Latin School, where, under Johann Christoph Reinemann, conrector from 1712 to 1729, there had been a tradition of performing early-eighteenth-century Thuringian cantatas. Moreover, Reinemann's predecessor, Johann Heinrich Schuchardt (conrector from 1663 to 1712), was the son of Theodor Schuchardt, who had been cantor from 1643 to 1671 at Johann Sebastian Bach's baptismal church, St. George's, in Eisenach and whose colleague as organist was none other than Johann Christoph Bach, Johann Michael's brother.[33]

The Works of Georg Andreas Sorge

The five organ chorales of Sorge appear to be inserted and added, respectively, as a supplement to the principal repertoire in LM 4708. They represent by far the youngest stylistic layer in the collection and were taken over from Sorge's published collection of eight chorale preludes: *Erster Theil der VORSPIELE vor bekannten Choral-Gesängen in 3 stimmiger reiner Harmonie gesetzt, welche so wohl auf der Orgel als auch auf dem Clavier zur Übung nützlich können gebraucht werden . . . Im Verlag Balthasar Schmids Erben in Nürnberg. No. XXX.* [1750].[34] (See Figures 9.3–9.5.)

These three-part chorale settings form a closed group at the end of the manuscript, nos. 79–82; no. 25 was apparently entered on a page that had originally been left empty. It is unclear why only five of the eight chorales in the Sorge print were copied into the volume. Since the page following page 149 remained blank, it is unlikely that the remaining Sorge chorales were entered on the pages that were later cut out. (See above for a description of the physical layout of the manuscript.) Had the Sorge print been in Neumeister's possession there would then have been no need to copy this material, but it must have been made available to him, since he copied the five pieces in exactly the order of the print (LM 4708, no. 25 = Sorge, p. 1; no. 79 = p. 2; no. 80 = p. 3, and so on).

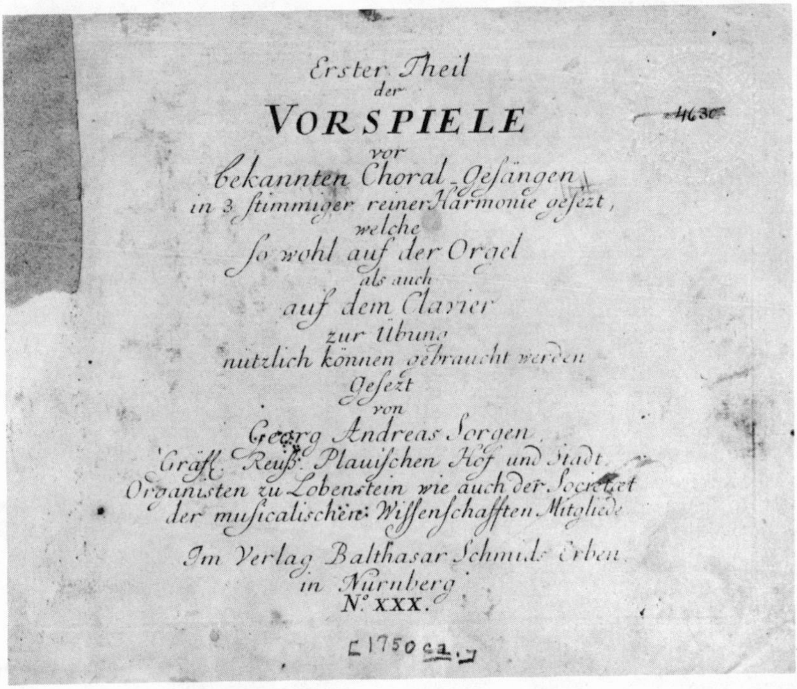

Figure 9.3. Sorge, *Erster Theil der Vorspiele* (1750), title page.

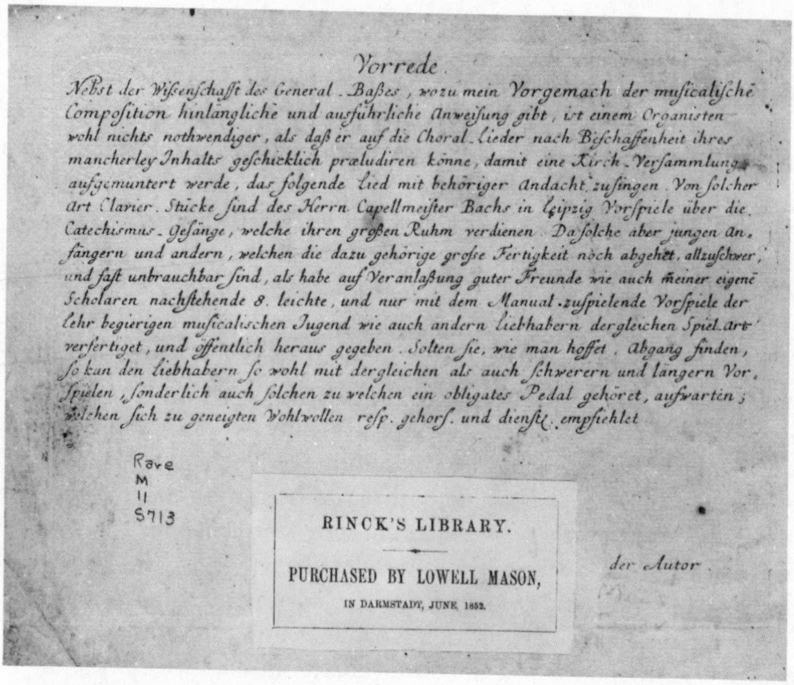

Vorrede.

Nebst der Wiſſenſchafft des General-Baſſes, wozu mein Vorgemach der muſicaliſchē Compoſition hinlängliche und ausführliche Anweiſung gibt, ist einem Organisten wohl nichts nothwendiger, als daß er auf die Choral-Lieder nach Beſchaffenheit ihres mancherley Inhalts geſchicklich præludiren könne, damit eine Kirch-Verſammlung aufgemuntert werde, das folgende Lied mit behöriger Andacht zuſingen. Von ſolcher Art Clavier-Stücke ſind des Herrn Capellmeiſter Bachs in Leipzig Vorſpiele über die Catechismus-Geſänge, welche ihren großen Ruhm verdienen. Da ſolche aber jungen Anfängern und andern, welchen die dazu gehörige groſſe Fertigkeit noch abgehet, allzuſchwer, und faſt unbrauchbar ſind, als habe auf Veranlaßung guter Freunde wie auch meiner eigenē Scholaren nachſtehende 8. leichte, und nur mit dem Manual zuſpielende Vorſpiele der lehr begierigen muſicaliſchen Jugend wie auch andern Liebhabern dergleichen Spiel-art verfertiget, und öffentlich heraus gegeben. Solten ſie, wie man hoffet, Abgang finden, ſo kan den Liebhabern ſo wohl mit dergleichen als auch ſchwerern und längern Vorſpielen, ſonderlich auch ſolchen zu welchen ein obligates Pedal gehöret, aufwarten; welchen ſich zu geneigten Wohlwollen reſp. gehorſ. und dienſtl. empfiehlet

der Autor.

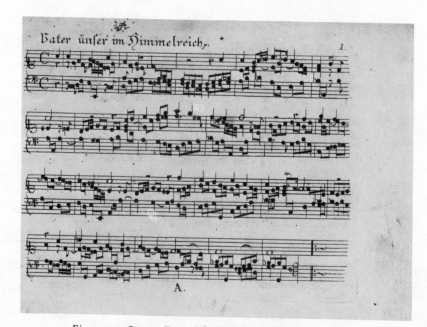

Figure 9.4. Sorge, *Erster Theil der Vorspiele* (1750), preface.

Figure 9.5. Sorge, *Erster Theil der Vorspiele* (1750), page 1.

Sorge's preface discusses the function of the three-part manualiter chorale settings, compares them in general with the difficult and demanding organ chorales in Johann Sebastian Bach's Clavier-Übung III (1739), suggests the possibility of performing them on both organ and clavier (harpsichord, or another keyboard), and by analogy refers to the overall purpose of the Neumeister collection:

> Next to the knowledge of figured bass, to which my "Vorgemach der musicalischen Composition" [Lobenstein, 1745–1747] gives sufficiently comprehensive and detailed instructions, nothing is more important to the organist than he be adroit in preluding to the various chorales, according to their particular content, so that the congregation will be stimulated to sing the subsequent chorale with appropriate devotion. The preludes on the Catechism Chorales by Herr Capellmeister Bach in Leipzig are examples of this kind of keyboard piece that deserve the great renown they enjoy. But because works such as these are so difficult as to be all but unusable by young beginners and others who may lack the considerable proficiency they require, I have prepared, at the suggestion of my good friends as well as my own pupils, the following eight simple preludes, to be played only on the manuals, and I herewith publicly present them to those members of our musical youth who are eager to learn and to all devotees of this type of playing.

The Works of Johann Christoph Bach, Pachelbel, Erich, and Zachow

This small group of compositions, three by Johann Christoph Bach (1642–1703), four by Friedrich Wilhelm Zachow (1663–1712), and one each by Johann Pachelbel (1653–1706) and Daniel Erich (1646–1712), complements the larger work groups of Johann Michael and Johann Sebastian Bach and points to the general significance of LM 4708 in that it largely comprises uniquely transmitted material. The works of both Johann Christoph Bach and Daniel Erich[35] survive in no other source; the same applies to two of the four Zachow works (nos. 9 and 61).[36]

The three chorale preludes of Johann Christoph Bach, "the great, expressive composer"[37] and perhaps most significant member of the Bach family before Johann Sebastian, are of particular importance since they supplement his rather insignificant and small-scale forty-four "Choraele zum Praeambuliren" by a more sophisticated compositional style and represent the two preeminent types of Thuringian organ chorale preludes: *fugirte* and *variirte und figurierte Choräle* [fugued as well as varied and figured chorales].[38] Pachelbel's piece as a "figured chorale" (for him a rather rare type) also fits in the Middle German style. Pachelbel had spent a considerable portion of his professional life in Thuringia, and specifically the years 1677–1678 in Eisenach as a colleague of Johann Christoph Bach. During his Erfurt years he taught Johann Sebastian's elder brother, Johann Christoph, who in turn was the first teacher of Johann Sebastian.[39] Erich's chorale prelude with it fantasy-like and more virtuosic approach clearly follows the North German mold, most typically represented in the works of Dietrich Buxtehude, with whom Erich had studied.[40] The presence of a work by Erich, a distinguished composer whose output has been only very sparsely preserved, again speaks well for the authoritative nature of the Neumeister collection and relates it to the mixed Middle and North German repertoire so characteristic of the Bach family manuscripts (Andreas Bach Book and Möller Manuscript), which also contain an unusually large number of uniquely transmitted materials.[41]

The Works of Johann Michael Bach

The hitherto known keyboard output of Johann Christoph Bach's slightly younger brother, Johann Michael (1648–1694) of Gehren, was limited to eight chorale preludes,[42] which hardly permitted us to establish the historical position of this composer, particularly vis-à-vis Johann Sebastian Bach, who in 1707, shortly after his move from Arnstadt to Mühlhausen, married Johann Michael's orphaned daughter. Maria Barbara Bach had since 1704 also lived in Arnstadt, and it is possible that Johann Sebastian Bach became acquainted with the full extent of Johann Michael's oeuvre only through her.[43] It must be assumed, however, that Johann Michael Bach's reputation as a major composer of chorale preludes was firmly established by the end of the seventeenth century. Thus Johann Sebastian would most likely already have become familiar with this material during his Ohrdruf study years. Ernst Ludwig Gerber[44] refers to a volume of 246 pages from the Bach family estate (at the time in his possession, now lost) that contained more than five hundred *figurirte und fugirte Choräle,* including compositions of practically all the composers to be found in LM 4708: Johann Christoph, Johann Michael (with seventy-two chorale preludes the most prominent name in this manuscript), and Johann Sebastian Bach, Pachelbel, and Zachow. This congruence of composers indicates a close connection with the Neumeister collection, although there is no reason to suggest more than an indirect relationship of the sources.

The repertoire in LM 4708 adds significantly to the known works of Johann Michael Bach and permits us now to see in him one of the major seminal figures who established the style and typology of the late-seventeenth-century Middle German chorale prelude. That, simply in terms of age, he preceded Pachelbel is obvious. But the musical quality and variety of his organ chorales suggests that he might well have outweighed Pachelbel as a composer in this genre of fugued and figured chorales. The so-called Pachelbel type[45] of fugued chorale prelude (melody in the upper voice and preimitation of each *cantus firmus* line) is well represented among Johann Michael's pieces, without any indication that he was depending on Pachelbel as a model. As foreshadowings of Johann Sebastian Bach the more important chorale settings can be found in Johann Michael's varied and figured chorales, which are more imaginatively treated. In these the *cantus firmus* (upper voice) has a texturally flexible and expressive accompanimental underpinning; in some the chorale melody is treated in a sophisticated polyphonic manner through all voices and is combined with highly unified and motivically controlled accompanimental figuration (no. 6, for example).

The attribution of twenty-five chorale preludes in LM 4708 to Johann Michael Bach is unequivocal and, therefore, clarifies a number of questions of authenticity. For instance, the setting "In dulci jubilo" (no. 12) was previously known only from the Mempell-Preller collection, where it is identified simply as "di Bach." It was ascribed to Johann Sebastian Bach[46] and listed as BWV 751, but its authenticity was always considered doubtful. LM 4708 solves the problem by attributing BWV 751 to its true author. The Plauen Organ Book contains as no. 186 the chorale setting "Mag ich Unglück nicht widerstahn" without any attribution. Seiffert ascribed it to Pachelbel on stylistic grounds,[47] whereas LM 4708 attributes it to Johann Michael Bach. There is no reason to doubt the reliability of Neumeister's source. This has also major implications for the authenticity of a number of chorale preludes attributed or ascribed to Pachelbel. The Thuringian manuscript sources traditionally contributed to the confusion by usually spelling Pachelbel's name *Bachelbel* (see no. 34) and by using the abbreviation *Bach:* and the initials *J. B.* or just *B.,* which easily lend themselves to mistaken identifications, Pachelbel for Bach and vice versa. Johann Michael Bach's oeuvre in particular seems to have suffered from this situation. LM 4708, as the now most extensive source[48] of Johann Michael Bach's keyboard music, helps to return to his list of works five chorale preludes that were previously ascribed to Pachelbel (nos. 4, 6, 29, 37, and 39), so that this composer's historical position can now be more adequately defined.

The Works of Johann Sebastian Bach

The thirty-eight chorale preludes of Johann Sebastian Bach, thirty-three of which were previously unknown, open a number of significant perspectives, especially on the early Bach. The context of the Neumeister collection, the reliability of LM 4708, and the concordances with five compositions (BWV 601, 639, 719, 737, and 742), as well as two compositional sections from BWV 714 and 957, cast no doubt on their attribution.[49] Stylistic and notational characteristics suggest that the origin of this repertoire (with the exception of BWV 601 and 639) definitely precedes the Weimar Orgel-Büchlein by a considerable margin. But both BWV 601 and 639 not only represent a later appendix to the repertoire, they also most likely belong to the earliest layer of the Orgel-Büchlein and therefore provide an important link with its hitherto unknown prehistory.[50] (A later-eighteenth-century Bach imitation would certainly have been based on his widely disseminated mature organ chorales rather than on compositions reflecting the formative stages.) Furthermore, the fact that few of Bach's organ chorales from the Neumeister collection are transmitted in the major group of manuscript copies of works from the Weimar period (copies by Johann Gottfried Walther, Johann Tobias Krebs, or Johann Peter Kellner)[51] suggests not only pre-1708 origin in general, but early pre-Weimar origin in particular. Bach apparently did not make these works readily available to his students and colleagues since he had in the meantime reached a higher level of proficiency. Therefore these works began their very limited circulation most likely only after 1750, perhaps originating primarily from the part of Bach's estate inherited by Wilhelm Friedemann.[52] The situation is quite similar of that of other very early Bach compositions.[53]

The body of thirty-six chorales (all but BWV 601 and 639) indeed appears to belong to the earliest stratum of Bach's compositional experience, probably even reaching back into the Ohrdruf study years with his brother, the former Pachelbel pupil Johann Christoph. The writing of *fugirte, variirte und figurirte Choräle* was a traditional part of the fundamental training in composition. It may not be a coincidence that the first twenty-five measures of the setting of "Christe, der du bist Tag und Licht" (no. 20) are transmitted in an early-eighteenth-century manuscript, apparently under Pachelbel's name. This seems to indicate Pachelbel's influence on the chorale style of the early Bach. Could Bach perhaps have taken a concrete Pachelbel model as a point of departure and expanded on it? Although this is quite possible as a study method, the music of LM 4708, no. 20, does not bear this out; it suggests rather a corrupted version in the Königsberg manuscript.[54] It is by no means clear that Pachelbel had a hand in the piece; it may well have been Johann Michael Bach. However, if one can trust the source at all, its spelling ("Bach:" or some variant?) can no longer be verified, since the manuscript is lost. At any rate the style of Johann Michael Bach's chorales seems to have had a more direct and lasting impact on Johann Sebastian's organ chorale composition.

The connections between Johann Michael's and Johann Sebastian's chorale preludes cannot be underestimated. They may be found in the basic format, layout, and solid contrapuntal texture, and particularly in the expressive language. However, the younger composer almost invariably surpasses his models in terms of formal and structural flexibility, innovative elements (primarily harmonic design), and systematic logic (especially motivic construction and distribution). Johann Sebastian's thoroughly original approach is characterized particularly by his integration of North German manners, to which he was exposed in Lüneburg at the very latest. An example of a direct link provides the beginning of "Herzlich lieb hab ich dich, o Herr" (no. 68) with its elaboration of a Buxtehudian thematic model, the Praeludium in C Major (BuxWV 137),[55] which, incidentally, is transmitted solely in the Andreas Bach Book. Strong influences also come from Georg Böhm, as can be seen in chorales such as nos. 14, 16, and 36, which can be compared with the stylistic level of the partita "Ach, was soll ich Sünder machen" (BWV 770).

Figure 9.6. Bach, "Jesu, meine Freude" BWV 1105 (copied by J. G. Neumeister in his collection of organ chorale preludes, page 93).

Bach's application of the more unpredictable and expressive North German harmonic language, together with its more expansive fantasia- and partita-like formal concept, to the Middle German format of organ chorales resulted in a remarkable and unparalleled variety of chorale settings. In fact, the degree of individuality to be found among the works of Johann Sebastian Bach in the Neumeister collection provides the strongest style-critical evidence for their authenticity. One need only examine in "Wir Christenleut" (no. 14) the combination of the partita-like features to create a diversified yet unified whole; in "Jesu, meine Freude" (no. 51) the ingenious migration of the *cantus firmus* in the first six measures from soprano to bass (Fig. 9.6); in "Wir glauben all an einen Gott" (no. 31) the inventive harmonic progressions, mm. 16–27; and in general, the deliberate search for an unusual treatment and/or sophisticated contrapuntal (including canonic) treatment of the melodic material, the emphasis on highly diversified formal and textural design (often with double or even multiple treatment of chorale lines, alternating chordal and imitative fabric), and the nonrepetitive, indeed particularly creative cadential shaping of the endings of the chorales. The Johann Sebastian Bach repertoire in the Neumeister collection may be best described as representing the preparatory middleground between the large-

Table 9.1. Projected Orgel-Büchlein chorales

LM 4708 number	Chorale headings
18	O Jesu, wie ist dein Gestalt
21	O wir armen Sünder [Ehre sei dir, Christe]
17	Herzliebster Jesu, was hast du verbrochen
60	O Herre Gott, dein göttlich Wort
31	Wir glauben all an einen Gott
32	Aus tiefer Not schrei ich zu dir
33	Allein zu dir, Herr Jesu Christ
35	Ach, Gott und Herr
67	Herr Jesu Christ, du höchstes Gut
36	Ach Herr, mich armen Sünder
50	Wenn dich Unglück tut greifen an
52	Gott ist mein Heil, mein Hilf und Trost
69	Was Gott tut, das ist wohlgetan
73	Wie nach einer Wasserquelle
48	Erhalt uns, Herr, bei deinem Wort
40	Du Friedefürst, Herr Jesu Christ
64	Nun laßt uns den Leib begraben
65	Christus, der ist mein Leben
68	Herzlich lieb hab' ich dich, o Herr
71	Mach's mit mir, Gott, nach deiner Güt
59	Ach Gott, tu dich erbarmen
75	Christ, der du bist der helle Tag
20	Christe, der du bist Tag und Licht
72	Werde munter, mein Gemüte

format Eighteen Chorales (BWV 651–668) and the small-format Orgel-Büchlein chorales (BWV 599–644).

The conceptual connection with the Orgel-Büchlein is particularly close since the type of chorale setting found there appears to be the end product of a systematic process, in which the idea of the varied and figured chorale is embodied in a musical structure that could be made neither more expressive nor more compact. The occurrence of BWV 639 and 601 in LM 4708 may actually suggest that the Orgel-Büchlein was planned as a more systematically organized collection of *alio modo* settings of chorale preludes already at hand, so that the overlap of the Neumeister collection with the projected chorales in the Orgel-Büchlein is anything but a coincidence (see Table 9.1). This list demonstrates that the sequence of the Neumeister collection very closely resembles that of the Orgel-Büchlein.

The collection in LM 4708 appears to represent the remainder of a more extensive chorale portfolio of Johann Sebastian's, the original size of which can hardly be determined today.[56] Its primary function, besides providing pieces for service playing, seems related to learning the art of preluding and to consolidating his compositional craftsmanship (he shied away from neither difficult *cantus firmi* such as "Ach Gott, tu dich erbarmen"[57] nor simple but popular melodies such as "Was Gott tut, das ist wohlgetan"), as well as to experimenting with the possibilities of a given small-scale format. The chronology of what appears to be Bach's first study and practice collection of chorale preludes can only be hypothetically determined, but the general time frame 1695–1705 seems to be the most reasonable one on biographical and stylistic grounds, and also with respect to the lack of the obbligato pedal.

The Unattributed Works

The scribe of LM 4708 carefully copied from his source the author's name for nearly all pieces, and the reliability of the attributions can in many cases be verified through concordances. In only six instances (nos. 22, 41, 43, 44, 62, and 80) is no composer indicated. The absence of the composer's name in no. 80 is clearly due to an oversight (all the Sorge pieces must have been copied from the same print), and a similar negligence may have been the reason for the other missing names. In that case it is quite likely that the names left out are closely related to the composers in the immediate vicinity; that is, the missing name probably should be the composer of the piece preceding or following the anonymous entry. This line of reasoning results in the following tentative attributions:

No. 22—J. S. Bach or J. M. Bach
No. 41—J. S. Bach or J. M. Bach
No. 43—J. M. Bach
No. 44—J. M. Bach
No. 62—F. W. Zachow or J. M. Bach

The stylistic evidence helps to clarify the situation in that nos. 22, 43, 44, and 62 can hardly be works of Johann Sebastian Bach, but rather must have been composed by a musician of the elder generation. Here the most likely candidate is Johann Michael Bach, though for no. 62 Zachow cannot be excluded. A solution for no. 41 cannot easily be arrived at. It resembles those compositions of Johann Sebastian Bach in LM 4708 that display a more conservative mold, such as nos. 59, 69, or 73, and therefore it may well have been written by him. But there is no decisive evidence to tip the balance clearly toward Johann Sebastian rather than his father-in-law.

Synopsis of Chorale Preludes in the Neumeister Collection

This synopsis presents the contents of LM 4708 in the order of the manuscript and includes in abbreviated form information on the relevant concordances, where such are traceable. It incorporates results of research completed since the original publication of this chapter as an introduction to the 1985 facsimile edition of the LM 4708. See also the preface and critical notes to my edition of Johann Michael Bach, *Sämtliche Orgelchoräle, mit einem An-hang (Orgelchoräle des Bach-Kreises, hauptsächlich aus der Neumeister-Sammlung)* (Neuhausen-Stuttgart, 1987); my article, "From Berlin to Lódz: The Spitta Collection Resurfaces," *Notes* 46 (1989), pp. 311–327; and Harry Joelson-Strohbach, "Nachricht von verschiedenen verloren geglaubten Handschrif-ten mit barocker Tastenmusik," *Archiv für Musikwissenschaft* 44 (1987), pp. 91–140. I am indebted to Harry Joelson (Zurich) and Dominik Sackmann and Jean-Claude Zehnder (both of Basle) for the exchange of pertinent infor-mation.

Chorale titles are listed in modern orthography to facilitate hymnological identification. Within the synopsis, references to editions for purposes of the identification of individual pieces are limited to: DTB IV/1, for Johann Pachelbel, *Orgelkompositionen,* ed. Max Seiffert, in *Denkmäler der Tonkunst in Bayern,* IV/1 (1903); and JMB, for Johann Michael Bach, *Sämtliche Orgelcho-räle* (see above). The compositions of Zachow are included in Lohmann's edi-tion (see note 10). The hitherto unpublished chorale preludes by J. S. Bach (BWV 1090–1120) are collected along with BWV 714, 719, 742, and 957 in Johann Sebastian Bach, *Orgelchoräle der Neumeister-Sammlung,* ed. Chris-toph Wolff (Kassel and New Haven, 1985). The pieces known previously, that is, nos. 49, 77, and 78 (BWV 639, 601, and 737), are published in *NBA* IV/1 (ed. Heinz-Harald Löhlein, 1984) and *NBA* IV/3 (ed. Hans Klotz, 1961). All additional unpublished compositions found in LM 4708 by Johann Christoph Bach and Daniel Erich, as well as several unattributed works, are included in the appendix to the 1987 edition, mentioned above, of the complete organ chorales of Johann Michael Bach (JMB App.).

Key to Abbreviations

*	no concordances known
attr.	attributed to
Dröbs	manuscript compiled by J. A. Dröbs (1784–1825): SPK, Mus. ms. 30245 (SPK, Mus. ms. Bach P 806, is a copy thereof)
DTB IV/1	*Denkmäler der Tonkunst in Bayern* IV/1 (1903)
HfM	Berlin, Hochschule für Musik (now Hochschule der Künste), manuscripts lost or inaccesible [W film]
JMB; JMB App.	Johann Michael Bach, *Sämtliche Orgelchoräle* (Neuhausen-Stuttgart, 1987)
PO	Plauen Organ Book, lost; photostatic copy in DSB, Fot. 129/2 (Bückeburg); see note 29
Rinck Cat	C. H. Rinck, *Verzeichnis von alter Musik* (manuscript cata-logue of organ music with incipits), Yale University, Music Library, LM 2769
Ritter Cat	A. G. Ritter, *Katalog der Orgelkompositionen* (manuscript catalogue of organ music incipits, in part dependent on Rinck Cat), Archabbey St. Martin, Beuron, Von Werra-Ritter Collection, Mus. 159; see note 24

Schneider   Max Schneider, "Thematisches Verzeichnis"; see note 35
scr.   scribe
Sorge *Vorspiele*   G. A. Sorge, *Erster Theil der Vorspiele vor bekannten Choralge-*
sängen (Nuremberg, 1750); see note 34
Thomas   Günter Thomas, *Friedrich Wilhelm Zachow* (Regensburg,
1966)
W film   Stadtbibliothek Winterthur, Karl Matthei Collection,
films of lost or inaccessible manuscripts
Walther A   manuscript compiled by J. G. Walther (1684–1748): formerly Königsberg (Kaliningrad), Universitätsbibliothek,
Ms. Gotthold 15839 [W film]
Walther B   manuscript compiled by J. G. Walther: Den Haag, Gemeente Museum, 4.G.14 (for an inventory, see *NBA* IV/3,
Krit. Bericht, pp. 19–29)
Walther C-I, C-II, C-III   manuscript compiled by J. G. Walther: DSB, Mus. ms.
22541/1–3 (for an inventory, see *NBA* IV/2, *Krit. Bericht,*
pp. 26–35)

No.	Page	Composer	Work (Location of work)
1	1	J. M. Bach	*Nun komm, der Heiden Heiland (JMB 1)
2	2	J. M. Bach	*Meine Seele erhebt den Herren *or* Gott, sei uns gnädig und barmherzig (JMB 2)
3	5	J. M. Bach	*Herr Christ, der einig Gottes Sohn (JMB 3)
4	6	J. M. Bach	Nun freut euch, lieben Christen gmein [I] (JMB 4; DTB IV/1, no. 49)
			Concordance: HfM, Ms. Seiffert, pp. 82f. (anonymous)
5	8	J. M. Bach	Nun freut euch, lieben Christen gmein *or* Es ist gewißlich an der Zeit [II] (JMB 5 = Schneider 52)
			Concordances:
			1. Walther A, p. 113 (anonymous)
			2. HfM, Spitta Collection, Ms. Ritter
6	10	J. M. Bach	*Gott hat das Evangelium [I] (JMB 6)
7	12	J. M. Bach	Gott hat das Evangelium [II] (JMB 7; DTB IV/I, no. 32)
			Concordances:
			1. Walther B, pp. 235f.; version in B minor (attr. Pachelbel)
			2. Walther C-II, pp. 49f.; version in B minor (attr. Pachelbel)
			3. Dröbs (anonymous)
			4. DSB, Mus. ms. 30280 (attr. Pachelbel)
8	14	J. M. Bach	Gelobet seist du, Jesu Christ (JMB 8 = BWV 723)
			Concordances (attr. J. S. Bach):
			1. Leipzig, Musikbibliothek, Poel. Mus. ms. 39 [scr. J. N. Gebhardi, ca. 1800]
			2. Leipzig, Bach-Archiv, Go. S. 25 [scr. G. Hohlstein, ca. 1840–45]
			3. SPK, Mus. ms. Bach P 409 [ca. 1800]
9	16	F. W. Zachow	*Gelobet seist du, Jesu Christ (Thomas 61)
10	17	F. W. Zachow	Vom Himmel hoch, da komm ich her (Thomas 82)
			Concordance (version in C major): Walther C-II, p. 74

No.	Page	Composer	Work (Location of work)
11	18	J. S. Bach	Der Tag, der ist so freudenreich *or* Ein Kindelein so löbelich (BWV 719) *Concordances:* see *Bach Compendium* II/1 *Incipit:* Ritter Cat, nos. 25 and 399
12	20	J. M. Bach	In dulci jubilo (JMB 9 = BWV 751) *Concordance* (attr. "di Bach"): Leipzig, Musikbibliothek, Ms. 7 [scr. J. G. Preller, 1727–1786]
13	22	D. Erich	*Christum wir sollen loben schon (JMB App. 39)
14	24	J. S. Bach	*Wir Christenleut (BWV 1090) *Incipit:* Ritter Cat, no. 26
15	26	J. S. Bach	*Das alte Jahr vergangen ist (BWV 1091) *Incipit:* Ritter Cat, no. 27
16	28	J. S. Bach	*Herr Gott, nun schleuß den Himmel auf (BWV 1092)
17	30	J. S. Bach	*Herzliebster Jesu, was hast du verbrochen (BWV 1093) *Incipit:* Ritter Cat, no. 28
18	32	J. S. Bach	*O Jesu, wie ist dein Gestalt (BWV 1094) *Incipit:* Ritter Cat, no. 29
19	34	J. S. Bach	*O Lamm Gottes unschuldig (BWV 1095)
20	36	J. S. Bach	Christe, der du bist Tag und Licht *or* Wir danken dir, Herr Jesu Christ (BWV 1096; DTB IV/I no. 12) *Partial concordance* (mm. 1–25, substantial variants): Walther A, p. 322 (attr. "JP" [Pachelbel] as later addition by Walther)
21	38	J. S. Bach	*Ehre sei dir, Christe, der du leidest Not (BWV 1097)
22	40	anonymous [Pachelbel]	Christ lag in Todesbanden (JMB App. 27 = Schneider 6) *Concordances:* 1. Walther C-I, p. 121 (attr. J. H. Buttstedt) 2. HfM, Ms. 1491, pp. 250f. (attr. Pachelbel) 3. HfM, Ms. Spitta 1440 [scr. J. E. Rembt, 1749–1810], p. 94f. (attr. "HB" = Buttstedt, not Heinrich Bach) 4. Yale University, LM 4983 [scr. J. C. Bach, 1673–1727], 52 (attr. Pachelbel)
23	42	J. M. Bach	*Jesus Christus, unser Heiland, der den Tod überwand (JMB 10)
24	44	J. M. Bach	*O Herre Gott, Vater in Ewigkeit (JMB 11)
25	47	G. A. Sorge	Vater unser im Himmelreich *Concordance:* Sorge *Vorspiele*, p. 1
26	48	J. M. Bach	Der du bist drei in Einigkeit (JMB 12) *Partial concordances* (mm. 12–43 only): 1. PO, p. 161 (anonymous) 2. Walther A, p. 54 (anonymous) 3. Dröbs, p. 13 (anonymous)
27	50	J. C. Bach	*Allein Gott in der Höh sei Ehr (JMB App. 35)
28	52	J. M. Bach	Allein Gott in der Höh sei Ehr (JMB 13 = Schneider 51) *Concordances:* 1. Walther A, p. 278–280 2. Walther B, pp. 5f.
29	54	J. M. Bach	Mag ich Unglück nicht widerstahn (JMB 14; DTB IV/I, no. 47) *Concordances:* 1. PO, p. 186 2. Walther A, pp. 31f. (anonymous) 3. Walther B, p. 223 (attr. Pachelbel)

No.	Page	Composer	Work (Location of work)
30	56	J. M. Bach	Dies sind die heilgen zehn Gebot (JMB 15 = Schneider 49)
			Concordances (all in G major):
			1. PO, pp. 60 and 249
			2. Walther A, p. 6
			3. Berlin HfM, Ms. Spitta 1439 [scr. M. G. Fischer, 1793]
			4. Dröbs
31	58	J. S. Bach	*Wir glauben all an einen Gott (BWV 1098)
32	60	J. S. Bach	*Aus tiefer Not schrei ich zu dir (BWV 1099)
33	62	J. S. Bach	*Allein zu dir, Herr Jesu Christ (BWV 1100)
34	64	J. Pachelbel	Allein zu dir, Herr Jesu Christ
			Concordances:
			1. PO, p. 240
			2. Dröbs (version in B flat major)
35	66	J. S. Bach	Ach, Gott und Herr (BWV 714)
			Partial concordances (mm. 38ff. only; NBA IV/3, *Krit. Bericht*, p. 39):
			1. Walther A, p. 217
			2. DSB, Mus. ms. P 802 [scr. J. T. Krebs, 1690–1762]
36	68	J. S. Bach	Ach Herr, mich armen Sünder (BWV 742)
			Concordance: SPK, Mus. ms. 40037 [scr. J. C. Sasse, 1721–1794], p. 46
37	70	J. M. Bach	Auf meinen lieben Gott *or* Wo soll ich fliehen hin (JMB 16; DTB IV/I, no. 11)
			Concordance (substantial variant version; first section = mm. 1–23a recomposed, 7 mm. shorter): Ms. Seiffert [W film], p. 89 (anonymous)
38	72	J. S. Bach	*Durch Adams Fall ist ganz verderbt (BWV 1101)
39	74	J. M. Bach	Nun laßt uns Gott, dem Herren *or* Wach auf, mein Herz, und singe (JMB 17; DTB IV/I, no. 51)
			Concordance: Walther A, p. 92 (anonymous)
40	76	J. S. Bach	*Du Friedefürst, Herr Jesu Christ (BWV 1102)
41	78	anonymous [Pachelbel]	Was mein Gott will, das g'scheh allzeit (JMB App. 28)
			Concordance: SPK, Mus. ms. 11419 [scr. J. C. Kittel], p. 111 (attr. Pachelbel)
42	80	J. M. Bach	*Kommt her zu mir, spricht Gottes Sohn (JMB 18)
43	82	anonymous	*Ich ruf zu dir, Herr Jesu Christ (JMB App. 29)
44	83	anonymous	*Ich ruf zu dir, Herr Jesu Christ (JMB App. 30)
45	84	J. M. Bach	*Der Herr ist mein getreuer Hirt (JMB 19)
46	85	J. M. Bach	*Warum betrübst du dich, mein Herz (JMB 20)
47	86	J. M. Bach	Von Gott will ich nicht lassen (JMB 21 = Schneider 47)
			Concordances:
			1. PO, p. 182
			2. Dröbs
48	88	J. S. Bach	*Erhalt uns, Herr, bei deinem Wort (BWV 1103)
49	90	J. S. Bach	Vater unser im Himmelreich *or* Nimm von uns, Herr, du treuer Gott (BWV 737)
			Concordance: Walther B, p. 109 (see NBA IV/3, *Krit. Bericht*, p. 59)
			Incipit: Ritter Cat, no. 288
50	92	J. S. Bach	*Wenn dich Unglück tut greifen an (BWV 1104)
51	93	J. S. Bach	*Jesu, meine Freude (BWV 1105)

No.	Page	Composer	Work (Location of work)
52	94	J. S. Bach	*Gott ist mein Heil, mein Hilf und Trost (BWV 1106)
53	96	J. M. Bach [read: J. H. Buttstedt]	Ach Gott, vom Himmel sieh darein (JMB App. 31) *Concordances:* 1. PO, p. 180 (attr. J. H. Buttstedt) 2. Walther A, p. 25 (attr. Buttstedt)
54	98	J. M. Bach	*Es spricht der Unweisen Mund wohl (JMB 22)
55	99	J. M. Bach	Wo Gott, der Herr, nicht bei uns hält *or* Ach lieben Christen, seid getrost (JMB 23 = Schneider 45, in G minor) *Concordances* (all in G minor): 1. PO, p. 209 2. Walther A, pp. 278–280 (anonymous) 3. Walther B, p. 243 (anonymous) 4. Dröbs, p. 21
56	100	J. C. Bach	*An Wasserflüssen Babylon (JMB App. 36)
57	102	J. S. Bach	*Jesu, meines Lebens Leben (BWV 1107)
58	104	J. S. Bach	*Als Jesus Christus in der Nacht (BWV 1108)
59	106	J. S. Bach	*Ach Gott, tu dich erbarmen (BWV 1109)
60	110	J. S Bach	*O Herre Gott, dein göttlich Wort (BWV 1110)
61	112	F. W. Zachow	*Wie schön leuchtet der Morgenstern (Thomas 88)
62	114	anonymous [F. W. Zachow]	Heut triumphieret Gottes Sohn (JMB App. 32) *Incipit:* Rinck Cat, no. D/3 (attr. F. W. Zachow)
63	116	J. M. Bach	Wenn mein Stündlein vorhanden ist (JMB 24 = Schneider 46) *Concordances* (variant version): 1. PO, p. 190 2. Walther A, p. 229 3. Walther B, p. 321 4. Dröbs *Incipit:* Ritter Cat, no. 30 (attr. J. S. Bach)
64	118	J. S. Bach	*Nun laßt uns den Leib begraben (BWV 1111)
65	120	J. S. Bach	*Christus, der ist mein Leben (BWV 1112)
66	122	J. S. Bach	*Ich hab' mein Sach Gott heimgestellt (BWV 1113)
67	124	J. S. Bach	*Herr Jesu Christ, du höchstes Gut (BWV 1114)
68	126	J. S. Bach	*Herzlich lieb hab' ich dich, o Herr (BWV 1115)
69	128	J. S. Bach	*Was Gott tut, das ist wohlgetan (BWV 1116)
70	130	J. S. Bach	*Alle Menschen müssen sterben (BWV 1117)
71	132	J. S. Bach	Mach's mit mir, Gott, nach deiner Güt (BWV 957) *Partial concordance* (mm. 25–34 missing): Frankfurt, Mozart-Stiftung, 140 *variirte Choräle von Joh. Sebastian Bach* [in the possession of J. N. Schelble, 1789–1837; F. X. Gleichauf, 1801–1856] (ms. lost)
72	134	J. S. Bach	*Werde munter, mein Gemüte (BWV 1118)
73	136	J. S. Bach	*Wie nach einer Wasserquelle (BWV 1119)
74	138	J. C. Bach	*Wer Gott vertraut (JMB App. 37)
75	140	J. S. Bach	*Christe, der du bist der helle Tag (BWV 1120)
76	142	F. W. Zachow	Erbarm dich mein, o Herre Gott (Thomas 58) *Concordances:* 1. PO, p. 227 2. Walther B, pp. 122f. 3. Dröbs

No.	Page	Composer	Work (Location of work)
77	144	J. S. Bach	Ich ruf zu dir, Herr Jesu Christ (BWV 639) *Principal concordances* (minor variants; see *NBA* IV/1, *Krit. Bericht*, p. 119): 1. DSB, Mus. ms. P 283 [scr. J. S. Bach] 2. DSB, Mus. ms. P 802 [scr. J. T. Krebs]
78	145	J. S. Bach	Herr Christ, der einig Gotts Sohn (BWV 601) *Principal concordances* (minor variants; see *NBA* IV/I, *Krit. Bericht*, p. 118): 1. DSB, Mus. ms. P 283 (see no. 77, above) 2. DSB, Mus. ms. P 802 (see no. 77, above) 3. DSB, Mus. ms. P 801 [scr. J. T. Krebs] 4. Walther B, p. 198
79	146	G. A. Sorge	Auf Christenmensch *Concordance:* Sorge *Vorspiele,* p. 2
80	147	anonymous [G. A. Sorge]	Wo Gott, der Herr, nicht gibt sein Gunst *Concordance:* Sorge *Vorspiele,* p. 3
81	148	G. A. Sorge	Herr Jesu Christ, du höchstes Gut *Concordance:* Sorge *Vorspiele,* p. 4
82	149	G. A. Sorge	Freu dich sehr, o meine Seele *Concordance:* Sorge *Vorspiele,* p. 5

10

Bach's Audition for the St. Thomas Cantorate:
The Cantata "Du wahrer Gott und Davids Sohn"

"ON SUNDAY LAST in the morning the Hon. Capellmeister of Cöthen, Mr. Bach, gave here his test at the church of St. Thomas's for the hitherto vacant cantorate, the music of the same having been amply praised on that occasion by all knowledgeable persons . . ." Thus opens the report in the public press of 15 February 1723.[1] The question of which "music" of Bach's met with such "ample praise" has occupied scholarship again and again, and varying answers have been provided. A particular problem arises from the fact that two "test" cantatas are under discussion: "Jesus nahm zu sich die Zwölfe" BWV 22 and "Du wahrer Gott und Davids Sohn" BWV 23. Did both works or only one of them serve for the cantorate audition on the Sunday of Estomihi, 7 February 1723?

Spitta ascertained, on the basis of his source studies, that Cantatas 22 and 23 must have been written toward the end of Bach's Cöthen tenure, evidently with the cantorate audition in mind. He believed, however, that Cantata 22, better suited to "the taste of the Leipzig public" than the "somber, profoundly and artfully conceived" Cantata 23, was given preference and that Cantata 23 was not heard until 1724.[2] Spitta's opinion has generally taken hold in the Bach literature, but minor modifications have been voiced concerning the reasons for putting aside Cantata 23.[3]

The modern source studies by Alfred Dürr and Georg von Dadelsen seemed to agree with Spitta in principle, though their investigation of the original performance material preserved for BWV 23 yielded no conclusive result.[4] Although a major share of the parts had been prepared for a performance in 1723, a presentation of the cantata in its original form of three movements (in C minor, using oboes) apparently did not take place. Rather, it seemed that the work was offered first in a longer version including the figural chorale "Christe, du Lamm Gottes" (transposed to B minor, with oboes d'amore, cornetto, and trombones) on Estomihi Sunday (the Sunday before Lent, also known as Quinquagesima) 1724. On the basis of inserted leaves in the vocal parts, a later performance of the cantata was established, with key and instrumentation remaining uncertain, for the period between 1728 and 1731.

Through further research, Alfred Dürr has been able to advance our knowledge of the perplexing performance history of BWV 23 by a decisive step.[5] His critical evaluation of preserved performance material for the two test pieces written by Bach's competitor for the post, Christoph Graupner—"Lobet den Herrn, alle Heiden" and "Aus der Tiefen rufen wir"[6]—has led to the observation that the two principal copyists for the performance parts of BWV 23 also served as copyists for Graupner's works; both hands show the same early characteristics of script. Dürr's corrected calendar for the performance of Bach's vocal works in Leipzig gives the following entry for the Sunday of Estomihi 1723:[7]

BWV 22 [. . .]
Presumably also BWV 23, documented by
Performing parts St 16: Watermark IMK (oboe d'amore in D Minor, copies duplicating Violins I, II, both Violoncello parts). Copyists: principal copyists A, B (earliest script forms).
Score and remaining parts (oboes in C Minor, vocal parts, strings), except for inserted leaves in the final chorale, on Cöthen paper. The continuo part listed in *BG* 5/1 in A Minor is lost.
A performance—after the sermon—of this cantata, prepared in Cöthen in the version in C Minor and without final chorale, was apparently now presented in B Minor and included the final chorale (supported by trombones), the chorale having been added in Bach's hand to the instrumental parts from Cöthen.
Repeat performance, 1728–31 with newly added vocal parts (for the final chorale), documented by watermark MA in the form reflecting the middle period of its use (the parts that had been added earlier apparently having been lost or used elsewhere).

Through a fortunate coincidence, the source situation for BWV 23 has recently been substantially improved. Unexpectedly, three parts belonging to the performance material of the cantata, but for more than seventy years unidentified, have turned up (the long-missed A minor continuo part and two further parts, of whose existence nothing had been known: *Violoncello,* in Bach's hand, and *Baßon è Cembalo,* written by a copyist).[8] They confirm Dürr's findings and offer, in addition, most welcome evidence regarding the overall performance history of BWV 23.

Through analysis and interpretation of sources now available I will attempt here to clarify—to the degree possible—the performance history of Cantata 23.[9] What questions have remained unanswered so far will readily be seen from Dürr's resumé quoted above. In view of the complexity of sources it will not seem surprising that clarification of all remaining details may be unattainable and that, in fact, new problems may move into focus.

Since there can be no further doubt about the performance of both Cantata 22 and Cantata 23 on the Sunday of Estomihi 1723,[10] their origin as audition pieces requires further investigation. Research is rendered problematic, however, by the fact that we have no documentation regarding the exact circumstances and dates of Bach's application for the St. Thomas cantorate. Precise documentation of Bach's name first appears in this connection in the town council proceedings of 21 December 1722.[11] Here Bach is named, together with Graupner, at the head of the list of seven contestants "to be subjected to examination for the Cantorate." Graupner's audition took place on 17 January 1723, the last Sunday after Epiphany. And since the Leipzig town council did not decide before 15 January[12] that "Bach was also to be admitted for the audition," word concerning approval of his candidacy and a date for his audition could not have reached Bach until after this date—just three weeks before 7 February.

The fact that Graupner and Bach were the preferred candidates may seem evident from the granting of two cantata performances to each, whereas the other candidates had to be content with that of a single cantata. Georg Friedrich Kauffmann and Andreas Christoph Tufen, on the first Sunday in Advent 1722, were even obliged to divide a musical service between them,[13] which caused Kauffmann to ask "that he be admitted for audition again."[14]

In the interest of continuity and in order to preclude undesirable surprises, the choice of texts was likely not left to the applicants. Ever since Kuhnau's tenure it had, in fact, become a practice to determine the texts for a considerable number of Sunday services ahead of time and to have them printed in collections.[15] While the post was vacant, some minor changes in the selection might have had to be accommodated, but hardly any major ones. The presence of ministry, school authorities, and choir prefects must have insured a certain stability. Thus we may conclude that, with the notification of admittance to the audition, Bach received the texts for the cantatas in question. Linguistic consistencies suggest that they were written by the same poet;[16] furthermore, there are no models in Bach's earlier cantatas for these texts, whereas they are closely related to those for BWV 75 and 76, the first two cantatas written after Bach had assumed the Leipzig office in 1723.[17] Both structural and literary similarities between the texts for Bach's and Graupner's test pieces make it appear even more likely that the choices were not made by the candidates.

Bach must have traveled to Leipzig in good time prior to the date of the audition to prepare the performance of his test pieces, particularly since he was not familiar with local conditions.[18] With some assurance we may conjecture that he was present on the preceding Tuesday, 2 February (the Feast of the Purification of Mary), to attend the cantorate audition of Georg Balthasar Schott at St. Nicholas's[19] and that he thus received a direct impression of the vocal and instrumental forces. In view of the fact that Schott's audition took place only a few days before the date set for Bach, it is unlikely that Bach was able to avail himself of the help of St. Thomas students prior to Wednesday, 3 February, for copying performance material or rehearsing his cantatas. In this respect, he was at a distinct disadvantage in comparison with Graupner, who had arrived in Leipzig before the Christmas season of 1722,[20] or with Schott, who lived there.[21]

That Bach decided, in spite of the pressure of time, to enlarge Cantata 23, so to speak at the last minute, by a fourth movement is remarkable; he must have had good reasons for doing so. The details for his decision remain unknown. It is possible, however, that he learned only after he arrived in Leipzig what amount of time was allotted for a cantata to be performed after the sermon. It seems impossible, however, that he would have composed the movement "Christe, du Lamm Gottes" after his arrival. Unfortunately, the original score for the piece has not survived.[22] It must have formed an insertion in the score of Cantata 23, for the manuscript concludes with the movement "Aller Augen warten auf dich," at the end of which is expressly noted "Il Fine." Clearly Bach had planned a three-movement work, but even before his departure for Leipzig he must have weighed the possibility of enlarging it and given thought to a suitable setting. It can be shown (see below) that the figural chorale "Christe, du Lamm Gottes" goes back to a work from Bach's Weimar period. The choice of this movement may have been prompted by the use of the same *cantus firmus* in the recitative of BWV 23. In any event, the German Agnus Dei was liturgically most befitting for a cantata after the sermon, that is, for a communion piece,[23] quite apart from its significance for the season of the church year.

As is shown by the extant performance material for Cantata 23 (see Table 10.1), Bach had written out the vocal parts and—with the exception of duplicates for the strings and organ—the instrumental parts as well. In the instrumentation of the two test pieces Bach had adopted the standard scoring (strings, oboes); he obviously did not wish to take chances. A decision about the size of the performance ensemble could not have been made before his arrival in Leipzig. Thus the execution of duplicate parts for violins 1, 2, and violoncello by the Leipzig copyists Kuhnau and Meissner is easily explained. In the case of Graupner's test pieces we find the same logical division of labor between composer (for the principal parts) and copyists (for the duplicates); see Table 10.2. A further similarity between Graupner's and Bach's performance material arises from the *colla parte* trombone parts. Their use (in Graupner's works consistently for all choral movements) served entirely for the support of the choir and thus offered welcome security for the performance of the test pieces.

Both Cantata 22 and its sister work BWV 23 are so designed in their choral movements that the instruments play *colla parte* with respective sections of the choir: BWV 22/1 (strings), BWV 23/3 (strings), BWV 23/4 (cornetto, three trombones). Had Bach composed the movement BWV 23/4 specifically for the cantata, he would have taken care to write the vocal parts

Table 10.1. The original sources for BWV 23

"Du wahrer Gott und Davids Sohn" SPK, P 69; DSB, St 16	Watermark	Scribe: mvts. 1–3	Scribe: mvt. 4
Score (P 69)	X	JSB	—
Parts (St 16):			
Soprano	X	JSB	—
Alto	X	JSB	—
Tenore	X	JSB	—
Basso	X	JSB	—
Oboe 1	X	JSB	JSB
Oboe 2	X	JSB	JSB
Violino 1	X	JSB	JSB
Violino 2	X	JSB	JSB
Viola	X	JSB	JSB
*Violoncello	X	JSB	JSB (fig.)[a]
Cornetto ⎫	Y	—	JSB
Trombone 1 ⎪ *(colla parte)*	Y	—	JSB
Trombone 2 ⎬	Y	—	JSB
Trombone 3 ⎭	Y	—	JSB
Oboe d'amore 1 ⎫ (substitute	Y	JSB	JSB
Oboe d'amore 2 ⎬ parts)	Y	JSB	JSB
Violino 1 ⎫	Y	CGM	JSB
Violino 2 ⎪ *(duplicate parts)*	Y	CGM	JSB
Violoncello ⎬	Y	CGM, Anon.[b]	CGM
Violoncello ⎭	Y	JAK	CGM
*Bassono[c] [è Cembalo][d](fig.)[e]	Y	JAK	JAK
*Continuo (fig.)[e]	Y	JAK, CGM	JAK
Soprano ⎫	Z	—	JSB
Alto ⎪ (insertions)	Z	—	JSB
Tenore ⎬	Z	—	JSB
Basso ⎭	Z	—	JSB

a. Only the fourth movement is figured; see note 38.
b. Anonymous hand, not listed in Dürr *Chr* or Dürr *Chr* 2.
c. Title in Bach's hand.
d. Autograph addition to the title.
e. Mainly in autograph.

Key:
X = Wild man with tree branch (Cöthen paper); see Weiss, no. 1.
Y = "IMK"; see Weiss, no. 97; Dürr *Chr*, pp. 123ff.
Z = "MA" (intermediate form); see Weiss, no. 122; Dürr *Chr*, pp. 138ff.
JSB = Johann Sebastian Bach.
JAK = Johann Andreas Kuhnau (principal copyist A in Dürr *Chr* 2, p. 163).
CGM = Christian Gottlob Meissner (principal copyist B in Dürr *Chr* 2, p. 163).
* = Sources recently located again.
fig. = Thorough-bass figures.

Table 10.2. The original sources for Graupner's audition pieces

"Lobet den Herrn" (Mus. ms. 431/1)[a]	Scribe	"Aus der Tiefen" (Mus. ms. 431/2)[a]	Scribe
Score[b]	CG	*Score*[c]	CG
Parts:[c]		*Parts:*[c]	
Canto	JAK	Canto	CG
Alto	JAK	Alto	CG
Tenore	JAK	Tenore	CG
Basso	JAK	Basso	CG
Canto in ripieno	JAK	Canto in ripieno	JAK
Alto in ripieno	JAK	Alto in ripieno	JAK
Tenore in ripieno	JAK	Tenore in ripieno	JAK
		Basso in ripieno	JAK, CG
Oboe 1	JAK	Oboe 1	CG
Oboe 2	JAK	Oboe 2	CG
Clarino 1	JAK		
Clarino 2	JAK		
Tamburi	JAK		
Violino 1	JAK	Violino 1	CG
Violino 2	JAK	Violino 2	CG
Viola	JAK	Viola	CG
Continuo	JAK	Violone	CG
Violino 1 ⎫	JAK	Violino 1 ⎫	JAK
Violino 2 ⎬ (duplicate parts)	JAK	Violino 2 ⎬ (duplicate parts)	JAK
Continuo ⎭	JAK	Violone ⎭	CGM
		Clarino ⎫	CG
Trombono 1 ⎫	CG	Trombono 1 ⎬ (colla parte)	CG
Trombono 2 ⎬ (colla parte)	CG	Trombono 2 ⎪	CG
Trombono 3 ⎭	CG	Trombono 3 ⎭	CG
Continuo ⎱ (transposed	JAK	Continuo ⎱ (transposed	CG
Continuo ⎰ and fig.)	Anon. Ic, JAK	Continuo ⎰ and fig.)	JAK

a. Darmstadt, Hessische Landesbibliothek.

b. Watermark: Deer/"IAI"; see Weiss, no. 6—and "IMK"; see Weiss, no. 97; Dürr *Chr*, pp. 123ff.

c. Watermark: "IMK"; see Weiss, no. 97; Dürr *Chr*, pp. 123ff.

Key:
CG = Christoph Graupner.
JAK = Johann Andreas Kuhnau.
CGM = Christian Gottlob Meissner.

either in *stylus simplex* (as in BWV 22/5) or with doubling strings (as in BWV 22/1 and BWV 23/3). The use of cornetto and trombones suggests that Bach had no other choice, a disposition of string parts having already been made for this movement, but it also suggests that he (like Graupner) did not want to forgo the support for the chorus. The added movement meant additional rehearsal time for the singers. Yet the inclusion of trombones, though involving additional work, must have seemed indispensable to Bach.

Cornetto and trombone pitch in Leipzig was a whole tone above Kammerton pitch, in conformance with the pitch of the organ. The G/C minor chorale "Christe, du Lamm Gottes" would accordingly have had to be played in F/B♭ minor. But since this was hardly possible, the whole cantata had to be transposed down a half-tone in order to allow the cornetto and trombone parts to be played in E/A minor. The strings, therefore, had to tune down half a step, a practice that is variously documented for Bach's performances.[24] For this reason, oboes (with the lowest tone c′) could not be used and had to be supplanted by oboi d'amore. A new pair of parts was thus needed and, because of the transposition (concert pitch b, written as d) Bach wrote them out himself, as he did with the cornetto and trombone parts.

Bach may not have minded the employment of oboi d'amore, since this afforded him a change of sonority from that of BWV 22. Furthermore, so far as we know, he had not used the oboe d'amore in any of his earlier vocal works, so the change offered the attraction of novelty.[25]

Included in the copyists' work was the preparation of continuo parts, which Bach had not written out in Cöthen, likely because of the changes of Chorton pitch from place to place. Owing to the transposition of Cantata 23, a new organ part in A minor was required. This was prepared mainly by Johann Andreas Kuhnau, the experienced copyist, and based on the autograph violoncello part which bears Bach's copying directive "*NB. Eine 3 minor tiffer | als Chorton*" (a minor third down, in accordance with the Chorton). That is, the part was to be written in A minor (representing the Chorton pitch for B minor), a minor third lower than the C minor notation of the violoncello (which had to be tuned down a half-step).

Within the entire set of performance parts in the Deutsche Staatsbibliothek (St 16), the only one written, and meant to sound, in B minor is a bassoon part.[26] The addition of this part to organ and violoncello[27] suggests an especially strong continuo scoring. It is curious that the bassoon part contains continuo figuring (largely in autograph) as well as the superscription (also in Bach's hand) "*è Cembalo*" following that of "*Baßon.*" Whether this notation, recognizable as a later addition,[28] applied to the first performance of the cantata, in 1723, cannot be ascertained. In this connection, the existence of two figured continuo parts in the performance material for Graupner's test pieces gains significance, for it indicates dual keyboard accompaniment. The appearance of both organ and harpsichord parts,[29] to be found in other sets of performance material for works by Bach, seems to prove the double accompaniment, though the entire question needs further clarification. The unusually rich continuo section for Cantata 23 renders the practice of using two keyboards entirely plausible.

Dual keyboard accompaniment would, in fact, fit particularly well the picture unfolding from the evidence of the extant performance material of BWV 23 prepared for the cantorate audition of 1723. This shows how much

Bach must have been concerned with creating an impression in Leipzig. Exuberant sonority, such as Graupner's use of trumpets and kettledrums, was precluded by the somber character of the Lenten season. Yet within this restriction, Bach made the most of the volume of sound. The orchestra may have numbered no less than nineteen to twenty-two players. If the performers that can be documented for trumpets and drums in Graupner's audition were assigned to string parts in Bach's, the number would be even higher. What is not clear is the size of the choir. Curiously, no vocal *ripieno* parts, as they appear for Graupner's work, are found for Bach's. Whether this proves an uncommonly large choral ensemble for Graupner's cantorate audition remains an open question. For regular Sunday services the St. Thomas cantor had the twelve to sixteen singers of the principal Kantorei at his disposal. If vocal *ripieno* parts for BWV 23 have been lost, Bach may have had sixteen or more singers. Considering the seemingly complete set of performance parts, however, such a loss is not very likely. (Concerning the loss of the leaves inserted in the vocal parts and containing the chorale, see below.)

Because of the lack of source material for the performance of Cantata 22[30] it is not possible to arrive at a precise description of its presentation. Its performance forces may have been largely the same as those for BWV 23. The disposition of sonorities and the design of the two cantatas are different, but the pair of works composed for the cantorate audition represents a broad and highly integrated spectrum of Bach's vocal art: choral fugue with solo exposition (BWV 22/1B), concerted choral movement (BWV 23/3), straightforward hymn setting (BWV 22/5), figural chorale (BWV 23/4), *secco* recitative (BWV 22/3), recitative with instrumental *cantus firmus* (BWV 23/2), dialogue (BWV 22/1A), aria in trio setting (BWV 22/2), duet in a five-part setting (BWV 23/1), aria with full string accompaniment (BWV 22/4), grouping of lower solo voices (alto, tenor, bass in BWV 22), grouping of higher solo voices (soprano, alto, tenor in BWV 23). The fine balance of parts within the total picture attests to Bach's artistic judgment, a judgment that was not lacking in adroit calculation, considering the "finale" effect, so unusual in Bach's cantata oeuvre, of the chorale fantasy BWV 23/4. It doubtless formed the climax, from the point of view of both invention and sound, of the cantorate audition that earned such "ample praise."

II

A repeat performance of Cantata 23 is verified by the insertion in the vocal parts of four leaves whose watermarks enable us to ascertain a date between the years 1728 and 1731. It stands to reason, however, that an earlier repeat performance might have taken place as well. Evidence that would support this assumption is the revival of Cantata 22, which can be assigned to the date of Estomihi 1724 through a printed wordbook.[31] That this book omits the text for Cantata 23 is of no consequence: according to the Leipzig practice observed in the issuing of wordbooks, the texts for the music to be performed after the sermon were not included.[32] On the other hand, there is

no proof that the pairing of the two cantatas for Estomihi 1723 was maintained. The idea of pairing is, moreover, complicated by the absence of proof
that BWV 22 was resumed in performances after 1724. If Cantata 23 was
performed with Cantata 22 in 1724, its bassoon part may have been revised
to serve additionally as harpsichord part on this occasion.

It is possible that the harpsichord was employed in lieu of the (then unusable?) organ in 1724—a hypothesis that might be advanced as an alternative to the suggestion of dual accompaniment in 1723. Only a few weeks
after Estomihi, in connection with the first performance of the St. John Passion on Good Friday 1724, there is mention of the fact that "the *Clav-Cymbel*
will require some repair."[33] It is not possible, however, to determine whether
the harpsichord part prepared for the Passion music, but now lost, was intended as substituted or added accompaniment. Since the performance of the
St. John Passion was at St. Nicholas's, whereas that of Cantatas 22 and 23
likely took place at St. Thomas's, no direct analogy can be suggested; but
the practice of harpsichord accompaniment is worth noting. In the end, it
cannot be determined whether BWV 23 was presented on Estomihi 1724
with harpsichord continuo only or with both harpsichord and organ. The
key for the performance may have been B minor, and it remains uncertain
whether *colla parte* support of trombones was involved, for their presence was
not absolutely required.

A further revival of Cantata 23 could not have taken place before 1727,
because performances of other works are documented for Estomihi 1725 and
1726.[34] And the vocal-part insertions dated by watermark to the period
1728–1731 make a repeat performance date of 1727 seem unlikely (and
1729 may be excluded as well since Cantata 159 was most probably performed on Estomihi Sunday of that year.)[35] The contents of the insertions,
pertaining to the fourth movement only, are an important key for understanding the assumption that a new performance occurred in the period between 1728 and 1731, a performance that deviated in some crucial points
from the earlier one (or earlier ones). The *colla parte* brass parts and the vocal

Example 10.1.

Example 10.2.

parts show different readings in numerous spots, which means the use of the respective sets of parts on one and the same occasion would not have been possible. As an illustration of the predominantly declamatory variants, the third line of the second chorale stanza is quoted (Ex. 10.1). This passage actually requires a reexamination of the history of the chorale setting. In 1725 it was incorporated in the revised form of the St. John Passion as a final movement. By providing a frame for the Passion music through the large figural chorale settings "O Mensch bewein dein Sünde groß" (BWV 245/1^II) and "Christe, du Lamm Gottes" (BWV 245/40^II = 23/4) and adding an aria with chorale (BWV 245/11^+), Bach deliberately integrated the work in the chorale cantata cycle of 1724–25. That the chorale "O Mensch bewein dein Sünde groß" goes back to an earlier Passion work by Bach has been convincingly shown by Arthur Mendel[36] on the basis of a suggestion supplied by Alfred Dürr. The same applies to three new arias in the second version of BWV 245. Stylistic features, as well as features pertaining to structure and the technique of writing, link the movements "Christe, du Lamm Gottes" and "O Mensch bewein dein Sünde groß" and make their derivation from a lost Weimar Passion setting likely (one might compare especially the treatment of chorale sections and the juxtaposed textures of wind and string scoring).[37] Thus all five additions to the second version of BWV 245 might go back to the same origin—an entirely persuasive conjecture.

The version of the chorale "Christe, du Lamm Gottes" as given in the extant vocal parts for the St. John Passion corresponds exactly to the brass parts for the cantata version of 1723 (see Ex. 10.2). Bach clearly decided upon a revision of the vocal parts when he removed the chorale setting from the St. John Passion and reassigned it to the cantata. This necessitated the preparation of new copies for the insertions. The insertions formerly used were no longer needed; it is possible that they had finally served as *ripieno* parts for the second version of the St. John Passion. The new vocal parts for the cantata rendered the use of the *colla parte* brass impossible—and so transposition of the cantata from C minor to B minor became unnecessary.

As a matter of fact, a return to the "Cöthen key" of the work—in which it had never been heard—can be variously proved. The "Cöthen" oboe parts, written in C minor, did not contain the 1723 chorale, whereas in the oboe d'amore parts it was included from the outset. Figure 10.1 demonstrates how the notation of the chorale was directly joined to the preceding move-

Figure 10.1. Cantata 23, movement 4: *Hautbois d'Amour*, folio 1v (detail).

Figure 10.2. Cantata 23, movement 4: *Hautbois Ire*, folio 1v (detail).

ment. Conversely, Figure 10.2 exhibits by fermatas, placed above and below the double bar, the explicit indication for an ending of the work at the conclusion of the third movement. The chorale emerges as a subsequent entry, since the end of its first line is written over the original marking for the close. Differences in writing also indicate that the chorale was not added in the oboe parts until preparation of a new performance in the period between 1728 and 1731. Thus the oboe parts were first copied for a performance of the work in its four-movement form, presumably to supplant those written for the oboi d'amore. The performance in C minor also made the A minor organ part unusable. In order to avoid having to prepare a new B♭ minor organ part, Bach availed himself of the extant B minor bassoon/harpsichord part. As is clearly shown in Figure 10.3, the B minor key signature was changed by the respective entries into a B♭ minor key signature. The placement of note heads and the like required no change. Only the accidentals and the corresponding figure notation had to be adapted to the new key.

The revision of the former B minor version precluded the use of harpsichord, unless the harpsichordist played from a score.[38] The data compiled in Table 10.3, comparing the two performance versions of the work, make it clear that a major portion of the performance material could no longer be put to use. Bach had reduced the performance forces and returned to the established norm. That he resumed Cantata 23 after 1731 in what was now its

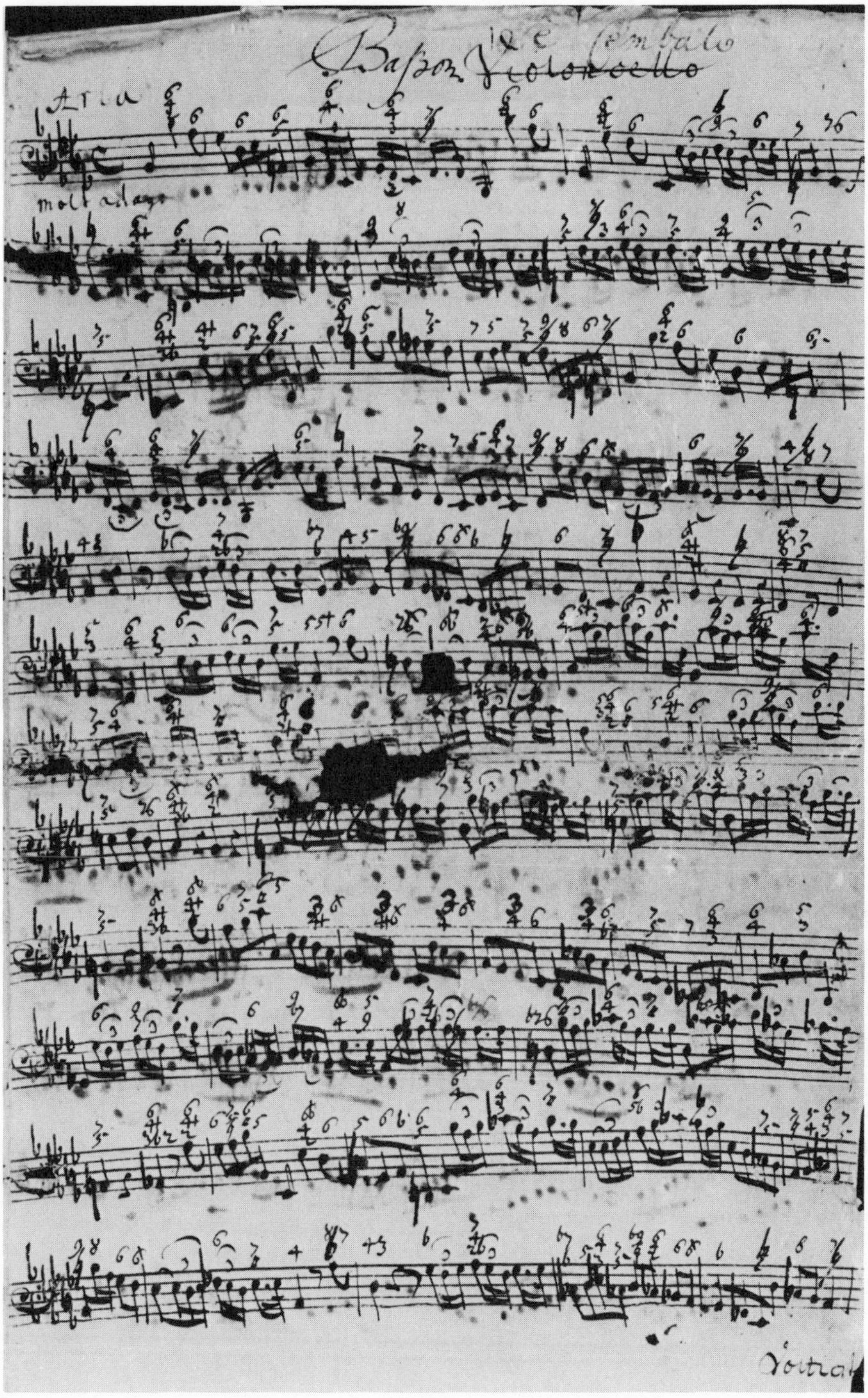

Figure 10.3. Cantata 23, movement 1: *Baßon è Cembalo*, folio 1v.

Table 10.3. Keys for performances of BWV 23

Performance key	Parts	Notated pitch	Concert pitch
B minor	Vocal parts	C minor	B minor[a]
	Strings	C minor	B minor[b]
	Oboe d'amore 1, 2	D minor	B minor
	Bassoon/harpsichord	B minor	B minor
	Continuo (organ)	A minor	B minor
	Cornetto, trombone 1–3	A minor	B minor
	Not usable:		
	Oboe 1, 2	C minor	C minor
C minor	Vocal parts	C minor	C minor
	Strings	C minor	C minor
	Oboe 1, 2	C minor	C minor
	Continuo (organ)	B minor	C minor
	Not usable:		
	Oboe d'amore 1, 2	D minor	B minor
	Bassoon/harpsichord	B minor	B minor
	Continuo (organ)	A minor	B minor
	Cornetto, trombone 1–3	A minor	B minor

a. By transposing at sight.
b. By tuning down (see also note 24).

final form is possible, even probable, though no evidence can be cited. There are no traces of further changes or modifications.

It is remarkable that the final version reverts to the original conception of the work, both in the choice of key (C minor) and sonority (regular oboes). This return constitutes a certain parallel to the St. John Passion, whose last version, after several intermediate ones, was also largely adapted to the original form. The metamorphoses of the cantata "Du wahrer Gott und Davids Sohn"—which like those of a number of other Bach works can be deduced from the original sources—are linked to practical performance considerations, yet at the same time they reflect the primacy of Bach's artistic judgment when the substance of a work was the issue.

11

Origins of the Kyrie of the B Minor Mass

THE MUSICOLOGICAL DEBATE over Bach's B Minor Mass has been going on ever since Friedrich Smend's edition of the "Missa. Symbolum Nicenum. Sanctus. Osanna, Benedictus, Agnus Dei et Dona nobis pacem" (BWV 232).[1] The focus has been almost entirely on philological source studies, with questions of source criticism and chronology, arising from original performance material and especially from the autograph score,[2] in the foreground. I shall not confront the problems connected with the genesis of the four segments of the work. Bach's inexhaustible *opus summum* presents further unanswered questions as well, questions that are not without significance for a historical perspective on and perception of the B Minor Mass.

We are here concerned with the historical background, especially of the Missa (Kyrie and Gloria), which Bach submitted as a completed work on 27 July 1733 to the Dresden court with a formal request for the title of Royal Polish and Electoral Saxon Court Composer. I will explore not only the historical background as constituted by dates, facts, and archival sources,[3] but also the musical origins of the great work. Among Bach's five extant Masses, this Missa is the earliest, possibly his very first setting of the time-honored texts "Kyrie eleison" and "Gloria in excelsis Deo."[4] It is for this reason in particular that Bach's interest in the Mass composition of other masters must be considered of importance. For during his Leipzig period Bach was intensely occupied with the study of Masses by various composers, probably foremost among them Palestrina and Antonio Lotti.[5] Some copies of these works, partly in Bach's autograph, can be dated about or before the year 1730, and thus they enter—quite generally—into the musical origin of the Missa. Among them, however, a small and so far unknown work, a Mass in G Minor by the Palatine Electoral court composer Johann Hugo von Wilderer,[6] is especially revealing with regard to the conception of the work with which, in 1733, the Thomascantor re-entered the scene of major church composition after his three monumental Passion settings, the Passions according to St. John, St. Matthew, and St. Mark.[7]

"*Missa a 2 Violini 2 Viole Bassono 4 Voci Cont. di Sig. Wilderer*" is the title under which the Deutsche Staatsbibliothek Berlin has preserved the manuscript of Wilderer's score, which is of special value since it appears throughout in Bach's hand.[8] The manuscript, bearing the signature Mus. ms. 23116/10, consists of eight leaves of four pages each. Page 1 recto to page 4 recto (upper brace) contains the Kyrie, with the Gloria appearing on page 4 recto (lower brace) through page 8 verso (upper half of the page, the lower half having been left blank). The watermark of the paper, barely recognizable, shows the Electoral Saxon coat of arms.[9] Because this was so widely used, over a long period and in several variant forms, it is not possible to assign the paper to a definite period. Some of the characteristics of Bach's handwriting would place the manuscript into the second half of the 1720s at the earliest. A date that would link this manuscript to other copies of Mass compositions, approximately within the three-year span 1730–1733, seems plausible inasmuch as a *terminus ante quem* is clearly given by Bach's Missa (first half of 1733), as is to be explained below. After Bach's death the manuscript passed into the possession of Carl Philipp Emanuel Bach, and in the listing of his estate of 1790 it is recorded under the title "*1 Messe von Wilderez, Partitur und Stimmen.*"[10] From the autograph collection of Georg Poelchau it went, after the latter's death in 1836, to the Royal Library in Berlin.[11]

The first question we must consider is where Bach may have obtained the model for his copy. It must have been in score format, for the appearance of Bach's manuscript rules out any likelihood that it was scored from parts. No further source for Wilderer's work has so far been located, so it has not been possible to trace a derivation of manuscripts. We are left to conjecture. A feasible possibility is that Bach used material that came from Dresden holdings.[12] His connections to that city were strong; for the period before 1733 there is documented interchange with Georg Pisendel, Jan Dismas Zelenka, Johann Gottlieb Graun, and Johann David Heinichen as well as Johann Adolf Hasse, though Hasse did not assume his office as Dresden court composer until December 1733. Bach traveled to Dresden for concert performances on the city's Silbermann organs between 1725 and 1731.[13] Altogether, the links were so substantial that—as related by Johann Adolph Scheibe— "almost any day they would have provided Leipzig with reliable and abundant news about the Dresden court orchestra."[14]

We do not know why and at what point Bach began to plan the composition of a Mass of rather unusual dimensions and the submission of this work—not the more likely choice of a cantata or an instrumental piece— with his request for the title of Dresden court composer.[15] Yet a remark in the dedicatory letter that accompanied the parts for the Missa, as they were sent to Dresden, seems of significance: "and I offer myself in most indebted obedience to show at all times, upon Your Royal Highness's Most Gracious Desire, my untiring zeal in the composition of music for the church as well as for the orchestre, and to devote my entire forces to the services of Your Highness."[16] Bach's words suggest that he had informed himself about the performance of sacred music at the Dresden court. Why might it not have been for this purpose that he obtained, together with other works, a number of Mass compositions—among them the one by Wilderer—from the rich Dresden repertoire? The Dresden works must have held an interest for him quite different from the appeal of the extensive but somewhat outdated collection of choral music at St. Thomas's in Leipzig.[17]

The very careful design and execution of the copy attest to the attention Bach paid to the Missa of Johann Hugo von Wilderer. The work was doubtless used not only for study but also for performance in the service. The fact that a set of parts was originally preserved with the score speaks for this; and its clear structure rendered the Missa particularly suitable for use in the liturgy. Yet our principal interest is in its implication for the plan of Bach's Missa. What—possibly numerous—influences entered into this work can probably never be determined. Much is bound to remain in the dark—as with most works of art—but as I intend to show, Wilderer's Missa must be considered one of the most important documents to have a bearing upon the musical origin of the B Minor Mass. There are manifest connections between the two works, which will be explored on the basis of the autograph manuscripts.

The Mass in G Minor by Wilderer—a student of Giovanni Legrenzi and younger colleague of Agostino Steffani, who, especially in his operatic work, stands on the borderline between Venetian and Neapolitan schools[18]—shows definite traits of the early Neapolitan Mass style. One characteristic of the work is highly varied orchestral writing with its obbligato textures. The closed form of the solo aria is not yet employed, but smaller and larger solo sections (though without use of the da capo pattern)[19] are in evidence. The Kyrie is in tripartite form (Kyrie-Christe-Kyrie), the Gloria (beginning with "Et in terra pax" and obviously introduced with an intonation by the liturgist) follows a continuous structure, though without any apparent sectional division. On the whole the work is tersely designed, clearly aimed at liturgical use. The following measure count is merely intended as a means of general orientation—Kyrie I, 31; Christe, 28; Kyrie II, 40; and Gloria, 110—yet it clearly suggests the general proportions of Bach's work.

In its design Wilderer's Kyrie, in fact, is comparable to Bach's, whereas the Gloria is not. A tripartite form for the Kyrie is, of course, traditional and a logical reflection of the text; but more far-reaching correspondences suggest a correlation of the two works, which we shall trace section by section, beginning with the prefatory Kyrie statement. A block-like "antecedent" of the Kyrie movement is not in itself unusual among the many possibilities of musical settings, but in the series of Bach's copies of Mass compositions preceding his own, this feature appears only in the one by Wilderer.[20] As we follow the details of musical patterns, we find surprising similarities between Wilderer's and Bach's work in the few opening measures, similarities that exceed the immediately startling similarity of manuscript appearance in the opening pages for both works (see Figures 11.1 and 11.2).[21] A tabulation of details will illustrate this clearly:

Figure 11.1. Wilderer, Missa in G Minor (copied by Bach), page 1.

Figure 11.2. Missa in B Minor BWV 232[1] (autograph score), page 1.

Wilderer	*Bach*
(a) Adagio Introduction (beginning on the offbeat) in 4/4.	Adagio Introduction[22] (beginning on the downbeat) in 4/4.
(b) Threefold "Kyrie" invocation.	Threefold "Kyrie" invocation.
Three "blocks" unified in text and music and set off by rests.	Three unified "blocks" linked by upbeat figures (S I, II). Tripartite arrangement of the text strictly carried out in T and B.
(c) Broadly designed Phrygian cadence on the dominant (VI–V).	Broadly designed Phrygian cadence on the dominant.
First invocation: a chord, sounded three times in succession (—∪—).	First invocation: a chord sounded twice, then departure from the tonic pattern (—∪—). Intensification of the newly reached 6th chord through 7th suspension.
Second invocation: preparation of the Phrygian cadence through the bass descent from the upper octave of the tonic to VI.	Second invocation: stepwise motion to the subdominant through its leading tone.
Third invocation: cadence, after renewed ascent of the bass from the leading tone of the subdominant.	Third invocation: return to the upper octave of the tonic (through its leading tone), then descent of the bass to the half-cadence.
(d) Orchestration adjusted to the vocal setting, not designed in obbligato manner. Placement of the two violin parts above the upper vocal part, the continuo representing a foundation kept consciously tranquil in rhythmic deviation from the vocal bass.[23]	Orchestration adjusted to the vocal setting, not designed in obbligato manner. Placement of the intensified two violin parts above the upper vocal part, the continuo representing a foundation kept consciously tranquil in rhythmic deviation from the vocal bass.
(e) Ascending, pointedly triadic motif (as upbeat figure) g′-b′-d″ in Violin II, m. 5.	Ascending triadic motif (as upbeat figure), a♯′-c♯″-e″ / b′-e″-g″ / f♯′-a♯′c♯″, as an essential factor in the design of S I and II.

From this comparison of the two Kyries it becomes evident where the concordances are to be found, and at the same time where the unmistakable individuality of Bach's art lies. For instance, in the design of a bass line (and thus of the harmonic structure) that is gradually rising—almost beyond its given confines—then falling, Bach achieves an arch of immense, consistent tension. Bach's Kyrie introduction "presses forward" with a driving force that culminates in the Phrygian cadence leading into the stately flowing fugue. By comparison, Wilderer's introduction is much more contained and without dynamic propulsion. Nevertheless, the common idea that connects the two pieces is not lost in this difference. Nor is it correct to say that Bach's version represents a revision or merely an adaptation of a model. His composition shows an unmistakable integral originality, but the formal planning and musical impulse of the other work somehow remain in the background. In fact, it becomes difficult to think of the opening four measures of Bach's B Minor Mass without reference to Wilderer's Missa.

We must now turn our attention briefly to the highly complex problem of the origin of this Kyrie introduction in particular, leaving aside for the moment the reference to Wilderer's work. Arnold Schering[24] suggested as a source the passage in mm. 11–14 of the opening chorus from the Funeral Ode "Laß, Fürstin, laß noch einen Strahl aus Salems Sterngewölben schießen" BWV 198 for the late Electoress Christiane Eberhardine (1727).[25] Schering's reasoning is that the Missa dedicated to the ruler suggested in its Kyrie the "character of a Requiem" founded in the "solemn mood of the continuing weeks of mourning." The somewhat debatable interpretation aside,[26] a certain affinity to the measures referred to by Schering, underlined by the like harmonic structure,[27] is true to fact. The relationship, however, is more evident to the eye than to the ear, for the aural perception of the four-part vocal writing in these measures, owing to the unusual instrumentation[28] with its bizarre rhythmic character, remains opaque. By contrast, vocal and instrumental part writing in the Kyrie introduction of the B Minor Mass clearly correspond to one another. The instrumental texture moves largely *colla parte,* especially in the support given by Flauto traverso I and Oboe d'amore I to Soprano I, which thus obtains a certain *cantus firmus* character. This correspondence of parts leads to the following observation: moving in half-measure units, the tones of the opening invocation present (transposed) the melodic line of the Kyrie in Martin Luther's *Deutsche Messe* (1524); they assume, in fact, the manner of a sparsely embellished *cantus firmus.*[29] The same melody of the first psalm tone furnishes the basis for the German Agnus Dei, "Christe, du Lamm Gottes." This liturgical *cantus firmus* is also used elsewhere by Bach: together with the Kyrie intonation of Luther's German Litany in the Kyrie section of the Mass in F Major (BWV 233) and in his single Kyrie "Christe, du Lamm Gottes" (BWV 233a).[30] The fact that these Kyrie settings by Bach contain the traditional *cantus firmus* must be considered of significance for the composition of the B Minor Mass (Ex. 11.1). In summary, we might say that the following components have a bearing upon Bach's Kyrie introduction: first, the Kyrie by Wilderer, with respect to its formal design and motivic detail; second, Luther's Kyrie from the *Deutsche Messe,* with respect to the melodic shape of its prominently supported highest vocal part; and third, if one accepts Schering's argument, the opening chorus (mm. 11–14) of the Funeral Ode BWV 198, with respect to its harmonic pattern.

Resuming the comparison of Wilderer's and Bach's Masses, we note additional similarities in the main part of Kyrie I. In Wilderer's fugal movement, the theme is first presented by the instruments, then by the voices whose successive entrances start in m. 11. The beginning of the theme is identical

Example 11.1.

Example 11.2.

with that of Bach's monumental fugue (Ex. 11.2). A relationship of the themes can also be seen in their formation after the manner of psalm-tone recitation. Both themes ascend stepwise, following the metric accents, to the beginning of the second measure;[31] they do not exceed the interval of the fourth and, toward the end, grow into a density of sixteenth-note motion. Bach's individuality comes to the fore again in the compelling melodic tension and more dynamically drawn declamation, particularly in the departures from the recitation tones c♯ and d to the progression g-f♯, the second of them not returning to d but d♯. Thus he obtains a greater intensity in expressing the meaning of "eleison" than does Wilderer. Yet the incentive given by the latter's work remains noticeable in such details as the thematic entrance itself, which is not unaccompanied but surrounded by instrumental harmony above a steadily moving basso continuo.

Both composers created further a musical connection between introduction and main part of the Kyrie but with different means: Wilderer, by a pointed anticipation of the thematic beginning in the third measure of the introduction; Bach, by a suggestive sequence of melodic accents from the opening bass part in pivotal tones of the fugal theme (b-c♯-d♯-e-a♯-b).

The ensuing Christe eleison is in both Masses a soloistic movement in the key of the relative major, B♭ major and D major (Ex. 11.3). The solo setting for three voices (alto, tenor, and bass) in Wilderer's work favors changing duet combinations, supported by a third part in each case through consistent syncopation in larger note values. The duet texture is taken up, with the same motivic material, by the two violin parts in brief, continuo-sustained ritornello sections. Bach's corresponding setting takes over the striking characteristic of linking the duet parts in long progressions of parallel thirds and sixths. The prevailing passages in dotted rhythm are likewise not without relevance to Bach's duet.[32]

In comparison with Bach's work, Wilderer's is of course more simply fashioned, applying as it does parallel motion as a principle from beginning to end. Such joining of the voices is variously suspended in Bach's setting, though it is mirrored in the canonic technique, which ties the voices even more closely to one another. What is involved here is a device similar to that which we have observed in the heightening of the recitation structure in the preceding section. Bach commands a greater wealth of means. Still, the suggestion of such unusually pronounced duet writing remains perceptible.[33] With regard to the structure, as well, there are similarities, particularly in

Example 11.3.

the division of the vocal setting into three segments separated by instrumental episodes, by no means a matter of course.

The next movement, Kyrie II, is in Wilderer's Missa a motet-like structure, with basso continuo. In its clearly archaic texture and its refined imitation technique, involving stretto and inversion, it moves into the orbit of the *stile antico*. The instrumental writing is entirely adapted to the vocal writing; the form of the written and aural images is the same. Surprising, again, is the correspondence to Bach's Kyrie II, which requires no further discussion. Yet in a strictly musical sense, Bach shows total independence, as becomes apparent from a comparison of the opening themes[34] (Ex. 11.4), both of which are accompanied by continuo, as is the main part of Kyrie I. Bach is bolder and more progressive in his harmonic language and control of technical means, though on the whole more conservative. This Kyrie II, especially, shows how Bach, quite differently from Wilderer, recaptures the spirit of classical vocal polyphony.[35] It becomes clear that Wilderer's work is merely one in the series of Masses which Bach copied, studied, and performed. Noticeable also is how the congruence between Bach and Wilderer decreases from one movement of the Kyrie to the next. Bach departs from his recollection of the Missa by another composer the more he becomes involved in the composition of his own work—a process we can recognize generally in Bach's parody technique when comparing his work to the model. Together with growing detachment, adaptation from Bach's own work sets in—in the Gloria as early as the first movement.[36] The model of the Kyrie in early Neapolitan style is thus relinquished.

In Johann Hugo von Wilderer's Missa in G Minor we have found an essential component for the history of the origin of Bach's B Minor Mass, more precisely of its opening movements, both with regard to technical details of composition and overall layout of form. For no other work from Bach's collection of various Mass compositions shows the same characteristic design: Kyrie I (brief Adagio introduction with Phrygian cadence, fugal main part, tutti scoring, minor mode); Christe (soloistic duet setting, threefold presen-

Example 11.4.

tation of the text "Christe eleison," relative major); Kyrie II (motet-like texture in *stile antico,* tutti scoring, minor mode). The principal task of this small contribution to the study of Bach's Kyrie was in comparing the two related works by way of detailed discussion. A historically oriented analysis, however, can never ignore the musical character of the work, and I have included comparative interpretation wherever it seemed indicated. The procedure of placing side by side pieces that are logically linked to one another is apt to guide us toward a deeper understanding of Bach's artistic devices. In this manner characteristic details are brought to the fore that would have eluded us without such a comparison. Wilderer's Missa was in this discussion by no means to be judged by the standard of Bach's work, to be relegated to the status and function of stepping stone. This would be inadmissible inasmuch as the two artists were speaking in entirely different languages. After all, Bach himself considered the Mass worthy of copy and study. Had he not, his B Minor Mass would doubtless not have had—at least in its Kyrie section—the structure we have before us. It is remarkable to what extent even the greatest masters, in their seemingly utter independence of creation, remain indebted to existing material while at the same time rising above it.

12

The Reformation Cantata "Ein feste Burg"

BACH'S REFORMATION CANTATA, "Ein feste Burg" BWV 80, has always claimed a special place within his cantata oeuvre. It was printed in score by Breitkopf and Härtel, Leipzig, in 1821[1] and thus its publication not only represented the first of any Bach cantata but also preceded the publication of Bach's Passion settings and B Minor Mass. Its appearance contributed decisively to the fact that next to the awareness of his significance as a composer of instrumental music Bach's prominence as a composer of vocal music gained definition in the view of the Romantic era. Friedrich Rochlitz paid tribute to the publication in words of hymnic praise:

> The work abounds in profound, highly original and—one might say—unimaginable wealth of sound [*Vollstimmigkeit*—'this word to be understood in its highest and strictest meaning']; it abounds an unparalleled inventiveness in exploring these means; in amazing skill and sureness of marshalling these means; in a greatness and austerity of conception that aspires to nothing but the spiritual substance and that eschews anything that might detract from this ideal. One speaks of musical art and artists, and Johann Sebastian Bach remains not only unique—as is understood in the case of any original genius—but he remains the foremost, the highest, set apart from all who preceded, surrounded, and followed him. Each of the major works preserved from his hand attests to this, as does the present one, in the rarest and most gratifying manner.[2]

In the course of subsequent decades, the publication of "Ein feste Burg" was followed by that of further cantatas which were revived for the propagation of Bach's work. Yet the adopted repertoire of Bach cantatas continued to be so relatively small throughout the nineteenth century that "Ein feste Burg" acquired not only the character of prototype for Bach's church cantata but also that of paragon of Protestant chorale composition. What doubtless contributed to this situation was the fact that the hymn which served as its basis had become the musical symbol of Lutheranism. Only in this sense can we understand, for instance, Mendelssohn's incorporating the melody in his

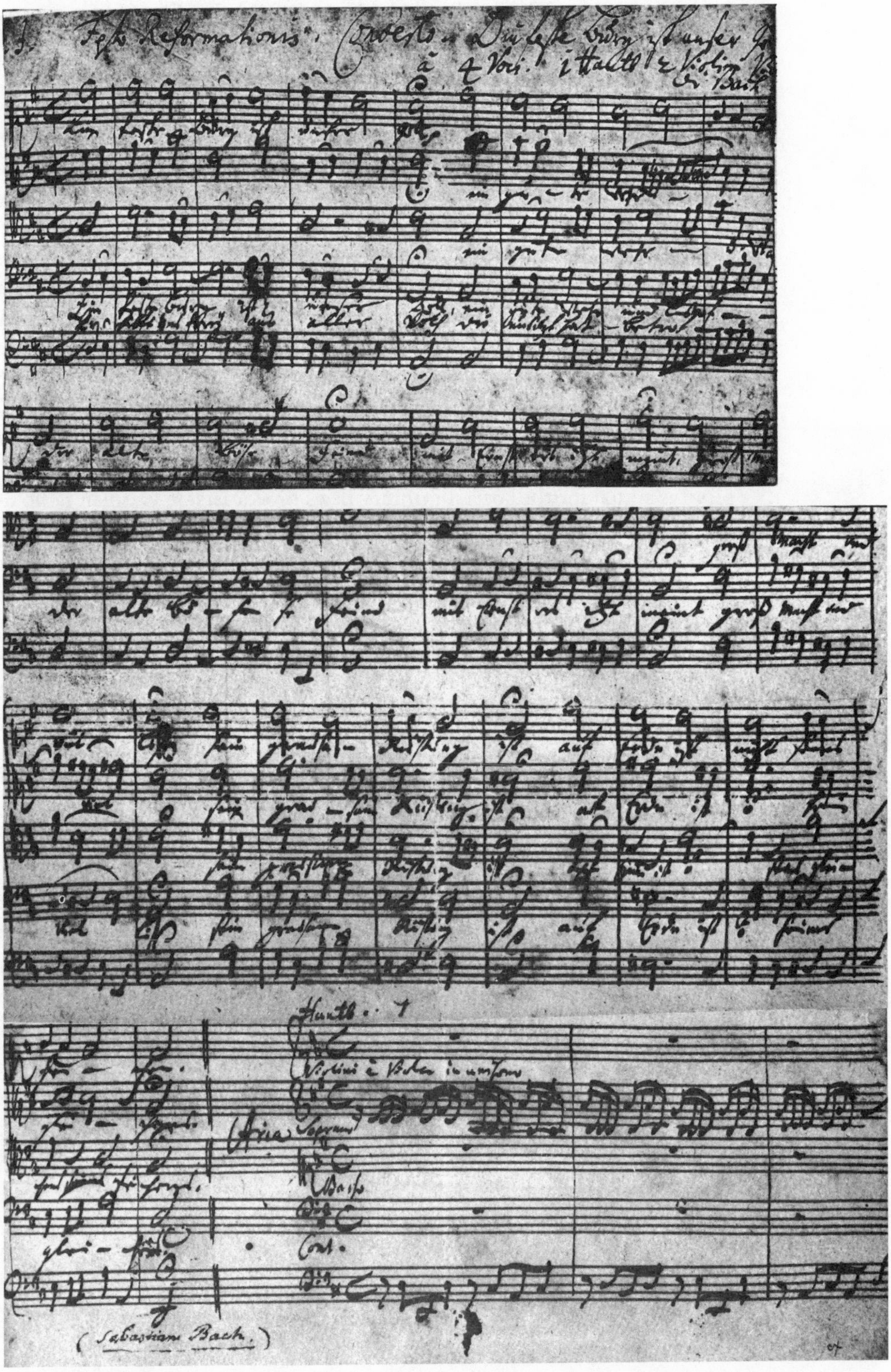

Figure 12.1. A composite facsimile of the autograph score of the interim version of Cantata 80, movement 1; the three fragments come from the Musée Adam Mickiewicz, Paris; the Saltykov-Shtshedrin Library, Leningrad; and the Scheide Library, Princeton. See the Postscript to this chapter for more details.

Fifth Symphony ("Symphony in celebration of the Church Revolution," namely, the tercentenary of the *Confessio Augustana* in 1830).

Its new publication as Cantata 80, with enlarged orchestration (trumpets and timpani), issued in volume 28 of the Bach-Gesellschaft edition in 1870,[3] enhanced the popularity of the work, yet it also marked the beginning of embarrassing tendencies in its reception. The victory fanfares of the opening chorus and the unison presentation of Martin Luther's "revolutionary hymn" were appropriated by the rise of hybrid national sentiments in the wake of the German-French War of 1870–1871. The concluding line of Luther's hymn, "Ours remains the Kingdom," became the quintessence of an all-German secularized Protestantism and thus took its place of final emphasis in Fritz Volbach's interpretation of Bach's cantata.[4] And just as religious nationalism turned into noisy proclamation of faith in World War I with a Patriotic Overture, op. 140 by Max Reger ("dedicated to the German Army, 1914–15") in which "The Watch on the Rhine" and "Nun danket alle Gott" were casually combined, the opening of Bach's Cantata 80 was degraded to serve as signal for the special military news broadcasts on German radio during World War II. The sound pattern of Bach's cantata consequently assumed the nature of a concrete image that grew to excesses in the quoted examples yet nevertheless became symptomatic. And it is only against the background of nationalistic aberration that one can explain the fact that, against better knowledge, Cantata 80 is still normally performed in the version propagated by the Bach-Gesellschaft edition. Bach research has long recognized that the addition of trumpets and drums and its suggestion of bombastic gesture derives from a later hand.

A thorough revision of current performance practice seems as overdue in the case of Cantata 80 as a new critical edition, based on solid source study—which is to be expected in the context of the *Neue Bach-Ausgabe*. The following remarks are concerned with some of the crucial problems presented by the score of this work; these, however, can in no way be treated exhaustively in such a brief study, and it should also be pointed out that the questions addressed here give only an incomplete impression of the scope of existing issues.

The Interim Version of 1723: BWV 80b

It has long been known that the cantata "Ein feste Burg" (BWV 80) of the Leipzig period represents a revision of the cantata "Alles, was von Gott geboren" written in Weimar for a service on the third Sunday of Lent (BWV 80a). A tabulation of the movements will illustrate the interrelationship of the two versions.

BWV 80a (music lost)

1. Aria: "Alles, was von Gott geboren"

BWV 80

1. Chorale motet: "Ein feste Burg"
2. Chorale aria: "Alles, was von Gott geboren/Mit unsrer Macht"

2. Recitative: "Erwäge doch"	3. Aria: "Erwäge doch"
3. Aria: "Komm in mein Herzenshaus"	4. Aria: "Komm in mein Herzenshaus"
	5. Chorale aria: "Und wenn die Welt"
4. Recitative: "So stehe denn"	6. Recitative: "So stehe denn"
5. Aria: "Wie selig sind doch die"	7. Aria: "Wie selig sind doch die"
6. Chorale: "Mit unsrer Macht"	8. Chorale: "Das Wort sie sollen"

Whereas the Weimar cantata can be assigned a date of 1715,[5] we are left to conjecture in the case of the Leipzig cantata, since no original sources for this version have survived. The anniversary year of the Augsburg Confession, 1730, has been suggested by way of plausible hypothesis,[6] although this assumption may have been guided by analogy with the choice of date for Mendelssohn's Reformation Symphony. The question of date, however, has appeared in a totally different light since it has become evident through recent source studies that we must differentiate between two versions of the Leipzig Reformation Cantata "Ein feste Burg." Two fragments, which add up to a leaf of an autograph score, so far totally unknown, can be assigned to the year 1723 on the basis of watermarks, thus curiously confirming a theory that dates back to the middle of the nineteenth century.[7]

The two fragments form the upper[8] and lower half,[9] respectively, of the first leaf belonging to the original autograph score; inscribed "*J[esu] J[uva]. Festo Reformationis. Concerto. Ein feste Burg ist unser Go[tt] /à 4 voci. 1 Hautb. 2 Violin Vio[la e Cont.] di Bach*," it contains the first movement of the work as well as the beginning of the second. While the latter is identical with the second aria of BWV 80, the first movement is a hitherto unknown piece, surprisingly a straightforward four-part chorale harmonization—a highly unusual cantata opening. The two fragments show the chorale in almost complete form; the few missing passages can easily be filled in (Ex. 12.1). A remarkable feature of the chorale setting is its sparse but unmistakable interpretation of the text. We encounter harmonic gestures at the beginning of the second section ("der alte böse Feind"—the inveterate old enemy), in mm. 13–14 ("mit Ernst er's jetzt meint"—in earnest he presses on), in mm. 19–20 ("grausam Rüstung"—grim armor); and there are rhythmic gestures in mm. 2–3 (bass: "Burg"—fortress; tenor: "feste"—firm), in m. 7 (alto: "Wehr"—defense), and in mm. 7–8 (bass: "Waffen"—weapon).

This interim version documented by a fragment raises several questions that cannot be fully answered. Why, for instance, did Bach write a new score rather than merely inserting the new chorale into the score of the Weimar version? The design of a new score suggests that Bach was faced with a certain requirement. Presumably the revision of movements contained in the Weimar version (of which only the verbal text remains) was more thorough than has been guessed so far. Thus the version BWV 80a would be less easily reconstructed than has been assumed. One of the open questions is its key, which probably was not D major. This may be concluded from one fact alone, namely that Bach had no oboe da caccia among the instruments available to him at Weimar.[10]

Example 12.1. Cantata 80 (interim version), opening chorale; the small print is a reconstruction of missing notes

Example 12.1. (continued)

The fact that Bach wrote out a new score for the Reformation Cantata can be related above all to the consideration that as early as 1723, and with this work, he may have anticipated the composition of the later series of chorale cantatas.[11] He had placed the first two stanzas of Luther's hymn text in the first two movements and had presumably replaced the original closing chorale of BWV 80a "Mit unsrer Macht") with the last stanza ("Das Wort sie sollen lassen stahn"). What remained, therefore, was the third stanza of Luther's hymn, and we can reasonably assume that the version of 1723 contained the chorale aria no. 5, probably with the accompaniment of strings only. It is also likely that in this version the *cantus firmus* part did not as yet appear doubled in octaves. A later single source,[12] in the hand of Johann Philipp Kirnberger, identifies this movement as a "church piece for solo bass."

The Oboes in Movements 1 and 5 of BWV 80

The second Leipzig revision of the cantata contained above all a newly composed large-scale chorale setting, which replaced the simple chorale of the 1723 version. An immense chorale motet of 228 measures, it is one of Bach's most elaborate choral compositions and one of the most impressive high points in the history of the chorale cantata. The piece is written in what is an actual seven-part texture made up of three components: a two-part canonic framework in the outer voices (stretto at the octave with entrances at the distance of a whole note); a four-part imitative setting of individual chorale phrases in motet style, and a continuo part, inexorably moving to join sections and provide continuity for the entire setting. Bach's choral language is not concerned here with technical virtuosity but with an expression of the incontestable might of the word of God—central concept of the Reformation.

In this utterly strict design of the score, the trumpets and drums of the version contained in volume 28 of the Bach-Gesellschaft edition appear as a foreign element, one that is difficult to comprehend despite its effective sound. A widespread misunderstanding has arisen, namely that we are dealing with a version of the cantata that Wilhelm Friedemann (as suggested, even at his father's request) wrote out with the addition of trumpets and drums. The fact is that Friedemann (who had inherited the chorale cantata cycle containing this work) extracted, for a purpose unknown, two movements from the cantata and adapted them to a new text and a new instrumentation. Movement 1 received the Latin text "Gaudete omnes populi" and Movement 5, the Latin text "Manebit verbum Domini." In both cases, he added three trumpets and timpani to the score. The remaining movements of the cantata were not used.

The original sources for both arrangements have been preserved;[13] they show only the trumpet and timpani parts in Friedemann's hand. The main body of the score was copied by an unidentified scribe, probably from Johann Sebastian Bach's own autograph. The additional parts were newly composed by Friedemann into this copy, as we can gather from various changes he made. Thus the evidence from the sources clearly disproves the hypothesis of a BWV 80 version made by Friedemann. What we have in reality are reorchestrated parodies of two movements from the cantata. The trumpet parts are alien to Movement 1, especially when one considers the opening fanfares of Friedemann's parody against the retrospective motet style in his father's composition. Similarly, in Movement 5, the brass parts cover up the opening ritornello motif derived from the chorale (mm. 1–2), which Bach wished to emphasize by his unison writing in the strings. Finally, neither Bach's own practice nor that of his sons bears out a neglect of the tutti ensemble sound in a final movement. The concluding chorale in the hypothetical trumpet/timpani version of BWV 80 seems anticlimactic and discloses this version's fictitious character.

The oldest and most reliable source of BWV 80 is a copy written by Bach's son-in-law Johann Christoph Altnikol.[14] The opening chorus is here marked *Choro Alla Capella,* underlining the *stile antico* manner,[15] which is also suggested by a metric pattern governed by the unit of the half note (4/2 instead of 4/4). The canonic top part is assigned to oboes only. Volume 28 of the

Example 12.2. Cantata 80 (later version), conclusion of opening movement

Bach-Gesellschaft edition calls for two oboes played in unison (except for a brief *divisi* section in the final measures)—as do some more recent editions. This seems incongruent with Bach's use of three oboes in Movement 5. A close examination of the Altnikol copy, in fact, shows the use of three oboes also for the opening movement—a point that has not been taken into consideration in any edition so far. Because of lack of space on the manuscript page, the third oboe part was placed in the system of the first violin part, though it was clearly marked for oboe. Viewed in the context of the entire score, the third oboe part actually functions as second, and vice versa, so that a corresponding exchange is feasible in a modern rendering of the score (see Ex. 12.2). This source finding offers not only a perfection of the sonority in the final measures (compare, for instance, the less satisfactory "open" sixth interval between oboe I and II in measure 227, contained in all editions of BWV 80) but also a strengthening of the *cantus firmus* and thus a better balance of the canonic voices.

Altnikol's score contains no oboe parts for Movement 5. This may be taken to mean that Bach had originally planned the movement without oboes. Their eventual function was only a doubling, and it is conceivable that Bach never entered this into his score but merely wrote out oboe parts for Movement 5 in connection with his new composition of the opening movement.

The Basso Continuo in Movement 1 of BWV 80

One of the unusual features of the newly composed opening chorus is its twofold bass part: *cantus firmus* and continuo. This pattern must be considered unique; it is prompted by the contrapuntal design of the piece. The canonic bass *cantus firmus* could not function as a continuo part as well. Bach was therefore compelled to differentiate clearly between two bass parts, and the resulting independent continuo part took on a form by which it became indispensable to the total fabric, especially in view of the polyphonic texture maintained in the vocal parts.[16]

Bach fuses the first two chorale lines into a unified setting for the first section of the movement (comprising phrases 1–4 of the chorale in 118 measures); see Example 12.3. The individual melodic lines represent paraphrases of the *cantus firmus* sections in the style of florid counterpoint. Bach's declamation suggests a fine distinction between phrase 1 (= a) and phrase 2 (= b) through the melismatic beginning of phrase 1 ("feste"—firm) and the melismatic ending of phrase 2 ("Waffen"—weapon). While this underlines the meaning of the text words concerned, it enhances the contrapuntal merging of the two phrases which appears first in m. 6 and returns regularly, eventually also in double counterpoint. In mm. 32ff. phrase 1 is presented first above phrase 2 (soprano/alto), then below it (bass/soprano). This procedure, however, results in problems of part-writing, such as hidden successions of octaves and fifths (mm. 36–37, 41–42) whose sound is so exposed that it needs to be covered by the continuo part: Bach must have considered the addition of a continuo part to the *cantus firmus* bass indispensable in order to absorb or conceal flaws arising from the complex contrapuntal texture of this opening chorus.

There was also a need for a continuo part because of the variety of chorale

Example 12.3.

phases serving as a basis for the motet setting; beginning with m. 119 the thematic material constantly changes, and its configuration is subject to further change through the interpretation of key words from phrase to phrase (see, for instance, the chromaticism used for "der alte böse Feind"—the inveterate enemy; or "sein grausam Rüstung ist"—is his grim armor). Only the continuo part could therefore supply a consistency that would lend sufficient unity to the movement. The manner in which the duplicity of bass parts is rendered in the existing editions obscures the source situation. Altnikol's score is unequivocal in this respect; the next-to-last line, the actual continuo part, is designated *Violoncello e Cembalo* and the bottom line (the canonic part), *Violone e Organo.* Thus the *Cembalo* continuo is intended to sound in 8′ register, the organ bass in 16′ register.

What was evidently a special arrangement is found in a further source (an anonymous copy of the score from the second half of the eighteenth century).[17] Here the two bass parts are distributed over manual and pedal systems of an organ part (with the notation "*Posaune* 16′"), doubtless because no second keyboard instrument was available. Consequently, this arrangement may be understood to reflect a makeshift solution arising from a particular performance situation, not Bach's own practice. The latter may be considered documented in Altnikol's copy.

Bach's use of a differentiated double accompaniment in BWV 80 offers possibilities for conclusions regarding the origin of the newly composed opening chorus. A notable example of twofold continuo accompaniment occurs in the 1736 version of the St. Matthew Passion, where a consistent antiphonal scoring is introduced. And in the late 1730s and 1740s we find various instances for the combination of harpsichord and organ in Bach's work.[18] It would be entirely plausible to link the first chorus of BWV 80 to these cases. Stylistic criteria support this interpretation: the canonic treatment and the retrospective motet style suggest an affinity of this movement to the culmination of Bach's involvement in the *stile antico* about 1740 and to the onset of his systematic exploration of canonic art in Clavier-Übung III.

13

The Handexemplar of the Goldberg Variations

THE PERSONAL COPY of a printed work a composer retained as Handexemplar for his own use must arouse the keen interest of source-critical research. It may contain the only documentary evidence of his later thoughts on, and relationship with, the finished opus, the publication of which ordinarily marks the end of its compositional genesis. Unlike an autograph, the Handexemplar will not reveal any information on the various developmental stages of the work; rather, it exclusively discloses corrections made after publication as well as the composer's afterthoughts of varying degrees of significance. Hence, one might find simple emendations of errors and misprints, supplementary instructions about performance and interpretation, or—in certain instances, perhaps—additions and more substantial changes adjusting or improving the musical text. A full constellation of sources, however, comprising sketches, drafts, composing score, fair copy, performance parts, proof sheets, original print, revised editions, and even the composer's conducting score can, of course, rarely be found even under the most favorable conditions.

In the case of those of Bach's instrumental works that were published during his lifetime[1] the lack of primary sources other than the prints themselves is particularly distressing. Except for a manuscript of the Variations on Vom Himmel hoch[2] and some fragmentary material for the first part of the Clavier-Übung,[3] the Musical Offering,[4] and the Art of Fugue,[5] no autographs have survived. Each of these manuscripts, moreover, owes its preservation to special circumstances. The early versions of two partitas from the first part of the Clavier-Übung were written into the Clavier-Büchlein for Anna Magdalena Bach of 1725 and remained protected as part of that collection. The autograph keyboard score of the six-part ricercar from the Musical Offering provided a practical alternative to the open-score version of the piece in the original print. Similarly, the autograph of the Vom Himmel hoch variations, in which the canonic parts appear fully written out, served as a supplement to the abridged notation of the printed edition. Finally, the extant autograph material of the Art of Fugue must have been treasured by the Bach family after the composer's death for sentimental reasons and deemed worthy of preservation. In general, however, the autographs were considered superfluous after the publication of a work, and it is not surprising, therefore, that such primary material for the vast majority of compositions printed in the Baroque has disappeared.

As for Bach's printed works, the scarcity of both autograph manuscripts and apograph sources derived from autograph material makes those copies of the original editions that can be identified as personal copies all the more important. Without a doubt, such copies once existed for all of Bach's publications, but unfortunately only four are known to have survived:

1. London, British Library, K.8.g.7—a copy of the first edition (1735) of the second part of the Clavier-Übung containing substantial corrections and additions in Bach's hand. They were incorporated into a second edition of the work, which appeared about a year after the initial publication.[6]

2. Berlin, Staatsbibliothek Preußischer Kulturbesitz, DMS 224676(3)— Bach's personal copy of the third part of the Clavier-Übung containing only insignificant manuscript corrections.[7]

3. Princeton, private collection of William H. Scheide—Bach's personal copy of the *Sechs Choräle von verschiedener Art,* the so-called Schübler Chorales, containing a number of very important corrections, textual improvements, as well as performance instructions (for example, distribution of manuals and pedals).[8]

4. Paris, Bibliothèque Nationale, Ms. 17669, formerly Strasbourg, private library of Paul Blumenroeder—a copy of the original edition of the fourth part of the Clavier-Übung, the so-called Goldberg Variations BWV 988, discovered only recently and submitted to the Johann-Sebastian-Bach-Institut (Göttingen) in February 1975 for authentification of the numerous manuscript entries.[9] Work then in progress on the edition of the Goldberg Variations for the *Neue Bach-Ausgabe*[10] enabled this copy to be identified as Bach's Handexemplar. This new source is far more significant than the other personal copies, for it not only contains corrections and supplementary material for the Goldberg Variations but also has an appendix consisting of a previously unknown set of fourteen canons. For this reason the Handexemplar of the Goldberg Variations must be considered the most important Bach source that has come to light in a generation.[11]

The provenance of this source can be traced back no further than the late nineteenth century. Franz Stockhausen (1839–1926), director of the Strasbourg Conservatory and brother of the famous singer Julius Stockhausen (one of the cofounders of the Neue Bachgesellschaft), owned the annotated edition. But when and where he obtained it remains totally unclear. Neither the copy itself nor its wrapper gives any hint whatsoever about the matter. As for the other Handexemplare, it is known that the copies of the first[12] and third parts of the Clavier-Übung and the Schübler Chorales were once in the possession of Johann Nicolaus Forkel, who had bought them from Carl Philipp Emanuel Bach in 1774.[13] There is no evidence, however, connecting Bach's personal copy of the Goldberg Variations with Forkel's collection of Bachiana.

The present essay endeavors to summarize the new material contained in this copy,[14] to comment upon some specific features of the fourteen canons,[15] and to offer a concise critical inquiry into the historical significance of the new source with respect to some crucial aspects of Bach's late works.

FIRST TO BE DISCUSSED are Bach's handwritten annotations that appear within the text of the Goldberg Variations. Most of these entries were made in red rather than black ink, obviously to set off the corrections and additions for some reason. Perhaps a second edition was planned at one point, though it never materialized. Bach's emendations and additions fall into six categories:

1. Cosmetic mending. Bach removed a number of minor engraving mistakes by blackening note heads, erasing ink spots, changing stemmings, and so on.

2. Key signatures. He added flats and sharps after clef changes where key signatures had been left out. These meticulous and rather pedantic corrections demonstrate that Bach wanted to possess a perfect copy.

3. Textual corrections. He rectified certain misprints and omissions, adding accidentals in m. 17 of the seventeenth variation—to cite one instance—in order to achieve a more compelling modulation from D major to G major (see Ex. 13.1).

4. Articulation marks. Bach added a number of slurs and staccato dots to elucidate the manner of performance. In mm. 9–12, 15–16, 25–28, and 31–32 of the fourteenth variation, for example, he put in supplementary staccato marks, which are of particular importance, mm. 15–16 and 31–32 (see Ex. 13.2).

5. Tempo specifications. Bach placed the indication *"adagio"* before the twenty-fifth variation (Ex. 13.4) and *"al tempo di Giga"* before the seventh. In the latter, he must have realized that the 6/8 time signature was ambiguous, allowing an interpretation either as a gigue or a siciliano. He clarified the matter, therefore, by stipulating the intended faster tempo of a gigue.

6. Ornamentation. Bach added a number of ornaments (trills, mordents, appoggiaturas, slurs) to variations 10, 25, and 26 (Exx. 13.3–13.5). Espe-

Example 13.1. Variation 17

Example 13.2. Variation 14

Example 13.3 Variation 10

Example 13.4. Variation 25

Example 13.5. Variation 26

Figure 13.1. Fourteen Canons BWV 1087 (autograph), in Bach's personal copy of Clavier-Übung IV (Nuremberg, 1741), folio 18r.

cially interesting are the appoggiaturas and mordents which appear, respectively, in measures 2, 4, 6, 10–16, and 17–27 of the twenty-sixth variation. Here Bach obviously meant to intensify the 3/4 meter of saraband rhythm by stressing the second beat of the measure. This refinement is important because it clearly implies a moderate tempo and underlines the rhythmic and metric conflict between the two parts. Johann Friedrich Agricola stated that Bach did not like declamatory adjustments in simultaneous combinations of 3/4 time with 6/16, 9/16, and other compound times, a comment that gains new credence from Bach's annotations mentioned above.[16] Furthermore, Johann Philipp Kirnberger specifically refers to the twenty-sixth variation and emphatically says that the part in 18/16 time is to be played as a line free of accent, thus not interfering with the prevailing saraband rhythm.[17]

The examples given above—though representing only a small selection of Bach's entries—illustrate how important this new source is for the establishment of a definitive text of the Goldberg Variations.

AT THE VERY END of the Handexemplar, on the inner side of the back cover of the edition (folio 18r) facing the quodlibet (page 32), we find a set of fourteen enigmatic circle canons, written by Bach himself and entitled "Verschiedene Canones über die ersteren acht Fundamental-Noten vorheriger Aria von J. S. Bach" (Diverse canons on the first eight notes of the ground of the preceding aria by J. S. Bach—see Fig. 13.1). The subject of the entire series (Ex. 13.6b) is derived from the first eight measures of the unembellished ground of the aria (Ex. 13.6a).[18]

Example 13.6.

The whole cycle of perpetual canons, therefore, is thematically related to the set of variations. In terms of actual musical content and contrapuntal treatment, however, they represent an approach to canonic writing of a primarily theoretical nature. The fourteen canons encompass nearly all types of canonic technique and are arranged in order of increasing contrapuntal complexity. The series begins with a retrograde canon and concludes with a quadruple proportion canon; simple and multiple canons intervene and introduce various kinds of highly refined devices. The enigmatic notation, the style, the character, and the organization of these canons immediately call to mind the similarly numbered series of "Canones diversi" of the Musical Offering (see Fig. 13.2). It seems obvious that the fourteen canons form the hitherto unknown but direct and logical link between the Goldberg Variations and the Musical Offering.

The fact that the total of numbered canons comes to fourteen is not without significance. This number represents Bach's name (BACH = 2 + 1 + 3 + 8 = 14) according to the numerical alphabet,[19] which was often referred to in Baroque cabalistic *lusus ingenii* (although admittedly such numerological interpretations have occasionally engendered unreasonable speculations in the Bach literature). In the present case, however, there can be no doubt that Bach chose this number deliberately, for the canons could have been counted in other ways (for example, by combining the first and second pairs of canons according to the procedure displayed in no. 10), which would have led to a different total. Moreover, at the end of the last canon appears the abbreviation *"etc.,"* which shows clearly that the composer could have continued with further canons had he wanted to. Thus by decorating his Handexemplar with fourteen canons, Bach personalized his own copy of the last part of the Clavier-Übung in a most extraordinary fashion.

Two canons of the series, nos. 11 and 13, are already familiar to us. They occur, in slightly revised version, in two datable sources, thus providing important evidence for the chronology of Bach's entry of the canonic appendix in his Handexemplar. No. 13 appears as the "Canon triplex a 6 Voc.," BWV 1076, held by Bach on the famous portrait painted by Elias Gottlob Haußmann in 1746 (Fig. 13.3a). This same canon was subsequently printed in 1747 and presented as a special gift to the members of the Correspondierende Societät der Musicalischen Wissenschaften, which Bach had joined in June of that year (see Fig. 13.3b). No. 11 is the "Canone doppio sopr' il Soggetto," BWV 1077, which Bach entered in the album of the Leipzig divinity student Johann Gottlieb Fulde on 15 October 1747 (Fig. 13.4).[20] Until recently these pieces had to be considered independent dedication or presentation canons, a type of theoretical canonic style for which only eight examples by Bach were known to exist. The discovery of the new cycle, however, doubles the size of this small repertoire[21] and, at the same time, reveals the true context of BWV 1076 and 1077. The date of the revised version of Canon no. 13 (1746) determines the *terminus ante quem* for the Handexemplar appendix, whereas the *terminus post quem* is provided by the

Figure 13.2. Original print (1747) of the Musical Offering BWV 1079 (= Section D, folio 1r): "Canones diversi."

Figure 13.3a. Canon BWV 1076 as seen in Haußmann's famous portrait of Bach; this detail is from a 1748 replica of the portrait.

Figure 13.3b. Canon BWV 1076, original print (1747) for the members of the Correspondierende Societät der musicalischen Wissenschaften.

publication date of the Goldberg Variations (1741 or the spring of 1742 at the very latest).[22] Thus, the set of fourteen canons can be assigned to the period ca. 1742–1746. The well-known characteristics of Bach's late handwriting style appear in the appendix and further confirm this conclusion (note especially the typical late form of the C clef).[23] Unfortunately, there are no other criteria that might set a more precise date for the autograph page at the end of the Handexemplar.

Figure 13.4. Canon BWV 1077 (autograph) from J. G. Fulde's album *PATRONIS / FAUTORIBUS atque AMICIS*.

The entire cycle of canons can be divided into three parts: simple canons using thematic material exclusively (nos. 1–4); simple canons combining the subject with canonic free counterpoint (nos. 5–10); and multiple canons (nos. 11–14). It is within each of these individual groups that the canons are arranged according to increasing contrapuntal complexity. No. 1 opens the cycle by demonstrating a special feature of the soggetto: when read forwards and backwards it produces a perfect two-part setting whose first half forms the mirror image of its second half (Ex. 13.7). Although the theme, as such, was not designed by Bach, no one before him seems to have recognized its inherent canonic potential. The subsequent treatment of the subject alone is extended to include inversion (no. 2), and combinations of *modo recto et contrario* (nos. 3–4). Canon no. 5 stands as the stylistic intermediary between nos. 1–4 and 6–10, for it incorporates canon no. 3 as its subject. In canons 6–10, the entry points of the canonic voices vary, with the narrowest stretto occurring in no. 9. Canon 10 employs very sophisticated contrapuntal writing—in the *evolutio* the two voices are inverted at the same time as their position is reversed—and serves as a natural transition to the final group of pieces. No. 11 is a chromatic double canon, and its counterpart, no. 12, introduces the principle of mensural proportioning in the bass (augmenta-

Example 13.7.

tion of the original quarter-note mensuration of the subject) and in the incip-its of both upper voices (twofold diminution of the subject; see also the di-minished versions of the subject at the beginning of the canonic counterpoints in nos. 7 and 8). In canon 13 the eight notes of the subject are combined with another established soggetto—one that was widely used in seventeenth-century imitative keyboard music. This theme also appears as a subject of study in several chapters of Johann Joseph Fux's *Gradus ad Parnassum*[24] (Ex. 13.8a) and was utilized by Bach in the Fugue in E Major, BWV 878, from the second part of the Well-Tempered Clavier (Ex. 13.8b).[25] Finally, no. 14, a quadruple proportion canon, whose material is derived exclusively from a single line by means of augmentation, diminu-tion, and inversion, serves as the culmination of the cycle.

The resolutions of most of the canons do not present any real difficulty. The necessary clues have been provided by Bach himself: titles in Latin or Italian or both stipulate the kind of canonic treatment and the number of voices required, and *signa congruentiae* prescribe the exact point at which the responding parts should enter. Not indicated, however, is the melodic direc-tion of the canonic *comes,* though upon close inspection it quickly becomes obvious that in most instances the *comes* represents the inversion of the *dux.*[26]

No. 10 is somewhat unusual because it is more an example of invertible double counterpoint than an actual canonic setting. Although strictly speak-ing no. 10 may not be a canon, the reference "alio modo" in its title clearly points to the close relationship between this piece and the preceding set-tings, no. 9 in particular. Indeed, no. 10 might be resolved as a three-part *canon in unisono*—the solution intended for no. 9—especially in view of the harsh dissonances, a typical feature of writing *per syncopationes et ligaturas* (Ex. 13.9). The designation *"à 2"* at the beginning of the staff in the autograph, however, speaks against this three-part solution. Unless one presumes that this indication is a slip of Bach's pen on an otherwise flawless page, canon no. 10 must be resolved in two voices. Bach may have intended a three-part solution at one point, but the unavoidable parallel fifths that occur in the outer voices of the *evolutio* (Ex. 13.9b, mm. 5–6) probably compelled him to reject his original plan. The parallels are certainly not of a totally objection-able kind by baroque standards, but they must have irritated Bach's sense of perfection, particularly in this context.

a.

b.

Example 13.8.

Example 13.9. Canon 10

Canon no. 14 presents a different problem. Here the composer gives no hint at the resolution except for the indication "per Augmentationem et Diminutionem." This means, of course, that both augmented and diminished forms of the subject are to be employed. Furthermore, since it is a four-part canon and, as the very last entry, certainly was intended to exceed in complexity the similarly devised canon no. 12, a resolution using four different mensural degrees seems to be in order. The given theme (Ex. 13.10a) having undergone inversion, augmentation, and diminution, two suitable parts in half notes and eighth notes (the bass and alto, respectively) are easily found (Ex. 13.10b). For the quarter-note form of the subject two possibilities occur: either the incipit (the first nine notes of the given theme) can be transposed down a fourth to A, a procedure never required elsewhere in the canonic series, or the second phrase of the subject (notes 10–24 of the given material), which is already transposed to A, can be used.

The second solution is identical to the first for the opening two measures (the continuation of the first solution is given on the small staff in Ex. 13.10b, mm. 4–5). Moreover, the second solution has an advantage over the first in that it provides a more satisfying harmonic structure (note the clash between a' and g in m. 4 of the first resolution) and a more complete texture in m. 5. Thus resolved, the last canon is a model of perfect balance. The lengths of the voices are well proportioned (see the diagram over Example 13.10a; the parts in half notes and quarter notes together extend to the same length as the voice in eighth notes, which, in turn, is one half the length of the given theme). The two inverted lines (alto and bass) complement the two forms of the subject in *modo recto* (soprano and tenor). The motivically significant octave leap (bracketed in Ex. 13.10b) corresponds in a striking manner to similar leaps in all four voices at the end of the setting. Together these traits result in a specimen of canonic composition that is unique in Bach's work and perhaps the entire eighteenth century.

BACH'S Handexemplar of the Goldberg Variations must be regarded as an important new source in many respects, not least in regard to our knowledge and understanding of several crucial stylistic trends and historical developments in his late works. Two specific aspects are of particular concern here: Bach's concept of monothematic design in multimovement compositions and his systematic involvement with canonic art, both of which now appear in a considerably more transparent outline.

Each of the four major instrumental works of Bach's last decade—the Goldberg Variations, the Musical Offering, the Variations on Vom Himmel hoch, and the Art of Fugue—is based on a single principal subject. The unprecedented series of works is inaugurated by the Goldberg Variations. Bach's interest in monothematicism is apparent here, but his serious concern for this clearly innovative venture becomes even more evident when one considers the supplementary cycle of fourteen theoretical canons. He had writa.

b.

Example 13.10. Canon 14

ten thirty variations on the aria ground of unusual length, thereby virtually exhausting the material. But his high standards obviously demanded that he elaborate the ground even further, this time restricting himself to just the first eight notes of the ground and composing on an entirely different contrapuntal level as well. So he proceeded to write a carefully structured series of miniature canons, quickly realizing, however, that even this small portion of the original subject offered unlimited potential. Thus he confined the set to fourteen pieces and referred to the possible but speculative continuation by placing "etc." instead of the conventional "fine" at the end of canon no. 14. This annotation has very human connotations, for it reveals Bach's resignation to incomplete mastery of the chosen task. Or, perhaps, he simply wished to go no further: after all, fourteen different canonic elaborations represented a sensible and well-rounded—perhaps even an optimum—musical choice. In any event, the "etc." signifies the composer's insight that perfection is limited. He made the conscious decision to leave the appendix of the Handexemplar as an open-ended compositional problem.

The contents of the Handexemplar allow one to draw some general conclusions about Bach's compositional behavior in the later 1740s. During this period Bach drastically reduced his work load:[27] the only major project from these years besides the monothematic instrumental works mentioned above is the completion of the B Minor Mass, an undertaking that relies heavily on parody technique. The significant reduction in productivity—to which developing eye trouble may have contributed—parallels a certain shift of emphasis in Bach's fundamentally encyclopedic disposition. He began at this time to treat compositional material in much greater depth, turning away from his previous habit of exploring a multitude of subjects and incorporating all types of styles and genres as was still displayed in works such as the third part of the Clavier-Übung or the second part of the Well-Tempered Clavier. On the basis of this somewhat hypothetical presumption, two provocative questions can be formulated whose answers cannot easily be given:

1. Did Bach find it difficult in his later years to invent new and stimulating musical subject matter and decide, therefore, to concentrate on a different goal: that of concentrating on the contrapuntal elaboration and refinement of a single musical idea with the aim of exhausting its content?

2. Did Bach, in his immense compositional expertise, feel challenged by the complex nature of the few subjects he dealt with in the monothematic works,[28] so challenged that he wished to treat these ideas in every manner possible and thereby demonstrate their inexhaustible wealth?

Bach's growing interest in the use of concentrated material—a concern clearly demonstrated in his *stile antico* studies[29] and, oddly enough, paralleled by his increasing adoption of more up-to-date stylistic trends[30]—culminated in the systematic exploration of canonic technique. This exploration began with the Goldberg Variations, a work in which only one canonic species is employed, namely the interval canon in semistrict realizations. Within the overall structure of the Goldberg Variations, these canons provide both variety and continuity. Bach's thinking process, however, did not

Example 13.11.

cease with the completion of the thirty variations. On the contrary, his theoretical reflection resulted in the fourteen perpetual canons, a development that seems only logical in retrospect.

Before writing this canonic cycle Bach had never shown any propensity for strict canonic art: his few enigmatic album canons do not represent more than *parerga*. In the fourteen canons, however, he systematically applied the various techniques of canonic art, thereby producing masterly examples of the most important traditional canonic types. The primary function of these pieces is not performance but intellectual challenge. By comparison, the canonic writing found in the Musical Offering and in the Variations on Vom Himmel hoch seems far less comprehensive and, at the same time, less theoretical. Nevertheless, it is now evident that the canons in these two works could not have been written without the essay in canonic art at the end of the Handexemplar. The links between these compositions are obvious. Especially the Variations on Vom Himmel hoch (written presumably before the Musical Offering) benefit directly from the experience with the fourteen canons. Actually, the thematic relationship between the two works suggests that the idea to elaborate the Christmas *cantus firmus* originated as an afterthought in connection with the fourteen canons (Ex. 13.11). The melodic and rhythmic structure of the first and last lines of the chorale (Ex. 13.11, a and b, in particular is nearly identical with that of the subject of the eightnote ground bass, and the harmonic implications are the same in both instances. The Musical Offering, on the other hand, uses much the same devices as the cycle of fourteen canons, though it employs a far more complex soggetto. The only kind of canon found in the Musical Offering that is not included in the other work is the modulation canon "per tonos."

The Handexemplar of the Goldberg Variations contains the earliest evidence of Bach's serious concern for theoretical reflection and, therefore, adds a new perspective to our understanding of this facet of his creativity. To judge from the Handexemplar, Bach's penchant for theoretical reflection begins on a tentative and rather private basis. The Goldberg Variations and the manuscript canonic appendix display a certain bipolarity of practice and theory. In the Musical Offering, the coexistence of pieces of a primarily practical character with settings of a primarily theoretical nature appears as an official principle of design. In the Variations on Vom Himmel hoch, however, and even more distinctly in the Art of Fugue, practice and theory are not only manifest, they actually merge into one integrated and unified artistic and didactic concept.

14

Bach's Personal Copy of the Schübler Chorales

DURING THE REDACTING of the original Bach prints for the Bach-Gesellschaft edition, only one of the composer's personal copies, or Handexemplare, was known to exist: that for the "Six Chorales of diverse kinds," the so-called Schübler Chorales, BWV 645–650. Friedrich Conrad Griepenkerl brought it into consideration for the first time in volumes 6 and 7 of his edition of the organ works published by Peters in 1847. Wilhelm Rust also used it for his editorial work on volume 25 of the Bach-Gesellschaft edition in 1878.

Since that time Bach's personal copies of almost all the other original prints have been located and identified,[1] so the Handexemplar of the Schübler Chorales must relinquish its position of singularity. But despite its relatively early utilization by Griepenkerl and Rust, it never really lost its significance, especially because of the unusually encompassing and instructive additions and corrections it contains. On the contrary, the Handexemplar of the Schübler Chorales attained an almost legendary fame, for it disappeared without a trace in the 1850s and was considered a lost source, unavailable to Bach research, for more than a century.

Rust, who had inspected the Schübler print in 1852, while it was owned by Siegfried Wilhelm Dehn in Berlin (Dehn had obtained it from Griepenkerl's estate), lamented its later disappearance in his foreword: "Whoever is now the fortunate owner, is anyone's guess."[2] In the summer of 1975 Bach's personal copy of the Schübler Chorales came to light once again in the international book dealers' market. The generosity of the present owner[3] has made possible new study and appraisal of this long-vanished "relic."

I

Indeed, "precious relic" was the term used for the Handexemplar of the Schübler Chorales by Philipp Spitta, while he had access to it for a brief time in 1882 through arrangements made by Joseph Joachim.[4] In two letters that accompany the print today, Spitta attempted to clarify the provenance of the copy and to confirm its identity as the Griepenkerl-Dehn source. His primary concern was to determine whether a second Handexemplar might exist. Spitta's initial letter runs as follows:

Berlin W., Burggrafenstr. 10
30.1.82

My Esteemed Sir,

My friend Professor Joachim has shown me the original print of the six Bach chorales, of which you are the owner. In the annotations written in ink I perceive Bach's own hand, and I believe, as you do, that you are in possession of a precious relic.

What also arouses my special interest is the following circumstance. There was once a copy of the six chorales with Bach's handwritten corrections throughout. Griepenkerl, the editor of the Bach instrumental works at Peters in Leipzig, owned it. After Griepenkerl's death, it went into the possession of Professor S. W. Dehn here in Berlin, who apparently still possessed it in 1852. Thereafter it disappeared.

Is your copy the one owned by Griepenkerl? Certain facts lead me to doubt that it is. I would be very grateful to you, Esteemed Sir, if you could tell me what you know about the past fortunes of your relic. Joachim said to me that you obtained it from Princess Czartoryska, who in turn received it from the Duke of Aumale in Paris. He couldn't specify, however, how and when these transactions took place.

In looking forward to receiving helpful particulars from you, I am

With high esteem,
Yours respectfully,
Philipp Spitta
Prof.

Apparently this letter, whose addressee was not named, went unanswered, for a half year later Spitta again picked up his pen:

Berlin W., Burggrafenstr. 10
14.6.82

My Esteemed Sir,

In January of this year Professor Joachim, upon returning from Krakow, brought me a copy of the six organ chorales of Bach belonging to you—a copy which contains corrections in the hand of the master. This print awakened a great interest in me, for at the beginning of the '50s just such a print was owned by Prof. Dehn in Berlin. In the meantime, this print has disappeared. It seems quite possible that Dehn's copy is identical with yours. In order to enter into greater certainty on the matter, I turned to you in a letter of January 30 with the request for further information. My letter remains unanswered. Might I be so bold as to approach you once more about this matter. I do not conceal the fact that I run the danger of appearing to be importunate. I find an excuse solely in the circumstance that this concerns a master to whose life and works I have dedicated a portion of my own.

Professor Joachim mentioned to me that the print was given by the Duke of Aumale (perhaps after it had been owned by Chopin) to Princess Czartoryska in Warsaw, who in turn presented it to you. It is very important to me to ascertain when, by chance, this may have happened, and if the transmission of the manuscript can perhaps be traced back even further, and if the title page was already lost, as it came into your hands. Anything else you might be able to say about it would be of great interest to me.

As soon as I know that this letter has safely reached its address, I will hurry to return the precious relic to you.

With high esteem,
Yours faithfully,
Professor Dr. Spitta

Sometime thereafter Spitta must have received a response, which may have been lost, for he returned the source to its Polish owner. Spitta's remarks and conjectures about the print's change of owners give us the occasion to go briefly into the question of its provenance. Joachim's information appears to be reliable. To judge from his report, Henri Eugène Philippe Louis d'Orléans, Duke of Aumale (1822–1897), gave the Handexemplar to Marcelline Czartoryska, née Princess Radziwill (1817–1894), a student of Chopin's and a much-celebrated pianist. From her it went to the unnamed recipient of the two Spitta letters, a citizen of Krakow.[5] We do not know when or how the print came into the duke's hands. One can rule out Joachim and Spitta's hypothesis that it came via Chopin, for the pianist died in 1849, just a few months after Griepenkerl, and it is beyond question that the print went from Griepenkerl's estate to Dehn's collection without detour. Since it was still in Dehn's possession in 1852, according to Rust, it could only have changed ownership once again between this date and the year of Dehn's death, 1858.

During the last years of his life, Dehn gave away various items from his valuable collection. On 1 October 1857, for instance, he presented the manuscript of the "Small" Magnificat, BWV Anh. 21, attested to be a Bach autograph, to the Russian composer Alexis von Lwoff.[6] Since at that time Dehn was on bad terms with the Bach-Gesellschaft, it would not be surprising if he wished to keep the Schübler Handexemplar out of its reach by passing it on to a foreigner. Possibly Dehn intended to give it to the pianist Czartoryska, which means that the Duke of Aumale would have served chiefly as a "middleman." This theory is compelling, since Dehn's contacts with eastern Europe were very close at all times. Thus he was united in a warm friendship with Glinka; Anton Rubinstein was one of his composition students; and he gave the supposed Magnificat autograph to a Russian musician.

The details of the travels of the Schübler print after its separation from the Dehn library will probably never be clarified. And in the long run, they are of little significance to the actual value of the score. It is unfortunate, however, that the first page of the Handexemplar has been lost.[7] It was still present, with the title of the collection on the front side and the beginning of the musical text on the back, when Rust inspected the source in 1852, but it was absent by the time Spitta looked at it in 1882. The title side may have contained lines of dedication or other remarks about earlier owners. The initial page may have been removed because it was an especially attractive collector's item, or in order to "hush up" the lineage of the copy in question.

II

With regard to the provenance of the Handexemplar, the first century after Bach's death is incomparably more important than the period after 1852. Up to 1852 the line of descent seems to be clear and without gaps. In 1750 the print was inherited by Carl Philipp Emanuel Bach, who sold it in 1774 to Johann Nicolaus Forkel. Griepenkerl procured it from Forkel's estate in 1819, and after his death in 1849 it went to Dehn along with other "Griepenkerliana." According to an exchange of letters between C. P. E. Bach and Forkel on the occasion of the sale of the Schübler print, the Handexemplar of the Schübler Chorales was bound with the Handexemplar of Clavier-Übung III. In a letter to Forkel on 26 August 1774, Emanuel wrote: "Find hereby enclosed the two volumes, the correct payment for which I heartily thank you. To the back of one you will find bound the six printed chorales."[8] In an earlier letter he had already indicated that the print of Clavier-Übung III was "the copy which he [J. S. Bach] used to have for his own use."[9] But when was Bach's personal copy of the Schübler Chorales separated from the volume obtained by Forkel, and what happened to his personal copy of Clavier-Übung III? In the 1819 catalogue of Forkel's estate, the two are still listed together:

> (Clavierübung) 3 Thl. Consisting of diverse preludes on chorales for the organ, in 4. Bound to it are 6 chorales for an organ with 2 manuals and pedal.[10]

Ever since the publication of Georg Kinsky's bibliographical study of the Bach original prints,[11] it has been assumed that Bach's Handexemplar of Clavier-Übung III is the copy in the Staatsbibliothek Preußischer Kulturbesitz in West Berlin, DMS 224676(3), which went to the Berlin Staatsbibliothek via Georg Poelchau. A connection between Forkel and Poelchau cannot be verified, however. As far as we know, Forkel did not own a second copy of Clavier-Übung III, and, as it has been unequivocally demonstrated, the Forkel copy mentioned above was obtained by Griepenkerl. It is inconceivable that the question of provenance was not taken up anew by Manfred Tessmer in the *Kritischer Bericht* of the *Neue Bach-Ausgabe,* where the Berlin copy (Source A1) is unambiguously labeled "with all certainty . . . stemming from J. S. Bach's estate."[12]

Also overlooked is the fact that the print of Clavier-Übung III, once owned by Rust and now in the Musikbibliothek der Stadt Leipzig under the shelfmark PM 1403, has a more striking and significant clue about the provenance of the Schübler Handexemplar. On the pasteboard binding, covered with brown paper with parchment edges and corners, there is a faded ink notation in Griepenkerl's hand:

> Third Part / of the / Clavier-Übung / and / Six Chorales / NB: the corrections in the 6 chorales are in J. S. Bach's / own hand.[13]

This print, therefore, is the true Handexemplar of the composer, and we can disqualify the Berlin copy. The binding also shows traces that it was originally fashioned for thicker contents. Hence the Schübler Chorales were probably removed after Griepenkerl's death, possibly so that the two prints could be sold separately.[14]

There remains one interesting detail. The back flyleaf of the Leipzig binding,[15] which appears to stem from the second half of the eighteenth century, bears a Berlin watermark: a crowned double eagle with breastplate; in the breastplate, F[ridericus] R[ex]. From this watermark we can conclude that C. P. E. Bach had the two prints of organ chorales stemming from his father's estate bound together during his years in Berlin.

III

Bach's handwritten additions and corrections in his personal copy of the Schübler Chorales have been very carefully described and evaluated by Griepenkerl and above all by Rust. Five categories can be distinguished:

1. Corrections of printing errors. Examples: the erasure of a tie in m. 2 of "Meine Seele erhebt den Herren," BWV 648 (Fig. 14.1); correction of the first note in m. 2 of "Kommst du nun, Jesu, vom Himmel herunter," BWV 650 (d″ instead of c″; Fig. 14.3); correction of the last two notes in m. 15 of the same piece (c″–b′ to b′–a′; Fig. 14.4).
2. Filling in of accidentals and articulation marks. Example: legato indications in mm. 1–5 of "Meine Seele erhebt den Herren" (Fig. 14.1).
3. Improvement of readings. Example: modification of the arpeggiated figure in m. 2 of "Kommst du nun, Jesu" (Fig. 14.3). See also below.

Figure 14.1. "Meine Seele erhebt den Herren" BWV 648, mm. 1–5 (autograph addenda in Bach's personal copy of the original edition of the Schübler Chorales).

Figure 14.2. BWV 648, mm. 9f. (autograph addendum and emendations).

Figure 14.3. "Kommst du nun, Jesu, vom Himmel herunter" BWV 650, mm. 1–3 (autograph addenda).

Figure 14.4. BWV 650, mm. 13–17 (autograph addendum and emendations).

4. Performance and registration indications. Examples: indication of how the voices are to be distributed, on manual or pedal (Figs. 14.1, 14.3, and 14.4); indication of the pitch of stops to be used (*"Ped. 4 F. u. eine 8tav tiefer"* [Pedal 4 foot and an octave lower]; Fig. 14.4), as well as degree of prominence (*"destra forte"* [right hand forte]; Fig. 14.2).

5. Clarification of the rhythmic notation. Example: indication of rhythmic sharpening in m. 13 and of triplets in m. 16 of the middle voice of "Kommst du nun, Jesu" (Fig. 14.4).[16]

This is not the place to enumerate the various small details that were overlooked previously or to enlarge upon Rust's critical report in the Bach-Gesellschaft edition. Nevertheless, several observations of a general nature should be made.

Bach's handwriting, which can be seen most clearly in the written comments, appears to stem from the last years of his life and may even be one of the latest preserved samples of his script. It exhibits the distinctive features delineated in Bach's late handwriting by Georg von Dadelsen.[17] For instance, the discontinuity of the ductus is unmistakable. The segregation of the individual letters within words and the uneven slant of the letters is striking. See, for example, the *s* leaning strongly to the right, followed by the *i* leaning strongly to the left in *"Sinistra"* (Fig. 14.3). Along with this go the clublike corrections of the noteheads (see especially Fig. 14.3). The absolute *terminus ante quem non* for the completion of the Schübler Chorale print is the second half of 1746.[18] In all likelihood, however, the edition was not issued before 1748.[19] Thus Bach's handwriting characteristics may reflect the period 1748–1750, possibly even 1749–1750.

The state of m. 2 of the chorale "Meine Seele erhebt den Herren" (Fig. 14.1) allows us to draw certain inferences about the manuscript (now lost) from which it was engraved. The reading *ante correcturam* is shown in Example 14.1. The tie between the third and fourth notes is engraved (and appears in all other copies of the Schübler print), but during the "filling-in process" it was changed by Bach into an articulation sign. The printing mistake most certainly goes back to a handwritten model and can be explained in the following way: The handwritten model was apparently copied from the autograph score of Cantata 10, "Meine Seel' erhebt den Herren," written in 1724. The fifth movement of this work represents the original, aria form of the organ chorale prelude. In Bach's score of Cantata 10 (now in the Library of Congress, Washington, D.C., under the shelfmark ML

Example 14.1.

Example 14.2. (1) BWV 137/2; (2) BWV 650 (ante correcturam);
(3) BWV 650 (post correcturam)

30.8b.B2M4), the articulation mark in m. 2 is misplaced to the degree that it can easily be misinterpreted as a tie. Such an error would certainly not be made by Bach. Thus the handwritten manuscript of the Schübler Chorales used in the production of the print must have been made by a copyist, at least for this piece. Bach must have given the copyist instructions to write out the movement without articulation marks, for the mistake in m. 2 of the print can only be explained as a misunderstood tie. Similar errors traceable to copying mistakes are found in other places in the print. A further sign of copyists at work is the layout of the voices, which are taken over in a mechanical way from the cantata scores, with the result that the parts in the individual preludes are often set out in a manner poorly suited to the organ (see Figs. 14.3 and 14.4). One can thus conclude that Bach was probably not closely involved in the printing of the six chorales. This assumption adds strength to the time-honored belief that the prelude "Wo soll ich fliehen hin," BWV 646, also represents a movement drawn from a cantata score. Hence in this piece we have a fragment of a lost work.

The corrections in the print, taken as a whole, show that Bach scrutinized the text of the Schübler Chorales not only in terms of orthography and mistakes of secondary consequence but also from the standpoint of a composer giving his work a critical appraisal. An especially characteristic example can be seen in m. 2 of the prelude "Kommst du nun, Jesu" (see Fig. 14.3), where Bach used the correction of a printing mistake as an opportunity to ponder anew the motivic consequences of the arpeggiated figure in the right hand. The three different readings given in Example 14.2 document the metamorphosis of the motive.

Reading 1 represents the passage as written for solo violin in the chorale setting from Cantata 137, "Lobe den Herren," of 1725. Reading 2 corresponds to the uncorrected state of the organ prelude, in which neither the first note nor last two notes can be viewed as a revision of Reading 1. Rather they are printing and copying mistakes, respectively.[20] Reading 3, finally, gives Bach's last version of the text, as found in the Handexemplar. The

Example 14.3.

initial shape of the sixteenth-note figure, as set forth in m. 1, was repetitive, with a repeated d″ as the top tone (shown in Ex. 14.3).

This shape was initially maintained in m. 2, with a repeated a″ as the top tone (see Readings 1 and 2, in Ex. 14.2), but then softened into a more melodically flexible version (Reading 3). The highest tone now moves down, b″–a″–g″, complementing the movement of the bass. As his personal copy of the Schübler Chorales aptly demonstrates, when Bach set his indefatigably self-critical hand in motion, there seemed to be no such thing as an "untouchable" text, whether manuscript or print.

❖   ❖   ❖

"OLD" SOURCES REVISITED:
NOVEL ASPECTS

15

The Clavier-Übung Series

The Overall Plan

IT WAS NOT WITHOUT careful consideration that Bach chose the title *Clavier-Übung* for his most extensive publication project. When, in 1726, he issued the first partita under this title, he had only recently assumed the post as cantor and music director of Leipzig—a position previously held by Johann Kuhnau. In the years 1689 and 1692, while still organist at St. Thomas's Church, Kuhnau had published two prints respectively entitled *Neuer Clavier-Übung Erster Theil* and *Andrer Theil,* each containing seven partitas. These two works were closely related: the first issue contained partitas set in ascendingly ordered major keys (C, D, E, F, G, A, and Bb); the second, those in ascendingly ordered minor keys (c, d, e, f, g, a, and b). Evidently, Bach picked up the thread of Kuhnau's works for he took over not only the title but their contents and dimensions as well. According to an announcement of the single issue of the fifth partita in the Leipzig *Post-Zeitungen* on 1 May 1730, Part I of Bach's Clavier-Übung should also have contained seven partitas: "Inasmuch as the fifth suite of Bach's *Clavier-Übung* is now finished, and with those last two still remaining will, at the coming Michaelmas fair, bring the whole work to an end, then such be known to amateurs of the clavier." [1]

We do not know why the planned seventh partita was not published. At any rate, according to Bach's well-ordered tonal plan, it must have been intended to be set in F major. But unlike Kuhnau, Bach employed both major and minor modes in his key scheme. As the following chart shows, he also did not use an ascendingly ordered succession of keys as he had in the Well-Tempered Clavier and the Inventions and Sinfonias; instead he chose a sequence based on gradually expanding upward and downward intervals:

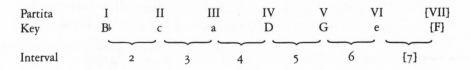

Partita	I	II	III	IV	V	VI	[VII]
Key	Bb	c	a	D	G	e	[F]
Interval		2	3	4	5	6	[7]

Without the seventh partita, the consistent logic of the original plan was, of course, destroyed. Yet, the end result forms a hardly less logical order: one piece in the major mode followed by two in minor modes for the first half of the work, two pieces in major followed by one in minor for the second half, for a total of three pieces in major and three in minor modes.

Kuhnau was probably the first to use the term *Clavier-Übung* ("keyboard exercise") for a publication of keyboard music. He did this evidently in imitation of the Italian term *essercizi* dating back to the early seventeenth century, a term also used by Domenico Scarlatti (*Essercizi per gravicembalo;* London, 1738) and Georg Philipp Telemann (*Essercizii musici;* Hamburg, 1739–1740). The first one to follow Kuhnau's examples from 1689 and 1692, Johann Krieger published a collection of organ compositions (with ricercars, preludes, fugues, and other types of pieces) under the title *Anmuthige Clavier-Übung* (Nuremberg, 1699). This kind of title proved to be extraordinarily flexible in terms of its range of application because it could be used to refer not only to all the diverse keyboard instruments but also to different compositional genres. Vincent Lübeck's *Clavier-Übung* (Hamburg, 1728), for example, which includes a chorale prelude to "Lobt Gott, ihr Christen allzugleich" as well as free-setting types such as prelude, fugue, allemande, and courante, exemplifies the usefulness of the title as a "neutral" name for a heterogeneous collection of keyboard music. Bach was undoubtedly aware of this advantage when he published the first partita in 1726 under this same title. Nonetheless, it is unlikely that he had the entire multi-part series containing a broad spectrum of compositional forms in mind at that time.

In fact, that Bach was being especially cautious when he first published his partitas separately before collecting them together in 1731 as a single opus certainly argues against an early conception of an extensive publication project. It seems that Bach first wanted to test the market and hence issued the partitas in a piecemeal way, which was still no small financial risk—especially since he functioned as his own publisher. Moreover, he must have been intensely aware of the fact that these partitas were difficult of perform and that hardly any similarly demanding keyboard music was then available. He could not, therefore, have expected a great number of customers from the start. Nevertheless, the sales must eventually have been good enough for Bach to risk the collected edition, in the hope that it would be a somewhat profitable endeavor. In 1731 he declared his intention to deliver a multi-part series by calling the collected edition of the partitas his *Opus 1,* clearly implying that other numbers would follow. We cannot infer how detailed a concept was in his mind at that time. Presumably, the complete work, finished ten years later, took on its final form only over the course of time and, for that matter, unhindered by the great flexibility of its title. Further evidence supporting the gradual crystallization of the large-scale project is that each of the later parts conforms to Bach's compositional interests as they unfold with time. A work such as the Goldberg Variations could hardly have been projected as early as 1731.

Bach was not alone in his time in planning and executing an ambitious musical publication with several sequels. Georg Philipp Telemann had a similar intention, though in a completely different area, with a series of works begun in 1728 and published in installments under the elaborate title:

> The True Music Master in which are arranged for singers as well as for instrumentalists all types of musical pieces for different voice parts and nearly all commonly-used instruments and containing moral, operatic, and other arias as well as trios, duets, solos etc., sonatas, overtures etc., and also fugues, counterpoints, canons etc., hence all the most current music according to the Italian, French, English, Polish etc., manners both serious as well as spirited, and lighthearted, . . . you might conceive of performing . . . [2]

In 1733, Telemann published a less comprehensive collection entitled *Musique de Table,* which nevertheless contained in its three *Productions* three altogether different examples each for the major genres of instrumental ensemble music (overture, concerto, quatuor, trio, duo, and solo sonata). But in the realm of keyboard music there was no analogous, representative collection and so it remained for Bach to undertake such a task. His already undisputed fame as a distinguished virtuoso of the organ and other keyboard instruments seemed to make him predestined for such a project. It was not by chance, for instance, that a newspaper review of Bach's organ recital in Dresden on 14 September 1731, which was "attended by all the court musicians and virtuosos," ended with a poem of praise:

> Tis said, when Orpheus did his lyre string awake,
> All creatures in the forest answered to the sound;
> But sure, 'twere better that such praise of Bach we spake,
> Since he whene'er he plays, doth each and all astound. [3]

Bach was clearly aware of his standing and renown and, thus, it cannot be considered a mere coincidence that the four-part Clavier-Übung originated in the same period during which he devoted his professional skills particularly to instrumental virtuosity. Indeed, from 1729 to 1740 the Collegium Musicum and its weekly concerts in Leipzig stood at the center of his Leipzig activities.

The overall design of the Clavier-Übung, in which Bach exhibited an encyclopedic survey of his artistry in the field of keyboard music for "amateurs and especially for connoisseurs of such work to refresh their spirits," [4] was aimed at several different levels. First of all, the most important keyboard instruments were paid attention to: one-manual harpsichord (Part I), two-manual harpsichord (Parts II and IV), and large organ as well as organ without pedals (Part III). Then, the most important styles and types of composition were represented: as an exemplary case, the contrasting of the leading national styles (Part II); the enormously rich stylistic spectrum in both Part III (ranging from the *stile antico* of the large Kyrie settings to the modern mannerism of the "Vater unser" chorale) and Part IV (from the intricate canonic movements to the burlesque Quodlibet). In the end all the standard genres, forms, and categories were represented: suite, concerto, prelude, fugue, chorale settings of all kinds, and variations. All fundamental compositional techniques could also be found: from free-voiced improvisatory pieces to movements using all sorts of imitative polyphony through strict canon; from two-voice settings to a piece exhibiting six obbligato voices (the organ chorale "Aus tiefer Not" from Part III); all possible *cantus firmus* techniques; and, finally, a wide choice of movement dimensions, levels of difficulty, and keys and modes (within the still-prevailing system of unequal temperament, that is, containing generally no more than three sharps or flats).

The relative scarcity of fugues or preludes with fugues—which are generally so prominent in Bach's keyboard music but in the Clavier-Übung are found only in the several preludes without fugues (Part I), in a few chorale fugues, and in the Prelude and Fugue in E♭ (Part III)—raises the question of whether the Goldberg Variations ought indeed be considered the closing statement of the series. Studies of the sources offer no conclusive answer to this problem. It is quite conceivable, however, that Bach intended to conclude with Book II of the Well-Tempered Clavier. Yet there is no indication whatsoever that this work, although completed around 1740, was ever intended for publication. Moreover, its wide range of tonalities would have made the printing of that work extraordinarily difficult. In this regard the Art of Fugue could be imagined as perhaps a more suitable component fitting the overall publication project. Yet its strongly didactic concept and its exclusive preference of "connoisseurs" as opposed to "amateurs"—in open contradiction to the more generous wording of the various Clavier-Übung title pages addressing both constituencies—speaks against that possibility. Be that as it may, there can be no other choice but to consider the four parts of the Clavier-Übung as a unified whole, not as an incomplete project in need of supplementation.

The well-thought-out design of the complete work is mirrored in the careful planning and formation of its individual parts, each of which represents a well-rounded entity. Regarding Part I, next to the above-mentioned order of keys (spanning the interval of the tritone, B♭ to e), it is particularly noteworthy that though all six partitas conform to the same fundamental suite scheme, each (according to the principle of variety) possesses its own special individuality. Here we find six different and, hence, differently named opening movements (Praeludium, Sinfonia, Fantasia, Ouverture, Praeambulum, and Toccata) as well as diverse interspersed gallantry movements (Rondeau, Capriccio, Burlesca, Scherzo, and so on). In Part II, the predominant national styles, Italian *Gusto* and French *Manier,* are juxtaposed in several ways: three-movement concerto form versus an eleven-movement suite structure; F major versus B minor, that is, opposite modes and tritone interval (attained by means of transposing the earlier C minor version of the

French overture). Part III presents a multi-layered formal organization, which is held together by a striking frame device (Prelude and Fugue in E♭). Within this frame are to be found nine (three times three) chorale preludes to the German Kyrie and Gloria as well as twelve (six times two) Catechism chorales. Each large-sized chorale has a corresponding small-sized pendant (in this sense the four two-voice duets function as corresponding *cantus firmus* free pieces to the Prelude and Fugue in E♭). These smaller, less difficult settings certainly played a role also in Bach's publication goals for Part III of the series, for he would have found much fewer buyers for a work that contained only lengthy, elaborate, and extraordinarily difficult pieces for large church organ with pedals. In fact, the systematic interspersal of smaller-sized pieces made the collection accessible to a broader circle of customers. Not only the large church organ, but also the keyboard instruments normally found in the home were considered.[5] Finally, Part IV as a large-scale but unified monothematic performing cycle contrasts with the character of the preceding parts as collections. Here, a chain of thirty variations is placed between an opening Aria and its repetition at the end, marking both the point of departure and the point of arrival for the work. An overture designates the beginning of the second half of the cycle (fulfilling the same function as the overture of the fourth partita in Part I). The internal arrangement of the variations is punctuated by canons which end each of the ten threefold groups of pieces; the canons themselves are arranged in ascendingly ordered imitation intervals (unison to ninth) leading up to the Quodlibet, with its tuneful *Kehraus* melodies and its most special application of combinatorial (stretto) techniques, as final culmination point.

Bach's Clavier-Übung must be viewed as an all-encompassing monument of clavier and organ music that in this form was unparalleled at the time and that had neither an immediate predecessor (works like Kuhnau's *Clavier-Übung* or Nicholas de Grigny's *Livre d'orgue* can be considered only as indirect and partial models) nor a direct successor. With this kaleidoscope of keyboard music, Bach composed nothing short of a memorial to his own artistry. As his obituary, published in 1754, declared: "Bach was the greatest organ and clavier player that we have ever had."[6]

The Technical Aspects of Printing

In the secondary literature one continually finds reports that Bach practiced the art of engraving and that he produced at least a large number of pages of Clavier-Übung III himself. Indeed it was quite typical during Bach's lifetime for a composer to engrave his own work in copper and to have it printed. Telemann, for example, attended to the engraving of his own music on a large scale. Wilhelm Friedemann Bach also tried his hand at it. A publication announcement of his Sonata in D Major (Dresden, 1745) mentions this explicitly: "The skillful musician, Herr Bach in Dresden, has completed a composition for solo harpsichord and, assisted by the Royal Court Engraver, Signor Zucchi, has engraved it in copper himself."[7] His younger brother, Carl Philipp Emanuel, was also involved with similar endeavors at least once in his youth. In his informative autobiographical sketch related to us by Charles Burney, he refers to a "Minuet with crossed hands" saying, "This Minuet I etched in copper myself."[8] There is no documentary evidence, however, to support the claim that Johann Sebastian ever engraved any part of his works. The theory that Bach participated in the manufacture of several pages of Clavier-Übung III is founded exclusively on the similarity that exists between the image of several printed pages and Bach's own handwriting. As will be shown, it is this very observation that speaks against the case of "Bach the engraver."

With the sole exception of the vocal parts to the 1708 cantata "Gott ist mein König" (BWV 71), all of Bach's music that was published during his lifetime was printed from copper plates. This procedure had proved to be especially propitious for the printing of clavier and organ music, because a satisfactory method for printing polyphonic music with type had not yet been perfected. For single lines of music, as in the case of the parts to Cantata 71, printing with type was the simpler, more sensible method commonly used since 1500. Printing music from copper plates as first developed in Italy at the beginning of the seventeenth century was then confined virtually exclusively to soloistic literature for keyboard and lute instruments. Here one must distinguish between two different methods: engraving, that is, incising a mirror image of the musical text directly into a copper plate, and etching, that is, transferring the musical text onto a copper plate by means of a corrosive acid.

The original editions of Bach's instrumental works were all etched. This method, most commonly used for the reproduction of paintings and other works of art, had been extraordinarily refined since the seventeenth century; it was possible for the resulting image to conform extremely closely to the manuscript score. The more skilled the etcher was, the more accurate the reproduction would be. This can be illustrated by comparing samples of Bach's music hand with the first page from Part III of the Clavier-Übung. How could it have been possible for Bach, unaccustomed to this technically complicated process, to reproduce the very characteristic fluent and bold strokes of his handwriting style? Not all etchers of music thought it important to reproduce an exact copy of the so-called Stichvorlage. Many developed their own mannerisms, eventually leading to a uniform and stylized notation.[9] Yet, anyone who could have produced a facsimile of Bach's handwriting was doubtlessly quite accomplished in the art of reproducing works of art. The latest research concerning this subject indicates that this person may have been an etcher from Johann Gottfried Krügner's workshop in Leipzig.[10] He also apparently worked on the Schemelli Gesang-Buch, which was printed by Breitkopf of Leipzig in 1736.[11] Krügner himself was also active in engraving reproductions, as his famous engraving of the St. Thomas courtyard shows.[12]

Figure 15.1. Clavier-Übung (Partita II, single edition of 1727), page 12: an autograph manuscript addition in the bottom staff.

Several different features of the printing process may actually be seen in Bach's original prints. The plate-marks, which result from pressing the paper onto the plate, are physically recognizable and unmistakable in any original copy. Some details, however, may be clearly seen also in facsimile editions: scratches and smudges caused by an imperfect copper plate; uneven staff lines or note signs due to careless correction; and inverted placement of accidentals resulting from an error in copying directly onto the plate.

As Bach's original editions show, correction of the actual plates was either too time-consuming, too troublesome, or too costly an undertaking. At any rate, most of the necessary corrections were entered on the printed copies by hand and in ink. These corrections, evidently made from errata lists, were made either in the printer's workshop or in Bach's house. Simple erasures and smaller improvements were in most instances not made by Bach but by assistants. Autograph corrections, especially of small details, are generally difficult to detect. Yet, Bach's hand is clearly visible in a more extended passage on the last page of a single issue of the second partita from 1727, where, because the imprint was too faint, a larger section had to be copied over (see Figure 15.1).[13] Here we find an especially characteristic example of Bach's participation in the manufacture of his printed compositions. It becomes apparent that his work did by no means end after the preparation of the Stichvorlage, but usually continued through the inspection and revision of the printed and finished copies.

In 1731, Bach published as his Opus 1 a collected edition of the six partitas that in previous years had been issued in separate installments. Like the single issues, this collected edition was also entitled Clavier-Übung. Bach followed the same procedures in printing both the single issues and the collected edition; accordingly, all the title pages include the indication, *In Verlegung des Autoris* (published by the author). With the exception of the two ceremonial cantatas of 1708 and 1709, respectively (BWV 71; the other one is lost), which were paid for by the town council of Mühlhausen, no other works by Bach had heretofore been printed. It must have been in his own best interest, therefore, to secure his place as a famous and influential virtuoso of both the clavier and organ and to establish a larger following with the publication of appropriate works. Bach could be especially sure of the compositional quality of the partitas since the work dealt with a genre of keyboard music which he had already tried out extensively and had brought together in two earlier complete series, the so-called English and French Suites. Thus he began the publication of his Clavier-Übung with what was in every respect a seasoned effort.

Much of the composition of the partitas took place before the single publication in 1726 of the first one. In fact, early versions of Partitas III and VI open the second Clavierbüchlein for Anna Magdalena Bach of 1725. Moreover, variants of two movements of Partita VI (Courante and Tempo di Gavotta) appear in an older manuscript source[14] of the Violin Sonata in G Major (BWV 1019: there as the third and fifth movements). This only proves that the genesis of at least some if not all of the partitas took place originally without regard to the planning of their publication. The thorough revision of the early versions of Partitas III and VI, however, bears witness to the great care Bach took in improving them for publication.

It is difficult to explain the relatively irregular dates of publication of the single issues, the first of which was announced in the late fall of 1726 in the Leipzig *Post-Zeitungen* as follows:

> The Capellmeister to the Prince of Anhalt-Cöthen and Director Chori Musici Lipsiensis, Herr Johann Sebastian Bach, intends to publish a colleciton of clavier Suites of which the first Partita has already been issued, and, by and by, they will continue to come to light until the work is complete, and as such will be made known to amateurs of the clavier. Let it be known that the author is himself the publisher of his work.[15]

The next two partitas were evidently published to coincide with the following year's Easter and Michaelmas fairs, respectively, for it was announced that "the continuation is taking place at both fairs."[16] Partita IV followed in 1728; none were published in 1729, and no explanation for the interruption of the series was offered; finally, Partitas V and VI came out in 1730. However, since Partita VI was composed much earlier, the reason for its late pub-

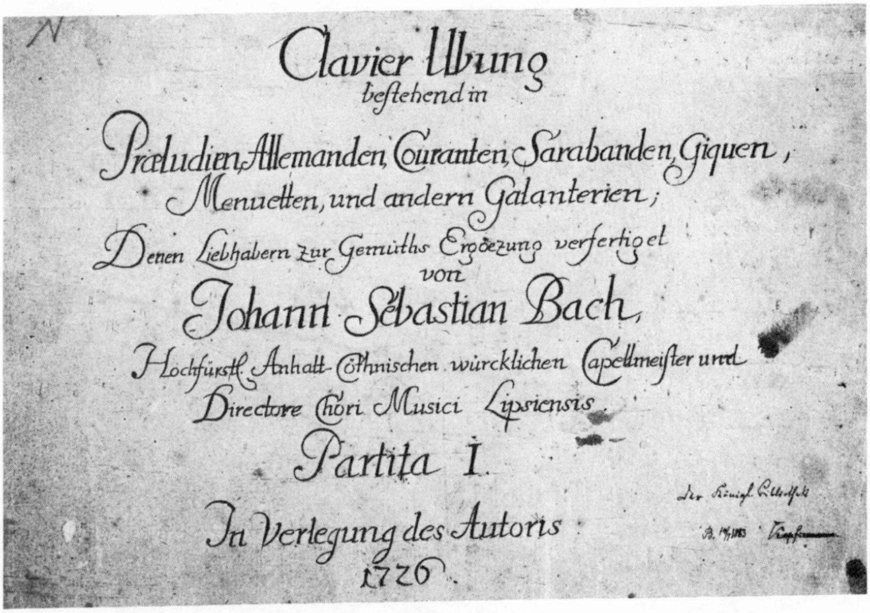
Clavier Übung
bestehend in
Præludien, Allemanden, Couranten, Sarabanden, Giquen,
Menuetten, und andern Galanterien;
Denen Liebhabern zur Gemüths Ergoezung verfertiget
von
Johann Sebastian Bach,
Hochfürstl. Anhalt-Cöthnischen würcklichen Capellmeister und
Directore Chori Musici Lipsiensis.
Partita I.
In Verlegung des Autoris
1726.

Figure 15.2. Clavier-Übung (Partita I, single edition of 1726), title page.

lication could not have stemmed from the composer. Rather, it would have been the result of technical or publishing difficulties; for, beginning with Partitas II and III, a change of engravers was made. Whether there also may have been a problem in selling the works is difficult to say. In any case, to insure the distribution, Bach started to make use of commission sales, for in the publication announcement of the second and third partitas, dated 19 September 1727, he notes that:

> they may be obtained from not only the author, but also from 1) Herr Petsold, the Royal, Polish, and Electoral Saxon Chamber Musician in Dresden; 2) Herr Ziegler, Direct. Musices and Organist at St. Ulrich in Halle; 3) Herr Böhm, Organist at St. Johann in Lüneburg; 4) Herr Schwaneberg, Chamber Musician to the Prince of Brunswick; 5) Herr Fischer, City and Council Musician in Nuremberg; and 6) Herr Roth, City and Council Musician in Augsburg.[17]

Bach was probably accustomed to such a complicated system of distribution, since he himself was numbered among the commissioned salesmen of Johann David Heinichen's *Der General-Baß in der Composition* (Dresden, 1728). Understandably, he entrusted the sale of the 1731 collected edition of the partitas to the well-known Boetius book dealership in Leipzig. Hence a one-line notice was engraved at the foot of the title page of part of the edition: "Leipzig, distributed by the orphaned daughter of the deceased Boetius, near the town hall." Obviously, this information is also important in view of the production of not only the collected edition, but of the single issues as well, for the daughter of Johann Theodor Boetius (d. 1722), Rosine Dorothee, had

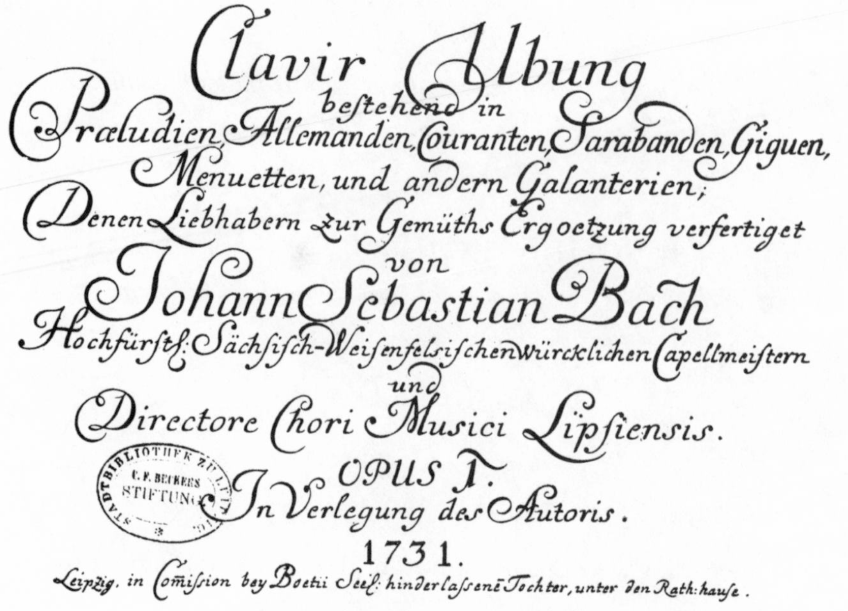
Clavir Ubung
beſtehend in
Præludien, Allemanden, Couranten, Sarabanden, Giguen,
Menuetten, und andern Galanterien;
Denen Liebhabern zur Gemüths Ergoetzung verfertiget
von
Johann Sebastian Bach
Hochfürſtl: Sächſiſch-Weiſenfelſiſchen würcklichen Capellmeiſtern
und
Directore Chori Muſici Lipſienſis.
OPUS I.
In Verlegung des Autoris.
1731.
Leipzig. in Comiſsion bey Boetii Seel: hinderlaſsenē Tochter, unter den Rath:hauſe.

Figure 15.3. Clavier-Übung I (1731), title page.

married in 1726 the engraver Johann Gottfried Krügner, who was also active as a music engraver.[18] Krügner has been established as the engraver of the title page of the collected edition, as well as of the individual titles of the partitas and their pagination. He must also be credited with having engraved the movement headings for the last three single issues of the Partitas, thus suggesting that all the printing work of the partitas was carried out in Krügner's Leipzig workshop.[19]

The first print of the 1731 collected edition of all six partitas is made up of thirty-eight leaves, measuring 23.5 × 29 cm, containing seventy-four printed pages (title page and seventy-three pages of music). As was usual for oblong-sized prints, the plates were pulled by individual leaf, not folded sheet. Therefore, there is no gathering structure, but only a collection of single leaves, usually stitched together. The sizes of the plates vary between 16 × 23 cm and 17 × 24 cm. With the exception of the newly engraved title page, the plates from the single issues were reused (for the musical text). Only the head titles for the individual works (Partita I, Partita II, and so on) had to be added, and, beginning with the second partita (page 11), the pagination was changed so that it would be consecutive. All of these changes, including the new title page, were the work of Krügner. His part in the production of the single issues of Partitas IV to VI is evidenced by his engraving the titles of the movements. Whether he was involved in further work on the partitas must remain an open question because we lack sufficient evidence for comparison. The earliest signed example of Krügner's music engraving is Georg Friedrich Kauffmann's collection of chorale preludes, *Harmonische Seelen Lust,* which was also published by Krügner in installments beginning in 1733. In any case, it is virtually certain that Krügner's connection with Clavier-Übung I began prior to 1731. Indeed it is highly probable that the single issues were also produced by engravers from his workshop.

Just the fact that the plates for the title pages of the first two partitas were reused after only slight retouching for the remaining partitas (the first place for Partitas I and V, the second for Partitas II, III, and IV) speaks for the manufacture of the single issues in one and the same workshop. No copy of the single issue of the sixth partita survives. Yet, on the basis of indirect evidence (the reference in Walther's *Musicalisches Lexicon* of 1732, for example),[20] it too must have been issued separately.

The title pages of Partitas III through VI (as well as several movement headings for the first two partitas) were produced by an engraver who was obviously fairly inexperienced at first, though in the later partitas the quality of his work progressively improved. The engraving of Partitas I and II, on the other hand, was carried out by another co-worker from the same workshop, who apparently was quite experienced. A third engraver may possibly have contributed some of the movement headings.

Whereas for each of the single issues only one printing is traceable, it appears that the collected edition went through three printings. The first

Figure 15.4. Clavier-Übung I (1731), page 1.

edition is set apart from the later reprints by the reference on the title page to the Boetius bookshop, but no clues of any kind for the dating of the later editions are to be found. The second edition contains several corrections made on the plates, which are different from the handwritten corrections on the single copies. The third edition is characterized by alphabetically ordered letters, which appear in the lower left or right corner of the plates.[21]

In the six partitas of Clavier-Übung I, Bach exhibited his mastery of the suite form. As he did in the English Suites, he began each piece with a large-scale free prelude, though he varied each work by introducing new types of movements. Bach's suites generally conform to the scheme Allemande-Courante-Sarabande-Gigue (although the last is missing from the second partita), but he expanded the form by integrating a large number of fashionable gallantry pieces like Capriccio, Burlesca, and Scherzo, and also by inserting more conventional suite movements like Aria, Minuet, Rondeaux, Passepied, and Gavotta. The resulting flexibility of the overall design enabled Bach to impart a maximum degree of individuality to each work, emphasized by tonal differentiation, textural diversification, and a broad spectrum of musical affects and expressions.

Clavier-Übung, Part II

Part II of the Clavier-Übung, containing the Italian Concerto and the French Overture, appeared in Leipzig during the 1735 Easter fair from the publishing firm of Christoph Weigel, Jr. of Nuremberg. Although no publication date is given on the title page (among Bach's original prints, only in Clavier-Übung I is this the case), the date is known from other documentary evidence. A marginal reference in Johann Gottfried Walther's personal copy of his *Musicalisches Lexicon* (Leipzig, 1732) indicates that the above-mentioned "two pieces . . . came to light at Easter, 1735 . . . by means of copper engraving," and this is corroborated by publication announcements appearing in both Nuremberg and Leipzig.[22] From these announcements we also learn that in addition to the publisher Weigel, Johann Meindel of Leipzig was also involved as a co-distributor of the print.

How Bach came to be associated with the Nuremberg publisher remains unknown. Occasions for contact may have arisen in Leipzig, where Weigel regularly maintained an office during the fairs. And since there were no printers and publishers of repute specializing in music in Leipzig during Bach's time and, furthermore, since his experience with the production of Clavier-Übung I in Leipzig was probably not too favorable, Bach may well have wished to turn to a better-known and expert outside firm.

Christoph Weigel, Jr. (1702–1777) was the son of the well-known Nuremberg engraver and art dealer Johann Christoph Weigel (1661–1726). The elder Weigel had published compositions by Johann Pachelbel and a book of plates, *Musicalisches Theatrum* (ca. 1725), which is of great socio-historical and organological importance. In 1734, the young Christoph left the family business, which was being carried on by his mother after his father's death, to set up his own firm. Bach's Clavier-Übung II was probably his first publication of music.

The sale of the first edition must have been successful, for after a short time a new edition became necessary. This new edition, containing numerous corrections, must have been begun in the fall of 1736 at the latest. The date can be deduced from the fact that Bach was still designated on the title page as titular capellmeister at the court of Weissenfels, as he had been before, but not yet as Electoral Saxon court composer. The Dresden court title was awarded to him on 19 November 1736 and Bach would certainly not have hesitated to make public this new and especially high honor if it had already been bestowed on him (especially given the fact that he took pains to have a minor spelling error *verferdiget* corrected to *verfertiget*). Therefore, it is possible that the new edition appeared as late as 1736. The unusually quick sale of the first printing indicates the special popularity of this work of Bach's, which in both editions must have enjoyed great vogue. This is also confirmed by the writings of Bach's harshest critic, Johann Adolph Scheibe, who, in a review in 1739, wrote enthusiastically about the Italian Concerto (the French Overture was not mentioned):

> Pre-eminent among works known through published prints is a clavier concerto of which the author is the famous Bach in Leipzig and which is in the key of F major. It is arranged in the best fashion which is applicable alone in these pieces. This clavier concerto is to be regarded as a perfect model of a well-designed solo concerto.[23]

The original print comprises fourteen leaves (a title page plus twenty-seven numbered pages of music) in upright folio format measuring 34.5 × 25 cm with the gathering structure: binio, binio, ternio. The plates vary in size between 30–31 cm in height and 20–21 cm in width. According to the different notational styles, at least four engravers participated in the fabrication of the print. From Engraver I stems the complete Italian Concerto (pages 1–13); from Engraver II, pages 14–16, 18, and 21–27; from Engraver III (an apprentice), pages 17 and 20; and from Engraver IV, page 19. In addition to these engravers, Weigel's co-worker, Balthasar Schmid, can be identified as the engraver of the title page (as well as the later title pages of Parts III and IV of the Clavier-Übung and the Canonic Variations of Vom Himmel hoch). The fact that Engraver II was also active in Krügner's workshop[24] raises the question whether the manufacture of Part II was at first planned for Leipzig. It is more probable, however, that Engraver II moved to Leipzig around or after 1736 (he is first proven there in Sperontes' *Singende Muse an der Pleisse* of 1736). In any case, these initial demonstrable connections between Leipzig and Nuremberg become important, as we shall see, for Clavier-Übung III.

The second edition of the Clavier-Übung II print is, on the whole, identical with the first. Several corrections were incorporated and pages 20–22

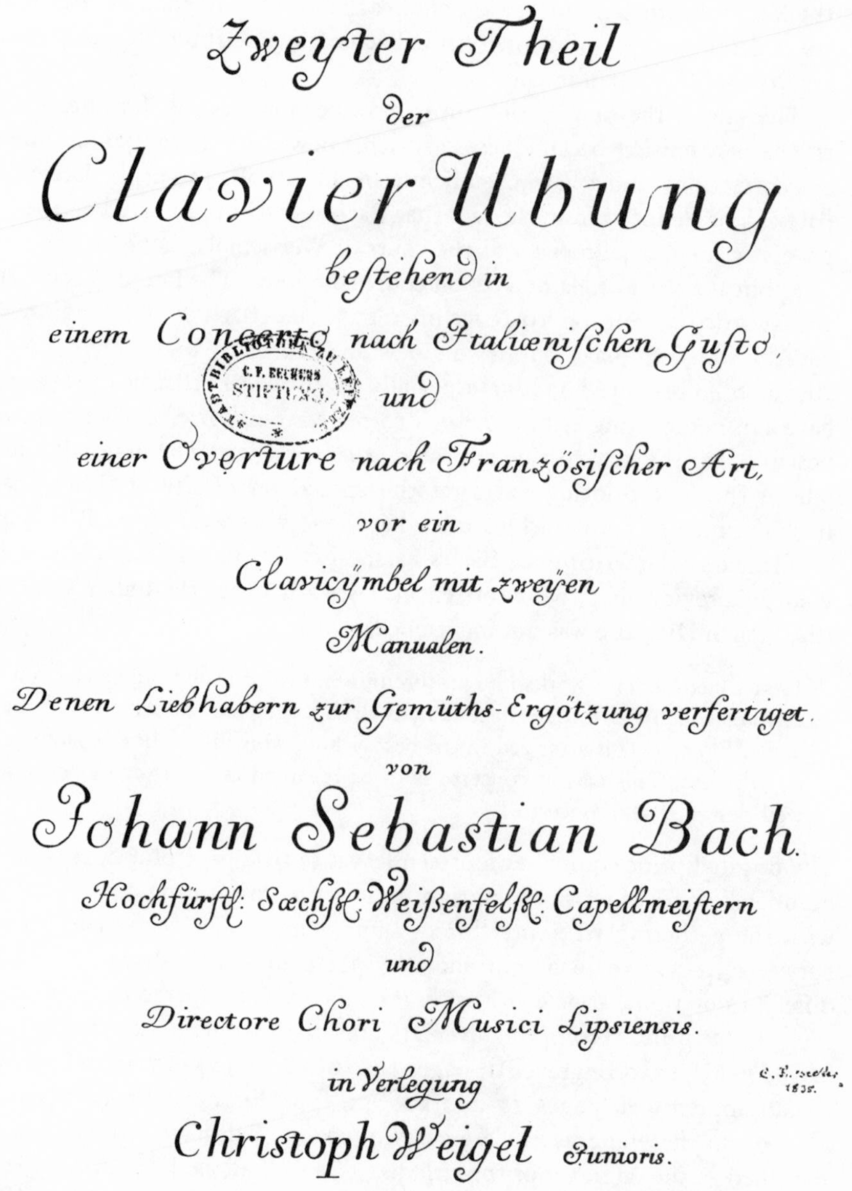

Zweyter Theil

der

Clavier Ubung

bestehend in

einem Concerto nach Italiænischen Gusto,

und

einer Overture nach Französischer Art,

vor ein

Claricymbel mit zweyen

Manualen.

Denen Liebhabern zur Gemüths-Ergötzung verfertiget.

von

Johann Sebastian Bach.

Hochfürstl: Sæchsl: Weißenfelsl: Capellmeistern

und

Directore Chori Musici Lipsiensis.

in Verlegung

Christoph Weigel *Junioris.*

C. F. Becker
1825.

Figure 15.5. Clavier-Übung II (1735), title page.

were newly engraved (so that the Gavotte II could now be played without turning a page). Many of the corrections may have followed the markings in Bach's extant Handexemplar of the first edition.[25] Not all of them were made on the plates, however. Handwritten corrections in ink form a distinct layer of the edition, as they do in the other original prints of Bach's works.

The origins of both compositions in Clavier-Übung II evidently go back

Figure 15.6. Clavier-Übung II (1735), page 1.

to a point in time considerably earlier than the publication date of the first printing. This is clearly the case with the French Overture, for which an original manuscript source survives. This manuscript[26] was prepared around 1730 by Anna Magdalena Bach (the title, *Ouverture pour le clavecin par J. S. Bach,* and the titles of the individual movements are in Johann Sebastian's hand) and is certainly a transcription of an autograph copy. The composition presumably dates from the same time as the genesis of the partitas, that is, the middle to the late 1720s. Among the most important features of the early version are its different key (C minor) and the simplified notation of the slow sections of the Overture. An undatable early version of the Italian Concerto is indicated by a pre-1762 manuscript copy[27] made by Johann Christoph Oley with the title *Concerto in F dur Del Sigr: Johann Sebastian Bach*. The variants in this source probably stem from an older version of the concerto that is now lost. Moreover, it is noteworthy that this concerto was written for a harpsichord that had a compass extending only to c′′′ (see the skip of a seventh in the otherwise strictly motivic voice-leading in the last movement, m. 138). Whether or not this means that the concerto predates Partitas II, III, and V, which exceed this range, is uncertain. In any case, we can be sure that in laying out the print of Clavier-Übung II, Bach referred back to two pre-existing compositions which required only minor revisions.

In the publication of these two works Bach contrasted the two leading national styles of the Baroque in exemplary compositions. The Italian Concerto recalls Bach's Weimar settings for organ and harpsichord of Italian instrumental concertos by Vivaldi, Marcello, and others. Nonetheless, its content is surely original and particularly well suited for the keyboard, and, as such, it remains unique among Bach's keyboard music. The French Overture has no direct counterpart. It follows the specific French notions of style and

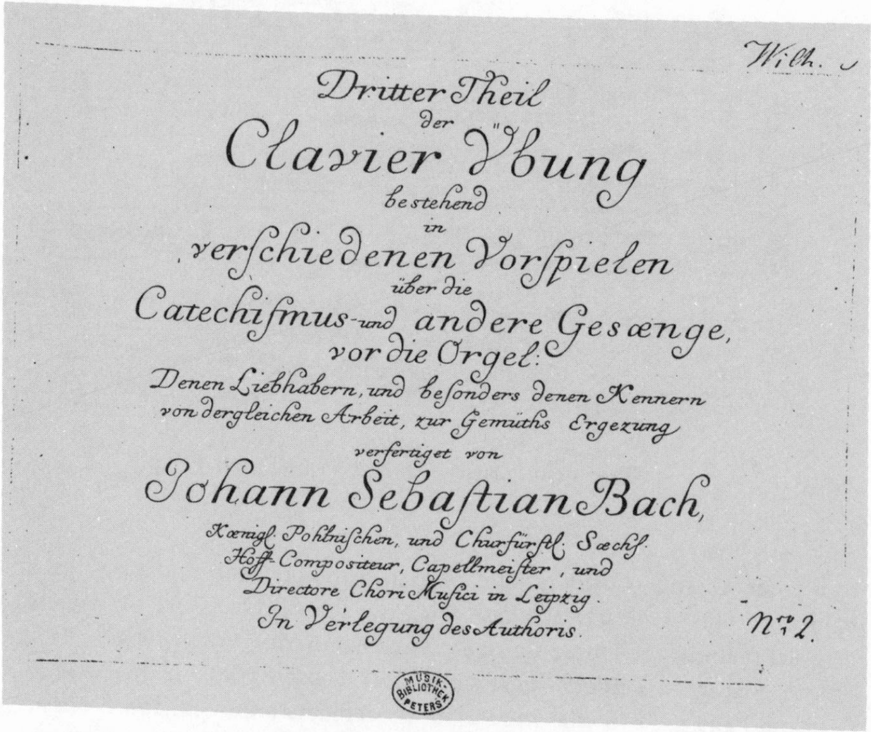

Figure 15.7. Clavier-Übung III (1739), title page of Bach's personal copy.

"OLD" SOURCES REVISITED: NOVEL ASPECTS

Figure 15.8. Clavier-Übung III (1739), page 1.

manner much more closely than the partitas do, and, with its eleven movements, it far exceeds the usual format of Bach's suite compositions.

Clavier-Übung, Part III

Part III of the Clavier-Übung most probably appeared at the Michaelmas fair
of 1739, for on 28 September 1739 Johann Elias Bach, who at the time was
acting as private secretary to the cantor of St. Thomas, informed Johann
Wilhelm Koch, cantor at Ronneburg, "that the work of my cousin engraved
in copper is now ready and a copy may be had from him for three reichs-
thaler."[28] Evidently, the work was to have been published earlier, for in a
previous message dated 10 January of the same year, Johann Elias Bach mentioned "that my honored cousin will bring out some pieces for keyboard
which are principally intended for organists and are exceedingly well-
composed. They will probably be ready in time for the coming Easter fair
and make up some 80 pages."[29] The delay in publishing this extensive work
was most likely due to the fact that Bach, again his own publisher, changed
engravers after more than half the plates had been completed. According to
the latest research,[30] the work was not wholly engraved by Balthasar Schmid
as was hitherto thought—for if that were the case it probably would have
been published by him as well. The engraving of the music was begun in
Krügner's workshop in Leipzig by an engraver who had also worked on the

Schemelli *Gesang-Buch* for Breitkopf of Leipzig. The few extant copies of the work contain Leipzig paper for those pages engraved at Krügner's shop and Nuremberg paper for those pages engraved by Schmid. This suggests that for the first edition, the sheets were pulled in different locations.

Krügner's workshop was extremely busy, though rarely with music. It is possible, therefore, that Bach's Clavier-Übung befell a fate similar to Johann Gottfried Walther's variations on "Allein Gott in der Höh sei Ehr." On 26 January 1736 Walther wrote to Heinrich Bokemeyer in Wolfenbüttel regarding certain problems in the printing of his variations:

> Herr Krügner of Leipzig was introduced and recommended to me by the Capellmeister Bach, but he [Krügner] had to excuse himself because he already had accepted the Kauffmann pieces for publication and would not be able to complete them for a long time. Also the costs run too high.[31]

The seventy-eight plates of Bach's entire project may, then, have overtaxed Krügner's capacity. Whatever the causes for Krügner's not having completed the engraving of Clavier-Übung III, the problems must have already arisen in 1738. When Johann Elias Bach in January 1739 reckoned that the work would appear at the Easter fair, Krügner (having completed at most forty-three plates) could no longer have been involved. Schmid, however, evidently could not meet the Easter deadline. These details concerning the pre-publication history of the work, though still unclear, are nonetheless of the highest relevance to our understanding of the genesis of Bach's composition. They show that the work was probably composed significantly earlier than is generally assumed, perhaps as early as 1737–38 or even 1736–37, certainly much closer in time to the 1735 publication date of Clavier-Übung II.

The first edition comprises thirty-nine leaves with a title page and seventy-seven numbered pages of music. The surviving copies have been differently trimmed and so the sizes of the leaves vary, measuring between 22.5 × 28.5 cm and 25.5 × 30.5 cm (oblong format). The sizes of the plates are 16–16.5 cm × 23–23.5 cm, that is, about the same size as for the partitas, an indication that the design of the print originated with Krügner. For Bach's Nuremberg publications, Clavier-Übung II and IV, larger plates were used, in anticipation of their design in upright format. The engraving work was distributed as follows: the engravers from Krügner's workshop, who were evidently skilled reproduction engravers and who successfully produced a striking facsimile of Bach's Stichvorlage (see Fig. 15.8),[32] took care of pages 1–18, 20, 22, 24, 30–34, 37–46, 48–53, and 55 (for a total of forty-three); Balthasar Schmid engraved the title page (Fig. 15.7), as well as pages 19, 21, 23, 25–29, 35–36, 47, 54, and 56–77 (for a total of thirty-five). It can be assumed that Schmid worked from the same autograph Stichvorlage, yet as a specialized craftsman he had developed his own typographical style of notation that can be seen in his other publications.

Among the extant copies of the original print we can differentiate between two editions that are, for the most part, textually identical. Few corrections were made on the plates themselves; a much larger number were made in ink by hand, after the printing had been completed.[33]

Within the complete four-part Clavier-Übung series, Part III is specifically devoted to the organ and, accordingly, Bach selected a typical organ repertoire, mainly chorale settings. These represent the main focus of the collection and, at the same time, determine its overall organization, for Bach sets two different categories of church hymns: first, German chorale versions of the Kyrie and Gloria of the Mass and, second, Martin Luther's Catechism chorales. In both groups pre-Reformational and classical Lutheran hymn repertoire is dealt with exclusively. Thus Clavier-Übung III demonstrates Bach's continuing preference for sixteenth-century chorale material, which he had also used in the 1724–25 cycle of cantatas. Moreover, Bach's choice of hymns seems to have implied some crucial aspects of compositional technique as well, especially with regard to the emphasis on church modes. Bach was now able to explore modal harmony in a rather systematic way, thereby extending the limited tonal vocabulary of the major and minor modes.[34] The conception of Clavier-Übung III stands also in the context of Bach's growing interest in Mass composition, following the Missa BWV 232^1 (Kyrie-Gloria) dedicated in 1733 to the Dresden court, which stimulated him to come to terms with the history of this venerable genre. Bach's study of the masses of Palestrina, Lotti, Caldara, and other *stile antico* masters is a reflection this historical interest, and it influenced the retrospective style of composition to be found in the large chorale settings of the three Kyrie stanzas and in "Aus tiefer Not." While the two preceding parts of the Clavier-Übung contrasted a wide range of modern keyboard music, Part III added a truly historical dimension: old techniques (motet style, modality, canon) blended with examples of modern compositional idioms (epitomized particularly in the French-style organ chorale "Vater unser im Himmelreich").

Considering the historical orientation of Clavier-Übung III, it is significant that—in conjunction with Johann Adolph Scheibe's critical assaults against Bach—Johann Abraham Birnbaum, Bach's "spokesman," defended the composer in his *Unpartheyische Anmerkungen* (Impartial Comments) published in early 1738 by explicitly referring to the *Livres d'orgue* (Organ Masses) of Nicolas de Grigny (1700) and Pierre Du Mage (1708) as well as to compositions of Palestrina and Antonio Lotti.[35] These references, then indicate that Bach was apparently concerned with the works of these masters at that time. Indeed we know that he possessed not only works by Palestrina and Lotti, but also a copy of de Grigny's *Livre d'orgue* in his own hand, and there appears to be little doubt that the conception of Part III was influenced by it.

To what extent all of this can illuminate the genesis of Part III may be hinted at by the following speculative considerations. On 1 December 1736, Bach, in connection with his being named Electoral Saxon court composer, "was heard with special admiration on the new organ" at the Frauenkirche in

Dresden.[36] Would it be too far off the mark to suggest that Bach, since his 1733 application for a court title included a concerted Missa (Kyrie and Gloria), may have performed an Organ Mass (Kyrie and Gloria) at the recital subsequent to his appointment? Whether or not any compositions from Clavier-Übung III were actually played at the concert remains open. Yet, the fact that the work was composed considerably earlier than 1739 speaks for the hypothesis.

The succession of movements within the original edition evidently conforms to a precise plan. On the one hand, Bach ordered the chorale settings according to large and small types. However, whether this arrangement was intended from the beginning is by no means clear. There exists the possibility, at least, that Bach, after preparing the Stichvorlage, was annoyed by several half-empty and some only partly used pages and subsequently decided to insert the small settings as "stopgaps." The absolutely precise fit of such small pieces as those on pages 29, 39, 46, and 50 suggests such a conjecture. On the other hand—and this likewise speaks in favor of this suggestion— the arrangement of the Catechism chorales was evidently determined by the large settings alone: in the first three-piece group, two movements with a *cantus firmus* canon enclose one setting for *organo pleno;* in the second three-piece group, two organ chorales with pedal *cantus firmus* frame a setting for full organ.

The grouping of large and small settings—and here the four duets function to a certain extent as the "small," non-*cantus firmus* counterparts to the large Prelude and Fugue in E♭—also ensured that the collection would be accessible to a wider circle of users. The most demanding work was certainly intended primarily for professional musicians who had access to a large church organ. It did not exlude, however, those who wished to perform examples of Bach's artistry in chorale setting on domestic keyboard instruments. It is thoroughly characteristic of Bach to have combined both abstract and pragmatic considerations.

In Clavier-Übung III Bach created not only his most extensive, but also his most significant organ work. It stands on the threshold of his late style and was produced at a time when organ composition was no longer at the center of his activities. Nevertheless, Lorenz Christoph Mizler remarked correctly in his 1740 review: "The author has here given proof that in this field of composition he is more skilled and more successful than many others. No one will surpass him in it and few will be able to imitate him."[37]

Clavier-Übung, Part IV

The weighty conclusion of the four-part series constitutes a large-scale set of variations, which since the nineteenth century has been known as the Goldberg Variations. Curiously enough, the specification "Part IV" is missing from the title page, an omission probably related to factors concerning its publication. This set of variations was the first of Bach's works to be published by Balthasar Schmid, who presumably would not have wished to begin his association with Bach by printing just the concluding part of a series of works. True, Schmid had been involved in the preparation of the two immediately preceding Clavier-Übung parts as one of the engravers, but now he took over the entire manufacture, printing, and distribution of the new work. There is no documentary verification of its exact publication date. Since Schmid used different series of plate numbers concurrently, the number of the Goldberg Variations (No. 16) offers no precise time frame, although only the early 1740s come into consideration. A comparison of the technical execution in the print of Bach's work with several other unequivocally datable examples from Schmid's workshop (especially Johann Ludwig Krebs's *Andere Piece* and *Dritte Piece,* with forewords dated 3 January and 11 September 1741, respectively) leads to the conclusion that the production of Bach's print must have been undertaken during the first half of 1741. This would suggest a release date during the 1741 Michaelmas fair, although because of possible delays in work on the print the 1742 Easter fair cannot be entirely ruled out.

The original print comprises eighteen leaves, 31–32.5 × 20 cm in size (upright format). The leaves form one enclosed fascicle of nine interlaid bifolios, and the outer bifolio, printed only on the front side, serves as a title wrapper. Incidentally, the title page does not resemble any other of Bach's first editions, for it is ornamented by a cartouche. The music makes up eight folios printed on all thirty-two sides. The sizes of the plates are as follows: 23.5 × 16.5 cm (title page); 26–26.5 × 16.5 cm (music). The engraving is of a piece, the work of Balthasar Schmid himself throughout, and here he produced a particular masterpiece of his craft.

Nothing is known about the size of the print run, nor is there any trace of further editions. But since there are more extant copies of Clavier-Übung IV (18) than of Part II (13), which went through two editions, one can conclude that the Goldberg Variations had a least a comparable if not larger circulation. A hint at the planning of a new, improved edition may be offered by Bach's extant Handexemplar,[38] which contains several corrections and additions not encountered in any other surviving copy. Moreover, it contains an autograph appendix with a cycle of artful circle canons (BWV 1087) set to the opening ground bass of the Aria.[39]

In the absence of autograph manuscript sources, the date of origin and the genesis of the Goldberg Variations can only be hypothetically discussed. That a copy of the Aria in the hand of Anna Magdalena Bach may be found in her second clavier book (1725) has for a long time furnished the argument that the Aria was written down during the 1720s and moreover that it should be considered a copy of a work not by Bach. Our knowledge of the handwriting style of Bach's second wife reveals that this Aria could hardly have been entered before 1740, however, and that it was probably included in a series of later additions made on unused pages of the book. Therefore, the decisive criterion which led to the belief that the composition and pub-

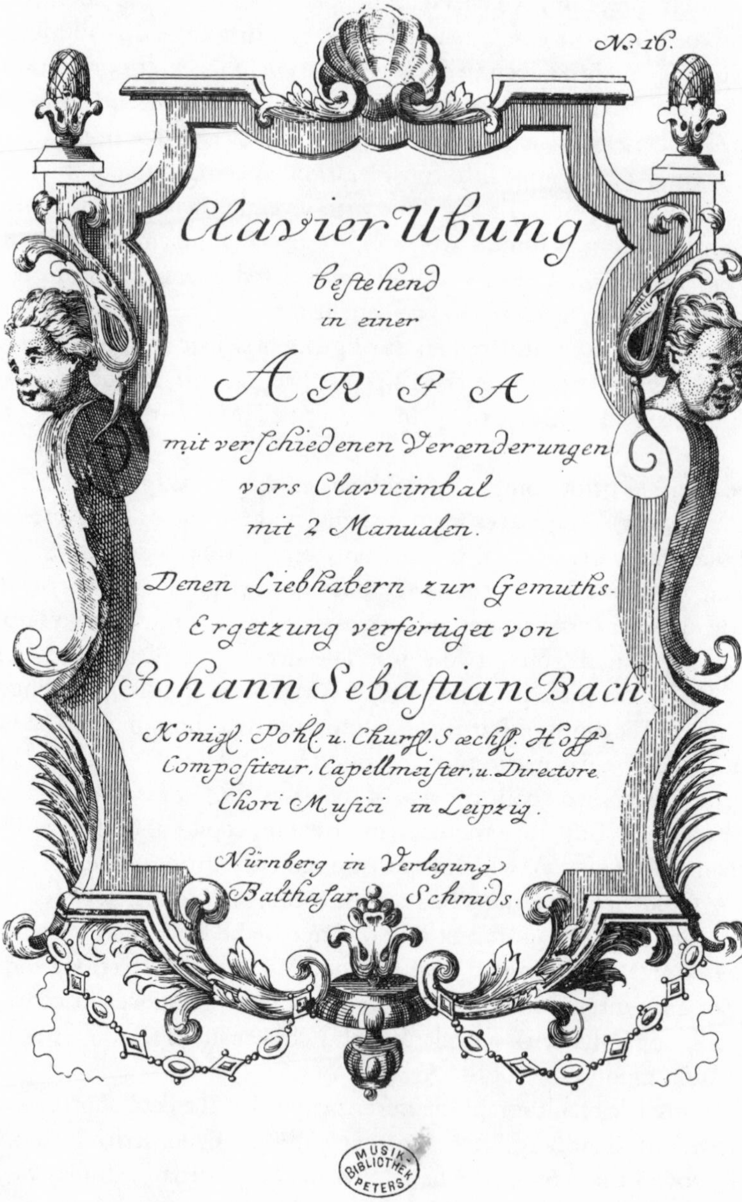

Figure 15.9. Clavier-Übung IV (1741), title page.

Figure 15.10. Clavier-Übung IV (1741), page 1.

lication of the Goldberg Variations were separated by several years is not valid. Anna Magdalena's copy, which had the right-hand part notated in soprano clef (instead of treble clef, as in the print), must be either a copy of the first edition or, more likely, a copy of an autograph manuscript. Thus, the decisive argument against the authenticity of the Aria is likewise invalid, because the piece can no longer be considered with the context of the other aria pieces by different composers (Stölzel, Giovannini) in the second Clavier-Büchlein—it clearly belongs to another species. No firm argument against the authenticity of the Aria from the Goldberg Variations can be put forth. Bach took the fundamental bass line of an early seventeenth-century soggetto (which underlies the Canons BWV 1087) and extended it considerably. Expansions of this kind were very customary. For instance, Johann Christoph Bach (1642–1703) wrote an Aria in G Major with twelve variations on the same theme, which may well have served as a stimulus for Johann Sebastian. Nonetheless, the thirty-two-measure bass line of the Goldberg Variations is unique. The melodically elegant and richly ornamented, rhythmically accentuated grace of the treble voice corresponds to the upper voice of the early Aria Variata in A Minor (BWV 989), inasmuch as it balances an otherwise excessive concentration on the bass line.

Bach had shown little interest in the genre of variations since his youth and took it up again only in the last decade of his life. The principle of variation now becomes an integral component of the predominantly monothematic concept that characterizes Bach's late instrumental style. This monothematic concept together with the appearance of retrospective elements (canonic technique, for example) as well as stylistic modernisms (such as the use of popular tunes in the Quodlibet, which also occur in the Peasant Cantata BWV 212 of 1742) make it improbable that the Goldberg Variations were composed substantially earlier than the time of their going to press. The overall stylistic orientation suggests that the variation cycle originated shortly after Clavier-Übung III, that is, about 1740.

The story that the work came into being at the request of the then Russian envoy to the Dresden court, Hermann Carl Reichsgraf von Keyserlingk, goes back to Johann Nicolaus Forkel, who wrote in his 1802 biography:[40]

> The Count once said to Bach that he should like to have some clavier pieces for his Goldberg, which should be of such a soft and somewhat lively character that he might be a little cheered up by them in his sleepless nights. Bach thought that he could best fulfill this wish through variations, which, on account of the constant sameness of the fundamental harmony, he had hitherto considered as an ungrateful task.

Actually, there is no documentary evidence to support Forkel's statement. On the contrary, a number of facts show Forkel's account to be rather untrustworthy. For one thing, for a commissioned work not to include an official dedication in its published version contradicts eighteenth-century custom. The original print contains no trace of a dedicatory inscription (see Fig.

15.9). Also, the age of the doubtlessly gifted Johann Gottlieb Goldberg (1727–1756), who was brought to Bach in Leipzig by Keyserlingk in 1737 for instruction and was subsequently engaged as the latter's house harpsichordist, would seem to make it highly improbable that Bach had him, barely thirteen years old, in mind when he planned the work. On the other hand, it is certainly conceivable—and here may lie the true seed of Forkel's anecdotal remark—that after the publication of the work Bach may have dedicated a freshly printed copy of the work to his patron, the count, from which Goldberg later may frequently have played to while away the sleepless nights of his master. It can be proven that Bach stayed at Keyserlingk's Dresden house in November 1741, and it seems highly plausible that Bach gave him on that occasion a presentation copy of the last part of the Clavier-Übung hot from the press.

All internal and external clues indicate that the so-called Goldberg Variations did not originate as an independently commissioned work, but were from the outset integrated into the overall concept of the Clavier-Übung series, to which they constitute a grandiose finale.

16

Text-Critical Comments on the Original Print
of the Partitas

THE STUDY OF THE ORIGINAL PRINTS of Bach's works received a solid foundation through Georg Kinsky's pathbreaking monograph more than forty years ago,[1] yet about three decades passed before detailed bibliographical and text-critical research of the prints was undertaken in connection with the *Neue Bach-Ausgabe*. In the process it became clear—and the editorial work done for Clavier-Übung III and the Musical Offering[2] was especially convincing in this respect—that a descriptive bibliographical analysis as well as a critical evaluation of the musical text required a collation of all extant copies of the prints concerned. The original editions contained not only variants due to the existence of different printings, but also an unexpectedly large number of manuscript corrections and other entries, the authenticity of which could not be doubted. Evidently, in an attempt to avoid cumbersome and doubtlessly expensive revisions in the engraver's plates, copies of the original prints were often touched upon through erasures or annotations in ink. This was apparently done on the basis of errata sheets, which, however, did not always seem to present the complete picture, since we often can recognize different layers of correction.

The special significance of Bach's personal copies arises from the fact that they contain entries that go beyond mere correction; there are also directions for tempo, registration, added ornaments, articulation, or alterations in the musical text. Through fortunate circumstances, it has become possible to evaluate the information contained in Bach's personal copies of the Goldberg Variations and the Schübler Chorales, which are particularly interesting and informative and which were hitherto unknown or inaccessible.[3] Yet a comparison of Bach's personal copies, to the extent that these can be traced,[4] shows also how differently they were marked. His copy of Clavier-Übung III,[5] for instance, contains no entries of any consequence and yields less evidence of proofing than other revised copies of the work. A rather plausible explanation is that the composer himself was not in need of a corrected copy; he would have spotted mistakes in any event. On the other hand, we need to realize that we still know as little about the function of the so-called Handexemplare as we do about their number. It is possible, in fact likely, that Bach retained several copies of each print for his own use. What purpose would they have served? Certainly not that of archival so much as practical material, to be used for performance, instruction, and correction (correction to be applied to further copies or preparation for a new edition). Yet a combination of these three functions is not in evidence in any of the extant copies classified as Handexemplare. One can suppose that in the course of time Bach may have given away one or the other copy that had been used for a given purpose. Still the meaning of the "acknowledged" Handexemplar remains relative.

In his "Critical Report" for volume V/1 of the *Neue Bach-Ausgabe* (1978), Richard D. Jones has thoroughly dealt with the source situation for Clavier-Übung I, and he has made a good case for the conjecture that a copy preserved in the British Library (source G 23) was originally in the possession of the composer, though the details of provenance remain unexplained. G 23 contains systematic corrections and "no patently spurious entries" (p. 29). There are, however, three further copies in existence, namely G 24 (Staats-bibliothek Preußischer Kulturbesitz, Berlin), G 25 (Library of Congress, Washington, D.C.), and G 26 (University of Illinois Library, Urbana, Illinois), whose comparable yet less extensive manuscript entries[6] represent the same phase of revision (designated "Korr III" by Jones). That the emendations in these four copies do not overlap in every respect is hardly surprising in view of similar discrepancies found in other original Bach prints. Jones considers the possibility that "Bach may have corrected some of the newly printed copies by memory, the slightly varying entries perhaps having been transferred by sons and students to further copies" (p. 29), but the significance of revisions contained in the four mentioned copies is accepted by him without doubt. For this reason it is doubly puzzling why, in his *recensio* of the sources, the corrections and additions in G 23—hypothetically assigned the status of Handexemplar—are referred to almost exclusively, whereas those in G 24 to G 26 (whenever not identical with those in G 23) are used only in exceptional instances, and this for no obvious reason.[7] Aside from the fact that there is no philological argument for a differing evaluation of the four sources with their invariably consistent and systematic though— given the imponderabilia of transference—not strictly parallel revisions, the inadequate attention given to copy G 25 from the Library of Congress[8] is to be especially regretted.

This copy contains corrections and additions dealing in particular with the second and third partitas. The majority of them is concerned with matters of practical use—in distinction to entries in G 23, 24, and 26—leading to the conclusion that the copy may have served for performance and instruction in Bach's presence. In view of their minute and highly restricted nature, it is not possible fully to identify the corrector who made these entries. Yet they doubtlessly come from the same hand, at least so far as notations in

Table 16.1. Variants in Partitas II and III; only those corrections and additions which have been disregarded in *NBA* V/1 are included. All emendations refer—unless noted differently—to the source G 25.

Measure	Part	Readings emended

Partita II (BWV 826):

1. Sinfonia

28	—	*allegro* (entered in red ink)
29	—	*adagio* (entered in red ink)
	S	♩. 𝅘𝅥𝅯𝅘𝅥𝅯𝅘𝅥𝅯𝅘𝅥𝅯 ♩. changed from 𝅘𝅥𝅯𝅘𝅥𝅯𝅘𝅥𝅯𝅘𝅥𝅯𝅘𝅥𝅯.

2. Allemande

Upbeat	S	*Tr* added to note 2 (in pencil)
2	S	∿ changed from *Tr*
8	A	*M* added to the penultimate note (b♭')
16	S	2nd eighth note: arpeggio marking (in pencil, gone over in ink)
Upbeat	S	*Tr* added to note 2 (in pencil)
17	S	*Tr* added to the penultimate note
22	S	*M* added to the 3rd quarter (f")
32	S	Grace note f" added to the 3rd eighth note (e♭") (in pencil, gone over in ink)

3. Courante

1	S	Grace note d" added to note 8 (c"); *M* added to note 9 (a♭")
2	A	*M* added to note 3 (e♭");
	T	Grace note d' added to note 8 (c')
6	S	*M* added to the penultimate note (b♭")
8	B	Grace note c added to note 8 (B♭)
14	S	Arpeggio marking added to the chord
16	S	*Tr* added to the 2nd eighth note
	B	Grace note d added to note 8 (c)

4. Sarabande

4	S	Grace note a' added to the last note (g')
5	S	*Tr* added to note 5 (a♭')
6	S	*Tr* added to note 5 (g)
7	S	Grace note e♭" added to the penultimate note (f")
8	S	*M* added to the middle note of the final chord
9	S	*Tr* added to note 5 (b♭')

Table *16.1.* (*continued*)

Measure	Part	Readings emended
		5. *Rondeaux*
18–20	S	*M* added to note 5 of each measure
98	S	Grace note f″ added to the 1st note
99–103	S	Slur placed above groups of three notes each
106	S	Grace note f′ added to the 1st note

Partita III (BWV 827):

Measure	Part	Readings emended
		7. *Gigue*
25	B	Notes 5 and 11: f (see note a)
27	S	Notes 5 and 11: b♭ (see note a)
	B	Notes 5 and 11: d (see note a)
34	S	Notes 5 and 11: f′ (see note a)
39	T	Note 5: a; note 10: d′ (see note b)
40	T	Note 5: g; note 10: c′ (see note b)
41	T	Note 5: f♯; note 11: b (see note b)
42	S	Notes 5 and 11: c″ (see note a)
	B	Notes 2 and 5: e (see note a)
44	S	Second quarter: the turn a″–g(g♯)″–f♯″–g(g♯)″, written out as 𝄾 ♫♫ for 𝄾 ♫ ; (see note c); last quarter: the turn b″–a″–g♯″–a″, written out as ♩ ♫♫ for ♩ ♪ ♪ (see note d)
	A	Notes 5 and 11: f′ (see note a)
45	S	*Tr* above the 1st note; second quarter: the turn d″–c(c♯)″–b′–c(c♯)″ (as in m. 44, second quarter), written out as ♩ ♫♫ for ♩ ♪ ♪ (see note e)
	B	Notes 5 and 11: b♭ (see note a)

a. As in G 26 and G 28, in the Hoboken Collection, Österreichische Nationalbibliothek, Vienna.

b. As in G 28; G 26 shows no correction.

c. As in G 28; in G 26 eighth notes: g♯″–a″.

d. The last two eighth notes in G 26: a″–b″; G 28 shows no correction.

e. The last two eighth notes in G 26: d″–e″; G 28 shows no correction.

Key:

S = Soprano/top part.

A = Alto/second part from the top.

T = Tenor/second part from the bottom.

B = Bass/bottom part.

Tr, *M* = Trillo, Mordent, which here are used for ∿, ∿.

black-brown ink are concerned. The same seems to apply to the small number of pencil entries,[9] since their style of writing does not markedly depart from that of the ink entries. Besides—and this may be a unique case—several pencil annotations were subsequently gone over in ink and unquestionably represent the same phase as the other ink corrections and additions, establishing the fact that the ink and pencil entries must have come from the same hand. It should be added that the annotations show, in their entirety, such a striking resemblance to those in G 23 (as well as to those of Bach's personal correction copies for Clavier-Übung II and IV)[10] that the identity of the corrector seems entirely persuasive.

Notable also are three entries in red ink, which again constitute a parallel with Bach's copy of the Goldberg Variations.[11] Involved are a correction in the penultimate measure of the Gigue from the sixth partita and the only two notations of G 25 (as well as G 23, 24, and 26) that are spelled out in letters, the tempo indications *"allegro"* and *"adagio"* in the sinfonia of the second partita (see Figure 16.1).[12] Once again, there is a certain risk in declaring them as clearly coming from Bach's hand; yet their autograph character could not with any more certainty be denied. The corrections and additions, taken in their entirety, well fit the picture of the so-called Handexemplare and of the other copies of original prints bearing authentic corrections.[13] The entries in G 25 exhibit neither paleographical nor musical characteristics of the period after 1750, as Jones (also with regard to G 24 and G 25) seems to imply.[14] Conspicuous among the added embellishments in G 25 is the frequency of grace notes, again in conformance with Bach's personal copy of the Goldberg Variations.

Figure 16.1. Partita II, Clavier-Übung I (1731), page 12: autograph addenda in copy G 25.

The total extent of text revisions may be gathered from the listing of variants in Table 16.1; in the following I shall discuss merely a selection of typical examples.

1. The concluding passage of the Andante section in the sinfonia of Partita II can be recognized in its function as a transition to the fugue section, even without a given tempo indication. Yet the added tempo markings reveal very definite intentions as to declamation and structuring; they identify a quicker and slower phrase each, which would not be necessarily understood as such (Ex. 16.1). Added to this is the more highly defined rhythmic formation for

Example 16.1.

Example 16.2.

the second quarter of m. 29,[15] which, in its correspondence to the ending of the figure on the preceding quarter-note value, shows an obvious improvement as compared with the uncorrected version of the engraving and that given in the *Neue Bach-Ausgabe;* it seems also to agree well with the entry of a trill (*accent u. trillo,* according to the ornamentation table in the Clavierbüchlein for Wilhelm Friedemann Bach) found only in G 25.[16] The entire revision in G 25 offers welcome directions for the realization of this passage in performance.

2. The embellishments entered in the Courante of Partita II serve to emphasize the *style brisé* manner of this movement and to accentuate its rhythmic structure (Ex. 16.2). The imitative treatment of the opening motif (mm. 1–2, upper voice of right and left hands, respectively) is heightened by the added grace note for the last of the eighth notes, as is the stress given to the melodic high point through the aid of the mordent. The musical inconsistency of the text given by Jones is borne out in that, with disregard

Example 16.3.

Example 16.4.

for the motivic imitation expressed by the placing of all embellishments for
mm. 1 and 2 in G 25, only the mordent of measure 2 is included (since it is
the only one contained in G 23, designated as the authoritative Handexemplar).

3. The most serious flaw of text criticism occurs in the second half of the
Gigue in Partita II. Whereas all other corrections in G 25 belong to the
category of musical *executio,* here we are clearly concerned with a further step
toward compositional *elaboratio.* In accordance with the contrapuntal conception of the fugato setting, the second half of the Gigue is based upon the

inversion of the theme presented in the first half. The original print of 1731, like the earlier version of the third partita in the Clavier-Büchlein for Anna Magdalena Bach of 1725, shows the two thematic beginnings as shown in Example 16.3. The inversion is not strictly carried out, but the second and fourth quarter groups, respectively, correspond to one another in the leading-tone function g♯–a (in A minor) and d♯–e (in E minor). The correction in G 25, cleanly adjusted to the appearance of the engraving (see Figure 16.2), restores the exact "thema inversum." It leads to a series of further changes in non-thematic contrapuntal lines (for example, in mm. 27 and 41–42), among which those in measures 44 and 46 are the most striking (Ex. 16.4). Through the revision of the inverted theme arise more cogent modulations to D minor (mm. 27ff.), to A minor (mm. 34ff.), and to E minor (mm. 42ff.); in addition, the sixteenth-note figuration in measures 44 and 46 fits smoothly into the 12/8 motion, resulting in a certain rhythmic climax toward its end.

The change in the thematic material, which is also handed down through the manuscripts G 26 and G 28[17] and thus receives important documentary

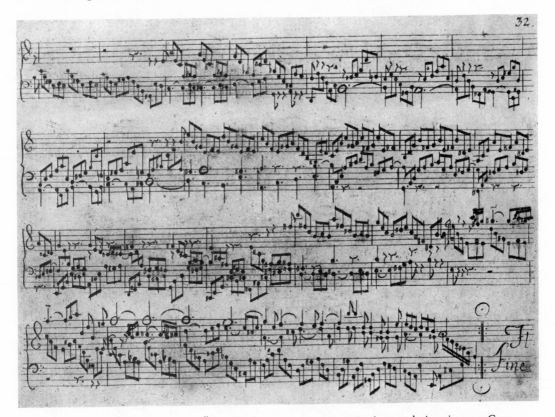

Figure 16.2. Partita III, *Clavier-Übung* I (1731), page 32: autograph emendations in copy G 25.

support, establishes a later version, not fashioned before the appearance of the second, undated edition of Clavier-Übung I.[18] Evidently the "Fassung letzter Hand" (that is, representing the composer's definitive version), this revision does not necessarily invalidate the older form. But it takes its place next to it as a variant which is to be accorded validity and which proves that contrapuntal logic, wherever it might seem indicated and appropriate even within the liberal stylistic domain of the suite, remains a mandate for Bach.

17

Bach's Leipzig Chamber Music

BACH THE CANTOR and Bach the capellmeister are usually seen in opposition to one another. Traditionally this view focused on the differences between Bach's activities and creative output as Hofcapellmeister in Cöthen (1717–1723) on the one hand, and as "Cantor & Director Musices" in Leipzig from 1723 on the other. Hence, with apparent logic, Bach's repertoire of chamber compositions has generally been considered to have originated largely in conjunction with his six-year capellmeistership at the Cöthen court. Bach biography for a long time has taken the extremely schematic view that Bach's career is to be divided, essentially, into three periods: the years as organist from Lüneburg to Weimar (1700–1717), the time as capellmeister in Cöthen (1717–1723), and finally the twenty-seven years as cantor at St. Thomas's in Leipzig. On a strict analogy between Bach's current post and his output,[1] his compositional activities supposedly reflected more or less accurately his official responsibilities, so that his chamber music would quite naturally fall primarily into the Cöthen period. Listings of Bach's chamber compositions in Schmieder's Bach-Werke-Verzeichnis [BWV] almost mechanically, and with very few exceptions, refer to the Cöthen period as their time of origin.

That such a rigid view can no longer be upheld has become increasingly clear in recent years. The worklist in the *New Grove*[2] has therefore already introduced some notable, though insufficient, modifications to Schmieder's BWV chronology. As this essay will point out, a systematic and thorough review of this matter is long overdue. Although Bach's vocal works have been the focal point of substantial chronological revisions that have forced us to rethink major aspects of Bach's stylistic evolution, the instrumental works should not remain unaffected by these developments in Bach scholarship. For a number of reasons, however, research into the chronological problems of Bach's instrumental music has proceeded along rather restricted lines by concentrating on source-critical as well as stylistic investigations of limited repertoires (such as keyboard music, works with obbligato harpsichord, and flute sonatas) or specific genres (such as organ preludes, concertos, and suites). Although most of these studies have resulted in important findings and significant—if often hypothetical—chronological revisions,[3] we do not, as yet, possess a reliable chronological frame of reference for Bach's instrumental output in general and for his chamber music in particular.

It seems clear nevertheless that the familiar and seemingly self-explanatory synchronization of the Cöthen years with Bach's output of chamber music is a notion to which we can no longer adhere. In particular, it is Bach's activities as director of the Leipzig Collegium Musicum that have to be taken into consideration, activities which have often and misleadingly been regarded as being limited mainly to the secular cantatas and the harpsichord concertos. However, to limit Bach's involvement with chamber music in Leipzig to his years with the Collegium (1729–1741) would be as wrong as to disclaim the Cöthen period as a crucial and productive phase in his chamber music output. In the interests of a more accurately balanced biographical picture I propose to replace the deep-rooted dichotomy between cantor and capellmeister with more varied relationships between the many facets of Bach's rich personality. The attitudes and ambitions of a capellmeister penetrated Bach's tenure at St. Thomas's, although this merely complemented other lifelong characteristics of the composer's artistic mentality, which ranged widely from prodigious virtuosity to profound musical scholarship.

THE RELATIVELY SMALL number of chamber ensemble works that have been preserved—especially in the most popular trio and quartet genres—gives a deceptive picture of the original repertoire that must once have existed. The oldest list of works, compiled for the obituary notice for Johann Sebastian—drawn up shortly after his death by his son Carl Philipp Emanuel and his student Johann Friedrich Agricola[4]—mentions "various concertos for one, two, three, and four harpsichords" (the only orchestral works listed) after entry no. 15, and under no. 16 summarily: "Endlich eine Menge anderer Instrumentalsachen, von allerley Art, und für allerley Instrumente" (Finally, a mass of other instrumental pieces of all kinds and for various kinds of instruments). Apparently the material was so abundant that a more detailed specification could not be given.

The reference to "various kinds of instruments" assumes importance because the extant chamber music for two or three instruments with basso continuo or obbligato harpsichord is limited to violin, viola da gamba, and transverse flute. The importance of the violin is self-evident both from its dominating role in contemporary musical practice and the special position accorded it by Bach. However, it does not seem plausible that the transverse flute, which became important in Germany only from around 1720, should alone have represented the wind instruments in Bach's chamber sonatas. Rather, the presence of this instrument must be due to one of the many coincidences which occurred in the transmission of works after Bach's death.

In addition to the flute, the oboe and recorder hold such an important place in the scoring of Bach's vocal works that their absence from his sonatas is simply inconceivable. Furthermore, the unusually broad spectrum of instrumental sonorities displayed in the six "Brandenburg" *Concerts avec plusieurs instruments* itself suggests the use of "various kinds of instruments" for other concertos: a matter which for the time being must remain hypothetical.

To take up the other point in the obituary worklist, namely the reference to "a mass of . . . instrumental pieces," it is indeed a strange fact that, of Bach's total output of works for instrumental ensemble, a little over forty have survived, of which about sixteen exist, definitely or most probably, in two or three versions. So the basic repertoire comprises about twenty-four original compositions for various-sized ensembles, and hence the losses must have exceeded by far those in, for instance, Bach's vocal music. The reason for this state of affairs is not entirely clear, but among the contributory factors is the division of Bach's estate. The bulk of the vocal works were inherited by the elder brothers, whereas the younger sons, Johann Christoph Friedrich and Johann Christian, seem to have been the primary recipients of the chamber works. The material inherited by the younger sons has, with few exceptions, not survived.

There are two factors which appear to have influenced the survival of Bach's music: first, a selection process favoring works of original design or of special interest (for example, works with obbligato harpsichord, or the unaccompanied string compositions, BWV 1001–1006 and 1007–1012); and second, mere coincidences in the dissemination and transmission of the manuscript sources. A striking example of the latter is the survival of the Brandenburg Concertos solely in the autograph score dedicated to Margrave Christian Ludwig: had we depended on the distribution of Bach's estate alone, the collection as a whole would probably have been lost.

It is virtually impossible to find information on the original size of Bach's chamber music repertoire that is even remotely reliable. One has to assume that Bach began to write ensemble sonatas and similar works in order to supplement his personal collection of works by other composers, such as the trio sonatas of Albinoni, Corelli, Legrenzi, or Reinken. Moreover, quite apart from personal taste and his training in the context of a professional musical family, Bach's first positions at court in Weimar (in 1703 as well as from 1708–1717) were largely concerned with chamber music. Here he must have enjoyed many opportunities not only to participate in the performance of chamber music, but also to produce a substantial number of sonatas and concertos. However, there is hardly enough extant material even to speculate about Bach's early, pre-Cöthen, chamber works. The earliest extant piece might be the Fugue in G Minor for Violin and Continuo BWV 1026, the only source of which is a copy, ca. 1710, in the hand of Johann Gottfried Walther.[5] As for Bach's pre-Cöthen concertos, no sources survive and stylistic argument has been fierce: there can be no firm conclusions.

The years as capellmeister at Cöthen have always been considered the classic period of Bach's chamber music activities, and they must indeed have represented a point of culmination in this area. Nevertheless, a closer scrutiny of those years reveals that problems occurred which led Bach, as early as 1720–1721, to seek positions in Hamburg and Berlin. Reductions in the personnel and, apparently, the budget of the court capelle prompted him to invest less in the production of works for larger ensembles such as the Brandenburg Concertos and to turn, instead, to solo and, primarily, keyboard composition.[7]

One traditional misconception in Bach biography is the view that Bach's move to Leipzig coincided with a fundamental shift of emphasis from instrumental toward vocal composition. Despite Bach's serious, primary commitment to the creation of a cantata repertoire for the Leipzig churches, fulfilling the desire of the town councillors for Bach to treat his duties as those of a capellmeister rather than those of a schoolmaster, evidence strongly suggests that he continued to engage in instrumental performance and composition. So his appointment in 1729 as director of the Collegium Musicum was but a logical step.[8]

This Collegium Musicum, a bourgeois concert enterprise drawing on university student musicians and both amateur and professional forces, had been founded in 1702 by Georg Philipp Telemann (then music director at the Neukirche, Leipzig) and was subsequently directed by his successors at the Neukirche, Melchior Hoffmann (1704–1715), Johann Gottfried Vogler (1716–1720), and Georg Balthasar Schott (1720–1729). After Schott's departure from Leipzig to Gotha in March 1729, Bach assumed the organizational and artistic leadership. What had hitherto been known as the "Telemannische Collegium Musicum" soon gained an even more distinguished reputation as the famous "Bachische Collegium Musicum."[9] It clearly represented the focus of Bach's activities for well over a decade until the death (30 May 1741) of the long-time host of the Collegium concerts, coffee-house owner Gottfried Zimmermann. Shortly after Bach's retirement the Collegium reorganized itself under the direction of Bach's former student and assistant Carl Gotthelf Gerlach (music director at the Neukirche) as Neues Concert, the immediate forerunner of the Gewandhaus Concerte and perhaps the most distinguished series of public concerts in eighteenth-century Germany.

An important question is whether or not Bach already played a role, perhaps even a decisive one, in the Collegium Musicum before the year 1729; although documentation is unclear, circumstantial evidence may well point in that direction. Such evidence includes the composition of some chamber works dating from before 1729, shown in Table 17.1, as well as a notable emphasis on large-scale orchestral sinfonias to the cantatas between 1726 and 1729, which probably required the participation of the Collegium Musicum.[10] Perhaps the most revealing document, however, is the reference in the Leipzig academic chronicle to Bach's first official cantata performance on

30 May 1723: he is mentioned there as "der neue Cantor u. Collegii Musici Direct."[11] Even allowing for the possibility of journalistic error, such a comment is not without significance.

THE COLLEGIUM MUSICUM was without a doubt the principal forum for Bach's chamber music activities in Leipzig. Indeed, our knowledge of the frequency and general schedule of performances is in marked contrast to our lack of certainty about the details of Bach's direction of activities at Cöthen. The Leipzig Collegium offered its concerts on a very regular basis: once a week on Fridays at the Zimmermannische Coffee-Haus (during the summer in the afternoon from four until six, and on winter evenings from eight until ten) and twice weekly on Tuesdays and Fridays during the weeks of the spring and autumn trade fairs. The programs of these *Ordinaire Concerten* are unknown, but they must have consisted largely of a variety of solo and ensemble instrumental music as well as vocal chamber pieces. The Collegium performances of large-scale congratulatory or dedicatory secular cantatas took place as *Extra-ordinaire Concerten* on specific occasions, such as the visit of a member of the Dresden electoral family. Among the vocal compositions which must have belonged to the Collegium's repertory are the *dramma per musica*, "Der Streit zwischen Phoebus und Pan" BWV 201 (1729), Bach's "aesthetic credo" from the initial phase of his Collegium activities, and also the so-called Coffee Cantata BWV 211 (1734–1735), a work not without promotional interest for Zimmermann's coffee-house.

The Collegium concerts often featured guest artists, and it is very likely that most of the musicians who reportedly came to visit Bach in the 1730s (including Johann Adolph Hasse and Faustina Bordoni, Silvius Leopold Weiss, and others)[12] also made appearances there. Vocal and instrumental pieces by a great variety of composers must have been included. Traceable among the surviving pertinent performing materials are, for example, compositions by Johann Bernhard Bach,[13] George Frideric Handel,[14] Pietro Locatelli,[15] and Nicola Porpora.[16] Further, Bach's name can be found on the list of subscribers to Telemann's flute quartets (Paris, 1738),[17] and one can safely assume that it was in Bach's interest to supply the Collegium with the best of the newest music available to him. The central repertory for the *Ordinaire Concerten*, however, must have comprised Bach's own compositions, mainly works for keyboard and instrumental ensemble. While it may be accepted that most, if not all, of Bach's keyboard pieces from at least 1729 to 1741 (Clavier-Übung I and II to the Well-Tempered Clavier II and the Goldberg Variations) were presented at Collegium events, it is the second group—chamber ensemble works—that we shall examine in closer detail in order to determine the extent of the surviving materials and, as far as possible, a chronology.

Table 17.1 lists all the works for instrumental ensemble whose extant sources are certainly, or possibly, of Leipzig origin. It becomes clear imme-

Table *17.1*. Bach's Leipzig works for instrumental ensemble

BWV	Title, key	Scoring	Date (approximate)	Watermark type (see Weiss)
	Sonatas			
1014–19	b, A, E, c, f, G	vn, hpd	completed ca. 1725[a]	—
1021	G	vn, bc	1732–35[b]	no. 121
1023	e	vn, bc	after 1723[c]	—
1027–29	G*, D*, g*	va da gamba, hpd	1736–41 (G, from BWV 1039)	no. 67
1030–33	b*, E♭, A, C*	fl, hpd	ca. 1736 (C), 1730–34 (E♭), ca. 1736 (b, A)[d]	nos. 46, 56, 122
1034–35	e, E	fl, bc	ca. 1724 (e), 1741 (E)[e]	—
1038	G*	fl, vn, bc	1732–35 (bc from BWV 1021)	no. 121
1039	G	2 fl, bc	1736–41	no. 62
	Concertos			
1041	a	vn; str, bc	ca. 1730	nos. 56, 122
1043	d	2 vn; str, bc	ca. 1730–31	no. 122
1044	a*	fl, vn, hpd; str, bc	1729–41[f]	—
1052–56 and 1058	d*, E*, D*, A*, f*, g*	hpd; str, bc	completed ca. 1738 (D, from BWV 1042; g, from BWV 1041), 1734 (D: BWV 1052), ca. 1737 (A)	nos. 48, 63
1057	F**	hpd, 2 rec; str, bc	ca. 1738–39 (from BWV 1049)[g]	—
1060	c*	2 hpds; str, bc	ca. 1736	[see *NBA* VII/7, *Krit. Bericht*]
1061	C	2 hpds; str, bc	1732–35	121
1062	c*	2 hpds; str, bc	ca. 1736 (from BWV 1043)	86, 95
1063	d*	3 hpds; str, bc	ca. 1730	[see *NBA* VII/6, *Krit. Bericht*]
1064	C*	3 hpds; str, bc	1729–41	[see *NBA* VII/6, *Krit. Bericht*]
1065	a*	4 hpds; str, bc	ca. 1730 (after Vivaldi)[h]	no. 122

diately that this repertory represents the bulk of the known chamber music of Bach and, thereby, raises some rather crucial questions. For example, where is the necessary source-critical evidence for what is generally considered Bach's Cöthen and pre-Cöthen ensemble chamber music? Positive evidence relating to the Cöthen period is indeed limited to the Brandenburg Concertos and for the pre-Cöthen years to the Fugue, BWV 1026. There are no further pre-Leipzig autograph manuscripts, which, coupled with the absence of any relevant scribal copies, suggests that scores and performing parts of instrumental ensemble music must, in general, have been carefully guarded during Bach's lifetime in order to prevent any unauthorized use. As

Table 17.1. *(continued)*

BWV	Title, key	Scoring	Date (approximate)	Watermark type (see Weiss)
	Suites			
1066	C	2 ob, bn, str, bc	ca. 1725[i]	no. 94
1067	b	fl; str, bc	ca. 1738–39	no. 105
1068	D	3 tpt. timp, 2 ob, str, bc	spring 1731	no. 122
1069	D*	3 tpt, timp, 3 ob, bn, str, bc	ca. 1725 (BWV 110/1), 1729–41	[see *NBA* VII/1, *Krit. Bericht*]
1079	Musical Offering	fl, 2 vn, bc, kbd	1747 (original edition)	[see *NBA* VII/1, *Krit. Bericht*]

*Entirely/partially based on earlier work(s).
**Source of pre-Leipzig work extant.
a. H.-J. Schulze, *Studien zur Bach-Überlieferung im 18. Jahrhundert* (Leipzig, 1984), pp. 110–119.
b. Dating primarily on the basis of the types of paper used by Bach; for watermark information, see Weiss.
c. Dresden, Sächsische Landesbibliothek, Mus. 2405-R-1 (copyist A of the Hofcapelle).
d. Marshall *Bach.*, pp. 201 ff.
e. Ibid.
f. See the preface by H.-J. Schulze to Peters Edition 9383 (Leipzig, 1974).
g. A. Glöckner, "Neuerkenntnisse zu J. S. Bach Aufführungskalender zwischen 1729 und 1735," *BJ* 67 (1981), pp. 66ff.; Schulze, *Studien,* pp. 143f.
h. Schulze, *Studien,* pp. 147ff.
i. Ibid., pp. 101, 122.

Key:

bc	basso continuo	rec	recorder
bn	bassoon	str	strings
fl	flauto traverso	timp	timpani
hpd	harpsichord	tpt	trumpet
keybd	keyboard instruments	va	viola
ob	oboe	vn	violin

can be shown for the Leipzig repertory, scribal copies before and even shortly after 1750 were usually limited to the inner Bach circle.

There remains the possibility of course, that some of those works surviving among post-1750 sources (such as the Violin Concerto in E Major BWV 1042) or, at least in some form, in the Leipzig repertory itself (such as some of the models for the harpsichord concertos or also those for the organ trio sonatas BWV 525–530) were composed at Cöthen or earlier. However, for the time being only stylistic criteria can help to differentiate between earlier and later works; and furthermore, these criteria must be applied primarily to works which have not come down to us in their original version. Since Bach usually made considerable adjustments and changes whenever he reworked a piece, it becomes extremely difficult to define stylistic details of a lost original version. Nevertheless, Bach scholars have been rather generous in allocating lost sonatas and concertos to the Weimar and Cöthen periods, so that a careful reappraisal is in order.

The chronology presented in the table primarily reflects datings on the basis of performing materials, since autograph scores have survived only for some exceptional items, namely the harpsichord concertos BWV 1052–1058 and the harpsichord-flute sonatas BWV 1030 and 1032, all of which, being genuine working scores, show a considerable amount of compositional activity. Thus the time of origin can be fixed, at least in relation to the earlier sonatas and concertos of which they are reworkings.

Bach's involvement with the Collegium prior to 1729 remains an open question, though he obviously composed and performed instrumental ensemble works. The sonatas for violin and harpsichord may well, in part, have originated in Cöthen; however, the completion of the set and also the composition of the most mature pieces (such as the B Minor Sonata) most certainly occurred in Leipzig. The two E Minor Continuo Sonatas BWV 1023 and 1034 also seem to belong to the early Leipzig years, although there is no source evidence to corroborate this. However, for the orchestral Suites nos. 1 and 4, BWV 1066 and 1069, respectively, original sources do exist. At the least, they confirm early Leipzig performances, but neither suggests nor excludes a Leipzig origin. Although not datable on the basis of the manuscript sources, the Triple Concerto BWV 1044 and the later version of BWV 1069 would both, on general grounds, belong more naturally to the earlier rather than the later 1730s.

The extant original sources of some of Bach's Leipzig chamber music provide us with some welcome material regarding performance practice, particularly in regard to articulation. However, I should like to single out the only surviving set of original parts for one of Bach's harpsichord concertos. The parts for the A Major Concerto BWV 1055 had been used for the Bach-Gesellschaft edition, but they were not available for nearly thirty-five years after the Second World War. They reveal some important details about Bach's continuo practice that cannot be gathered from the autograph score.

First, Bach wrote out a figured "Continuo" part (see Figure 17.1), indicating a presence of a second harpsichord for continuo purposes (a function that it seems unlikely could be fulfilled by a lute or any other instrument). It would be logical to conclude that this would also be required for the other harpsichord concertos, since there is no reason why this concerto should represent an exception rather than the norm. In fact, this practice is also supported by the evidence in the cantatas with obbligato organ, where we also find separate figured continuo parts. Second, Bach differentiated carefully between the participating basso continuo instruments by designating a separate violone part (presumably harpsichord and violoncello shared the continuo part). This "Violone" part (see Figure 17.2) is no mere copy of the continuo part, but shows that the violone participates primarily in the tutti passages. Again, there seems to be no reason why this registral differentiation between 16′ and 8′ should not also apply to the other harpsichord concertos for which we have no original parts.

IT WOULD BE MISLEADING to assume that Bach's composition and performance of chamber music during his Leipzig period would have been limited to the Collegium. Although the latter was, undeniably, the focal point of his activities for well over a decade, there were numerous other opportunities and venues for chamber music. An obvious place is Bach's home and the family circle, frequently complemented or amplified by students, colleagues, and friends. What Bach describes in his 1730 letter to Erdmann ("I can assure you that I can already form an ensemble both *vocaliter* and *instrumentaliter* within my family")[18] is essentially a new situation that developed only in Leipzig. While we can be sure that Bach also performed chamber music at home with relatives, friends, and professional colleagues during his pre-Leipzig years, by 1730 the elder sons had become professional musicians in their own right, and at the same time Bach was surrounded by an ever-increasing number of excellent students and assistants, some of whom even lived with him. The incentive and need for chamber music had never before been greater.

The same is true for Bach's activities as a traveling virtuoso, which increased substantially during his Leipzig years, particularly with regard to his formal responsibilities as honorary capellmeister at Cöthen (from 1723), Weißenfels (from 1729), and Dresden (from 1736). Of special significance must have been his connections with the musicians of the Electoral court, which certainly predate his 1736 appointment and which were clearly intensified after Wilhelm Friedemann Bach obtained a position at Dresden in 1733, the year in which Bach dedicated the Missa in B Minor to the Elector and offered to compose not only church pieces but specifically music "*zum Orchestre*."[19] It is probably not just a coincidence that the last two datable chamber works by Bach, the Flute Sonata in E Major (1741) and the Musical Offering (1747), originated in connection with Bach's visiting a court as a distinguished guest performer: in both cases the court of Frederick the Great in Berlin.

To summarize, the Leipzig years provided Bach with ample opportunity to broaden the scope of his chamber music beyond his work in Cöthen, through the Collegium Musicum, the circle of family, students, and friends, and finally through involvements outside Leipzig. The traditional view of the Cöthen capellmeister years as the principal, if not exclusive, period of Bach's writing chamber music clearly seems based on false premises. As to the question of the Leipzig origin of chamber music works, we must differentiate between two categories: (1) compositions which are reworkings of pre-Leipzig works and (2) compositions newly written in Leipzig. The first

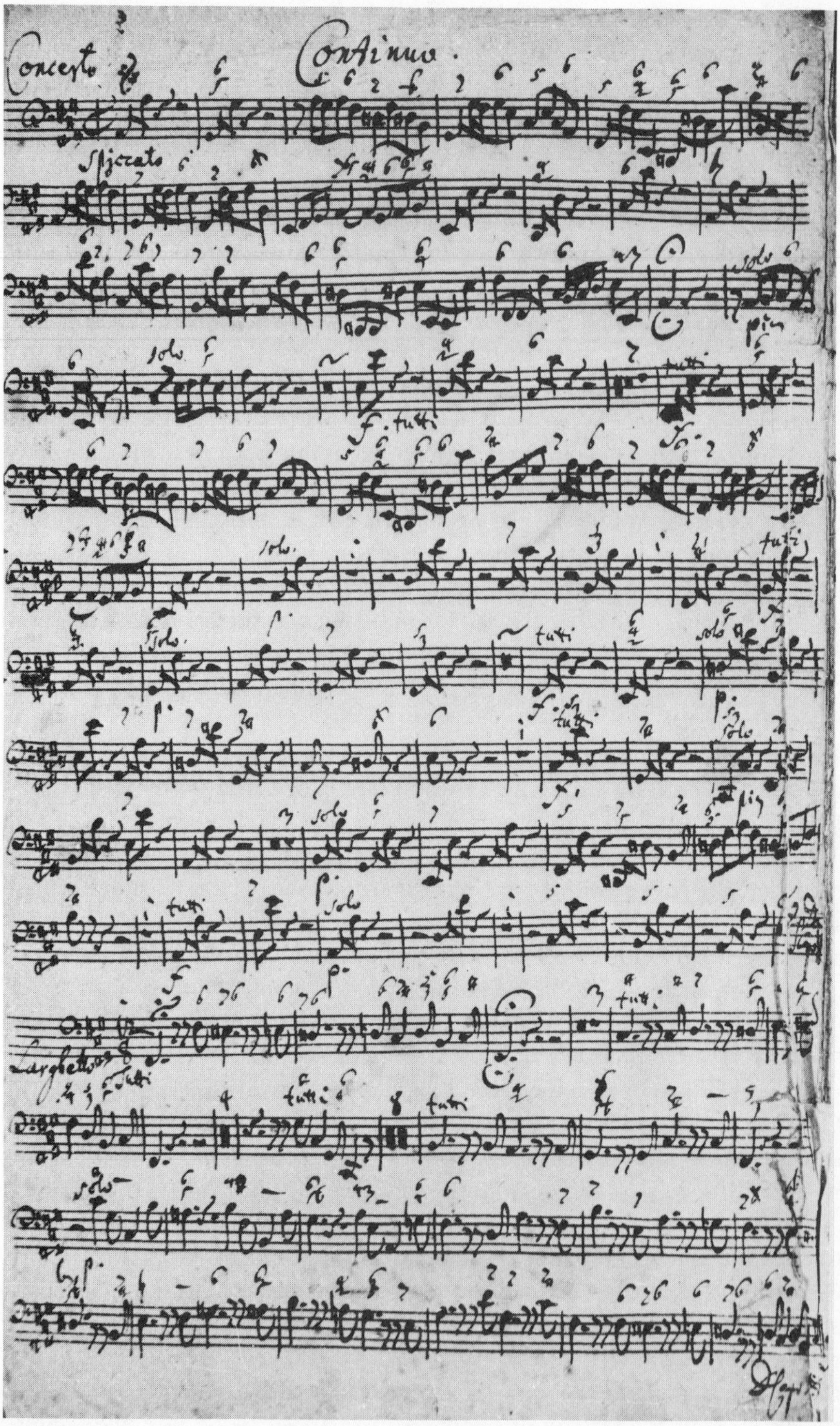

Figure 17.1. Harpsichord Concerto in A Major BWV 1055: autograph continuo part, page 1.

Figure 17.2. Harpsichord Concerto in A Major BWV 1055: violone part, page 1 (with autograph heading and revisions).

category, however difficult to define, is by no means a negligible quantity. Most of the harpsichord concertos appear to be part of this group, although evidence for a Cöthen origin exists only in the case of BWV 1057, and the earlier cantata sinfonia versions of BWV 1052 and 1053 are at least strongly suggestive of pre-Leipzig origins. It is also clear that the Leipzig transcriptions of earlier works incorporate a considerable degree of compositional reshaping, including stylistic adjustments, making detailed reconstructions of lost models extremely difficult. Of most importance, with respect to Bach's ever-changing creative orientation, are those compositions of the second category, not based on any pre-Leipzig versions.

I should like to single out five works which are traditionally regarded as Cöthen works but for which we possess strong source- and style-critical evidence that suggests an origin in the 1730s. A brief summary of the arguments in favor of this theory will have to suffice here.

(1) *Sonata in B Minor for Flute BWV 1030.* Robert Marshall[20] has already presented a very convincing case for the origin of this piece around 1736. With some justification he doubts a Cöthen origin for the G minor version, which he dates ca. 1729–1731 on the basis of a thematic connection with the Cantata BWV 117. Although this latter point is not particularly persuasive and, therefore, I prefer a slightly extended time scale for the G minor version (perhaps 1729–1736), it should be emphasized that the overall format of this sonata, particularly the expansive design of its first movement, has no parallel in any pre-Leipzig instrumental composition.

(2) *Sonata in G Major for Viola da Gamba BWV 1027.* In the preface to his edition,[21] Laurence Dreyfus argues for a Leipzig dating not only for this piece, but for all three sonatas for viola da gamba and harpsichord. I fully subscribe to his theories and, in particular, to his reasoning on the grounds of style (related, for instance, to the principle of the "Sonata auf Concerten-Art") that the lost trio sonatas which served as models originate from the Leipzig period. On the basis of the surviving authenticated materials for the G Major Sonata as it appears in BWV 1027 and 1039, I see no philological or stylistic merit in the common presupposition that both versions originate from an earlier model, and much less, from the Cöthen period. It seems that BWV 1027 and BWV 1039 are two different means of expressing the same idea and that they clearly belong to the same period. The older hypothesis of a common model is perpetuated primarily by the mistaken idea that Bach did not write original chamber music while in Leipzig, rather only—or at least primarily—transcriptions.

(3) *Concerto in A Minor for Violin BWV 1041* and (4) *Concerto in D Minor for Two Violins BWV 1043.* The possibility of a Leipzig origin for these concertos has, I believe, never been given serious consideration. However, for both pieces we have the original and largely autograph performing parts (see Figures 17.3 and 17.4 for the autograph manuscript of BWV 1043, charac-

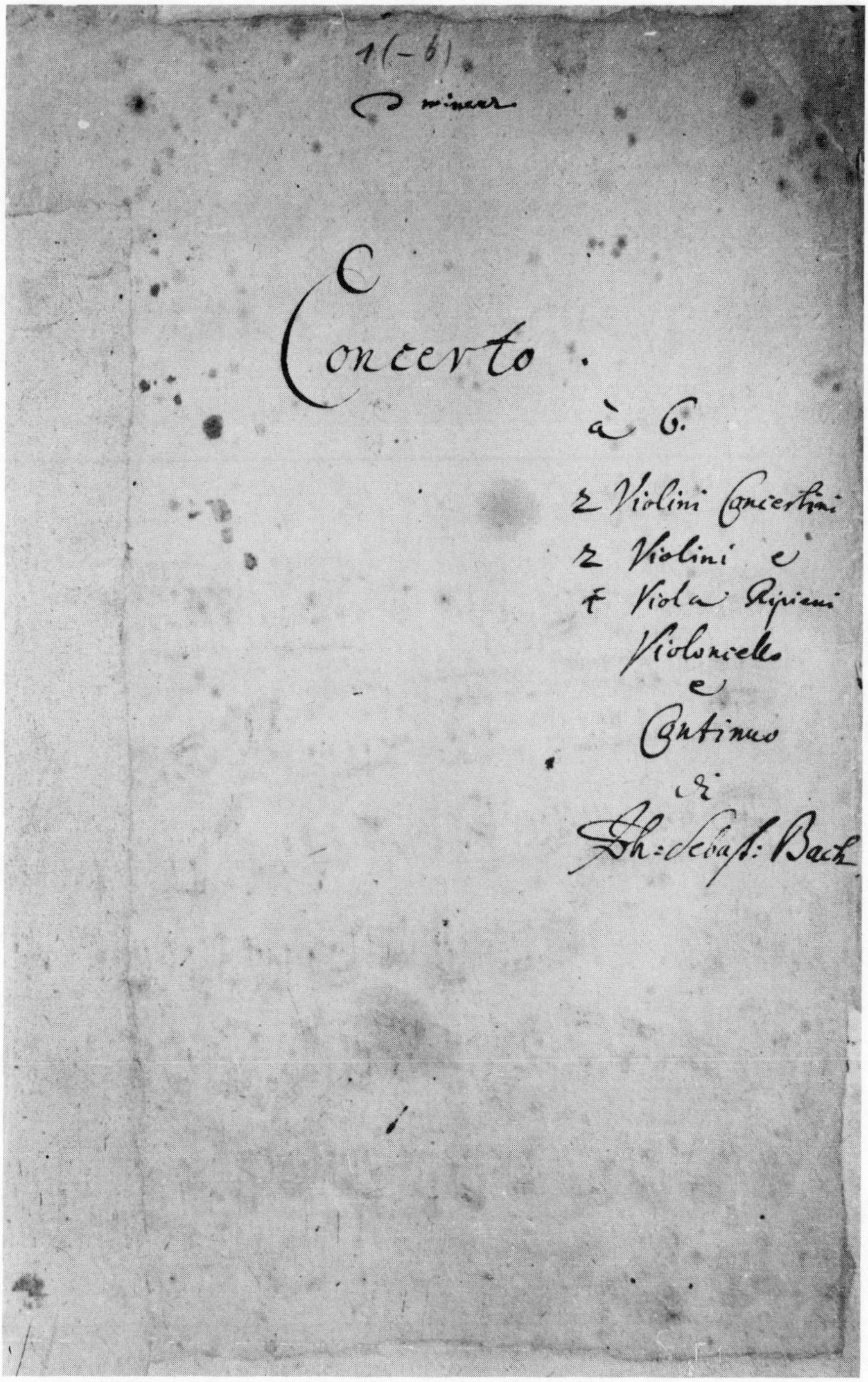

Figure 17.3. Concerto for Two Violins in D Minor BWV 1043: autograph title page.

Figure 17.4. Concerto for Two Violins in D Minor BWV 1043: autograph Violino 1 concertino part, page 1.

"OLD" SOURCES REVISITED: NOVEL ASPECTS

teristically labeled by Bach *"Concerto à 6"*), which can be dated only to the first years of Bach's Collegium Musicum activities. Had the concertos been composed in Cöthen, these parts would have to be interpreted as replacements for "lost" sets. We do not have any conclusive evidence, since neither autograph fair scores nor composing scores—which would provide definitive clues—have survived. However, there are stylistic criteria which clearly separate both concertos—BWV 1043 even more than BWV 1041—from what we know about Bach's pre-Leipzig concerto writing.

In particular, the thoroughly contrapuntal design and extent of the ritornello structure in these concertos displays a maturity of writing that may well have benefited from Bach's composition of large-scale instrumental ritornellos and sinfonias for cantatas. In this respect the A Minor Concerto differs quite significantly from its companion work, the earlier Concerto in E Major BWV 1042. Both harmonic planning and the shape and gesture of the extended melodic phrases in the slow movement of the double Concerto BWV 1043 provide further considerations which would make it very difficult to extricate this work from the context of the "progressive" style of the middle Leipzig years. It would be premature on the basis of these observations to draw any specific conclusions regarding the overall development of Bach's concerto style, but a thorough rethinking of Bach's concerto chronology in conjunction with a more sophisticated analytical approach is now necessary.

(5) *The Ouverture in B Minor BWV 1067*. A comparison of the flute parts of the fifth Brandenburg Concerto of 1721 (the early version of 1719 is probably Bach's first extant instrumental composition involving transverse flute) and BWV 1067 demonstrates immediately that there are worlds between them, but not merely on technical grounds. There is no indication that Bach experimented in Cöthen with hybrid forms combining the idea of a suite with that of a concerto, and from this point of view the B Minor Suite is clearly the latest of the four orchestral overtures. The conflation of genres in BWV 1067 seems to reflect a trend characteristic of Bach's compositional concerns in the later 1730s, namely, that of presenting unprecedented and often daring approaches to musical genres of a rather conventional nature, be it keyboard variations, a concerto, suite, sonata, organ chorale, or fugue. Apart from such general tendencies, various features of this intricate, polyphonic score—namely, a fine balance between dense and transparent textures, rhythmic refinement, and penetrating use of dissonance and consonance, especially in the Grave of the *Ouverture*—show a degree of sophistication without equal in any earlier period of Bach's creative life.

It must be emphasized that the preceding suggestions on chronology are presented as working hypotheses. In the absence of any unquestionably documented dates, they cannot be considered definitive. On the other hand, it is likely that this kind of definitive evidence may never materialize, and a chronology must be formed from an assessment of contemporary scholarship.

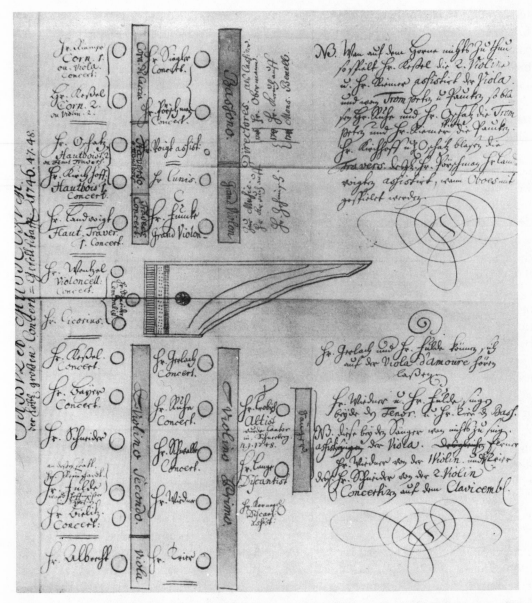

Figure 17.5. The membership and layout of the Leipzig "Große Concert-Gesellschaft" during 1746–1748, a few years after Bach's student C. G. Gerlach took over its direction.

Of course, it is impossible, as well as illegitimate, to proceed with the dating of individual works and the interpretation of stylistic developments without regard for the wider context. The purpose of this essay has been to raise precisely this issue and to stress that the wider context of Bach's chamber music unquestionably comprises the Leipzig years—all of them, and not just the Collegium Musicum period.

18

New Research on the Musical Offering

IN OUR FAMILIAR PICTURE of Johann Sebastian Bach the years of his late works are surrounded by a mysterious veil. His labors appear to be closer to heaven than earth, and so, for instance, it is said that some of his late compositions—among them the Art of Fugue and the Musical Offering—do not require any earthly instruments for their realization in sound. They rather represent pure, abstract music: *musica sui generis.* And looking behind the mysterious veil of the composer's esoteric last works becomes a kind of sacral act.

But one does not bring into question Bach's greatness by stating that this picture is more in accord with a certain ideology, idolization, and speculation than with reality. The prevailing reasons for this misconception are grounded in some basic misunderstandings which arise to a great extent from ignorance of the source material in its entirety. Despite the many valuable discoveries and contributions concerning Bach's last works, our efforts have been burdened with too many hypotheses, particularly in the case of the Musical Offering. Though the work has undergone much scholarly scrutiny, previous research was confined to only a part of the sources. Consequently, many questions had to remain open. Aiming at reliable answers to the central questions, new research has had to start with a complete re-examination of the known sources in connection with a thorough investigation of neglected or newly discovered material. I should like to present here the most important findings of the recent source studies concerning history, text, order, and performance problems of one of Bach's major late works, with particular regard to controversial issues.[1]

I

The composition of the Musical Offering was inspired by a fugue subject given by Frederick the Great to Bach when he visited the Prussian court at Potsdam in May 1747.[2] The work, consisting of two ricercari of three and six parts, a trio sonata of four movements, and ten canonic settings, is among the very few compositions of Bach that were printed in his lifetime. It was humbly dedicated to the king of Prussia and became well-known apart from the widely circulated original print,[3] in numerous manuscript copies.[4] Parts of the work, mostly canons, appeared in treatises of the later eighteenth century,[5] and unlike most compositions of Bach the entire work was even reprinted twice in the nineteenth century prior to its publication in the Bach-Gesellschaft edition.[6] But no questions were raised about the homogeneity of the work, its cyclical order, instrumentation, and chronology until Philipp Spitta critically studied its history and its nature with special attention to the original print of 1747. Most scholars more or less closely followed the basic results of Spitta's research,[7] among them (to mention only the most important) Alfred Dörffel, the editor of the Musical Offering in the Bach-Gesellschaft edition,[8] Ludwig Landshoff with his new edition and critical commentary,[9] and Georg Kinsky in his book on the original prints of Bach's works.[10] Hans Theodor David was the first one to contradict Spitta's views on some crucial points in an article published some thirty years ago in the *Musical Quarterly*[11] and later on in a remarkable monograph supplementing his practical edition of the Musical Offering.[12] There he laid the foundation for later, smaller studies by Rudolf Gerber[13] and Wilhelm Pfannkuch.[14]

The many arguments about the Musical Offering in the Bach literature to the present day, making this one of the most difficult and delicate issues in Bach research concerning a single work, boil down to the following essential questions: (1) What is the explanation for the peculiar and puzzling arrangement of the original print? (2) Is the work conceived as a unity? (3) What is the original order of the pieces? (4) What instruments are required for the performance? The first question is undoubtedly the central one and its answer determines the solution to most of the others. The print of 1747 offers the key for understanding as well as for misunderstanding the work. According to the critical investigations since Spitta, the structure and layout of the original print has been described as follows (see Table 18.1 and Figs. 18.1, 18.2, and 18.4–18.6).[15]

The original print consists of five separate sections or printing units (the letters A–E serve as reference codes to them) that show a great deal of inconsistency, especially in the use of different formats (A, B, E: oblong; C, D: upright), pagination (B: 1–4; C: 1–4; E: 1–7), and numbering (D: canons numbered 1–5). Section A, containing the title and preface (dedication), was printed by Breitkopf in Leipzig. The bulk of the print containing the musical pieces was engraved by Johann Georg Schübler in Zella as his signature on the bottom of page 7 in E shows. B embodies the three-part ricercar followed by a single canon; C, the three instrumental parts of the trio and another single canon; D, a group of five canons and a canonic fugue with the acrostic printed on a small strip of paper and pasted on the blank folio 1 recto; and E, the six-part ricercar and two more canons.

The traditional source description, as well as all source studies, was based exclusively on the following copies of the original print: the so-called dedi-

Table 18.1. Traditional description of the original print

New sigla	Lieferung (Spitta)	Section (David)	Paper format	Folio	Original pagination	BWV	Contents
A	I	—[a]	oblong	1r		1079	*Musicalisches Opfer . . .* (title)
				1v			(blank)
				2r			*Allergnädigster König . . .* (preface)
				2v			*bewerkstelliget worden . . .* (preface continued)
B	I	1	oblong	1r			(blank)
				1v	1	1	*Ricercar à 3,* mm. 1–60a
				2r	2		mm. 60b–110
				2v	3		mm. 111–156
				3r	4	2	mm. 157–185; *Canon perpetuus super Thema Regium*
				3v			(blank)
D	I	2	upright	1r			*Regis Iussu Cantio Et Reliqua Canonica Arte Resoluta*
				1v		3	*Canones diversi super Thema Regium*
						a	*1. à 2* (cancrizans)
						b	*2. à 2 Violin: in Unisono*
						c	*3. à 2 per Motum contrarium*
						d	*4. à 2 per Augmentationem, contrario Motu*
						e	*5. à 2* (per tonos)
						4	*Fuga canonica in Epidiapente,* mm. 1–9a
				2r			mm. 9b–78
				2v			(blank)
C	III	3	upright	1–2	1–4	8,9	*Traversa.* (Trio[b]); *Canon perpetuus*
				1–2	1–4	8,9	*Violino.* (Trio[b]); *Canon perpetuus*
				1–2	1–4	8,9	*Continuo.* (Trio[b]); *Canon perpetuus*
E	II	4	oblong	1r	1	5	*Ricercar à 6,* mm. 1–17
				1v	2		mm. 18–33a
				2r	3		mm. 33b–51a
				2v	4		mm. 51b–67a
				3r	5		mm. 67b–79
				3v	6		mm. 80–95
				4r	7	6,7	mm. 96–103; *Canon à 2. Quaerendo Invenietis; Canon à 4; J. G. Schübler sc* (engraver's signature)
				4v			(blank)

a. Hans Theodor David, *J. S. Bach's Musical Offering: History, Interpretation, and Analysis* (New York, 1945), pp. 8f., assumed that the blank page at the beginning of section B was intended to receive the title and that the separately printed title (section A) was perhaps a later idea of Bach's.

b. Title unknown.

Muſicaliſches

Opfer

Sr. Königlichen Majeſtät in Preußen ꝛc.

alleruntertpänigſt gewidmet

von

Johann Sebaſtian Bach.

Figure 18.1. Musical Offering BWV 1079 (original print of 1747): section A, folio 1r.

Figure 18.2. Original print of 1747: section B, folio 1v.

"OLD" SOURCES REVISITED: NOVEL ASPECTS

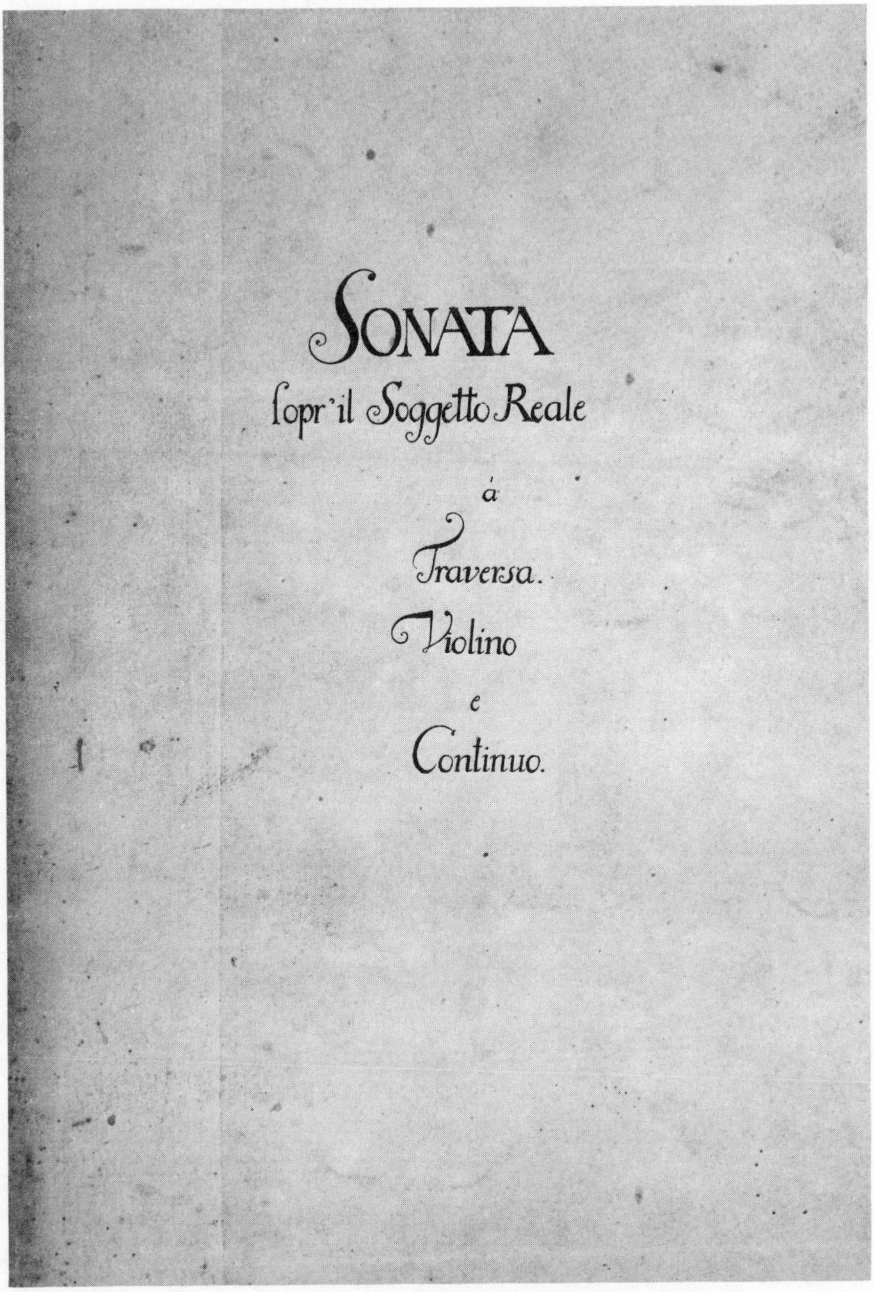

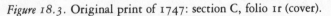

SONATA
fopr'il Soggetto Reale

à

Traversa.

Violino

e

Continuo.

Figure 18.3. Original print of 1747: section C, folio 1r (cover).

Figure 18.4. Original print of 1747: section C, folio 1r (flute part).

Regis Iussu Cantio Et Reliqua Canonica Arte Resoluta.

Figure 18.5. Original print of 1747: section D, folio 1r.

Figure 18.6. Original print of 1747: section E, folio 1r.

cation copy, which was presented to Frederick and contained all five sections (nos. 1 and 2 of Table 18.2), a second copy in Berlin with sections A, B, and E, and a third in Berlin with section C only (nos. 3 and 4 of Table 18.2). Though Kinsky[16] lists seven additional copies of the original print, nobody has ever collated them. Even David, who apparently knew the copy in the Library of Congress containing sections A, B, D, and E (no. 17 of Table 18.2),[17] did not make use of it for the chapter on textual criticism in his book.[18] Thus the dedication copy, as the only complete source, played a major role. Unlike the others, this special copy contains the sections A, B, and D on luxurious paper of unusually large size (ca. 29 × 45 cm) and fine quality; C and E, however, are of the same size and quality as the ordinary copies (ca. 22.5 × 36 cm). A and B are bound together in elegant brown leather, whereas the remainder consists of loose leaves (D and E) or bifolios (C), as Table 18.3 may demonstrate.[19]

The dedication copy also shows some calligraphic inscriptions: on folio 1 recto of B the R-I-C-E-R-C-A-R acrostic and in D on folio 1 recto (the place of the acrostic in the ordinary copies) *Thematis Regii Elaborationes Canonicae;* also in D, on folio 1 verso at the margin the complimentary annotations *Notulis crescentibus crescat Fortuna Regis* and *Ascendenteque Modulatione ascendat Gloria Regis* (belonging to canons 4 and 5). There are further differences between the dedication copy and the ordinary copies,[20] but we can disregard them here.

Spitta and his followers drew the following conclusions from their source

Table 18.2. Surviving copies of the original print

	Library	Included sections
1	DSB, Am. B. 73	A,B,D,E
2	DSB, Am. B. 74	C
3	DSB, Mus. 0.9525 R	A,B,E
4	DSB, Mus. 11531 R	D
5	Fulda, Hessische Landesbibliothek, K.W.F. 138/84	A,B,E
6	Leipzig, Musikbibliothek der Stadt Leipzig, III.6.17	A,B,D,E
7	Leipzig, Musikbibliothek der Stadt Leipzig, PM 5696	A,B,D,E
8	Munich, Bayerische Staatsbibliothek, Mus.pr. 2°,777	C
9	Vienna, Österreichische Nationalbibliothek (Hoboken Collection), Copy A	A,B,D,E
10	Vienna, Österreichische Nationalbibliothek (Hoboken Collection), Copy B	A,B,E
11	Vienna, Österreichische Nationalbibliothek (Hoboken Collection), Copy C	B,E
12	Berea (Ohio), Riemenschneider Memorial Bach Library	A,B,E
13	Bologna, Civico Museo Bibliografico, Biblioteca Musicale G.B. Martini, DD 73, 75, 76	B,C,D,E
14	The Hague, Gemeente Museum, Bach-Doos, Nr.III	B,D,E
15	London, British Library, K.10 b.28	A,B,E
16	Rochester, N.Y., Eastman School of Music, Sibley Music Library, M3.3.B 118	B,E
17	Washington, D.C., Library of Congress, M 3.3.B 2	A,B,D,E

Table 18.3. Schematic layout of the dedication copy

DSB call no.	Layout	
Am. B. 73	A + B (luxurious paper) : bound	
Am. B. 73	D (luxurious paper) : separate, annex to A + B	
Am. B. 73	E (ordinary paper) : separate, annex to A + B	
Am. B. 74	C (ordinary paper) : separate	

examinations.[21] Bach sent to Frederick in July 1747 (the preface is dated: "7. Julii 1747") a volume containing the title, the preface, and the three-part ricercar (sections A and B) bound in leather along with the two loose canon leaves (D). These three sections form the first installment (Lieferung I) of the work, the respective sections of the ordinary copies corresponding to the sections of luxurious paper in the dedication copy. "All the rest of the music which is now included under the title *Musical Offering* does not strictly speaking belong to it, but was composed by Bach afterwards and sent to the king without any formal dedication."[22] Therefore the sections C and E of the dedication copy consist of the same ordinary paper as all the other copies.

According to Spitta, E formed the second and C the third installment, which were issued in the later months of 1747 or possibly in 1748. "As the whole collection now exists it is a strange conglomerate of pieces, lacking not only internal connection but external uniformity. . . . In this work Bach renounced the introduction of any comprehensive idea which would unify the separate artistic creations."[23] While most later authors agree with Spitta's view about the sources, they believe in the possibility of a hidden artistic concept unifying the entire work despite the peculiar and disconcerting layout of the original print, and this they take as a point of departure for the construction of grand hypotheses on the internal and external order of the Musical Offering and as justification for all sorts of arrangements for practical performances.[24]

David also emphasizes throughout his book the structure, scope, and integration of the work as a whole; he is, however, the first scholar to oppose strongly Spitta's source interpretation and correct some of the latter's conclusions regarding the dedication copy. For example, he proves that the leather binding was not provided by Bach but done much later for the library of Princess Anna Amalia, Frederick's sister. Thus the main argument for Spitta's so-called Lieferungstheorie was based on the wrong assumption, at least so far as sections A, B, D, and E are concerned. David offers, in addition, a new hypothesis to explain the change of paper quality in the dedication copy, suggesting that this might be the result of a lack of fine paper furnished by the Prussian court for the print. He also points out that the odd and messy appearance of the print must have been primarily Schübler's fault rather than Bach's, because Schübler tried to save expenses by filling empty spaces left on the plates (for example, at the end of the two ricercari) with canons, misunderstanding Bach's intentions and mixing up the originally well-planned order. "Schübler tried hard to do his best although he did not realize that here for once the order of movements in a collection of independent compositions was a matter of importance."[25]

II

David's plausible arguments for the artistic unity of Bach's conception as evident in the "original" comprehensive structure and order must remain hypotheses too, as long as they fail to explain major details of the appearance of the original print. For instance, why does it have separate pagination for sections B and E? Could Schübler really have so mixed up the work without Bach's having corrected it in proof? As a possible solution for this question it was suggested that the Musical Offering was published piecemeal (the installment theory) so that its individual sections could be sold separately.[26] But why then is the composer's name found only on the title page and not at the beginning of each section? The distribution and sale of pieces without mention of the author is unthinkable. Finally, the explanation has been offered that Bach obviously intended to publish the work with a deliberate lack of order, rather like a puzzle corresponding to the enigmatic notation of the canons. In this connection Bach's use of the term *ricercar* (Italian for "to search/research") was understood as an important hint.[27] But why then the clear original numbering 1 to 5 of the canons in section D?

The list of questions and doubts is indeed endless, because explanations of the odd appearance of the print still remain unsatisfactory despite so many sharp-witted and penetrating attempts. The failure arose from the methodological assumption that collating all traceable copies of the same print was unnecessary. But it is now common knowledge that source criticism often meets the same difficulties with original printings as it does with original manuscripts—as in the case of the Frescobaldi sources. Since all previous editions and studies of the Musical Offering have used as a basis only the Berlin copies with their varying states of completeness and incompleteness, they came inevitably to erroneous conclusions. The weakness of this basis can be fully realized only after collating the eighteen extant copies (see Table 18.2), eleven of which were already listed by Kinsky.[28] The total number of copies per section is: eleven for A, fourteen for B, three for C, eight for D, and fourteen for E.

The existence of three copies of the trio parts is surprising, since copies of this section of the Musical Offering have been considered lost.[29] The two unknown copies provide an original engraved title cover for the trio, which the Berlin copy does not have. Here we learn for the first time the full title for the piece that was cautiously entitled "Trio" in the Bach-Gesellschaft edition: *Sonata sopr' il Soggetto Reale a Traversa, Violino e Continuo*. The title cover for the sonata parts forms a bifolio and belongs as such to section C:

upright format, fol. 1r: *Sonata* . . . (title)
              fol. 1v: blank
              fol. 2r: blank
              fol. 2v: blank

Of similar importance was the discovery that one copy (Table 18.2, no. 9) shows section A consisting of a bifolio, the title and preface on one piece of paper with the fold on the upper long side. All other copies of section A were cut on the fold for binding purposes in the later eighteenth, nineteenth, or even twentieth century, thus destroying the original layout. In some copies section D, which also formed originally a bifolio, suffered the same mutilation.

It follows that the 1747 print must have shown uncut bifolios for A, C, and D, as well as loose single leaves for B and E. This can be verified by checking the paper and its watermarks in all copies. without going into the details here,[30] the three diverse uses of the paper for the printing can be described as in Figure 18.7 (X and Y marking the two folios of a double leaf).

This at first puzzling use of double and single leaves in oblong and upright position actually turns out to be very efficient. We have three unbound fascicles arranged in the following manner: A functions as main title for the

DOUBLE LEAVES (BIFOLIOS)

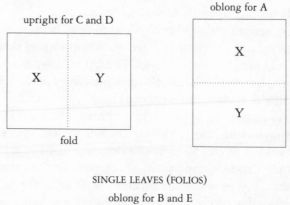

upright for C and D

oblong for A

X   Y

X

Y

fold

SINGLE LEAVES (FOLIOS)

oblong for B and E

X   Y

Figure 18.7. The different paper sizes used in the 1747 print.

entire work and provides the cover for B. Now we really understand the preface, which strangely enough mentions only the three-part ricercar and none of the other settings, thus demonstrating that these two items (A and B) belong together. Section C, the second fascicle, contains in a title cover the parts of the sonata. The publication of the sonata in parts was much better for practical use than a score would have been. For this reason Bach gave up the printing of an open score, which would have facilitated the publication of the entire Musical Offering in a simple standard volume like the Clavier-Übungen, the Schübler Chorales, or the Art of Fugue. D is the third title cover, containing E. The acrostic[31] functions as a subtitle explaining that the enclosed six-part ricercar represents the piece that the king wanted Bach to play after he finished the three-part fugue. But not daring to improvise a six-part keyboard fugue on the complicated royal theme, Bach chose a subject himself[32] and delivered the required piece later with the ingenious words of the acrostic: "At the king's command, the song [referring to the fugue] and the remainder [referring to the canons of section D] resolved with canonic art." The fascicle structure also explains the use of three independent paginations for the two ricercari and the sonata.

What seemed previously only peculiar now appears as an admirable solution to the difficult assignment of finding an appropriate way to publish a work which represents a mixed repertoire of keyboard and ensemble pieces, a problem which Bach and his printers did not face when planning the publication of pure keyboard music. There was no piecemeal delivery of the separate sections of the work, no errors by the engraver, no puzzle, and no mysterious intentions, but, on the contrary, a very smart and practical layout (the arrangement shown in Table 18.4).

It is necessary to return briefly to the special case of the dedication copy mentioned above.[33] In addition to David's findings it can be shown that the present sections E and C did not originally belong to the dedication copy but apparently were later replacements for the lost originals. These must also have been printed on luxurious paper like the present sections A, B, and D, but they were somehow lost, very probably before the dedication copy was given to the library of Princess Amalia. The fine paper used for this special copy was available only in single sheets and not in bifolios. Thus there was no possibility for forming three fascicles with separate title covers as in the ordinary copies. We see now the reasons for the different makeup and particularly for the handwritten inscriptions that are to be found only in the dedication copy. Since the fascicle structure was inapplicable and consequently the acrostic could no longer function as subtitle for the third fascicle, Bach put the acrostic on the blank folio 1 recto of section B, at the beginning of the entire work. He obviously did not want to abandon the brilliant idea of the acrostic. Because the paper strip with the engraved acrostic was disproportionately small for the large folio, the calligraphic handwriting was substituted. As a result of this shift, folio 1 recto of section D received a new inscription avoiding any reference to the six-part ricercar, namely, *Thematis Regii Elaborationes Canonicae.*

Table 18.4. Arrangement of fascicles in the 1747 print

Fascicle 1		
	A: fol. 1	Title: *Musicalisches Opfer . . .*
	B: fol. 1	
	fol. 2	Ricercar à 3, Canon (pp. 1 – 4)
	fol. 3	
	A: fol. 2	Dedication (preface)
Fascicle 2		
	C: fol. 1	Subtitle: *Sonata . . .*
	fol. 1	Traversa (pp. 1 – 4)
	fol. 2	
	fol. 1	Violino (pp. 1 – 4)
	fol. 2	
	fol. 1	Continuo (pp. 1 – 4)
	fol. 2	
	fol. 2	
Fascicle 3		
	D: fol. 1	Subtitle: *Regis Iussu . . ./Canons*
	E: fol. 1	
	fol. 2	
	fol. 3	Ricercar à 6, Canons (pp. 1 – 7)
	fol. 4	
	D: fol. 2	

One of the crucial points in connection with the original print has always been the date of the composition and publication. Spitta surmised that several months or perhaps a year elapsed from the first to the last installment. David rejected this, but he himself remained unclear about the chronology. Three exact dates have been known for a long time: 7 May 1747, the day of the visit in Potsdam, as the *terminus post quem;* 7 July, the date of the preface; 10 July, a date in the records of Breitkopf saying that Bach had to pay two Thaler and twelve Groschen for two hundred copies of a title "Musicalisches Opfer genannt."[34] But these dates do not indicate when the publication actually appeared.

The engraved sections show without any doubt that the printing was done hurriedly. For example, we find an unusual number of unclean spots on the pages, originating from scratches on the plates where the engraver's tools slipped. If there had been time, the flaws could easily have been corrected on the plates before printing began. More important, however, is the fact that there also was obviously no time to correct mistakes in the musical text. Thus the final proofreading took place after the plates went to press, the corrections being made in handwriting with brown ink. Most of these corrections as well as many other details about the engraving (etching) have not yet been noted.[35] Here, too, only the collation of all extant copies could yield satisfactory findings.

The proofreading and correcting procedures show how hastily the edition was prepared and published. Furthermore, the paper proves that the printing was done in one working procedure and, surprisingly, not at two different places but obviously at one, since the paper used for section A (set up in type by Breitkopf in Leipzig) and for the musical sections (engraved by Schübler of Zella) is identical in all copies, including the dedication copy. Very probably the plates were pulled in one of the Leipzig copper presses that worked with Breitkopf.[36] This was important for the timing of the publication, which in fact did not have to suffer from difficult communications among composer, engraver, and printer, as was previously thought.

All things considered, there is no indication whatsoever that the composing and publishing could not have been completed within the summer of 1747. A new archival document finally verifies the date.[37] In a supplement to the *Leipziger Zeitungen,* "Extract der eingelauffenen Nouvellen," from 30 September 1747, Bach made the following announcement, telling the public that the Musical Offering would be ready for sale at the upcoming St. Michael's Fair:

> Since the Royal Prussian Fugue Theme, as announced on May 11 of the current year by the Leipzig, Berlin, Frankfort, and other gazettes, has now left the press, it shall be made known that the same may be obtained at the forthcoming St. Michael's Fair from the author, Capellmeister Bach, as well as from his two sons in Halle and Berlin, at the price of 1 imperial taler. The elaboration consists 1.) in two fugues, one with three, the other with six obbligato parts; 2.) in a sonata for transverse flute, violin, and continuo; 3.) in diverse canons, among which is a *fuga canonica.*

The relevance of thorough critical investigations of the sources may be briefly exemplified by two controversial issues of more immediate musical significance: the questions of instrumentation and cyclical order. Previous attempts to solve these and other problems of the Musical Offering had proceeded from the supposition that the appearance of the original print was scarcely explainable, thus inviting all sorts of hypotheses. The results of new research, however, ascertain the well-planned arrangement of the print, thus cutting the ground from under some unprovable theses.

The ostensible lack of specified instrumentation for the Art of Fugue and the Musical Offering has stimulated the fantasy of many musicians and scholars concerning performance. This was not an issue in the eighteenth or nineteenth century; it became one only in 1924, when Wolfgang Graeser with his orchestration and arrangement of the Art of Fugue started what is still a flourishing pastime and set a precedent for similar undertakings of questionable scholarly pretension.[38] The confusion and muddle caused by the numerous arrangements and their often contradictory justifications eventually led some musicologists to the view that these last compositions of Bach did not call on instruments at all. They represent ideal and pure *ars musica*.[39] But the original print of the Musical Offering does not conceal the instrumentation, though specific instruments are mentioned only in the three parts of the sonata and in the canon no. 2 (*à 2 Violini in unisono*) of section D. Thus it amounts to a total of five instruments: flute, two violins, and the continuo instruments. A question that has never been articulated is: Can one possibly perform the entire work with only these instruments? The answer is positive.

Starting with the canons, it should be noted, the composer's first concern is the theoretical, contrapuntal solution of the canons in abbreviated or enigmatic notation. But this does not mean that the settings are merely paper music. No conflict existed for Bach between theory and practice. Nevertheless, the performance aspect is a secondary one and is, moreover, dependent on the available instruments. Therefore, it would seem to be quite natural for Bach to avoid prescribing specific instruments. The only exceptions are the *canon perpetuus* following the sonata and the *canon à 2 Violini in unisono*. But they give two important and necessary hints. First, the canonic settings are ensemble pieces, as is the sonata. Second, an additional violin is required whenever the range of the flute is exceeded. The compulsory assumption for the realization of the bulk of the canons by the aforementioned instruments rather than by using additional instruments not named in the original (such as viola or oboe da caccia) is the employment of the obbligato right and left hand on the keyboard instrument, which is so often to be found in Bach's works. Sources from the C. P. E. Bach circle already suggest this practice for the canons.[40] And since the canonic pieces which require the two keyboard parts are not thoroughbass settings, there is no musical contradiction. The choice of either flute plus violin, two violins, or just one flute or violin, respectively, in addition to the harpsichord remains, then, solely a matter of the number and range of the canonic parts and the availability of the respective instruments.

The two ricercari are indisputably keyboard pieces despite the open-score notation of the six-part ricercar. As in the Art of Fugue and the Canonic Variations on Vom Himmel hoch, Bach followed here the traditional manner of notation for compositions in the strictest contrapuntal style. The comparison between the two ricercari poses an interesting question. The strong stylistic contrast between them is obvious and seems to be underlined by the deliberate application of the ambiguous term *ricercar,* labeling free, improvisatory style as well as extremely strict polyphonic writing. Johann Gottfried Walther's *Musicalisches Lexicon* (1732)[41] points out the terminological details.[42] But shouldn't this contrast perhaps be reinforced with a contrast in the performing medium?

We know that Bach improvised a fugue on the given theme on one of the king's fortepianos at Potsdam. According to the *Spenersche Zeitung* of 11 May 1747, the king "went at Bach's entrance to the so-called forte and piano, condescending also to play, in person and without any preparation, a theme to be executed by Capellmeister Bach in a fugue. This was done so happily by the aforementioned Capellmeister that not only His Majesty was pleased to show his satisfaction thereat, but also all those present were seized with astonishment."[43] The free treatment of the fugal principles in the three-part ricercar is unique among Bach's fugues. There is no question that it represents the worked-out version of the improvisation, as the preface of the print suggests. However, the piece not only reflects improvisatory manners (as indeed do other Bach fugues) but also seems to develop and expand typical motivic elements of the *galant* and *empfindsame Stil* in the unusually extensive and lengthy interludes (see Exx. 18.1 and 18.2). The third movement of the sonata stresses even more the references to this characteristic style of the

Example 18.1. Ricercar à 3, mm. 37–44

Example 18.2. Ricercar à 3, mm. 107–116

Berlin school in the 1740s and 1750s (see Ex. 18.3). Here we have the only pieces of Bach in which he uses the delicate expressive musical language of the generation of his sons. That he does it in one of his last works is surprising but may well demonstrate again the broad horizon of his artistic genius at a time when he was very much oriented toward stylistic and technical musical concepts of the past.[44] These stylistic elements of the Empfindsamkeit, which manifest how well the old capellmeister understood the music of the young Berlin court musicians, are in agreement with the sound ideal of the fortepiano. Performance of the three-part ricercar on the fortepiano seems to be strongly indicated. This becomes even more likely when we add to the musical evidence the fact (known from recently discovered Polish archival material)[45] that in his last years Bach acted as sales agent for Silbermann fortepianos in Leipzig.[46] If one accepts this convincing hypothesis, the three-part ricercar may be considered a composition inspired by and conceived for the fortepiano and its new sound effects, whereas the six-part ricercar truly reflects the traditional world of conservative fugal style in Baroque harpsichord and organ music.

   The second major controversial issue concerns the conception of the Musical Offering as a unity, which was denied by Spitta but strongly affirmed by David and which, as we have seen, can be justified although from a different basis. The particular layout of the original print makes it very clear that the idea of a sophisticated cyclical structure to be realized in a cyclical performance has to be rejected.[47] There is no doubt, of course, that the work was planned in a well-balanced way: two corresponding ricercari *à 3* and *à 6,* five thematic and five contrapuntal canons (as a total of ten symbolizing the number of the Law), and the sonata as central piece and special homage to the flute-playing king. But such a conception is quite in keeping with Bach's characteristic behavior in compiling and grouping compositions with some inner connection in order to form an *opus perfectum.* Three examples from

Example 18.3. Sonata, beginning of third movement

Bach's last period illustrate the various degrees of ordering principles to be found in his major handwritten or printed collections of matching compositions.[48]

The *Clavier Übung bestehend in einer Aria mit verschiedenen Veraenderungen vors Clavicimbel mit 2 Manualen* (the Goldberg Variations) establishes an overall form in which a sequence of thirty pieces arranged with a logical climax are framed by two identical settings which mark beginning and end of a musical idea (see Table 27.3). Within this frame we find 3 × 10 groups, each ending with a canonic variation. These ten canons are arranged according to ascending intervals with the quodlibet as culmination point. The center of the long sequence of movements is emphasized by an *ouverture* which opens the second half of the work. The order as a whole presents 10 (5 + 5) small climatic units within an overall climax held together by the aria.[49]

The second example, *Dritter Theil der Clavier Übung bestehend in verschiedenen Vorspielen über die Catechismus- und andere Gesaenge, vor die Orgel*, establishes a much more refined order by combining various complementary principles of organization. The Prelude and Fugue in E♭ functions as a frame enclosing three different groups of pieces: Missa chorales, catechism chorales, and duets. The first group of 9 (3 × 3) shows a rational planning of three climactic units. The first two contrast in style and format, the third one stresses the middle piece (*pedaliter*). The catechism chorales (see Table 27.2) contain six, or better 2 × 3, pairs of pieces (a longer and a shorter setting of each hymn). The two poles are formed by *organo pleno* settings, each of them framed by two settings either with canonic *cantus firmus* or with *cantus firmus* in the pedal. Finally, the group of duets which, as free pieces, are the smaller pendants to the framing prelude and fugue display ordering devices of multiple interlocking relationship.[50]

The last example differs essentially from the first two. The *Sechs Choräle von verschiedener Art auf einer Orgel mit 2 Clavieren und Pedal vorzuspielen* (see Table 27.1) display no particular principle of ordering but instead the idea of variety ("von verschiedener Art"). Nevertheless, the settings belong very closely together. All six of them (six is the standard number for a closed musical opus) are compositions requiring two manuals and pedal and they all exhibit the same style of plain *cantus firmus* treatment as model samples for chorale preludes. At least five of them are transcriptions of cantata movements, which distinguishes the so-called Schübler Chorales from any other chorale collection of Bach. Thus there is without doubt a planned coherence here too.[51]

Tectonic-order principles as used by Bach are based on framing, axial, symmetric, or climactic devices with systematic arrangements of groups, pairs, or contrasting pairs. Every single collection of pieces placed together either in a printed opus or in a handwritten fair copy manifests in a different way the incredible powers of organization of the composer's mind. Only in exceptional cases, however, does the formal arrangement require a cyclical performance. The Goldberg Variations are such an exception; the logical compositional sequence of movements becomes immediately comprehensible for player and listener, whereas the structure of Clavier-Übung III and the Schübler Chorales carries the idea of a compulsory cyclical performance ad absurdum.

The homogeneity and cohesiveness of the Musical Offering lies in its conception as the exposition of various possibilities of dealing with the royal theme. But there is no hint whatsoever at any intended order for a complete cyclical performance. The most likely original order of the fascicles of the print as suggested above (A + B first because of the main title, D + E last because of the engraver's signature) may show that the grand pieces display a symmetric arrangement: ricercar–sonata–ricercar. The canonic pieces are placed as practically as possible: the *canon perpetuus* that could not be notated in abbreviated manner was put with the sonata parts, the two *quaerendo invenietis* canons at the end of the six-part ricercar, and the remaining *canon perpetuus* in abbreviated notation at the end of the three-part ricercar. Finally, the main body of the canons got its own section, containing the group of five numbered canons in a climactic sequence followed by a canonic fugue as highlight. Thus each of the three fascicles contains at least one canon. Indeed these little pieces run through the entire work like a red thread or like an ingenious ornamentation of the print. If Bach had wanted them and the grand pieces in a specific order he would have used any opportunity for making his desires clear. He himself, for instance, listed the contents of the work in the above-quoted newspaper advertisement in a systematic order—two fugues, a sonata, various canons—demonstrating that the sequence of movements was not a matter of great importance. But he did give emphasis to the three grand pieces, and his contemporaries obviously understood their primary weight, as is shown by a letter of Lorenz Mizler. On 1 March 1752, Mizler wrote to Meinrad Spiess, a member of the Societät der Musicalischen Wissenschaften: "What the late Herr Bach has played for the king of Prussia is now engraved in copper and obtainable in Leipzig: it is [consists of] three pieces. A trio, a ricercar, and a fugue, and I shall write to Leipzig so that you may receive a copy, at the Easter Fair."[52]

The strict historical standpoint that rejects a complete cyclical performance in favor of an ad libitum performance of single pieces does not necessarily affect the question of a modern cyclical performance of the entire work. But it should be pointed out that it was simply not Bach's intention to perform the complete Musical Offering, or the complete Well-Tempered Clavier, the Brandenburg Concertos, the Partitas, or the Art of Fugue, as monumental concert cycles.

19

Bach's Last Fugue: Unfinished?

THERE SEEMS TO BE but one answer to the question why the last piece of
the Art of Fugue is unfinished: Bach's illness and subsequent death prevented
him from completing his last major work and from supervising the final
stages of the printing procedure. The matter does not appear quite so
simple, however, if we direct special attention to the very spot in the autograph manuscript of the Art of Fugue[1] where Bach actually stopped writing.
For page 5 of Appendix 3 of the manuscript score (see Fig. 19.1) holds a
hitherto unnoticed key position in regard to the above question.

Figure 19.1. The Art of Fugue: end of the unfinished fugue BWV 1080/19 (autograph).

Figure 19.2. The Art of Fugue: beginning of the unfinished fugue (autograph).

It has been taken for granted that Bach put aside his pen at m. 239 be-cause he became unable to continue composing, and C. P. E. Bach's *nota bene*[2] is usually cited as supporting evidence even though he was not in Leip-zig during his father's last months. But the appearance of page 5 shows very clearly that Bach obviously had never planned to fill the sheet from top to bottom in other words that he stopped writing deliberately at m. 239. The irregular and faulty ruling of the lower staff lines on page 5 did not permit the use of this part of the page for a dense fugal setting. Bach would never have started on such an untidy piece of paper had he planned to fill a larger portion of it than he did. Pages 1–4 of the appendix (see Fig. 19.2, which shows page 1) demonstrate that Bach aimed at a neat layout and clean musi-cal text for this fugue. (It had to be easily legible for the copyist, who even-tually had to transcribe it into open score for the printer's copy.) Surely Bach used the last page only because he needed a sheet of music paper for just a few bars; since he never wasted paper, such a piece could serve his purpose.

All five pages of the appendix are recto sides of single folios with blank verso sides, the type of paper that was used for the engraver's copy (Ab-klatschvorlage). But the last page differs from the preceding ones insofar as the first four are ruled with ten staves *à 2* (like the paper for the printer's copy of the canons, Appendix 1) whereas page 5 bears twelve staves (like the paper for the contrapuncti).[3] The fact that the paper must have been left over from a supply of ruled paper for the engraver's copy permits a significant chronological conclusion: Appendix 3 was written at a time when the preparation for the printing was already in progress—even more precisely, while or after the printer's copies of the canons were made.[4]

That Appendix 3 represents the composition manuscript of the fragmentary last fugue is shown by some characteristic corrections and the overall graphic appearance. It comprises three complete sections (mm. 1–115: exposition of theme I; 115–193: exposition of theme II and combination with theme I; 193–233: exposition of theme III, "B-A-C-H") and the transition to a fourth and probably final section, which begins immediately with the combination of themes I–III (mm. 233–239). There can be no doubt that the piece was to be a quadruple fugue—a movement of extraordinary length—and as such the culmination of the entire Art of Fugue. Theme IV would have been the principal unifying subject found throughout the work, producing stretto combinations such as that in Example 19.1.[5]

For the composing of a polythematic fugue it is absolutely necessary first to try out the combinatorial possibilities of the various subjects. As a matter of fact, the subjects themselves have to be designed according to the rules of quadruple counterpoint. Therefore Bach had no choice but to start with the combinations of the four themes before writing the opening sections of the fugue. Consequently, it is unthinkable that Bach composed the surviving fragment (Appendix 3) before he had worked out, or at least sketched, the combinatorial section of the quadruple fugue in a manuscript (hereafter designed fragment x) that originally belonged together with Appendix 3 but is now lost. There are indeed two bits of evidence for the one-time existence of such a fragment x: (a) the appearance of page 5 of Appendix 3 and (b) the report, in Bach's obituary,[6] of a projected closing for the Art of Fugue.

Concerning (a), it has been demonstrated above that Bach could never have planned to use page 5 for a major text portion of the concluding section of the fugue: he stopped at m. 239, the point of the retransition from the dominant to the tonic key, because the continuation of the piece was already written down elsewhere, namely in fragment x. Bach's revision of Contra-

Example 19.1. The combination of four subjects in the unfinished fugue

Example 19.2. Contrapunctus 10, mm. 21–22 (a), and the Unfinished fugue, mm. 232–233 (b)

punctus 14 (BWV 1080:10a) of the Art of Fugue offers an interesting parallel. To it he added the extra exposition of the second theme, which now forms the beginning of Contrapunctus 10 (BWV 1080: 10, mm. 1–22; the remainder is identical to 10a, except for the transitional bars 23–26). The autograph of these twenty-two bars has not survived, but it must have been a "fragment"—similar to Appendix 3—which had to be pieced together, by a copyist, with the original version of the double fugue in the autograph (P 200, pp. 14–16) to produce the printer's copy. The joint between the old and the new parts (mm. 21–22) is very similar to the corresponding spot in the quadruple fugue (mm. 232–234; see Ex. 19.2).

With respect to (b) it should be noted that the obituary by C. P. E. Bach and J. F. Agricola mentions a draft (Entwurf), according to which the last fugue "was to contain four themes and to have been afterward inverted note for note in all four voices." This means that C. P. E. Bach, whose later ownership of the printing plates of the Art of Fugue implies a participation in the editing of the work after his father's death, must have known of or even seen fragment x, the complete draft of the combination of the themes and their inversions; the phrase "note for note" clearly refers to an elaborate musical text. But what happened to it?

We know that those responsible for the editing of the Art of Fugue were startlingly unfamiliar with the composer's plans and intentions. Fundamental errors such as the senseless inclusion of Contrapunctus 14, the earlier version of Contrapunctus 10, prove their incompetence and carelessness. Therefore their failure to recognize the connection between the fragmentary Appendix 3 and fragment x is not surprising. They considered the two fragments as representing two different pieces, which explains the mention of two concluding fugues in the obituary:

His last illness prevented him, according to his draft, from bringing the next-to-the-last fugue to completion and working out the last one, which was to contain four themes and to have been afterward inverted note for note in all four voices.[7]

Hence the "unfinished" Appendix 3 (taken for the next-to-last piece) was published as a triple fugue and the only movement of the whole work without the principal theme, the essential unifying element of the Art of Fugue. The Italian title given to it, *Fuga à 3 Soggetti,* departs from Bach's concept of naming the fugues plainly "contrapunctus," without reference to the number of subjects. Furthermore, mm. 233ff. were cut off in order to avoid too abrupt an ending. The fragment x (taken for the draft of a concluding fugue), with its combination of four subjects and their inversions but obviously without a beginning, was not at all considered for publication. The editors knew what to do with a piece without an end, but they did not know how to handle a piece without a beginning, and there may well have been further deficiencies in the fugal setting.

Figure 19.3 illustrates the suggested relationship of the two fragments and outlines the presumable overall structure of the quadruple fugue (I = theme I, etc.; I^i = theme I inverted, etc.; I/II = theme I and II combined, and so on). As a result of most unfortunate and unknown circumstances, the last part of the quadruple fugue, fragment x, became lost. Also lost were other important autograph materials, including complete movements, such as Contrapunctus 4 and the canons *alla decima* and *alla duodecima,* as well as fragments like the concluding bars of Contrapuncti 1, 2, and 3 and the opening of Contrapunctus 10, and, finally, the entire printer's copy (except that of the augmentation canon).[8]

Returning to the question posed at the beginning, our answer to a large extent can only be hypothetical. But it seems that the surviving source material offers no better solution to the problem than the following: Appendix 3 (mm. 1–239 of the last fugue) was originally to be supplemented by another manuscript with the remainder of the piece, comprising the combination of the four subjects, which had to be composed first. The last fugue was not left unfinished as it appears today and, in fact, the Art of Fugue must have been a nearly completed work when Bach died.

fragment Appendix 3				fragment x
m.1	115	193	233	239
$I\text{-}I^i$ (mm. 21ff. passim)	II-II/I (mm. 148ff.)	$III\text{-}III^i$ (mm. 213ff.)	I/II/III	$/IV\text{-}I^i/II^i/III^i/IV^i$

Figure 19.3. A possible structure for the quadruple fugue.

Appendix

During a close reexamination of P 200 in Berlin during the summer of 1973, infra-red photography produced a clear picture (see Fig. 19.4) of a faded, now barely visible, pencil entry, obviously in the hand of J. S. Bach, on page 25, just above the beginning of Contrapunctus 8. The note, reproduced here courtesy of the Deutsche Staatsbibliothek, reads: "Folgendes muß also geschrieben werden" (the following must be written thus; see Ex. 19.3).

This pencil note represents an instruction to the scribe of the printer's copy to double the note values of the first triple fugue, as shown in the original edition. We now have sufficient evidence that Bach himself was responsible for the notational changes found in the print: besides this instruction, there is a similar one in ink for the first double fugue (on the fourth system of page 10 of P 200), and the augmentation canon with doubled note values was written out in its entirety by J. S. Bach.[9] Thus, one of the most significant departures from the autograph found in the original edition, once regarded as a falsification by H. T. David and others,[10] can be authenticated as intended by Bach.

Example 19.3.

Figure 19.4. The Art of Fugue: triple fugue BWV 1080/8, detail (pencil instruction for copyist, autograph).

20

The Compositional History of the Art of Fugue

THE ART OF FUGUE has long been one of the most fascinating yet vexing objects of Bach research. An aura of the unfinished and an uncertainty with regard to Bach's ultimate artistic goal have combined to direct the focus of practical, theoretical, aesthetic, and historical studies to *res facta*—to the concrete aspects of the work before us—rather than to a serious investigation of its origin.

To a large extent the first edition of the Art of Fugue was regarded as an authoritative musical text, though it became increasingly apparent that the extant autograph furnished contradictory evidence. Yet the ostensible discrepancies between these two authentic sources were almost invariably attributed to the torso character of the work and presumably pressing circumstances in the face of the composer's approaching death. The juxtaposition of both original print and autograph as documents from Bach's waning years prompted a puzzled and speculative approach.

The following reflections on the origin of the work deal with a critical examination of the traditional dating and suggest a new chronology that presents the compositional history as well as the nature of the Art of Fugue in a new light, of relevance moreover for the general view of the last decade of Bach's life.

I

The printing of the Art of Fugue was initiated by Bach himself and in large part was also supervised by him. After his death on 28 July 1750 it was hastily concluded, so that the original edition could appear as early as the spring of 1751. The editorial tasks seem to have fallen principally to Carl Philipp Emanuel Bach and his Berlin colleague Johann Friedrich Agricola, both of whom were also responsible for the formulation of Bach's obituary. Completed in 1750, though not published until 1754, the obituary contains the earliest catalogue of works, in which the Art of Fugue is described as "the last work of the author."[1] Conscious of the incomplete state of the work and in an attempt to compensate for its unfinished form, the editors added the organ chorale "Wenn wir in höchsten Nöten sein" at the end, a work taken from a collection of chorale settings in which Bach had evidently worked until his last days. They explained, in a terse statement in the prefatory notice of the original print, that "it was wished to compensate the friends of his Muse by the four-part church chorale added at the end, which the deceased man in his blindness dictated on the spur of the moment to the pen of one of his friends."[2] This was not meant to add a touch of mystery to the work; it was left to posterity to arrive at such an interpretation. The peculiar notions of an inner connection between the Art of Fugue and the chorale and the speculations as to performance medium and movement sequence are of recent origin.

The posthumous publication of a fragmentary work in particular was bound to give rise to the thought that the Art of Fugue was a testament of the great master of fugue, a legacy inseparably connected with Bach's very last years. The Art of Fugue was seen as a climactic phase in the development of the concept of a cyclic structure for monothematic instrumental works realized first in the Goldberg Variations and further evolved in the Musical Offering and the Canonic Variations on Vom Himmel hoch. Philipp Spitta also saw a certain affinity between the Art of Fugue and the Musical Offering, especially on the basis of thematic correlation, and suggested that the Musical Offering seemed to emerge as a preliminary "study for a greater work."[3] This idea further suggested a frame for dating. Since the inception of the Musical Offering was tied to the Potsdam visit to Frederick the Great in May 1747, the beginning of Bach's work on the Art of Fugue could hardly have taken place before the latter half of that year. A *terminus ante quem* was given with the summer of 1749, when the cantorate test for Bach's successor took place; extensive work on the composition after that date would have been unlikely, given the state of Bach's health.

The newest attempt at dating the Art of Fugue is still largely determined by the traditional time frame as set by Spitta, though it is connected with a new hypothesis for the work's origin: it assigns to the Art of Fugue the purpose of essay for Lorenz Christoph Mizler's Societät der musicalischen Wissenschaften. Bach had joined the society in 1747, and in the guise of essay the work would have served the function of obligatory contribution for the year 1749, a most weighty tribute to the society's goals, which the composer was unable to complete. The relevant points were thoroughly expounded and substantiated by Hans Gunter Hoke in the commentary for the facsimile edition of the Art of Fugue.[4]

Doubts regarding the accepted dating, which was not questioned by Hoke, were raised, probably for the first time, in 1966 by Hans-Joachim Schulze[5] and subsequently more fully discussed on a broader and systematic basis in one of my doctoral seminars at Columbia University in 1973–74.[6] In past decades research dealing with the Art of Fugue had become locked into the problems of order and performance medium, and analytical studies had receded into the background. The exploration of sources, as well, was guided by the question of sequence. In discussions of order the autograph and original print were at times interpreted as alternate solutions, but the printed edition was usually seen as the version representing Bach's final intentions, at least in general outline.

It is on this issue that the work of Wolfgang Wiemer[7] provided special clarification, even though its title, referring to the "restoration of the original order" of the work, seems rather too presumptuous. A series of open questions remains, especially with regard to the placement of the canons.[8] Nevertheless, the order of fugues I through 13 in the original edition can now assuredly be considered authentic.

The customary view that both autograph and print belonged to the final period of Bach's life had the damaging effect that they were considered of practically equal text validity. This in turn implied a license for rearranging the order of the work, for Bach was presumably undecided to the last. Now, while the importance Bach attached to a fixed order has never been doubted, we are nevertheless not concerned with invariable factors. We need merely refer to the extensive changes of movement sequence in the parodies of cantatas or—closer to the Art of Fugue—in the Canonic Variations on Vom Himmel hoch BWV 769. Bach was always as precise about numbering and paginating in such works or work versions as he was in the cases of the Art of Fugue or the Musical Offering. No clever hypothesis[9] can alter the fact that the original sources for Bach's works speak an unmistakable language.

The dilemma of the seemingly contradictory numbering of movements in the Art of Fugue can be resolved without difficulty once a precise distinction of layers in the source material is recognized. That the extant sources might represent different layers of a process of composition extending over a long period of time is a matter so far hardly considered, let alone systematically explored. It seems therefore advisable to review the entire source material, particularly in relation to the work's genesis, with critical scrutiny.

The sources can be divided into two clearly distinguishable groups: (1) the original print (minimal differences between the first edition of 1751 and the second edition of 1752 being irrelevant in this context); and (2) the autograph manuscripts. For the investigation of the work's origins, only the latter are of significance, and our first task is to describe and classify the existing material.

The autograph in the possession of the Deutsche Staatsbibliothek Berlin consists of two units: a forty-page fascicle, whose pages are stitched together, and an appendix of three sections, all of them made up of single leaves (Table 20.1).[10] The main portion of the autograph shows the title *Die Kunst der Fuga / di Sig. Joh. Seb. Bach* in the hand of Johann Christoph Altnikol and contains on pages 2 through 38 fourteen movements entered consecutively, namely twelve fugues and two canons, nos. I–XIV. On page 38 begins a thorough revision (no. XV) of the augmentation canon no. XII. The three sections of the appendix appear in a wrapper inscribed by Johann Christoph

Table 20.1. The original sources and their contents

Autograph score (DSB, P 200)	BWV 1080	Printed score (Leipzig, 1751)
I	1	Contrapunctus 1
II	2	Contrapunctus 2
III	3	Contrapunctus 3
IV	4	Contrapunctus 4
V	5	Contrapunctus 5
VI	6	Contrapunctus 6. a 4 in Stylo Francese
VII	7	Contrapunctus 7. a 4 per Augment: et Diminut:
VIII	8	Contrapunctus 8. a 3
IX	9	Contrapunctus 9. a alla Duodecima
X	10	Contrapunctus 10. a 4 alla Decima
XI	11	Contrapunctus 11. a 4
XII	12	Contrapunctus inversus 12. a 4
XIII	13	Contrapunctus inversus [13] a 3
XIV	10a	Contrapunctus a 4
———	14	Canon per Augmentationem in Contrario Motu
XVᵃ	15	Canon alla Ottava
———	16	Canon alla Decima in Contrapunto alla Terza
Appendix 1ᵇ	17	Canon alla Duodecima in Contrapunto alla Quinta
Appendix 2ᶜ	18	Fuga a 2 Clav:
Appendix 3ᵈ	19	Fuga a 3 Soggetti
	668	Choral. Wenn wir in hoechsten Noethen

Note: Roman numerals here and in the text denote the movements (fugues and canons) of the autograph version. This table also serves as a concordance for the two versions; arrows clarify the reorganization of movements: I = early version of Contrapunctus 1; II = early version of Contapunctus 3; there is no early version of Contrapunctus 4; and so on. See also Table 27.8.

    a. Variant (first revision) of the augmentation canon no. XII = BWV 1080/14.

    b. Engraver's copy (second revision) of the augmentation canon BWV 1080/14.

    c. Arrangement for two keyboards of the mirror fugue BWV 1080/13.

    d. Unfinished fugue.

Friedrich Bach with the title *Die Kunst der Fuge / Von J. S. Bach*. As is to be shown, originally a larger amount of material must have been inserted in the wrapper, for the three sections do not represent a unit that is in any way complete. Appendix 1 is the engraver's copy for the original print of the augmentation canon no. 14 (three single proof sheets whose verso pages are blank); Appendix 2 consists of two leaves containing the three-part mirror fugue arranged for two keyboard instruments; and Appendix 3 contains, on five single leaves, the unfinished fugue.

An analysis of these autograph manuscripts as to their respective shares in the genesis of the work results in the following picture (as summarized in Table 20.2; see also the Postscript to this chapter). The main portion of the autograph—referred to as P 200, after its call number—represents a fair copy which must have been preceded by a "working copy" or composing score. Nothing in the physical appearance of the fourteen movements points to essential changes that would imply the act of composition. What corrections are there were evidently made in the process of proofreading. Whereas the fair copy (source B) is preserved, the working copy (source A) must be considered lost. Thus we can arrive at no conclusions about the working copy, except that it was probably a manuscript notated on two staves. Directly derived from source B is the appended arrangement of the mirror fugue (source C). A fourth layer, finally, is made up of a group of working copies containing movements not in existence when source B was compiled. Among these copies, representing source D, is the revision of the augmentation canon (source D1) and the manuscript of the unfinished fugue (D1); what must have been lost are the autographs for Contrapunctus 4 (D2), the opening twenty-two measures of Contrapunctus 10, and the canons at the

Table 20.2. Derivation and stemma of sources

[A]	Working copy: lost (nos. I – XIV)
B	Fair copy: DSB, P 200, pp. 1–38 (nos. I – XIV)
C	Arrangement: DSB, P 200, Appendix 2 (*Fuga a 2 Clav.*)
D1	Working copy: DSB, P 200, pp. 38 – 39 (no. XV, first revision of augmentation canon = D1a) and Appendix 3 (*Fuga a 3 Soggetti* = D1b)
[D2]	Working copy: lost (Contrapunctus 4; Contrapunctus 10, mm. 1 – 22; canon at the tenth; canon at the twelfth; quadruple fugue, mm. 239ff.)
E1	Engraver's copy: DSB, P 200, Appendix 1 (augmentation canon, final version)
[E2]	Engraver's copy (principal portion): lost (Contrapuncti 1–14, canons 1–3)
F	Original edition of 1751
G	Second printing of 1752 (with preface by Friedrich Wilhelm Marpurg)

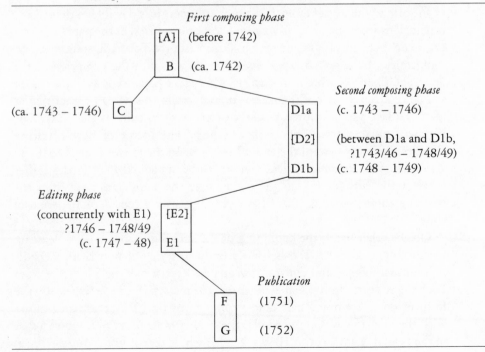

First composing phase

[A] (before 1742)

B (ca. 1742)

Second composing phase

(ca. 1743 – 1746) C D1a (c. 1743 – 1746)

[D2] (between D1a and D1b, ?1743/46 – 1748/49)

D1b (c. 1748 – 1749)

Editing phase

(concurrently with E1) [E2]
?1746 – 1748/49
(c. 1747 – 48) E1

Publication

F (1751)

G (1752)

tenth and twelfth, as well as the draft for the combination of themes in the quadruple fugue. Lost as well is the engraver's copy for the original print (source E2), with the exception of the mentioned leaves for the augmentation canon (E1). The original edition (source F) and its reprint (G) could not have been based upon the sources B, C, or D, but must go back to a complete proof copy comparable to source E1.

The evidence of the extant autograph material clearly reveals its fragmentary character: three large portions are missing. These are the original working copy A, the working copies for the movements subsequently composed (D2), and a major part of the engraver's copy (E2). Thus an investigation of the work's origin is hampered by significant lacunae. And the vestiges of lost material offer little help. Among these must be counted the wrapper inscribed by Johann Christoph Friedrich Bach, which possibly contained the engraver's copy. A hint of merely literary nature as to its former whereabouts is the mention in 1845 by the erstwhile Berlin librarian Siegfried Wilhelm Dehn[11] of a note in the hand of Carl Philipp Emanuel Bach, originally enclosed in the autograph P 200, "Herr Hartmann hat das eigentliche" (has the actual copy). This might refer to the engraver's copy that could have come into the possession of the Elbingen publisher Friedrich Traugott Hartmann, who, through earlier collaboration with Friedrich Wilhelm Marpurg (author of the preface for the second edition of the Art of Fugue, issued in 1752) would have been in communication with Carl Philipp Emanuel Bach.[12] For the latter had made public, in a 1756 announcement addressed to "publishers of musical works," that he intended to sell the engraver's plates for the Art of Fugue.[13]

In spite of the loss of essential original sources, it is possible to draw some conclusions from the existing material. An examination of the paper used for the main portion of the autograph P 200 (source B), for instance, shows uniformity of the watermark ("double eagle"),[14] with the exception of the last leaf ("Eger"),[15] which, in turn, is of the same paper type as that used for source C (arrangement of the mirror fugue). From this we can gather that at least the last part of source B was written close in time to source C. The handwriting seems to support this finding. The nature of Bach's writing changes markedly toward the end of source B. In the mirror fugues XIII and XIV the notes are smaller, less regular, and less slanted than in the earlier parts of the autograph—an indication that the transfer process from the working copy (source A) must have extended over a considerable period of time.

On the other hand, the beginning of the autograph (source B), at least up to movement no. VIII, shows a fairly uniform style of handwriting, a calligraphic assuredness and dynamic sweep characteristic of the fair copies from Bach's best years. Individual elements of the manuscript style (especially the form of down-stemmed half notes) conform to Bach's practices beginning with the mid-1730s. On the whole, the quality of manuscript is close to that of the Peasant Cantata score (BWV 212),[16] whose date is fixed (August 1742) and with which source B also shares the "double eagle" watermark (see Figs. 20.1 and 20.2). The same watermark,[17] however, appears also in the score of the St. Matthew Passion copy of 1736 and in other instances, so the congruence with BWV 212 is by no means isolated. Yet paper and manuscript findings, taken together, suggest that an origin of at least two-thirds of source B in the early 1740s is not only not to be dismissed, but is actually likely.

This deduction is supported by the appearance of Appendixes 1 and 3: sources E1 and D1. The character of Bach's writing is here quite different (and the paper types are different from any of the others); it is rougher, in D1 occasionally cramped. Among the autographs that can be dated, source B1 comes closest to the six-part ricercar from the Musical Offering (1747). No ready parallel can be quoted for source D1 (the unfinished fugue), and it is entirely possible that here we are dealing with one of the last documents of Bach's handwriting. There is no doubt that the period concerned is 1747–1749, the same years in which Bach undertook the publication, and it seems plausible that source E1 belongs to an early and source D1 to a final phase.

To summarize the results so far: the autograph material, taken as a whole, is of entirely heterogeneous nature and reflects diverse phases of the work's origin, phases that must have covered many years. The oldest source is manuscript B, from the period 1740–1742, and it must have been preceded by a working copy A. The latter cannot be dated, but it must go back to about 1740 at the latest, more likely to the end of the 1730s. This means that we must take leave of the time-honored idea that the Art of Fugue was Bach's "swan song."

It is true that Bach was occupied with the work until the last, but apparently above all with seeing it through the press. The conception of the work and the essential creative process go back at least another decade.

II

We must now deal with the history of the work's composition. "Compositional history" rather than "genesis" is here used advisedly. The notion of genesis is too much obscured by the problem of dates, whereas the compositional history can be traced in its main phases and tendencies.

The investigation of the autograph material leads beyond the problem of dates to further observations regarding the work's origin. What emerges first of all is a revision, quite evidently undertaken in connection with the printing; it includes the completion of new versions for some movements as well as a change of the total design. Table 20.1 shows how the work was reorganized and which pieces had not yet been included in the autograph. But before we turn to the details of the revisions that must have proceeded in stages beginning about 1747, it is necessary to give separate consideration to the version represented by the autograph fair copy B. For there is no doubt that source B stands at some distance, both with regard to date and conception, from the original print. Nor is there any doubt about the fact that

Figure 20.1. The Art of Fugue: section of counterfugue BWV 1080/5 (autograph).

Figure 20.2. Cantate burlesque BWV 212: autograph score, page 15.

source B, the main portion of the autograph, forms an integral unit. We are by no means concerned with an ex post facto collection of single leaves but a carefully planned manuscript, executed with prior knowledge of its total extent. This is shown by the leaf gatherings, the numbering, and the entire calligraphic design. And this early version shows how the form of the work originally unfolded (see Table 20.3, left section).

The beginning is formed by three fugues (I–III) in simple (that is, not in invertible) counterpoint. They are followed by six fugues in double counterpoint (IV: counterpoint at the octave; V: counterpoint at the twelfth; VI: counterpoint at the tenth; VII: counterpoint at the octave in diminution; VIII: counterpoint at the octave in diminution and augmentation; IX: perpetual canon at the octave). Next are three fugues written in triple counterpoint, after which follows a perpetual canon in augmentation. The conclusion is formed by two mirror fugues (XIII in single counterpoint; XIV in double counterpoint). Without going into further detail, one can recognize from this sequence that the work was planned according to the principles of contrapuntal types, in an order of progressive complexity. To speak of categories of fugues, as has been the custom, seems imprecise at best: for instance, at the beginning of the work, we are not concerned with "simple fugues" so much as with "fugues in simple counterpoint."

Another principle by which Bach is guided in this early version in particular is that of variation, applied on several levels. It becomes evident in the rising rhythmic complexity of the theme. As shown in Example 20.1, the rhythmic-melodic contours of the theme change in the sense of variations. Thus there is a gradual departure from the initial model, proceeding in two clearly distinguished sections (see Table 20.3). In the groups A and B (movements I–VIII of the early version), the variation process remains deliberate and substantial changes are eschewed. By contrast, in groups D and E (movements IX–XIV) the thematic metamorphosis becomes conscious. This mounting variation principle was abandoned by Bach in the later version, as is made clear by the rearrangement of movements.

That Bach's early version of the Art of Fugue is guided by the concept of variation—interestingly enough, Forkel, who knew only the printed version, speaks also of "Variationen im Großen" (variations on a grand scale)[18]— becomes apparent from the very fact that Fugue no. III ended originally on the dominant, that is, in A major. This can only mean that Fugue no. IV was to follow directly in order to lead back to the original key. Bach departed later from a strict sequence of variants. Yet it is important to take into account that the initial conception of the work was guided by such a principle.

The development of countersubjects, too, plays an important role in this connection (see Ex. 20.2). In Angelo Berardi's *Documenti Armonici* (Bologna, 1687),[19] for instance, a carefully planned arrangement of countersubjects is discussed: "alla zoppa" (syncopated), "alla diritta" (stepwise), "saltando" (in disjunct progression), and so on. Bach seems to pursue a similar disposition of types. Thus he proceeds slowly in the development from movement I to

Table 20.3. Design of movements

Earlier version	No.	Later version	No.
A. *Contrapunctus simplex*		A. *Contrapunctus simplex*	
Th/R: ASBT; Cs/diatonic	I	a. Th/R: ASBT; Cs/diatonic	1
Th/I: TASB; Cs/dotted	II	Th/R: BTAS; Cs/chromatic	2
		b. Th/I: TASB; Cs/dotted	3
Th/R: BTAS; Cs/chromatic	III	Th/I: SATB; Cs/syncopated	4
B. *Contrapunctus duplex*		B. *Contrapunctus duplex*	
a. Th/I + R: ABST; Cp/8	IV	a. Th/I + R: ABST; Cp/8	5
Th/R + Cs A/R; Cp/12	V	Th/R + I; dim.; Cp/8	6
Th/I + Cs B/R; Cp/10	VI	Th/I + R; dim./augm.; Cp/8	7
b. Th/R + I; dim.; Cp/8	VII	b. Th/I + Cs C/R, D/R; Cp/8	8
Th/R + I; dim./augm.; Cp/8	VIII	Th/R + Cs A/R; Cp/12	9
		Th/I + Cs B/R; Cp/10	10
C. *Contrapunctus duplex* (Th/var)		Th/R + Cs C/I, D/I, E/R + I;	
Canon perp: Th/I + R; Cp/8	IX	Cp/8	11
Th/I + Cs C/R, D/R; Cp/8	X		
Th/R + Cs C/I, D/I, E/R + I;		C. *Contrapunctus inversus*	
Cp/8	XI	Th/R; Cp/simplex	12
Canon perp: Th/R + I; augm.;		Th/R + I; Cp/duplex	13
Cp/8	XII		
		D. *Canon, Contrapunctus duplex*	
D. *Contrapunctus inversus*		Canon perp: Th/I + R; Cp/8	15
Th/R; Cp/simplex	XIII	Canon perp: Th/I + R; Cp/10/3	16
Th/R + I; Cp/duplex	XIV	Canon fin: Th/R; Cp/12/5	17
		Canon fin: Th/R + I; augm.;	
		Cp/8	14
		E. *Contrapunctus duplex*	
		[Th/R + I] + Cs F/R + I, G,	
		H/R + I	18

Key:
Th/R = Thema rectum (normal form of the principal theme)
Th/I = Thema inversum (inverted form of the principal theme)
Cs = Contrasubject
A–H = Secondary subjects A, B, C, D, E, F, G, H
R = Normal form of subject
I = Inverted form of subject
I + R = Normal and inverted forms combined
Cp/8 = Counterpoint at the octave; Cp/10 at the tenth, etc.
SATB = Soprano, alto, tenor, bass
dim. = diminution
augm. = augmentation

Example 20.1. Rhythmic metamorphoses of the principal theme

movement III (see Ex. 20.3), in the rhythmic as well as the melodic and even the harmonic conformation (compare the chromaticism in movement III). Contrapunctus 4 of the later version offers special insight into the harmonic dimension of Bach's working process in the course of the work's evolution. The harmonic language unfolds with increasing complexity, as is shown especially by the intensification of chromaticism. Contrapunctus 4, newly composed for the later version, shows an entirely novel combination of thematic entrances, nowhere to be found in the early version; through the inser-

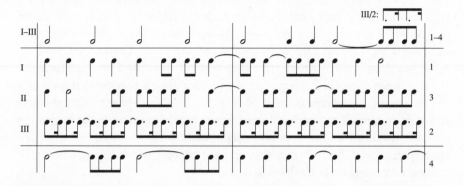

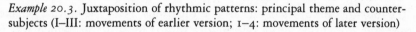

Example 20.2. Dux and comes versions of the principal theme

Example 20.3. Juxtaposition of rhythmic patterns: principal theme and counter-subjects (I–III: movements of earlier version; 1–4: movements of later version)

tion of the seventh, the fugal answer gains in this case a modulatory quality (Ex. 20.2). This leads to surprising harmonic progressions (such as in mm. 77ff.), foreign in kind to the early version. It seems indeed that the contrapuntal principle was the predominant one in the early version (even vis-à-vis the harmonic development). The contrapuntal categories outbalance all other structural considerations, without ever descending to didactic pedantry.

It cannot be considered accidental that Bach used the designation *contrapunctus* for individual fugues in the printed edition. A brief review of specific connotations of the term *contrapunctus* in Bach's time might here be of help. In the writings of Fux, Mattheson, or Heinichen, for instance, *contrapunctus* applies simply to part-writing in a contrapuntal manner. Mattheson defines contrapunctus in the chapter on *Symphoniurgie*—the art of perfect part-writing—as "the adroit combination of several melodies sounding simultaneously, whereby manifold euphony arises conjointly."[20] This formulation recalls Johann Abraham Birnbaum's characterization of Bach's concept of harmony (as stated in his defense of Bach written in 1738): "Harmony becomes far more complete if all the voices collaborate to form it. Accordingly this is not a failing but rather a musical perfection."[21]

We would therefore not go wrong in assuming that, at least in his conception of the early version, Bach was not concerned so much with the genre of fugue (as in the Well-Tempered Clavier) as with a demonstration of "harmony" as the essence of music, harmony conceived on the basis of contrapuntal writing and with the object of "musical perfection" in mind.

Harmony being obtained through the joint motion of voices, it follows logically, for instance, that the first setting in double counterpoint using three themes is written in three voices only; a fourth voice would be superfluous from the point of view of contrapuntal texture—it would serve merely a supplemental function.

In the revision of the work, as presented in the original print, the determining principle of design becomes that of fugal manners (see Table 20.3). And this is given special emphasis through the addition of newly composed pieces. The beginning is now formed by four fugues in simple counterpoint but duplicity of theme formation (rectus and inversus). They are followed by three counterfugues in which the expositions of rectus and inversus forms of the theme are combined. Next in order are four double fugues with from two to four themes (Contrapunctus 2 adds to the principal three further themes) and four canons. The conclusion is formed by the quadruple fugue, which was left unfinished. Yet it is not only possible, but even likely, that this incomplete form of the fugue does not correspond to what was actually in existence at the time of Bach's death.

The conception of a quadruple fugue commences necessarily with a draft for the four themes in their various combinations. Now the obituary makes unmistakable mention of an "Entwurff" (draft) for a fugue "which was to contain four themes and to have been afterward inverted note for note in all four voices."[22] It can be ascribed only to lack of understanding on the part of the editors that this draft (perhaps even fully executed) was not added to the opening portion written out on five leaves. For it is easily seen that Bach planned to stop where he did. The page consists of paper on which the five-line systems were poorly marked, and it left room only for a small additional entry. Had Bach intended to continue the composition, he would have used another, cleanly prepared piece of music paper. We can thus surmise that the state of the Art of Fugue at the time of Bach's death was less incomplete than the traditional accounts relate.[23] Carl Philipp Emanuel Bach's note, "While working on this fugue, in which the name *B A C H* appears in the counter-subject, the author died," ostensibly entered as late as ca. 1780, has misguided posterity and created the impression that death stayed the composer's pen at this passage.[24] Our explanation is bound to be less "romantically" formulated: Bach interrupted the manuscript at that point because its continuation was unequivocal; the remainder had at least been sketched, complete in outline.

III

The new dating of the Art of Fugue and the distinction to be observed between the two versions lead to conclusions of decisive importance for our understanding of the works from Bach's last period. The Art of Fugue, together with other works, marks the beginning of that epoch in Bach's life (to sketch briefly the biographical context) in which he was concerned with the thought of gaining freedom to pursue projects of his own choosing. For this reason he reduced the duties of the St. Thomas cantorate essentially to administrative matters: he created hardly any new works for the service; and for Passiontide he fell back on such works as Telemann's *Seliges Erwägen* during the 1740s, rather than completing a revision of his own St. John Passion, begun about 1738. The activities of the Collegium Musicum, which had commanded his full attention after 1729, were also no longer of interest to him; in 1741 he resigned its direction for good.

His concentration was now devoted to works stimulated by his own imagination. Official verdicts had no further influence upon them. Were the concept of artistic autonomy not so foreign to Bach's time, it would apply here. For this is precisely what is involved in such works as the Art of Fugue and the other late instrumental works—compositions undertaken without commission, without model, and without popular appeal (because of technical demands they were strictly for professional not to say virtuoso performers) or financial interest (since they hardly covered costs).

The Art of Fugue was not the utmost and final goal representing Bach's concept of the monothematic cycle of instrumental music but rather its point of departure. Because of the absence of a working copy, the start of Bach's work on the Art of Fugue cannot be determined. Since, however, the fair copy for the earlier version must go back to the early 1740s, the origin of the Goldberg Variations (printed 1741) must be seen as closely connected with the Art of Fugue, especially inasmuch as the latter shares the variation principle with the former. A further point of orientation is given through the completion of Well-Tempered Clavier II toward the end of the 1730s.

Whereas that work deals with fugue as a genre, the Art of Fugue is concerned with fugal setting as a contrapuntal principle. Yet the preoccupation with fugal composition forms an obvious connecting link between these two major works, similar to the one that arises with Clavier-Übung III (1739). It is not only the concept of variation which is also present there (multiple forms of chorale settings) but the thoroughly explored spectrum of strict and free, retrospective as well as modern instrumental forms which is analogous to the design of the Art of Fugue.

The opening movements of the Art of Fugue show the contrapuntal style par excellence, polyphony in the traditional vocal style, the symbol of the "time-honored majesty of music" (Lorenz Christoph Mizler),[25] serving as point of departure, not as end goal. The gradual departure from the retrospective manner of the *stile antico* in the course of the work and the growing integration of other, increasingly personal style elements can only be understood in a symptomatic sense. And the final fugue reflects the same process in summary form. The total work thus emerges as a document of systematic exploration of the foundations of contrapuntal composition, with particular reference to instrumental art. A parallel in the vocal domain is Bach's increasing involvement in the setting of the Mass text during the 1730s, culminating in the completion of the B Minor Mass. The correlation is evident. The Mass, as the vocal genre richest in tradition, played for a long time an important role in Bach's work. This applies especially to the B Minor Mass and its design in setting forth *exempla classica* of vocal composition, for the latter purpose is doubtless an essential characteristic of the B Minor Mass, in contradistinction to stylistically more homogeneous works such as the St. Matthew Passion. The Art of Fugue appears thus as an instrumental counterpart to the B Minor Mass.

Without doubt the Art of Fugue must be considered the principal project of composition during the last decade of Bach's life, one that grew and variously changed in the course of time. It was an achievement that exerted its influence upon other projects, especially the Musical Offering and the Canonic Variations on Vom Himmel hoch, and it was the work in which Bach merged the monothematic concept in the most concentrated and consistent manner with contrapuntal texture. Moreover, it was the work in which the theoretical component of Bach's thought became most manifest, without ever freezing into mere theory. The development from the first version of the Art of Fugue, as an "Art of Counterpoint in the Form of Variations," to the formation of the final version, as a "Study of Fugue and Canon" arranged, as it were, in chapters, may have been guided by theoretical motives; but it resulted, in Carl Philipp Emanuel Bach's words, in "the most perfect practical fugal work."[26] Theory and practice merge, old and new techniques of composition as well as elements of style are integrated and thus embody the universality of Bach's art in the most unmistakable and inimitable manner. The Art of Fugue thus stands before us as the most comprehensive and seemingly also the most personal document of the aged Bach's instrumental language. That he wove the letters of his name into the final movement is surely more than a touch of fanciful imagination.

Finally, there is no mistaking the fact that the Art of Fugue, well-nigh the prototype of a work free of ties imposed by commission, shows Bach as a composer taking the decisive step toward what might be called—with a grain of salt—the autonomous work of art. And again the B Minor Mass may be understood to figure as the relevant counterpart—a work unparalleled in dimensions and artistic challenge. Yet the language of the Art of Fugue, despite the extent of its stylistic palette, is marked by greater concentration, abstraction, and individualism—one is tempted say: originality. While the individuality of genius is a concept foreign to Bach and his time, the response to Bach's instrumental music was later to become one of the cornerstones of the aesthetics of genius. But even Bach's contemporaries recognized, as early as the 1730s, the different quality of his music as considered against the general norms of taste. It is mentioned repeatedly that in his works one encounters an "astonishing mass of unusual and well-developed ideas" (Birnbaum, 1739),[27] and the obituary states summarily that his music was "resembling that of no other composer." [28] This, however, does not refer to dissimilarity so much as to uniqueness—originality. [29]

The evolution of Bach's creative career, spanning close to fifty years, is without parallel. By way of comparison, Handel's first operas and last oratorios, for instance, show a much greater affinity than Bach's earliest and last works. Viewed from this vantage point, the Art of Fugue, in spite of the fact that it is not Bach's very last work, represents the attainment of an ultimate goal, the "be-all and end-all" of an extraordinarily strong-willed artistic personality.

21

The Deathbed Chorale: Exposing a Myth

WHEN, shortly after Bach's death, a chorale setting was joined to the original edition of the Art of Fugue, the object was neither one of sanctifying Bach's lifework nor one of creating a myth. The reason for adding to the print the four-part organ chorale "Wenn wir in höchsten Nöten sein" (When we are caught in dire distress) BWV 668 is given in a terse annotation placed by the anonymous editor on the verso page of the title: ". . . it was wished to compensate the friends of his Muse by the four-part church chorale added at the end, which the deceased man in his blindness dictated on the spur of the moment to the pen of one of his friends."[1] In a rather similar form this notice appears within the more extended preface that Friedrich Wilhelm Marpurg wrote for the second edition of the Art of Fugue, which was issued under his editorship (Leipzig, 1752): "But we are proud to think that the four-part church chorale added here, which the deceased man in his blindness dictated on the spur of the moment to the pen of one of his friends, will make up for his lack, and compensate the friends of his Muse."[2]

These are the earliest literary sources relating to the origin of this chorale setting. They also provide clarification as to the fact that the chorale was not essentially connected with the Art of Fugue but merely joined to it by a pious gesture to offset the lack of a conclusion for the final fugue.

It is strange that the obituary compiled in 1750[3] by Carl Philipp Emanuel Bach and Johann Friedrich Agricola, which represents the first authentic biographical account, is silent on the question of the chorale and its remarkable genesis. Were they not informed about it, or did its history not seem sufficiently important to them? Further mention is made, however, in a discussion of Bach's last contrapuntal works, especially the Art of Fugue, contained in Johann Michael Schmidt's *Musico-Theologia* (Bayreuth and Hof, 1754): "or, which is even more miraculous, the chorale: 'Wenn wir in höchsten Nöten sein' dictated in his blindness to someone else's pen."[4] Schmidt's formulation is obviously based on the notice contained in the original print of the Art of Fugue; merely the words "on the spur of the moment" are omitted. On the other hand, he introduces the quotation with an appraisal of awe and admiration ("which is even more miraculous").

The next literary documentation to follow is found approximately half a century later in the work of Johann Nicolaus Forkel. It appears not in the biographical section of his 1802 book but in the catalogue of Bach's works. Here the following is stated in connection with the Art of Fugue:

> To make up for what is wanting to the last fugue, there was added to the end of the work the four-part Chorale: *Wenn wir in höchsten Nöthen seyn &c.* Bach dictated it in his blindness, a few days before his death, to the pen of his son-in-law, Altnikol. Of the art displayed in this Chorale, I will say nothing; it was so familiar to the author that he could exercise it even in his illness. But the expression of pious resignation and devotion in it has always affected me whenever I have played it; so I can hardly say which I would rather miss— this Chorale, or the end of the last fugue.[5]

Forkel was supposedly in the possession of more information than was available to the editor of the Art of Fugue, though on the whole his account followed the traditional wording, as may be seen from a comparison of the portions in question: "dictated in his blindness to the pen of one of his friends" (Art of Fugue, 1751); "dictated in his blindness, a few days before his death, to the pen of his son-in-law, Altnikol" (Forkel, 1802). Forkel gives a more definite date for the dictation as well as the name of the one who took it. Where did he get this information? As he attested, he received important biographical detail from the two oldest Bach sons. This can be clearly verified from his text.[6] Nevertheless, Forkel says nothing about the chorale dictation in the passage dealing with Bach's death (and containing a faulty date: 30 July 1750). Had he received an authentic report, it would doubtless have been incorporated there. As it is, the story appears in the worklist (the items of which show no other suggestion of communications received from the Bach sons), in fact patently derived from the formulation in the original Art of Fugue edition. It gives the appearance of a historical record rounded out or substantiated by Forkel himself.[7] He sketches a vivid picture of Bach's demise which does not conceal his emotional response.

Philipp Spitta aligns the description given in his fundamental biographical work (1880) with that of Forkel; indeed he elaborates upon its features:

> By his deathbed stood his wife and daughters, his youngest son Christian, his son-in-law, Altnikol, and his pupil Müthel. He had been working with Altnikol only a few days before his death. An organ chorale composed in a former time was floating in his soul, ready as he was to die, and he wanted to complete and perfect it. He dictated and Altnikol wrote. "Wenn wir in höchsten Nöten sein" was the name he had originally given it; he now adapted the sentiment to another hymn and wrote above it "Vor deinen Thron tret ich hiermit."

This small excerpt is entirely characteristic of Spitta's working method. On the one hand, he exhibits a familiarity with historical dates and facts regarding Bach's life and work such as no one before him was able to command. On the other hand, he integrates them as components placed within a broad canvass designed according to his ideals and goals, but in a manner contradicting historical exactness and the array of actual events. For instance, he takes over from Forkel's presentation both the name and date connected with the scene of dictation. They prove, however, insufficient for the outline of historical scene; and it is with this that he is concerned. Thus he includes further personages he assumes to have been present and gathers them around the deathbed, though without a basis of documentary evidence. Yet his knowledge enables him to interpolate what was unknown to Forkel and apparently also to the editor of the Art of Fugue, namely the connection between the "deathbed chorale" and an earlier work. He is referring to the short chorale setting "Wenn wir in höchsten Nöten sein" BWV 641 from the Weimar Orgel-Büchlein.

Spitta, in turn, is superseded in his novel-like narration and poetic style by Wilhelm Rust, principal editor of the old Bach edition for more than a quarter of a century. In his critical commentary to the Bach-Gesellschaft edition (1878) of Bach's organ chorales Rust gives free rein to fantasy:

> But the benighted body remained imbued with, and inspired by, the glory of the divine strength that raised him to his station of musical apostle. It was to speak and give witness once more and took recourse to a song from bygone days to render it in perfected and transfigured form. Was he guided in his choice by the remembrance of his first wife whom he had left in good health as he embarked on a journey, only to find her slumbering in the graveyard as he returned without premonition? Was the original form in the Orgelbüchlein a commemorative tablet dedicated to her which he recalled on his own deathbed? At the time he had the spiritual poem "Wenn wir in höchsten Nöten sein" in mind; but now he had the superscription changed by his son-in-law to whose pen he dictated the chorale, with significant reference to the song "Vor deinen Thron tret ich hiermit." Unfortunately the end of the dictation that in its total form amounts to twenty-five and a half measures has been lost. But even up to this point the writing displays all the interruptions of the ailing as well as the obstacles the writer had to surmount in the room of the blinded. From day to day the ink begins to run dry. Heavily veiled windows and subdued light impair the distinctness of the notes—a melancholic picture that conveys to the beholder the impression of the master's world coming to an end and eternal rest.[9]

Rust, the philologist, now even describes the manuscript as well as the course of the dictation. The copy is a fragment of the so-called Leipzig original manuscript, to which we will have to return. Yet this leaf shows neither the hand of Altnikol nor does it represent the dictation. In addition, Rust's remarks concerning interruptions and the failing ink are entirely without foundation.[10]

As we trace the evolution from the initial almost insignificant notice in the original print of the Art of Fugue to the inflated narration of Rust—a development unsupported by any added documentation—we are bound to conclude that we are faced with the growth of a legend. All the telltale characteristics are here: a small germ, a mention of fact given without comment, grows into a concretely perceived report with intensely religious overtones. Nor has the myth of Bach's death chamber, touched by the breath of eternity, reached its final expression in the sources quoted. But there is no need to pursue the trail from Albert Schweitzer's interpretations[11] to the expressions of popular historiography whose repercussions have remained alive. The course was set in the late nineteenth century. With the authoritative writings of Spitta and Rust, the concept of the "Fifth Evangelist" was preordained.[12]

Our critical inquiry, however, is not so much concerned with the formation of the myth (to be sure, this is not the first and only case of an idealized or even ideological Bach image), but with the verified written account, as it appears in the original print of the Art of Fugue in relation to the preserved musical sources. Neither Spitta nor Rust had consulted the original manuscripts; they were rather enthralled by a fascination which in view of the spirit of their time cannot be held against them. The factual basis is formed by three sources:

1. The chorale setting of nine measures "Wenn wir in höchsten Nöten sein" BWV 641 from the Orgel-Büchlein (abbreviated O in the following).[13]

2. The chorale setting of forty-five measures "Wenn wir in höchsten Nöten sein" BWV 668a appended to the Art of Fugue (here abbreviated W).

3. The fragmentary chorale arrangement of twenty-five and a half measures "Vor deinen Thron tret ich hiermit" BWV 668 appearing at the end of the so-called Leipzig autograph album (here V).[14]

Spitta and Rust had pointed out the correlation of V and O, describing V as an enlarged version of O. Curiously they make no mention of W. Hans Klotz[15] has explained that W is an older version of V, thus establishing a chronology moving from O through W to V. This chronology invalidates Rust's claim that V is the dictated version. According to Klotz, the place of the dictated version is taken by W, whereas V assumes that of a later revision.[16] The time Klotz assigns to W is "towards the end of his life, while Bach was bedridden," and the one he assigns to V is "shortly before his death."

This schedule would be plausible enough, were it not for the critical interdependence of O and W. A detailed investigation reveals that the essence of the two settings is identical. The four-part setting from the Orgel-Büchlein recurs in the "deathbed chorale" note-for-note, except for the omitted ornamentation of the *cantus firmus* in the top part and slight deviations in the lower parts. The synopsis given in Example 21.1 bears this out. The larger

Example 21.1. Synopsis of BWV 641 (= O) and BWV 668 (= W)

"OLD" SOURCES REVISITED: NOVEL ASPECTS

Example 21.1 (continued)

structure of versions W and V is based on interpolated imitative phrase introductions whose motivic substance and contrapuntal treatment (melodic inversion) are derived from the Orgel-Büchlein chorale (see Fig. 21.1).

But how is one to understand the idea of a blind Bach dictating, with exactness, large sections of a composition written probably more than thirty years ago? Even considering Bach's virtuosity in the craft, the borderline of probability would here seem to have been crossed. Today we have attained a familiarity with Bach's working procedure that tells us that even in his prime he rarely relied entirely on his memory. For instance, in drawing parts from a score just finished, or in dealing with parodies or transcriptions of existing works, he used the original manuscripts as a working base.[17] How much more plausible would it be that on the spur of the moment Bach might have created a completely new variant by dictation, without having to strain his memory!

Our doubt regarding the impromptu dictation, however, also casts doubt upon the oldest literary documents. The possibility that Carl Philipp Emanuel Bach may have been the editor of the Art of Fugue, which must be considered with reasonable certainty,[18] is here in conflict with our definite knowledge that at the time of his father's death, or immediately prior to it, he was not in Leipzig. Thus he could have known only secondhand about the chorale dictation. To this consideration must be added that of the prevailing animosity concerning the problems of dividing Bach's estate. An additional question regarding the information at the disposal of the editor for the Art of Fugue would be: Why did he choose version W instead of the earlier version V with its title so much more obviously suited to the nature of a swan song? This could have happened only because he had no knowledge of version V, for he evidently had no access to the manuscript P 271. The problems arising from the unfavorable source situation and the numerous unknown factors seem beyond solution, and a final answer can indeed not be given. Yet this does not rule out conjectural arguments that may at least pave the way toward such an answer.

The methodical basis for the following analysis is an exploration of the relationship existing between the three extant musical sources. The scheme given in Figure 21.2 reflects a reconstruction of the derivation of versions as

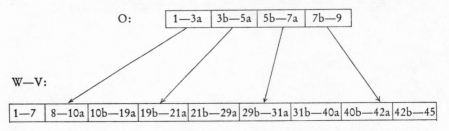

Figure 21.1. A comparison of measures from the Orgel-Büchlein chorale and versions W and V.

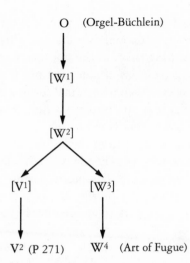

O (Orgel-Büchlein)

[W^1]

[W^2]

[V^1]   [W^3]

V^2 (P 271)   W^4 (Art of Fugue)

Figure 21.2. A possible derivation of the sources.

evident from the manuscripts, the apparently lost or unknown links being marked by brackets. [W^3] and W^4, as posthumous creations, must be separated from the original sources: W^4 represents the chorale published with the Art of Fugue, [W^3] is the four-part scoring furnished as printer's copy and devised supposedly by the editor of the Art of Fugue or his anonymous scribe from a notation on two staves in [W^2].[19] [W^2] must have been the source known to the editor as the chorale arrangement "which the deceased man in his blindness dictated on the spur of the moment to the pen of one of his friends." Accordingly it was not a manuscript written by Johann Sebastian Bach, for as such it would certainly have been identified within the inner Bach circle. [W^2] renders the enlarged version of O in precisely the form that has come down in W^4. Since we may rule out editorial changes, W^4 and [W^2] must have been identical readings. Yet the version of W^4 and V^2, and correspondingly of [W^2] and V^2, differ in critical points to be discussed below. On the other hand, the fragment in P 271, representing version V^2, is a fair copy executed, without corrections, by the copyist "Anonymous 12"[20] and thus must have been based upon an earlier copy. This could not have been [W^2], for it was not subjected to proofing and the resulting changes which undoubtedly would have been taken over in [W^3]. The place of an intermediate source must have been taken by [V^1], a complete or fragmentary copy of [W^2], with the corrections entered or with a list of corrections given merely in the letter notation of organ tablature.

The derivation of V^2 from [W^2] may thus be traced in outline. But what is the origin of [W^2] as key source? We have expressed doubt that version [W^2] was produced by dictation. It seems more justified to view the provenance of [W^2] in the context of the other seventeen chorales in the so-called Leipzig original copy. Likely it is not without reason that the fair copy of V^2

appears in the volume P 271, separated from the seventeen chorales only through the autograph of the Canonic Variations on Vom Himmel hoch.[21]

A common distinguishing factor of the so-called Great Eighteen Chorales is that they all represent revisions of older settings from Bach's Weimar period. The "deathbed chorale," whose original form is contained in the Weimar Orgel-Büchlein, fits logically into the series. It is not possible to consider it an isolated work that stands apart from the other seventeen chorales, for we know of no single instance from the last decade of Bach's life in which (other than in correlation with the chorale collection in P 271) he dealt with the revision or a new version of a composition going back to the Weimar period. It is even harder to imagine that the blind composer suddenly remembered the small Weimar work so vividly that he could dictate it without deviation.

If we thus link the "deathbed chorale" to the seventeen chorales, it appears as a striking circumstance that the sixteenth and seventeenth chorales (BWV 666 and 667) are not written out by Bach himself but by Altnikol. In resurrecting the pieces from old copies or new sketches, Bach availed himself of help. In a similar manner V^2 was entered in the volume, as in the case of Altnikol, by the hand of an organist.[22] A further connection arises from the fact that the seventeenth chorale goes back to a model in the Orgel-Büchlein as well. It constitutes the only such case within the group of seventeen chorales, and it can hardly be considered accidental that the two pieces from the same source stand, so to speak, side by side.

It was originally a large complex of manuscripts in single pages or leaves, containing sketches and earlier versions, that formed the chorale collection in the Leipzig original manuscript. After their contents were entered into the fair copy, they were apparently destroyed by Bach or otherwise lost. Only one leaf for BWV 660a was preserved and bound into P 271.[23] [W^2] might have been a similar leaf, possibly also copied by Altnikol, the copyist of the other setting that is an enlarged version of an Orgel-Büchlein chorale.[24] Altnikol's work as Bach's assistant was apparently linked to the period of his studies, 1744 to 1747. The fact that Bach placed the Canonic Variations BWV 769 in his own hand after Altnikol's last entry in P 271 would fit with these dates. And the *terminus ad quem* or *post quem* is Bach's admittance in June 1747 to Mizler's Societät der musicalischen Wissenschaften, for which Bach had submitted the canonic work. The process of compiling a fair copy of the revised Weimar chorales must accordingly have ceased in 1746–47 at about the time Altnikol relinquished his duties. If we count the "deathbed chorale" as the eighteenth in this collection, the manuscript [W^2], whether or not copied by Altnikol, would have to be dated at the time the Weimar organ chorales were revised.

Since [W^2] is not an autograph, it must have been based on an original manuscript [W^1], whose nature, in contrast to that of [W^2], cannot be further determined. Likely it was a first draft containing various corrections, or merely a sketch limited to the additions to O, for otherwise there would have been no need for the copy [W^2]. [W^1] must go back to Bach's own hand. But when were the additions to O, entered for the first time in [W^2], conceived? In the case of "Komm, Gott Schöpfer, heiliger Geist" BWV 667 it has been ascertained on the basis of the existing sources that the extended version effected through a second *cantus firmus* elaboration, with the chorale in the bass, dates back to Weimar.[25] The same might apply to [W^1]. What speaks against this conjecture is that, in distinction to BWV 667, no copies from the Weimar period, such as were normally distributed among the members of the Bach circle of those years, can be verified. All seventeen chorales have come down in such copies,[26] and it seems likely that no expanded form derived from the Orgel-Büchlein for [W^1] was then in existence.

It is equally likely that [W^1] originated later than most of the Weimar chorales, which, in large part, can be dated to the early Weimar years before 1714, and thus it was not available for the copyist. A number of settings from the Orgel-Büchlein have not been preserved in copies, for they were entered by Bach in the later Weimar years. And O belongs to this later group.[27] Another explanation for the absence of copies based on [W^1] might arise from the fact that [W^1], being an incomplete draft (see above), was not suitable for copy.

Criteria of style analysis do not enter here. The motivic material for the added sections of W is totally drawn from the original version O, as is indicated by the brackets in Figure 21.1. The harmonic structure does not suggest a stylistic phase departing from the seventeen chorales or the Orgel-Büchlein. It is true that the consistency of motivic elaboration and the logic of part-writing points beyond the scope of the seventeen chorales to a stage of greater maturity. This was reached with the unparalleled concentration of musical substance found in the Orgel-Büchlein, which forms a notable contrast to most of the seventeen chorales.[28] Seen in this perspective, a date for the first version of W close to that of O seems entirely plausible. The analogous case of BWV 667 may be remembered here. Nevertheless, a dating within the last decade of Bach's life can be ruled out by arguments of neither source nor style criticism. Only the rhythmic uniformity and a certain unevenness of character (as represented by the slackening of motion in m. 32; see the discussion below) give rise to some reservation as to a collocation with Bach's last works.

Yet there is no doubt that Bach dealt with W during the last decade of his life. There is no other way to explain the inclusion of V in P 271, following the canonic work BWV 769, nor the notice in the original print of the Art of Fugue. For the decisive step leading from the older version [W^2] to the final version V^2, I might advance the following hypothesis. Bach was occupied with unfinished works during the time of his illness,[29] and it is possible that he returned to the collection of chorales contained in P 271 with a view toward publication. A person from among those closest to Bach plays version [W^2] for the blind composer. Bach listens intently and dictates important revisions, which are taken down by the helper onto [V^1]. The emendations move on a plane characteristic for the highly refined style of the late works and serve as a basis for the fair copy V^2.

The first of the corrections intensifies the rhythmic-melodic texture in the last measure of the first interpolation (m. 7) by adjusting the tenor in a manner corresponding to that of the alto. The entrance of the *cantus firmus* (c.f.) thus becomes more compelling (Ex. 21.2). The second correction is likewise of rhythmic nature, since the bass line in m. 9 avoids, through an anticipation of the connecting formula in the *cantus firmus,* an unvarying connection of the head motif with the consistent succession of eighth notes (Ex. 21.3). The third correction, in m. 10, eliminates a close repetition of the cadence in G major. The first cadence in W was directly taken over from O, causing a renewed return to G major at the introduction of the second interpolation. V now leads through a deceptive cadence in E minor to the full cadence in G major and thus lends a sense of totally different elegance to the harmonic structure (Ex. 21.4). The last correction occurs in m. 26, immediately before the fragment in P 271 breaks off. Again Bach alters the rhythmic nature and changes the steadily rising succession of eighth notes, thus bringing about a pointed climax by which the melodic high point reached in the second half of the measure is introduced with greater tension (Ex. 21.5). The remaining part of the final version is unfortunately lost, which limits our awareness of Bach's finishing touches to the extent here discussed. But even the preserved fragment shows the superior quality of craftsmanship in the final version V as compared with the older version W, regardless of the unchanging basic substance of the setting. This may raise new doubt as to a later origin of [W²].

What cannot be overlooked is the change of title in V. It is understandable that the ailing Bach, perhaps after the unsuccessful eye operation,[30] was given to thoughts of the beyond. And only with the most somber thought can one regard his choice of the emphatically eschatological chorale which, at a morning, noon, or evening prayer, was traditionally sung on the melody "Wenn wir in höchsten Nöten sein."[31]

Our deliberations upon the questions concerning the constellation of the three surviving sources, questions that arise from an extended line of circumstantial evidence, leads to the reconstruction for the filiation of derivative versions shown in Figure 21.3.

The course of our investigations for an explanation of the genesis of the "deathbed chorale" consisted of a chain of hypothetical conclusions placed in logical order. It is to be understood that these hypotheses are partly subject to doubt, yet they offer fewer points of argument than the earlier suggestions for the origin of the "deathbed chorale."

The principal result is founded in the justified contention that this so-called deathbed chorale was never "dictated . . . on the spur of the moment," but that Bach dictated in his blindness revisions for an existing composition. It is possible that this was his last creative expression. The editor of the Art of Fugue received word of the last work, though not of the precise circumstances under which it was written. And the situation in the family after Bach's death—the lawsuit over inheritance claims, the quarrel of the older

Example 21.2.

Example 21.3.

Example 21.4.

Example 21.5.

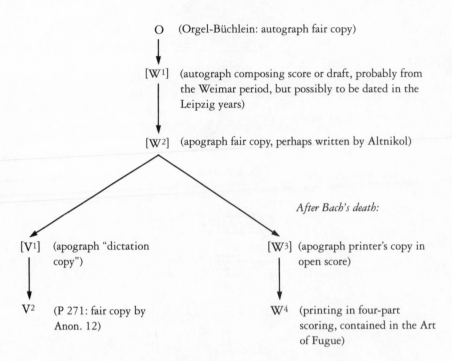

O   (Orgel-Büchlein: autograph fair copy)

[W^1]   (autograph composing score or draft, probably from the Weimar period, but possibly to be dated in the Leipzig years)

[W^2]   (apograph fair copy, perhaps written by Altnikol)

After Bach's death:

[V^1]   (apograph "dictation copy")

[W^3]   (apograph printer's copy in open score)

V^2 (P 271: fair copy by Anon. 12)

W^4 (printing in four-part scoring, contained in the Art of Fugue)

Figure 21.3. A more detailed scheme for the derivation of the sources.

Bach sons with Anna Magdalena and her children—was a poor basis for a clear account of Bach's last weeks and months, if such was sought to begin with. In any event, P 271 with its final version of the chorale was not available, for this important collection of organ works likely went to Wilhelm Friedemann Bach, the organist, just as the autograph and engraver's plates for the Art of Fugue went to Carl Philipp Emanuel, the harpsichordist and theorist. This might explain the strange fact that the older version W was published with the original print of the Art of Fugue—the version with which evidently vague reports of a dictation were associated.[32]

The point of departure for our critical study was the myth that gradually surrounded the "deathbed chorale." The thought that Bach dictated on his deathbed a swan song in which not the composer so much as the "divine strength that raised him to the station of musical apostle . . . was to speak and give witness" (in Rust's words) calls forth associations with the classic mythical image of Pope Gregory the Great, who dictated to the pen of a monk the chorale melodies handed down by the Holy Spirit in form of a dove. An undoing of the familiar reverential myth becomes unavoidable. The remaining hard core, however, is more than an obscured fact. The sources indisputably verify Bach's artistic involvement to his last moment. The emendations that elevate the final version "Vor deinen Thron tret ich hiermit" from the earlier form of "Wenn wir in höchsten Nöten sein" are the last reflection of a lifelong striving for an *ars perfecta*.

❖   ❖   ❖

CONCEPTS, STYLE,
AND CHRONOLOGY

22

Chronology and Style in the Early Works: A Background for the Orgel-Büchlein

POSSIBLY THE LARGEST grey area in the exploration of Bach's music is that of the composer's early work. This fact gravely impedes any discussion of the development leading to the young Johann Sebastian's relatively isolated works of unquestionable mastery. Works such as the "Actus Tragicus" BWV 106 or the ceremonial cantata "Gott ist mein König" BWV 71 for the 1708 inauguration of the Mühlhausen town council seem to stand apart, and even the cantatas "Aus der Tiefen rufe ich" BWV 131 or "Christ lag in Todesbanden" BWV 4, with their highly individual level of perfection, fail to explain how Bach reached the Parnassus of sacred cantata composition at such an early age or how he arrived at original solutions in the genre.

It is entirely possible that one or another early vocal work was lost. The likelihood of major losses, however, is negligible—prior to 1714 Bach apparently wrote only a few vocal pieces; and it is safe to assume that he had ample time for the composition of such works. This is doubtless true for those works that show a superior measure of elaboration, such as BWV 71 as well as the "Actus Tragicus." The composition of the latter, for example, could hardly have been a command performance, given the invariably short time span between actual dates of death and memorial service; the hypothesis, in itself not convincing, that BWV 106 was written in tribute to Bach's uncle Tobias Lämmerhirt (d. 10 August 1707) seems unfounded.[1] There exists no documentation on this matter, and we are also left in the dark about the possible early date of the original version of the cantata "Ich hatte viel Bekümmernis" BWV 21. The uncertainties in the limited and relatively clear domain of vocal composition are numerous and consequential, yet they add up to a situation considerably more favorable to interpretation than that in the domain of instrumental music.

The beginnings of Bach's work as a composer of chamber music, for instance, are totally obscure. The Violin Fugue in G Minor BWV 1026, transmitted in a copy by Johann Gottfried Walther from ca. 1710, is but one example; entirely without parallel, it adds to many open questions a further riddle (regarding origin as well as function): When (in Weimar or earlier?) did Bach begin to take an interest in the composition of instrumental ensemble works (sonatas and concertos)? His relatively early clavier and organ arrangements of works by Legrenzi, Corelli, Albinoni, Reinken, and others suggest an extensive acquaintance with this literature.

With regard to keyboard music, finally, we have at our disposal a large, even very large repertoire, which, however, because of the lack of autograph manuscripts, is encumbered with questions of chronology and authenticity. It is difficult to escape a vicious circle, for the absence of a dependable frame of chronology makes it impossible to fix points of stylistic orientation from which to establish uniform criteria.

Though major progress has been made, above all in the studies of Hans-Joachim Schulze,[2] Elke Krüger,[3] Hermann Zietz,[4] Hartwig Eichberg,[5] and George B. Stauffer,[6] much work is still to be done. Results such as those of Eichberg's investigations with regard to critical questions of authenticity remain relative, for example, because of the lack of conclusive research in the history of Bach's earliest clavier suites.[7] And the point of departure for a chronology and stylistic evolution of the free forms of organ music loses its validity with the argument that Buxtehude's influence upon Bach's work did not commence with the journey to Lübeck in 1705–1706 but earlier.[8]

The greatest problem, however, arises in connection with the genre of the organ chorale, the one that may be considered predominant in the work of the young Bach. Among the very earliest compositions of Bach are generally counted the chorale partitas. For stylistic reasons (adherence to the model set by Georg Böhm), their origin in Lüneburg seems probable, yet not the slightest documentary proof for this general date exists. Furthermore, we do not know when the young Bach began to compose: in Ohrdruf or in Lüneburg?—hardly thereafter, and doubtless not as late as in Arnstadt.[9] Yet on this question hinges the premise of either a longer or a shorter maturing process of Bach's compositional experience.

Considering that there are so many elements of uncertainty, special significance must be attributed to the first work that bears the unquestionable stamp of Bach's individual style, namely the Orgel-Büchlein. Ever since the writing of Philipp Spitta, the Orgel-Büchlein has occupied the position of a key work in the evolution of the chorale setting marked by consistent motivic elaboration and an expressive, highly individual idiom. But when did Bach arrive at such an achievement? Whereas Wilhelm Rust assumed (in the process of preparing the first critical edition of the work) that the Orgel-Büchlein, in accordance with its title signature, belonged to the Cöthen period,[10] it was clear to Spitta that it must have originated in the last Weimar years, though he was unable to corroborate this by source evidence.[11] It was not until the beginning of the 1960s that Georg von Dadelsen advanced philologically convincing arguments that the origin of the Orgel-Büchlein can by no means be placed in the later Weimar period. His 1713–1714 dating[12] for the beginning of Bach's work on the autograph of the Orgel-

Büchlein has been generally accepted, and it has received concrete support through Heinz-Harald Löhlein's grouping of three manuscript phases (Advent 1713 to Pentecost 1714; Advent 1714 to Easter 1715; and Christmas 1715 to Passiontide 1716).[13]

The question, however, arises whether the time of the Orgel-Büchlein does essentially coincide with the beginning of Bach's cantata production. Although the determining graphological arguments for the dating of the Orgel-Büchlein were oriented by fairly secure dates for autograph scores of the Weimar cantatas,[14] the basis for the studies involved has been somewhat broadened since the time of Dadelsen's writing. To be included in the discussion are in particular Bach's autograph copies of the *Livre d'Orgue* by Nicolas de Grigny and of other French keyboard works (Stadt- und Universitätsbibliothek, Frankfort, Mus. Hs. 1538), his share in the copies of orchestral material for a Telemann concerto (Sächsische Landesbibliothek, Dresden, Mus. 2392-0-35a), or his copy of Tomaso Albinoni's op. II, no. 2 (Stadtarchiv Leipzig, Go.S. 301), as well as Bach's autograph tablature of the Fantasia in C Minor (BWV Anh. 205/Anh. II 45→) from the so-called Andreas Bach Book. Moreover, a major vocal score, the autograph of Cantata 131, which was inaccessible for a long time, turns out to be of particular importance for the investigation of Bach's early manuscript characteristics. Finally, a series of Bach copies for vocal works by other composers (Johann Baal, Marco Gioseffo Peranda, Johann Christoph Schmidt)[15] requires comparison in the process of analyzing Bach's handwriting. From this material it becomes evident that Bach's writing between the years 1708 and 1715 (and perhaps beyond this period in both directions) remained remarkably unchanged.

Given the fact that Bach's manuscript style does not suggest precise confines, the thought of setting a beginning for the Orgel-Büchlein closer to the early Weimar period, approximately 1708 to 1710—thus linking it to the court organist's need for a repertoire—becomes tempting. Bach took up his service at Weimar in the summer of 1708, and he may have made the first entries in the Orgel-Büchlein during the Advent and Christmas seasons of 1708–1709; the major share of the work may have been completed before 1714 (excepting the small number of additions proved to have been entered at a later time). The watermark (Arnstadt paper mill) of the autograph does not contradict this supposition.[16] Whether further individual manuscript phases could be exactly dated remains doubtful in view of the sparseness of comparable autograph sources. Yet in whatever manner one proceeds to date the Orgel-Büchlein and its contents, the problem of the relative isolation of the Orgel-Büchlein chorale as a genre of composition persists. Is it possible that we are dealing with a prototype that has no antecedents?

The great organ chorales, in particular the Weimar versions of the chorales in the Leipzig autograph album (the Great Eighteen), have no conceptual affinity to the Orgel-Büchlein and belong presumably to a later period. The singly transmitted organ chorales issued in series IV, volume 3 of the *Neue*

Bach-Ausgabe are too heterogeneous in nature, and the number of small chorale arrangements is too insignificant, to serve as plausible background for the Orgel-Büchlein. In this connection a manuscript from the Lowell Mason Collection of Yale University, with the shelfmark LM 4708, which so far has not been taken into consideration by Bach scholarship, assumes major significance; it contains, among others, thirty-eight organ chorales attributed to Bach, including two belonging to the Orgel-Büchlein ("Herr Christ, der einig Gott's Sohn" BWV 601 and "Ich ruf zu dir, Herr Jesu Christ" BWV 639, both in patently older versions). In addition, there is a series of single chorales, heretofore largely unknown and primarily of Johann Michael Bach's authorship. The manuscript LM 4708 was written by Johann Gottfried Neumeister, a Thuringian who was a student of Georg Andreas Sorge and whose name had remained unknown in Bach studies; it was apparently compiled shortly after 1790 in Friedberg (Hesse).[17]

Since we are dealing here with a late-eighteenth-century secondary source, for the most part lacking any concordances, we can omit a critical description of the manuscript as well as a discussion of its repertoire, of further identification of the scribe, of authenticity and dating of its contents, and of the problems involved in an edition. What I propose to do is to establish the relationship of the repertoire of LM 4708 to the Orgel-Büchlein in an attempt to illuminate the background of the latter.

The repertoire of LM 4708 follows the usual type of brief variation and fughetta chorales, as it was prevalent, above all, in central Germany about 1700. LM 4708 seems to present a choice made from a collection, originally larger, the extent of which we can no longer estimate. As is known, the Orgel-Büchlein, too, was meant to include 182 chorales, but less than a quarter of the total number was completed. It is yet to be considered whether Bach's design for 182 chorale titles within the Orgel-Büchlein was not so much oriented by a concrete hymnal index (which, for that matter, cannot be identified)[18] as it might have been by a large compilation for study and performance, from which Bach selected examples for the Orgel-Büchlein, partly revising them and partly creating *alio modo* versions of the newer types to fit the Orgel-Büchlein.

The so-called Plauen Organ Book, now lost,[19] represents with its 280 chorales the model of such a Thuringian collection, presumably the typical counterpart to manuscripts of the circle closest to Bach (such as the Möller Manuscript and the Andreas Bach Book). Since these, almost without exception, contain literature not directly tied to the chorale melodies, there may have been a need at the time for a chorale anthology (possibly consisting of several volumes) that would have served the purpose of a supplement to the repertoire. In any event, a collection of this sort for use in the worship service might suggest the origin for Bach's involvement in the composition of organ works. It is not possible to determine to what extent the general design of the Orgel-Büchlein was guided by these collections. More likely, the organization was not based so much upon a concrete model as upon the plan to

Example 22.1. "Wir Christenleut" BWV 1090

compile a "portfolio," the contents of which were dictated by purely practical considerations.

The musical style of the Orgel-Büchlein points with unmistakable consistency to a systematically developed type of embellished hymn setting, especially one including the use of obbligato pedal. The manifest maturity of creative expression suggests that Bach had gathered experience by consistent and intense improvisatory probing as well as written elaboration—vestiges seem to be preserved in LM 4708. Nor can it be considered accidental that the two concordances between LM 4708 and the Orgel-Büchlein, BWV 601 and 639, include the only piece whose texture is unusual, namely the three-part setting "Ich ruf zu dir, Herr Jesu Christ" BWV 639. It might be understood as an indication that older material was absorbed.

As one of the works ascribed to Bach, the Neumeister Collection represents a rather broad spectrum of compositional approach and apparent experimentation. There are settings, for instance, in which the pattern of the multi-movement partita is projected upon the elaboration of a single chorale verse. An example of this form is the tripartite setting of "Wir Christenleut" (Ex. 22.1). The first section of this work is characterized by the rhythmic exchange of sixteenth-note passages; it is followed by a section in 12/8, and the concluding section is marked by consistently dotted-eighth-note motion. Further, there are chorales determined by the style of chordal hymn setting, which continue either in strict polyphonic or free improvisatory manner; the chordal beginning of "Aus tiefer Not schrei ich zu dir" (Strasbourg melody version), for instance, leads to a canonic *cantus firmus* setting[20] (Ex. 22.2), whereas in the chorale "Jesu, meine Freude," the hymn melody leads in unbroken succession from soprano to tenor and bass, then giving way to a free fantasy with suggestions of the *cantus firmus* (see Fig. 9.6).

Next to the numerous chorales elaborated in a fugal manner (usually anticipating the melodic shape for a verse line in imitative entrances) stands the example of an almost equally important type of varied hymn setting in which the melody is accompanied by the lower voices in motet-like manner. Here the style of composition is most closely related to that of the Orgel-Büchlein. The pieces in the Orgel-Büchlein can be seen to be usually derived from settings marked by simple polarity, as a rule through added motivic elaboration. This is evident especially in the autograph of the chorale "Der Tag der ist so freudenreich" BWV 605, where the unadorned appearance of the outer parts (the soprano in quarter-note and the bass in eighth-note motion) suggests a primary phase of manuscript. Such a procedure applies even to the few chorales with an embellished *cantus firmus*—which turns out to represent an advanced form of what was originally a plain *cantus firmus* melody. An extreme example is the chorale "O Mensch, bewein dein Sünde groß" BWV 622.

This type of varied hymn setting, otherwise very rare in the singly preserved organ chorales by Bach,[21] appears with frequency in LM 4708, though in differently conceived and executed forms. In the same category must be counted a variety of chorale elaboration, at first glance seemingly rudimentary and inconsistent, in which motivic material and texture of part-writing are subjected to constant changes (the chorale verse lines with their respective textual meaning showing an affect-oriented differentiation); an example is the chorale "Herzliebster Jesu, was hast du verbrochen" (Ex. 22.3). A direct text interpretation, with intensely chromatic definition of the final line "und du mußt leiden" (and thou must suffer) stands out above all in the constantly varying tretment of chorale segments (the compositional technique here recalls seventeenth-century models, apparent for instance in Sweelinck's *Fantasia chromatica*).

The chorale "Das alte Jahr vergangen ist" BWV 614—well-known from the Orgel-Büchlein—which appears in a rather different (though equally expressive) form in LM 4708, shows that, on the whole, the Orgel-Büchlein tends more toward a terse type of setting recognizable even in the notation of the chorale melodies, which in turn influences the character of elaboration. The *cantus firmi* of the Orgel-Büchlein move in quarter notes, whereas the majority of chorale melodies in LM 4708 are set in half notes.

The level of technical execution represented by the motivically strict style of the Orgel-Büchlein settings is reached in principle in the chorale "Als Jesus Christus in der Nacht." The unity of its construction, which leads into a *Variatio,* is derived from the last *cantus firmus* line. This line consists of a

Example 22.2. "Aus tiefer Not schrei ich zu dir" BWV 1099

Example 22.3. "Herzliebster Jesu, was hast du verbrochen" BWV 1093

step-wise ascending and an intermittently descending phrase (Ex. 22.4); it furnishes the material for an ascending four-note motif, its inversion, and intervallic variant, and their combination produces the polyphonic fabric of the accompaniment in the lower parts. Thus the entire setting can be reduced to a germinal element in the *cantus firmus* (Ex. 22.5).

The few examples given here are intended to illustrate how the repertoire of LM 4708 may have paved the way toward the concentrated and compact settings of the Orgel-Büchlein. The chorales are marked above all by a systematic probing of harmonic possibilities inherent in the hymn melodies (at times by the dual elaboration of a verse line, as it appears, for instance, in "Ich hab mein Sach Gott heimgestellt" BWV 1113), and often by surpris-

Example 22.4.

Example 22.5. "Als Jesus Christus in der Nacht" BWV 1108

ingly unusual harmonic turns as well as density of the total contrapuntal texture. Beyond this, the Neumeister Collection strengthens a documentation of the influence emanating from Johann Michael Bach, Bach's first father-in-law (by virtue of more than twenty additions to the oeuvre of the Gehren organist). This applies especially to the terse as well as expressive type of hymn setting, for which Johann Michael provided the model, as is shown in the contents of LM 4708. Yet the pronounced interest of the young Johann Sebastian to merge north and central German prototypes and to reach beyond them is borne out in the highly individual manner of the Neumeister Chorales. No such variety of original solutions can be found in the work of any of his contemporaries.

The chorales from the manuscript LM 4708 add a major component to the picture of the young Bach. At the same time they discredit all the more plainly an unsatisfactory analytical manner that has been applied to well-known material—including those Bachiana designated as doubtful by the totally inappropriate methods of stylistic analysis applied by Johannes Schreyer[22] and Werner Danckert[23] and (especially as a consequence of incorporating the Schreyer and Danckert findings in Schmieder's BWV) largely excluded from the canon of accepted Bach works. There is much that needs to be reviewed if we are to arrive, on the one hand, at a more apt definition of the corpus of Bach's early compositions (not only in the domain of the organ chorale) and, on the other, at a better understanding of the technical process by which the style of these compositions took shape. The exploration of Bach's earliest works remains a particularly urgent desideratum, since only here is it possible to obtain a vantage point from which clearly to view Bach's artistic development.

23

The Architecture of the Passacaglia

THAT ARCHITECTURE represents music turned to stone is a simile prompted in particular by the comparison of Baroque edifices and works of music from the same period. From a historical point of view, the comparison, which links two arts categorically, is not without danger. But if one takes the differences into account it is surely justified to speak at times of musical elements in architecture and, correspondingly, of architectonic elements in music, and to take advantage of such analogies in the attempt to define genres or individual achievements. In music, reflection on architectural traits is useful especially where fixed and transferable components are concerned. These components appear in large format in multi-movement works like opera, oratorio, suite; in smaller format they are found in single works marked by multiple subdivisions, as in variations, fugues, preludes, fantasias, and particularly in the special case of ostinato variations that we encounter in Bach's Passacaglia in C Minor BWV 582.

The structure of a passacaglia or chaconne is determined by the principle of apposition of ostinato variations. Apposition is accomplished in various ways: for example, by gradually increasing technical difficulty; by harmonic, rhythmic, or melodic designs; or by rise and fall of sonority or texture. In every instance the ostinato theme acts as the audible pulse for the entire compositional structure. Yet hardly ever will a mere auditive or visual count of constant recurrences suffice to allow me to grasp the artistic intent of an edifice or composition. Organists, in particular, are faced with the task of further probing, since to them the analysis of the work is a basis for appropriate registration. A step-by-step change of stops from section to section will never do—whether one deals with a work by Frescobaldi or Reger. It is essential to recognize structures extending beyond the sectional arrangement.

The structure of Bach's Passacaglia has often been subjected to investigation, ranging in scope from the organist's practical interest to a search for hidden secrets. Hermann Keller was of the opinion that such discussions, in view of the highly differing results, might be summarized categorically as follows: "A number of scholars have tried to interpret the design of Bach's twenty variations; yet its concealed laws cannot be rationally grasped!"[1] Indeed, the known solutions remain largely unsatisfactory; they are apt to be rigidly systematic,[2] to represent arbitrary decisions lacking in imagination, or—as in most cases—to arrive at a compromise between these two extremes.[3] Yet what is presented as a perplexing or even unsolvable problem will become intelligible to eye and ear when one desists from doing violence to the musical text or capitulating before it, rather letting it speak in all its fine details.

The Passacaglia consists of two parts, variations and fugue. These two parts are preceded by the theme of the work in unaccompanied form—a feature not found in keyboard passacaglias and chaconnes before Bach. Not only is its initial appearance unique for its time, but the theme itself represents an innovation in that it is constructed as a genuinely melodic subject. Ostinato "themes" of earlier keyboard music, by contrast, were no more than short harmonic or melodic patterns, almost invariably consisting of four measures in triple time, as they are found in the works of Kerll, Krieger, Pachelbel, Buxtehude, and numerous other masters (Ex. 23.1). More extensive ostinato themes before Bach's time appear only in the works of Purcell and Muffat. Yet even Muffat's theme does not compare to Bach's, the first theme truly formed as an eloquent statement with clearly defined beginning, middle, and end as well as a subtle balance of rising and falling cadential steps (see Exx. 23.2 and 23.3).

As is known, the opening four measures of Bach's Passacaglia theme came from an organ Mass by André Raison.[4] Yet it is not actually possible to speak of two halves, one to be considered original and the other not. For the theme in its entirety, homogenous from the first tone to the last, reflects new di-

Example 23.1. Buxtehude, Ciacona in C Minor BuxWV 159

Example 23.2. Muffat, Passacaglia in G Minor

Example 23.3. Bach, Passacaglia C Minor BWV 582

mensions, in its length of eight measures as well as its ambitus of more than two-and-a-half octaves. Here already, in the nucleus of the work, the composer emerges as architect, weighing with absolute clarity the disposition of a theme which thereafter, in a set of variations, is to reappear in all imaginable rhythmic, melodic, and harmonic permutations, and eventually in the contrapuntal configurations of a fugue.

Focusing on the architecture of the Passacaglia, I shall deal here primarily with the twenty ostinato subdivisions of its variation part. The form analysis will proceed along a number of questions aiming at basic structural elements: placement of the theme; alterations of the theme; motivic design in terms of rhythmic-melodic or harmonic aspects; contrapuntal elaboration; and number of voices.

In the attempt to place the data thus obtained in the context of the total work, I shall outline the structure of the entire variation part (see the tabulation of variation incipits in Ex. 23.4). My concern will not be with detailed analysis of individual variations so much as with the larger scope of their collective appearance as principal components of a large edifice.

Section I (Variations 1–2)

Consistently sequential motivic formation in the parts above the ostinato bass (four-part texture); resolutions of syncopated suspensions entering upon quarter-note upbeats; differentiated rhythmic-melodic patterns in the three upper parts, forming uninterrupted sequences. A difference between the two variations lies in the register: the upper range of the first variation covers the second octave above middle c; that of the second variation, the first octave above middle c.

Section II (Variations 3–5)

Logically developed rhythmic-melodic motifs above the ostinato bass (four-part writing); the upper part in Variation 3 are primarily made up of eighth notes moving step-wise. Variation 4 sustains the linear motion, though reinterpreting it, in complementary patterns, to anapest norm (two sixteenth notes followed by one eighth note). Variation 5 retains this rhythmic model, but the melodic progressions are split into larger intervals (mostly through descending skips in sixteenth notes). The pedal ostinato is now drawn into the motivic work of the upper parts, in correspondingly diminished rhythm (see asterisks in Ex. 23.3).

Section III (Variation 6–9)

Development of motivic material that is rhythmically uniform and constant but varying in its melodic direction (four-part writing). The rhythmic design of this variation group, again in complementary patterns, is based on a steady and uninterrupted flow of sixteenths. The melodic design is as follows.

Variation 6: Sequential upbeat motifs of three sixteenth notes each, ascending step-wise.

Variation 7: Sequential upbeat motifs of three sixteenth notes each, descending step-wise.

Variation 8: Sequential upbeat motifs of three sixteenth notes each, pairs of voices ascending and descending step-wise in contrary motion.

Variation 9: Sequential upbeat motifs of three sixteenth notes each, now rising and falling in melodically disjunct motion (thirds); the ostinato bass is adjusted to the motivic patterns of the upper voices in corresponding rhythmic diminution (compare the concluding variation of Section II).

Section IV (Variation 10–11)

The two central variations of the work are linked in double counterpoint. The same flowing sixteenth-note line serves in one case as upper counterpart (C) to the ostinato bass (the theme, T) and in the other as lower counterpart to the ostinato placed in the soprano, so that here, by mirror symmetry, the two halves of the entire composition are defined and joined.

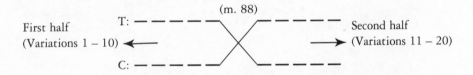

This central point of the work is marked in various other ways. In the first half the ostinato remains in the bass register; thereafter, through a device of contrapuntal technique, it is organically transferred to the opposite register. In Variation 10 (four-part texture) the ostinato functions finally as a bass support for chordal strokes, accentuating the clearly stressed ostinato tones before leaving this register, not to reach it fully again until Variation 16. Variation 11 presents the ostinato in its original guise, but in the upper part, introducing the second half of the work without a break. The two-part texture of this variation indicates that from now on the regularly applied four-part writing in the first half will no longer be the rule.

Section V (Variation 12–15)

The connections among these four variations are based on the following elements: descent of the ostinato from the top to the bottom register; decrease of part texture from four parts to a single line; progressively embellished dissolution of the ostinato theme. Variation 12 begins with the statement of

Example 23.4. Survey of the Passacaglia variation structure

the ostinato in the upper part, whereas the three lower parts form a dense texture of a predominantly descending "step-pattern" motif. Compared to the first half of the work, there is a reverse arrangement of parts. The full texture and plenum character of this variation is given emphasis through the contrast with the preceding two-part variation. Variation 13 turns to three-part texture, the ostinato moving into the middle register (alto range). Variation 14 reduces the texture to two parts, with the ostinato in the lower part (tenor range, 8' register). The concluding Variation 15 retains but a single part, the ostinato being formed by pointed sixteenth notes on beats three and one in alternating soprano and bass registers. The transformation of the original ostinato theme is subtly suggested as early as Variation 12 (m. 99),

Example 23.4. (continued)

the following variation showing an ornamental alto version of the ostinato, whereas in Variation 14 its melody is dissolved into arpeggios and in Variation 15 it is wholly divided into top and bottom spheres (see the corresponding asterisked markings in the example). At the same time, beginning with Variation 13, there is a gradual integration of the broken ostinato theme with the texture of the other voices.

Section VI (Variation 16–18)

This group of variations (in three- to six-part texture) returns to the pedal ostinato. The coherence of these variations is founded on a dualism of chordal and linear principles. The vertical principle appears in strict form in Variation 16, with its acciaccatura-like, successive "clusters" of six-part chords. The linear principle emerges in the ensuing three-part setting with its brilliant concertato duo of the upper parts. Both principles, chordal writing impeded by syncopation and fluent melodic writing in sixths and tenths, are joined in Variation 18, kept in four parts; the pedal bass marks the conclusion of the group once again in motivic adaptation (compare the ending variations for Sections II and III).

Section VII (Variation 19–20)

The last variation group consists of two settings containing identical motivic material, in four and five voices respectively, in correspondence to the arrangement in the first group. Both settings are based on a syncopated chordal structure enhanced by circular and sequential sixteenth-note elaboration. Variation 19, with its upbeat beginning, distributes the sixteenth-note motion over the upper and lower manual parts, whereas the last variation, again with upbeat beginning, combines the outer and inner manual parts in complementary manner, widening the texture to five parts in final climactic sonority.

FROM THESE ANALYTICAL OBSERVATIONS there emerges a structure of the work that, in its staggered sequence of variation groups, proves to be clearly symmetrical:

1–2	3–5	6–9	10–11	12–15	16–18	19–20
I	II	III	IV	V	VI	VII
2 –	3 –	4 –	2 –	4 –	3 –	2

Three groups of two (I, IV, VII)—marking beginning, middle, and end of the variation part—constitute a scheme of paired variations, in each of which the motivic material remains identical. Theirs is a strong static function; they serve as cornerstones, so to speak, and their conjunction is in each case readily perceptible to the listener. The groups joining three or four variations represent developmental units of a more dynamic character. Their most important architectural element is the detailed, brick-like motivic work. Of similar structural significance, however, is the placing (that is, the register) and treatment (diminution) of the ostinato theme, as well as the deviations, commencing in the second half of the work, from four-part writing as the norm for the entire work including the fugue. From the varying combinations of such compositional elements Bach derives a carefully designed symmetrical frame[5] comparable to that not infrequently found in the structures of Baroque architecture; we might refer here to the large scope of

Example 23.5.

castle construction, or the smaller one of organ façades. Fervent imagination, paired with musical logic and architectural reasoning, furnished the driving artistic impulse.[6]

AS WE TURN to the fugue, it may at first seem surprising that there is no similar framework. But precisely this fact speaks for Bach's architectonic sensitivity. Symmetry is a static element, applicable to music only when correspondent components are involved, as is the case in the variation part of the Passacaglia. In distinction, fugue, by its nature, is developmental in structural design, the only potential element of symmetry being in a congruence of beginning and end, as for instance in the *da capo* form of Bach's great E Minor Organ Fugue BWV 548. Yet this is no more than the mere suggestion of a framework by which no symmetry of further, let alone all, components is implied.

The musical intent inherent in the fugue segment of the Passacaglia is now subjecting Raison's original theme—that is, the first half of Bach's ostinato theme—to contrapuntal elaboration. Bach inscribed this final portion of the entire work *thema fugatum*,[7] indicating that, in contrast to the preceding variation part, the treatment of the theme will be fugal and in strict four-part writing. And Bach chose an especially complicated fugal manner—not the least of the reasons being the consideration of balance against the variation segment—namely the conjuncture of the derived subject with two original subjects (see Ex. 23.5). Thus he proceeds in multiple counterpoint, that is, the theme (A) is heard, in each of its entries, together with the two countersubjects (B and C) in various combinations. Based on these combinations, the outline of the fugue structure is as follows:

Measure	169	174	181	186	192	198	209	221	234	246	256	272
Soprano		A	B	C	—	C	B	C		A	—	A
Alto	A	B	C	—	A	B	A	B	C	—	B	B
Tenor	B	C	—	A	B	A	C	—	A	B	C	—
Bass			A	B	C			A	B	C	A	C
Harmonic plan	c	g	c	g	c	E♭	B♭	g	c	g	f	c

The first section (ending in m. 197, after all three subjects have appeared at least once in all parts, last in the pedal) complies in its regulated sequence of the different subjects with the principle of the permutation fugue that served Bach in his vocal works, particularly those of the early period.[8] Bach departs from a systematically applied permutation principle after what might be considered the first exposition, which moves back and forth between tonic and dominant harmonies, eschewing wider modulation. He continues in a more liberal manner (for instance, using the theme also in the major modes, E♭ and B♭) and with more extensive interpolations between combined entries of A, B, and C, which, however, do not grow into genuine episodes. Rather, the interpolations involve intense modifications, fragments, or elaborations of B and C. With the increasing separation of the combined entries, the harmonic palette and dynamic intensity increase as well, yet without producing a clearly sectional pattern. The fugue ends after a climactic deceptive cadence, introducing the Neapolitan sixth and leading into a free coda that contains neither theme nor countersubjects yet culminates for the last three measures in seven-part texture.

THE QUESTION of a realization of these musical structures in actual performance naturally arises, above all with regard to the architectonic conception of the work's variation part. There are numerous musical structures whose realization in sound is obvious, but there are also those which require conscious shading. The latter situation may be taken for granted for the passacaglia and chaconne repertory beginning with the middle of the seventeenth century, especially in the case of organ music where the fact of variously modified color of sound is presupposed.[9]

It need not be stressed that the realization of an organ work in performance—the registration and manual changes—must be based on its structure. This being such a fundamental requisite, early organ music could forego special indications. In Bach's works original performance directions appear only sparingly; examples are found in the "Dorian Toccata" BWV 538/1, in the Prelude in E♭ BWV 552/1, and in various chorales. If directions by the composer are absent, analysis of form becomes the point of departure for an image in sound. It falls to the organist to determine and observe, on the basis of such analysis, the guiding principle of the work—to subject his interpretation to it in a fine balance of musical imagination and clear comprehension of the work's architecture. Merely to render a methodical analysis in performance or to succumb to an arbitrary display of effects—to name the extremes—can never be the artistic goal of performance.

A few points, limited to purely structural matters, might be gathered from the above discussion[10] for the preparation of a performance. More detailed registration and interplay of dynamics will depend upon different considerations: the individual attitude of the performer vis-à-vis the work, the instrument, hall, and acoustics.

A well-known performance problem is the transition from the variation to the fugue part. The problem arises from the fact that the first note of the fugue subject is not given in separate notation but rather included in the final C minor chord of the last variation, thus seemingly depriving the fugue of its upbeat beginning. There is every reason to regard this manner of notation as the original one, since Friedrich Conrad Griepenkerl made his edition published by C. F. Peters (Leipzig, 1844) in conformance with the autograph, now lost, and since it also occurs in the oldest source of the work in the Andreas Bach Book.

The primary reason for this form of transition, unique for Bach, is evidently the composer's intention to have the beginning of the fugue, arising from the last variation—the unmistakable joining of the two segments—confirmed even in the written form of the transition. The opposite extreme is seen in the Prelude and Fugue in E♭ Major BWV 552, as they appear in the original print of Clavier-Übung III, where the patent separation of prelude and fugue creates a frame for the entire work and does not negate their essential connection yet suggests the possibility of individual existence—a situation that would be unthinkable in the case of the two Passacaglia parts: whereas the Prelude and Fugue in E♭ Major, like other preludes (fantasies, toccatas) and fugues by Bach, are not necessarily performed in uninterrupted succession, this is mandatory for the Passacaglia. However, the absence of a double bar or any other clear marking for an end or a new beginning in the notation of the transition (m. 168) need not be interpreted so literally in performance that the fugue is deprived of its upbeat beginning. It is rather to be understood in the sense of a strict attacca connection.

Thus there are two possibilities open to the organist: either to hold middle c, as the beginning of the theme, from the final chord of the previous section, letting its isolated sound appear as a quarter-note upbeat, or else to begin, after the chord, with the unabridged *thema fugatum*. The former solution will be defeated in most cases by the acoustical properties of the room, in that the upbeat of the fugal theme will be absorbed by the reverberation of the closing plenum chord. Yet the rhythmic impulse of the upbeat is indispensable. The latter possibility is therefore usually to be preferred, provided that due advantage is taken of the musical tension between termination of the chord (not being a final ending) and entrance of the fugue theme (not being an "absolute" beginning).

To make brief mention, finally, of the question of sonority in the fugue itself, we revert to the fact that the analysis yields no genuine sections for any corresponding distinction in sound; there are no full cadences to mark fugal sections. This suggests that the entire fugue should be played on one manual,[11] in plenum sound, the coda perhaps receiving additional emphasis (for instance by coupling the manuals). Special conditions might on occasion require alternate solutions. Considering the work as a whole, the changing sonorities of the variation part will find a convincing conclusion only with an even level of sound for the fugue, for the formal and textural contrast will in principle require a corresponding expression in sound. The highly articulated variation part finds its complement in the expansively unified contrapuntal nature of the fugue, which does not lend itself to sectionalizing. The artful building process of the variation architecture leads to a culminating fugal finale, rounding out the entire composition by its unrestricted rule of musical laws.

Viewing the complete work, we realize that architectural structures such as that of the variation part can only be an aspect, never the total content of a composition or of musical thought in general. In this respect we stand merely at the beginning of a long road that the interpreter must travel in his attempt to comprehend the nature of Bach's Passacaglia as a musical work of art.

24

The Organ in Bach's Cantatas

THE CULMINATION POINT in the history of the organ and organ music in the Baroque era is inseparably bound up with the name of Johann Sebastian Bach, and this by no means only on account of his independent organ repertoire. The prominent role vested in the organ in Bach's vocal church music is not exhausted in its practical application as an accompanying or concertato instrument, for it is precisely at the level of compositional arrangement and modes of behavior that the alternating pervasion of vocal and organist traditions becomes manifest. The so-called Schübler Chorales (BWV 645–650), published in the last years of Bach's life as transcriptions from vocal movements, place on record the especial affinity of organ-style and cantata-style chorale arrangement. Similarly, in the orchestral treatment, not infrequently typical organ-like registration of the instruments is evident, as for example in the final duet (*gli stromenti all' unisono*) of the cantata "Tritt auf die Glaubensbahn" BWV 152. Further connections can be cited which reflect the creative dualism emanating from Bach's experiences as organist and cantor.

With regard to the performance forces in the cantatas, the organ already occupies a dominating position if only because of its function as an obligatory thoroughbass instrument. It took on further emphasis under the performance conditions of the Bach period in as much as the cantata, as the main music ("Haupt-Music") and musical core of the Lutheran service, was introduced by usually freely improvised organ playing. Accordingly a note written by Bach with reference to the Leipzig liturgy says: organ "preludes for the main music" (following reading of the Gospel).[1] During this prelude the choir and orchestra formed a group on the musicians' gallery, the so-called pupils choir, and the instruments' pitch was checked with the final chord of the organ. The chief organists under Bach during his period in Leipzig were Christian Heinrich Gräbner (St. Thomas's Church, until 1729), Johann Gottlieb Görner (St. Nicholas's Church, until 1729; St. Thomas's Church from 1729), and Johann Schneider (St. Nicholas's Church, from 1729). They would in general have taken over the organ part of the cantatas, although Bach most likely also occasionally observed the practice (exercised regularly by his predecessor in office, Kuhnau) of enlisting "the pupils and students who are well practised in organ playing."[2] This probably applied particularly to the pieces with a concertato organ part.

Traditionally, the organ was the thoroughbass keyboard instrument of church music. For secular cantatas, however, the harpsichord was always used, from where Bach (at least from time to time), in the manner of an orchestra leader, conducted the performance. This would not have been possible from the organ, since he would have his back to the musicians. A contemporary report on the performance of the Funeral Ode BWV 198 in the academic obsequies for the death of Electress Christiane Eberhardine on 17 October 1727 expressly mentions the "Clave di Cembalo, which was played by Herr Bach himself."[3] The use of the harpsichord in Leipzig church music was not restricted, as previously assumed, to accompanying the Sunday introit motets. Dual accompaniment involving the participation of both organ and harpsichord seems to have been exercised frequently if not regularly in Leipzig during Bach's time. Quite possibly Bach played the harpsichord accompaniment from his autograph score. A number of continuo parts specifically designated for harpsichord have survived, but the extent of the harpsichord use cannot be fully documented. However, virtually all surviving original performing materials for Bach's church music include organ parts. Even if they are not specifically designated for *Organo,* continuo parts containing thoroughbass figures and notated a whole step lower than in the score, explained by the higher so-called choir pitch of the Leipzig organs, show clear proof of its use by the organist.

An early example of Bach's organ expertise indicates the importance he placed upon the organ's accompaniment function. When his Mühlhausen organ was being reconstructed in 1708, he ordered that the Brustwerk (choir organ) that was to be newly built should especially have a "Stillgedackt 8 foot which thus fully accords with the music [motets, vocal concert or cantata] and shall be made of quality wood and must sound much better than a metal Gedackt [stop]."[4] In the Baroque organ, which is composed of sections ("Werke"), unified cabinets which are of different sound character and played by their own manuals or pedals, the Brustwerk—a special group of smaller pipes in the middle of the front of the organ between the large pedal pipes— is regarded as a favorable accompanying section because of its immediate spatial contact with the choir and orchestra. In addition to the typical Gedackt (or stopped) 8' register, it normally contains a series of further advantageous accompanying stops. The Brustwerk of the great organ of St. Thomas's Church from the year 1525, which has not been preserved, had the following disposition after its renovation in 1720–1721; the stops which would primarily be used for accompanying purposes are marked with an asterisk.

*Grobgedackt 8'	*Cymbel (II ranks)
Principal 4'	Sesquialtera
*Nachthorn 4'	Regal 8'
Nazard 3'	Geigen Regal 4'
*Gemshorn 2'	

Authentic registration details by Bach are sparse and have been preserved in only a few special cases, but these provide welcome orientation points. Regarding the organ version of the lute part of the arioso "Betrachte meine Seel" from the St. John Passion, Bach remarks for a performance in the 1740s: "Is played on the organ with 8' and 4' Gedackt."[5] The two Brustwerk stops thus guarantee clarification of the important part but at the same time maintain their discreet and unobtrusive tonal character. On the other hand, Bach's registration direction "*Rückpositiv* [positive organ]: *sesquialtera*" for the *cantus firmus* reinforcement in the introductory chorus of the St. Matthew Passion points to the strong tonal emphasis necessary at this point, evidently with inclusion of the Rückpositiv.[6] Also comparable is the registration direction "*Sesquialtera ad Continuo*" in the opening chorus of the Weimar cantata "Komm du süße Todesstunde" BWV 161.[7]

The manner of registration, as well as of the organ accompaniment as such, is primarily dependent upon the particular type of movement. A difference has to be made here between on the one hand elaborate movements, such as chorus, chorale, aria, and arioso, and on the other recitatives with the more loosely knit supporting chordal structure (secco recitative). In the latter case the organ is called upon to provide only short supporting chords in order to ensure a basis for the free declaiming singing voice and (together with the melodic fundamental instruments, such as violoncello, violone, and, if necessary, bassoon) to give the grammatical construction of the text an underpinning with the aid of cadential formulae. Expressive passages are distinguished by the fact that the harmonic rhythm is more tightly textured and consequently the chordal contribution of the organ is also more intensive. As opposed to this, in the elaborate movement types the organ operates as a subordinate instrument, serving fusion of the voices and their interaction by way of chordal consolidation. Its presence is also essential here, and there are only very few pieces where omission of the organ is demanded. This occurs in the bassetto ("Bassettchen") arias, movements with high-pitched continuo (which is normally performed by alto instruments, such as viola or oboe da caccia).[8] Over and above this there are in some thin-textured middle movements of cantatas from the period around 1732 (BWV 5, 9, 94, 97, 129, 139, 177) original tacet directions for the organ, the significance of which is not quite clear. Should perhaps the harpsichord or lute take over the thoroughbass at this stage?

Of particular importance in Bach's cantata works is the enlistment of the obbligato organ as a solo, in a manner which was otherwise completely un-

Example 24.1. Vocal solo section with obbligato organ (BWV 71/2)

known at that time. This proves Bach's special interest in his favorite instrument, but also his striving to create original instrumental combinations in cantata composition. The beginnings of this trend go back as far as the Mühlhausen period. The town council election cantata "Gott ist mein König" BWV 71 for the first time features in the second movement a partially obbligato organ voice. The thoroughbass accompaniment alternates with the motif insertions answering the vocal part in echo style (Bach's direction "Positiv" indicates manual change to the Rückpositiv; see Ex. 24.1). Otherwise no documented examples of obbligato use of the organ have been preserved from the pre-Leipzig period. It is not until the end of the first Leipzig annual cantata cycle that a single case occurs, in the Whitsun cantata No. 172 "Erschallet, ihr Lieder." In the Leipzig repeat performance of this work, composed in 1714, the obbligato oboe is replaced by the organ in the second movement. It thus serves to represent a melody instrument; in other words, it is not employed because of the keyboard instrumental possibilities. Accordingly the obbligato organ in the second movement of Cantata No. 47 "Wer sich selbst erhöhet," composed in 1726, can also be replaced by a violin (as in a performance which took place after 1734). Similarly exchanging of the *cantus firmus* part in the introductory movement of Cantata No. 73 "Herr, wie du willt" between horn (1724) and organ Rückpositiv (1732–1735), as well as the *cantus firmus* reinforcement in the introductory chorus of Cantata No. 80 "Ein feste Burg," can be understood as meaning that the organ takes over the role of a melody instrument. This applies in principle also to the following group of cantatas, which make generous use of the obbligato organ:

No. 146 "Wir müssen durch viel Trübsal" (Jubilate 1726): movements 1 (sinfonia) and 2 (chorus), arranged after the original version (violin concerto) of the Harpsichord Concerto in D Minor (BWV 1052/1–2).

No. 170 "Vergnügte Ruh" (sixth Sunday after Trinity, 1726): movements 3 (aria) and 5 (aria).

No. 35 "Geist und Seele wird verwirret" (twelfth Sunday after Trinity, 1726): movements 1 (sinfonia), 2 (aria), 4 (aria), and 5 (sinfonia); movements 1, 2, and 5 arranged after the original version of the fragmentary Harpsichord Concerto in D Minor (BWV 1059).

No. 169 "Gott soll allein mein Herze haben" (eighteenth Sunday after Trinity, 1726): movements 1 (sinfonia), 3 (aria), and 5 (aria); movements 1 and 5 arranged after the original version (oboe concerto?) of the Harpsichord Concerto in E Major (BWV 1053/1–2).

No. 49 "Ich geh und suche mit Verlangen" (twentieth Sunday after Trinity, ca. 1726): movements 1 (sinfonia; arranged after the original version of BWV 1053/3), 2 (aria), and 6 (chorale arrangement).

No. 188 "Ich habe meine Zuversicht" (twenty-first Sunday after Trinity, ca. 1728): movements 1 (incompletely preserved sinfonia; arranged after the original version of BWV 1052/3) and 4 (aria).

No. 120a "Herr Gott, Beherrscher aller Dinge" (Wedding Mass, ca. 1729): movement 4 (sinfonia; arranged after the prelude of the third partita for solo violin in E major (BWV 1006/1).

No. 29 "Wir danken dir, Gott" (town council election 1731): movement 1 (sinfonia; arranged after BWV 120a/4).

It is conspicuous that most of the cantatas belong to 1726 and thus are an integral part of the third annual cycle. Admittedly we do not know whether there was a definite reason for the frequency of organ solos in the Trinity period of 1726, or whether perhaps Wilhelm Friedemann Bach, sixteen years old at that time, was the performer of the virtuoso passages. An examination of the individual movements discloses that the figurative importance of the concertato organ part lies almost throughout on the right hand, while the left follows the basso continuo. This applies both to those sections which were arranged after missing solo concertos for violin and oboe and to the original organ passages in the arias of BWV 170, 35, 169, 49, and 188. A certain exception is provided only by the isolated quartet movement of the alto aria from Cantata No. 27 "Wer weiß, wie nahe mir mein Ende" (sixteenth Sunday after Trinity, 1726) for obbligato harpsichord (replaced by the organ around 1737), oboe da caccia, and thoroughbass. Whereas in the case of the solos specifically composed for the organ the generally richly figured work is definitely conceived for the keyboard, this does not necessarily apply to the transcribed concerto movements. It becomes evident here that it is

Example 24.2. Sinfonia of Cantata 169 (a), and the first movement of the Harpsichord Concerto in E Major BWV 1053 (b)

only the rearrangements of the movements as harpsichord concertos, carried out in the later 1730s, that take on a more idiomatic keyboard quality, and that they do so because of the emancipation of the left hand and general figurative refinements (see Exx. 24.2 and 24.3).

Taking over already existing material is by no means, however, a mechanical process. This becomes especially clear in those movements where one or several vocal parts are freshly added to the obbligato organ (BWV 146/2, 35/2, and 169/5). The subtler manner with which a vocal insertion of this kind is effected (see Ex. 24.3) reveals a characteristic trait of Bach's arrangement technique, which is not restricted to mere exploitation of what is available but aims at further exploration, enrichment, and perfection of the compositional material. In this respect these pieces are equal in value to those original compositions which are counted among Bach's most artful cantata movements, in particular the bass/soprano duet "Dich hab ich je und je geliebet" BWV 49/6, where the obbligato organ has a major share in bringing out the chorale substance.

stirb ———————— in mir ——— stirb ——— in mir, Welt ————

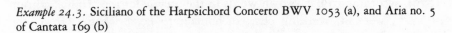

Example 24.3. Siciliano of the Harpsichord Concerto BWV 1053 (a), and Aria no. 5 of Cantata 169 (b)

25

Apropos the Musical Offering:
The Thema Regium and the Term *Ricercar*

I

FROM THE VERY outset, the focus and aim of the Musical Offering (BWV 1079), according to Bach's own words in the preface for the original edition of 1747, were in "working out," in homage to Frederick the Great, the king's "right Royal theme more fully and then make it known to the world." "Working out" refers to the various compositions written in elaboration of the theme. Accordingly, Bach's publication announcement of 30 September 1747 reads: "The elaboration [of the theme] consists of 1. two fugues . . . 2. one sonata . . . 3. various canons."[1] The idea of the work's conception unfolded in reaction to the unusual quality of the royal theme. The *Berlinische Nachrichten von Staats- und gelehrten Sachen* of 11 May 1747 contained in its report of Bach's visit at the Potsdam court the news that "Her Bach found the theme submitted to him *so exceedingly beautiful* [so ausbündig schön] that he wishes to write out a formal fugue based upon it, to be subsequently engraved in copper."[2] The dedicatory preface refers later to the "so *excellent* theme" as the "*noblest* part" of the work. No other theme in Bach's works was ever singled out by the composer in like manner.

Together with these unusual appraisals we encounter a highly imaginative rhetoric in the description of the theme. It is called a "right royal theme" in the preface and a "royal Prussian fugue theme" in the publication announcement mentioned above. The Latin version *Thema Regium* is found in the canonic movements (*Canon perpetuus super Thema Regium; Canones diversi super Thema Regium; Thematis Regii Elaborationes Canonicae*), and the Italian form *Soggetto Reale* appears in the title of the trio sonata (*Sonata sopr' il Soggetto Reale . . .*). Ostensibly the choice of languages corresponds to that of the genres of composition. The learned Latin is reserved for the movements of an essentially theoretical character,[3] whereas Italian, generally suggesting the solo and ensemble sonata of Italian origin, is applied to the typical sonata da chiesa. The German language is associated, according to the prefatory dedication, with the "Fuge auf dem Clavier," apparently referring to the three-part ricercar and likely also to the one written in six parts, though here the connection is not as obvious as it is in the cases involving Latin and Italian usage.[4]

The preface for the original print and the newspaper report concur in the statement that Frederick played for Bach the "theme for a fugue" on the fortepiano. The newspaper report stresses that this was done "without any preparation." According to Wilhelm Friedemann Bach's account as related by Forkel,[5] "he [J. S. Bach] asked the king for a fugue theme," implying that Frederick would indeed not have had any time for preparation.[6] There is no reason to doubt this point of the historical record inasmuch as Bach's request for a fugal theme should be understood as a special gesture toward the musically knowledgeable young monarch.

Nevertheless, the uncommonly finished and balanced form of the theme, as published in the Musical Offering, invites a questioning of the extempore formulation, especially since neither the structure nor the musical content show an affinity with the stylistic ideals of the Prussian king, as they can be easily gathered from his compositions and various utterances. Frederick's taste was formed primarily by the Italian opera of his time. One tends toward the conclusion that, in designing a theme so persuasively "Bachian," he may have consulted with members of his court orchestra, such as C. P. E. Bach or Bach's student, Johann Christoph Nichelmann. If so, it would mean that the king prepared himself for the assignment of the theme well ahead of time. Yet the sources in no manner support such a hypothesis.

Philipp Spitta[7] has called attention to the finale of Frederick's flute sonata in C minor, whose theme is the only one within the Prussian king's known oeuvre to come close to the Thema Regium (Ex. 25.1). Furthermore, the entire movement is contrapuntal to a degree quite unusual for Frederick—though not fugal—and Spitta concluded that the composition could have originated only under the immediate impression of the Musical Offering. Taking his point of departure from Spitta's statement, Hermann Keller draws the opposite conclusion.[8] He believes that this sonata movement was composed before the Musical Offering[9] and that Frederick would have played its theme, or one quite close to it, for Bach. Under Bach's hands the theme would then have grown into the true Thema Regium, and it would have been mere flattery "that he ascribed the excellence of this theme to the king."[10] This conjecture is subject to doubt for various reasons. First, the elements of the theme for the sonata movement (melodic motion by scale or chord formation) are placed in an order opposite to that appearing in the Thema Regium. Second, the sonata theme lacks chromaticism, an essential characteristic of the Thema Regium, which, in Frederick's own words, rep-

Example 25.1.

resented a "sujet de Fugue chromatique." [11] Finally, it is hardly imaginable that Bach would have departed so far from the king's suggested theme. The object of the fugue improvisation, requested in the presence of the court orchestra members, was certainly not to disfigure the assigned theme almost beyond recognition, in order then to derive a fugue from it. To do this would have been tantamount to declaring that he could not solve the task as posed, and it would have meant a disqualification of the formulation for the royal theme and thus a disavowal. We must therefore assume that Bach held to the theme as played by the king—although this does not exclude some slight revisions in using it, similar perhaps to the manner in which Bach adapted chorale incipits in fugal elaboration.

The elements of the Thema Regium (Ex. 25.2) are derived from conventional soggetto motifs (Ex. 25.3), as they are frequently found in imitative keyboard pieces of the seventeenth century. [12] The harmonic pattern (Ex. 25.4) appears with greatest frequency in two basic forms. [13] The chromatically descending tetrachord represents a convention which, above all as a recurring lament motif, retained currency until the late eighteenth century. [14] That Frederick, a well-informed musician, was familiar with these models can be taken for granted, particularly since he himself used the model of the descending diminished seventh in his flute sonata. A plausible explanation for the extempore presentation of the Thema Regium would thus be that Frederick, wanting to give the aged Bach as complex a task as possible, joined the two time-honored soggetto types to a fugue theme somewhat of this kind (Ex. 25.5). This reduced form of the Thema Regium, which might be considered the minimum of Frederick's share in its formulation, would have served several requirements implied in the situation. It is archaic and thus conceivably a gesture toward the conservative tastes of the St. Thomas cantor. Its character calls for strict contrapuntal elaboration. Its chromatic harmony presumes total command of compositional technique, and its sheer length challenges the improvisor to utter concentration.

The originality of the six-measure model is in a deft and unprecedented combination of two soggetti that establishes both the interesting and difficult aspects of the theme. The three-part ricercar, evidently a written elaboration of the Potsdam improvisation, presents at some points the two soggetti as single motifs (mm. 115ff.) and even combines two forms of rhythmic diminution (Ex. 25.6) The difference between the model cited above as the conjectured original form of the Thema Regium (Ex. 25.5) and its final formulation (Ex. 25.7) is in two points. The rhythmic modification of the passage connecting the two soggetti (X) results in a more compelling junction of the two theme components. The two-measure insert (Y), elegantly introduced by way of a suspension, leads into the ensuing smaller note values and then reverts directly to the melodic line of the basic pattern; it serves not merely for elongation but, by virtue of the interpolated smaller note values, imparts to the theme a new dynamic quality and the plagal ambitus of a widened melodic scope (Ex. 25.7).

Example 25.2.

Example 25.3.

Example 25.4.

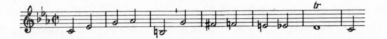

Example 25.5.

Example 25.6.

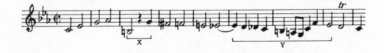

Example 25.7.

To what extent the theme extemporized by the king might have combined the elements X and Y in their suggested, rudimentary form is beyond any speculation. Yet it is precisely in these elements that we may recognize the hand of Bach, as might be shown by two related examples. The two thematic segments of the B♭ Minor Fugue BWV 867, with their contrasting rhythmic motion, are linked in similar manner (Ex. 25.8). In the contrapuntal continuation of the theme for the E Major Fugue BWV 878 from the Well-

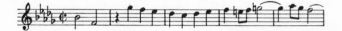

Example 25.8.

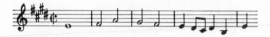

Example 25.9.

Tempered Clavier II we encounter the same descent toward the lower fourth at the first return of the tonic, coupled with the same intensified rhythmic declamation (Ex. 25.9). There is every indication that the final form of the Thema Regium was crafted by Bach's hand. It is marked by a balance, combining clarity with flexibility, of melodic, harmonic, and rhythmic tensions not inherent in the hypothetical basic pattern of the theme.

The actual form in which the Thema Regium was cast by Frederick on that memorable evening at the Potsdam castle cannot in the end be verified. But in an analytical distinction between reduced and final forms, a sense of Frederick's and Bach's respective shares in the formulation of the theme seems to emerge with a certain transparency. On the basis of such reasoning, roles of author and editor appear in characteristic partnership. If one views the Musical Offering in its entirety, it is difficult to regard its unique theme as "something in its given form extraneous, placing one's total impression of the work not so much upon an original form as upon the art by which it is subjected to varied treatment. Bach's instant realization in Potsdam, on the other hand, of the theme's potential far beyond the possibilities of improvisation, and his resolve for extended compositional elaboration, support the maxim that an artistic *sujet* belongs to him who knows best how to evaluate it." [15] In this sense a further clarification of the royal theme's origin might rightly be considered a problem of secondary importance.

II

Among the major sections of Bach's Musical Offering are two extended fugal movements—one in three and the other in six parts, both of them designated a ricercar (BWV 1079/1 and 5). That Bach chose a heading that otherwise—so far as we know—never appears in his works gives us pause, and the question arises why he revived the title with these two particular pieces. It is curious that two works so radically different in character, structure, and musical content should bear the same heading (see Figs. 18.2 and 18.6). It seems rather unlikely that we are dealing with thoughtlessness on the part of the composer; rather we are bound to conclude—especially since a publication of obviously distinguished nature was involved—that he very deliberately selected a designation he had never used elsewhere.

The divergence of texture that exists between the two ricercari impressed Spitta.[16] He found the appellation completely justified in the case of the six-part setting but, in viewing the other, says: "To a much lesser degree does the three-part fugue seem to conform to the essence of a ricercare." If we take the norm of the sixteenth- and seventeenth-century ricercar as a point of comparison—as Spitta undoubtedly does[17]—it seems entirely plausible to assign the name to the *Ricercar à 6* and its patently motet-like characteristics, despite the fact that it is carried out in the manner of a monothematic fugue.[18] Conversely, the three-part setting, judged from this perspective, does not seem to deserve the epithet *ricercar* at all. Considering its free, unusually loose structure, one would hardly dare—in view of other fugues by Bach—to call it a fugue. But what could have prompted Bach to name this piece "Ricercar"?

Our question might appear in more salient form when linked to a quotation from Landshoff's edition, by which the current view is expressed.[19] "Bach may have named the three-part and six-part fugues 'Ricercar' for purely external reasons: the letters of the word could be used for the anagram: 'Regis Iussu Cantio Et Reliqua Canonica Arte Resoluta' which forms, as it were the opening motto of the work, and the work's archaic character was thus emphasized." Both assumptions can be clearly disproved. First, as shown by the sources, the acrostic ("anagram" is not applicable in this case) did not occur to Bach until after the *Ricercar à 3,* complete with its title, had been engraved. This explains the manuscript entry of the acrostic in the dedication copy and its belated imprint on a label to be inserted. The hypothesis of "opening motto" is, in view of the source situation, untenable. Second, an "archaic character" can be associated only with the *Ricercar à 6.* The musical texture of the three-part setting is totally different, and its playfully varied design is devoid of archaic tendencies. The correlation of the two pieces is, in fact, founded on their very contrast.

Since the choice of the term *ricercar* cannot be rationalized in any such manner, we must attempt to solve the problem by other means—by means of terminological considerations.[20] The original meaning of the term *ricercare* was in "searching out again, testing the tuning,[21] probing the key of the piece to follow, intone," and thus it was initially applied to instrumental compositions in the style of the *intonatione.* The early ricercar is closely related to pieces of different designations, all of which, however, also conform to the "intonatione" character: *praeambulum, prooemium, fantasia, toccata, tastata, tiento, arpeggiata,* and others.[22] By name and musical function the ricercar was a priori a free improvisation. In the course of time, however, the term underwent a change in meaning by which its original sense was transformed.[23] Thus in Bach's time it served almost exclusively for the title of a strict and, in its polyphonic texture, highly elaborate fugue. This connotation evolved from the tradition of the imitative ricercar of the sixteenth and seventeenth centuries that is connected with such names as Willaert, Palestrina, Gabrieli, Hassler, Frescobaldi, Froberger, and others. The definition of *Ricercata oder Kunstfuge* in the writing of Heinrich Christoph Koch,[24] quoted in this connection by Eggebrecht[25] and characteristic of the eighteenth-century interpretation, can be found in precise formulation as early as the writing of Friedrich Wilhelm Marpurg,[26] editor of the second printing of Bach's Art of Fugue (1752). In discussing the genre of strict fugue Marpurg writes:

> If such a strict fugue is carried out at length, and if it contains a number of contrapuntal artifices such as various kinds of imitation, double counterpoint, canonic writing, and modulations, it may be given the Italian name *ricercare* or *ricercata*—a fugue showing utmost skill, a master fugue. Such are most of the fugues by J. S. Bach.

Next to this prevalent meaning of *ricerar* there is, however, one based on another eighteenth-century connotation of the term, as can be seen in the widely used dictionaries by Sébastien de Brossard[27] and Johann Gottfried Walther.[28] Here *ricercare* is interpreted as the searching for "harmonic progressions and designs," reverting to the original definition of *ricercare* in the sense of "probing the key," which later was even extended to "motivic searching."[29]

Because of its special importance, we turn to the entry—slightly shortened—in Walther's 1732 *Lexicon,* which, in its terminological information, was the most authoritative work of its kind in Bach's era:

> Ricercare, pl. Ricercare (It.), a word used by Galilei . . . as well as Penna . . . Johann Krieger . . . and Praetorius . . . as a noun, by the latter two especially in the sense of an elaborate fugue; otherwise ricerare is a verb, meaning to investigate, query, inquire, search out with diligence—actions, which indeed are needed in a good fugue, for by them all musical imagination might be judged, whenever a fugue, adapted to the nature of a given mode, results and shows fine and laudable coherence. Others use the forms Ricercata (It.), Recherche (Fr.), the latter being described by Brossard[30] as a Prelude, or a kind of Fantasy, to be performed on the organ, harpsichord, theorbo, or the like; pieces which give the appearance of the composer's searching for harmonic passages or patterns that might be applied to the work to be produced. Such is normally done extempore and without preparation and thus calls for considerable practice. It seems to me that a proper distinction between the two terms could be made: one could call that which is still subject to searching Ricercare, but that which has been duly searched and composed with much thought rightly a Ricercata.[31]

Walther's terminological glossary seems to provide a key for the explanation of what at the outset strikes one as a curious divergence of the two ricercari in the Musical Offering, namely, that totally different musical contents claim one and the same term. Indeed, the obscurity beclouding the implication of title for the two pieces is removed once Walther's definitions are applied to them.

The *Ricercar à 3* represents a subsequent elaboration of Bach's improvisation upon the Thema Regium. Bach's choice of superscription represents concrete reference to this fact: *Ricercar* is here used in the meaning of "Prelude, or a kind of Fantasy." That it is a fugue in basic design does not contradict the fact. The development of ever new motivic ideas, unusual by comparison with other fugues by Bach, and the frequent episodes devoted to contrapuntal or harmonic patterns clearly point to fantasy-like improvisation, which "is normally done extempore and without preparation." In particular, the probing of different subjects and countersubjects becomes noticeable, as does the searching for harmonic "designs."[32] There can be no question that Bach here proved his "considerable practice." He met with corresponding acclaim in Potsdam.

The six-part fugue refers in its superscription to the other meaning of the term *ricerar*. In this work we have before us the prototype of an "elaborate fugue," the character of which is considerably reinforced by the archaic tendency of the *alla breve* setting. In its conception one recognizes clearly the model of the seventeenth-century imitative ricercar in the manner of Frescobaldi. With all its contrapuntal interweaving, the structure shows an unequaled equilibrium. And even without a particular concentration upon strictly thematic treatment, the ricercar attests to Bach's mastery of the strict fugue in every respect. It truly appears as a work that "has been duly searched and composed with much thought." That which Bach, doubtless with good reason, did not attempt to extemporize is here subsequently presented as an addition to the Musical Offering for the Prussian king.

The ambivalence of the term *ricercar,* as evident from Walther's dictionary entry, is put to use by Bach in his description of the two keyboard fugues.[33] It is not an arbitrary but a pointed designation that suggests a reflection upon the events in Potsdam.[34] Most likely, Bach could expect that his implication was grasped by Frederick II, who was highly educated in musical matters. The terminological explanations of Brossard, Walther, and other authors were without question not unfamiliar to musicians of the period, whereas today, the multiple meanings of the term *ricercar* having long lost currency, the titles used in the Musical Offering are no longer readily understood. "Comprehending the termini musicae, an apperception of terminology, not only in the sense of accurate translation and transfer into the right context, but especially in the sense of a proper understanding of such context—one of the surest ways to perceive history in a historical sense, to discern past musical reality as reality come to fresh life—is the ubiquitous task of musicology."[35]

The true purpose of terminological research in music does not rest at the cognizance of a given term as a piece of musical vocabulary. It is rather the genuine relationship between term and substance that is at issue, in our case the actual correlation of the two movements from the Musical Offering here examined as to their name. For an awareness of such correlation—a correlation consciously drawn by the composer—forms part of our awareness of the work of art and its essence.

26

The Agnus Dei of the B Minor Mass:
Parody and New Composition Reconciled

THE AGNUS DEI belongs not only to that major portion of the B Minor Mass which in 1748–49 expanded the 1733 Missa to a complete Mass cycle but also, as the penultimate movement of the entire work, to the very final phase of Bach's completion of the score. An exact and detailed chronology of the events leading to the completion of the Mass cannot be established, but it seems clear from the autograph score that Bach entered the movements in the manuscript one after another, that is, according to the liturgical order of the Mass ordinary. The only piece entered outside this sequence, the "Et incarnatus est" of the Symbolum Nicenum, was quite definitely an after-thought. It was a newly composed piece, certainly entered after the completion of the rest of the Symbolum Nicenum (Part II of the B Minor Mass), and perhaps even after the completion by October 1749[1] of the entire Mass with the Sanctus (Part III) and the Osanna, Benedictus, Agnus Dei, and "Dona nobis pacem" movements of Part IV.

Along with the "Et incarnatus est," the Agnus Dei represented not only the final steps in the completion of the entire work, but also Bach's last major efforts with respect to vocal composition in general. The parody procedure in the Agnus Dei involved an unusually large measure of new composition, whereas the writing of the "Dona nobis pacem"—likewise a parody piece—primarily meant copying an older setting and accommodating a new text underlay.

Beginning with the Osanna, the movements of Part IV of the B Minor Mass are without exception parody pieces.[2] Largely for that reason, this concluding section of the B Minor Mass has been criticized as not quite meeting the highest musical standards represented elsewhere in the Mass, and Friedrich Smend specifically referred to "the decline of artistic quality"[3] toward the end of the work. There are at least two major problems with such a viewpoint. First, the composition of the B Minor Mass in its entirety is dominated by parody procedure; hence the concluding movements must not be singled out. Second, the nature and quality of Bach's parody process, which varies from case to case, reflect generally in the B Minor Mass an extremely careful handling.

The present essay addresses a number of crucial points related to Bach's parody procedure in the Agnus Dei, which particular reference to its pivotal position as the penultimate movement of the entire Mass, but also to its identification with the latest layer of Bach's compositional style.

I

The parody movements chosen by Bach for the B Minor Mass represent a broad spectrum of compositional types and originate from very different periods in Bach's creative life. For instance, in 1748–49 he picked for the "Crucifixus" the thirty-five-year-old cantata chorus "Weinen, Klagen, Sorgen, Zagen" (BWV 12/2). The choice indicates not only the remarkable capacity of his memory, his detailed knowledge and control of his own vast compositional output, but also—at least on a selective basis—his general aesthetic acceptance of older stylistic premises for a new work. In the case of the "Crucifixus" Bach of course made several important adjustments to the older piece, among them chiefly the redressing of the instrumentation, the intensification of the rhythmic pulse of the ostinato bass, the insertion of a four-measure instrumental introduction, and the addition of a textually motivated a cappella concluding phrase (". . . passus et sepultus est") that modulates from E minor to G major; however, the compositional substance of the older piece as well as its sequence of measures remain essentially unaltered.

The "Crucifixus," incidentally, offers some useful insight into Bach's requirements for selecting a parody model. The principal criteria include primarily technical aspects, such as propriety of affect as well as applicability of prosodic and declamatory structure. In this respect the original "Weinen, Klagen" movement ideally suited the needs of a "Crucifixus" setting. The adjustments made by Bach were not at all necessary for the borrowing procedure as such, but they were essential for contextual purposes, specifically the placing of the movement between the "Et incarnatus est" and "Et expecto resurrectionem" settings.

The criteria of selection also seem to have involved considerations regarding compositional quality and suitability of genre. Thus the B Minor Mass clearly focuses on a broadly diversified collection of highly elaborate vocal settings: realizations of representative compositional types (choruses as well as arias) that stand out in terms of sophistication and quality. And, as the result of further compositional refinements, the Mass movements whose parody models are known invariably surpass the pieces on which they are based. This is true not only of the portions beginning with the Symbolum Nicenum but of the 1733 Missa as well. In fact, in the B Minor Mass Bach exemplifies, even surmounts, the practice he also pursues in the four Kyrie-Gloria Masses (BWV 233–236) of circa 1738–39.

For the five Mass compositions of the 1730s Bach reworked a great number of vocal pieces of various kinds and of exceptional quality, suitable and worthy of further elaboration. They include some of the finest concerto choruses, choral fugues, arias, and duets taken mainly from regular Sunday and feast-day cantatas, in a few instances also from secular cantatas. Bach provided a new context for these highly select pieces written for specific occasions. What happens here is, in fact, nothing less than an elevation of several compositions from the liturgical (and "secular," respectively) Proper to the more universal level of the Ordinary. Incidentally, a parallel tendency can be observed in the third part of the Clavier-Übung (1739), whose chorale preludes, unlike those of the Orgel-Büchlein, do not belong to the proper of the liturgical year but to the Mass and the Catechism, that is, to the Ordinary.

With the exception of the dedication of the 1733 Missa, we have no evidence concerning the original destination either of the Kyrie-Gloria Masses or, for that matter, of the enlarged B Minor Mass itself. Nevertheless, the aspect of preserving a representative body of elaborate vocal settings with German text in the functionally much less restricted and more widely accepted genre of the Latin Mass must have played a role in the conceptual planning. In addition, the particularly precious musical substance of the chosen parody models must have occurred to Bach not only as eminently suitable for textual, expressive, and interpretive purposes, but also from a merely musical perspective as a set of intriguing possibilities for further improvements and elaboration.[4]

II

Bach scholars have often discussed the relationship of the Agnus Dei to its parody models, the arias "Entfernet euch, ihr kalten Herzen" (BWV Anh. 196/Anh. I 14→; libretto by Johann Christoph Gottsched, 1725)[5] and "Ach bleibe doch, mein liebstes Leben" (BWV 11/4), but almost exclusively for two purposes: to emphasize the derivative nature of the Agnus Dei and to reconstruct the lost music for the Gottsched text of the Wedding Serenata "Auf! süß entzückende Gewalt."

The issue of the quality of the parody movements in Bach's Masses has already been questioned above. And as for the second aspect, Alfred Dürr has argued convincingly that any attempt to reconstruct an authentic version of the lost serenata aria on the basis of either BWV 11/4 or BWV 232^{IV}/3, or both, is bound to fail because of Bach's substantial alterations in the Ascension Oratorio aria as well as in the Agnus Dei.[6] He also suggests, in contradiction to Smend, that the Agnus Dei was parodied after the serenata aria of 1725 rather than after the oratorio aria of 1735,[7] indeed a very plausible assumption. This means, however, that any detailed comparison between the Agnus Dei and BWV 11/4 is limited to the extent that the two pieces are not directly related but, rather, independently based on a common model. Nevertheless, since the music of the 1725 serenata has not survived, BWV 11/4 has to serve as a legitimate, albeit deficient substitute for the lost parody model.

The texts of the three interrelated pieces[8] indicate some significant elements of common properties as well as major differences:

    I. *1725: Serenata (BWV deest), third movement*

      Entfernet euch, ihr kalten Herzen!   [A]
        Entfernet euch, ich bin euch feind.
      Wer nicht der Liebe Platz will geben,   [B]
      Der flieht sein Glück, der haßt das Leben
        Und ist der ärgsten Torheit Freund:
      Ihr wählt euch selber nichts als Schmerzen.   [C]
      Entfernet euch, ihr kalten Herzen!   [A]
        Entfernet euch, ich bin euch feind.

    II. *1735: Ascension Oratorio (BWV 11/4)*

      Ach, bleibe doch, mein liebstes Leben,   [A]
        Ach, fliehe nicht so bald von mir!
      Dein Abschied und dein frühes Scheiden   [B]
      Bringt mir das allergrößte Leiden,
        Ach ja, so bleibe doch noch hier:
      Sonst werd ich ganz von Schmerz umgeben.   [C]
      Ach, bleibe doch, mein liebstes Leben,   [A]
        Ach, fliehe nicht so bald von mir!

    III. *1748–49: B Minor Mass (BWV 232^IV/4)*

      Agnus Dei,   [1]
      qui tollis peccata mundi,   [2]
      miserere nobis.   [3]

The poetic texts I and II share the same metric scheme and rhyme order, whereas form, length, and prosody of the short liturgical prose text III are completely different. All three texts, however, focus on a very similar affect, effectively identified by the key word *Schmerz* (pain) in line 6, that is, the crucial part [C] of the aria form-scheme of texts I and II. The highly expressive key word is featured most prominently in conjunction with the principal motivic material of the oratorio aria (mm. 49–53) and most likely it functioned in an analogous manner in the serenata aria (Ex. 26.1). In the Agnus Dei the pertinent musical material is assigned most fittingly to text phrases [2] ("qui tollis peccata mundi") and [3] ("miserere nobis"), referring to Christ's suffering in line 2 as well as the call for mercy in line 3 (Ex. 26.2).

The short Agnus Dei text—applied to the music originally written for the aria texts I and II—necessitates a greater number of text repeats, which results, in turn, in a higher concentration of intense exclamations and closely corresponding expressive musical gestures. In other words, Bach manages to transform the prosodic incompatibility of texts I and II on the one hand, and III on the other, into a genuine enhancement of the coordination of words and music in the Agnus Dei.

Bach's choice of the parody model for the Agnus Dei could hardly have

Example 26.1. Aria no. 4 from the Ascension Oratorio BWV 11

Example 26.2. Agnus Dei BWV 232^{IV}/4

CONCEPTS, STYLE, AND CHRONOLOGY

been better. Yet, the degree of his compositional reworking of the entire piece raises at least the question of whether it would not have been much easier, let alone faster, for Bach to compose a new piece from scratch. Why he actually decided against composing an entirely new movement in this case (or, for that matter, in many other comparable cases) will never be definitely known. To be sure, however, one reason (of maybe several reasons) must have been his declared desire to preserve a particularly exquisite piece, to elaborate and improve on it.

The further elaboration of the aria involves three major aspects:

1. Redesign of form. The parody model (we may reasonably assume that BWV 11/4 represents essentially the structure of the serenata aria of 1725) consists of 79 measures, of which the Agnus Dei discards no fewer than 40 measures, that is, slightly more than half of the original substance. Eliminating the entire B-material, Bach retains exclusively the bulk of the A-material of the original *da capo* structure[9] and, along with this, gives up the conventional A-B-A form as entirely unsuitable for the liturgical prose text of the Agnus Dei. The new and asymmetric formal design of the Agnus Dei is based on the combination of the "old" A-material with entirely new X-material. (The measures marked *R* in the diagram below are ritornellos based on material from vocal section *A*. The musically identical portions of the two aria versions are bracketed.)

```
                              BWV 11/4
  R              A           R                   B       A        R
|1–8|         9–14      |15–24|   |25–28|      29–58  |59–70|  71–74  |75–79|

|1–8|  9–12   |13–22|   |23–26|  27–33              |34–44|          |45–49|
  R    X         A         R       X                  A                R
                           BWV 232ᴵⱽ/3
```

2. New composition. The most striking feature of the musically reorganized Agnus Dei is the strong thematic contrast between the opening instrumental ritornello and the subsequent first vocal section. The initial three continuo chords of mm. 1 and 9 (as well as mm. 23 and 27) are identical, but the upper voices differ considerably, both in terms of melodic contour and rhythmic shape and with respect to contrapuntal writing (Ex. 26.3).

The newly composed and interpolated mm. 9–12 and 27–33, respectively, focus on text phrases [1] and [2], that is, first on the invocation "Agnus Dei" and then on the relative clause "qui tollis peccata mundi," which also serves as opening text for the ritornello theme first recurring in m. 13. This results in a tightly interlocking device:

Measures	9–12	13–22	27–33	34–44
Musical material	new	old	new	old
Text phrases	1 + 2	2 + 3	1 + 2	2 + 3

The newly composed measures present in the two upper voices a dense contrapuntal texture that begins with a canon in the lower fifth (mm. 9–11)

Example 26.3. Comparison between ritornellos, BWV 11/4 and BWV 232^{IV}/3

and undergoes several imitative permutations. Taken separately the newly composed sections correspond to one another in a symmetrical manner:

mm. 9–12 | 27–30 | 31–34

The newly introduced fermata in m. 34, however, not only accentuates the return to the home key (in conjunction with the reappearance of the primary thematic material) but also generally supports the sectionalized habit of the entire movement structure that provides for well-balanced alternation between the ritornello sections (R) and the vocal passages (A and X): R–X–A–R–X–A–R. Moreover, the emphasis on polyphonic texture in the newly composed sections finds its repercussion in some revisions of the interrelationship between the solo voice and the instrumental obbligato (for example, in mm. 15–16). In general, the Agnus Dei is a much more thematically controlled piece of music than its parody model.

Contrapuntal sophistication and canonic technique are the common hallmark of the major newly composed movements of the Symbolum Nicenum ("Credo in unum Deum," "Et incarnatus est," and "Confiteor"). The addition of new compositional material in the Agnus Dei that resembles the conceptual premises of those Symbolum movements means nothing less than a deliberate aesthetic rapprochement and musical integration of the Agnus Dei in the large-scale structure of the B Minor Mass.

3. Contextual aspects. The newly composed sections of the Agnus Dei along with the substantial revisions of its parody model show some very strong indications of Bach's interest in creating not only a *Missa tota* as a

unified whole but also a sequence of movements that fit well and tightly together. The Agnus Dei provides a case in point particularly for this important aspect.

The key of the Agnus Dei (G minor) happens to be the only flat key in the entire work. The key thus enriches the overall harmonic plan of the Mass, especially toward the end with its heavy emphasis on D major. More than that, it creates a very special relationship with the only other place in the entire Mass in which a flat-key area is sustained for a short section: the Adagio ending of the "Confiteor" movement (mm. 121–145) with its sudden harmonic shift from sharps to flats on the word "peccatorum" (mm. 121–122). The textual link with "Agnus Dei, qui tollis peccata [!] mundi" could hardly be stronger.

Apart from these large-scale considerations, Bach seems to have paid attention also to the immediate connection of the Agnus Dei to its two framing tutti movements in the key of D major ("Osanna" and "Dona nobis pacem"). A comparison between the basically identical ritornellos of BWV 11/4 and of the Agnus Dei reveals a number of striking details in the instrumental obbligato (Ex. 26.3). First, the treatment of the obbligato part in the opening ritornello shows an important pitch adjustment. The piece was transposed down from A minor to G minor and, since the violins could not go below g, a portion (mm. 5b–7a) had to be played an octave higher. This being a routine adjustment for technical reasons, the changes made in the concluding ritornello are made on completely different grounds. Bach condensed the final ritornello from eight to four measures (with a completely rewritten, contrapuntally more active continuo line); furthermore, the highly expressive breakings of the melodic contours in the last three measures provide the movement with an unexpected instrumental culmination point that in a way compensates for the equally surprising vocal fermata in m. 34. The quick descent from $b^{\flat\prime\prime}$ to g by means of extremely disjunct interval leaps results in a most unusual, highly mannered reshaping of an otherwise rather traditional cadential formula. The low open-string g of the obbligato part ideally suits the low-register fugal opening (d–e–f♯–g) of the immediately subsequent "Dona nobis pacem" and, therefore, the two last movements of the completed Mass are particularly closely linked together.

This link, however, becomes obvious, let alone audible, only in a performance. Parody and new composition, different processes that find their reconciliation in Bach's Agnus Dei, cannot at all be regarded as abstract exercises. They are instead an exemplary case of a practical, effective, and performance-oriented artistic commitment. We have no documentation for a performance during Bach's life of the entire B Minor Mass nor of its Parts II–IV, but if he had not had the benefit of an actual "hearing," Bach must at least have had a very concrete idea in mind about how the work should sound.

27

Principles of Design and Order in Bach's Original Editions

ONLY A SMALL NUMBER of Bach's works appeared in print during his life.[1] As is characteristic of music printing in the eighteenth century, Bach's publications consisted almost entirely of keyboard works; vocal and instrumental ensemble music was rarely published at the time. Not the least of the results of these keyboard publications was the influence they exerted among Bach's contemporaries in forming a view by which—as the obituary expresses it—Bach was seen as "the strongest performer on the organ and the clavier that was ever known."[2] We are not aware of any particular circumstances that might have prompted the issue of specific works, and thus we are led to conclude that Bach published when he considered one or another work worthy of publication, or that he planned certain works with publication in mind. It seems important to stress the author's total independence in this matter. He was not guided by official duties, by available performance forces, by liturgical considerations, or by given texts for vocal works. He was free to pursue his own artistic ideas and plans, with the principal goal of composing "for Music Lovers, to Refresh their Spirits."

It would be wrong, however, to assign the printed works a place of qualitative priority. The technical and financial difficulties, as well as difficulties of distribution, for a work like the St. Matthew Passion are immediately apparent. But why was it that the Well-Tempered Clavier—to which no such publisher's consideration applied—was denied a printing? We do not know but are led to conclude that publication did not necessarily signify a selective artistic choice. The printed works do not constitute a category to be ranked above all others but claim equal value with a large number handed down only in manuscript. Why Bach designated certain works to be engraved thus remains obscure. The publications are of interest to us because they are the parts of his creative work through which he appears before the musical public of his time. They make up a body of creative work, arising from thoroughly independent thought and conception, that was refined to the last detail and—whenever we are dealing with works consisting of several parts—placed in a carefully designed selection and order.

Our attention is drawn to the principles of design and order by which individual works and the sequence of individual movements may have been planned. What immediately moves into the center of interest is the problem of order, or rather disorder, in two major works of Bach's last years, the Musical Offering and the Art of Fugue. This question suggests an obvious point of departure for the issue under consideration: Did definite principles of disposition guide Bach in the compilation of his printed works? What is the nature of these principles, their purpose, and their significance? And do they throw light on the implied design of those works that have come down to us in prints seemingly devoid of any intended order?

Order is especially relevant with regard to cyclic works, works that exhibit an overall construction of content or thematic unity; less so, with regard to compositions presented in print on the basis of more external considerations of form. It becomes evident to which of the prints our study should be devoted; and some works that remain in manuscript will have to be included in an attempt to trace precepts of order and to weigh the arguments for them from case to case. The goal envisaged here is to clarify and grasp the basis for such precepts in their given context through comparison and synopsis; what is not intended is to suggest new and more or less speculative constructions or reconstructions of sequence arrangements—for instance for the Art of Fugue, where such ventures have developed into a favorite pastime of arrangers.[3]

In order to view the various design possibilities and their fundamental implications, it is necessary at the outset to establish the factors through which an articulate succession of movements is accomplished. How are musical elements deployed to bring about a cyclic or noncyclic order by means of variation or tectonic and architectonic procedures? I shall list some of those that are of importance in Bach's oeuvre, citing examples of collective works preserved only in manuscript but closely related in method to the prints.[4]

1. Form and style. The original manuscripts of the solo works for violin are so arranged that each of three four-movement sonatas forms a pair with a partita made up of a larger number of movements (see also section 5, below). In this case the difference in general form of sonata and partita becomes a primary factor of consideration. It is a variance in style—involving special stylistic features within the personal style—that becomes the criterion for a distinction of types among the preludes of the Well-Tempered Clavier (for example, the arpeggio style in BWV 846 and 866, the siciliano style in BWV 854, or the overture manner in BWV 885). Here the sequence of pairs in contrasting styles (prelude and fugue, representing free and strict genres) assumes a conspicuous function.

2. Extent. The principal difference between the collections of the English

and French Suites is in the grouping of larger suites in one case and smaller ones in the other. Similarly, the length of individual compositions constitutes the difference between the chorale arrangements in the Orgel-Büchlein and the Leipzig manuscript of the so-called Eighteen Chorales; one collection is comprised of short, the other of extended chorale preludes.

3. Technique of composition. Within the organ chorale collections, successive pieces are distinguished by texture of setting (placement of the chorale in the soprano, alto, tenor, or bass; canonic *cantus firmus* treatment; or embellished or plain cantus firmus). Thus both collections encompass a compound repertoire of chorale elaborations.

4. Sonority. Here we are dealing with the possibility of compiling works in like scoring (as in the sonatas for harpsichord and violin or viola da gamba) or differentiated scoring (as in the Brandenburg Concertos), according to the particular purpose of a given collection. In the Brandenburg Concertos, for instance, the aim is to present different examples for the genre of the concerto grosso, the concerto "avec plusieurs Instruments." In a similar manner, the number of parts plays a role in group designs, for instance in the series of trio sonatas for organ, all of which are written "a 2 Clav. e Pedal," or in the consistency of two-part or three-part scoring, respectively, for the Inventions and Sinfonias.

5. Choice of keys. The preludes and fugues in both parts of the Well-Tempered Clavier are arranged in their rising order of keys "through all tones and semi-tones." The same principle is found in the arrangement of the Inventions and Sinfonias. They were taken from the older versions as preambles and fantasies of the Clavier-Büchlein for Wilhelm Friedemann Bach and placed in an ascending and descending order of keys. The two schemes (illustrating the principles of increase and symmetry, respectively) are here placed side by side for comparison:

	⟶
Inventions and Sinfonias	C – c – D – d – E♭ – E – e – F – f – G – g – A – a – B♭ – b
Preambles and Fantasias	C – d – e – F – G – a – b – B♭ – A – g – f – E – E♭ – D – c
	⟶ ⟵

A totally different disposition of keys, oriented in a decidedly architectonic manner, is observed in the original succession of the solo violin works: Sonata I and Sonata III, like Partita I and Partita III, are the keys a fifth apart, a situation that equally applies to the central pair formed by Sonata II and Partita II (g–C, b–E, a–d). Furthermore, Sonata II and Partita I, like Partita II and Sonata III, are in keys a second apart (a–b, d–c), and Partita I and Sonata I, like Sonata III and Partita III, are in keys a third apart (b–g, C–E). Thus there arises a symmetrical order, tightly organized by key relationships (see Fig. 27.1).

Such principles of order appear as early as in printed manuscript collections of the seventeenth century. An arrangement devised by the variety of

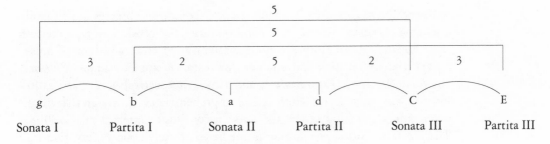

Figure 27.1. The key relationships of the solo violin works.

form and style plays a distinct role in Frescobaldi's *Il primo libro di Capricci, Canzon Francese e Recercari* (1626), as does the sequence of nine psalm tones in the Magnificat settings in the third part of Scheidt's *Tabulatura Nova* (1624). Bach's practice therefore forms no exception, but his command of specially planned designs is greater than that of almost any other musician of his time or the past. Very rarely do we encounter an arbitrary order in his works, as in the Clavier-Büchlein for Anna Magdalena Bach or for Wilhelm Friedemann Bach, which in the succession of their components represent conglomerates of larger and smaller pieces collected over a period of time. The types of arrangement listed above are based on specifically musical considerations. There are, however, also arrangements based on extramusical considerations, as for instance that of the Orgel-Büchlein, in which the individual settings follow the course of the church year.

In questioning the intent and purpose of different orders—without going into the facets of larger or smaller principles of structure involved—we find that two immediate answers offer themselves. On the one hand, there is the composer's wish to design his works in a manner of lucid exposition governed by discernible principles as model collections. On the other hand, didactic aims—especially in the keyboard works—guide the composer; the Orgel-Büchlein, for instance, is compiled with a view of "instruction" for the "Beginner at the Organ," the Inventions and Sinfonias for the "Lovers of the Clavier, and especially those desirous of Learning," and the Well-Tempered Clavier "For the Use and Profit of the Musical Youth desirous of Learning."

WHEN WE CONSIDER the printed works as a defined group within Bach's total oeuvre, our initial interest must be directed to cases of unproblematic order. One of these is the first publication issued in 1731 by Bach himself and designated by him as Opus 1: *Clavier Übung, bestehend in Praeludien, Allemanden, Couranten, Sarabanden, Giguen, Menuetten, und anderen Galanterien.*[5] The partitas included here had previously appeared in single issues, beginning in 1726, and it stands to reason that Bach had not planned their compilation as Opus 1 at the outset: it would have been a publishing risk, even though the title, complying with the taste of the time, paid obeisance to the notion of gallantry. The collection of six partitas observes quite plainly a scheme of works, alike in form and quality, "For Music Lovers, to refresh their Spirits." Apart from certain deviations as to order and type of movements (the six opening movements, for instance, are *Praeludium, Sinfonia, Fantasia, Ouverture, Praeambulum,* and *Toccata,* respectively), all partitas follow the same basic form. There is no comprehensive cyclic design that might determine a grouping of the six works according to internal relationships. The prevailing principle of order is one based entirely upon variety, that is, a joining of works of similar kind and rank that differ merely as to their musical character. The same principle applies to the series of Bach's organ chorales issued some time after 1746 by Schübler: *Sechs Choräle von verschiedener Art auf einer Orgel mit 2 Clavieren und Pedal vorzuspielen.*[6] Again we find in this collection the total number of six (the titles are given in Table 27.1), favored by Bach and his contemporaries. It contains chorale settings, five of which patently go back to earlier cantata movements. Possible correlation among the works, however, was doubtless of no interest to the organist of the time—if indeed he was aware of it in the first place. What mattered was that model chorale settings "of various kinds" were here published, without the suggestion of a performance cycle. This point is also borne out by the absence of a grouping according to the church year.

In 1735 a print appeared under the title of *Zweyter Theil der Clavier Übung bestehend in einem Concerto nach Italiaenischen Gusto und einer Overture nach Französischer Art, vor ein Clavicymbel mit zweyen Manualen,*[7] in which Bach departed from a grouping based purely upon variety. In this case it is the combination of pieces in contrasting genre (concerto and overture) and contrasting style (representing the Italian and French manner). The varying works of Clavier-Übung II were placed side by side with these contrasts in mind. Bach was evidently guided also by a didactic consideration. He wished to offer model examples for the two national genres and styles so highly regarded in the music of the Baroque and to show the divergence between pattern and style of individual expression. The conscious opposition of the two works for a two-manual instrument (again without any implied order of performance) is stressed by the tritone distance of the keys of F major and B minor. Key gains in importance when one considers that the older autograph version of the overture was written in C minor[8] and was transposed evidently only with reference to this publication.

Table 27.1. Contents of the Schübler Chorales

---

1. Wachet auf rufft uns die Stimme
2. Wo soll ich fliehen hin [*or* Auf meinen lieben Gott]
3. Wer nur den lieben Gott laesst walten
4. Meine Seele erhebt den Herren
5. Ach bleib bey uns Herr Jesu Christ
6. Kommst du nun Jesu vom Himmel herunter

Table 27.2. The design of Clavier-Übung III

Contents	Comments
Praeludium (pro Organo pleno)	
Kyrie, Gott Vater	*Cantus firmus* in soprano
Christe, aller Welt Trost	*Cantus firmus* in tenore } *stile antico*
Kyrie, Gott heiliger Geist	Con Organo Pleno
Kyrie, Gott Vater	3/4 time
Christe, aller Welt Trost	6/8 time } versets
Kyrie, Gott heiliger Geist	9/8 time
Allein Gott in der Höh	Trio in F Major, Manualiter
Allein Gott in der Höh	Trio in G Major, *a 2 Clav. e Ped.*
Allein Gott in der Höh	Trio in A Major, Manualiter, Fughetta
Dies sind die heilgen zehn Gebot	*a 2 Clav. e Ped. Cantus firmus in Canone*
Dies sind die heilgen zehn Gebot	Manualiter
Wir glauben all an einen Gott	In Organo pleno
Wir glauben all an einen Gott	Manualiter
Vater unser im Himmelreich	*a 2 Clav. e Ped. Cantus firmus in Canone*
Vater unser im Himmelreich	Manualiter
Christ, unser Herr, zum Jordan kam	*a 2 Clav. e Cantus firmus in Ped.*
Christ, unser Herr, zum Jordan kam	Manualiter
Aus tiefer Not schrei ich zu dir	In Organo pleno
Aus tiefer Not schrei ich zu dir	Manualiter
Jesus Christus, unser Heiland	*a 2 Clav. e Cantus firmus in Ped.*
Jesus Christus, unser Heiland	Manualiter
Duetto I	(E minor, 3/8 time)
Duetto II	(F major, 2/4 time)
Duetto III	(G minor, 12/8 time)
Duetto IV	(A major, 2/2 time)
Fuga (a 5 voci. Pro Organo Pleno)	

In the collection published by Bach in 1739 as *Dritter Theil der Clavier Übung bestehend in verschiedenen Vorspielen über die Catechismus- und andere Gesaenge, vor die Orgel*[9] we can recognize for the first time a cyclic order. The contents appear in their original sequence as in Table 27.2. Plainly perceptible is the function of frame design, in which the Prelude and Fugue in E♭ Major surround three groups: the chorale settings related to the Mass text; those related to Catechism texts; and the duets. The individual groups show multiple substructures guided by a variety of principles. The division of the first group into nine components, by a grouping of 3 × 3 settings, reflects a play on numbers not directly suggested by the texts. The beginning is formed by three chorale arrangements written in the style of classical vocal polyphony and growing in texture from *cantus firmus* treatment in soprano, tenor, and pedal bass (consistently skipping the intervening voice registers) to a plenum setting. They are followed by three small and uniformly verset-like Kyrie movements that are related to one another by proportional meters: 3/4–6/8–9/8. Three settings of the German Gloria conclude the group. Here Bach forgoes a division into two self-contained groups of large and small settings that he had observed for the Kyrie movements (there prompted predominantly by a *cantus firmus* distributed over three chorale stanzas) but rather surrounds a setting with pedal by two that are kept manualiter. Next to the symmetric disposition, it is the sequence of keys, rising from trio to trio by three steps, that shows the tight organization of this group.

The section of twelve Catechism chorales is strictly articulated in six pairs. The smaller settings are interrelated in that they are all written in a fugal manner, whereas the larger settings follow a varying pattern of structure. It is from the point of view of compositional techniques that we can here recognize a systematic order. There are two groups, of three components each, whose pivot points are marked in each case by a plenum setting. In the first group, this central setting is surrounded by two chorale elaborations using canonic *cantus firmus* treatment; in the second group, by chorale elaborations with the *cantus firmus* placed in the pedal. The involved interrelationships of the Catechism chorales therefore yield a multiplicity of recognizable orders: 6 × 2, 3 × 2, 2 × 3, and 2 × 6.

By a similarly complex grouping the duets are related to one another. The predominant factor here is that of a choice of keys arranged in step-wise rising succession. This diatonic sequence receives symmetrical form in that two pieces in major keys are placed within a pair of pieces in minor keys. Furthermore, the duets are linked by an order of meters: the first and third are in triple and compound meter, respectively, unlike the second and fourth, which are in duple meter.

In Clavier-Übung III we thus encounter a summation encompassing various principles of disposition: pivotal arrangement; arrangement in groups of corresponding or contrasting pairs; arrangement in intensifying the symmetrical sequence. These are all joined in an overall framework of architectonic conception in which smaller groupings follow their own respective orders. The manifold combinations arising from purely musical considerations are enhanced by extramusical ones, namely the distinction of Mass and Catechism settings. The duets form again a distinct group, whether or not they are to be interpreted as communion music; it stands to reason that they do not represent a merely expletive addition.

Not the least aspect of Bach's profoundly organized structure is that of the symbolism of numbers.[10] The nine (3 × 3) Missa settings doubtless refer to the glorification of Trinity in the Mass service, whereas in the case of the Catechism chorales it is evidently the ecclesiastical number of twelve to which reference is made. The entire work consists of twenty-seven (3 × 3 × 3) movements adding up to a thoroughly cyclic structure. Yet, as in the other editions of the Clavier-Übung, this does not mean a performance cycle. Not only artistic reasons would speak against it—for no cogent musical development is implied—but also historical reasons. Such performance cycles had never existed, nor does Bach's work offer liturgical or other arguments for such a concept. Apparently we are dealing with a kind of compendium of organ music for the worship service, combining all genres for which the organist of the time would have had use: large and small free-prelude forms, as well as large and small chorale preludes.[11] According to the amount of time available, the organist would have been in need of shorter or larger preludes for the service, and Bach's sense of proportion predicated manualiter performance for the smaller and the extension to pedaliter performance for the larger works. In this sense, too, the place of the duets within the total scheme may be clarified. Possibly they are free preludes in the manner of *intonationi* (for the preferred octave species on E, F, G, and A), which as models of the small form are to be grouped with those of the large (Prelude and Fugue in E♭ Major). The organist could choose, as from a manual—practical as well as theoretical—according to what might be required for use in the service, or for instruction in composition, or for a demonstration of the possibilities existing for the liturgical organ practice. This was evidently Bach's intention, and special emphasis is placed in his dedicatory title upon the formulation "For Music Lovers and especially for Connoisseurs of such Work"—a formulation conspicuously absent from the other parts of his Clavier-Übung.

The so-called Goldberg Variations published in 1741 as *Clavier Übung bestehend in einer Aria mit verschiedenen Veraenderungen vors Clavicimbel mit 2 Manualen*[12] exhibit in the thirty-two movements a comparable, though independently designed structure (see Table 27.3). The aria forms beginning and end. Within this frame are 10 × 3 groups, each concluding with a canonic variation. The canons themselves are written at intervals arranged in rising order, from the unison to the ninth, with a climactic Quodlibet representing a canonic rarity.

The number of ten is doubtless not accidental but alludes to the symbol of law, the plausible multiplication by three producing the total of thirty variations. The movements not written in canon show no apparent sequence construction corresponding to that of the canons, though the process of variation develops in a perceptibly planned manner. The evident intensification of virtuosity and purely technical demands at the conclusion of individual groups, for instance, enters here as a factor. And beyond the comprehensive pattern established by the canons, we can recognize a smaller formative pattern related to their order but arising in the succession of the other movements. A variation written in the manner of the French Overture forms the center of the work (incidentally, corresponding to the centrally placed Overture from Clavier-Übung I as well as to the small Credo setting, written in the French style, from Clavier-Übung III); it is accordingly entitled in the original print and represents an important formal accent, as the beginning of the second part of the work, equally manifest to the reader and listener. The only other movements with original title designations are Variations 10 and 22, both placed at the distance of six movements from the Overture as

Table 27.3. The design of the Goldberg Variations

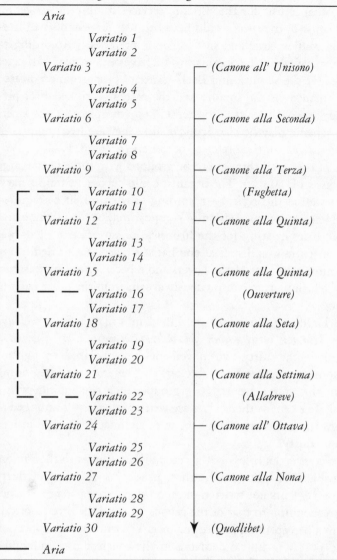

Aria	
Variatio 1	
Variatio 2	
Variatio 3	(Canone all' Unisono)
Variatio 4	
Variatio 5	
Variatio 6	(Canone alla Seconda)
Variatio 7	
Variatio 8	
Variatio 9	(Canone alla Terza)
Variatio 10	(Fughetta)
Variatio 11	
Variatio 12	(Canone alla Quinta)
Variatio 13	
Variatio 14	
Variatio 15	(Canone alla Quinta)
Variatio 16	(Ouverture)
Variatio 17	
Variatio 18	(Canone alla Seta)
Variatio 19	
Variatio 20	
Variatio 21	(Canone alla Settima)
Variatio 22	(Allabreve)
Variatio 23	
Variatio 24	(Canone all' Ottava)
Variatio 25	
Variatio 26	
Variatio 27	(Canone alla Nona)
Variatio 28	
Variatio 29	
Variatio 30	(Quodlibet)
Aria	

pivotal point. And both stand, like the Overture, for a fixed form or genre, one of them being a fughetta and the other an imitative *alla breve*.

In distinction to all the other works mentioned, however, Clavier-Übung IV—the Goldberg Variations—combines with its frame structure the concept of a performance cycle. It is an integral piece, its firm structure encompassing a well-designed development outlined by the canonic movements and enriched by the more loosely varied noncanonic movements. A consistent unfolding process is founded in the total plan of the work: from the aria bass, as constant factor, are derived thirty variations in ever growing organic and forceful musical logic.

IN THIS DISCUSSION of principles of design in the original prints of Bach's works, we have so far not questioned the logic, or even the authenticity, of a given printed order. We are unavoidably confronted with such questions when it comes to the prints of the Canonic Variations on Vom Himmel hoch,[13] the Musical Offering, and the Art of Fugue.

The Vom Himmel hoch variations, composed for Lorenz Christoph Mizler's Correspondierende Societät der Musicalischen Wissenschaften (which Bach joined in June 1747), consist of five movements, each of which contains two canonic voices in its elaboration. As he did in the Goldberg Variations, Bach honors the number of ten, as the symbol of law, by the disposition of canonic parts in five movements. In its order of movements, the original edition, published in 1748 under the title *Einige canonische Veränderungen über das Weyhnachts-Lied: "Vom Himmel hoch da komm ich her"* is unequivocal, given the fact that the individual settings are numbered in continuity (see Table 27.4). Doubts arise only in consulting a later version preserved in autograph[14] and the sources connected with it. For here the order is slightly though decidedly changed (see Table 27.5).

The order of the engraved version reflects a gradual increase in contrapuntal complexity. It begins with a canon at the octave, proceeds to canons at the fifth and seventh, and leads to an octave canon in augmentation. These four movements show a contrapuntal fabric distributed over three levels of sound: two manuals and pedal. The *cantus firmus* remains unaltered in all four settings as a *cantus planus* in half notes, placed either in the lowest or highest

Table 27.4. The printed version of the Canonic Variations

Variatio 1.	in Canone all' Ottava à 2 Clav. et Pedal.
Variatio 2.	Alio Modo in Canone alla Quinta à 2 Clav. et Pedal.
Variatio 3.	Canone alla Settima.
Variatio 4.	à 2. Clav. et Pedal. per augmentation. in Canone all' ottava.
Variatio 5.	L'altra Sorte del Canone all' rovercio, 1) alla Sesta. 2) alla Terza. 3) alla Seconda è 4) alla Nona.

Table 27.5. The autograph version of the Canonic Variations

(a)	Canone all' Ottava. Pedal Canto fermo.
(b)	Canone alla Quinta. Canto fermo in Pedal.
(c)	Canto fermo in Canone. alla Sesta e al rovescio. alla Terza. alla Seconda. alla Nona.
(d)	Canon alla Settima. (a 2 Clav. et Ped.)
(e)	Canon per augmentationem. a 2 Clav. et Pedal.

voice. Not until the final movement is the *cantus firmus* incorporated in the canonic procedure. Paired with the contrapuntal intensification involving the *cantus firmus* (canons at four different intervals, with inversion in each case) is an increase in dynamics specified in the original: first the right hand changes to the forte manual, then the left, until toward the end of the movement both hands are placed on the forte manual, leading to a rising plenum sound. The growing intensity comes to a climax at the end of the concluding movement (after a brief *diminutio* passage) with an extraordinary expression of contrapuntal density marked *alla Stretta* (original inscription) culminating in six-part texture. The stretta (mm. 54ff.) is made up of a combination, or superimposition, of all *cantus firmus* phrases that prior to this were introduced as separate soggetti. A comparison with the canonic climax in Clavier-Übung IV is instructive: the stretta is related in kind to the Quodlibet. The same principle of contrapuntal procedure, the combination of several themes locked in close canonic entries, in both works mark the point of finality and the crowning of the total structure.

In contrast to the printed version, in which the form of the work is guided by consistently rising intensity, the autograph—the authentic version emanating directly from the composer—shows a symmetric form. The crucial point moves from the end to the middle of the canonic work, which is to be surrounded by two movements each in canonic counterpoint. The central position of the former final movement is underlined by the new titles. It is now expressly stated that this movement takes up the *cantus firmus* in canon, a situation that does not apply to the other settings. Friedrich Smend has convincingly shown how the plan of the work is revealed in its overall structure. As he points out, the beginning is formed by a canon in purely contrapuntal play, a canon that accompanies the *cantus firmus* but is motivically independent. The ensuing movement is a similar canon, but the chorale melody relinquishes its isolation and becomes involved in reflective gestures through the rhythmic and melodic fabric of the contrapuntal parts. The middle movement, finally, presents the *cantus firmus* itself in canonic form, in a full setting that stands in contrast to the earlier trio settings. The next-to-last movement leads away from this concentration of sonority and contrapuntal texture, relegating the canonic setting to the accompanying parts again, though the chorale still influences their motivic shape. The last movement rounds out this development by loosening the contrapuntal writing, with a return to the canon at the octave, now in augmentation and with *cantus firmus* phases spaced widely apart.

The different placement of movements in print and autograph can, in the last analysis, be derived from two totally different concepts in Bach's thought. We see no other solution than to accept either version, in its given formal logic, as authentic. [15] The printed version is determined by expansion of contrapuntal and dynamic means, whereas the autograph version stresses the function of the chorale in relation to its various contrapuntal elaborations. The printed sequence finds a more immediate response in modern ears influenced by the anticipation of a finale effect; Bach may have given preference to the autograph sequence, its climax being both central and symbolic in that the chorale emerges clearly as basic substance of the canonic work. Yet it becomes evident that the compositional process was not at the outset guided by Bach's insistence on an unequivocal order. An initial order of intensification could be changed to an order of symmetry—a process which may have presented a most earnest challenge to the composer's sense of form. In viewing the two solutions, perhaps considered equally valid by Bach, one cannot escape a comparison between natural and constructed form. It is readily understandable that in the hands of the composer as performer there arose a form based on growth, but a more contemplative attitude—once he gained a certain distance from the work—prompted a restructuring.

Probably the most difficult problem in the interpretation of design is posed by the original edition of the Musical Offering, issued in 1747.[16] It consists of several independent printing units which, strangely, offer no hint as to their correlation (see Table 27.6). The units A, B, and E are in oblong folio, C and D in upright folio format; B and E show the paginations 1–4 and 1–7, respectively; C consists of separate part books, that is, separate folders for flute, violin, and continuo, with a title cover.

An autograph, from which an explanation could possibly have been derived, is not preserved—merely an autograph copy of a later version for the six-part ricercar.[17] Thus we are faced with the question whether a specific order was intended in the first place, and if so, of what kind. Arguments for an integral coherence of the work are: (1) the connection of all parts with the Thema Regium; (2) the distribution of canonic movements over three printed units, bearing out at least a closer relationship of these units; (3) the obvious grouping of the three-part and six-part ricercari by choice of term;[18] (4) the fact that only once, at the end of unit D, does the engraver's identification, *J. G. Schübler sc*[ulpsit], appear; and (5) principles of arrangement

Table 27.6. The original edition of the Musical Offering

A	Title page (*Musicalisches Opfer* . . .) and dedication
B	*Ricercar à 3*
	Canon perpetuus super Thema Regium
C	*Sonata sopr' il Soggetto Reale*
	Canon perpetuus
D	*Canones diversi super Thema Regium*
	Canon 1. à 2 (cancrizans)
	Canon 2. à 2 Violini in Unisono
	Canon 3. à 2. per Motum contrarium
	Canon 4. à 2. per Augmentationem, contrario Motu
	Canon 5. à 2. (per tonos)
	Fuga canonica in Epidiapente
E	*Ricercar à 6*
	Canon à 2. Quaerendo invenietis
	Canon à 4.

that may appear plausible by analogy to other printed works by Bach. The two ricercari (the first of which must form the beginning in any event, as is evident from the origin of the work) may be placed together as a pair of contrasting pieces or apart as a frame for the entire work. The canons suggest a close relationship; their total number of ten, by comparison with the works just discussed, seems hardly accidental. A reference to the Canonic Variations on Vom Himmel hoch may be seen in the distinction between purely contrapuntal canons and canons directly related to the theme itself, in the Musical Offering resulting in two groups of five each. Finally, the sonata may be seen as the pivotal section of a symmetrical form or final section in a sequence governed by consistent intensification. Judging by the designs of Bach's other printed works, we arrive at the following two basic possibilities of arrangement (see Table 27.7). Which canon group is to be placed first, and what sequence is to be chosen within each canon group will at first be open to question. With reference to the basic possibilities mentioned above, it seems equally feasible to employ the principle of increasing contrapuntal complexity or the principle of axial symmetry.

With regard to a division of the total number of canons into two groups, we might note that the preserved dedication copy for Frederick the Great bears, next to the engraved title *Canones diversi super Thema Regium,* an added calligraphic inscription reading *Thematis Regium Elaborationes Canonicae.* What is apparently designated here are the two canonic techniques concerned: on the one hand, canonic treatment of contrapuntal voices placed freely upon a theme serving as *cantus firmus*; and on the other, canonic writing involving the thematic *cantus firmus* itself.

In considering the options for the order of movements within the Musical Offering, we arrive, curiously enough, at the same conclusions as drawn for the printed and autograph versions of Vom Himmel hoch. We assumed there that the printed version likely corresponded to the process of composition; a parallel may be seen in the Musical Offering, in that version A may also represent the sequence in which the movements were written. To be sure, this is a matter of conjecture, but one supported by arguments whose full discussion exceeds the present scope (for a more detailed discussion see Chapter 18). Version B—and this is again conjectural—might represent a plan arising during the genesis of the work or after its completion. Both the expanding form A and the free form B possess their own logic, the latter with

Table 27.7. Two possibilities for the order of the Musical Offering

Version A	Version B
Ricercar à 3	*Ricercar à 3*
Ricercar à 6	5 contrapuntal canons
5 contrapuntal canons	*Sonata . . .*
5 thematic canons	5 thematic canons
Sonata . . .	*Ricarcar à 6*

its emphasis upon the sonata as a gesture of homage to the royal flautist perhaps claiming preference.[19]

But why does the print give no clue as to an initially intended order of movements?[20] That there must have been such an order remains a hypothesis founded more or less on deductions of varying cogency. A contrary argument, however, that there was no planned order at all would be equally difficult to prove. My assumption of an existing definite design is based on comparison with analogous situations. The possible reasons a design was not expressed in the printed edition remain, once again, conjectural. We might list them briefly.

In the first place, there was a time interval of two months between the Potsdam visit and the date of dedication. Thus the printing process must have been fairly hurried. This is borne out by the evident manuscript corrections in the preserved print copies; apparently there was no time for correcting the engraver's plates. It should be mentioned too that the acrostic *Regis Iussu Cantio Et Reliqua Canonica Arte Resoluta* was glued in only afterward, on a separate slip of paper, and in the dedication copy it was entered in manuscript.

Second, it was doubtless very difficult, in terms of typographical layout, to find a solution of uniform format for printing a series of movements highly divergent as to the number of parts and instruments required—a problem that did not exist in the case of any other of Bach's original prints. Bach must have been concerned about keeping the printing costs as low as possible since he could not count on a large income from sales; indeed, he later said that most of the printed copies "were distributed *gratis* to good friends."[21]

Finally, Bach may not have been particularly interested in a precise reflection of his idea of design because its realization would have been most unwieldy. It would have represented merely a graphic form, without musical consequences in actual performance, for the movements of the Musical Offering, like those of Clavier-Übung III, were not conceived as components of a performance cycle. A print arranged according to an envisioned order would thus have been tantamount to luxury. An inherent order, however, retains validity, even though it is barely or inadequately suggested in the print.

The Art of Fugue appeared posthumously, edited by Carl Philipp Emanuel and, in a second edition (1752), by Friedrich Wilhelm Marpurg.[22] Determining an intended order for this volume of keyboard fugues is problematic mainly in that we are dealing with a torso whose printed guise leaves some doubt as to an authentic conception of form. Questions that in part defy final answers arise—as with the Musical Offering—from a comparison with the autograph,[23] which in itself presents an incomplete picture of the work and which documents totally different phases of origin. By way of an account of the contents I present the two primary sources in comparative tabular listings (see Tables 27.8 and 27.9). We may take it for granted that Bach had in mind a definite order for the printed form, an order which could be carried out without difficulty. It could not have been otherwise in view of

Table 27.8. The autograph version of the Art of Fugue

Movement number	Description	Corresponding piece in the printed version
I	Fugue, thema rectum	*Contrapunctus 1.*
II	Fugue, thema inversum	*Contrapunctus 3.*
III	Fugue, thema rectum	*Contrapunctus 2.*
IV	Counterfugue	*Contrapunctus 5.*
V	Double fugue	*Contrapunctus 9.*
VI	Double fugue	*Contrapunctus 10.* (variant)
VII	Counterfugue	*Contrapunctus 6.*
VIII	Counterfugue	*Contrapunctus 7.*
IX	*Canon in Hypodiapason* (enigmatic notation)	*Canon alla Ottava*
—	*Resolutio canonis* (resolved)	
X	Triple fugue	*Contrapunctus 8.*
XI	Triple fugue	*Contrapunctus 11.*
XII	*Canon in Hypodiatesseron . . .* (resolved)	
—	Augmentation canon (enigmatic notation)	*Canon per Augmentationem*
XIII	Mirror fugue (synoptic notation)	*Contrapunctus 12.*
XIV	Mirror fugue (synoptic notation)	*Contrapunctus 13.*
XV	Augmentation canon (first revision)	*Canon per Augmentationem*
	Appendix 1: Augmentation canon (engraver's copy)	*Canon per Augmentationem*
	Appendix 2: *Fuga a 2 Clav.* (arrangement)	*Contrapunctus 13.* (variant)
	Appendix 3: *Fuga a 3 Soggetti*	*Fuga a 3 Soggetti*

the didactic purpose of the work as a compendium of fugues. In probing for recognizable principles of order, we find that the engraved version suggests, at least in general, a detailed disposition. Four fugues based on single themes form the beginning of the work and are followed by three counterfugues, double and triple fugues, mirror fugues, four canons, and finally the unfinished quadruple fugue. This sequence, however, is disturbed by additions whose relation to the total work is questionable (such as the two arrangements of the mirror fugues); the additions may have been included through a misunderstanding of the details involved (such as the variant of the second double fugue) or represent an editorial supplement (the reverentially attached "deathbed chorale" intended as an expression of the composer's legacy). Disregarding these movements, we can identify a tangible structure based on the principle of grouping sections by fugal techniques and placing them in the order of intricacy. Apparent also are smaller structural gestures, such as the pairing of fugues on single themes, the growing complexity in the sequence of counterfugues as well as their symmetrical arrangement (obtained by placing the movement in French style in the center), the symmetrical arrangement of the double and triple fugues, and the pairing of contrasting mirror fugues.

A detailed discussion of the authenticity of such an order would lead us beyond the present scope (see, however, Chapter 20). Yet a few doubts must be mentioned, even with regard to the first half of the work, despite the fact that Bach scholarship has so far considered the sequence leading from Contrapunctus 1 to 12 (this is the extent of numbered movements in the engraving) as the original one. Doubtful above all is the placement of the canons. Were they meant directly to precede the quadruple fugue? Furthermore, by contrapuntal logic, the canon in augmentation should follow the canon at the twelfth. The pairing of contrasting mirror fugues seems feasible, though not as persuasive as the superimposition of forma recta and inversa in autograph; yet it is unlikely that Bach wished to place the forma inversa in each case before the forma recta. Questionable, finally, is the grouping of double and triple fugues. The symmetrical arrangement seems to have a meaning, but an arrangement by pairs seems preferable in view of the increasing level

Table 27.9. The printed version of the Art of Fugue

Title	Description
Contrapunctus 1.	Fugue, thema rectum
Contrapunctus 2.	Fugue, thema rectum
Contrapunctus 3.	Fugue, thema inversum
Contrapunctus 4.	Fugue, thema inversum
Contrapunctus 5.	Counterfugue
Contrapunctus 6. a 4. in Stylo Francese	Counterfugue
Contrapunctus 7. a 4. per Augment et Diminut:	Counterfugue
Contrapunctus 8. a 3.	Triple fugue
Contrapunctus 9. a 4. alla Duodecima	Double fugue
Contrapunctus 10. a 4. alla Decima	Double fugue
Contrapunctus 11. a 3	Triple fugue
Contrapunctus inversus. 12 a 4	Mirror fugue, forma inversa
Contrapunctus inversus. 12 a 4	Mirror fugue, forma recta
Contrapunctus inversus [13] a 3	Mirror fugue, forma inversa
Contrapunctus inversus [13] a 3	Mirror fugue, forma recta
Contrapunctus [14] a 4.	Variant of Contrapunctus 10
Canon per Augmentationem in contrario motu.	Augmentation canon
Canon alla' Ottava	Canon at the octave
Canon alla Decima {in} Contrapuncto alla Terza	Canon at the tenth
Canon alla Duodecima in Contrapuncto alla Quinta	Canon at the twelfth
Fuga a 2 Clav.	Arrangement of Contrapunctus 13, forma inversa
Fuga a 2 Clav:	Arrangement of Contrapunctus 13, forma recta
Fuga a 3 Soggetti	Unfinished quadruple fugue
Choral. Wenn wir in hoechsten Noethen	

of technical difficulty. The questions must remain unanswered, yet we must keep in mind that the uncertainties were created by Bach's executors and editors, not the composer himself.

There is an illuminating manuscript annotation—rarely considered and never fully interpreted—by Johann Friedrich Agricola (who apparently assisted Emanuel Bach in the preparation of the edition). It is contained in a third attachment to the autograph and reads: *"und / einen andern / Grund Plan."* This is a clear indication that the editors had knowledge of at least two basic plans, which undoubtedly go back to Bach himself. It is only from these plans that they could have gathered the information they related in the obituary (formulated jointly by Emanuel and Agricola) that "his last illness prevented him from completing, in accordance with his design, the next-to-last fugue as well as from working out the last one, which was to contain four themes and was to be inverted in all four parts note-by-note."[24] What is here described as design must be identical with one or the other ground plan, for these—since lost—would once have been the only source of an intended form for the complete work. The design, however, would not have been unequivocal, for we know that at least two basic plans existed. And it stands to reason that they, being drafted for the composer's own use, were not readily understandable to the editors. They may have been difficult to decipher and may have contained ambiguous notations or directions for change of placement, thus causing mistakes in the print.

It is possible that the autograph offers hints of "the other" basic plan, divergent from that of the engraved version. Here we find, at least in one spot, an obvious departure from the principles governing the order of the print. In its total form the autograph does not suggest any patterned sequence, for it is a mixture of proof copy, fair copy prepared for the engraver, and original composing copy, the order of movements being largely arbitrary. Only the movements surrounding the two triple fugues show a carefully thought-out structure, namely that of a double frame. This, nevertheless, has only visual significance: the canon notation in a single part recurs in symmetrically corresponding places. It can no longer be ascertained whether this represents a one-time experiment, or whether Bach meant to apply a similar scheme to other groups of movements. The printed version shows no trace of the double frame. Bach may have discarded the other plan, or he may not have worked it out. We do not know, as we will never know, what final form Bach's last work would have had if it could have been completed.[25] It would be futile to discuss the possibilities of reconstruction—more appropriate than a reconstruction or hypothetical solution is the guide of Bach's principles of design, as it emerges even in this torso. A comparison of the principles apparent in the two sources shows how Bach tested the available options in striving for a well-directed and logical form. Again we can recognize in the autograph and in the print a balance held by building intensity (increase of demands in fugal technique) and pivotal symmetry—manners of design which do not imply the performance sequence but which do reflect an order of the work's innate conception.

OUR OBJECT was necessarily not a detailed discussion of structural problems in Bach's work or of the highly specialized issues of source study posed by the Musical Offering and the Art of Fugue; not a small number of questions must therefore remain unanswered, not a small number of points must remain in need of clarification. Our attempt, prompted by the manifold possibilities of comparison, was to investigate the principles of design and order in Bach's original prints. These principles arise above all from the use of integral musical components to mark groups, sections, or correspondences. What results are expressions of limited structural articulation (similar or contrasting pairs, groups formed in symmetrical or expanding sequence), their sum or combination forming larger architectonic designs (cycles governed by the principle of intensification, frame or multiple frame structures).

The printed works as such do not assume an extraordinary position within Bach's oeuvre, yet because of their choice and special preparation as works to be placed before the public, they form a more or less defined group in themselves. Furthermore, beginning with Clavier-Übung III, a certain relatedness of idea marks the conception of the printed works of Bach's later years, in which a special intricacy begins to rule the structural planning. The monothematic variation works above all (Clavier-Übung IV, Vom Himmel hoch, the Musical Offering, and the Art of Fugue) reveal an inner connection which to a large extent is manifested in like principles of design. These principles are never imposed at random but grow from the musical conception. It is for this reason that the Schübler Chorales and Clavier-Übung I represent merely diversified collections of kindred pieces. Since the works were not planned on the basis of inner relationships, a structuring of the total sequence would have had no meaning. Conversely, in works with movements bearing a direct connection one to another, diligently structured designs play a decisive role in giving the inherent conception perceptible expression. As examples from Clavier-Übung III may be cited the Missa and Catechism chorales, the grouping of large and small settings for each *cantus firmus,* as well as the gathering of the total work as a compendium of organ liturgy, which is not devoid of didactic implications. Similarly, Clavier-Übung IV is characteristic of a variously yet progressively unfolding, logically articulated variation form; the Canonic Variations on Vom Himmel hoch are indicative of a consciously graded probing and systematic demonstration of the forms of freely contrapuntal or strictly thematic canons upon a recurring *cantus firmus.* The Musical Offering exhibits, in tribute to the king, the Thema Regium as a rich source for the development of highly varied strict and free polyphonic forms, be they sparsely or densely voiced keyboard fugues in modern or traditional manner, diverse types of canon, or a chamber music work. The guiding thought of the Art of Fugue, finally, is the construction of a gigantic work of pedagogy in which the different possibilities of fugal composition are displayed in keyboard models, the contrapuntal intricacies being introduced one by one in a continuity formed on the basis of instructional logic. The principles of design are oriented by such a generic concept in order to attain the greatest possible congruity of internal and external structure—an idea that again and again must have posed the composer problems difficult to overcome, as is evident especially in the cases of Vom Himmel hoch and the Art of Fugue.

The cyclically arranged printed works (perhaps with the exception of Clavier-Übung IV and Vom Himmel hoch) were never intended to present the variety and specific cogency required for a performance sequence. Even the example of Vom Himmel hoch shows that such a sequence was a secondary consideration, since the purely musical dynamics reflected by the natural logic in the succession of movements was later renounced in favor of an order constructed with a view to symbolic implications. Bach's cyclic dispositions emanate apparently from the thought that the microcosmic order must be mirrored in a macrocosmic order in rational correspondence. Thus he adds to the audible order of the work, unfolding in time, an inaudible order that is static. This produces a quality of immense density: the work lives both in the dimensions of time and space, in an audible as well as in a visual world. It is above all in the last printed works that Bach is concerned with a reciprocity of internal and external structure. A concept of *ars musica* is revealed that reaches beyond the sound of the musical composition toward depths of the no longer directly perceptible and the symbolic.

Yet in reality this remains only a partial aspect of Bach's artistic conception; it seems worth recalling the words of E. T. A. Hoffmann (1826): "To build a house, one needs a frame. Yet it would be unusual to discover the architect's merit in the framework rather than in the house." Bach knows no purely speculative esoteric craftsmanship aimed at strictly representational exhibit and abrogating reality of sound. His last works may suggest some such fascination, but the Schübler Chorales draw us back to the basis of reality—that is, to practical performance. This collection of organ works from Bach's last years, totally devoid of any conjectural elements, stands as a monument of the musician first and foremost devoted to practice who is in no way confined by abstract and artificial symbolism. Wherever we encounter particular principles of order in Bach's work they are founded in an organic unity of the art of invention and the art of design, enriching the immediate aural impression, for they serve "for Music Lovers, to Refresh their Spirits."

28

Toward a Definition of the Last Period
of Bach's Work

THAT PHASE of Johann Sebastian Bach's life work which, widely and frequently, is referred to as the composer's last proves—on closer examination—neither a unified nor an unproblematic entity. This is so because answers to three principal questions can be provided only with great difficulty; (1) What are the criteria for the organization of biographical phases by which such a period can be declared and justified? (2) What are the works that form its repertoire and character? (3) How can its artistic and stylistic qualities be identified? I shall explore these questions in an attempt to probe possible interpretations.

I

The story of Bach's life, especially during the Leipzig years, from 1723 to 1750, is unusually scant in significant dates. A division into designated periods of creativity is therefore dependent, in the last analysis, upon the achievements resulting from the manifold musical responsibilities of the St. Thomas cantorate. That the interrelation of office and mandate, in itself open to question, applies only in a most limited sense to the Leipzig period is well documented for the 1720s and 1730s. To the cantor's tasks of instruction and church music was added after 1729 the direction of the Collegium Musicum, the new position signifying the ascendancy of civic music practice and considerably enlarging his duties. Next to the responsibilities pertaining to Sunday and feast-day services now stood that of regular concert programs once a week (and, during the time of the Leipzig Fair, twice a week). Bach's work schedule was further complicated by the fact that he undertook major publication projects (the Clavier-Übung series, 1731 to 1741, was the principal result).

In the later 1730s it was determined also by extensive obligations to the Dresden Court. In the dedication of his Missa in B Minor, Bach had offered his services to the electoral court "in the composition of music for the Church as well as for the Orchestra" with the goal of joining a wider corollary to the sphere of his responsibilities in Leipzig. Official recognition was given his request by his appointment in 1736 as "Electoral Saxon and Royal Polish Court Composer." Since Wilhelm Friedemann Bach became organist in Dresden's church of St. Sophia's in 1733, there arose many possibilities for Bach to participate in, and profit from, the attractive Dresden scene. It is probably accidental that his guest engagements as organist in Dresden are verified only for the years 1731 and 1736; we may assume more frequent appearances. Beyond this, we know of his performance as soloist in other locations (for instance in 1733, for the dedication of the organ at St. Martin's in Kassel).

Everyday life in Leipzig included many administrative details for Bach, not least of them the lending of instruments and the sale of music publications. Both were firmly anchored in Bach's primary interests: he was deeply committed to the technical and artistic aspects of instrument building (his organological expertise was evident ever since his Arnstadt days, and in the 1730s he became involved in the construction of fortepianos by Gottfried Silbermann); and he was ever curious about any news of the music market (the geographical confines stipulated by his working situation notwithstanding, his knowledge of musical literature apparently knew no bounds). The picture would not be complete without a mention of the steady comings and goings of colleagues (in later years, Carl Philipp Emanuel Bach related recollections of his parental home as a veritable beehive); among the prominent visitors were the Dresden capellmeister Johann Adolf Hasse and his wife, the famous primadonna Faustina Bordoni.

More important than ever before were Bach's extensive teaching activities. The students from the 1730s included musicians who subsequently gained distinction in their own right as music theorists: Lorenz Christoph Mizler, Johann Friedrich Agricola, Johann Philipp Kirnberger. Here we may recognize also a closer relationship to the university circles which decisively influenced the intellectual climate of Leipzig, and it was not by chance that the interest became mutual: Bach needed the contact with professionally oriented music students; with private pupils of means, many of them scions of the nobility; and with members of the faculty. The latter, in turn, sought the connection with Bach as a virtuoso well known in circles extending far beyond Leipzig and as an authority on musical matters—about the year 1740, the Leipzig Professor of Physics Johann Friedrich Mentz asked Bach, apparently as a matter of course, for the favor of offering a solution to a riddle canon by the Renaissance composer Teodoro Riccio, contained in an album collection.

Bach's family situation entered a new phase in the 1730s in that he could witness his older sons' entering the profession—with pride (in the case of Wilhelm Friedemann) as well as with concern (in the case of Johann Gottfried Bernhard). It became clear that the talent of "the many members of the Bach family who have excelled in practical music" [1] continued in the youngest generation. It is particularly in this context that Bach's turning to the documentation of a family genealogy, about the year 1735, might be seen— a documentation that added commentary to the *Alt-Bachisches Archiv,* his treasured collection of works by members of the family. One cannot overlook the fact that—at the age of fifty, and with sons leaving the home—Bach realized a historical perspective in which he felt bound to place himself.

Perhaps it was this manifest "changing of the guard" that prompted at the end of the 1730s a gradual decline in Bach's observance of regular duties, in no way abrupt yet perceptible. He resigned the direction of the Collegium Musicum between the spring and fall of 1739, to resume it temporarily prior to his official withdrawal after 1742. Nevertheless, since the new director, Carl Gotthelf Gerlach, organist at the New Church, was a student of his, we may surmise that Bach was connected with the continuing organization, constituted under the name of "Grosses Concert" in 1743–1744, and remained so until the end of his life.

There was also, even before 1740, a certain reorientation, doubtless initiated by Bach, in the conduct of the office of the cantorate. The argument over proper authority flaring up in the fall of 1736 between Bach and the St. Thomas School Rector Johann August Ernesti, in office since 1734—an argument about the appointment of choir prefects—must have brought home to Bach the limitations of his jurisdiction and independence. It is true that in the 1730s he had invested a noticeably smaller total creative effort in the church music carried out by the St. Thomas School ensembles, as compared especially with the production of close to four year-cycles of church cantatas at the beginning of his cantorate. Yet we cannot speak of a retirement from church music activities either in the 1730s or the 1740s. Consider the groups of works in the genres of oratorio and Mass from the years 1733–1735 and beyond; nor was there a cessation of cantata composition. On the other hand, a fact such as that the revision of the St. John Passion was abandoned about 1740 (whereas a new, revised, and expanded version of the St. Matthew Passion was completed in 1736) signifies a change in Bach's priorities, above all with regard to official duties versus free artistic inclination.

A further given and biographically important date during the 1730s is found in the literary-critical dispute, beginning in 1737, between Johann Adolph Scheibe and Johann Abraham Birnbaum regarding the quality and challenges of Bach's music. From the very fact that he sought an eloquent and effective spokesman in Birnbaum, a lawyer and university lecturer on rhetoric, it becomes evident how offended Bach must have been by Scheibe's charge that he removed "the natural element in his pieces by giving them a turgid and confused style" so as to "darken their beauty by an excess of art." But this did not mean that Bach ceased to be concerned with showing in his creative work—perhaps more pointedly than ever before—what aspects of his music mattered to him. In order to trace and understand this development, it is necessary in the first place to clarify the particular repertoire involved.

II

It would be wrong to equate Bach's reaction to Scheibe's criticism—a reaction for which we can give hypothetical reasons at best—with the inception of a late period. Yet toward the middle and end of the 1730s there is a perceptible change in Bach's orientation, a change that, regardless of all continuity of Bach's highly developed idiom, gives a characteristic stamp to the works of the last twelve years. It would have been unlikely that such a change could have been initiated by Scheibe, for it arose logically from the aging Bach's increasingly systematic realization of a synthesis of his rich creative experience and his manifold musical interests.

The works traditionally considered typical of his last period, the great monothematic instrumental cycles, such as the Goldberg Variations, the Musical Offering, or the Art of Fugue, nevertheless represent only a partial and relatively one-sided share of the repertoire in question. Obviously it is not insignificant to an understanding of Bach's old age—more and more given to instrumental conception—that keyboard and chamber music became an essential and influential component of his works of the 1730s.

A counterpart to the four issues of the Clavier-Übung series (concluded in 1741 with the so-called Goldberg Variations) is the large project of the Well-Tempered Clavier II, whose major portion was probably completed about 1739 or 1740. Scattered single works such as the Fantasy in C Minor BWV 906 of about 1738 (with a fragmentary fugue) suggest serious losses of the total output. The most momentous keyboard work of the late period is doubtless the Art of Fugue, which—as recent research has shown—goes back to about 1740. The work has come down in an early version (in manuscript, but complete) from before 1745; the revision, printed in (incomplete) enlarged form, kept Bach occupied until close to the end of his life. The two ricercari of the Musical Offering date from 1747, the one written in three parts having probably been conceived for the fortepiano, in which Bach was especially interested during that time.

The organ works likewise assume a major place among the late works. Their actual beginning is probably the third part of the Clavier-Übung (twenty-one Mass and Catechism chorales, Prelude and Fugue in E♭ Major, four duets), which is the most extensive of all of Bach's organ projects. Next to it stand two other printed works, the Canonic Variations on Vom Himmel hoch and the "Six Chorales of Various Kinds" (the so-called Schübler Chorales), arrangements of chorale cantata movements. An emphasis upon the extended organ chorale within the late works is reflected also in the repeated revision of works from the Weimar period, resulting in the Eighteen Chorales as the most representative collection. But free forms of organ music were also resumed by Bach in revised versions, among them those of the great Prelude and Fugue in G Major BWV 541 (about 1742), as well as probably the early Passacaglia BWV 582.

Closely related to the keyboard works are Bach's compositions for lute, the most important of which (Partita in C Minor BWV 997 and Prelude, Fugue and Allegro in E♭ Major BWV 998) date from about 1740: they presumably emanate from Bach's association with the Dresden lute virtuosos Silvius Leopold Weiß and Johann Kropffganss, whose performances include the participation in a 1739 musical gathering in Bach's home.

In the 1730s, chamber music and music in the home seems to have moved, more strongly than at any other time (including the Cöthen years), into the center of Bach's activity. This change in focus was due not only to the work with the Collegium Musicum, but also predominantly to the many opportunities that arose, "vocaliter and instrumentaliter," in the circles of students, colleagues, and family, with children now having come of age. It appears that the major portion of the extant chamber music actually derives from the Leipzig period. Among the late works must be counted the three viola da gamba sonatas BWV 1027–1029 and the G major trio sonata for flutes BWV 1039 (1736–1742), the flute sonata in E major BWV 1035 (probably 1741), and the trio sonata from the Musical Offering (1747); among the works of larger scoring, mainly the harpsichord concertos (ca. 1738) and, from the period 1738–1739, the B Minor Suite BWV 1067, likely the last of Bach's orchestral pieces.

The vocal works of the last period form as broad a spectrum as the instrumental works. From the secular compositions must be singled out the wedding cantata "O holder Tag" BWV 210 and the cantata burlesque "Mer hahn en neue Oberkeet" BWV 212 (1742). A major segment of this repertoire, however, will have to be considered lost, such as the cantata on a text by Gottsched, "Willkommen! Ihr herrschenden Götter der Erden" BWV Anh. I 13 (1739), which according to a contemporary statement "was written entirely in accordance with the latest taste, and was approved by everyone. So well does the Hon. Capellmeister know how to suite himself to his listeners"[2]—a patent innuendo directed by Bach's student Mizler at his critic Scheibe.

The losses of sacred music are evidently no less serious, and an overview of the last vocal works is even more restricted than that of the instrumental works. Fragments such as the aria "Bekennen will ich seinen Namen" BWV 200 or the Sinfonia for a cantata BWV 1045 (both from the period 1742–1746) indicate a much larger original scope. Revisions of existing works, sometimes far-reaching, play a certain role in this connection; mention should also be made of the cantata for St. John's Day, "Freue dich, erlöste Schar" BWV 30 (1738–1742), based on a secular congratulatory work), the new version of the opening chorus for the cantata "Ein feste Burg ist unser Gott" BWV 80 (before 1744), and the last version (1748–1749) of the wedding cantata "Dem Gerechten muß das Licht immer wieder aufgehen" BWV 195. Even the relatively late funeral motet "O Jesu Christ, mein's Lebens Licht" BWV 118 (about 1736–1737) exists in a subsequent version dating from the years 1746–1747. In general, occasional works like the wedding cantata "Gott ist unsre Zuversicht" BWV 197 (1736–1737) seem to have made up an increasing part in Bach's output.

The Mass is the focus of Bach's vocal oeuvre from the later years. In connection with his Missa "solemnis" in B Minor (Kyrie and Gloria), dedicated to the Dresden court in 1733, Bach wrote the four "ferial" Kyrie-Gloria Masses in A Major, G Major, F Major, and G Minor (largely based on earlier compositions). The intensity of Bach's focus on the Mass genre and other forms of Latin church music is documented in the numerous copies, performances, and arrangements of works by other composers (ranging from Palestrina's "Missa sine Nomine" to Pergolesi's "Stabat Mater") as well as in continued work on his own compositions. Thus he drew the cantata for the Feast of the Nativity, "Gloria in excelcis Deo" BWV 191 (1743–1746), from three movements of the Gloria of the Missa of 1733. Probably the same period (possibly even the same Christmas service) saw a revival of the Sanctus in D major, written as early as 1724. We may assume that it was in this connection that Bach resolved to link this Sanctus setting closely with the Missa of 1733. His ostensible plan was to expand this Mass, originally consisting only of the Kyrie and Gloria sections, to a "Missa tota." We know nothing of a reason, let alone a commission, for the creation of such a work—although some such motive may be presumed. Nor do we have any knowledge of a performance of the composite work during Bach's life; yet he was concerned with its completion until the years 1748–1749, which means that it must be counted among Bach's very last creative tasks–to all appearances, Bach composed no further works after the "Et incarnatus est."

III

There are two works that, in special measure, aid a definition of the last phase of Bach's creativity: the Art of Fugue and the B Minor Mass. Both are compositions that evidently were not written in a short time but required an uncommonly extensive process of development. In the case of the Art of Fugue, composition required at least ten years. In the case of the B Minor Mass, the span of time must be set more widely; here we have to take into account that a work finished in 1748–1749 absorbed movements (as in the case of the "Crucifixus") whose original conception went back as far as thirty-five years ("Weinen, Klagen, Sorgen, Zagen" BWV 12 of 1714). This proves first of all the conspicuous continuity of the essence of Bach's language—a continuity expressed also in the fact that he maintained his judgment of Weimar organ chorales as valid works, to be revised only with great care (the Great Eighteen), and of movements from the early Leipzig cantatas as requiring almost no change (Schübler Chorales). The correlation with existing work applies especially to the Art of Fugue. Its proximity to the fugues of the Well-Tempered Clavier II (as well as those of the preceding part) is as manifest as that to the Clavier-Übung, especially so far as the principle of diversity, so consistently applied in the Goldberg Variations, is concerned. Such tangible connections bear out again that the unmistakable characteristics of the last works are anticipated in the compositions of the 1730s and their context.

In carrying out his duties, Bach had managed from the first to keep from being confined by official assignments, above all from being subjected to aesthetic dictates. In consequence Bach enjoyed unusual freedom in pursuing projects not tied to any model. His striving for innovation (be it in the year-cycle of chorale cantatas, the St. Matthew Passion, the trio sonatas or great preludes and fugues for organ, the solo works for violin, or the so-called Brandenburg Concertos) is even more pronounced in the late works. Here are some typical examples:

1. Clavier-Übung III. True, comparable "Livres d'orgue" can be found (and Bach knew even the more remote literature, such as the organ books of Frescobaldi and de Grigny). But an organ collection as systematically arranged, well-rounded, and varied as this had not existed before—and Bach new this best.

2. The harpsichord concertos. Examples for the concertato use of the harpsichord were there before and next to Bach's works. But Bach's concertos (especially BWV 1052–1059, preserved in autograph score) demonstrate how technical refinement and new idiomatic conception of the solo parts (based upon earlier concerto scores) could provide the basis for a genre that held promise of a great future.

3. The opening chorus of Cantata BWV 80. Figural chorale settings serving as opening choruses were in a way a specialty of Bach's which had been extensively tested in the second Leipzig year-cycle. But in the reworked large chorale setting of "Ein feste Burg" (228 measures) for the cantata of the same name, Bach joins the most diversified elements—the polyphony of a highly integrated motet-like vocal scoring is combined with the instrumental *cantus firmus* canon involving an obbligato basso continuo—and thus achieves a hitherto unattained degree of monumental scope and expression.

The Art of Fugue and the B Minor Mass conform to this striking Bachian trait of "intending to excel above others and oneself." The Art of Fugue is linked to earlier fugue compositions yet moves to a level that is novel in principle. The entire multi-sectional work is derived from the same thematic material, a musical plan that presupposes a far-reaching process of thought with regard to the harmonic-contrapuntal implications of the chosen theme. The result is more than a study of fugue: a compendium of the range offered by utmost concentration and highest technical demands of instrumental counterpoint. The B Minor Mass figures in this respect as a fully comparable counterpart. Its dimensions correspond to those of the St. Matthew Passion, but the B Minor Mass stands out by virtue of its concentration upon the contrapuntally integrated soloistic and choral vocal texture (with and without obbligato instruments); recitative and note-against-note setting of chorales vanish. And the genres, structures, and manners of vocal writing reach an optimum multiformity (ranging from the motet and fugue through passacaglia and concerto to totally free forms).

The working process and style of composition in Bach's later years (after the end of the 1730s) is marked by the following characteristics: a theoretical component, a tendency toward melodic writing in cantabile style (without abandoning harmonic-contrapuntal elaboration), an integral stylistic plurality, and a historically-oriented dimension.

A certain penchant toward theoretical permeation of the compositional process was apparently present from the outset (possibly an underlying tenet of his largely unaided early training), and it grew through his steadily increasing pedagogical work, perhaps also through the academic-scholarly climate in Leipzig. As a basis for composition, however, theoretical speculation was essentially limited to the canonic art. The canon, as strictest form of imitative counterpoint, takes an especially noticeable place in the later works (chorale settings of Clavier-Übung III, Goldberg Variations with the Fourteen Canons BWV 1087, Vom Himmel hoch BWV 769, Art of Fugue, Musical Offering, "Ein feste Burg" BWV 80, "Confiteor" of the B Minor Mass). Yet the principle of canon (beyond its significance as a genre) doubtless served Bach as well in exploring the basic substance of a theme or musical thought. In this respect the emphasis on canonic writing in Bach's late works reflects his concern with economy and concentration. Of theoretical impact also is Bach's expansion of major-minor tonal harmony through the systematic inclusion of the church modes. This trait, appearing in the four-part chorale settings of his cantatas at an early time (about 1724), provides new initiative in the composition of Clavier-Übung III, its overt consequences reaching as far as the enharmonic chromaticism and modal harmony of the Art of Fugue and the Symbolum Nicenum of the B Minor Mass.

Among the palpable differences between the two parts of the Well-Tempered Clavier is the increase of the cantabile quality in the melodies of the contrapuntal fabric. In Bach's polyphonic texture, a "principal part," so epitomized by Scheibe, does not normally exist. Even within the polarity of such a melodically attractive setting as that of the Air in the D major orchestral suite BWV 1068 (1731), which heralds the cantabile manner of the late works, Bach cannot forgo a weighty contrapuntal treatment of inner voices. The same applies to the mature style of the four-part chorale settings (such as found in the Christmas Oratorio of 1734–1735), in which strong melodic interest is paired with polyphony. In this context belong also such heterogeneous elements as the vocal-melodic quality of the *stile antico,* as it appears in the Credo intonation of the B Minor Mass and in the theme for the Art of Fugue, or the popular song quality to which Bach turned in the Goldberg Variations and the Peasant Cantata. Ranging from the chorale melodies of Schemelli's *Musicalisches Gesang-Buch* (1736) to arias, choruses, preludes, fugues, and dances, a tendency arises and leads to many-sided new cantabile manner.

Stylistic pluralism is indicative of the German musical scene of Bach's time, and Bach from early on was adept at handling the vocabulary of the French and Italian tastes as well as that of various fusions (including exotic genera such as the Polish manner). In the late period there enters, however, a strong sense of integration stressing not only the coexistence of contrasting styles (including the period styles "antico" and "moderno") as it appears first in Clavier-Übung III (though persisting in the Art of Fugue, Musical Offering, and B Minor Mass) but also the musical coherence and aesthetic unity of otherwise divergent manners. As a characteristic example we might quote the merging of French suite and Italian concerto principles in the Orchestral Suite in B Minor. Bach seems consciously to avoid the traditional style models (still existent in Clavier-Übung II) in a formal continuity. Thus he does not write a set of Goldberg Variations "alla maniera italiana" or a B Minor Mass in *stile antico*. The different styles are used for highly differentiated expression and thus form an important factor of structural universality.

Bach was also able to draw on the new musical tendencies of the younger generation for positive aspects of his own work, never compromising his harmonic-contrapuntal orientation. A movement such as the E♭ Major Andante of the trio sonata in the Musical Offering, which is deeply indebted to the fashionable Berlin style of the 1740s, rises in the hands of the aging Bach to an exceedingly complex structure in which brief "sigh" motifs with conscious dynamic shades join with consistent polyphony and modulation-laden harmony. Similarly the "Et incarnatus est," presumably the last vocal setting of Bach, breathes in its confluence of unorthodox polyphony and expressive gestures a progressive sense of style. It is all the more remarkable how this movement is conjoined with the oldest segment of the B Minor Mass, the "Crucifixus"—yet not without Bach having previously imparted to the "Crucifixus" an updated garb by means of more sensitive continuo declamation and richly differentiated instrumentation in the upper parts.

It is especially such an example that shows with what keen awareness Bach lived through the change of generations. Just as Bach could state in 1730 that "the former style of music no longer seems to please our ears" (with reference to the Kuhnau generation),[3] he would have had to include his own manner of writing, at least of the period before Leipzig, in speaking from the vantage point of his old age. It is true that he could not accept the often provocative simplicity of the new musical styles and their ideals and felt compelled to observe a critical distance. Yet the style of his later years can hardly be seen as an obstinate "contrast program": his musical intuition and his mastery of composition enabled him to blend tradition and modernism. What emerges is a quasi-historical attitude that leads Bach into the musical past (to Palestrina and the forebears of the Bach family) as well as bestowing upon him, especially through the exchange with his students and sons, a foretaste of future developments.[4]

From such a perspective, Bach was able, in wholesome self-assurance, to fix his own historical position, at the time assigning himself the task of the teacher who realized the dialectical principle inherent in the association of tradition and modernism and who knows how to pass this on. Hardly in any other way can the artistic bequest of the Art of Fugue and of the B Minor Mass be understood. Bach, in his old age, wrote music more advanced than ever before, as was proved to later generations through its enduring vigor.

❖   ❖   ❖

EARLY RECEPTION AND
ARTISTIC LEGACY

29

On the Original Editions of Bach's Works

THE PUBLIC AWARENESS of the name and stature of a composer is in general inseparably connected with the distribution and performance of his works. And it is by no means merely a modern thought that a great composer's life work must be available in a printed "complete edition." As early as the sixteenth century we encounter quite a few nearly complete editions of works published during their composers' lifetimes. Among these are to be counted those by Palestrina, Monteverdi, Praetorius, and Schütz. The distribution in contemporary prints of their essential oeuvre, undertaken primarily at their own initiative, contributed rather decisively to the propagation and acceptance of their music. By comparison, Bach's publishing effort seems to have been remarkably limited, and only a disproportionally small number of his works appeared in print during his life. Most of his works, preserved only in manuscript, remained restricted to his close circle of students and colleagues, at least in the period before 1750. The object of greatest interest in this respect was the clavier and organ music; other instrumental works, as well as the vocal works, received notably smaller attention. Bach evidently did not do anything in particular to alter this situation. Only on rare occasions did he lend performance material for any of the larger pieces to colleagues and acquaintances (and he usually retained the full score).[1] Moreover, only a few of his compositions were dedicated to eminent persons in other places,[2] without any appreciable results as to wider performances. Yet the relatively scant number of extant original Bach prints and a correspondingly narrow choice of preserved manuscript copies of works from the time before 1750 should not prevent us from assuming a much larger original number from which major losses may have occurred.

The difference in the second half of the eighteenth century is unmistakable. The situation changed abruptly with the almost desultory increase in the distribution of manuscripts, especially of Bach's keyboard works, but also, to a degree that should not be underestimated, of his vocal works.[3] Manuscripts prepared by professional copyists now became available in the trade. This is amply documented in the voluminous catalogues of the firms Breitkopf in Leipzig; Westphal in Hamburg; or Traeg in Vienna.[4] The early propagation of Bach's music was stimulated by the publication of the four-part chorales, issued first in two volumes by Birnstiel (Berlin, 1765 and 1769) and close to twenty years later in a new edition, enlarged to four volumes, by Breitkopf (Leipzig, 1784–1787). Yet as early as 1781, before the appearance of this edition, a connoisseur such as Johann Friedrich Reichardt was able to describe the composer of these chorales as "the greatest harmonist of all times and nations."[5] The quotations of examples drawn from Bach's instrumental and vocal works in numerous books on music, both in Germany and abroad, aroused further interest and underlined the composer's steadily growing recognition.[6]

As a logical consequence, individual works began to appear in print even before the beginning of the nineteenth century. An edition of the *Oeuvres complettes* for clavier and organ was projected by Hoffmeister & Kühnel in Leipzig and Vienna; it commenced in 1800 but ceased as early as 1803 after the fourteenth issue. Separately from this project, editions of vocal works were undertaken by various publishers: in 1802–1803 an edition of all motets appeared in two volumes (including "Ich lasse dich nicht, du segnest mich denn" BWV Anh. III 159, later ascribed to Johann Christoph Bach). In 1811 the Magnificat followed (in the E♭ major version BWV 243a), in 1818 the A Major Mass (BWV 234), later, as the first cantata, "Ein feste Burg" (BWV 80), and in 1830, the St. Matthew Passion—to name only the most important titles. In 1818 the Zurich publisher Hans Georg Nägeli announced his first edition of the B Minor Mass as that of the "greatest musical work of art of all times and nations" (an echo of the statement by Reichardt mentioned above); this edition, however, required two phases of publication (1833 for the Kyrie and Gloria; 1845 for the remainder of the Mass).

In some measure, the growing attention to Bach's music after his death was doubtless prompted by his own publication and distribution of the most important keyboard works, which even during his life earned him legendary fame. Thus it is not surprising that a commentator of the rank of the Bolognese music scholar Padre Martini, having received a copy of the Musical Offering in the spring of 1750,[7] sent the following statement to Germany: "I consider it superfluous to describe the special merits of Mr. Bach. He is well known and admired not only in Germany but throughout our own Italy; I only wish to say that I would consider it difficult to find a teacher who would surpass him; he can lay claim to being one of the foremost in all of Europe."[8]

There are a number of reasons why relatively few of Bach's works were published in his lifetime. One of them is the decline of the music trade in central Germany after the Thirty Years War. There was a dearth of financial support from aristocratic and civic sources which had been of such importance for the earlier flowering of music printing. Another reason was the very costly production (by movable music type) of polyphonic keyboard music, which was most readily reproduced by the process of engraving, at that time rarely practiced in Germany. Finally, because it was highly innovative and technically demanding, Bach's music attracted only a limited, commercially insignificant clientele.

The first of Bach's works to be printed, in 1708, was a cantata, namely "Gott ist mein König" (BWV 71), written for the installation of a new town council. Its publication may be ascribed to the ambition of the young composer, not to the initiative of the free imperial city of Mühlhausen, since that might have been seen as setting a precedent for issuing works by Bach's predecessors and successors in office. The import of this edition can be fully measured only when one considers that no other composer of Bach's generation (including Telemann and Handel) was at that time represented by the publication of a vocal work in Protestant Germany. For the election of the Mühlhausen town council of 1709, Bach again furnished a celebratory cantata. This work, also printed, is documented merely in the civic files, but no copy has survived.[9] Thus the earlier piece remained the only extant contemporary print of a vocal composition by Bach and, for nearly twenty years, of any of his published works.[10] Furthermore, it was the only original Bach edition set in movable type. All works published subsequently were produced by copper engraving, the process particularly suited for keyboard music. For these editions the manuscript copy was etched into a metal plate in mirror image, gone over with a graver's chisel, and reproduced by a paper impression taken under a copper press.[11]

In the fourth year of his Leipzig tenure Bach began to take an interest in the thorough and systematic publication of his keyboard works. In 1726 he had his first partita engraved and printed. Although at least two more partitas were ready at the time,[12] Bach was cautious in testing the market. It was also necessary to create a carefully planned chain of distributors. This becomes apparent from a 1727 publication notice for Partitas II and III, which states that they are "available not only from the author, but also from 1) Mr. Petzold, Royal Polish and Electoral Saxon Chamber Organist in Dresden; 2) Mr. Ziegler, Director Musices and Organist at St. Ulrich's in Halle; 3) Mr. Böhm, Organist at St. Johannis in Lüneburg; 4) Mr. Schwaneberg, Chamber Musician at the Ducal Court of Brunswick in Wolfenbüttel; 5) Mr. Fischer, Civic Musician and Town Council Musician in Nuremberg and 6) Mr. Roth, Civic and Town Council Musician in Augsburg."[13] Thus the partitas appeared at first in single issues though they were eventually published collectively as Opus 1, initially by the author and subsequently in a licensed edition by Boetius of Leipzig.[14]

The series of original editions that followed was thus launched with a highly representative opening volume. The repertoire seems to have been consciously limited to keyboard music, except for the ensemble movements from the Musical Offering and the six-part canon BWV 1076, issued in a special printing for the members of Mizler's Societät der musicalischen Wissenschaften. Bach apparently presented in these editions the major part of his organ and clavier works written in Leipzig.[15] The publishing activities involved must, in fact, have constituted one of his major interests during the 1730s and 1740s. The four-fold series of the Clavier-Übung shows Bach's concern to represent the almost encyclopedic scope of his compositions for keyboard instruments. All varieties of instruments (harpsichord with one or two manuals, small or large organ) were included, as were all the usual genres, textures, and styles of clavier and organ music. And the conspicuous increase in printed editions during Bach's last years—the Canonic Variations on Vom Himmel hoch, the so-called Schübler Chorales, and the Art of Fugue—suggests that he may have had further publication plans (possibly the Well-Tempered Clavier II or even the harpsichord concertos), some of them connected with the critical review of earlier works (such as that resulting in the Great Eighteen Chorales).

The declaration in the obituary of 1754 that Bach was "the greatest organist and clavier player we have ever had"[16] may be understood in the context of the publicity Bach generated as composer of brilliant and erudite keyboard music. The master of vocal music, by contrast, was hardly recognized. He had published none of his Leipzig cantatas, and the reason is easily comprehended. The vocal performance forces reflected conditions in Leipzig, which were almost without parallel in Protestant Germany. It is, moreover, particularly in these works that a tendency toward the unusual and unaccustomed is expressed; and their complexity of texture and technical demands made them less accessible to the general practice of church performance. In this conscious exclusiveness Bach's work is clearly distinguished from that of his contemporaries. Telemann, for instance, aimed his cantata publications carefully at average conditions. The style and technical requirements of his works clearly reflect his own advice that "He who proves to be of use to many acts more wisely than the one who addresses his writing to a chosen few; what is easily perceptible will always serve everyone."[17]

An orientation toward the tastes and needs of a wider public seems to have been entirely foreign to Bach. Otherwise he would hardly have had the idea of compiling, in the so-called Brandenburg Concertos, six pieces of radically different texture and scoring, to say nothing of their exacting demands on performers. A collection of this kind did not lend itself to publication. And Bach was evidently not moved to compromise in order to gain the scope of distribution readily open to Vivaldi's concertos *L'Estro armonico* (1711) or Handel's Concerti Grossi Op. 6 (1739) with their standard scoring. Any average orchestra could immediately include these in its repertoire, whereas Bach's concertos could be played only by an elite ensemble. The degree of performance skill required was also presumably the reason both parts of the Well-Tempered Clavier were never printed. Here a market might be more easily found. Yet how many, outside of Bach's circle of students, would have been ready to tackle keys with up to seven accidentals?

It is not surprising that in his printed works Bach scrupulously avoided exceeding the conventional limit of three sharps or flats; but other than that he made no concessions to the amateur. It was for this very reason that an author like Georg Andreas Sorge, in his collection of *Drittes halbes Dutzend Sonatinen vors Clavier nach Italienischen Gusto* published by Balthasar Schmid (Nuremberg, ca. 1744) and dedicated to Bach, reassured the "Hon. Court Composer" in the preface that he "would be able to work out something more artful and difficult," adding that "this time such was in no way my purpose, but I wanted to provide Music Lovers . . . with something for their pleasure, something which they could read without trouble and for which they might show some greater appreciation than for my Preludes in D♭ and G♭." [18] His words clarify what was required for a successful distribution. In view of this conflict between musical and economic considerations, it seems almost miraculous that Bach managed to market more than a dozen large and ambitious publications.

Printed editions in early-eighteenth-century Germany were entirely dependent upon the initiative of the composer. There were hardly any printers or publishers who would approach musicians with a request to publish their works, as was the rule in Italy, France, the Netherlands, and England. Even Telemann was obliged to remain his own publisher until about 1740. Bach had the good fortune of working closely with printers in the environment of Leipzig, a university town and the home of a trade fair as well as a center of the book trade. His regular business dealings with the local print shops of Tietze, Breitkopf, and others who took care of the routine publications of cantata librettos brought him also into contact with the allied trades of engravers and music printers. Boetius and Krügner, both of them printers and engravers, were directly involved in the production of Clavier-Übung I and III. Johann Gottfried Krügner, primarily an art engraver, was responsible for the facsimile-like reproduction of Bach's manuscript; the high quality of his work indeed led to the erroneous conclusion that Bach himself participated in the engraving of Clavier-Übung III. [19] Weigel and Schmid, both in Nuremberg, had given good care to Clavier-Übung II. Schmid himself later functioned as publisher for Part IV of the collection (Goldberg Variations), as well as for the Canonic Variations on Vom Himmel hoch. The Schübler brothers in Zella took on Bach's last three printing projects, the Musical Offering, the "Six [Schübler] Chorales," and the Art of Fugue. The firm of Breitkopf, with which Bach had been regularly connected through the prints of his cantata librettos, had shown at that time only limited involvement in the music trade (though having acted as publisher for the so-called Schemelli Hymn Book in 1736). With the print for the title of the Musical Offering, however, the firm took a further step toward the auspicious music publishing enterprise to which Bach, with his prints of the 1720s, had made a decisive contribution. [20]

The actual direction of the various printing projects remained in Bach's hands. Not infrequently, and especially at the beginning, he had to assume the role of publisher as well. In matters of distribution he could rely on various helpers, including members of the family, as the title page of the

Schübler Chorales indicates: "Available in Leipzig from Capellmeister Bach; from his sons in Berlin and Halle; and from his publishers in Zella."[21] In similar manner he had taken over the distribution, on commission, of works by others (his sons as well as a number of colleagues) and of some theoretical works (for example, Johann David Heinichen's *Der General-Bass in der Composition*, Dresden, 1728, or Johann Gottfried Walther's *Musicalisches Lexicon*, Leipzig, 1732).[22] Small commercial enterprises of this sort were at that time part of the life of many a musician, and thus also of the Thomascantor.

30

Bach's Vocal Music and Early Music Criticism

CRITICAL, EVALUATIVE COMMENT on topical events in musical life was one of the earliest and most lasting features of the age of enlightenment in Germany. As early as 1720 Johann Mattheson of Hamburg had made a name for himself as a critic with some writings. This even preceded developments in France and England, where enlightening tendencies on the whole were considerably more advanced and where, in the middle of the eighteenth century, Jean-Jacques Rousseau, Friedrich Melchior von Grimm, and Charles Avison had set in motion literary discussions on style, taste and compositional technique. In particular with his book *Das Beschützte Orchestre* (1717) Mattheson made himself the eloquent and militant spokesman of the younger generation of musicians who, conscious of the impending far-reaching historical, social, and intellectual changes of the time, were bent upon indicating a new direction to music in practice and theory. Successors soon followed in Mattheson's wake, especially since, with his publication in 1722 of the first musical journal *Critica Musica,* he had created an exemplary and above all popular model of a specialist literary mouthpiece. Johann Adolph Scheibe with his *Critischer Musicus* (1737 et seq.) and Lorenz Christoph Mizler with his *Musikalische Bibliothek* (1736 et seq.) were among the most prominent of Mattheson's successors. Strangely enough both of them came from the circle around Johann Sebastian Bach, although the goals to which they aspired were different from Bach's. Bach's music had seen neither objective appreciation nor criticism during the composer's lifetime. This is less due to the fact that one might have had too little viewing distance in relation to his works (Telemann or Handel were, as contemporaries, certainly objectively and, to a large extent, justly appraised) than the fact that Bach fitted into none of the category systems. The complexity of his manner of composing was beyond the reach of contemporary critics in as much as it did not provide them with adequate standards of values. Thus it was only symptomatic of the understanding of his art that the obituary, written immediately after his death but not published until 1754 in Mizler's *Musikalische*

Bibliothek, referred in the heading to Bach as a man "world famous in organ playing."[1] In his day, Bach the composer had always stood in the shadow of Bach the organ and clavier virtuoso, without anybody properly combining these two aspects of his creative personality.

It is all the more astounding that the first literary reference to Bach mentions the keyboard music with his sacred vocal works in one breath. In 1717 Mattheson wrote in *Das Beschützte Orchestre*: "I have seen things by the famous organist in Weimar, Herr Joh. Sebastian Bach, both for the church [cantatas] and for the fist [keyboard music] which are certainly of such a quality that one must highly esteem the man."[2] This exclamation testifies on the one hand as to how well informed Mattheson was, and on the other as to how little one-sided his considerable evaluation of the young Weimar maestro was.

That his knowledge of vocal music was very much broader than generally assumed is proved by a section in volume 2 of his *Critica Musica* (1725), in which he most sharply criticizes Bach's text repetitions in the cantata "Ich hatte viel Bekümmernis" BWV 21 and compares Bach to the elder Friedrich Wilhelm Zachow. There is no indication as to how Mattheson acquired such precise knowledge of the Bach score. (The work had been composed 1713–1714 in Weimar and was performed for the first time in Leipzig in 1723; it is conceivable, although there is no documentary evidence of the fact, that the work was performed in Hamburg in connection with Bach's application for the post of organist at St. Jacobi in 1720).[3] It is just as difficult to draw conclusions as to whether Mattheson took this negative attitude toward Cantata No. 21 as an individual case or whether it referred to all of the Bach vocal works known to him. Mattheson wrote: "In order that the good Zachau (Handel's teacher) should have some company and not be so entirely alone, he is to have another otherwise well-behaved *practicus hodiernus* at his side who keeps repeating: Ich, ich, ich, ich hatte viel Bekümmerniß, ich hatte viel Bekümmerniß, in meinem Hertzen, in meinem Hertzen. Ich hatte viel Bekümmerniß :|: in meinem Hertzen :|: :|: Ich hatte viel Bekümmerniß :|: in meinem Hertzen :|: :|: Ich hatte viel Bekümmerniß :|: in meinem Hertzen :|: :|: :|: :|: :|: Ich hatte viel Bekümmerniß :|: in meinem Hertzen :|: etc. And then like this: Seufzer, Thränen, Kummer, Noth (pause), Seufzer, Thränen, ängstlichs Sehnen, Furcht und Tod (pause) und erfreu mit deinem Blicke (pause) komm, mein JEsu, (pause) komm, mein JEsu, und erquicke, und erfreu . . . mit deinem Blicke diese Seele etc."[4] [My heart and soul were sore distrest, my spirit troubled; but Lord, by Thy comforting my spirit is delighted. Sighing, weeping, sorrow, care, / anxious yearning, fear of death / nag and gnaw my aching heart, / tear my troubled soul apart. Come, now my Jesus and restore me / shed Thy grace and gladness o'er me]. These quotations, which accord precisely with the Bach text declamations, reveal how little Mattheson was capable of appreciating the musical context. He is concerned with the principle of natural speech declamation in a transparent musical setting with "unaffected" melody bearing. It was thus inevitable that he would thoroughly misunderstand Bach's intentions (the comparison with the conservative Zachow is extremely superficial) with regard to the poetical-rhetorical intensification of language-content by way of extraordinarily varied repetition of text sections in conjunction with the concertante style of the musical setting.

It is hard to estimate how Bach's Leipzig audiences received his cantatas. Although there would certainly have been no stormy enthusiasm or deeper understanding of his music, there was no sign of any kind that Leipzig's citizens were perhaps dissatisfied. The first press report on Bach's audition for the cantor's post on Estomihi Sunday 1723 (the cantatas played before and after the sermon were "Jesus nahm zu sich die Zwölfe" BWV 22 and "Du wahrer Gott und Davids Sohn" BWV 23) was markedly positive, indeed far more so than Bach's fellow applicants: "On the past Sunday in the forenoon the prince-appointed capellmeister of Cöthen, Mr. Bach, gave an audition here in the church of St. Thomas in respect of the still vacant post of the cantor, and the music he made on that occasion was highly praised by all those who esteem such things."[5] Subsequent newspaper reports, mainly concerning Bach's performances of grand secular cantatas given on special occasions within the framework of his Collegium Musicum concerts, contained similar words of praise and approval. Nevertheless, these reviews are all of an extremely general nature, as for instance the remark on the performance in 1734 of the homage cantata "Preise dein Glücke, gesegnetes Sachsen" BWV 215, to the effect that "His Royal Majesty, together with his Royal Wife and Royal Princes, did not leave the window as long as the music lasted, but most graciously listened to it and His Majesty found pleasure in it."[6]

Reports of this kind provide no indication of the reception and appraisal of Bach's music in expert circles. Here too one has to assume that to a large extent approval was cloaked in literary silence. What can be found in Telemann's "Sonnet to the late Herr Capellmeister Bach" (1751)[7] in the way of verses of praise is perhaps more directed toward the instrumental musician than the vocal composer:

> O faded Bach! Alone from thine organ playing
> Did you get long since the noble, favoured word, the Great;
> Your art with quill to paper nimbly set,
> Envious masters themselves evaluate.

After all, Telemann must by and large have been on the side of Scheibe when the latter launched his massive criticism, mainly aimed at Bach's vocal works, in his publication *Der Critische Musicus* (sixth number, 1737) and thus triggered what was probably the most significant aesthetic controversy in German music prior to 1750. Scheibe, to whom Bach in 1731 had issued a sympathetic and favorable testimonal, complained—while acknowledging the composer's extraordinary adroitness as an organ and harpsichord virtuoso—of Bach's compositions that he "deprived them of the natural element by a bombastic and confused nature, and obscured their beauty by far too much art." Bach must have been greatly hurt by this criticism; for he had distributed among friends and acquaintances in answer to Scheibe's attacks a defense by the Leipzig lecturer in rhetoric Johann Abraham Birnbaum, published in the spring of 1738. If Bach had not in fact suggested this reply, he must at least have supplied Birnbaum with material that would not otherwise have been accessible to the latter. Birnbaum first countered Scheibe's aspersion, which ran as follows: "Because he [Bach] judges according to his fingers, these pieces are extremely difficult to play; for he demands of the singers and instrumentalists that they should by way of their throats and instruments do precisely that which he can play on the harpsichord. However, this is impossible. All the mannerisms, all the little embellishments, and everything that one understands by the method of playing, he expresses with actual notes; and this not only removes from his pieces the beauty of the harmony, but also makes the singing absolutely incomprehensible."[8] With regard to the writing out of the ornamentations, Birnbaum first refers to the *Livres d'Orgue* by Grigny and Du Mage, copies of which Bach possessed (thus the reference to them probably comes from him), and states: "Now experience has also shown that in most cases their application [i.e. of the ornamentation etc.] is left to the free will of the singers and instrumentalists. If these were sufficiently informed of everything that is in the method, which would certainly be wonderful, they would know at all times the place at which they could use the main melody to provide actual ornamentation and particular emphasis . . . However, the least of them possess sufficient knowledge of this; by inappropriate application of their method they spoil the main melody. They even quite often use such passages which . . . can easily be regarded as a mistake on the composer's part. Therefore any composer, and certainly the court composer, is entitled—by prescribing a correct method according to his intention—to direct the erring performers onto the proper path."[9] Another of Scheibe's main contentions was: "All the voices have to cooperate with each other, and with the same difficulty, and one does not recognize a main voice among them . . . one admires the arduous task and exhausting effort, which, however, is applied in vain because it runs contrary to nature."[10] Birnbaum made his point with partial repetition of the criticism "that all one cannot recognize a main voice, which presumably is supposed to mean the upper voice. The fact alone that the melody must by all means lie in the upper part, and that all the cooperation of the parts is a mistake—I have not been able to discover any adequate grounds for this. Rather the opposite flows from the nature of the music; for this consists of the harmony. The harmony is far more perfect when all the voices cooperate with each other . . . The author needs only to refer to the old Praenestini, to the newer Lotti [Bach possessed copies of Masses by Palestrina and Lotti, and thus probably here too the reference to the historical context of his compositions came from him], and other works and he will see that not only all voices work consistently but also that each one of them has its own melody

Example 30.1. Bach, "Mit Fried und Freud ich fahr dahin" BWV 382

Example 30.2. Vogler's correction ("Verbesserung") of Bach's harmonization

quite well harmonising with all the others."[11] A reasonable compromise between the two contrary views was hardly possible, since in this case the style
ideals were obviously on an irreconcilable collision course. Thus the controversy dragged on for years without any conclusive discussion of the problem.
The Societät der musicalischen Wissenschaften headed by Mizler as the main
spokesman eventually came out clearly on Bach's side, and in 1745 Scheibe
followed suit with a conciliatory review of the Italian Concerto BWV 971,
praising it as "a perfect model" of its kind.[12]

The younger generation, whose aims, ideals, and views became the supporting foundations of blossoming music reviewing, were actually incapable
of understanding Bach's music, particularly his vocal works, and merely admired them as a curiosity. In the later eighteenth century the highly elaborate nature of Bach's compositional art, and especially his fugues, was also
regarded as exemplary and—within the scope of strict counterpoint—as
something worthy of emulation. The discussion concerning the alleged faul-
tiness of Bach's four-part chorales in Abbé Georg Joseph Vogler's *Choral-
System* (1800) is further evidence of the lack of understanding of Bachian
harmony and voice-leading in simple, upper-voice-emphasized composition:
"The surprise over the absurdity . . . is without end . . . All of this is in
exalted church music—to a noble, simple chorale—how unbecoming; how
absurd!"[13] This head-shaking lack of comprehension forms the basis of Vogler's "improvements" of the Bach chorales (see Exx. 30.1 and 30.2). It was
only the subsequent period, in particular the period of Romantic histori-
cism, which created the basis for a gradual change in the interpretation of
Bach's art. After all, music criticism of the nineteenth century played a decisive part in deepening the understanding of specifically Bach's vocal works,
although admittedly the appreciation of Bach was subordinate to the prevailing aesthetic concepts and their transformations. Only in this way was Bach's
vocal music able to become generally accepted. There had never been any
comparable obstacle with regard to his organ and harpsichord works.

31

On the Recognition of Bach and "the Bach Chorale":
Eighteenth-Century Perspectives

I

IT IS FOR GOOD reasons that the early nineteenth century receives primary attention in the study of the appreciation of Bach's work. German Romanticism, after all, initiated an aesthetic premise for the unparalleled reception of Bach's music. Turning our attention here to the eighteenth century is not so much prompted by routine method of historical inquiry as it is a matter of genuine necessity, for it stands to reason that the roots of the decisive Bach revival arising in the early nineteenth century bear investigation. Indeed, in view of current Bach research, the aesthetic response of the eighteenth century (I refer to its first as well as to its second half) calls for fresh exploration.

It cannot be considered a mere curiosity that Frederick Christoph Kollmann, a native German who was active for many years in England as a performer and theorist, designed in the last year of the eighteenth century—1799—the diagram of a "sun of composers" (Fig. 31.1) which he had published by Johann Nicolaus Forkel in the *Allgemeine Musikalische Zeitung*.[1] In the center of the many rays emanating from the sun there is an equilateral triangle—in iconographical terms evidently a symbol for the eye of Yahweh—and along its sides are entered the names Handel, Carl Heinrich Graun, and Haydn; in the middle, however, forming the pupil of the eye, as it were, appears the name Johann Sebastian Bach. It seems superfluous in this context to offer an analysis of the time-bound evaluation of the first garland of rays (Gluck, Carl Philipp Emanuel Bach, Hiller, Mozart) or the second (Stölzel, Quantz, Abel, Hasse). What matters is the center of the hierarchy—above all its focal point, Bach.[2]

The illustration cannot be understood as suggesting that Bach had already become a favorite of the public. Quite the contrary: public concert life of the late eighteenth century did not grant Bach more than the role of a marginal and somewhat odd figure. An actual public recognition of Bach's music did not begin to take shape until Mendelssohn's memorable and influential Berlin performance of the St. Matthew Passion in 1829. Yet neither can it be overlooked that in professional circles the name of Bach, even during the

Figure 31.1. Kollmann's "sun of composers" (1799).

composer's life (and even outside of Germany), was well known. Prior to 1750, Padre Giovanni Battista Martini of the Accademia Filarmonica at Bologna had referred to the "world famous Bach";[3] and the distribution of Bach's works, in manuscript and print, during the later part of the eighteenth century gives an indication, more recognizable today than any time before, of a wide general familiarity with Bach's keyboard music in particular. But Bach's vocal works as well, his oratorios, Masses, and cantatas (next to the four-part chorales and motets) were better known than has been hitherto assumed. The Berlin performance of the St. Matthew Passion emerges as a first high point, then, rather than the actual beginning, of a recognition of his vocal oeuvre.

The "latent" rise of Bach's fame, initially restricted to the sphere of professionals, led early to the epithet "Father of Harmony" (a concept that was gaining some definition even before 1780).[4] Bach now assumed a place in music comparable to that of Shakespeare in literature or Raphael and Michelangelo (in Germany also Dürer) in fine arts. The paradigm of Bach's art of composition had, no later than 1750, become a major influence, even incentive, in music theory. Of importance here as well is doubtless Bach's own pedagogical influence, for his numerous students played a preeminent role in German music theory of the later eighteenth century.

Needless to say, Bach cannot be reduced to a theoretical standard, for his significance, especially with regard to the rising theory of harmony, is founded in the rich variety and originality of his compositional grasp and procedure. Daniel Christian Friedrich Schubart's categorical characterization of Bach as an "original genius" (1784), the interpretation of which would require centuries,[5] is radically different in its implication from the recognition given Palestrina, the predominant element of which was the elevation of his work to a norm. As early as the obituary of 1750, emphasis is given to the fact that Bach's music is divergent, "unlike that of any other composer."[6] This divergence—or rather, originality—was soon perceived. In the end, however, it was this dissimilarity, the unusual quality of Bach's music, that made him an outsider. It became a factor that upset the logic in a musical historiography of the eighteenth century, a historiography by tradition unfortunately given to dividing the century at the midpoint, which happened to coincide with Bach's death. We should realize that such works as the Passion oratorios of Carl Heinrich Graun or Carl Philipp Emanuel Bach were relegated in conventional historical perspective to a "decline" only because they were placed against the works of J. S. Bach, the outsider, and thus deprived of their true context.

The realization of Bach's "dissimilarity," no matter to what extent it may seem definable in detail, calls for the analytical investigation of the "qualities" of his music. It is in this connection that a study of the impact of Bach's work after 1750 is of importance in clarifying his place in music and its history.

II

Three decades after Bach's death Johann Friedrich Reichardt announced, in veritably extolling terms, the second edition, enlarged to two volumes, of Bach's *Vierstimmige Choralgesänge*[7] in his *Musikalisches Kunstmagazin* (Berlin, 1781): "If ever a work deserved the earnest support of German connoisseurs, it is this one. The contents: chorales, the highest achievement of German art; the author of their harmonic accompaniment: Johann Sebastian Bach, the greatest harmonist of all times and nations."[8] Reichardt's absolute superlative anticipates a formulation of Hans Georg Nägeli, who in 1818 described the B Minor mass (in the subscription notice for his planned edition of the score) as the "greatest musical work of art of all times and nations."[9]

Several aspects move into focus here, the most important of which is perhaps the early recognition of Bach's universal significance. Reichardt's words also call to mind what we might refer to as the "latent" eighteenth-century Bach reception, which not only antedated the "public" Bach movement of the nineteenth century but also had considerable bearing upon the Romantic interpretation of Bach. For in the second half of the eighteenth century the name Bach had already become somewhat of a household word in professional music circles—not merely those in Germany, as has been variously suggested, but soon after 1800 in England, France, Italy, Russia, and even America.

The two editions of the four-part-chorales—the first of them issued by Birnstiel (Berlin, 1765 and 1769) and the second by Breitkopf (Leipzig, 1784–1787)—having formed the basis for numerous later ones,[10] occupy more than an accidental role in spreading Bach's fame. Being readily available, the four-part chorales not only offered access to a relatively large repertory of Bach works; they also—and above all—furnished "models of part-writing."[11] And as such they represented both the normative qualities and the originality of language inherent in Bach's art. This union of the archetypal and the individual became the cornerstone of the "latent," professionally oriented Bach reception and assured the rapidly gaining influence Bach exerted upon the history of composition. The quality of paradigm associated with the music of Palestrina, on the other hand—especially after its codification through Johann Joseph Fux[12]—was clearly limited to technical criteria of part-writing and is thus different from the normative character imparted to Bach's music.

That which today appears as an unquestionable concept, "the Bach chorale," was a salient phenomenon as early as the eighteenth century. From the point of view of documentary evidence, the 370 or so published chorale settings present a modest remnant of the extensive vocal repertory of the cantor of St. Thomas's but they were "rescued" into a practice having different function by the separation of the chorales from their original context in cantatas, Passions, and oratorios. As a matter of fact, the context of original practice became irrelevant. It was the exemplary representation of a technique of writing that became more significant—a technique of writing whose live correlation was no longer felt. Whatever recitative, aria, and chorus had lost in vitality was made up for by the chorales through their quasi-timeless validity and—as cannot be overlooked, considering the period of the waning eighteenth century—the import of their melodies as a German national bequest.[13]

In the end, the critical element in the valuation of the chorales was the originality of their part-writing, for the chorales were published neither in the sense of a hymnal for practical use nor as vocal settings or accompanimental settings for organ. The aim of their publication was, as stressed even in Carl Philipp Emanuel Bach's preface to the Birnstiel edition, in presenting "master settings" that were to "demonstrate the unusual harmony and the natural flow of inner voices and bass."[14]

The "unusual" quality refers to a statement that Bach's son had made as early as in the obituary for his father, namely that it was "unlike that of any other composer."[15] While the originality of the four-part chorale settings can hardly represent Bach's style of composition as such, it nonetheless shows in an especially cogent manner the principles of his writing. It was not without reason that Bach himself based his "instruction in composition" upon the chorale, not upon the "stiff and pedantic manners of counterpoint."[16]

In viewing Bach's chorale writing within its original context, that is, as part of the cantata repertory, we can discern a definite line of development.

Although a comprehensive chronological survey of Bach's chorale style has not as yet been undertaken,[17] the clearly emerging tendency toward a consistently polyphonic design of texture cannot be overlooked.[18] A final phase—in a stylistic sense—is formed perhaps by the chorales in the Christmas Oratorio of 1734–1735, which appear as highly differentiated examples of part-writing and expression. The wide chronological span of Bach's chorale style is impressively illustrated by the difference between the four-part chorales of the St. John Passion of 1724 and its (incompletely) revised version from the period about 1740 (Ex. 31.1)[19] The later version of the chorale departs from the note-against-note style above all in its greatly varied melodic and rhythmic profiles of soprano and alto, in m.2 enhanced by the change of a full cadence from V–I to IV–V–I. Added suspensions, passing tones, and syncopations lend the setting an evenly flowing (complementary) eighth-note motion; at the same time the bass part, in its simplified melodic line, receives greater stringency.

It can be shown step by step—beginning with the earliest Weimar cantatas, that is, from the period 1713–1714 onwards[20]—how Bach steadily refined his chorale settings, how he worked on perfecting the compositional process, the individuality of part-writing and text expression. The actual origin, the inception of Bach's chorale style, however, cannot be fixed in time. The setting in BWV 18, the first one to be preserved yet not the earliest chorale to be composed by Bach, already displays in its texture the traits of a rather sophisticated personal style. The hymn settings of Bach's contemporaries, such as Telemann, Stölzel, or Graupner, are different: predominant is their note-against-note harmonization of a *cantus firmus* declaimed in half-note motion.

Bach's almost exclusive use of quarter-note declamation is not prompted by an external, notation-bound necessity. The setting in quarter notes has a different, "inner" motivation whose quality emerges as early as in the hymn

Example 31.1. "Dein Will gescheh, Herr Gott zugleich" BWV 245/5, the 1724 version (a) and one from ca. 1740 (b)

settings of the organ partitas, but especially in the embellished chorales of the Orgel-Büchlein. The integration of the chorale melody in a four-part polyphonic fabric, as an active contrapuntal part, is a notable characteristic. And the influence of the expressively polyphonic instrumental style of the organ chorale upon the four-part hymn settings is beyond question. It suggests that the provenance of Bach's chorales (in distinction to the hymn settings by Telemann and others) is of a nature primarily determined by the style of organ music. The interconnections with the embellished and varied organ chorale become innumerable, as is intimated by Example 31.2.[21] Clear expressions of this manner of organ-oriented hymn setting—a chorale style that is more severe yet more *cantabile* than, for instance, that found in Samuel Scheidt's Görlitz Tablature Book of 1650—appears in the works of such masters as Johann Christoph and Johann Michael Bach.[22] In this connection it might become a point of discussion whether the Bach chorale, as a genre, can, in fact, be considered a primarily vocal phenomenon. The Birnstiel and Breitkopf editions, in any event, propagated it as an "abstract" form of composition. Though most of the chorales come from the body of cantatas, their source does not define their contrapuntal and aesthetic derivation. It can also be shown that some of the settings are refined versions of chorales contained in the hymnal by Gottfried Vopelius (Leipzig, 1682).[23] And settings such as the chorales "Kyrie, Gott Vater in Ewigkeit" BWV 371 or "Wir glauben all an einen Gott" BWV 437, already included in the Birnstiel edition, can doubtless not be traced to the composition of cantatas. That they must have been designed as instrumental harmonizations is immediately evident from the passage in BWV 371 quoted in Example 31.3. It might be suggested, with due caution, that this and similar chorales represent examples from a collection of Bach works no longer extant in its entirety. For "Bach's Chorale Book"—somewhat like "Bach's Thorough Bass

Example 31.2. "Liebster Jesu, wir sind hier" BWV 706, keyboard harmonization (a) and the *alio modo* (alternative) version (b)

Example 31.3. "Kyrie, Gott Vater in Ewigkeit" BWV 371, mm. 22ff.

Instruction"—has so far remained a phantom, though such a collection may have served an important function as a working and teaching device.[24]

Carl Philipp Emanuel Bach confirms that his father started with four-part chorales for the instruction in composition.[25] It seems also plausible that they served as suitable exercises and ideal working material in dealing with the matter of keys, chord progressions, and cadences, as well as with specific and general questions of part-writing. And that his students soon copied out sets of models is shown by the earliest manuscript collection of Bach chorales, prepared in Leipzig in 1735 by the St. Thomas alumnus Johann Ludwig Dietel.[26]

Thus it is not surprising that in German music theory—especially that represented by the increasingly influential Bach school—"the Bach chorale" as a genre became a norm for harmonic elaboration no later than Marpurg's publication of 1758.[27] What plays a special role here is the variety in realization of one and the same melody, for Bach never repeats himself. In fact, the multiformity of harmonization for the same chorale is subjected to a veritable variation principle, evidently with the discovery of ever new progressions and harmonic interpretations as a goal. One may see here a direct link with the notion of harmony that Bach had expressed through the rhetoric of Birnbaum, Bach's advocate in matters of describing his personal style, namely that through harmonization in the sense of a polyphonic aggregate may be gained an "insight into the depth of world wisdom."[28] World wisdom ("Weltweisheit") as a term and concept is synonymous with philosophy in Bach's time (for example, in Johann Christoph Gottsched's *Erste Prinzipien der Weltweisheit*, Leipzig 1733) and has been defined by Christian Wolff as "the science of all things possible, exploring how and why they are possible."[29] Accordingly, the philosophy of Bach's musical procedure is in exploring the secrets of "harmony" (that is, the art of part-writing) in order to fathom its manner and reason, its origin and potential.

"The Bach chorale" demonstrates the merging of harmony and counterpoint within a continuity of musical logic, whereby the most unusual chord progressions might be rendered plausible within the narrowest context. To impart the stamp of originality upon the norm was Bach's aim, and this goal forms his challenge to later generations. That Bach's music could engender theory without ever freezing into theory in itself constitutes its historic stature. When Beethoven called Bach the "Urvater der Harmonie" (Progenitor of Harmony),[30] he doubtless had in mind the same idea that Johann Friedrich Reichardt expressed in his 1805 review of the first edition of Bach's solo works for violin, namely that they "may give the greatest example in any art form for a master's ability to move with freedom and assurance, even in chains."[31] "The Bach chorale" is the abstraction and essence of this creative ability in its most impressive form, and its influence abides in unbroken tradition until our day.

32

"The Extraordinary Perfections of the Hon. Court
Composer": An Inquiry into the Individuality
of Bach's Music

QUESTIONS CONCERNING a composer's artistic impulse necessarily lead
into the nebulous sphere of the psychology of creativity. The nature of creativity cannot be confronted without a fair measure of speculation, especially
in the case of a composer who has left little or nothing in the way of personal
statements dealing with his motivation, statements that would possibly
prove revealing. Its problematic aspects notwithstanding, an examination of
the specific conditions of artistic production and of the setting and orientation of the moment of creative impetus, as well as of its parameters, is not
only a legitimate but indeed a central concern of the scholar investigating
the essence of art.

With regard to music, the scope of exploration extends from general
premises, historical conditions, and basic questions of the compositional
practice through the biographical and personal implications of a composer's
work to detailed phases of its genesis. Merely an outline can be drawn, and
within it ever new problems inevitably arise. This holds true in particular
for the gray area of primary artistic conception preceding and attending the
act of composition. The manifest ideas at the root of a work of art cannot be
reduced to single elements. Sketches, drafts, and other vestiges of the compositional process provide no more than an insecure basis for a realization of
the composer's critical attitude. Yet the study of the individual work's origin
and of the growth of a comprehensive repertoire may contribute to a discovery of patterns and principles of composition that will help in defining the
idiom of a composer. Naturally, the search for consistent characteristics gains
meaning, and the results gain reliability, only to the extent that they are
integrated with considerations of a historical context for which the notion of
originality holds a certain validity as an aesthetic maxim.

The idea of the originality of genius ("Originalgenie") was in essence foreign to Bach's era, whereas in the later revival of his music the concept of
genius became a veritable cornerstone of aesthetics. In several respects, however, Bach cannot be regarded as a composer representative of his age. It is

part of the unusual quality of his music that it stands as the expression of a strongly self-willed and, for the first half of the eighteenth century, atypical artistic personality. In the roughly fifty years of Bach's creative career, his work underwent an evolution which is without parallel in its time. continuity and change play equally determining roles. A principal component of continuity in Bach's work is an uncompromising professional attitude. Bach never addressed the dilettante. His own virtuosity—it is not accidental that the concluding poem of his obituary speaks of the "hero of virtuosos"—was firmly rooted in the guild tradition of the family and is ever reflected in the difficulty of technical execution of his music, considered extreme in his own time. The factor of change in the development of Bach's work, on the other hand, is founded on an infinite thirst for knowledge, defying geographical limitations, regarding all facets of the art of composition. Bach's knowledge of the musical literature of his day and of past generations was exemplary, as was above all the manner in which he was able to integrate newly won insight as a diversifying and enriching element in his own writing. Viewing Bach's oeuvre in its entire chronological span, one realizes an incomparably differentiated spectrum extending from the earliest to the last works. It is formed equally by instrumental and vocal genres: one might compare, on the one hand, the "Capriccio sopra la lontananza del suo fratro dilletissimo" with the Art of Fugue and, on the other hand, the "Actus Tragicus" BWV 106 with the B Minor Mass. By contrast, the evolution of Handel's style— if we take the polarity of earliest operas and last oratorios as an example— seems considerably more concise, quite apart from a more compressed range of repertoire categories and compositional techniques.

From today's vantage point it is not difficult to discuss Bach's unusual position in his time. Yet a fairly clear awareness of the fact that his music was, as stated in the obituary, "unlike that of any other composer" evidently existed—at least in a close circle—even during Bach's life. It is true that the perception of art based integrally upon individuality and singularity of the artist is not in evidence before the aesthetic code of the Age of Idealism. And it has been recognized early and stressed repeatedly that the propagation of Bach's instrumental music in particular contributed in large measure to the rise of this perception and its philosophical foundations.[1] But it cannot be overlooked that an unquestionably nonconformist quality of Bach's music was determined prior to 1750. Herein lies the source of the famous controversy, frequently and variously analyzed and interpreted, between Scheibe and Birnbaum (speaking for Bach).[2] The reason for Scheibe's incomprehension and Bach's lack of compromise is actually founded on his work's claim to perfection. "Perfection" is, in fact, often alluded to in Birnbaum's argumentation, culminating in the plural form of his terse reference to "the Extraordinary Perfections of the Hon. Court Composer" (die sonderbaren, [unmistakable, distinctive] Vollkommenheiten des Herrn Hof-Compositeurs).[3] Bach's individualistic adherence to principle, utterly unsuited for debate, draws its legitimacy from his avowal of perfection.

Birnbaum's assertion concerning Bach's music (1738–1739) is paralleled in the obituary by a pronouncement of its absolute nature, as is abundantly clear from the passages quoted below, and it is pointed out in this connection that Bach's music "was unlike that of any other composer" (keinem andern Componisten ähnlich).[4] These tributes have no model in music history. The concept of "greatness" is applied to musical achievement as early as the Renaissance, but the predicate of the dissimilar and the incomparable—quite aside from that of the perfect and that of the absolute—appearing prior to the 1750 as a criterion for Bach's music anticipates the terminology of the later-eighteenth-century aesthetics of genius. Nothing essentially new is contained in Christian Friedrich Daniel Schubart's statement of 1784–1785: "Sebastian Bach was a genius of the highest degree. His spirit is so individual, so immense, that it will require centuries to reach it's equal."[5] Schubart refers specifically to the fact that "there is no mistaking the originality of Bach's genius."[6] The concept of originality of genius is new, its meaning in relevancy to Bach is not. Thus it seems that in the musical explication of the aesthetics of genius a key role, incipient even before 1750, must be assigned to Bach.

How is the dissimilarity, the originality, or the individuality of Bach's music to be grasped? Its generic aspects could hardly be formulated more precisely and concisely than was done in the obituary published by Carl Philipp Emanuel Bach and Johann Friedrich Agricola:

> If ever a composer showed polyphony ["Vollstimmigkeit"] in its greatest strength, it was certainly our late lamented Bach. If ever a musician employed the most hidden secrets of harmony with the most skilled artistry, it was certainly our Bach. No one ever showed so many ingenious and unusual ideas as he in elaborate pieces such as ordinarily seemed dry exercises in craftsmanship. He needed only to have heard any theme to be aware—it seemed in the same instant—of almost every intricacy that artistry could produce in the treatment of it. His melodies were strange, but always varied, rich in invention, and resembling those of no other composer. His serious temperament drew him by preference to music that was serious, elaborate and profound; but he could also, when the occasion demanded, adjust himself, especially in playing, to a lighter and more humorous way of thought.[7]

Somewhat by way of commentary, several passages may be drawn from Birnbaum's essay of defense to elucidate this concise yet well-balanced résumé of Bach's art of composition. This course seems the more strongly indicated since a number of Birnbaum's important factual statements must be considered as having come directly from Bach. This applies not only to references to literature contained in Bach's library (de Grigny, du Mage, Lotti, Palestrina)[8] and to passages that are evidently direct quotations (for instance: "that which I have achieved by industry and practice, anyone else with tolerable gift and ability can also achieve").[9] One may assume that Birnbaum served quite generally as a spokesman for Bach, whose literary power of expression and eloquence was limited.

According to the obituary, the central quality of Bach's music lies in its "Vollstimmigkeit," its harmonic and polyphonic conception. Bach's mastery of the "hidden secrets of harmony" is based on the most intimate knowledge of "many-voiced part writing, which is the true description of harmony." [10]

> It is certain, by the way, that the voices in the works of this great master of music work wonderfully in and about one another, but without the slightest confusion. They move along together or in opposition, as necessary. They part company, and yet all meet again at the proper time. Each voice distinguishes itself clearly from the others by a particular variation, although they often imitate each other. They now flee, now follow one another without one's noticing the slightest irregularity in their efforts to outdo one another. Now when all this is performed as it should be, there is nothing more beautiful than this harmony. [11]

Bach considers harmony as nature-given and sees the task of the composer in discovering this nature-given quality in order to gain "insight into the depth of world wisdom": [12]

> The praiseworthy efforts of the Hon. Court Composer are directed toward the end of presenting this natural element to the worlds, through his art, in its highest splendor . . . Now, the greater the art—that is, the more industriously and painstakingly it works at the improvement of Nature—the more brilliantly shines the beauty thus brought into being. Accordingly it is impossible that the greatest art should darken the beauty of a thing. [13]

It is here that we find the explanation for the application of "seemingly dry artifices" whose dryness was removed by Bach's "imaginative and strange thought." The aim is not—as Scheibe postulates in his advocacy of the modern composer, rebuked by Birnbaum as a "hack"—merely to place accompanying voices under a melody.

> Rather it is the exact opposite which flows from the very nature of music. For music consists of harmony, and harmony becomes far more complete if all the voices collaborate to form it. Accordingly this is not a failing but rather a musical perfection. [14]

Perfection is the goal that might be reached with the help of "the greatest possible art" that can be represented, which is beautiful and natural. Perfection implies the knowledge of "the most hidden secrets of harmony." This concept, dating from the seventeenth century, presupposes a given essence which has only to be rediscovered; it finds a corollary in the "dichotomy of *ingenium* and *studium*" of the rhetoric of antiquity and assumes a mastery "that, independent of all knowledge of rules, is the poet's nature." [15] It is only in this sense that Birnbaum's argument—apparently quoting Bach—can be understood: "One can do anything if only one really wishes to, and if one industriously strives to convert natural abilities, by untiring zeal, into finished skills." [16]

At this point we encounter a cleavage of theory and reality. Birnbaum was not familiar with the concept of the originality of genius and would obviously not have been able to comprehend Bach's artistry in the sense of later aesthetics—perfection and beauty were given standards, yet not in the context of a formulated aesthetic concept of genius ("Genieästhetik").

Lacking a frame of reference developed from such a concept, a description of Bach's originality was destined to remain incomplete. The obituary speaks of "strange ideas" (fremde Gedanken) and describes Bach's melodies as "uncommon," "always divergent," and "fanciful," "unlike that of any other composer." [17] Birnbaum praises "the astonishing mass of unusual and well-developed ideas; (die erstaunliche Menge seltener und wohlausgeführter Einfälle). [18] This does not refer to traditional invention, guided by an art of devising melodies and themes, one governed by musical and rhetorical models. Bach's art of invention clearly moves away from tradition toward original though not unconditioned creation. Just as he conceives of harmony as a nature-given essence whose secrets are to be explored, his invention is always derived from given premises; they seem to invite challenge. In this connection, an observation recorded in 1741 by a certain Magister Pitschel is of interest:

> You know, the famous man who has the greatest praise in our town in music, and the greatest admiration of connoisseurs, does not get into condition, as the expression goes, to delight others with the mingling of his tones until he has played something from the printed or written page, and has [thus] set his powers of imagination ["Einbildungskraft"] in motion . . . The able man whom I have mentioned usually has to play something from the page which is inferior to his own ideas. And yet his superior ideas are the consequences of those inferior ones. [19]

Now it would hardly seem right to generalize and draw far-reaching conclusions on the basis of this remark. Yet a tendency is suggested here that seems indeed characteristic of Bach's manner of composing and of the individuality of his music. What is involved is the principle of elaboration of given ideas in the sense of deeper penetration, the sense of discovery of "the most hidden secrets of harmony." An observation by Carl Philipp Emanuel Bach points in the same direction:

> Thanks to his greatness in harmony, he accompanied trios on more than one occasion on the spur of the moment and, being in a good humor, . . . converted them into complete quartets . . . When he listened to a rich and many-voiced fugue, he could soon say, after the first entries of the subjects, what contrapuntal devices it would be possible to apply and which of them the composer by rights ought to apply. [20]

It appears that the uncovering of secrets implicated in harmony was a veritable passion of Bach's. As a student of composition essentially self-taught, he "had learned chiefly by the observation of the works of the most famous and proficient composers of his day and by the fruits of his own reflecting upon them," the obituary says. [21] To this was added later: "Through his own study and reflection alone he became even in his youth a pure and strong fugue writer." [22] It was "his own reflection" (eigenes Nachsinnen) that complemented traditional study of *exempla classica* for Bach, especially in relation to fugue. From the very outset the composition of a setting in the sense of contrapuntal elaboration of a theme must have held Bach's intense interest. It was his ability, documented in the obituary, when hearing a theme, to be "aware—it seemed in the same instant—of almost every intricacy that artistry could produce in the treatment of it" which seems so eminently indicative of his working procedure—an *elaboratio* rather than a *creatio:* the potential for "intricate artistry" was implied, its discovery requiring only "reflection." Given Bach's patent phenomenal gift of combination, it became immaterial whether the theme was his own or that of another composer. In every instance, a theme presented a challenge to uncover its latent contrapuntal qualities. *Mutatis mutandis* this holds true for Bach's entire compositional procedure, not only for fugal writing. The principle of elaboration is an integral factor, whatever the genre, of Bach's art and personal style. It is deeply rooted in Bach's striving for the detection of "secrets of harmony," his search for the "perfection of harmony." But such perfection is attained only "when all parts work together" indeed "without any confusion"—"each part is distinguished by the other by special variety, even though they often imitate one another."[23]

The concept of variation often dominates this principle of elaboration, as is evident from the fact that fugal expositions are carried out in diversification (Birnbaum praises "the development of a single subject through the keys with the most agreeable variation").[24] The close association of variation and elaboration in the monothematic cycles of Bach's late instrumental works bears out a veritable fusion of these two concepts in his compositional thought. Growing elaboration of a given musical idea, testing its inherent harmonic constellations, decrees in fact a chain of variations.

The principle of elaboration based on variation may also be considered as governing Bach's technique of arrangement and transcription (whether or not the model is Bach's own) and, above all, his practice of parody. The process of transcription and parody presupposes an option, and (for whatever reason) need, of change through elaboration. Economy of working procedure remains a very limited argument for a motivating force in Bach's work. With justification, the "multi-potentiality" of Bach's writing and the "excess" of musical thought beyond the mere setting of text have been cited.[25] Defining parody as a kind of variation—that is, an elaboration of unexplored dormant qualities—is more apt for an interpretation of Bach's working attitude.

Also to be included in this manner of elaboration are successive different settings or harmonizations of a *cantus firmus* (ranging from the simple four-part chorale through the chorale prelude to the more complex types of "Choralbearbeitung"). Similarly beholden to the principle is Bach's design in series and work groups: the probing of an idea in multiformity and diversity of execution (the Orgel-Büchlein, harpsichord concertos, Well-Tempered Clavier, chorale cantata cycle). In the end it encompasses the general procedures of revision and correction so especially typical of Bach: proof of his continuing search for improved alternate solutions. This can only be understood as originating in his quest for perfection, the constant impetus for elaboration. Bach's manner of composition cannot be reduced to a formula, but the principle of elaboration based upon variation may be considered a decisive factor lending Bach's music its characteristic profile. This one factor, however, represents only a step toward an explanation of its individuality.

It is a moot point whether Bach himself might have accorded his works the attribute of "extraordinary perfection." Yet there is no doubt that perfection in the sense of natural beauty achieved by the highest art was to him a musical goal. It cannot be without reason that Birnbaum gave the word *perfection* a key role in the text of his argumentation. But what about the adjective "extraordinary"? There can be no proof that Bach was conscious of the originality and unmistakable character of his music, though it might almost tacitly be assumed. Speaking for Bach's awareness of this quality of his work is his conspicuous, though in view of the existing social situation invariably surprising, assuredness in claiming artistic freedom. Of significance above all is Bach's unusual familiarity with the broad musical spectrum of his time and with works of preceding epochs. It could not have escaped his capacity for distinction that his organ and clavier works, his cantatas and major choral compositions, as well as his instrumental ensemble works, taken singly and collectively, stood without parallel. This assessment applies in the first place to their supreme measure of artistic elaboration. A corollary to the degree of musical perfection is their preservation in print or fair copy. The fact that the making of copies was a matter of particular concern for Bach—especially with major works like the St. Matthew Passion or the B Minor Mass—might be perceived, at least in part, as recognition of their historic stature and a consciousness of posterity. Bach must also have been aware of the ancient maxim, as formulated by the Neoplatonist Plotinus, that perfection of idea stands in contrast to perfection in execution. Only in this sense can the following passage of Birnbaum's text be comprehended:

> It is true, one does not judge a composition principally and predominantly by the impression of its performance. But if such judgment, which indeed may be deceiving, is not to be considered, I see no other way of judging than to view the work as it has been set down in notes.[26]

"To view the work as it has been set down in notes" (die Arbeit, wie sie in Noten gesetzt ist, ansehen)—these words, quite possibly emanating from Bach himself, stress the intrinsic value of the musical score beyond its practical purpose in performance. The music as written offers not only the single truly reliable documentation of the "Extraordinary Perfections of the Hon. Court Composer" but also the decisive means of recognizing a composition as a perfected idea and thus arriving at a "sound judgment" of its special quality and in fact, its originality.

Notes and Postscripts

Postscripts are placed at the end of the notes of individual chapters wherever and whenever the present state of research calls for major corrections, additions, commentary, and important references for further reading. No attempt has been made, however, to provide a thorough bibliographical updating. For this the reader might consult: *Bach-Bibliographie. Nachdruck der Verzeichnisse des Schrifttums über Johann Sebastian Bach (Bach-Jahrbuch 1905–1984), mit einem Supplement und Register*, ed. Christoph Wolff (Kassel, 1985); and Rosemarie Nestle, "Das Bach-Schrifttum 1981 bis 1985," *BJ* 1989, pp. 107–189. For the most up-to-date information on Bach's works, see *Bach Compendium*.

1. New Perspectives on Bach Biography

1. *Dok* II, no. 477.
2. *Dok* I, no. 42; *Bach Reader*, pp. 160–162.
3. The Möller Manuscript and the Andreas Bach Book are collections of musical sources assembled by Johann Christoph Bach in the early 1700s. The contents of both are given in *NBA* IV/5–6, *Krit. Bericht* (ed. Dietrich Kilian, 1978), pp. 98–106 and 122–131, respectively. See also Hans-Joachim Schulze, *Studien zur Bach-Überlieferung im 18. Jahrhundert* (Leipzig, 1984), pp. 30–56.

POSTSCRIPT

This chapter was originally presented in 1984 as a public lecture at Lincoln Center in New York City. It represents a substantially condensed and modified version of a paper read at the 1978 Bach Symposium of the University of Marburg, which was published with references and notes: "Probleme und Neuan-sätze der Bach-Biographik," in *Bachforschung und Bachinterpretation heute. Bericht über das Bachfest-Symposium 1978 der Philipps-Universität Marburg*, ed. Reinhold Brinkmann (Kassel, 1981), pp. 21–31.

An important complementary study is Hans-Joachim Schulze, "Johann Sebastian Bach," in *Komponisten auf Werk und Leben befragt: Ein Kolloquium*, ed. Harry Goldschmidt et al. (Leipzig, 1985), pp. 13–30. General historical and important methodological aspects, with emphasis on several problems of Bach biography, are discussed by Hans Lenneberg, *Witnesses and Scholars: Studies in Musical Biography* (New York, 1988).

For a critical biographical overview and pertinent bibliographic references, see my "Johann Sebastian Bach," in *The New Grove Bach Family*, ed. Christoph Wolff et al. (London and New York, 1983), pp. 44–237.

2. The Family

1. *Dok* III, no. 666; *Bach Reader*, p. 215.
2. *Dok* II, no. 323. *Bach Reader*, pp. 199–211.
3. *Dok* I, no. 184. Subsequent remarks about individual family members are quoted from this document.
4. Forkel, pp. 3f.; *Bach Reader*, p. 301.
5. *Dok* III, no. 819.
6. Fritz Rollberg, "Johann Ambrosius Bach, Stadtpfeifer zu Eisenach von 1671–1695," *BJ* 1972, p. 142.
7. *Dok* I, p. 68; *Bach Reader*, p. 126.
8. Ibid.
9. *Dok* II, no. 17; *Bach Reader*, p. 53
10. *Dok* III, no. 779.

11. *Dok* II, no. 527.
12. *Dok* I, no. 175.
13. *Dok* III, no. 631.

POSTSCRIPT

Chapters 2–4 were originally published in a collection of essays by nine different authors under the title *J. S. Bach: Time, Life, Influence* (Kassel, 1976), a lavishly illustrated volume for a general audience. Since the pictures appearing in that book did not link up closely with the text of the essays (except for the genealogy, Figure 2.1), they were omitted from this volume.

Figure 2.2 is a new addition. This painting was sold at the London auction house of Bonham's in 1978, purchased by Gerd Nickstadt, a private collector in Munich, and in 1985 acquired by the Internationale Bachakademie in Stuttgart. Bonham's auction catalogue attributed the unsigned painting to Herman van der Myn and described it as "The Quartet-Group Portrait of a gentleman seated at a table holding a cello, his three sons beside him with violins and a piccolo, oil on canvas, in carved frame, 28 × 36 in. (71 × 91.5 cm)."

The provenance of the painting is unknown, but it apparently had been kept in private hands in Germany until the 1930s, or even later. There was a persistent but unsubstantiated claim that this group portrait actually depicted the Bach family. The portrait itself offers no specific clues to that effect, particularly since (1) there exist no likenesses of most of Bach's sons in their youth, (2) the only authentic portrait of J. S. Bach is that of Haußmann (from 1746 and 1748, respectively), and (3) the musical notation on the depicted music sheets had long been (deliberately?) erased. The Berlin art historian Helmut Börsch-Supan conducted some detailed research on the picture and reported his conclusions in an article, "Gruppenbild mit Musikern: Ein Gemälde von Balthasar Denner und das Problem der Bach-Ikonographie," *Kunst und Antiquitäten* 3 (1982), pp. 22–32. Börsch-Supan was able to attribute the painting with considerable certainty to one of the most distinguished portrait painters of the German Baroque, Johann Balthasar Denner (1685–1749) of Hamburg, and dated it to ca. 1730. Denner had portrayed several musicians on canvas, among them Handel and the Dresden lutenist, Silvius Leopold Weiss, and, according to Börsch-Supan, the newly identified Denner painting might well depict Bach with his sons, Wilhelm Friedemann, Carl Philipp Emanuel, and Gottfried Heinrich.

Mr. Nickstadt, the one-time owner of the portrait, subsequently consulted me regarding Börsch-Supan's findings, which, on art-historical grounds, I agreed were generally very persuasive. Disagreeing with the proposed identification of the three sons, however, I suggested that they might rather represent Emanuel (born in 1714), who played the violin, Gottfried Bernhard (born 1715), who played the flute, and Gottfried Heinrich (born 1724); the empty chair would represent the absent Wilhelm Friedemann, who in 1733 left Leipzig for Dresden. My reasons were based (1) on the known facts regarding the instrumental expertise of the sons (we have no positive evidence for J. S. Bach playing the cello except that his idiomatic handling of this instrument in the suites for violoncello solo demonstrates his intimate familiarity with cello playing) and (2) on the striking similarity between a pastel portrait of C. P. E. Bach from ca. 1733 and the violinist on the right-hand side of the Denner painting, and the dissimilarity between this violinist and a pastel portrait of W. F. Bach from ca. 1733. (The two pastel drawings are reproduced in Werner Neumann, *Bilddokumente zur Lebensgeschichte Johann Sebastian Bachs. Bach-Dokumente*, vol. 4, Kassel and Leipzig, 1979, p. 237.) The dating of the Denner group portrait would have to be slightly adjusted to ca. 1733.

Of course, these conclusions do not yet amount to positive evidence that the group portrait indeed represents the Bach family, but, it is worth mentioning that there exists an important reference to a Bach family portrait that was in the possession of family descendants in Leipzig until the 1820s. Max Schneider's 1905 survey of the Bach literature and related materials points at an interesting item (see *Bach-Bibliographie*, ed. Christoph Wolff [Kassel, 1985], p. 37): "*Originalmanuscripte, Denkmäler, Porträts, Geburts- und Sterbehäuser der deutschen Klassiker: Bach, Beethoven usw., in Photographien von Fr. Wendling-Wien* (Berlin 1878, no. 57; 2/1881, no. 37a): Bach, J.S.—Familien-Porträt, nach einem Ölgemälde, welches bis Anfang der 20er Jahre dieses Jahrhunderts im Erbbesitz der Bachschen Familie war."

Unfortunately, no copy of either the 1878 or the 1881 edition (in the form of a boxed set of photographic reproductions, also known under the secondary title, *Porträt-Galerie musikalischer Heroen*) containing the Bach family portrait could be located in the leading European or American libraries. If a direct link between the Denner portrait and this lost photographic reproduction from the late nineteenth century could be established, the authenticity problem of the Denner painting as a Bach family portrait could indeed be resolved.

For more detailed discussions of the Bach family and individual members thereof, including bibliographic references, see Christoph Wolff et al., *The New Grove Bach Family* (London and New York, 1983).

3. Decisive Career Steps

1. *Dok* III, no. 666; *Bach Reader*, p. 215. Subsequent quotations from the same document.
2. *Dok* II, p. 20; *Bach Reader*, p. 52.
3. *Dok* I, no. 1; *Bach Reader*, p. 60.
4. Ibid.
5. *Dok* II, no. 66.
6. *Dok* II, no. 83; *Bach Reader*, p. 228.
7. *Dok* II, no. 84.
8. *Dok* I, p. 67; *Bach Reader*, p. 125.
9. *Dok* II, no. 139.
10. *Dok* II, no. 326.
11. *Dok* II, no. 584.
12. *Dok* II, no. 612.

4. Employers and Patrons

1. *Dok* II, no. 6.
2. Quote from the 1754 obituary: *Dok* III, p. 83; *Bach Reader*, p. 218.
3. *Dok* I, p. 67; *Bach Reader*, p. 125.
4. *Dok* II, no. 91.
5. *Dok* I, no. 150; *Bach Reader*, pp. 82f.
6. *Dok* I, no. 67; *Bach Reader*, p. 125.
7. *Dok* I, no. 155; *Bach Reader*, pp. 82f.
8. *Dok* I, p. 84; *Bach Reader*, p. 220.
9. *Dok* III, p. 638.
10. *Dok* II, no. 388; *Bach Reader*, p. 151.
11. Forkel, pp. 51f.; *Bach Reader*, pp. 338f.
12. *Dok* I, no. 173; *Bach Reader*, p. 178.
13. *Dok* II, no. 16; *Bach Reader*, p. 52.
14. *Dok* II, no. 17; *Bach Reader*, p. 53.
15. *Dok* I, no. 1; *Bach Reader*, p. 60.
16. *Dok* III, p. 638.
17. *Dok* I, p. 63; *Bach Reader*, p. 123.
18. *Dok* II, no. 614; *Bach Reader*, p. 189.
19. Poem by Christian Gottlob Meißner; facsimile of the manuscript libretto in *Sämtliche von Johann Sebastian Bach vertonte Texte*, ed. Werner Neumann (Leipzig, 1974), p. 459.

Und dich, geliebter Handels Plaz
Will ich als einen theuren Schaz

In meiner Seele tragen
Und aller Welt von deinem Ruhme sagen.

20. Latin original (in Gesner's Quintilian commentary, Göttingen, 1738): *Dok* II, no. 432; *Bach Reader*, p. 231.
21. *Dok* I, no. 92; *Bach Reader*, p. 92.
22. For the order of the Sunday Service in Leipzig, see *Dok* I, nos. 178 and 181; *Bach Reader*, p. 70.
23. *Dok* II, no. 352.
24. See Figures 15.3, 15.5, 15.7, and 15.9.

5. Buxtehude, Bach, and Seventeenth-Century Music in Retrospect

1. Spitta, I, pp. 256ff.
2. *Dietrich Buxtehude's Orgelcompositionen*, ed. Philipp Spitta, 2 vols. (Leipzig: Breitkopf & Härtel, 1876–1878).
3. Carl Stiehl, "Die Familie Düben und die Buxtehudischen Manuscripte auf der Bibliothek zu Upsala," *Monatshefte zur Musikgeschichte* 21 (1889), pp. 2–9.
4. André Pirro, *Dietrich Buxtehude* (Paris: Fischbacher, 1913).
5. *Dietrich Buxtehudes Werke*, vols. 1–8, ed. Wilibald Gurlitt et al. (Klecken: Ugrino, 1925–1958); continued: *Dietrich Buxtehude: The Collected Works*, vols. 9ff., ed. Kerala Snyder et al. (New York: Broude, 1987–).
6. *Georg Karstädt, Thematisch-systematisches Verzeichnis der musikalischen Werke von Dietrich Buxtehude*, 2d ed. (Wiesbaden: Breitkopf & Härtel, 1985), hereafter cited as Karstädt, Bux WV.
7. Kerala Snyder, *Dieterich Buxtehude, Organist in Lübeck* (New York: Schirmer, 1987).
8. Reprinted in Wilhelm Stahl, *Dietrich Buxtehude* (Kassel: Bärenreiter, 1937), following p. 56.
9. See Walther's letter of 6 August 1729 to Heinrich Bokemeyer (*Johann Gottfried Walther, Briefe*, ed. K. Beckmann and H.-J. Schulze [Leipzig: Deutscher Verlag für Musik, 1987], p. 63).
10. *Musicalisches Lexicon*, reprint, ed. Richard Schaal (Kassel: Bärenreiter, 1953), p. 123.
11. Although Buxtehude's tablatures from Walther's collection have not survived, his own copies in staff notation transmit the majority of the Buxtehude chorales known today (cf. Karstädt, BuxWV).
12. Ernst Ludwig Gerber, *Neues historisch-biographisches Lexikon der Tonkünstler*, reprint, ed. O. Wessely (Graz, 1966), vol. 1, pp. 590ff.
13. The oldest extant copies of Buxtehude's Pre-

lude in F♯ Minor (Musikbibliothek Leipzig and Hessische Landesbibliothek Darmstadt, respectively; cf. Karstädt, BuxWV) attribute the work to J. S. Bach.

14. Of particular importance are two early anthologies compiled after 1700 by the Ohrdruf J. C. Bach (the so-called Andreas Bach Book and Möller Manuscript).

15. *Bach Reader*, p. 253.

16. *Bach Reader*, p. 123. Here Bach does not refer to the sixteenth- and seventeenth-century motet tradition, but to the vocal-instrumental concertato style of the time around 1700.

17. *Bach Reader*, p. 51.

18. Cf. Johann Mattheson, *Grundlage einer Ehrenpforte* (Hamburg, 1740; reprint, ed. Max Schneider, Kassel, 1969), p. 94.

19. Cf. P. Walker, "From Renaissance 'Fuga' to Baroque Fugue: The Role of the 'Sweelinck Theory Manuscripts,'" *Schütz-Jahrbuch* 7–8 (1985–1986), pp. 93–104.

20. Cf. K. J. Snyder, "Dieterich Buxtehude's Studies in Learned Counterpoint," *Journal of the American Musicological Society* 23 (1980), pp. 544–564.

21. Cf. Snyder, *Dieterich Buxtehude*, pp. 352ff.

22. The connection with operas on biblical subjects such as Johann Theile's *Der erschaffene, gefallene und auffgerichtete Mensch* (1678) or *Die Geburth Christi* (1681), appears to be particularly strong.

23. Cf. Robert S. Hill, "Stilanalyse und Überlieferungsproblematik. Das Variationssuitenrepertoire J. A. Reinkens," in *Dietrich Buxtehude und die europäische Musik seiner Zeit. Bericht über das Lübecker Symposium 1987*, ed. A. Edler and F. Krummacher (Kassel, 1990), pp. 204–214.

24. Reprint in G. Karstädt, *Die "extraordinairen" Abendmusiken Dietrich Buxtehudes*, Veröffentlichungen der Stadt Lübeck, Neue Reihe, vol. 5 (Lübeck: M. Schmidt-Römhild, 1962).

25. After the concluding aria, according to the libretto, "the act is concluded with the mourning chorale 'Nun laßt uns den Leib begraben' in which all organs, choirs, and entire Christian congregation and assembly participate" [Worauf dieser Actus, mit dem Gesang und Choral "Nun laßt uns den Leib begraben" von allen Orgeln und Chören, darin die ganze Christliche Gemein und Versammlung mit einstimmet, ganz kläglich beschlossen wird].

26. Cf. the text of Bach's "Staatsmotette" BWV 71, in whose concluding chorus Emperor Joseph I is addressed also.

27. Most likely this was the first time that Bach could experience recitative style. The earliest surviving sample of Bach's recitative composition can be found in the Hunting Cantata (BWV 208) of 1713.

28. "Castrum doloris" includes also an instrumental "Lamento."

6. Bach and Johann Adam Reinken: A Context for the Early Works

1. Spitta I, book 1, sec. 4–7.

2. See the figure sketched in Friedrich Blume, *Der junge Bach* (Wolfenbüttel and Zurich, 1967); Gustav Fock, *Der junge Bach in Lüneburg. 1700 bis 1702* (Hamburg, 1950); Elke Krüger, *Stilistische Untersuchungen zu ausgewählten frühen Klavierfugen Johann Sebastian Bachs* (Hamburg, 1970); Hartwig Eichberg, "Unechtes unter Johann Sebastian Bachs Klavierwerken," *BJ* 1975, pp. 7–49; Peter Williams, *The Organ Music of J. S. Bach* (Cambridge, 1980–84), vols. 1 and 2.

3. See the discussion by Christoph Wolff, "Probleme und Neuansätze der Bach-Biographik," in *Bachforschung und Bachinterpretation heute*, ed. Reinhold Brinkmann (Kassel, 1981), pp. 21–31; Chapter 1, above, is an abbreviated translation of this work.

4. Assembled by C. P. E. Bach and Johann Friedrich Agricola in 1750 and printed in 1754; *Dok*, III, p. 81.

5. Letter to J. N. Forkel, 13 January 1775, in *Dok* III, p. 288.

6. Facsimile in *Bach-Urkunden . . . Nachrichten über Johann Sebastian Bach von Carl Philipp Emanuel Bach*, ed. Max Schneider (Leipzig, 1917); *Dok* III, p. 290.

7. A newspaper announcement of 19 September 1727 states that the two partitas "may be obtained . . . not only from the author, but also . . . 3) from Herr Böhm, organist at St. John's in Lüneburg . . .", *Dok* II, no. 224.

8. *Dok* III, p. 82.

9. *Dok* II, p. 19.

10. *Bachiana I*, in *Allgemeine Musikalische Zeitung*, 1881, no. 47–48. Reprinted in Philipp Spitta, *Musikgeschichtliche Aufsätze* (Berlin, 1894), pp. 111–120.

11. *Dok* II, no. 102.

12. *Dok* III, p. 84.

13. On this occasion, Bach performed in Hamburg "before the Magistrate and many other distinguished persons of the town, on the fine organ of St. Catherine's, for more than two hours, to their general astonishment. The aged organist of this church, Johann Adam Reinken, who at that time was nearly a hundred years old, listened to him with particular

pleasure. Bach, at the request of those present, performed *ex tempore* the chorale *An Wasserflüssen Babylon* at great length—almost a half-hour—and in different ways . . . Particularly on this Reinken paid Bach the following compliment: 'I thought that this art . . .'; *Dok* III, p. 81.

14. Johann Joachim Quantz, *Versuch einer Anleitung die Flöte traversiere zu spielen* (Berlin, 1752); *Dok* III, p. 18.

15. *Dok* III, p. 32.

16. *Dok* III, pp. 423–24.

17. One can also not exclude the possibility that Böhm, who was born in the vicinity of Ohrdruf and raised near Gotha, had ties to the Bach family that Johann Sebastian could only take advantage of in Lüneburg.

18. Johann Gottfried Walther (in *Musicalisches Lexicon*, Leipzig, 1732) speaks of the "two extremely renowned organists, Herren Reinken and Buxtehude"; Johann Mattheson (in *Critica Musica*, Hamburg, 1722, p. 517) writes of Reinken's organ playing: "of the things in which he was versed, one knew nothing comparable in his time."

19. Karl Müller, "Der junge Bach," *Arnstädter Bach-Buch*, 2d ed., ed. Karl Müller and Fritz Wiegand (Arnstadt, 1957), p. 63.

20. *Dok* II, no. 5.

21. Fock, *Der junge Bach in Lüneburg*, p. 100.

22. *Dok* I, no. 38.

23. *Dok* III, p. 82.

24. *Dok* II, no. 7.

25. Ibid.

26. On the life of Johann Christoph Bach see Hans-Joachim Schulze, "Johann Christoph Bach (1671–1721), 'Organist und Schul Collega in Ohrdruf', Johann Sebastian Bachs erster Lehrer," *BJ* 1985, pp. 55–81.

27. J. S. Bach's beginning salary at Arnstadt exceeded his brother's highest income. See *Dok* II, p. 12; and Ferdinand Reinhold, "Die Musik-Bache in Ohrdruf," *Festschrift zum Bachjahr 1950* (Ohrdruf, n.d.), p. 14.

28. Reinhold, p. 14.

29. *Dok* III, p. 81.

30. Ibid.

31. Blume, *Der junge Bach*, p. 7.

32. Spitta I, p. 186.

33. See Robert Hill, "The Lost Clavier Books of the Young Bach and Handel," *Bach, Handel, Scarlatti: Tercentenary Essays*, ed. Peter Williams (Cambridge, 1985).

34. Formerly Mus. ms. 40 035 of the Preußische Staatsbibliothek in Berlin, now preserved in the Bib-

lioteka Jagiellońska, Crakow. The source had not been accessible since World War II. I should like to thank the director of the library, Dr. J. Pierozyński, for allowing me to examine the manuscript for the first time during my stay in Cracow in 1981 and for placing a microfilm of it at my disposal.

35. See the article "Eckelt" by Walter Blankenburg, in *Die Musik in Geschichte und Gegenwart*, vol. 3 (1954), cols. 1091–1093.

36. I should like to thank Hans-Joachim Schulze for his help in identifying Pachelbel's handwriting.

37. An entry on the recto side of leaf 18 reads: "The music to the chorales I bought from him."

38. A thorough discussion of the Eckelt tablature book must remain the object of a future study.

39. Max Seiffert, ed., *Denkmäler der Tonkunst in Bayern* II/1 (1901); IV/1 (1903).

40. Guido Adler, ed., *Denkmäler der Tonkunst in Österreich* 13 (1899); 21 (1903).

41. Spitta, I, p. 220.

42. Eichberg, "Unechtes," pp. 14–17. New perspectives on Bach's early compositional activities are provided by the organ chorales of the Neumeister Collection (Yale University, ms. LM 4708), edited by Christoph Wolff (New Haven and Kassel, 1985); and Wolff, introduction to the facsimile edition, *The Neumeister Collection of Chorale Preludes from the Bach Circle* (New Haven, 1985).

43. The contents of both sources are given in *NBA* IV/5–6, *Krit. Bericht* (ed. Dietrich Kilian, 1978), pp. 98–106 (Möller manuscript) and 122–131 (Andreas Bach Book). For a detailed discussion of the repertoire of the two manuscripts as well as the identification of the principal copyist, see Hans Joachim Schulze, *Studien zur Bach-Überlieferung im 18. Jahrhundert* (Leipzig, 1984), pp. 30–56.

44. Gustav Fock, *Arp Schnitger und seine Schule* (Kassel, 1974), p. 104.

45. Ibid., p. 105.

46. *Dok* III, p. 82; see also Hans-Joachim Schulze, "Der französische Einfluß im Instrumentalwerk J. S. Bachs," in *Studien zur Afführungspraxis und Interpretation von Instrumentalmusik des 18. Jahrhunderts*, vol. 16 (Blankenburg, 1981), pp. 57–63.

47. The Herzogliches Schloß am Markt, built in 1693–1696 by D. A. Rossi after a French model. Today it is the district court house.

48. Bach did not return to Arnstadt from this journey of three to four months until shortly before 7 February 1706.

49. See Georg Karstädt, *Thematisch-systematisches Verzeichnis der musikalischen Werke von Dietrich Buxtehude* ("Bux WV"; Wiesbaden, 1974), p. 132.

50. *Dok* III, p. 82.

51. The proposed date of 1707 for Cantata 106 connecting it with the memorial service for Bach's uncle Tobias Lämmerhirt, who died on 10 August of that year (see Alfred Dürr, *Die Kantaten von Johann Sebastian Bach*, 2nd ed. [Kassel, 1971], p. 611), is questionable. Bach would have had to finish the composition between the day of death and the memorial service. This period was not enough time for "an ingenious work, which has seldom been equaled by great masters and with which the twenty-two year old, with a single stroke, swept all his contemporaries behind him" (ibid., pp. 611–612). It is more likely that Bach wrote the "Actus Tragicus" on "advance notice," so to speak, creating a carefully worked-out presentation piece for some opportune occasion.

52. Dadelsen, *Chr*, p. 75.

53. In Schulze, *Studien zur Bach-Überlieferung*, it is dated "scarcely before 1705" (assuming a relatively late reception of Buxtehude's style by Bach), from which corresponding inferences are drawn for the chronology of the Möller Manuscript.

54. See also Russell Stinson, "Bach's Earliest Autograph," *Musical Quarterly* 71 (1985), pp. 235–263.

55. J. A. Reincken, *Sämtliche Orgelwerke*, ed. Klaus Beckmann (Wiesbaden, 1974), pp. 4–21 and 22–37.

56. See the article "Böhm" by Hugh J. McLean, in *The New Grove Dictionary of Music and Musicians* (London, 1980), vol. 2, pp. 852–853.

57. Reinken's organ had 58 stops, distributed among four manuals and pedal. For Buxtehude, the large organ in St. Mary's had 54 stops (on three manuals and pedal); however, in 40 years Buxtehude did not succeed in obtaining an overdue "thorough renovation" of the instrument. See Friedrich W. Riedel, *Quellenkundliche Beiträge zur Geschichte der Musik für Tasteninstrumente in der 2. Hälfte des 17. Jahrhunderts* (Kassel, 1960), p. 189.

58. *Dok* III, no. 739: "In the organ of St. Catherine's Church in Hamburg there are 16 reeds. The late Kapellmeister, Herr J. S. Bach in Leipzig . . . could not praise the beauty and variety of tone of these reeds highly enough" (1768).

59. See Christoph Wolff, "The Hamburg Group Portrait with Reinken and Buxtehude: An Essay in Musical Iconography," in *Program Book, Boston Early Music Festival and Exhibition, 8–14 June 1987*, pp. 102–112; revised and expanded German version in *Studien zur Musikgeschichte der Hansestadt Lübeck*, ed. A. Edler and H. W. Schwab, Kieler Schriften zur Musikwissenschaft, vol. 31 (Kassel, 1989), pp. 168–189.

60. Reinken's library contained, among other things, treatises by Zarlino and Poglietti (see Riedel, p. 190) as well as Frescobaldi's Second Book of Toccatas (see Wolff, "The Hamburg Group Portrait," p. 112).

61. Spitta I, p. 431.

62. *Dok* III, no. 803.

63. *Dok* III, p. 82.

64. The only extant complete copy is located in DSB.

65. Hermann Keller, "Über Bachs Bearbeitungen aus dem 'Hortus musicus' von Reinken," in *Kongressbericht Basel 1949*, pp. 160–161.

66. Ulrich Siegele, *Kompositionsweise und Bearbeitungstechnik in der Instrumentalmusik Johann Sebastian Bachs* (Neuhausen-Stuttgart, 1975), pp. 11–22.

67. DSB, P 803. See Hermann Zietz, *Quellenkritische Untersuchungen an den Bach-Handschriften P 801, P 802, und P 803 aus dem "Krebsschen Nachlass" unter besonderer Berücksichtigung der Choralbearbeitungen des jungen J. S. Bach* (Hamburg, 1969), p. 216.

68. SPK, P 804. See Paul Kast, *Die Bach-Handschriften der Berliner Staatsbibliothek* (Trossingen, 1958), pp. 48–49.

69. The title of BWV 574b in the Andreas Bach Book is *"Thema Legrenzianum. Elaboratum per Joan. Seb. Bach."* Robert Hill recently identified the thematic source of Bach's Legrenzi fugue, and I am grateful to him for having shared that information with me before publication of his report ("Die Herkunft von Bachs 'Thema Legrenzianum,'" *BJ* 1986, pp. 105–107).

70. Reinken's sonatas are much more indebted to Italian trio-sonata style than are the chamber sonatas of Buxtehude, for instance.

71. It is possible that Bach also tried his hand at composing chamber music at this time, even though no trace of that activity has survived unless one places the Fugue in G Minor for Violin and Continuo BWV 1026, in the early period (the piece is also handed down in DSB, P 801, in Walther's hand). The style of the Fugue does not speak against an early date.

72. The fact that the Legrenzi fugue survives in three different versions strongly suggests that the remaining fugues on themes by other composers also went through several stages of refinement. That would certainly reflect their role as study pieces.

73. The original has not survived. It is not from *"Hortus Musicus."*

74. See Hans-Joachim Schulze, "J. S. Bach's Concerto Arrangements for Organ—Studies or Commissioned Works?" *Organ Yearbook* 3 (1972), pp. 4–13.

75. See the discussion in Joseph Müller-Blattau,

Geschichte der Fuge, 3d ed. (Kassel, 1963), pp. 66–78.

76. *Dok* III, pp. 144–145. Translation from *Bach Reader,* p. 257.

77. Note, for instance, the use of permutation technique in the fugue of the Passacaglia in C Minor for Organ BWV 582, which in some sources (including the earliest manuscript copy, in the Andreas Bach Book) is called "fuga cum subjectis." The structure of the passacaglia fugue follows a strict permutation scheme (see Chapter 23, especially the table on page 313).

78. Werner Neumann, *J. S. Bachs Chorfuge. Ein Beitrag zur Kompositionstechnik Bachs,* 2d ed. (Leipzig, 1950), pp. 14–15.

79. See also Carl Dahlhaus, "Zur Geschichte der Permutationsfuge," *BJ* 1959, pp. 95–110.

80. See also Chapter 32, below.

POSTSCRIPT

Recent studies which shed further light on Reinken, North German, and other late-seventeenth-century influences on Bach are: Robert Hill, "'Der Himmel weiß, wo diese Sachen hingekommen sind': Reconstructing the Lost Clavier Books of the Young Bach and Handel," *Bach-Handel-Scarlatti: A Tercentenary Anthology,* ed. Peter Williams (Cambridge, 1985), p. 161–172; Christoph Wolff, "Johann Valentin Eckelts Tabulaturbuch von 1692," *Festschrift Martin Ruhnke zum 65. Geburtstag,* ed. Klaus-Jürgen Sachs (Neuhausen-Stuttgart, 1986), pp. 374–386; Robert Hill, *The Möller Manuscript and the Andreas Bach Book: Two Keyboard Anthologies from the Circle of the Young Johann Sebastian Bach,* Ph.D. diss., Harvard University, 1987; Karl Heller, "Norddeutsche Musikkultur als Traditionsraum des jungen Bach," *BJ* 1989, pp. 7–19; Paul Walker, "Die Entstehung der Permutationsfuge," *BJ* 1989, pp. 21–41.

7. Vivaldi's Compositional Art, Bach, and the Process of "Musical Thinking"

1. Peter Ryom, *Répertoire des Oeuvres d'Antonio Vivaldi. Les compositions instrumentales* (Copenhagen, 1986).

2. Arnold Schering, *Geschichte des Instrumental-Konzerts* (Leipzig, 1905; 2d ed., 1927; reprint, 1965).

3. Rudolf Eller, "Die Konzertform Antonio Vivaldis: Habilitationsschrift" (typescript: Leipzig, 1957); "Geschichtliche Stellung und Wandlung der Vivaldischen Konzertform," *Kongressbericht* (Vienna, 1956), pp. 150ff.; "Vivaldi-Dresden-Bach," *Beiträge zur Musikwissenschaft* 3 (1961), pp. 31ff.

4. Walter Kolneder, *Die Solokonzertform bei Vivaldi* (Strasbourg and Baden-Baden, 1961).

5. Michael Talbot, "The Concerto Allegro in the Early Eighteenth Century," *Music & Letters* 52 (1971), pp. 8ff., 159ff.

6. Peter Ryom, "La comparaison entre les versions différentes d'un concerto d'Antonio Vivaldi transcrit par J. S. Bach" *Dansk aarbog for musikforskning* 5 (1966–67), pp. 91ff.

7. *Bach Reader,* pp. 295ff.

8. Hans-Joachim Schulze, *Studien zur Bach-Überlieferung im 18. Jahrhundert* (Leipzig, 1984), pp. 146–173.

9. Cf. ibid. p. 161; only one Weimar autograph manuscript of a Vivaldi transcription (BWV 596) has survived.

10. Forkel, p. 24; *Bach Reader,* p. 317.

11. *Dok* III, no. 803; *Bach Reader,* p. 278.

12. *Dok* III, P. 82; *Bach Reader,* p. 217.

13. Cf. Christoph Wolff, et al., *The New Grove Bach Family* (London and New York, 1983), p. 122.

14. BWV 978 (= op. 3, no. 3), BWV 593 (= op. 3, no. 8), BWV 972 (= op. 3, no. 9), BWV 596 (= op. 3, no. 11), and BWV 976 (= op. 3, no. 12).

15. Cf. Johann Christoph Adlung, *Grammatisch-Kritisches Wörterbuch* (Leipzig, 1793).

16. Forkel, pp. 23f.; *Bach Reader,* p. 317.

17. Harmony resulting from accumulated counterpoint; e.g., "harmony becomes far more complete if all the voices collaborate to form it" (Die Harmonie wird weit vollkommener, wenn alle Stimmen miteinander arbeiten). Cf. *Dok* II, p. 305; *Bach Reader,* p. 246.

18. Michael Talbot, *Vivaldi* (London, 1979), chap. 5.

19. J. S. Bach, *16 Konzerte nach Vivaldi,* ed. A. Schering (Leipzig: Edition Peters, n.d.)

20. The primary source for BWV 978 is a fair copy in the hand of Bach's nephew, Johann Bernhard Bach, dated Leipzig 1739; *XII Concerti di Vivaldi. elabor: di J. S. Bach,* SPK, Mus. ms. Bach P 280.

21. Forkel, p. 24; *Bach Reader,* p. 317.

8. Bach and the Tradition of the Palestrina Style

1. Sebastian Hensel, *Die Familie Mendelssohn,* 5th ed. (Berlin, 1911), p. 190.

2. E. T. A. Hoffmann, *Schriften zur Musik,* ed. Friedrich Schnapp (Darmstadt, 1963), pp. 215f.

3. *Dok* III, p. 289; *Bach Reader,* p. 279.

4. An edition of Caldara's Magnificat, with Bach's arrangement of the "Suscipit Israel" move-

ment was published, ed. Christoph Wolff (Kassel: Bärenreiter, 1967).

5. Lorenz Christoph Mizler, *Neu eröffnete Musikalische Bibliothek*, vol. 2, part 1 (Leipzig, 1742), p. 292.

POSTSCRIPT

This chapter was originally presented as a public lecture in 1967 at the forty-second Bachfest of the Neue Bachgesellschaft in Wuppertal; portions of the lecture making specific references to the festival program have been removed from the present version.

Section II of the chapter summarizes the findings of my dissertation (Friedrich-Alexander-Universität Erlangen, 1966); the published version of the dissertation (Wolff *Stile antico*) was discussed extensively in an editorial by Paul Henry Lang in the *Musical Quarterly* 55 (1969), pp. 545–558, and reviewed, among others, by Alfred Dürr in *Die Musikforschung* 23 (1970), pp. 324–328, and Robert L. Marshall in *Notes* 27 (1970), pp. 33–34. A related but different style-critical approach, without discussion of sources, can be found in Christfried Lenz, *Studien zur Satztechnik Bachs. Untersuchung einiger vom Erscheinungsbild der Vokalpolyphonie geprägter Kompositionen* (Ph.D. dissertation, Heidelberg, 1970). Some new material and perspectives are offered by Kirsten Beißwenger, *Johann Sebastian Bachs Notenbibliothek* (Ph.D. dissertation, Göttingen, 1990) and "Bachs Eingriffe in Werke fremder Komponisten. Beobachtungen an den Notenhandschriften aus seiner Bibliothek unter besonderer Berücksichtigung der lateinischen Kirchenmusik," *BJ* 1991. For matters of context, results of further research, and some more differentiated conclusions, see also this volume, Chapter 28.

Regarding Table 8.1: My discussion of the extended chorale chorus "Ein fest Burg ist unser Gott" in the revised version of Cantata 80 from 1744–1747 or earlier (see Chapter 12) suggests that this movement ought to be included in the relatively short list of compositions in which Bach adheres in a particularly strict sense to genuine *stile antico* principles.

9. The Neumeister Collection of Chorale Preludes from the Bach Circle

1. Gerhard Herz, *Bach Sources in America* (Kassel, 1984).

2. See Henry Cutler Fall, "A Critical Bibliographical Study of the Rinck Collection," master's thesis, Yale University, 1958.

3. See Christoph Wolff, *The New Grove Bach*

Family (London, 1983), p. 13; LM 4983 was first discussed by Walter Emery in "An American Manuscript: Two Unknown Pieces by Bach?" *Musical Times* 95 (1954), pp. 428–430.

4. Yoshitake Kobayashi, "Der Gehrener Kantor Johann Christoph Bach (1673–1727) und seine Sammelbände mit Musik für Tasteninstrumente," in *Bachiana et Alia Musicologica: Festschrift für Alfred Dürr*, ed. Wolfgang Rehm (Kassel, 1983), pp. 168–177, see also Herz, *Bach Sources*, pp. 210–211.

5. It seems that the many anonymous works in the two volumes are actually compositions of Johann Sebastian's cousin, Johann Christoph Bach—a possibility that Kobayashi does not propose.

6. Herz, *Bach Sources*, pp. 254–256 (LM 5056).

7. See Fall, "Bibliographical Study," appendix a, appendix c (with thematic index of "Choräle di Bach" from LM 4843); see also Wolff, "Bach's Organ Music: Studies and Discoveries," *Musical Times* 126 (1985), p. 152 n. 6.

8. Now published as the *Bach Compendium*. For a preliminary discussion see Wolff, "Bach's Organ Music," and idem, preface to Johann Sebastian Bach, *Organ Chorales from the Neumeister Collection (Yale University Manuscript LM 4708)* (New Haven, 1985).

The discovery of the Bach chorale preludes was announced on 17 December 1984, jointly by Harold E. Samuel, music librarian at Yale, and myself. Only in late December did we learn that the West German organist Wilhelm Krumbach had apparently examined LM 4708 independently on the basis of a microfilm and had drawn similar conclusions regarding the authenticity of the Bach works; he actually announced on January 5, 1985, that he had discovered some sixty unknown Bach organ chorales in three manuscripts, including LM 4708. This is misleading, however, for the other sources (LM 4803 at Yale and R 24 at the Musikbibliothek Leipzig) are well known to Bach scholars and in no way comparable in quality with LM 4708.

9. Fall, "Bibliographical Study," appendix a.

10. See Günter Thomas, *Friedrich Wilhelm Zachow* (Regensburg, 1966), and Zachow, *Gesammelte Werke für Tasteninstrumente*, ed. Heinz Lohmann (Wiesbaden, 1966).

11. See Robert Grosse-Stoltenberg, "Papiermühlengeschichten," *Zeitschrift für Papiergeschichte* 22 (1972), pp. 46–59. I wish to thank Dr. Wolfgang Schlieder, Deutsches Buch- und Schriftmuseum (at the Deutsche Bücherei), Leipzig, for his kind advice.

12. Friedrich-Wilhelm Donat, *Christian Heinrich Rinck und die Orgelmusik seiner Zeit* (Bad Oeynhausen, 1931); Herbert S. Oakeley and John Warrack,

"Rinck," in *The New Grove Dictionary of Music and Musicians*. 20 vols. (London, 1980), 16:43–44.

13. Hans Theodor Tiemann, *Geschichte der allgemeinen Bürgerschule zu Homburg v.d.H.* (Homburg vor der Höhe, 1881); Wilhelm Diehl, et., *Hessisches Lehrerbuch. Vierter Teil*. vol. 12 of *Hassia sacra* (Darmstadt, 1951), p. 380; and Friedrich Lotz, *Die Landgrafen-Zeit*, vol. 2 of *Geschichte der Stadt Bad Homburg vor der Höhe* (Frankfurt am Main, 1972), 372–374.

14. Fall, "Bibliographical Study," 1–12; Harry Eskew, "Lowell Mason," in *The New Grove Dictionary*. II:749.

15. Johann Philipp Diefenbach, *Die Augustiner-Schule zu Friedberg* (Friedberg, 1825); Georg Windhaus, *Geschichte der Lateinschule zu Friedberg* (Friedberg, 1893); Heinrich Müller, *Stadtkirche zu Friedberg; Feier des 25-jährigen Bestehens der Chorschule* (Friedberg, 1907); and Karl Schmidt, *Beiträge zur Kenntnis des musikalischen Lebens in der ehemaligen Reichsstadt Friedberg i.d.W.* (Leipzig, 1918).

16. Karl David Neumeister was born 1754 at Ebersdorf and died 1839 at Frankfurt. (Information kindly supplied by Karin Carl of the Stadtarchiv Frankfurt am Main.)

17. Stadtarchiv Friedberg. (I wish to thank Herr Keller of the Stadtarchiv for his kind assistance.) Schmid (1748–1811) occasionally served as librettist for church cantatas; see Schmidt, *Beiträge*, pp. 57, 59.

18. A Herrnhutter congregation was founded at Ebersdorf, Neumeister's birthplace, by Count Zinzendorf in 1732.

19. Neumeister is not mentioned in Schmidt.

20. Stadtarchiv Friedberg.

21. George J. Buelow, "Sorge," in *The New Grove Dictionary*, 17:537–538.

22. See Grosse-Stoltenberg, "Papiermühlengeschichten," p. 57.

23. See Robin A. Leaver, "Bach and Hymnody: The Evidence of the Orgelbüchlein," *Early Music 13* (1985), pp. 227–236.

24. See Michael Schneider, *Die Orgelspieltechnik des frühen 19. Jahrhunderts in Deutschland*, vol. 6 in *Kölner Beiträge zur Musikforschung* (Regensburg, 1941). A. G. Ritter had assembled for *Zur Geschichte des Orgelspiels im 14. bis 18. Jahrhundert* (Leipzig, 1884) an extensive incipit catalog (see synopsis), which includes references to seven compositions from LM 4708. Ritter must have had access to this source while it was in Rinck's possession. (For the Ritter-Rinck connection, see Spitta II, p. 633.) It remains unclear, however, why Ritter did not include all of the material from LM 4708. There is, of course, the remote possibility that Ritter took his information from a different source which is no longer extant. See also the synopsis of chorale preludes at the end of this chapter.

25. The context and influence of their widespread activities have yet to be fully examined.

26. Rinck probably received the volume before 1830. He apparently based his edition of Johann Michael Bach's chorale "Nun freut euch, lieben Christen gmein," *Orgel-Journal I, no. 7* (Mannheim, 1830–1831), on LM 4708, no. 5; see Spitta I, p. 119.

27. The numerous missing ties for syncopated and tied-over notes are another clear indication against tablature notation.

28. See Wolff, preface to *Organ Chorales*.

29. Max Seiffert, "Das Plauener Orgelbuch von 1708," *Archiv für Musikwissenschaft 2* (1919–1920) pp. 371–393. The Plauen Organ Book contains 37 chorale preludes by Pachelbel, 11 by Zachow, 6 by J. M. Bach, 1 by Erich, 3 by J. S. Bach (BWV 739, 735a, 720), and 49 anonymous works.

30. Musikbibliothek Leipzig, Becker Collection III.8.3.

31. SPK, Mus. ms. 40644. For a close discussion of these two manuscripts and the identification of their main scribe, see Hans-Joachim Schulze, *Studien zur Bach-Überlieferung im 18. Jahrhundert* (Leipzig 1984), pp. 30–55.

32. Schulze, *Bach-Überlieferung*, pp. 50–56.

33. See Schmidt, *Beiträge*, pp. 32–34, 46–51.

34. Yale University Music Library, LM 4630. (This is the only surviving copy, according to *Repertoire des Sources Musicales*, A/I/8 [Kassel, 1980], S 3980). Sorge's Sonatinen (Nuremberg, circa 1745) were dedicated to Bach; see *Dok* II, no. 526. There is no reference in this work to the publication of Sorge's chorale preludes.

35. See Max Schneider, "Thematisches Verzeichnis der musikalischen Werke der Familie Bach," *BJ 4* (1907), pp. 109–177 (work-list of J. C. Bach) and Hugh J. McLean, "Erich," in *The New Grove Dictionary*, 6:228. Most of Erich's works were transmitted in the Königsberg manuscript (see synopsis).

36. See Thomas, *Zachow*, pp. 261–271.

37. See Carl Philipp Emanuel's characterization in the obituary notice for his father, *Dok* III, no. 666.

38. Fritz Dietrich, *Geschichte des deutschen Orgelchorals im 17. Jahrhundert* (Kassel, 1932).

39. See Hans-Joachim Schulze, "Johann Christoph Bach (1671–1721), 'Organist und Schul Collega in Ohrdruf,' Johann Sebastian Bachs erster Lehrer," *BJ 71* (1985), pp. 55–81.

40. See McLean, "Erich."

41. See Schulze, *Bach-Überlieferung*, pp. 41–50.

42. See Max Schneider, "Thematisches Verzeichnis" (worklist J. M. Bach).

43. Karl Müller and Fritz Wiegand, *Arnstädter Bachbuch*, rev. ed. (Arnstadt, 1957), pp. 114–117.

44. Ernst Ludwig Gerber, *Neues historisch-biographisches Lexikon der Tonkünstler*, vol. 1 (Leipzig, 1812), pp. 208, 213.

45. Spitta I, pp. 108–110.

46. By Max Seiffert, ed., *J. S.Bachs Orgelwerke*, vol. 9 (Leipzig, 1904), pp. 53–55.

47. Seiffert, "Das Plauener Orgelbuch," p. 386.

48. A hitherto unnoticed keyboard suite *(Parthie Spinetto ex A Moll)* by J. M. Bach is transmitted in LM 4693 (Yale University).

49. I wish to thank Hans-Joachim Schulze for his identification of this piece as a chorale prelude. On the lost Schelble-Gleichauf volume containing a corrupted version of BWV 957, see Schulze, *Bach-Überlieferung*, pp. 26–27.

50. This matter is discussed in this volume, Chapter 22.

51. See critical reports in *NBA* IV/2–3; see also Hermann Zietz, *Quellenkritische Untersuchungen an den Bach-Handschriften P 801, P 802 und P 803 aus dem "Krebs'schen Nachlaß" unter besonderer Berücksichtigung des jungen J. S. Bach* (Hamburg, 1969).

52. A manuscript with predominantly early Bach chorale preludes copied by Christoph Sasse (1721–1794), organist at St. Lawrence's in Halle and a frequent substitute for Wilhelm Friedemann, points in this direction: SPK, Mus. ms. 40037 (see LM 4708, no. 36). Connections between W. F. Bach and Johann Georg Nacke (1718–1804) of Oelsnitz (Vogtland) helped to bring important Bach materials to Neumeister's native area; see Schulze, *Bach-Überlieferung*, pp. 21–22.

53. For example, the 'Actus Tragicus' (BWV 106), whose earliest source (SPK, Mus. ms. Bach P 1018) stems from 1768.

54. Only the first chorale line is treated, and mm. 25–29 conclude with a very clumsy cadence.

55. Curiously enough, also Johann Gottfried Walther's setting of the same chorale clearly alludes to this Buxtehude motif (or does Bach's piece provide the model for him?); see Walther, "Gesammelte Werke," *Denkmäler deutscher Tonkunst* 26–27 (1906); no. 48.

56. The preludes from LM 4708 and the related singly transmitted chorales published in *NBA* IV/3 represent only an inadequate picture.

57. Samuel Scheidt seems to have had problems with this most cumbersome melody when he treated it in his Görlitz Tabulaturbuch (1650).

POSTSCRIPT

According to the church records kept at the Evangelisch-lutherisches Pfarramt of Ebersdorf, Neumeister's date of birth is 24 February 1756. Accordingly, the year 1757 as reported in the Hassian schoolmaster chronicles (see above, note 13) needs to be corrected. His parents were the butcher, Friedrich Oswald Neumeister and Maria Barbara (née Schmidt). I am grateful to the parish of Ebersdorf for the kind permission to work at the church archives.

As for the problem of attribution discussed at the very end of the chapter, no. 41 ("Was mein Gott will, das g'scheh allzeit") can be positively identified as a work by Johann Pachelbel (cf. the synopsis of works in the Neumeister collection at the end of the chapter). For a more detailed stylistic discussion see this volume, Chapter 22. See also Russell Stinson, "Some Thoughts on Bach's Neumeister Chorales," *Journal of Musicology* 9 (1991), in press.

10. Bach's Audition for the St. Thomas Cantorate

1. See *Dok* III, no. 124.

2. Spitta II, pp. 679, 710f.

3. We might single out Bernhard Friedrich Richter ("Die Wahl Joh. Seb. Bachs zum Kantor der Thomasschule i.J. 1723," *BJ* 1905, pp. 48–67), advancing the hypothesis that Cantata 22 was written under supervised examination conditions; and—more recently—Martin Geck ("Bachs Probestück," in *Quellenstudien zur Musik: Wolfgang Schmieder zum 70. Geburtstag*, ed. Kurt Dorfmüller [Frankfort 1970], pp. 55–68), interpreting BWV 22 as "Cantor music" which, as a special gesture toward Leipzig authorities, was given preference to the "Capellmeister music" of BWV 23.

4. See Dürr *Chr*, p. 57 (mainly); Dadelsen *Chr*, pp. 93–97. The performance material for BWV 23 is preserved in SPK, Mus. ms. Bach P 69, and DSB, Mus. ms. Bach St 16.

5. Dürr *Chr* 2, pp. 163f.

6. Hessische Landes- und Hochschulbibliothek Darmstadt, Mus. ms. 431/1, 431/2. Cf. Table 10.2 and Friedrich Noack, "Johann Sebastian Bachs und Christoph Graupners Kompositionen zur Bewerbung um das Thomaskantorat in Leipzig 1722–23," *BJ* 1913, pp. 145–162.

7. Dürr *Chr* 2, p. 164.

8. See the report by Hans-Joachim Schulze, "Zur Rückkehr einiger autographer Kantatenfragmente in die Bach-Sammlung der Deutschen Staatsbibliothek Berlin," *BJ* 1977, pp. 130ff.

9. See the more recent studies mentioned in note 4 and the source description in *BG* 5/1 (Wilhelm Rust, 1855). For details beyond the present summary discussion and primarily dealing with documentation, see my critical report for *NBA* I/8 (forthcoming).

10. Thus the cantorate audition follows the practice of presenting within a single service two cantatas, or a cantata divided into two major sections—a practice to which Bach gave preference at the beginning of his Leipzig tenure in 1723: First Sunday after Trinity (BWV 75), Second Sunday after Trinity (BWV 76), Third Sunday after Trinity (BWV 21), Fourth Sunday after Trinity (BWV 185 and 24), etc. (see the listing in *BJ* 1976, p. 87).

11. *Dok* II, no. 119. See also H.-J. Schulze, "'. . . da man nun die besten nicht bekommen könne . . .' Kontroversen und Kompromisse vor Bachs Leipziger Amtsantritt," *Bericht über die Wissenschaftliche Konferenz zum III. Internationalen Bach-Fest der DDR, Leipzig 18./19. September 1975*, Leipzig, 1977, pp. 71–77.

12. *Dok* II, no. 121.

13. Press notice of 8 December 1722 (*Der Hamburgische Correspondent*); see Heinz Becker, "Die frühe Hamburgische Tagespresse als musikgeschichtliche Quelle," in *Beiträge zur Hamburgischen Musikgeschichte*, ed. Heinrich Husmann (Hamburg, 1956), p. 39.

14. *Dok* II, no. 119.

15. See Wolf Hobohm, "Neue Texte zur Leipziger Kirchen-Music,'" *BJ* 1973, pp. 5–32.

16. See Ferdinand Zander, *Die Dichter der Kantatentexte Johann Sebastian Bachs*, Ph.D. diss., University of Cologne, 1967, pp. 44, 50f.

17. Ibid.

18. A 1717 visit by Bach in Leipzig is documented (*Dok* I, no. 87). Even if this was not the only one, Bach's familiarity with conditions in Leipzig cannot be taken for granted.

19. Mentioned in the press notice for Bach's cantorate audition: *Dok* II, no. 124.

20. Richter, "Die Wahl Joh. Seb. Bachs."

21. Schott was organist at the New Church and director of the Collegium Musicum.

22. An autograph score by Carl Philipp Emanuel Bach (DSB, Mus. ms. Bach P 70) clearly shows the different readings of the original score.

23. Cf. my article, "Die Rastrierungen in den Originalhandschriften Joh. Seb. Bachs und ihre Bedeutung für die diplomatische Quellenkritik," in *Festschrift Friedrich Smend zum 70. Geburtstag* (Berlin, 1963), p. 85, n. 20. The conclusions with regard to the chronology of BWV 23 (pp. 86ff.) can no longer be considered valid.

24. Cf. Alfred Dürr in *NBA* II/3 (*Krit. Bericht*, 1955), pp. 34f., and *BJ* 1968, p. 91. The original parts for Cantata 194 (SPK, Mus. ms. Bach St 48), written in 1723 for the dedication of the organ at Störmthal, are expressly marked "tieff Cammerthon."

25. This situation still applied to the earliest cantatas in Bach's Leipzig tenure, where the instrument is given a certain preference.

26. Concerning the rearrangement of this part, adapting it to B flat minor, see below.

27. One of the parts was likely intended for Violone.

28. Cf. the illustration in *BJ* 1977, p. 133.

29. E.g., in the transcriptions of Palestrina's "Missa sine nomine" and Pergolesi's "Stabat mater"; see *BJ* 1927, p. 129, and *BJ* 1968, pp. 89ff.

30. Preserved are merely the autograph score (DSB, Mus. ms. Bach P 119) and a copy of the score in the hand of Johann Andreas Kuhnau (SPK, Mus. ms. Bach P 46). P 46 shows an entry, made by Johann Friedrich Agricola presumably about 1750: "N.B. Dies ist das Probestück in Leipzig" (This is the audition piece for Leipzig). Reasons why a copy of the score was made are not known. It is possible that a copy (now lost) was also made of BWV 23. Nothing is known about a later location of the parts for BWV 22 (which in 1790 were still listed in C. P. E. Bach's estate; cf. *Dok* III, pp. 498, 503).

31. Wolf Hobohm, "Neue Texte zur Leipziger Kirchen-Music,'" p. 16.

32. See William H. Scheide, "Zum Verhältnis von Textdrucken und musikalischen Quellen der Kirchenkantaten J. S. Bachs," *BJ* 1976, pp. 85–86; and Afred Dürr, "Bemerkungen zu Bachs Leipziger Kantatenaufführungen," *Bericht über die Wissenschaftliche Konferenz*, pp. 165ff.

33. *Dok* II, no. 179. Curiously, these documents are not mentioned in *NBA* II/4, ed. Arthur Mendel (*Krit. Bericht*, 1974).

34. Dürr *Chr*, pp. 79 and 85.

35. Ibid., p. 99.

36. Cf. the summary discussion (including further references) in *NBA* II/4, ed. Arthur Mendel (*Krit. Bericht*, 1974), p. 172, in which, however, the date for the composition of BWV 23 is given as "late in 1723 or early in 1724." *NBA* II/4, pp. 251–158,

contains the version of BWV 23/4 as it appears in the St. John Passion.

37. That is, the Weimar Passion music of 1717 mentioned by Hilgenfeldt (1850); cf. Hans-Joachim Schulze, program book for the Forty-ninth Bach Festival of the "Neue Bachgesellschaft" (Frankfurt an der Oder, 1974), p. 84. The hypothesis of a Weimar origin of BWV 23/4 was also advanced by Martin Geck, "Bachs Probestück," p. 67.

38. For the time being, there is no explanation for the figures given in the fourth movement of the autograph violoncello part. Possibly the part was here used as a harpsichord part in C minor; for movements 1–3, the harpsichord player might have used the score, which did not contain the fourth movement.

POSTSCRIPT

For a closer analysis of the continuo performance problems, see Laurence D. Dreyfus, *Bach's Continuo Group: Players and Practices in His Vocal Works* (Cambridge, Mass., 1987), pp. 33, 38, 42, 113.

Kobayashi *Chr*, p. 7, determined that the extant cornetto and trombone parts were added in 1724 and thus were not used in the 1723 performance. However, the participation of these instruments appears to have been necessary on two grounds. (1) The transposition to B minor can hardly have been necessitated by any other reason than the Chorton brass participation. (2) The sources of Graupner's audition pieces point to the "security blanket" value of *colla parte* accompaniment, especially for the purpose of an audition. The cornetto/trombone parts of 1724 might, therefore, be considered replacements for the lost 1723 parts, analogous to the function of the SATB insertions as a replacement for the 1723 set.

For Bach's "Weimar Passion" and the connection with BWV 23/4, see *Bach Compendium* I/3, D 1.

11. Origins of the Kyrie of the B Minor Mass

1. *NBA* II/1, (Kassel, 1955; *Krit. Bericht*, 1956).

2. SPK, Mus. ms. autogr. Bach P 180.

3. See Arnold Schering, "Die Hohe Messe in h-moll. Eine Huldigungsmusik und Krönungsmesse für Friedrich August II," *BJ* 1936, pp. 1ff. Of special significance is Schering's hypothesis, so far not disproved, that the *Missa* might have been first heard in the service in celebration of the new elector's accession to the throne, at St. Nicholas's in Leipzig, 21 April 1733. His assumption, however, that the entire B Minor Mass was intended as a Coronation Mass for the festivities on 17 January 1734 at the Cracow

Cathedral has since been shown to be erroneous in Friedrich Smend, "Bachs h-moll-Messe. Entstehung, Überlieferung, Bedeutung," *BJ* 1937, pp. 1–58.

4. A *terminus post quem* for the Masses BWV 233–236 is essentially given in various cases by the dates for the cantatas BWV 17, 40, 72, 79, 102, 138, 179, 187, and Anh. 18, single movements from which served for parodies. See also the dates given for the Masses in A Major and G Major in Dürr *Chr*, p. 116.

5. Spitta III, pp. 28f., and Wilhelm Rust, *BG* 11/1 (1862), preface, p. xiv. See also Wolff *Stile antico*, pp. 159–172.

6. A first compilation of source materials for the life and work of Wilderer is contained in Gerhard Steffen's *Johann Hugo von Wilderer (1670–1724). Kapellmeister am kurpfälzischen Hofe zu Düsseldorf und Mannheim.* Beiträge zur rheinischen Musikgeschichte, vol. 40 (Cologne, 1960). On pages 50 and 106 appear references to the Mass, which on pages 159–162, regrettably, is given only superficial and in part erroneous description (cf. note 23); nor are conclusions drawn from the fact that Bach dealt with this Mass.

7. There is a comparable background history for the Passion settings, in that Bach devoted detailed study to the genre prior to their composition, demonstrably having acquainted himself with texts by Christian Heinrich Postel, Salomo Franck, Barthold Heinrich Brockes, and Christian Friedrich Hunold, as well as with settings by Reinhard Keiser and Handel. See especially Alfred Dürr, "Zu den verschollenen Passionen Bachs," *BJ* 1949–50, pp. 82ff.; Friedrich Smend, *Bach in Köthen* (Berlin, 1951), pp. 123ff.; Walter Serauky, "Die 'Johannes-Passion' von Joh. Seb. Bach und ihr Vorbild," *BJ* 1954, pp. 29–39; Arthur Mendel, "Traces of the Pre-History of Bach's St. John and St. Matthew Passions," *Festschrift für Otto Erich Deutsch* (Kassel, 1963), pp. 31ff.

8. Paul Kast, *Die Bach-Handschriften der Berliner Staatsbibliothek*, Tübinger Bach-Studien, vol. 2/3 (Trossingen, 1958), makes no mention of this manuscript under the rubric "Fremde Kompositionen in der Handschrift J. S. Bachs" (p. 96).

9. Watermark: Saxon Electoral coat of arms (Weiss, no. 26). Variants of this watermark are found in Bach's letters of 7 September 1728 and 25 August 1733.

10. See the estate listing published by Heinrich Miesner in *BJ* 1939, p. 96. The performing parts mentioned there are no longer extant. A comparison with the autograph title of the score (see Fig. 11.1)

shows that, because of the form of the final *r*, the name, which had lost any degree of currency by 1790, was erroneously given as *Wilderez.*

11. The note *"Von Joh. Sebast. Bachs Hand,"* which appears in the manuscript on the first score page (see Fig. 11.1), is by Georg Poelchau.

12. A collection of music was dispatched in 1713 by the young Duke Johann Ernst of Saxe-Weimar to the Düsseldorf court, where Wilderer was active; see Alfred Einstein, "Italienische Musiker am Hofe der Neuburger Wittelsbacher," *Sammelbände der Internationalen Musikgesellschaft* 9 (1906–08), p. 413. The type of paper and forms of Bach's manuscript, however, preclude the assumption that this copy of the Mass could be dated as early as the Weimar period, an assumption that would be based on the Weimar-Düsseldorf connections. But it is possible that, aside from others, these connections served to supply Bach and Johann Gottfried Walther, both of them teachers of Duke Johann Ernst, as well as their circle with Italian literature in particular (Vivaldi, Marcello, Legrenzi, Corelli, etc.). The entry "Wilderer" in Walther's *Lexikon* (1732), however, makes no mention of this Mass.

13. See Werner David, *J. S. Bachs Orgeln* (Berlin, 1951), p. 58, and *Dok* I, p. 32.

14. Spitta III, pp. 226ff.

15. Schering's assumption (in "Die Hohe Messe in h-moll," p. 9), that the work was written on commission, must remain open.

16. *Dok* I, p. 74.

17. Cf. Arnold Schering, "Die alte Chorbibliothek der Thomasschule in Leipzig," *Archiv für Musikwissenschaft* 1 (1918–19), pp. 275ff.

18. See Steffen, *Johann Hugo von Wilderer.*

19. Nor does Bach's Missa include the genre of *da capo* aria, which in the opera, cantata, and oratorio of the period was customary. Bach is in this respect close to the Neapolitans who included the *da capo* aria in the free forms of church music, but not—save for some exceptions—in the setting of the Mass text. This distinction is strictly observed, for instance, in Hasse's entire sacred oeuvre, which, in distinction to his secular works, excludes the *da capo* aria altogether; cf. Walther Müller, *Johann Adolf Hasse als Kirchenkomponist* (Ph.D. diss., Leipzig, 1910), p. 11.

20. *Grave* introductions for the Kyrie are found in the Masses in G, C, D, F, and A major by Giovanni Battista Bassani. Bach's copies of six Bassani Masses from the latter's *Acroama Missale*, however, belong without doubt in the period of about 1740 and thus are not of consequence in this connection; cf. Georg von Dadelsen, "Eine unbekannte Messenbearbeitung

Bachs," *Festschrift für Karl Gustav Fellerer* (Regensburg, 1962), pp. 88ff. Slow introductions were also contained in two further sources: an undated and no longer extant continuo (violoncello) part for an unidentified Mass in C Minor (BWV Anh. 29) and a fragmentary bass part, probably belonging to an unidentified Kyrie; (cf. Alfred Dürr, "Marginalia Bachiana," *Die Musikforschung* 4 (1951), pp. 374f., and *NBA* I/2 (*Krit. Bericht*, 1957), pp. 8f.

21. An important consideration is that the autograph score (SPK, P 180) represents a composing score. The latter point has been convincingly stated by Friedrich Smend ("Bachs h-moll-Messe," *Krit. Bericht*, pp. 98ff.), with whose view Dadelsen *Chr*, p. 147, concurs.

22. The tempo indication *adagio* is not marked in the score but is contained in the original performance material preserved at the Sächsische Landesbibliothek Dresden, Mus. 2405 D 21, Aut. 2 (cf. Smend, p. 237).

23. Steffen, *Johann Hugo von Wilderer*, p. 162, is in error in his description of the Kyrie introduction when he says that "the word Kyrie, as an invocation, is first heard on three chords supported by the orchestral accompaniment colla parte." Other descriptions, as well, are incorrect, e.g., that "the orchestral texture is essentially a colla parte reinforcement," or that the violin parts represent predominantly an octave doubling of the inner vocal parts, or that "folk-like German melodies" might be discerned in the setting.

24. Ibid., p. 11, as well as Schering's monograph, *Johann Sebastian Bach und das Musikleben Leipzigs im 18. Jahrhundert*, Musikgeschichte Leipzigs, vol. 3 (Leipzig, 1941), p. 217.

25. This movement—as was not pointed out by Schering—returns as a parody, as early as 1728, in the opening chorus "Klagt Kinder, klagt es aller Welt" of the cantata written as a memorial tribute to Prince Leopold of Anhalt-Cöthen (BWV 244a); in 1731 it served again for a parody in the opening chorus "Geh, Jesu, geh zu deiner Pein" of the St. Mark Passion (BWV 247).

26. To apply terms of psychologizing, as it were, seems a rather questionable procedure as applied to Bach's creative work. Furthermore, the period of mourning here concerned relates to Augustus the Strong (d. 1 February 1733), not to his consort, whose death had occurred six years earlier. A direct connection with the Funeral Ode could therefore not possibly exist.

27. The recurrence of harmonic or rhythmic-melodic models in different works by Bach does not

necessarily signify a derivation of one composition from another; cf. Georg Reichert, "Harmoniemodelle in Johann Sebastian Bachs Musik," *Festschrift Friedrich Blume zum 70. Geburtstag*, ed. Anna Amalie Abert and Wilhelm Pfannkuch (Kassel, 1963), pp. 281ff., and Ulrich Siegele, "Von Bachschen Modellen und Zeitarten," *Festschrift Walter Gerstenberg zum 60. Geburtstag*, ed. Georg von Dadelsen and Andreas Holschneider (Wolfenbüttel, 1964), pp. 162ff.

28. Added to the normal string scoring are: Flauto traverso I/II, Oboe d'amore I/II, Viola da gamba I/II, and Liuto I/II.

29. The conformation of the two woodwind parts represents as such a somewhat simplified version of the vocal parts.

30. See the introduction to my edition, Johann Sebastian Bach, Kyrie "Christe, du Lamm Gottes" BWV 233a (Berlin: Merseburger, 1963).

31. The dominant-oriented opening of Wilderer's work involves a different placing of half-tone steps.

32. They are especially relevant to mm. 44ff. and 61ff. in Bach's duet.

33. Of relevance to the interpretation of the meaning of "Christe eleison" in Bach's work—which cannot be dealt with in greater detail within the present context—are the slightly later duets "Ich bin deine, du bist meine" from the Hercules Cantata BWV 213 and its parody "Herr, dein Mitleid, dein Erbarmen" from Part III of the Christmas Oratorio. There the solo voices are written in a correspondingly parallel motion; the texts themselves are related both to one another and to "Christe eleison." For an explanation of a basic "affection" linking the works, we might doubtless refer to the concept of "union," "affiance," and the like, in its sacred as well as secular connotations. Cf. Arnold Schmitz, "Die oratorische Kunst J. S. Bachs—Grundfragen und Grundlagen," *Bericht über den musikwissenschaftlichen Kongreß,* Lüneburg 1950 (Kassel, 1950), pp. 47f.

34. The theme for "Christe eleison" from Hasse's Requiem in C Major/C Minor (SPK, Mus. ms. 9475) shows an interesting similarity with Bach's theme, especially in its beginning (see example below). Hasse wrote this Requiem at the time of the death of Friedrich August II of Saxony (Augustus III of Poland), 22 November 1763 (cf. Walther Müller, *Johann Adolf Hasse,* p. 79). The work was addressed to the same ruler to whom Bach's Missa was dedicated thirty years earlier "in deepest devotion" and possibly performed in a service of homage at Leipzig.

Bach had gone to Dresden on the occasion of the 1731 premiere of Hasse's opera *Cleofide* (cf. Spitta III, p. 226). Forkel (p. 47; *Bach Reader,* p. 335) reports: "Hasse and his wife, the celebrated Faustina, had also come several times to Leipzig, and admired his great talents." We can assume that an exchange, at least with regard to some of their principal compositions, might have taken place, so that Hasse would have known Bach's Missa and various other works. It is also possible that some consultation with the principal employees of court music would have taken place in connection with the conferral of the title of court composer and that at such an occasion Hasse would have seen Bach's Missa. One might conjecture that Hasse, in composing a Requiem in memory of the ruler in whose honor Bach and he himself had written a number of celebratory works, consciously quoted his great Leipzig colleague in this small gesture—though we also may be dealing with a merely accidental conformance.

35. This spirit is evident even in the appearance of notation: Bach applies the breve as measure unit.

36. Three of the nine movements are parodies: Gloria, Gratias, and Qui tollis (cf. Smend, "Bachs h-moll-Messe," *Krit. Bericht,* table, p. 192).

POSTSCRIPT
The proposed dating, 1729–1731, of Bach's copy of the Wilderer Mass has been confirmed by Hans-Joachim Schulze, *Studien zur Bach-Überlieferung im 18. Jahrhundert* (Leipzig, 1984), pp. 107–108. See also "The Mass in B Minor: The Autograph Scores and the Compositional Process," in Marshall *Bach,* pp. 175–180. For further details regarding compositional and performance history of Bach's 1733 Missa, see *Bach Compendium* I/3, E1.

12. The Reformation Cantata "Ein feste Burg"

1. *"Ein feste Burg ist unser Gott." Cantata für vier Singstimmen mit Begleitung des Orchesters . . . nach J. S. Bachs Original-Handschrift.* The editor was J. C. F. Schneider, organist of St. Thomas's from 1813 to 1817, who in later years became well-known as an oratorio composer.

2. Friedrich Rochlitz, *Allgemeine Musikalische Zeitung* 30 (1822), p. 486.

3. Ed. W. Rust; Critical Report, pp. xxii ff.

4. Fritz Volbach, "Ein feste Burg ist unser Gott: Eine Studie," *BJ* 1905, pp. 68–75.

Chri - ste,   Chri - ste,   Chri - ste e - le - i - son,...

5. See entry in BWV; Alfred Dürr, *Studien über die frühen Kantaten Johann Sebastian Bachs* (Leipzig, 1951; rev. ed., Wiesbaden, 1977), pp. 64, 161ff.

6. See the entry in BWV and Werner Neumann, *Handbuch der Kantaten Johann Sebastian Bachs,* 4th ed. (Leipzig, 1971), p. 105.

7. Dürr *Chr,* p. 164; Carl Ludwig Hilgenfeldt, *Johann Sebastian Bachs Leben, Wirken und Werke* (Leipzig, 1850), p. 104.

8. Paris, Adam Mickiewicz Museum.

9. Leningrad, Saltykov-Shchedrin Library, discovered by Wolf Hobohm (Magdeburg). The provenance of the two joining fragments from the East suggests the same sequence of ownership as applies to several other Bach sources located in Poland and Russia (cf. this volume, Chapter 14). Grateful acknowledgment is made to the Johann-Sebastian-Bach-Institut, Göttingen, for permission to examine the source material for BWV 80.

10. Cf. Dürr, *Studien,* pp. 74ff.

11. The year cycle of chorale cantatas did not begin until the first Sunday after Trinity, 1724; it is possible that BWV 80 was subsequently revived.

12. DSB, Am. B. 556.

13. "Gaudete omnes populi," SPK, Mus. ms. Bach P 72; "Manebit verbum Domini," Library of Congress, Washington, D.C., ML 96, B 186, case.

14. SPK, Mus. ms. Bach P 177.

15. Wolff *Stile antico;* the list of *stile antico* compositions from the 1730s and 1740s, which provide the focus of this study, will have to be supplemented by the original version of BWV 80/1, for the chorale motet movement BWV 80/1 displays all the essential features of Bach's *stile antico* manner as discussed on pp. 36ff.

16. Among Bach's cantata movements there exists only one other setting with a comparable structure: the opening chorus of BWV 77, "Du sollt Gott, deinen Herren, lieben," of 1723. In this piece, the outer parts, Tromba da tirarsi and Continuo, constitute a canon of the fifth and, as in BWV 80/1, the continuo presents the canonic voice in augmentation. But unlike BWV 80/1 the continuo doubles the viola line in *bassetto* style during the non-canonic passages. Thus the continuo in BWV 77/1 alternates between *bassetto* function (free counterpoint; mm. 1–8, 15–24a, etc.) and genuine bass function (*cantus firmus;* mm. 9–14, 24b–30, etc.), whereas BWV 80/1, being the more sophisticated composition, operates throughout with two simultaneous bass parts.

17. SPK, Mus. ms. Bach P 71.

18. Cf. Laurence Dreyfus, "Zur Frage der Cembalo-Mitwirkung in den geistlichen Werken Bachs," in *Bachforschung und Bach-Interpretation heute*

(Conference Report of the Bach-Symposium held at the 1978 Bach Festival in Marburg), ed. Reinhold Brinkmann (Kassel, 1981), pp. 178–184.

POSTSCRIPT

A third clipping from the first page of Bach's autograph score turned up on the antiquarian market unexpectedly in 1983 and was subsequently acquired by Mr. William H. Scheide, Princeton, New Jersey, whom I wish to thank for giving me access to it.

With this addition, the first page of Bach's autograph score can now be almost completely restored (but there is still no trace of the whereabouts of the subsequent pages). Figure 12.1, replacing the single facsimile of the Paris fragment that appeared in the original article, represents a composite facsimile of all three fragments. As the emended score (Ex. 12.1) shows, the opening chorale can be restored nearly in its entirety; incidentally, the added third fragment basically corroborates my hypothetical reconstruction of 1982. Figure 12.1 and Example 12.1 are reprinted, with kind permission, from *NBA* I/31, which incorporates—in the passages marked by small print—my reconstruction.

The critical edition in *NBA* I/31 (ed. Frieder Rempp, 1987), pp. 67–70, presents for the first time what remains of the earlier version of the Reformation Cantata BWV 80b. For the sources and performance history of the various cantata versions see *Bach Compendium* I/2, A 183a–b.

13. The Handexemplar of the Goldberg Variations

1. See Georg Kinsky, *Die Originalausgaben der Werke Johann Sebastian Bachs* (Vienna, 1937), for a bibliographical overview.

2. DSB, Mus. ms. Bach P 271, pp. 100–106.

3. SPK, Mus. ms. Bach P 225, pp. 1–41 (early versions of BWV 827 and 830).

4. DSB, Mus. ms. Bach P 226, pp. 1–4 (early version of the six-part ricercar).

5. DSB, Mus. ms. Bach P 200.

6. For a detailed discussion, see J. S. Bach, *Klavierübung: Teil II und IV, NBA* V/2, *Krit. Bericht,* ed. Walter Emery and Christoph Wolff (Kassel, 1977).

7. See J. S. Bach, *Dritter Teil der Klavierübung, NBA* IV/4, *Krit. Bericht,* ed. Manfred Tessmer (Kassel, 1974), pp. 16f.

8. See *J. S. Bachs Kompositionen für die Orgel,* ed. Friedrich Conrad Griepenkerl and Ferdinand Roitzsch, vols. 6, 7 (Leipzig, 1845), preface. The copy was not available for scholarly investigations for well over a century and has only recently been ac-

quired by William H. Scheide. See this volume, Chapter 14.

9. I wish to thank Mr. Blumenroeder for his kindness in allowing me to examine his copy of this edition on various occasions during the spring of 1975 in Strasbourg and Freiburg. The Bibliothèque Nationale in Paris purchased the source in November 1975 and now lists it as MS 17 669.

10. *NBA* V/2.

11. For further details on the discovery of the source, see Olivier Alain, "Un supplement inédit aux 'Variations Goldberg' de Jean-Sebastien Bach," *Revue de musicologie* 61 (1975), pp. 244–294.

12. Possibly identical with the copy in London, British Library, Hirsch Collection, III.37; cf. J. S. Bach, *Klavierübung: Teil I, NBA* V/1, *Krit. Bericht*, ed. Richard Jones (Kassel, 1976).

13. See *Dok* III, pp. 227f. According to C. P. E. Bach's letter to Forkel of 9 August 1774, he kept his father's autograph (now lost) of the third part of the Clavier-Übung for himself.

14. For further details, see *NBA* V/2, *Krit. Bericht*.

15. The first critical edition of these canons was published by Bärenreiter-Verlag, Kassel, in the spring of 1976, prior to their appearance in *NBA*. They have been designated no. 1087 in the revised edition of the BWV by Wolfgang Schmieder.

16. Johann Friedrich Agricola, review of treatise by J. A. Hiller in *Allgemeine deutsche Bibliothek* 25, no. 1 (Berlin, 1775), p. 108.

17. Johann Philipp Kirnberger, *Die Kunst des reinen Satzes in der Musik*, II/1 (Berlin, 1776), p. 129.

18. For a discussion of the history of this subject, see Rudolf Flotzinger, "Die Gagliarda Italiana: Zur Frage der barocken Thementypologie," *Acta musicologica* 39 (1967), pp. 92–100; *NBA* V/2, *Krit. Bericht*. It should be noted that the total number of measures of the aria (thirty-two) concurs with the total number of movements in the entire work (including thirty variations plus the aria at the beginning and end). The composer thus seems to have sought a harmonious structural module in planning the design of this work.

19. Friedrich Smend, *J. S. Bach: Kirchen-Kantaten*, vol. 3 (Berlin, 1947), pp. 5–21.

20. The sources of BWV 1076 and 1077 are discussed in detail in J. S. Bach, *Kanons: Musikalisches Opfer, NBA* VIII/1, *Krit. Bericht* (Kassel, 1974), pp. 18–29.

21. BWV 1072–1078, 1083; Bach, *Kanons, NBA* VIII/1, *Krit. Bericht*, pp. 3–10.

22. See Walter Emery, "The Goldberg Engraver,"

Musical Times 104 (1963), p. 875; Emery, "Schmid and the Goldberg," *Musical Times* 105 (1964), 350.

23. See Dadelsen *Chr*, pp. 85ff.

24. Johann Joseph Fux, *Gradus ad Parnassum* (Vienna, 1725); annotated German trans., ed. Lorenz Christoph Mizler (Leipzig, 1742), plates 29, 27, 30. Cf. Wolff *Stile antico*, pp. 61f.

25. *The Well-Tempered Clavier* was completed by 1742 at the very latest, a fact that must be taken into account upon considering the chronological relationship of this fugue to the fourteen canons. On the date, see Dadelsen *Chr*, p. 109.

26. The principle of melodic inversion, incidentally, is not yet utilized substantially in the canonic movements of the Goldberg Variations, the only exceptions being variations 12 and 15.

27. See Dadelsen *Chr*, pp. 113ff.

28. In fact, three out of four subjects (those of the Goldberg Variations, Musical Offering, and Variations on Vom Himmel hoch) were not invented by Bach but, at least in their rudimentary forms, adopted.

29. See Wolff *Stile antico*.

30. Bach's attention to new trends is particularly evident in compositions such as the Prelude, Fugue, and Allegro for Lute BWV 998, the Peasant Cantata of 1742 BWV 212, or the slow movement of the trio sonata in *the Musical Offering* (1747).

POSTSCRIPT

The *Krit. Bericht* of my edition of the Goldberg Variations and the fourteen canons in *NBA* V/2 (1977), presents a more detailed account of the sources as well as the various philological and historical problems. Kobayashi *Chr* dates the autograph appendix to Bach's Handexemplar containing canons BWV 1087 to 1747–1748. For a discussion of canon 10, see Günter Hartmann, "BWV 1087/10: 'Evolutiones' eines Bach-Kanons," *Musiktheorie* 5 (1990), pp. 85–93.

14. Bach's Personal Copy of the Schübler Chorales

1. Around 1890 Bach's personal copy of Clavier-Übung II surfaced in Dresden (today it is in the British Library, London, under the call number K.8.g.7); see Walter Emery, *NBA* V/2, *Krit. Bericht* (1981). In 1975 the Handexemplar of the Goldberg Variations emerged (now in the Bibliothèque Nationale, Paris, under the call number Ms. 17 669); see Christoph Wolff, *NBA* V/2, *Krit. Bericht* (1981); and Chapter 13, above. Richard D. Jones presents arguments in *NBA* V/1, *Krit. Bericht* (1978), that

the copy of Clavier-Übung I in the British Library (Hirsch Collection III.37) is Bach's Handexemplar. On the supposed and actual composer's copy of Clavier-Übung III, see section II, below. For a related discussion of Bach's personal copies of his original editions, see also this volume, Chapter 16.

2. *BG* 25/2 (1878), p. xv. In the mid-1950s at the Bach-Archiv in Leipzig a certain Aleksaner Ewert from Poland was known as the owner of the *Handexemplar* in question. The original itself, however, was never seen (oral communication from Hans-Joachim Schulze).

3. William H. Scheide, of Princeton, obtained it from Albi Rosenthal, a book dealer in Oxford, England. Special thanks go to Mr. Scheide for his kind permission to examine the source and for providing the author with photographs of it.

4. Joseph Joachim was at that time director of the Musikhochschule in Berlin; Spitta had served the Musikhochschule as deputy director since 1879.

5. Perhaps the pianist and music historian Franciszek Bylicki, a student of Czartoryska (conjecture of Albi Rosenthal, Oxford).

6. See Hans-Joachim Schulze, "Das 'Kleine Magnificat' BWV Anh. 21 und sein Komponist," *Musikforschung* 21 (1968), p. 44.

7. In its present, unbound state, Bach's Handexemplar of the Schübler Chorales has the following structure:

```
┌ — — — (title page; musical text, page 1)
└——————— (musical text, pp. 2 – 3)
┌——————— (musical text, pp. 4 – 5)
│┌—————— (musical text, pp. 6 – 7)
│└—————— (musical text, pp. 8 – 9)
└——————— (musical text, pp. 10 – 11)
┌——————— (musical text, pp. 12 – 13)
└——————— (musical text, p. 14; reverse side, blank)
```

The pages were printed singly in oblong format (plate size: 17 × 28 cm). The appropriate pages were then glued together at the left vertical margins to form double pages. Finally, the double pages were folded and arranged in the manner shown above.

8. *Dok* III, no. 793.

9. *Dok* III, no. 792.

10. *Verzeichnis der von dem verstorbenen Doctor und Musikdirector Forkel in Göttingen nachgelassenen Bücher und Musikalien* (Göttingen, 1819), p. 136, no. 59.

11. Georg Kinsky, *Die Originalausgaben der Werke Johann Sebastian Bachs* (Vienna, 1937; Hilversum, Netherlands, 1968), p. 60.

12. *NBA* IV/4, (1974), p. 16. This view is also promulgated in the commentary to *Dok* III, no. 792, as well as in note 1 to Chapter 13, above.

13. Tessmer presents this copy of the print as Source A6 in the *Krit. Bericht* of *NBA* IV/4 without a more-detailed description. Peter Krause, in his catalogue *Originalausgaben und ältere Drucke der Werke Johann Sebastian Bachs in der Musikbibliothek der Stadt Leipzig* (Leipzig, 1970), clearly delineates the transmission of the copy from Griepenkerl to Rust (p. 77), but does not report Griepenkerl's remark on the cover and the descent of the print from Forkel's estate. In the foreword to vol. 6 of the Peters edition of the organ works (1847), Griepenkerl noted: "Nos. 2 and 3 [that is, Clavier-Übung III and the Schübler Chorales] are original editions from Forkel's estate and are now in my possession." The copy PM 1403 contains no striking autograph entries, but merits closer inspection in this regard. The Peters facsimile edition, edited by Christoph Wolff (Leipzig, 1984), is based on this copy.

14. Kinsky's comments *(Die Originalausgaben,* p. 60) on the Berlin copy—"Its present condition shows that a second print was bound to it and later cut out of the binding: the *Handexemplar* of the organ chorales"—remain enigmatic and could not be substantiated by Tessmer.

15. The front flyleaf has not survived.

16. The alignment of the sixteenth notes and the triplets in mm. 16, 26, etc., is misleading in the recently published *NBA* IV/1 (1983; pp. 99–100), ed. Heinz-Harald Löhlein. The sixteenth notes of the pedal are placed after the third note of each group of triplets, implying that the sixteenth notes are to be interpreted at face value, that is, as dotted figures falling after the last note of each triplet group. To judge from the manner in which such passages are aligned in other Bach works (the Prelude in C Minor, BWV 546/1, for example, where in manuscripts stemming from the Bach circle the sixteenth notes are placed directly above or below the third note of each triplet group) and from contemporary performance practices, it seems most likely that the sixteenth notes would be interpreted as the last third of a triplet figure, played in time with the triplets of the left hand.

17. Dadelsen *Chr,* pp. 113–118.

18. See the commentary to *Dok* I, no. 175.

19. Arguments for the appearance of the Schübler Chorales after the publication of the Musical Offering (1747), which was also printed by Schübler, are presented in *NBA* VIII/1, *Krit. Bericht,* ed. Christoph Wolff (1976), pp. 108–109.

20. Since the original score of Cantata 137, from which the manuscript copy for the print must have been made, is no longer available, one cannot ascertain if lack of clarity in the autograph was responsible for the error-ridden Reading 2 (see the case of the original score of Cantata 10, described above). Of the manuscripts used for writing out the Schübler transcriptions, only one besides the autograph score of Cantata 10 (the model for "Meine Seele erhebt den Herren" BWV 648) has survived: the original score for Cantata 6 (the model for "Ach bleib' bei uns, Herr Jesu Christ," BWV 649), preserved in Berlin, SPK, under the shelfmark P 44.

POSTSCRIPT
The new critical edition of the Schübler Chorales in *NBA* IV/1 (ed. Heinz-Harald Löhlein, 1983) takes Bach's Handexemplar into consideration. Its hitherto uncertain intermediate owner, who corresponded with Spitta, could recently be identified as Dr. von Bylicki of Krakow (Poland); see my article, "From Berlin to Lódz: The Spitta Collection Resurfaces," *Notes* 46 (1989), p. 319.

15. The Clavier-Übung Series

1. *Dok* II, no. 276.
2. Georg Philipp Telemann, *Der getreue / Musik-Meister / welcher so wol für Sänger als die Instrumentalisten / allerhand Gattungen musicalischer Stücke / so auf verschiedene Stimmen und fast alle gebräuchliche Instrumente / gerichtet sind / und / moralische, Opern- und andere Arien / desgleichen / Trii, Duetti, Soli etc. / Sonaten, Ouverturen etc. / wie auch / Fugen, Contrapuncte, Canones etc. enthalten / mithin / das mehreste, was nur in der Musik vorkommen mag, / nach Italiänischer, Französischer, Englischer, Polnischer, etc / so ernsthaft- als lebhaft- und lustigen Ahrt / . . . vorzutragen gedenket. . .* (Hamburg, 1728–1729).

3. Man sagt: Daß, wenn Orpheus die Laute
    sonst geschlagen,
Hab alle Thiere er in Wäldern zu sich
    bracht;
Gewiß, man muß diß mehr von unserm
    Bache sagen.
Weil er, so bald er spielt, ja alles
    staunend macht

(*Dok* II, no. 294; trans., *Bach Reader*, p. 226).
4. For the title pages of Parts I-IV, see Figures 15.3, 15.5, 15.7, and 15.9.
5. Compared with this more simple and

straightforward explanation, the often-propagated symbolic interpretation of the large and small chorale movements as relating to Martin Luther's two Catechisms, large and small, or the idea that the duets represent an allusion to the four elements, seem rather far-fetched.
6. *Bach Reader*, p. 223.
7. *Dok* II, no 527.
8. *Carl Burney's der Musik Doctors Tagebuch seiner Musikalischen Reisen,* vol. 3 (Hamburg, 1773; rpt., Kassel, 1959), p. 203.
9. As a consequence, the use of metal stamps with which to prick the plates was developed during Bach's time in London.
10. See Gregory G. Butler, "Leipziger Stecher in Bachs Originaldrucken," *BJ* 1980, pp. 9–26.
11. See Butler, "Leipziger Stecher," which refers to this artist as Engraver K III.
12. *Dok* IV, no. 264; see also nos. 126, 130, 413.
13. Musikbibliothek der Stadt Leipzig: Sammlung Becker, III.6.13.
14. DSB, Mus. ms. Bach St 162; copied in 1724–25 by Bach's nephew, Johann Heinrich Bach (formerly, principal copyist C).
15. *Dok* II, no. 224.
16. *Dok* II, no. 224.
17. *Dok* II, no. 224.
18. See section above, "The Technical Aspects of Printing."
19. See Butler, "Leipziger Stecher."
20. *Dok* II, no. 323.
21. For a discussion of the details concerning the differences between the various editions and the handwritten authentic corrections, see *NBA* V/I, *Krit. Bericht;* see also "Text-Critical Comments on the Original Print of Bach's Partitas," this volume, Chapter 16.
22. See *Dok* II, no. 323, as well as nos. 232, 366, and 370.
23. *Dok* II, no. 463; trans., *Bach Reader*, p. 234.
24. See Butler, "Leipziger Stecher," which refers to this engraver as Engraver K I.
25. London, British Library, K.8.g.7.
26. DSB, Mus. ms. Bach P 226 (cf. *NBA* V/2, *Krit. Bericht,* pp. 14–15).
27. Boston [Massachusetts] Public Library, Allen A. Brown Collection, MS M.200.12.
28. *Dok* II, no. 455.
29. *Dok* II, no. 434.
30. See Butler, "Leipziger Stecher."
31. *Dok* II, no. 377.
32. See Butler, "Leipziger Stecher" (Engraver K III).

33. See *NBA* IV/4, *Krit. Bericht*, pp. 14–16.

34. At a later point, in the early 1770s, Johann Philipp Kirnberger discussed Bach's treatment of the church modes in these chorale settings (see *Dok* III, no. 812).

35. *Dok* II, pp. 304f.

36. *Dok* II, no. 389.

37. *Dok* II, no. 481; trans., *Bach Reader*, p. 235.

38. Paris, Bibliothèque Nationale, Ms. 17669 (see this volume, Chapter 13).

39. *Vierzehn Kanons BWV 1087*, ed. C. Wolff, *NBA* V/2 (Kassel, 1977), pp. 119–28; see also the separate edition (Kassel: Bärenreiter, 1976).

40. *Bach Reader*, p. 339.

POSTSCRIPT

This chapter was originally written and published as introduction and commentary to a complete facsimile edition of the four parts of Bach's Clavier-Übung (Leipzig: Peters, 1984). Compared with the original version, the illustrations in this chapter have been reduced to two (Figs. 15.1 and 15.2); the title pages of the single issues of Partitas II–V were omitted. On the other hand, Figs. 15.3–15.10 (title page and first page of music from each part of the Clavier-Übung series) were added (reprinted from the facsimile edition, with the kind permission of the publisher).

The original version of this chapter included some supplementary bibliographical information: see Kinsky; Christoph Wolff, "Die Originaldrucke J. S. Bachs: Einführung und Verzeichnis," in *Die Nürnberger Drucke von J. S. und C. P. E. Bach* (Nuremberg, 1973), pp. 15–20; and Wolff, "Principles of Design and Order in Bach's Original Editions," this volume, Chapter 27. On printing technology, see Georg Andreas Böckler, *Radier-Büchlein* (Nuremberg, 1689); Abraham Bosse, *Gründliche Anweisung zur Radier und Etzkunst* (Nuremberg, 1761); Bosse, *Die Kunst in Kupfer zu stechen, sowohl vermittelst des Aetzwaßers als mit dem Grabstichel . . . ehemals durch Abraham Boße . . . herausgegeben. Jetzo aber aufs neue durchgesehen, verbeßert und um die Hälfte vermehret* (Dresden, 1765); Johann Samuel Halle, *Werkstäte der heutigen Künste* (Leipzig, 1761), vol. 1, pp. 195–240; and Christoph Wolff, *NBA* VIII/1, *Krit. Bericht* (Leipzig, Kassel, 1976), pp. 52–55. The Clavier-Übung collections were published by Peters in facsimile, with commentary by Christoph Wolff, under the title *Clavier-Übung. Teil I–IV* (Leipzig, 1984). See also *NBA* V/1 (Book I, ed. R. D. Jones), *Krit. Bericht* (1978); *NBA* V/2 (Books II and IV, ed. W. Emery and C. Wolff), *Krit. Bericht* (1977); and *NBA* IV/4 (Book III, ed.

M. Teßmer), *Krit. Bericht* (1969). Chapters 13 and 16 in this volume give additional details on the Goldberg Variations and Partitas I–VI, respectively.

For further points, see also my essay, "Johann Sebastian Bach's Third Part of the *Clavier-Übung*," in *Charles Brenton Fisk, Organ Builder*, vol. 1: *Essays in His Honor*, ed. Fenner Douglass et al. (Easthampton, Mass., 1986), pp. 283–291. My suggestion to consider the possibility of Bach's performing pieces from Clavier-Übung III at his organ recital on 1 December 1736 on the new Silbermann organ of the Dresden Frauenkirche needs to take into account the unequal temperament typical of Silbermann's instruments and the limitations resulting from it. This means that, for example, the Prelude in E♭ Major BWV 552/1 containing a section in B♭ minor would not have been playable.

As for the authorship of the "Goldberg" theme, questioned by Frederick Neumann, see the refutation of its "un-Bachian" qualities in Marshall *Bach*, pp. 57–58.

The publication date, 1741, of the Goldberg Variations has in the meantime been verified by Gregory Butler (who in 1968–69 took part in the first graduate seminar I taught in North America, at the University of Toronto), in "Neues zur Datierung der Goldberg-Variationen," *BJ* 1988, pp. 219–223. Butler has advanced research on Bach's original prints to a considerable degree during the past twelve years. From among his various individual studies, his recent monograph, *Bach's Clavierübung III: The Making of a Print, With a Companion Study of the Canonic Variations on Vom Himmel Hoch BWV 769* (Durham, N.C., 1990), provides particularly important and illuminating information; for instance, he was able to differentiate among three different engravers from the Krügner workshop in Leipzig. See also his article, "Clavier-Übung II and a Nuremberg-Leipzig Engraving Connection," in *A Bach Tribute: Essays in Honor of William H. Scheide*, ed. Paul Brainard and Ray Robinson (Kassel, 1991).

16. Text-Critical Comments on the Original Print of the Partitas

1. Georg Kinsky, *Die Originalausgaben der Werke Johann Sebastian Bachs* (Vienna, Leipzig, Zurich, 1937).

2. See *NBA* IV/1, ed. Manfred Teßmer (*Krit. Bericht*, 1974), and *NBA* VIII/1, ed. Christoph Wolff (*Krit. Bericht*, 1976).

3. See this volume, Chapters 13 and 14.

4. Aside from those mentioned, the following

copies are also considered Handexemplare: London, British Library, Hirsch III.37 (= Clavier-Übung I, see below); British Library, K.8.g.7 (= Clavier-Übung II); Musikbibliothek der Stadt Leipzig, PM 1403 (= Clavier-Übung III; see above, Chapter 14). No Handexemplare are known to exist for any of the remaining original Bach prints. As will be discussed below, the concept of "Handexemplar" requires new definition.

5. See *NBA* IV/1, p. 17. (It is A6, not A1, designated as a Handexemplar by Teßmer, which is involved.)

6. The corrections are limited to the first three partitas; cf. Richard D. Jones, *NBA* V/1, *Krit. Bericht* (1978).

7. Jones, pp. 29ff. In the specific annotations (pp. 55–67) the information given about the corrections found in the copies G 24–26 are similarly sparing.

8. Special thanks are due to the members of the Music Division, especially Mr. William Parsons, for their obliging help.

9. Also found in G 26; see *NBA* VI (*Krit. Bericht*), p. 28.

10. See *NBA* V/2, ed. Walter Emery and Christoph Wolff (*Krit. Bericht,* 1981). In both cases the execution of corrections and additions is confirmed as coming from Bach's hand. To what extent Bach himself undertook the mechanical correction of printing errors remains uncertain. Nevertheless, the mending of two faintly printed systems in one of the copies for the single edition of Partita II (Musikbibliothek der Stadt Leipzig, Sammlung Becker III.6.12, p. 12), ostensibly in Bach's own hand, corroborate Bach's personal involvement (see Fig. 15.1).

11. See this volume, Chapter 13, as well as *NBA* V/2. Corrections in red ink (though not including text) also appear in G 24.

12. Tempo indication in the Handexemplar for the Goldberg Variations: "*al tempo di Giga*" (Variation 7) and "*adagio*" (Variation 25).

13. Examples are cancelling or correcting wrongly placed stems, supplying directs that were omitted, and erasing blemishes in the engraving.

14. Jones assumes that "the numerous embellishments, in particular, . . . were added arbitrarily by early owners of the volumes" (p. 31). In contradiction to this appears his observation that G 23–26 on the whole belong to the same phase of correction (Korr III) and that the entries in G 25 go back "to a single person" (p. 28).

15. Incorrectly rendered in *NBA* V/1, p. 31. The musical text presented in the *NBA* volume

♫♫♪. , curiously, is in conformance with the manuscript source H 58 (Christian Friedrich Penzel, ca. 1755–1760).

16. This trill entered parenthetically in *NBA* V/1.

17. Vienna, Österreichische Nationalbibliothek (Hoboken Collection).

18. The copies G 8–26 represent (according to Jones) the second printing, the copies G 27 and 28, the third printing. Neither of the two editions, bearing actually the date of the first printing (1731) on their respective title pages, can be dated.

17. Bach's Leipzig Chamber Music

1. For a criticism of this analogy see this volume, Chapter 1.

2. C. Wolff, *The New Grove Bach Family* (London and New York, 1983), pp. 178ff.

3. For the chamber music see in particular H. Eppstein, "Studien über J. S. Bachs Sonaten für ein Melodieinstrument und obligates Cembalo," *Acta Universitatis uppsalensis,* new ser., 2 (Uppsala, 1966); R. L. Marshall, "J. S. Bach's compositions for solo flute," *JAMS* 32 (1979), p. 463; P. Ahnsehl, K. Heller, and H.-J. Schulze, eds., "Beiträge zum Konzertschaffen J. S. Bachs," *Bach-Studien,* 6 (1981); W. Breig, "Zur Chronologie von Johann Sebastian Bachs Konzertschaffen—Versuch eines neuen Zugangs," *Archiv für Musikwissenschaft* 40 (1983), pp. 77ff.

4. *Dok* III, no. 666.

5. DSB, Mus. ms. Bach P 801.

6. See Breig, "Chronologie."

7. U. Siegele, "Bachs Stellung in der Leipziger Kulturpolitik seiner Zeit," *BJ* 69 (1983), pp. 7ff; 70 (1984), pp. 7ff.

8. For the history of the Collegia Musica in Leipzig, see A. Schering, *Musikgeschichte Leipzigs,* vol. 3 (Leipzig, 1941), pp. 131–47; W Neumann, "Das 'Bachische Collegium Musicum,'" *BJ* 47 (1960), pp. 5ff.

9. J. H. Zedler, *Grosses Universal-Lexicon aller Wissenschafften und Kuenste,* vol. 22 (Leipzig, 1739), col. 1488, defines: "MUSICUM COLLEGIUM, ist eine Versammlung gewisser Musick-Verständigen, welche zu ihrer eigenen Ubung, sowol in der Vocal- als Instrumental-Musik, unter aufsicht eines gewissen Directors, zu gewissen Tagen und an gewissen Orten zusammen kommen, und musikalische Stücke aufführen. Dergleichen Collegia trifft man an verschiedenen Orten an. Zu Leipzig ist vor allen andern das Bachische Collegium Musicum berühmt"; *BJ* 70 (1984), p. 175.

10. Note especially the existence of 24 original

performing parts for "Ich liebe den Höchsten von ganzem Gemüte" *BWV*174 (*NBA* I/14, *Krit. Bericht,* pp. 67ff.) for Pentecost 1729, a few weeks after Bach had assumed the directorship of the Collegium.

11. *Dok* II, no. 139.

12. *Bach Reader,* p. 335.

13. A. Glöckner, "Neuerkenntnisse zu J. S. Bachs Aufführungskalender zwischen 1729 und 1735," *BJ* 67 (1981), pp. 66ff.

14. Ibid., p. 69.

15. H.-J. Schulze, "Ein apokryphes Händel-Concerto in J. S. Bachs Handschrift," *BJ* 66 (1980), pp. 27ff.

16. Glöckner, "Neuerkenntnisse," p. 74.

17. *Dok* II, no. 425.

18. *Bach Reader,* p. 125.

19. Dok I, no. 27; see also Marshall *Bach,* pp. 59–63.

20. See note 3.

21. Bach, *Drei Sonaten für Viola da gamba und Cembalo BWV 1027–1029* (Leipzig: Peters, 1985).

POSTSCRIPT

Kobayashi *Chr* provides a detailed chronological account with new information that permits more specific dates for the sources and re-performances, respectively, of the following works:

BWV 1027: ca. 1742 (autograph parts)
BWV 1030: 1736–37 (autograph score); flute part (apograph copy), ca. 1740–42
BWV 1031: 1748–1749 (score copy)
BWV 1041: ca. 1740–1742 (autograph title wrapper; re-performance?)
BWV 1055: ca. 1742 (violone part; re-performance)
BWV 1067: 1743–1746 (autograph viola part; re-performance)

See also the introduction to my facsimile edition of J. S. Bach, *Concerto à 6 BWV 1043* (New York: C. F. Peters, 1990).

18. New Research on the Musical Offering

1. Exact source descriptions, documentation, text-critical, and other particulars may be drawn from the *Kritische Bericht* of *NBA* VIII/1 ed. Christoph Wolff (Kassel, 1976).

2. Cf. the contemporary reports in *Dok* II, pp. 434f.; *Bach Reader,* pp. 176, 220, 260 (van Swieten), 305f. (Forkel).

3. At least 100 copies were printed. Cf. *Dok* I, p. 117 (Bach's letter from 6 October 1748).

4. For details see *NBA* VIII/1, *Krit. Bericht.*

5. Friedrich Wilhelm Marpurg, *Abhandlung von der Fuge,* Part II (Berlin, 1754); Johann Philipp Kirnberger, *Grundsätze des Generalbasses* (Berlin, 1779); A. F. C. Kollmann, *Essay on Practical Musical Composition* (London, 1799).

6. The first reprint was edited by C. G. Müller (Leipzig: Breitkopf & Härtel, 1831), the second by F. A. Roitzsch (Leipzig: Peters, 1866).

7. Spitta II, pp. 191ff., 292ff.

8. *BG* 31/2 (Leipzig, 1885).

9. Edition Peters No. 4202 (Leipzig, 1937); Ludwig Landshoff, *Beiheft zur Urtext-Ausgabe. Bemerkungen zur Textkritik und Darstellung des Werkes* (Leipzig, 1937).

10. Kinsky, pp. 62ff.

11. Hans Theodor David, "Bach's 'Musical Offering,'" *Musical Quarterly* 23 (1937), pp. 314–332.

12. Edition Schirmer No. 40062 (New York, 1944); Hans Theodor David, *J. S. Bach's Musical Offering: History, Interpretation, and Analysis* (New York, 1945).

13. Rudolf Gerber, "Sinn und Ordnung in Bachs 'Musikalischem Opfer,'" *Das Musikleben* 1 (1948), pp. 65ff.; "Das Musikalische Opfer," *Die Werke des Bach-Festes* [Göttingen] 1950 (Kassel, 1950), pp. 20ff.

14. Wilhelm Pfannkuch, "J. S. Bachs 'Musikalisches Opfer,'" *Die Musikforschung* 7 (1954), pp. 440ff.

15. Cf. Spitta II, pp. 292ff.; Landshoff, *Beiheft zur Urtext-Ausgabe,* pp. 7ff., Kinsky, pp. 63ff.; Pfannkuch, "J.S. Bachs 'Musikalisches Opfer," pp. 442ff.

16. Kinsky, p. 124.

17. David used the Washington copy for some facsimile reproductions in his book.

18. David, *Bach's Musical Offering,* pp. 153ff.

19. Cf. Spitta II, pp. 292f.; Landshoff, *Beiheft zur Urtext-Ausgabe,* pp. 7f.; Kinsky, pp. 63ff.; Pfannkuch, "J. S. Bachs 'Musikalisches Opfer,'" pp. 442ff.

20. See *NBA* VIII/1, *Krit. Bericht,* for details.

21. See note 19, above. Cf. the numbering of the movements and the brief source description in Schmieder's BWV (see Table 18.1).

22. Spitta III, p. 293.

23. Ibid.

24. See the literature mentioned in notes 9, 12–14, above; also Hans Joachim Moser and Hermann Diener, "Bachs 'Musikalisches Opfer' und 'Kunst der Fuge,'" *Jahrbuch der Staatlichen Akademie für Kirchen- und Schulmusik Berlin* 2 (Kassel, 1929), pp. 56ff.

(obviously inspired by David's arrangement of the Musical Offering and Art of Fugue for the Leipzig Bach-Feier, 1928, and for a Kiel performance in the same year); Alfred Orel, "Johann Sebastian Bachs 'Musikalisches Opfer,'" *Die Musik* 30 (19XX), 83ff., 165ff.; Erich Schenk, "Das 'Musikalische Opfer' von Johann Sebastian Bach," *Anzeiger der philosophisch-historischen Klasse der Österreichischen Akademie der Wissenschaften* (Vienna, 1953), pp. 51ff.

25. David, *Bach's Musical Offering*, p. 94. Cf. the chapter on "Erroneous Conclusions" (pp. 94ff.) for his general criticism of Spitta's research conclusions. As to the quality of paper and the binding, see pp. 91–92.

26. Cf. Joel Sheveloff, *Quaerendo Invenietis*, Masters thesis, Brandeis University, 1964.

27. Cf. Gerber, "Das Musicalische Opfer," pp. 22ff.

28. Kinsky, p. 124.

29. Kinsky, p. 66; David, *Bach's Musical Offering*, p. 91.

30. For diplomatic investigations, see *NBA* VIII/1, *Krit. Bericht*.

31. The acrostic is printed on a small paper strip and pasted on fol. 1r of section D in all copies. Spitta and David assumed that the acrostic was a later idea of Bach and was therefore subsequently added to the already finished printing. This cannot be upheld. A comparison between the engraved sonata title shows the practical purpose of the extra paper strip. Like the sonata title the acrostic was engraved on a much smaller plate (sonata: ca. 12.5 × 17 cm; acrostic: ca. 5.5 × 20 cm) than the musical parts (average size: ca. 20 × 34 cm). In order to avoid damaging the paper by pulling two plates of very different sizes for fol. 1r and fol. 1v of section D, the acrostic was printed on an extra piece of paper and neatly pasted on the proper place.

32. Cf. Forkel's report (according to Wilhelm Friedemann Bach): "The king admired the learned manner in which his subject was thus executed extempore; and, probably to see how far such art could be carried, expressed a wish to hear also a fugue with six obbligato parts. But as not every subject is fit for such full harmony, Bach chose one himself and immediately executed it to the astonishment of all present in the same magnificent and learned manner as he had done that of the king." *Bach Reader*, pp. 305f.

33. For details see *NBA* VIII/1, *Krit. Bericht*.

34. Cf. *Dok* I, no. 436.

35. See *NBA* VIII/1, *Krit. Bericht*.

36. E.g., for the edition of Sperontes's *Singende Muse an der Pleisse* (Leipzig, 1736–1751). The plates for the musical parts were engraved by J. G. Krüg-

ner, Jr. of Leipzig, and the text parts were set up in type by Breitkopf. For the printing (pulling) Breitkopf as the publisher had to call on a copper press, as the following note in the records of the old publishing house shows: "63 Rthr [Reichstaler] an Camann, Kupferdrucker, wegen der singenden Muse." Cf. Hermann von Hase, "Sperontes Singende Muse an der Pleisse," *Zeitschrift der Internationalen Musikgesellschaft* 14 (1912–1913), pp. 94ff.

37. "Da das unterm 11. May a.c. in denen Leipziger, Berliner, Franckfurter und andern Gazetten versprochene Königl. Preußische Fugen-Thema nunmehr die Presse paßieret; Als wird hierdurch bekannt gemacht, daß in bevorstehender Michaelis-Messe solches so wohl bey dem Autore, Capellmeister Bachen, als auch bey dessen beyden Söhnen in Halle und Berlin, zu bekommen seyn werde, a 1. thl. Die Elaboration bestehet 1.) in zweyen Fugen, eine mit 3. die andere mit 6. obligaten Stimmen; 2.) in einer Sonata, a Traverso, Violino e Continuo; 3.) in verschiedenen Canonibus, wobey eine Fuga canonica befindlich." I am indebted to Hans-Joachim Schulze of the Bach-Archiv in Leipzig for bringing this document (now published in *Dok* III, p. 656, no. 558a) to my attention. Cf. also *Dok* II, nos. 437, 454, 467, for other hitherto unknown archival sources concerning the history of the Musical Offering.

38. Wolfgang Graeser, "Bachs 'Kunst der Fuge,'" *BJ* 21 (1924), pp. 1ff.; the fact that Graeser's neoromantic arrangement was adopted as vol. 47 of the Bach-Gesellschaft edition (supplement) and in a special version as vol. 28 of the *Veröffentlichungen der Neuen Bachgesellschaft* (Leipzig, 1927) has given an unfortunate authority to Graeser.

39. Cf. Friedrich Blume, "Outlines of a New Picture of Bach," *Music and Letters* 44 (1963), p. 226: "Bach himself was not interested in whether they were performed or were capable of being performed. In them he wished to continue a tradition of consummate contrapuntal skill . . . It was . . . an 'esoteric' activity, this disinterested transmission of a purely abstract theory."

40. See *NBA* VIII/1, *Krit. Bericht*, for details about the manuscript tradition in the eighteenth century.

41. Johann Gottfried Walther, *Musicalisches Lexicon*, facsimile edition, ed. Richard Schaal (Kassel, 1953), pp. 525f.

42. Cf. this volume, Chapter 25, section II.

43. *Bach Reader*, p. 176.

44. Cf. Wolff, *Stile antico*.

45. A voucher from 9 May 1749 with the autograph signature of J. S. Bach: sale of a "Piano et

Forte" to Count Branitzky of Bialystok at a price of 115 Reichstaler. *Dok* III, p. 633, no. 142a.

46. Cf. also Johann Friedrich Agricola's report: "Mr. Gottfried Silbermann had at first built two of these instruments [fortepianos]. One of them was seen and played by the late Kapellmeister, Mr. Joh. Sebastian Bach. He had praised, indeed admired, its tone; but he had complained that it was too weak in the high register, and was too hard to play. This had been taken greatly amiss by Mr. Silbermann, who could not bear to have any fault found in his handiworks. He was therefore angry at Mr. Bach for a long time. And yet his conscience told him that Mr. Bach was not wrong. He therefore decided . . . not to deliver any more of these instruments, but instead to think all the harder about how to eliminate the faults Mr. J. S. Bach had observed. He worked for many years on this. . . . Finally, when Mr. Silbermann had really achieved many improvements, notably in respect to the action, he sold one again . . . Mr. Silbermann had also the laudable ambition to show one of these instruments of his later workmanship to the late Kapellmeister Bach, and have it examined by him; and he had received, in turn, complete approval from him." Cited in Jakob Adlung, *Musica mechanica Organoedi* (Berlin, 1768), pp. 116f.; *Bach Reader*, p. 259.

47. Two instructive examples:

David	BWV 1079	Landshoff	BWV 1079
Ricercar à 3	1	Ricercar à 3	1
Canon	2	Canon	2
Canon	3b	Canon	6
Canon	3c	Canon	7
Canon	3d	Canon	3a
Canon	3e	Canon	3b
Sonata	8	Canon	3c
Canon	9	Canon	3d
Canon	3a	Canon	3e
Canon	6	Fuga canonica	4
Canon	7	Ricercar à 6	5
Fuga Canonica	4	Sonata	8
Ricerar à 6	5	Canon	9

48. Cf. this volume, Chapter 27.
49. Cf. ibid., pp. 152ff.
50. Ibid., pp. 149ff.
51. Ibid., pp. 149, 165.
52. *Dok* III, p. 646: "Was aber Herr Bach seelig für den König in Preusen gespielt, das ist in Kupfer gestochen, u. in Leipzig zu haben: es sind 3 Stücke.

Ein Trio, ein Ricercar u. Fuge, u. will ich nach Leipzig schreiben, das Sie es bekommen können, auf die Ostermesse." I am indebted to Hans-Joachim Schulze of the Bach-Archiv in Leipzig for bringing this document to my attention prior to its publication.

POSTSCRIPT

Several paragraphs and all diagrams from the last section of the original version of this chapter, a paper read at the 1970 meeting of the American Musicological Society in Toronto, have been omitted because the discussion overlaps with pertinent sections of an earlier and related essay, included in this volume as Chapter 27.

For a more extensive discussion of the source-critical problems and findings, see my edition in *NBA* VIII/1 (1974; *Krit. Bericht*, 1976) and the commentary to my facsimile edition of the 1747 original print (Edition Peters: Leipzig, 1977).

A brief comment clarifying a detail regarding "printing unit A" of the 1747 edition is called for. Printing unit A (bifolio with title page and preface) fulfilled a practical double function. First, for regular "trade" copies it served as title wrapper (enclosing the separate pages of printing unit B = *Ricercar à 3*). Second, for purposes of binding, the bifolio would have to be cut, the two separate leaves then serving as front matter of a volume which—as the surviving copies demonstrate—ordinarily comprised the other two printing units in oblong format, that is, both keyboard ricercari.

On the issue of the fortepiano performance of the three-part ricercar, see my essay, "Bach und das Pianoforte," in *Bach und die italienische Musik—Bach e la musica italiana,* ed. Wolfgang Osthoff and Reinhard Wiesend, Centro Tedesco di Studi Veneziani—Quaderni, vol. 36 (Venice, 1987), pp. 197–210.

In "The Source for Bach's *Musical Offering:* The *Institutio Oratoria* of Quintilian," *Journal of the American Musicological Society* 33 (1980), pp. 88–141, Ursula Kirkendale presents the intriguing and imaginative hypothesis that the Musical Offering is based in form and content on Quintilian's famous treatise on rhetoric. Since her interpretation rests on a very specific sequence of movements for the entire work, which she accepts from the old collected edition (*BG* 31, 1885), she rejects my findings regarding the heterogeneous mixture of sizes, formats, paginations, and numberings in the 1747 print as well as my conclusions regarding the grouping of the work in three fascicles and the resulting editorial decisions. In short, she states that her study effectively invalidated my *NBA* edition. She posits a unified multi-movement structure that follows and displays exactly what she describes as Quintilian's rhetorical model:

Ricercar à 3	First exordium (principium)
Canon perpetuus	Narratio brevis
Canones diversi 1–5	Narratio longa
Fuga canonica	Egressus
Ricercar à 6	Second exordium (insinuatio)
Canon à 2, Canon à 4	Argumentatio
Sonata	First peroratio
Canon perpetuus	Second peroratio

There are numerous problems with her hypothesis that cannot be discussed in detail here. Suffice it to mention that, in comparison with Quintilian's model of rhetorical speech, the movements of Bach's composition completely distort the proportions of the section sizes of an oration ("narratio longa" and "argumentatio" are Quintilian's, not Bach's, centerpieces). Moreover, Bach's weightiest pieces (the two ricercari and the sonata) do not at all properly correspond to their alleged function within Quintilian's rhetorical scheme. Finally, a double peroration is quite an absurdity in general, and this all the more since Kirkendale deems the second one ("peroratio in rebus"), the concluding *canon perpetuus,* to be "the most extraordinary contrapuntal coup" (p. 125) and crowning of the entire work. This is simply not true, neither on the basis of compositional sophistication nor on the basis of musical content. After all, Bach did not even bother to mention this "most extraordinary" movement on the title wrapper for the sonata parts (cf. Fig. 18.3).

Kirkendale's interpretation borders on the characteristics of program music when she refers, for instance, to the representation of "epideictic virtues" (pp. 111ff.) in the *canones diversi.* Jupiter, Mars, and Neptune, along with Agamemnon, are supposed to determine the musical imagery of Bach's "operatic" instrumental pieces, in which "Jovian" thunderbolts, "Pyrrhic" rhythms, and "Martian" passages appear. The kind of relationship between music and rhetoric that is proposed here is fundamentally different from what is known about this relationship in the seventeenth and eighteenth centuries: nowhere are there parallels for the aspects of form (correspondence between a multi-movement musical structure and a rhetorical treatise) or the aspects of content (programmatic imagery). Since Kirkendale is unable to produce any hard evidence in favor of her hypothesis, she needs to assert that Bach deliberately kept his plan secret. The irregular makeup of the original print, which can under no circumstance be explained by means of rhetorical methods, then has to be understood as a major challenge for King Frederick and all other admirers of Bach's musical secrets.

At the 1980 meeting of the American Musicological Society in New York, where Kirkendale first presented her paper, I delivered a response which included some of the points presented above. For various reasons, however, I decided not to publish my response, which ultimately became obsolete after Peter Williams published two articles addressing very much the same issues: "The Snares and Delusions of Musical Rhetoric: Some Examples from Recent Writings on J. S. Bach," in *Alte Musik: Praxis and Reflexion,* ed. Peter Reidemeister and Veronika Gutmann (Winterthur, 1983), pp. 230–240; and "Encounters with the Chromatic Fourth . . . or, More on Figurenlehre," *Musical Times* 126 (1985), pp. 276ff. Williams summarizes: "J. S. Bach in particular is a beneficiary from or victim of (depending on one's viewpoint) wonderful hypotheses of this kind: I am thinking of such seductive but totally unfounded theories as that the Musical Offering is in some sense based on the writings of the Roman rhetorician Quintilianus" ("Encounters with the Chromatic Fourth," p. 276). He specifically takes issue with Kirkendale's convoluted terminology regarding the concept of "source" (that is, Quintilian's treatise), which "elevates an extra-musical conjecture to a position of influence which is not certifiable" ("Snares and Delusions," p. 236). His arguing some "of the many questionable claims" in Kirkendale's essay is meant "as a warning to those hoping to find in rhetoric a solution to musical problems, for it is characteristic of such approaches that they purport to solve even the large-scale problems of such works as the Musical Offering, e.g. what order its pieces should be in and what is its instrumentation. The query 'How did Bach come upon the idea of imitating Quintilian in music' [Kirkendale, p. 132] begs far too many questions for the student to be satisfied by being told that the composer is known to have been accustomed to 'conversing with rhetoricians on the relationship between rhetoric and music' [Kirkendale, p. 134]. Of course they are related, and of course a thinking composer will know that. But it is quite another matter to describe a specific piece of music in terms of a specific treatise. One cannot but be alarmed that the desk-bound ease with which such parallels are made will tempt others to propound similar ideas, seducing the student into thinking something has actually been said when an analogy is made or label fixed."

For a critical account of Bach's relationship with the rhetorical traditions and for a discussion of the problematic connection between compositional and rhetorical theories, see Arno Forchert, "Bach und die Tradition der Rhetorik," in *Alte Musik als ästhetische Gegenwart: Bach, Händel, Schütz. Bericht über den internationalen musikwissenschaftlichen Kongreß Stuttgart 1985*, ed. Dietrich Berke and Dorothee Hanemann, vol. 1 (Kassel, 1987), pp. 169–178.

19. Bach's Last Fugue: Unfinished?

1. The manuscript score is in DSB, Mus. ms. autogr. Bach P 200. It consists of a forty-page bound fascicle and an appendix in three sections (Appendix 1, Appendix 2, and Appendix 3). Facsimile edition: *Faksimile-Reihe Bachscher Werke und Schriftstücke*, vol. 14 (Leipzig, 1979). See Table 20.1 and accompanying text for more details regarding the autograph.

2. "N. B. While working on this fugue, in which the name BACH appears in the countersubject, the author died." *Bach Reader*, note to the facsimile facing p. 256. This note may have been written some years after 1750; see *Dok* III, p. 3.

3. The lack of the proper spacing between the staves (systems either *à 4* or *à 3*) was another reason for discarding the leaf as scrap paper. Bach had to skip the third staff in order to keep the systems clearly apart, while the layout of pages 1–4 was ideal for a keyboard score.

4. Of the engraver's copy only the three sheets of the augmentation canon have survived (Appendix 1). Their layout is identical with that of pages 1–4 of Appendix 3.

5. Gustav Nottebohm was the first to discover that the three themes of the last fugue could be combined with the principal theme (*Musik-Welt* 20, 1881, p. 234). For a complete list of combinatorial possibilities, see H. T. David's edition of the Art of Fugue (Leipzig: C. F. Peters, 1928), pp. 142–143. Most of the suggested combinations, however, fail to take into account the fact that the setting has to be playable for two hands on the keyboard.

6. Written by C. P. E. Bach and J. F. Agricola a few months after Bach's death (see *Dok* III, p. 7) and published in 1754 by L. Mizler (*Dok* III, pp. 80–93).

7. *Dok* III, p. 86 (translation mine):."Seine letzte Kranckheit, hat ihn verhindert, seinem Entwurfe nach, die vorletzte Fuge völlig zu Ende zu bringen, und die letzte, welche 4 Themata enthalten, und nachgehends in allen 4 Stimmen Note für Note umgekehrt werden sollte, auszuarbeiten."

8. The only trace of the lost material seems to be "a small . . . slip of paper, on which C. P. E. Bach has noted in his own hand: Herr Hartmann holds the real [perhaps the printer's copy, plus other autograph material?]" ("Noch ein kleines angeheftetes Zettelchen . . . , auf welchem C.Ph.E. Bach mit eigener Hand bemerkt hat: Herr Hartmann hat das eigentliche"). This note, originally attached to the blue title wrapper now enclosing the appendixes, has not been preserved, but it is referred to by S. W. Dehn, former librarian of the Royal Library at Berlin (*Caecilia* 24, 1845, p.22); see also *BG* 25/1 (1875), p. xix: Wilhelm Rust, the editor, reports that he was unable to find the slip of paper. In trying to fix the identity of "Herr Hartmann," Rust does not mention Friedrich Traugott Hartmann (1749–1833), publisher in Elbing (East Prussia) and at one time assistant to F. W. Marpurg, when the latter was director of the Royal Lottery-Office in Berlin (*Dok* III, p. 703). If he were indeed the "Herr Hartmann" in question, as his close association with Marpurg suggests, he may also have been the later owner of the copper plates of *Die Kunst der Fuge*, offered for sale by C. P. E. Bach to interested publishers (*Dok* III, pp. 113–114).

9. Thomas Baker, "Bach's Revisions in the Augmentation Canon," *Current Musicology* 19 (1975), pp. 67–71.

10. See David's introduction to his edition, p. lx.

POSTSCRIPT
Ulrich Siegele ("Wie vollständig ist Bach's 'Kunst der Fuge'?," in *Bericht über die Wissenschaftliche Konferenz zum V. Internationalen Bachfest der DDR*, ed. Winfried Hoffmann and Armin Schneiderheinze, Leipzig, 1987, pp. 219–225) disagrees with my view, put forth in this chapter, that the quadruple fugue in finished form actually constitutes the last "movement" of the entire work. According to Siegele's hypothesis Bach had planned altogether twenty-four movements for the work and, specifically, four fugues with four themes each, each one to be inverted. I consider this a misinterpretation of the rather clear statement in the obituary, which refers to a single fugue ("the last one") which "was to contain four themes and to have been afterward inverted note for note" (*Bach Reader*, p. 221).

20. The Compositional History of the Art of Fugue

1. *Bach Reader*, p. 221.
2. *Bach Reader*, p. 198.
3. Spitta III, p. 197.
4. *Faksimile-Reihe Bachscher Werke und Schriftstücke*, vol. 14 (Leipzig, 1979).
5. Hans-Joachim Schulze, "Beiträge zur Bach-Quellenforschung," in *Bericht über den internationalen*

musikwissenschaftlichen Kongreß Leipzig 1966 (Kassel and Leipzig, 1970), p. 272.

6. See Christoph Wolff, "Seminar Report: Bach's Art of Fugue—An Examination of the Sources," *Current Musicology* 19 (1975), pp. 47–77; cf. also this volume, Chapter 19.

7. Wolfgang Wiemer, *Die wiederhergestellte Ordnung von Bachs Kunst der Fuge* (Wiesbaden, 1979).

8. See my review in *Musica* 33 (1979), pp. 288ff.

9. Ursula Kirkendale, "The Source of Bach's Musical Offering: The *Institutio Oratoria* of Quintilian," *Journal of the American Musicological Society* 33 (1980), pp. 99–141.

10. Cf. also the facsimile edition (see note 4, above).

11. Report in *Caecilia* 24 (1845), p. 22; see also *BG* 25/1 (ed. Wilhelm Rust, 1875), p. xix.

12. See this volume, Chapter 19, note 8.

13. *Bach Reader*, p. 269.

14. Weiss, no. 67.

15. Weiss, no. 21.

16. J. S. Bach, *Cantate burlesque: "Mer hahn en neue Oberkeet"* (BWV 212), facsimile edition, ed. Wilhelm Virneisel (Munich, 1965).

17. See note 14.

18. *Bach Reader*, p. 340.

19. A complete manuscript copy of this treatise, supposedly in the hand of Johann Sebastian Bach, was acquired by Carl Friedrich Zelter from Bach's student Johann Christian Kittel (cf. Max Friedländer's catalog of Zelter's library, manuscript at the Nanki Library, Tokyo); this copy is now lost.

20. Johann Mattheson, *Der Vollkommene Capellmeister* (Hamburg, 1739; rpt., Kassel, 1954), p. 245.

21. *Bach Reader*, p. 246.

22. Ibid., p. 221.

23. For a more extended discussion of this point, see this volume, Chapter 19.

24. *Dok* III, no. 645.

25. *Musikalische Bibliothek*, vol. 2/4 (Leipzig, 1743; rpt., Hannover, 1965), p. 119.

26. *Bach Reader*, p. 269.

27. Ibid., p. 242.

28. *Bach Reader*, p. 222. See also this volume, Chapter 32.

29. See this volume, Chapter 32.

POSTSCRIPT
This chapter originated in a paper presented in 1979 at a Bach Conference in Leipzig and published in 1983; an abbreviated version appeared earlier under the title "Zur Entstehungsgeschichte von Bachs Kunst der Fuge," in *Bachwoche Ansbach 1981: Offizieller Almanach* (Ansbach, 1981), pp. 77–88. My critical two-volume edition of the Art of Fugue (Frankfurt, London, New York: C. F. Peters, 1987) includes as volume 1 the first edition of the early autograph version.

Kobayashi *Chr* generally and specifically confirms my datings, but provides some additional and important chronological details—ca. 1742: movements I to IX/without final section (= P 200, p. 1–24); ca. 1742–1746: movements IX/final section to XV (= P 200, pp. 25–40) and BWV 1080/18 (= P 200, Appendix 2); ca. 1747 to August 1748: BWV 1080/14 (= P 200, Appendix 1); and August 1748 to October 1749: BWV 1080/19 (= P 200, Appendix 3).

21. The Deathbed Chorale

1. 'Man hat . . . die Freunde seiner Muse durch Mittheilung des am Ende beygefügten vierstimmig ausgearbeiteten Kirchenchorals, den der selige Mann in seiner Blindheit einem seiner Freunde aus dem Stegereif in die Feder dictiret hat, schadlos halten wollen." *Dok* III, no. 645; *Bach Reader*, p. 198 (translation modified).

2. "Man hat indessen Ursache, sich zu schmeicheln, daß der zugefügte vierstimmig ausgearbeitete Kirchenchoral, den der selige Mann in seiner Blindheit einem seiner Freunde aus dem Stegereif in die Feder dictiret hat, diesen Mangel ersetzen, und die Freunde seiner Muse schadlos halten wird." *Dok* III, p. 15; *Bach Reader*, p. 267 (translation modified).

3. Published in Lorenz Christoph Mizler's *Musikalische Bibliothek*, vol. 4 (Leipzig, 1754). *Dok* III, no. 666; *Bach Reader*, pp. 213–224.

4. ". . . oder, welches ihm noch wunderbarer vorkommen muß, den in seiner Blindheit von ihm einem andern in die Feder dictirten Choral: Wenn wir in höchsten Nöthen seyn." *Dok* III, p. 73; *Bach Reader*, p. 256.

5. Forkel, pp. 53f.; *Bach Reader*, p. 340.

6. *Bach-Urkunden*, ed. Max Schneider, *Veröffentlichungen der Neuen Bachgesellschaft* 17 (Leipzig, 1916).

7. See note 24.

8. Spitta II, pp. 795f. [German edition]; Spitta III, pp. 274f. [English edition].

9. *BG* 25/2 (1878), pp. xxf.

10. See Dadelsen *Chr*, p. 114.

11. Albert Schweitzer, *J. S. Bach, le musicien-poète* (Leipzig, 1905; enlarged German and English trans., 1908 and 1911).

12. The notion of "Bach the fifth Evangelist" goes back to Nathan Söderblom, the Swedish theologian; cf. Hans Besch, *J. S. Bach. Frömmigkeit und Glaube,* 2d. ed. (Kassel, 1950), p. 3.

13. DSB, Mus. ms. autogr. Bach P 283.

14. DSB, Mus. ms. autogr. Bach P 271.

15. *NBA* IV/2, *Krit. Bericht* (1957), pp. 102 ff.

16. Both versions are printed in *NBA* IV/2.

17. See the *NBA* critical commentaries with corresponding detailed information for many works.

18. Both the engraver's plates and the autograph were in C. P. E. Bach's possession; see the critical commentary for *BG* 25/1 (Wilhelm Rust). See also this volume, Chapter 20.

19. The notation of V² is also on two staves.

20. Dadelsen *Chr,* p. 114. Anonymous 12 (= Anon Vr in Dürr *Chr*) appears as the copyist of continuo parts for such original manuscripts from Bach's last years in office as BWV 195, 245, and 232ᴵᴵᴵ. Presumably he was an organist.

21. P 271 contains the six trio sonatas for organ BWV 525–530 (pp. 1–57), the seventeen chorales BWV 651–667 (pp. 58–99), the Canonic Variations on Vom Himmel hoch BWV 769 (pp. 100–106), and an incomplete copy of the chorale "Vor deinen Thron tret ich hiermit" BWV 668 (p. 106). Except for the last two of the seventeen chorales (BWV 666–667) and the final entry (BWV 668), all appear in Bach's autograph.

22. See note 20.

23. See Klotz, *NBA* IV/2, *Krit. Bericht,* p. 5.

24. It is possible that Forkel's mention of Altnikol does go back to Carl Philipp Emanuel Bach. Emanuel may have identified Altnikol as the scribe of [W²] (which must have been known to him as the source for [W³] and W⁴) and thus linked his name to the dictation. Or else he may have confused the scribe of V² in P 271 (which source later came into his possession; see note 32) with Altnikol when he corresponded with Forkel in the 1770s; such an error may have been due to the two actual Altnikol entries in the volume.

25. See Klotz, *NBA* IV/2, *Krit. Bericht,* pp. 80f.

26. Ibid. The copies were made largely by Johann Gottfried Walther and Johann Tobias Krebs in the years 1710–1714; see the discussion by Hermann Zietz, *Quellenkritische Untersuchungen an den Bach-Handschriften P 801 und P 802 aus dem "Krebs'schen Nachlaß" unter besonderer Berücksichtigung der Choralbearbeitungen des jungen Bachs.* Hamburger Beiträge zur Musikwissenschaft, vol. 1 (Hamburg, 1969), pp. 30, 60, 137ff., who provides a much more detailed account than Klotz does.

27. Cf. Dadelsen *Chr,* p. 80; Ernst Arfken, "Zur Entstehungsgeschichte des Orgelbüchleins," *BJ* 1967, p. 50.

28. The majority of the seventeen chorales can definitely be dated prior to the Orgel-Büchlein; see Zietz, *Quellenkritische Untersuchungen,* pp. 137 ff. In matters of texture and declamatory style, the early organ chorale, "Ach Gott und Herr" (*per canonem*) BWV 714 is particularly close to this setting.

29. See Helmut Zeraschi, "Bach und der Okulist Taylor," *BJ* 1956, pp. 52–64.

30. According to Zeraschi, ibid., pp. 63f., the operations which eventually led to Bach's total blindness did not take place before April and May of 1750.

31. Cf. Albert F. W. Fischer and Wilhelm Tümpel, *Das deutsche evangelische Kirchenlied des 17. Jahrhunderts,* vol. 2 (Gütersloh, 1905; rpt., Hildesheim, 1964), p. 409, "At morning, noon, and evening one may sing: 1. 'Vor deinen Thron tret ich hiermit' . . . [15 verses]," first published in *New Ordentlich Gesang-Buch* (Hannover, 1646). The authorship of Bodo von Hohenberg (1604–1650) is uncertain.

32. P 271 was later in Emanuel's possession (according to the latter's *Nachlaß-Verzeichnis* of 1789). The volume had not been available to him immediately after Bach's death, as has been shown. He must have acquired it later, probably together with other manuscripts from Wilhelm Friedemann's share of their father's estate; see Dürr *Chr,* p. 9. A detailed study dealing with the provenance of Bach manuscripts inherited by Friedemann has not as yet been undertaken.

POSTSCRIPT

Kobayashi *Chr* (pp. 29–31) extensively discusses the work of the scribe, Anon. Vr (= Anonymus 12), who appears to have been active as a copyist from 1742 on, first in Leipzig under J. S. Bach and after 1750 in Berlin under C. P. E. Bach. He still cannot be identified by name, but it is entirely possible that he actually is the "friend" who—according to the notice in the Art of Fugue—took the dictation for [V¹] and, subsequently, prepared a fair copy of it, V². The dictation could have taken place only after Bach's eye operation in March 1750. The fair copy (in DSB, Mus. ms. Bach P 271), however, must have been completed in Leipzig before the division of J. S. Bach's estate (the album P 271 most likely did not then pass into C. P. E. Bach's hand but appears to have been acquired by him at a later point from another family member).

An expert ophthalmological and neurological

reexamination of the available medical information on Bach's illness (Detlev Kranemann, "Johann Sebastian Bachs Krankheit und Todesursache—Versuch einer Deutung," *BJ* 1990, pp. 53–64) came to the conclusion that both his eye problems (cataract) and handwriting difficulties (neuropathy and encephalosis) resulted from untreated diabetes.

Bach's revisional work on the "Great Eighteen" needs to be re-dated on the basis of a reevaluation (see Kobayashi *Chr*) of the scribal evidence in P 271: BWV 651–663 to ca. 1739–1742; BWV 664–667 to ca. 1746–1747. For the wider context, see also Werner Breig, "The 'Great Eighteen' Chorales: Bach's Revisional Process and the Genesis of the Work," *J. S. Bach as Organist: His Instruments, Music, and Performance Practices,* ed. George B. Stauffer and Ernest D. May (Bloomington, Ind., 1986), pp. 102–120; and Clark Kelly, *Johann Sebastian Bach's "Eighteen" Chorales, BWV 651–668: Perspectives on Editions and Hymnology,* D.M.A. diss., Eastman School of Music, Rochester, N.Y., 1988.

22. Chronology and Style in the Early Works

1. For the connection of BWV 106 with Tobias Lämmerhirt, see Alfred Dürr, *Die Kantaten von Johann Sebastian Bach* (Kassel, 1971; 5th rev. ed., 1985), p. 611; for the early vocal works in general, see Alfred Dürr, *Studien über die frühen Kantaten Johann Sebastian Bachs,* 2d rev. ed. (Wiesbaden, 1977).

2. Especially Hans-Joachim Schulze, *Studien zur Bach-Überlieferung im 18. Jahrhundert* (Leipzig, 1984).

3. Elke Krüger, *Stilistische Untersuchungen zu ausgewählten frühen Klavierfugen J. S. Bachs,* Hamburger Beiträge zur Musikwissenschaft, vol. 2 (Hamburg, 1970).

4. Hermann Zietz, *Quellenkritische Untersuchungen an den Bach-Handschriften P 801, P 802, und P 803 aus dem "Krebsschen Nachlaß" unter Berücksichtigung der Choralbearbeitungen des jungen Bach,* Hamburger Beiträge zur Musikwissenschaft, vol. 1 (Hamburg, 1969).

5. Hartwig Eichberg, *Johann Sebastian Bach: Einzelnstehende Suiten, Sonaten, Variationen und Capricci für Klavier, Untersuchungen zur Überlieferung und Edition* (doctoral diss., Tübingen, 1973); and "Unechtes unter Johann Sebastian Bachs Klavierwerken, *BJ* 1975, pp. 8–49.

6. George B. Stauffer, *The Organ Preludes of Johann Sebastian Bach,* Studies in Musicology, vol. 27 (Ann Arbor, Mich., 1980).

7. For the issues involved, see Robert Hill,

"Echtheit angezweifelt: Style and authenticity in two suites attributed to Bach," *Early Music* 13 (1985), pp. 248ff.

8. See this volume, Chapters 1, 5, and 6.

9. See Chapter 5.

10. *BG* 25/2 (preface), p. ixff. The autograph title page refers to the composer as *"Autore Joanne Sebast: Bach / p.t. Capellae magistri / S.P.R. Anhaltini- / Cotheniensis."*

11. Spitta I, pp. 597ff., 647ff.

12. Georg von Dadelsen, "Zur Entstehung des Bachschen Orgel-Büchleins," in *Festschrift Friedrich Blume zum 70. Geburtstag,* ed. Anna Amalie Abert and Wilhelm Pfannkuch (Kassel, 1963), pp. 74–79.

13. See the facsimile edition, *Orgel-Büchlein,* Faksimile-Reihe Bachscher Werke und Schriftstücke, vol. 17 (Leipzig, 1983), preface.

14. Dadelsen, "Entstehung"; Dürr, *Studien.*

15. Cf. the descriptions in Wolff *Stile antico,* pp. 159–172.

16. Weiss, no. 117.

17. For a more detailed discussion of the manuscript LM 4708, see this volume, Chapter 9.

18. Cf. Robin A. Leaver, "Bach and Hymnody," *Early Music* 13 (1985), pp. 227ff.

19. See Max Seiffert, "Das Plauener Orgelbuch," *Archiv für Musikwissenschaft* 2 (1920), pp. 371–402.

20. Consistently canonic is the elaboration of the chorale "Ach Gott und Herr" BWV 714. LM 4708 is the only source in which the chorale setting is preceded by a prelude in the manner of "durezze e ligature."

21. See the repertoire in *NBA* IV/3.

22. Johannes Schreyer, *Beiträge zur Bach-Kritik,* vol. 1 (Dresden, 1910), vol. 2 (Leipzig, 1913); and "Neue Beiträge zur Bach-Kritik," *Allgemeine Musikzeitung* 41 (1914), pp. 683–686, 923–926, 949–951, 976–978, 1006–1008, 1030–1031.

23. Werner Danckert, *Beiträge zur Bach-Kritik,* vol. 1 (Kassel, 1934); further volumes have not appeared.

POSTSCRIPT

For up-to-date information on the early vocal works, see *Bach Compendium* I/1–3. Authenticity issues of some key works, including what appears to be Bach's earliest cantata and his earliest motet, are discussed and resolved, respectively, by Andreas Glöckner, "Zur Echtheit und Datierung der Kantate BWV 150 'Nach dir, Herr, verlanget mich,'" *BJ* 1988, pp. 195–203; and Daniel R. Melamed, "The Authorship of the Motet 'Ich lasse dich nicht' BWV Anh. 159," *Journal of the American Musicological Society* 41 (1988), pp. 491–526. For the dating of the early Bach auto-graph sources, see generally *Die Notenschrift Johann Sebastian Bachs: Dokumentation ihrer Entwicklung, NBA IX/2* (ed. Yoshitake Kobayashi, 1989). An important study regarding the autograph transmission of Bach's early organ chorales is Russell Stinson, "Bach's Earliest Autograph," *Musical Quarterly* 71 (1985), pp. 235–263. See also the bibliographic references given in the Postscript to Chapter 6. Stinson's essay, "The Chronology and Compositional History of Bach's *Orgelbüchlein* Reconsidered," as yet unpublished, takes my discussion as a point of departure and argues, on the basis of detailed manuscript studies, that thirty-four entries in the Orgel-Büchlein may go back to the period 1708/09–1713/14, thereby substantially reducing the chronological gap between the Orgel-Büchlein and the early repertoire of Bach's organ chorales.

Stylistic features of the Neumeister Chorales are discussed extensively by Werner Breig, "Textbezug und Werkidee in Johann Sebastian Bachs frühen Orgelchorälen," in *Musikkulturgeschichte. Festschrift für Constantin Floros zum 60. Geburtstag,* ed. Peter Petersen (Wiesbaden, 1990), pp. 167–182. Breig's analytical studies support my suggestion that this earliest layer of Bach's composition of chorale preludes provides a decisive link to the Orgel-Büchlein.

23. The Architecture of the Passacaglia

1. Hermann Keller, *Die Orgelwerke Bachs* (Leipzig, 1948), pp. 96ff. From further literature concerning Bach's Passacaglia might be cited: Gotthold Frotscher, *Geschichte des Orgelspiels* (Berlin, 1934; 2d ed., 1959), vol. 2, pp. 883–886; Hermann Roth, "Bachs c-Moll Passacaglia und die verwandten Werke Dietrich Buxtehudes," *Monatsschrift für Gottesdienst und kirchliche Kunst* 20 (1915), pp. 18ff.; Werner Tell, "Das Formproblem der Passacaglia Bachs," *Musik und Kirche* 10 (1938), pp. 102ff.; Siegfried Vogelsänger, "Passacaglia und Chaconne in der Orgelmusik," *Musik und Kirche* 27 (1967), pp. 14ff.

2. Tell, "Das Formproblem," pp. 104f, probes number symbolism as a key to structure, proposing the view of a series of 7 × 3 sections, which is in no way supported in the work.

3. Siegfried Vogelsänger's analytical observations offer probably the best point of departure for an understanding of the structure. He groups the twenty variations in a pattern of 2–3–3–4–3–3–2, which, however, does not supply sufficient explanation for the three middle groups.

4. This is proved from the Christe (*Trio en Passa-caille*) of the "Messe du deuziesme ton" in Raison's *Livre d'Orgue* (Paris, 1688), ed. Alexandre Guilmant and André Pirro, Archives des maitres de l'orgue, vol. 2 (Paris, 1899).

5. See also this volume, Chapter 27.

6. In Buxtehude's work, too, we find distinct architectural structures, as for instance in his Passacaglia in D Minor, which is based on the following scheme: seven ostinato statements in D minor (the theme consists of four measures yet only seven notes); a short modulation (manualiter); seven ostinato statements in F major; a short modulation (manualiter); seven ostinato statements in A minor; a short modulation (manualiter); seven ostinato statements in D minor.

7. Also called *Fuga cum subjectis* in several manuscripts, according to Griepenkerl's preface for the Peters edition of Bach's *Orgelwerke* (Leipzig, 1844), vol. 1.

8. Cf. Werner Neumann, *J. S. Bachs Chorfuge* (Leipzig, 1938; 2d ed., 1950), pp. 14ff.; Carl Dahlhaus, "Zur Geschichte der Permutationsfuge," *BJ* 1959, pp. 95ff. The permutation structure of the fugue may aid the dating of the Passacaglia; cf. Dietrich Kilian's hypothesis, gained from source evidence and suggesting an origin of the work before the Weimar period, in his "Studie über Bachs Fantasie und Fuge c-Moll," in *Hans Albrecht in Memoriam,* ed. Wilfried Brennecke and Hans Haase (Kassel, 1962), pp. 134f. It poses an important question, but one that leads beyond the scope of our study.

9. Griepenkerl's work (*Orgelwerke* 1, p. 3) introduced to the literature the burden, derived from an erroneous interpretation of source material, of suspecting the Passacaglia as being a work originally intended for pedal harpsichord or pedal clavichord; cf. Winfried Schrammek, "Die musikgeschichtliche Stellung der Orgeltriosonaten Joh. Seb. Bachs," *BJ* 1954, pp. 8ff.

10. Though Hermann Keller (*Die Orgelwerke Bachs,* p. 97) claims: "The matter of registration in the twenty variations will tax the ability of every organist to the utmost; general suggestions are therefore here of least value."

11. This suggestion is found as early as in Griepenkerl's edition (*Orgelwerke* 1, p. 4). Dating from the beginning of the last century, and thus in some manner still connected with a living Bach tradition, his stand assumes a certain importance.

POSTSCRIPT

A short section suggesting manual changes and registration for the variation part of the Passacaglia has been deleted from this chapter. On the *organo pleno* designation of the Passacaglia and general questions of registration and manual change, see George B. Stauffer, *The Organ Preludes of Johann Sebastian Bach* (Ann Arbor, 1980), pp. 155–171.

Shortly after the original publication of this essay, Siegfried Vogelsänger, in his article, "Zur Architektonik der Passacaglia J.S. Bachs," *Die Musikforschung* 25 (1972), pp. 40–50, offered a different analytical approach in which he posits many analogies, correspondences, and symmetries between the variation and fugal sections of the Passacaglia. My critical comments ("Bemerkungen zu S. Vogelsängers Aufsatz 'Zur Architektonik der Passacaglia J.S. Bachs,'" ibid., pp. 488–490) stress the prevailing elements of formal and structural contrast intended by the composer. The material links between the two major sections are apparent because of the common musical subject and its peculiar design (consisting exclusively of accumulated cadential steps). See also Peter Williams, *The Organ Music of J. S. Bach,* vol. 1 (Cambridge, 1980), pp. 253–266.

Analysis filled with symbolic allusions have been offered by Piet Kee, "Die Geheimnisse von Bachs Passacaglia," *Musik und Kirche* 52 (1982), pp. 165–175, 235–244, and ibid., 53 (1983), pp. 19–28; "Maß und Zahl in Passacaglia und Ciacona—Astronomie in Buxtehudes Passacaglia," *Ars Organi* 32 (1984), pp. 232–241; and "Zahl und Symbolik in Passacaglia und Ciacona," *Musik und Kirche* 58 (1988), pp. 231–255.

24. The Organ in Bach's Cantatas

1. *Dok* I, pp. 248–249; cf. also Peter Williams, *The Organ Music of J. S. Bach,* vol. 3 (Cambridge, 1984), pp. 1ff. ("The Music in Service and Recital").

2. Spitta II, p. 860 [German ed.].

3. *Dok* II, no. 232.

4. *Dok,* I, pp. 152–153; cf. also Williams, *Organ Music,* vol. 3, pp. 141f.

5. See the facsimile of the autograph part in *NBA* II/4, p. xii.

6. See Winfried Schrammek, "Fragen des Orgelgebrauchs in Bachs Aufführungen der Matthäus-Passion," *BJ* 1975, pp. 114–123.

7. See *NBA* I/23, *Krit. Bericht,* ed. Helmuth Osthoff (Kassel, 1984), p. 14.

POSTSCRIPT
The original version of this essay contained no citation references. The short section discussing the role of the harpsichord vis-à-vis the organ has been rewritten.

The role of the organ receives a detailed asessment in Laurence D. Dreyfus, *Bach's Continuo Group: Players and Practices in His Vocal Works* (Cambridge, Mass., 1987), chap. 2 (which advances strong arguments in favor of dual accompaniment—organ and harpsichord—in church music and also deals with the *tacet*-indications in organ parts). On the issue of dual accompaniment, see also Hans-Joachim Schulze, "Zur Frage des Doppelaccompagnements (Orgel und Cembalo) in Kirchenmusik-Aufführungen der Bach-Zeit," *BJ* 1987, pp. 173–174, and the subsequent exchange in *BJ* 1989, pp. 227–233. Regarding Bach's use of concertato organ parts see Dreyfus, "The Metaphorical Soloist: Concerted Organ Parts in Bach's Cantatas," in *J. S. Bach as Organist: His Instruments, Music, and Performance Practices,* ed. George B. Stauffer and Ernest D. May (Bloomington, Ind., 1986), pp. 172–189.

25. Apropos the Musical Offering

1. *Dok* III (Appendix for II), no. 558A. For a description of the orginal print and the overall source situation, see my edition in *NBA* VIII/1 (*Krit. Bericht,* 1974).

2. *Dok* II, no. 554; italics added.

3. To be mentioned in this connection are also the allegorical Latin inscriptions for two canons in the dedication copy of the original print. In the *Fuga canonica* the interval distance of canonic entries is given in Greek terminology ("in Epidiapente").

4. Johann Mattheson's remark in connection with Bach's Art of Fugue comes to mind: "Germany is and remains the true organ and fugue country" (*Dok* III, no. 647).

5. Forkel, pp. 9f.

6. According to the press notice, the king played the theme immediately upon Bach's "entering."

7. Friedrich II. von Preußen, *Musikalische Werke,* vol. I (Leipzig, 1889), preface, p. viii.

8. Hermann Keller, "Das Königliche Thema," *Musica* 4 (1950), pp. 277–281.

9. Ibid., p. 279.

10. On the basis of available sources, the sonata cannot be exactly dated.

11. In conversation with Baron van Swieten; cf. *Dok* III, no. 790.

12. See Max Seiffert, *Geschichte der Klaviermusik* (Leipzig, 1899), pp. 203ff.

13. They appear, for instance, in the works of Froberger, Pachelbel, and others; see also BWV 534, 537, 546, 861, and 889; further examples in *BJ* 1924 (Supplement, Table III).

14. See the entry "Passus duriusculus," *Riemann*

Musik-Lexikon, 12th ed., *Sachteil,* ed. Hans-Heinrich Eggebrecht (Mainz, 1967).

15. Hans-Joachim Schulze in the program book for the 47th Bachfest of the Neue Bachgesellschaft, Leipzig, 1972. The author remains indebted to the late Professor Edward E. Lowinsky for a stimulating exchange (in 1970) concerning the subject of this study.

16. Spitta III, pp. 192f.

17. Beginning about the time of Girolamo Cavazzoni's *Intavolatura cioè Recercari Canzoni Himni Magnificat* (Venice, 1543), the imitation ricercar, somewhat in the form of a textless instrumental counterpart of the motet, became a prevalent type.

18. The monothematic ricercar appears, in fact, even before Bach, for instance in the works of Johann Jacob Froberger (*Denkmäler der Tonkunst in Österreich,* VI/1).

19. See Ludwig Landshoff in *Beiheft zur Urtext-Ausgabe* (Leipzig: Peters, 1937), p. 17. Even Hans T. David, in what was the first comprehensive study dealing with the Musical Offering, does not contribute toward a clarification or interpretation of the superscriptions "Ricercare" with regard to the differences of form and texture involved: *J. S. Bach's Musical Offering: History, Interpretation and Analysis* (New York, 1945), pp. 6ff. and 83ff.

20. For the evolution of the term *ricercar* see Hans Heinrich Eggebrecht, "Terminus 'Ricercar,'" *Archiv für Musikwissenschaft* 9 (1952), pp. 137–147; and *Studien zur musikalischen Terminologie,* Abhandlungen der Akademie der Wissenschaften und der Literatur in Mainz, Geistes- und sozialwissenschaftliche Klasse, vol. 1955, no. 10 (Wiesbaden, 1955; 2d ed., 1968).

21. See the entry "Ricercar' uno stromento" in Johann Gottfried Walther, *Musicalisches Lexicon* (Leipzig, 1732; rpt., Kassel, 1953).

22. Cf. Eggebrecht, "Terminus 'Ricercar,'" pp. 143–144.

23. As shown by Eggebrecht's investigations, it is to this process that so-called Bezeichnungsfragmente (fragmentary designations) such as *ricercar* (from the verb *ricercare*) are subjected in particular; cf. *Studien zur musikalischen Terminologie,* pp. 110ff.

24. Heinrich Christoph Koch, in the *Musikalisches Lexikon* (Frankfort, 1802; rpt., Hildesheim, 1964).

25. "Terminus 'Ricercar,'" p. 145.

26. Friedrich Wilhelm Marpurg, *Abhandlung von der Fuge* (Berlin, 1753), pp. 19f.; trans. Alfred Mann, *The Study of Fugue* (New York, 1965; 2d ed., 1987), p. 156.

27. Sébastien de Brossard, *Dictionnaire de Musique* (Paris, 1753; rpt., Amsterdam, 1964).

28. Walther, *Musicalisches Lexicon,* pp. 525–526.

29. Similar to its interpretation by Brossard and Walther is that by other authors: Marin Mersenne, *Harmonie universelle,* vol. 2 (Paris, 1636); Jean-Jacques Rousseau, *Dictionnaire de musique* (Paris, 1767); John Stainer and William Alexander Barret, *Dictionary of Musical Terms* (London, 1889). It is also in various compositions of fantasy or prelude-like character in later periods that the designation "Ricercar" is used in this meaning (e. g., by Georg Christoph Wagenseil, 1715–1777). See Eggebrecht, "Terminus 'Ricercar,'" pp. 145ff.

30. Brossard's entry reads: "RICERCATA veut dire, RECHERCHE. c'est un espece de Prelude ou de fantaisie qu'on joüe sur l'Orgue, le Clavessin, le Théodorbe, etc. où il semble que le Compositeur Recherche les traits d'harmonie qu'il veut employer dans les pieces reglées qu'il doit joüer dans la suite. Cela se fair ordinairement sur le champs & sans preparation, & par consequent cela demande beaucoup d'habilite" (*Dictionnaire de Musique*).

31. "Ricercare, pl. Ricercari [ital.] dieses Wort brauchet so wohl Galilei in seinem Dialogo della musica antica e moderna, f. 87. Tevo in seinem Musico Testore, p. 267. als Penna lib. 3. c. 1. delle Albori Musicali, Johann Krieger in seiner Clavier-Übung, und Praetorius, T. 3. c. 8. Syntagm. als ein Substantivum, und diese letztern beyde insonderheit von einer künstlichen Fuga; sonsten aber ist ricercare ein Verbum, und heisset so viel, als investigare, quaerere, exquirere, mit Fleiß suchen, als welches bey Ausarbeitung einer guten Fuge allerdings nöthig ist, nam ex hac omnium maxime musicum ingenium aestimandum est, si pro certa Modorum natura aptas Fugas eruere, arque erutas bona & laudabili cohaerentia rite jungere noverit. Andere brauchen und setzen davor: Ricercata [ital.]. Recherche [gall.] wovon Brossard schreibet: es sey eine Praeludien- oder Fantaisie-Art, so auf der Orgel, Clavicymbel, Théorbe, u.d.g. gespielt werde, wobey es scheine, ob suche der Componist die Harmonischen Gänge oder Entwürffe, so er hernach in den einzurichtenden Pièces anwenden wolle. Solches geschehe ordinairement ex tempore und ohne praeparation, und erfordere folglich einen starcken habitum. Mich deucht, man könne beyde terminos gar füglich also von einander unterscheiden: daß man dasjenige, so noch gesucht wird, ein Ricercare; hingegen das, so bereits gesucht und künstlich durch starckes Nachsinnen aufgesetzt worden, alsdenn mit gutem Recht eine Ricercata nenne."

The end of the entry contains the attempt, or suggestion, of a conceptual differentiation (*ricercare* and *ricercata*) conveyed by these two variant terms; yet

Walther evidently did not succeed in this respect. The terms *ricercar[e]* and *ricarcata* on the whole continued to be used synonymously. Even various copies of the *Ricercar à 6* show the heading *Ricercata,* as, for example, a manuscript by Johann Friedrich Agricola (DSB, Mus. ms. Bach P 667).

32. This probing can, in fact, be seen to a considerable extent in the *Ricercar à 3.* We might mention here not only the different harmonizations of the theme in various later movements of the Musical Offering but also the extensive harmonic digressions in the episodes, e.g., mm. 31–45. From the manner in which Bach here uses three diverse small patterns sequentially, one will easily conclude that during the improvisation of this episode his thoughts were already turning to the subsequent exposition of the theme in the dominant.

33. In conformance with the conclusion of Walther's entry (cf. note 31), one might call the three-part setting "Ricercare" and the six-part setting "Ricercata."

34. Other than in the original engraving, Bach seems to have referred to the works also as fugues. This applies at least to the *Ricercar à 6.* It is obviously this piece which is meant in the passage of the letter to his cousin Johann Elias Bach of 6 October 1748: "I cannot oblige you at present with the desired copy of the Prussian Fugue, the edition having been exhausted just today, since I had only one hundred printed, most of which were distributed *gratis* to good friends. But between now and the New Year's Fair I shall have some more printed, and if then my honored Cousin is still of a mind to have a copy, he need only give me notice upon occasion, sending me a thaler at the same time, and his wish shall be fulfilled" (*Bach Reader,* p. 182).

In Bach's autograph of the *Ricercar à 6* we find a heading in the hand of C. P. E. Bach, "*6stimmige Fuge, von J. S. Bach u. origineller Handschrift*" (cf. the facsimiles in *BG* 44, p. 134, and *NBA* VIII/1, pp. x-xiii).

35. Eggebrecht, *Studien zur musikalischen Terminologie,* p. 37.

POSTSCRIPT
This chapter combines two studies ("Überlegungen zum Thema Regium" and "Der Terminus 'Ricercar' in Bachs Musikalischem Opfer") that were written and published a few years apart. Part II, the terminological discussion, omits the first section of the original version—specifically *BJ* 1967, pp. 70–76. The contents of that introductory section, which described the original edition of the Musical Offering

according to an earlier state of scholarship (primarily the work of Philipp Spitta and Hans T. David), have largely been superseded by my own subsequent research. The omitted section is not relevant for the presentation of the central terminological argument. For a broader terminological and historical context, see also my article "Ricercar," in *Handwörterbuch der musikalischen Terminologie,* ed. Hans Heinrich Eggebrecht (Wiesbaden, 1974).

26. The Agnus Dei of the B Minor Mass

1. For the date, see Kobayashi *Chr.*
2. See Friedrich Smend, *NBA* II/1, *Krit. Bericht* (Kassel, 1954), pp. 178–184.
3. "Absinken der künstlerischen Qualität" (ibid., p. 189).
4. See also this volume, Chapter 32; and Hans-Joachim Schulze, "The Parody Process in Bach's Music: An Old Problem Reconsidered," *BACH: The Journal of the Riemenschneider Bach Institute* 20 (1989), pp. 7–21.
5. See Werner Neumann, *Sämtliche von J. S. Bach vertonte Texte* (Leipzig, 1974), p. 369.
6. Alfred Dürr, "'Entfernet euch, ihr kalten Herzen.' Möglichkeiten und Grenzen der Rekonstruktion einer Bach-Arie," *Die Musikforschung* 39 (1986), pp. 32–36.
7. Ibid., p. 34.
8. The text presented here follows the formal layout of Gottsched's original libretto, disregarded by Dürr (ibid.).
9. See Dürr (ibid.) for general form analysis.

27. Principles of Design and Order in Bach's Original Editions

1. See the listing and critical discussion of sources for all of Bach's printed works in Kinsky; cf. also Werner Neumann, "Einige neue Quellen zu Johann Sebastian Bachs Herausgabe eigener und zum Mitvertrieb fremder Werke," in *Musa-Mens-Musici: Festschrift für Walter Vetter* (Leipzig, 1969), pp. 165–168.

Aside from the works discussed here (Clavier-Übung I–IV, Musical Offering, Canonic Variations on Vom Himmel hoch, and Art of Fugue), the following works by Bach were printed in his lifetime: "Gott ist mein König," cantata written for the election of the town council, 1708; another cantata for town council election (now lost), 1709; several chorale settings for Schemelli's hymn book of 1736; and the *Canon triplex à 6 voci* for Mizler's musical society, 1747. See this volume, Chapter 29.

2. *Musikalische Bibliothek* IV/1, ed. Lorenz Christoph Mizler (Leipzig, 1754; rpt., Hannover, 1965), p. 171.

3. No detailed discussions dealing with the problem of design in the printed works (except for the Musical Offering and the Art of Fugue) are available. The principal studies approaching this complex of issues are cited below, though without critical assessment, since this essay is not directly related to most of them in orientation or purpose.

4. Concerning the question of formal design, especially in Bach's vocal works, cf. the fundamental studies by Friedrich Smend, "Die Johannes-Passion von Bach. Auf ihren Bau untersucht," *BJ* 1926, pp. 105–128, reprinted in Smend, *Bach-Studien*, ed. Christoph Wolff (Kassel, 1969), and "Luther und Bach," also in *Bach-Studien;* and W. Blankenburg, "Die Symmetrieform in Bachs Werken und ihre Bedeutung," *BJ* 1949–1950, pp. 24–39, and *Einführung in Bach h-Moll-Messe* (Kassel and Basel, 1950). See also Hans T. David, "The Structure of Musical Collections up to 1750," *Bulletin of the American Musicological Society* 3 (1939), pp. 2–5.

5. Cf. Kinsky, pp. 20–27. See also this volume, Chapter 14.

6. Cf. Kinsky, pp. 55–61.

7. Cf. Kinsky, pp. 25–33. See also this volume, Chapter 14.

8. DSB, Mus. ms. Bach P 226 (manuscript in the hand of Anna Magdalena Bach).

9. Cf. Wilhelm Ehmann, "J. S. Bachs Dritter Theil der Clavier Übung in seiner gottesdienstlichen Bedeutung und Verwendung," *Musik und Kirche* 5 (1933), pp. 77–87; Kinsky, pp. 38–47; Karl Ehricht, "'Die zyklische Gestalt und die Aufführungsmöglichkeit des III. Teils der Klavierübung von Joh. Seb. Bach," *BJ* 1949–1950, pp. 40–56; Gustav A. Trumpff, "Der Rahmen zu Bachs Drittem Teil der Klavierübung," *Neue Zeitschrift für Musik* 124 (1963), pp. 466–470. See also this volume, Chapter 15.

10. Concerning number symbolism in Bach's works, cf. Friedrich Smend, *Johann Sebastian Bachs Kirchen-Kantaten*, 3d ed. (Berlin, 1966), vol. 3, pp. 5–21, and vol. 4, pp. 5–21.

11. The argument that the chorales in Clavier-Übung III reflect Luther's Great and Small Catechisms (see Albert Schweitzer's *J. S. Bach* [Leipzig, 1980; German ed.], pp. 251f.) or that they mirror the Mass service (see Ehmann, "J. S. Bachs Dritter Theil") cannot be maintained.

12. Cf. Kinsky, pp. 48–54; Joseph M. Müller-Blattau, "Bachs Goldberg-Variationen," *Archiv für Musikwissenschaft* 16 (1959), pp. 207–219; Rudolf Steglich, "Warum eine Ouverture inmitten der Goldberg-Variationen?" *Musica* 15 (1961), pp. 627–629.

13. Cf. Friedrich Smend, "Bachs Kanonwerk über Vom Himmel hoch da komm ich her," *BJ* 1933, pp. 1–29, reprinted in *Bach-Studien;* Kinsky, pp. 67–71; Walter Emery, "A Note on the History of Bach's Canonic Variations," *Musical Times* 104 (1963), pp. 32f.; Hans Klotz, "Über J. S. Bachs Kanonwerk 'Vom Himmel hoch da komm ich her,'" *Die Musikforschung* 19 (1966), pp. 295–304.

14. DSB, Mus. ms. autogr. Bach P 271.

15. The authenticity of this sequence of sources was doubted by Smend, "Bachs Kanonwerk," p. 29.

16. Cf. Spitta III, pp. 191–197; Kinsky, pp. 62–66; Ludwig Landshoff, *Johann Sebastian Bachs Musikalisches Opfer* (Leipzig, 1937); Hans T. David, *J. S. Bach's Musical Offering: History, Interpretation and Analysis* (New York, 1945); Rudolf Gerber, "Sinn und Ordnung in Bachs Musikalischem Opfer," *Das Musikleben* 1 (1948), pp. 65–72; Erich Schenk, "Das Musikalische Opfer von Johann Sebastian Bach," *Anzeiger der philosophisch-historischen Klasse der Österreichischen Akademie der Wissenschaften* 3 (1953); Wilhelm Pfannkuch, "J. S. Bachs Musikalisches Opfer. Bemerkungen zu den bisherigen Untersuchungen und Neuordnungsversuchen," *Die Musikforschung* 7 (1954), pp. 440–51. See also this volume, Chapter 18.

17. DSB, Mus. ms. Bach P 226.

18. See this volume, Chapter 25, part II.

19. This basic order serves also as a point of departure for David's new interpretation, which is adopted by Gerber and Pfannkuch; conversely, Landshoff, Schenk, and others observe essentially the order of the original print (though transposing its units D–E to E–D).

20. Gerber, "Sinn und Ordnung," p. 68, advanced the thesis that the actual order might be determined according to the ricercare principle (*ricercare* = searching), in the manner of a musical conundrum. Schenk, "Das Musikalische Opfer," pp. 55ff., called attention to possible connections with the genre of the *Musikalische Kunstbuch*.

21. Letter to Johann Elias Bach in Schweinfurt; see *Bach Reader*, p. 182.

22. Cf. Spitta III, pp. 197–208; Wolfgang Graeser, "Bachs Kunst der Fuge," *BJ* 1924, pp. 1–104; Hermann Rietsch, "Zur Kunst der Fuge von J. S. Bach," *BJ* 1926, pp. 1–22; Hans T. David, "Zu

Bachs Kunst der Fuge," *Jahrbuch der Musikbibliothek Peters* 1927, pp. 55–63, and *Joh. Seb. Bach: Die Kunst der Fuge* (Leipzig, 1928; edition with commentary); Kinsky, pp. 74–81; Heinrich Husmann, "Die Kunst der Fuge als Klavierwerk. Besetzung und Anordnung," *BJ* 1938, pp. 1–61; Hans Gunter Hoke, "Studien zur Geschichte der Kunst der Fuge von J. S. Bach," *Beiträge zur Musikwissenschaft* 4 (1962), pp. 81–120; Roswitha Schlötterer-Traimer, *Johann Sebastian Bach: Die Kunst der Fuge,* Meisterwerke der Musik, vol. 4 (Munich, 1966). See also this volume, Chapter 20.

23. DSB, Mus. ms. autogr. Bach P 200.

24. *Musikalische Bibliothek* IV/1, p. 168.

25. We should refer here to the two most significant, though not unequivocal, new interpretations of the order, presented by David, "Zu Bachs Kunst der Fuge," and Husmann, "Die Kunst der Fuge als Klavierwerk"; the former takes its point of departure from the autograph and the latter, essentially from the printed version.

26. With particular skepticism, however, we must regard new interpretations devoted to the idea of a musically varied cyclic performance of the total work (compounded by expressly attractive instrumentation), an idea doubtless not in line with the intentions of the composer, here or in the cases of Clavier-Übung III and the Musical Offering.

POSTSCRIPT

The discussion of matters related to the Musical Offering and the Art of Fugue has been directly affected by my later and more intensive source studies in both works, some of which are included in this volume (Chapters 18 and 20). The nomenclature regarding the printing units in the original edition of the Musical Offering (Table 27.6) has been adjusted to be consistent with that in Chapter 18. While the results of my research have basically corroborated the principal thesis regarding principles of design and order in Bach's original editions, a number of conclusions must be modified and some specific details must be corrected. Much of it will be obvious to the reader, who is asked to consult Chapters 18 and 20 concurrently. I should like to single out two points, however.

Regarding the Musical Offering, I consider the differentiation between "contrapuntal" and "thematic" canons, first proposed by Hans T. David, no longer plausible—and this for both analytical and source-critical reasons. The group of "Canones diversi"—that is, nos. 1–5 in printing unit D, which are clearly numbered by Bach and form a logical sequence—should not be broken up. There seems to be no indication that Bach intended to make use of rigid symmetric devices in the Musical Offering.

As for the Art of Fugue, it is important to realize that the differences in movement order between the autograph manuscript and the original edition must not be considered as reflecting unresolved experiments in large-scale design. The order in the autograph definitely represents an earlier stage in the history of the work.

Gregory G. Butler, "Ordering Problems in J. S. Bach's Art of Fugue Resolved," *Musical Quarterly* 69 (1983), pp. 44–81, proposes that Bach planned to put the four canons at the very end of the work, that is, after the quadruple fugue—a hypothesis that, for lack of musical or source-critical evidence, I find difficult to accept. Observations with respect to both performance aspects and cyclical structures are made by Werner Breig, "Bachs Kunst der Fuge: Zur instrumentalen Bestimmung und zum Zyklus-Charakter," *BJ* 1982, pp. 103–123.

28. Toward a Definition of the Last Period of Bach's Work

1. From the obituary: *Bach Reader,* p. 215.

2. *Bach Reader,* p. 249.

3. *Bach Reader,* p. 123.

4. Readers interested in this aspect of Bach's work will find pertinent discussions in the following sources: Georg von Dadelsen, "Zu Bachs Leipziger Schaffen," in *Festschrift Martin Ruhnke zum 65. Geburtstag,* ed. Klaus-Jürgen Sachs (Neuhausen-Stuttgart, 1986), pp. 68–82; Alfred Dürr, "Gibt es einen Spätstil im Kantatenschaffen Bachs?" in *Bachtage Berlin. Vorträge 1970–1981,* ed. Günther Wagner (Neuhausen-Stuttgart, 1985), pp. 61–74; Rudolf Eller, "Gedanken über Bachs Leipziger Schaffensjahre," in *Bach-Studien,* vol. 5, ed. Rudolf Eller and Hans-Joachim Schulze (Leipzig, 1975), pp. 7–27; Kobayashi *Chr;* Marshall *Bach,* pp. 23–58; Wolff *Stile antico;* this volume, Chapters 1, 16, and 19.

POSTSCRIPT

This chapter was originally written as the introductory paper to the proceedings of the 1986 Bach Symposium devoted to the topic of Bach's late period; see also the contributions to related subject areas (continuity and change in Bach's style during the 1730s and 1740s; performance-related issues; opera and aesthetics) in *Johann Sebastian Bachs Spätwerk und des-*

sen Umfeld. Bericht über das wissenschaftliche Symposion anläßlich des 61. Bachfestes der Neuen Bach-gesellschaft, Duisburg 1986, ed. Christoph Wolff (Kassel, 1988).

29. On the Original Editions of Bach's Works

1. For instance, the performing parts for the Sanctus BWV 232[III]; cf. Bach's correspondence with Christoph Gottlob Wecker (*Dok* I, no. 20) and with Johann Wilhelm Koch (*Dok* II, nos. 475 and 484).

2. The Brandenburg Concertos, Kyrie and Gloria of the B Minor Mass, and the Musical Offering.

3. See Paul Kast, *Die Bach-Handschriften der Berliner Staatsbibliothek, TBSt 2/3* (Trossingen, 1958); *Handschriften der Werke Johann Sebastian Bachs in der Musikbibliothek der Stadt Leipzig,* ed. Peter Krause (Leipzig, 1964).

4. *Dok* III, nos. 711, 789, and 1027.

5. *Dok* III, no. 853.

6. The entire material concerned was first compiled in *Dok* III.

7. Martini also owned Part III of the Clavier-Übung.

8. *Dok* II, no. 600.

9. Ibid.

10. The *Musikalische Gesang-Buch,* whose edition was undertaken by Georg Christian Schemelli (Leipzig: B. C. Breitkopf, 1736) cannot be designated as an original Bach print in the true sense. Probably no more than three of the sixty-nine melodies are by Bach, and his collaboration in the publication of the *Gesang-Buch* was limited to the elaboration of the thoroughbass.

11. For a discussion of the technical process see this volume, Chapter 15.

12. They were included in the second Clavier-Büchlein for Anna Magdalena Bach, 1725.

13. *Dok,* II, no. 224.

14. The collection, following the model of Kuhnau's Clavier-Übung, was originally planned in seven issues; see *Dok* II, no. 276, and this volume, Chapter 15.

15. For the design of the prints, historical context, and bibliographical details, see this volume, Chapter 15.

16. *Bach Reader,* p. 223 (*Dok* III, no. 666).

17. Martin Ruhnke, "Telemann als Musikverleger," in *Musik und Verlag,* ed. Richard Baum and Wolfgang Rehm (Kassel, 1968), p. 504.

18. *Dok* II, no. 526.

19. See this volume, Chapter 15.

20. Concerning Bach's original prints, see the

standard work by Georg Kinsky, *Die Originalausgaben der Werke Johann Sebastian Bachs* (Vienna, Leipzig, and Zurich, 1937), and my article, "Die Originaldrucke Johann Sebastian Bachs" (Introduction and Catalogue, giving source locations), *Die Nürnberger Musikverleger und die Familie Bach* (Nuremberg, 1973), pp. 15–20; descriptions of the individual prints are in the critical reports of the respective *NBA* volumes.

21. *Dok* I, no. 175.

22. See Werner Neumann, "Einige neue Quellen zu J. S. Bachs Herausgabe eigener und zum Mitvertrieb fremder Werke," in *Musa—Mens—Musici. Gedenkschrift für Walter Vetter* (Leipzig, 1969), pp. 165–168; and *Dok* III, nos. 260, 363, and 373.

POSTSCRIPT

This chapter first appeared in the essay section of the exhibition catalogue, *300 Jahre Johann Sebastian Bach: Sein Werk in Handschriften und Dokumenten. Eine Ausstellung der Internationalen Bachakademie in der Staatsgalerie Stuttgart,* ed. Ulrich Prinz (Tutzing, 1985). References to the numbered items in the exhibition and to the catalogue entries and illustrations have been omitted from the present version.

Detailed information on the printing history of most of Bach's original editions has been made available by Gregory G. Butler; in addition to the bibliographical references in the Postscript to Chapter 15, see his "J. S. Bach and the Schemelli Gesangbuch Revisited," *Studi Musicali* 13 (1984), pp. 241–257.

30. Bach's Vocal Music and Early Music Criticism

1. *Dok* III, p. 80.

2. *Dok* II, no. 83.

3. For the performance history of Cantata No. 21, see *Bach Compendium* I/1, p. 405.

4. *Dok* II, no. 200.

5. *Dok* II, no. 124.

6. *Dok* II, no. 352; see this volume, Chapter 10.

7. *Dok* III, no. 636:

Erblichner Bach! Dir hat allein dein
    Orgelschlagen
  Das edle Vorzugs-Wort des Großen längst
    gebracht;
Und was für Kunst dein Kiel aufs
    Notenblatt getragen,
  Das wird von Meistern selbst nicht ohne
    Neid betracht't.

8. *Dok* II, p. 286; see this volume, Chapter 32.

9. *Dok* II, p. 286.

10. Ibid., p. 305.

11. Ibid., p. 305.

12. *Dok* II, no. 463; in the same year, 1745, Scheibe also issued an apology for his attacks on Bach (*Dok* II, no. 530).

13. *Dok* III, p. 603.

POSTSCRIPT

The original version of this chapter was published without notes.

31. On the Recognition of Bach and "the Bach Chorale"

1. Published in *Allgemeine musikalische Zeitung* 2 (Leipzig, 1799), cols. 103–104. See also *Dok* III, p. 586.

2. Forkel provides the following comment: "Our worthy Haydn is reported to have seen this piece himself and to have been not a little pleased by it, having not been ashamed to find himself a neighbor of Handel and Graun. Nor was he said to have questioned that Joh. Seb. Bach is the center of the sun and thus the man from whom all musical wisdom emanates" (*Dok* III, p. 587).

3. See *Dok* II, no. 600.

4. The implication (likewise in Beethoven's famous dictum), corresponding to the terminology of the time, is "Bach, the father of the art of composition"; see especially Johann Friedrich Reichardt's similar appraisement of Bach as harmonist (1782) with Goethe's impression of the Strasbourg Cathedral (*Dok* III, no. 864).

5. "Sebastian Bach was a genius of the highest degree. His spirit is so individual, so immense, that it will require centuries to reach his equal" (*Dok* III, no. 903); see this volume, Chapter 32.

6. Carl Philipp Emanuel Bach in the obituary; see *Bach Reader*, p. 222.

7. *Johann Sebastian Bachs vierstimmige Choralgesänge,* ed. Carl Philipp Emanuel Bach and Johann Philipp Kirnberger, vols. I–IV (Leipzig: Gottlob Immanuel Breitkopf, 1784–1787). A previous edition was *Johann Sebastian Bachs vierstimmige Choralgesänge,* ed. C. P. E. Bach, vols. I–II (Berlin: Friedrich Wilhelm Birnstiel: Berlin, 1765–1769). For the prefaces to these editions, see *Bach Reader*, pp. 270–275.

8. *Dok* III, no. 853.

9. Facsimile in *NBA* II/1, ed. Friedrich Smend (*Krit. Bericht,* 1956), p. 215.

10. See Gerd Wachowski, "Die vierstimmigen Choräle Johann Sebastian Bachs. Untersuchungen zu den Druckausgaben von 1765 bis 1932 und zur Frage der Authentizität," *BJ* 1983, pp. 51–79.

11. *Dok* III, no. 898.

12. *Gradus ad Parnassum* (Vienna, 1725). Facsimile edition with German and English commentary in: Johann Joseph Fux, *Sämtliche Werke,* series VII, vol. 1, ed. Alfred Mann; see also the latter's English translations in *The Study of Counterpoint* (New York, 1943; rpt., 1965) and *The Study of Fugue* (New York, 1965; rpt., 1987).

13. Johann Abraham Peter Schulz said in 1785: "Only Germany can call such a work its own" (*Dok* III, no. 906).

14. *Dok* III, no. 723.

15. *Dok* III, p. 87; see this volume, Chapter 32.

16. *Dok* III, no. 723.

17. See Werner Breig, "Grundzüge einer Geschichte von Bachs vierstimmigem Choralsatz," *Archiv für Musikwissenschaft* 45 (1988), pp. 165–185 and 300–319.

18. The line of development here suggested is neither direct (it includes above all the type of chorale setting with obbligato instruments from Bach's first year in the Leipzig office), nor can it—with the exception of certain tendencies—be determined in a strictly chronological sense. The major obstacle to such an analysis is the lack of available dates for the majority of the chorales contained in the Birnstiel and Breitkopf editions.

19. The two versions appear in *NBA* II/4 (ed. Arthur Mendel, 1974).

20. "Ich bitt, o Herr, aus Herzensgrund" (BWV 18/5).

21. The oldest source for BWV 706 is a copy by Johann Tobias Krebs, written no later than 1714 (DSB, Mus. ms. Bach P 801, pp. 24–25). Thus the origin of BWV 706 doubtless antedates that of BWV 18.

22. See this volume, Chapter 22.

23. See Emil Platen, "Zur Echtheit einiger Choralzätze Johann Sebastian Bachs," *BJ* 1975, pp. 50ff. Bach is also known to have used settings from the Dresden hymnal of 1694, from Daniel Vetter's *Musicalische Kirch- und Haußergötzlichkeit* (Leipzig, 1713), as well as those of Johann Pachelbel (1683); see *Bach Compendium* I/4, Work Group F.

24. The most concrete vestiges of chorale manuscripts not belonging to the cantata repertoire are found in the listing of C. P. E. Bach's estate (Hamburg, 1790), appendix to the Schemelli *Gesang-Buch* of "88 Fully Harmonized Chorales" (*Dok* III, p.

496); see also "J. S. Bachs vollständiges Choralbuch" (*Dok* III, p. 166) and the corresponding commentary in *Bach Compendium* I/4, pp. 1265–1274.

25. Letter to Johann Nicolaus Forkel: "His pupils had to begin their studies by learning pure four-part thorough bass. From this he went to chorales; first he added the basses to them himself, and they had to invent the alto and tenor. Then he taught them to devise the basses themselves . . . The introduction to chorales [is] without doubt the best method of studying composition, as far as harmony is concerned" (*Bach Reader*, p. 279).

26. Musikbibliothek der Stadt Leipzig, Ms. R 18; see Friedrich Smend, "Zu den ältesten Sammlungen der vierstimmigen Choräle Johann Sebastian Bachs," *BJ* 1966, pp. 5–40; and Hans-Joachim Schulze, "'150 Stück von den Bachischen Erben,' Zur Überlieferung der vierstimmigen Choräle Johann Sebastian Bachs," *BJ* 1983, pp. 81–100.

27. *Handbuch bey dem Generalbasse und der Composition*, Part III (Berlin, 1758): "The best models for this manner of writing, to be followed, are the elaborations of this kind of the late Hon. Capellmeister Bach" (German original quoted in *Dok* III, no. 697).

28. See this volume, Chapter 32.

29. Rudolf Eisler, *Wörterbuch der Philosophischen Begriffe*, 4th ed. (Berlin, 1929), vol. 2, p. 439.

30. Letter to Friedrich Hoffmeister, 15 January 1801; see *Ludwig van Beethovens sämtliche Briefe und Aufzeichnungen*, ed. Fritz Prelinger, vol. 1: *1783–1814* (Vienna and Leipzig, 1907), p. 65.

31. *Jenaische Allgemeine Literaturzeitung* 282 (November 1805), p. 391; I am indebted to Reinhold Brinkmann for this reference.

POSTSCRIPT

This chapter combines two essays which were conceived and published separately: Part I was originally presented in 1985 at the Bach Symposium of the International Congress of the Gesellschaft für Musikforschung in Stuttgart as an introduction ("Zur Rezeptionsgeschichte Bachs im 18. Jahrhundert") to the session discussing the eighteenth-century Bach reception. Part II originated as a paper ("Bachs vierstimmige Choräle. Geschichtliche Perspektiven im 18. Jahrhundert") given in 1985 at the Bach Symposium of the Wissenschaftskolleg Berlin.

Part I: The topic is explored more extensively by Ludwig Finscher, "Bach in the Eighteenth Century," in *Bach Studies*, ed. Don O. Franklin (Cambridge, 1989), pp. 281–296; see also my essay, "Bach und die Folgen: Überlegungen zu den Grundlagen und Anfängen der Bach-Rezeption," *Bachwoche Ansbach*

1989: Offizieller Almanach (Ansbach, 1989), pp. 23–34.

32. "The Extraordinary Perfections of the Hon. Court Composer"

1. See Carl Dahlhaus, "Zur Entstehung der romantischen Bach-Deutung", *BJ* 1978, pp. 192–220, and Martin Zenck, "Studien der Bach-Deutung in der Musikkritik, Musikästhetik und Musikgeschichtsschreibung zwischen 1750 und 1800," *BJ* 1982, pp. 7–32.

2. Cf. the summary discussion by Günther Wagner, "J. S. Bach und J. A. Scheibe," *BJ* 1982, pp. 33–49.

3. Johann Abraham Birnbaum, *Verteydigung seyner unpartheyischen Anmerkungen* (Leipzig, 1739), *Dok* II, p. 349 (*Bach Reader*, p. 239).

4. *Denkmal dreyer verstorbener Mitglieder der Societät der musikalischen Wissenschaften* (the section dealing with Bach written in 1750 by Carl Philipp Emanuel Bach and Johann Friedrich Agricola; published in 1754), *Dok* III, p. 87 (*Bach Reader*, p. 213).

5. C. F. D. Schubart, *Ideen zu einer Ästhetik der Tonkunst* (1784–1785), *Dok* III, p. 408.

6. Ibid., p. 409.

7. *Dok* III, p. 87 (*Bach Reader*, p. 222).

8. *Dok* II, pp. 304f. (*Bach Reader*, p. 246).

9. Ibid., p. 303 (*Bach Reader*, p. 245).

10. Johann Mattheson, *Der Vollkommene Capellmeister* (Hamburg, 1739; facsimile: Kassel, 1954), p. 245.

11. *Dok* II, p. 302 (*Bach Reader*, p. 244).

12. Ibid., p. 353.

13. Ibid., p. 303 (*Bach Reader*, p. 244).

14. Ibid., p. 305 (*Bach Reader*, p. 246).

15. B. Fabian, "Genie," in *Historisches Wörterbuch der Philosophie*, ed. Joachim Ritter, vol. 3 (Darmstadt, 1974), p. 279

16. *Dok* II, p. 303 (*Bach Reader*, p. 245).

17. *Dok* III, p. 87 (*Bach Reader*, p. 222).

18. *Dok* II, p. 300 (*Bach Reader*, p. 242). In substantiating his statements, Birnbaum refers to Bach's melodic style as "chromatic and dissonant," which he considers part of the "dissonant wealth of the Hon. Court Composer" (ibid., p. 354).

19. *Dok* II, p. 397 (*Bach Reader*, p. 290).

20. Letter to Johann Nicolaus Forkel (Hamburg, 1774), *Dok* III, p. 285 (*Bach Reader*, p. 277).

21. *Dok* III, p. 82 (*Bach Reader*, p. 216).

22. C. P. E. Bach's letter to Forkel (Hamburg, 1775), *Dok* III (*Bach Reader*, p. 278).

23. *Dok* II, p. 302 (*Bach Reader*, p. 244).

24. *Dok* II, p. 300 (*Bach Reader,* p. 242.)

25. Ludwig Finscher, "Zum Parodieproblem bei Bach," in *Bach-Interpretationen,* ed. Martin Geck (Göttingen, 1961), pp. 99ff.

26. *Dok* II, p. 355.

POSTSCRIPT

For a corresponding re-evaluation of Bach's use of parody, see Hans-Joachim Schulze, "The Parody Process in Bach's Music: An Old Problem Reconsidered," *Bach: The Journal of the Riemenschneider Bach Institute* 20 (1989), pp. 7–21. See also the essay "On Bach's Universality" in Marshall *Bach,* pp. 65–79.

Acknowledgments

The essays collected in this volume are listed below with their original titles and places of publication. Those that originally appeared in German and translated here by permission of the publishers, and those that were first published in English and are reprinted here with permission.

Essays Originally Published in German

TRANSLATED FOR THIS VOLUME
BY ALFRED MANN

Chapter 8: "Die Tradition des vokalpolyphonen Stils in der neueren Musikgeschichte, insbesondere bei Bach," *Musik und Kirche* 38 (1968), pp. 62–80.

Chapter 10: "Bachs Kantoratsprobe und die Aufführungsgeschichte der Kantate *'Du wahrer Gott und Davids Sohn'* BWV 23," *Bach-Jahrbuch* 64 (1978), pp. 78–94.

Chapter 11: "Zur musikalischen Vorgeschichte des Kyrie aus J. S. Bachs Messe in h-Moll," *Festschrift für Bruno Stäblein zum 70. Geburtstag,* ed. Martin Ruhnke (Kassel, 1967), pp. 316–326.

Chapter 16: "Textkritische Bemerkungen zum Originaldruck der Bachschen Partiten," *Bach-Jahrbuch* 65 (1979), pp. 65–74.

Chapter 20: "Zur Chronologie und Kompositionsgeschichte von Bachs *'Kunst der Fuge,'*" *Beiträge zur Musikwissenschaft* 25 (1983), pp. 130–142.

Chapter 21: "Bachs Sterbechoral. Kritische Fragen zu einem Mythos," in *Essays in Renaissance and Baroque Music in Honor of Arthur Mendel,* ed. Robert L. Marshall (Kassel, 1974), pp. 283–297.

Chapter 22: "Zur Problematik der Chronologie und Stilentwicklung des Bachschen Frühwerkes, insbesondere zur musikalischen Vorgeschichte des Orgelbüchleins," in *Bericht über die Wissenschaftliche Konferenz Leipzig 1985,* ed. Winfried Hoffmann and Armin Schneiderheinze (Leipzig, 1988), pp. 449–455.

Chapter 23: "Die Architektur von Bachs Passacaglia," *Acta Organologica* 3 (1969), pp. 183–194.

Chapter 25, part I: "Überlegungen zum 'Thema Regium'" *Bach-Jahrbuch* 59 (1973), pp. 33–38.

Chapter 25, part II: "Der Terminus 'Ricercar' in Bachs Musikalischem Opfer," *Bach-Jahrbuch* 53 (1967), pp. 70–81.

Chapter 27: "Ordnungsprinzipien in den Originaldrucken Bachscher Werke," in *Bach-Interpretationen,* ed. Martin Geck (Göttingen, 1969), pp. 144–167, 223–225.

Chapter 28: "Bachs Spätwerk: Versuch einer Definition," in *Johann Sebastian Bachs Spätwerk und dessen Umfeld: Perspektiven und Probleme. Bericht über das wissenschaftliche Symposion anläßlich des 61. Bachfestes der Neuen Bachgesellschaft, Duisburg 1986,* ed. Christoph Wolff (Kassel, 1988), pp. 15–22.

Chapter 29: "Zu den Originalausgaben Johann Sebastian Bachs," in *300 Jahre Johann Sebastian Bach. Ausstellungs-Katalog Stuttgart 1985,* ed. Ulrich Prinz (Tutzing, 1985), pp. 57–64.

Chapter 31, part I: "Zur Rezeptionsgeschichte Bachs im 18. Jahrhundert," in *Alte Musik als ästhetische Gegenwart: Bach, Händel, Schütz. Bericht über den internationalen musikwissenschaftlichen Kongreß Stuttgart 1985,* ed. Dietrich Berke and Dorothee Hanemann, vol. 1 (Kassel, 1987), pp. 162–164.

Chapter 31, part II: "Bachs vierstimmige Choräle.

Geschichtliche Perspektiven im 18. Jahrhundert," in *Jahrbuch des Instituts für Musikforschung der Stiftung Preußischer Kulturbesitz 1985–86,* ed. Günther Wagner (Kassel, 1989), pp. 257–263.

Chapter 32: "'Die sonderbaren Vollkommenheiten des Herrn Hofcompositeurs.' Versuch über die Eigenart der Bachschen Musik," in *Bachiana et alia musicologica. Festschrift Alfred Dürr zum 65. Geburtstag,* ed. Wolfgang Rehm (Kassel, 1983), pp. 356–362.

Essays Previously Published in English

Chapter 1: "Problems and New Perspectives of Bach Biography," *Proteus* 2 (1985), pp. 1–7.

Chapters 2–4: "The Family," "Events in His Life and Career," "Employers and Patrons," in *Johann Sebastian Bach: Life, Times, and Influence,* ed. Wolfgang Dömling and Barbara Schwendowius (Kassel, 1977), pp. 51–82.

Chapter 5: "Dietrich Buxtehude and Seventeenth-Century Music in Retrospect," in *Church, Stage, and Studio,* ed. Paul Walker (Ann Arbor, 1989), pp. 3–20.

Chapter 6: "Johann Adam Reinken and Johann Sebastian Bach: On the Context of Bach's Early Works," in *Bach the Organist,* ed. George B. Stauffer and Ernest May (Urbana-Champaign, 1985), pp. 57–80.

Chapter 7: "Vivaldi's Compositional Art and the Process of 'Musical Thinking,'" in *Nuovi Studi Vivaldiani,* vol. 1, ed. Antonio Fanna and Giovanni Morelli (Florence, 1988), pp. 1–17.

Chapter 9: "Introduction," in *The Neumeister Collection of Chorale Preludes from the Bach Circle (Yale University Manuscript LM 4708): A Facsimile Edition,* ed. Christoph Wolff (New Haven and London, 1986), pp. 1–14.

Chapter 12: "Bach's Cantata *Ein feste Burg*: History and Performance Practice," *American Choral Review* 24 (1982), pp. 27–38.

Chapter 13: "Bach's *Handexemplar* of the Goldberg Variations: A New Source," *Journal of the American Musicological Society,* 29 (1976), pp. 224–241.

Chapter 14: "Bach's Personal Copy of the Schübler Chorales," in *Bach the Organist,* ed. George B. Stauffer and Ernest May (Urbana-Champaign, 1985), pp. 121–132.

Chapter 15: "Commentary," in *Johann Sebastian Bach's Clavier-Übung,* Faksimile-Ausgabe, ed. Christoph Wolff (Leipzig, 1984), pp. 21–32.

Chapter 17: "Bach's Leipzig Chamber Music," *Early Music* 13 (1985), pp. 165–175. © Oxford University Press.

Chapter 18: "New Research on Bach's *Musical Offering,*" *The Musical Quarterly* 57 (1971), pp. 379–408.

Chapter 19: "The Last Fugue: Unfinished?" *Current Musicology* 19 (1975), pp. 71–77.

Chapter 24: "The Organ in Bach's Cantata Works," *Das Kantatenwerk,* vol. 13 (Hamburg: Teldec 6.35284–00–501, 1975), pp. 7–8.

Chapter 26: "The *Agnus Dei* of Bach's B Minor Mass: Parody and New Composition Reconciled," in *A Bach Tribute: Essays in Honor of William H. Scheide,* ed. Paul Brainard and Ray Robinson (Princeton, N.J., 1988).

Chapter 30: "Bach's Vocal Works and Early Music Criticism," *Das Kantatenwerk,* vol. 20 (Hamburg: Teldec 6.35362–00–501, 1978), pp. 6–7.

Illustrations

Various archives and libraries have granted their permission to reproduce here the autograph scores and other illustrative material in their collections. My thanks to all those who extended this courtesy:

Bayerische Staatsbibliothek, Munich: Figure 18.3 (Mus. pr. 2ᵉ 777

Biblioteka Jagiellońska, Kraków: Figures 17.1, 17.2 (Mus. ms. Bach St 127); 17.3, 17.4 (Mus. ms. Bach St 148)

Bibliothèque Nationale, Paris: Figure 13.1 (Ms. 17 669)

Deutsche Staatsbibliothek, Berlin: Figures 8.1 (Mus. ms. 16714, 15 [recto page]); 8.3 (Mus. ms. 2755 [inserted leaf]); 10.1–10.3 (Mus. ms. Bach St 16); 11.1 (Mus. ms. 23116/10); 15.2 (Mus. o. 73355 R); 18.1 (Mus. o. 9525 R); 18.2 (Am.B. 73); 18.4 (Am.B. 74); 18.6 (Am.B. 73); 19.1, 19.2, 19.4, 20.1 (Mus. ms. Bach P 200)

Internationale Bachakademie, Stuttgart: Figure 2.2

Johann-Sebastian-Bach-Institut, Göttingen, and Bach-Archiv, Leipzig: Figure 12.1 (originally published in *NBA* I/31).

Music Division, Library of Congress, Washington, D.C.: Figures 16.1, 16.2 (LM 3. 3B2. Case)

Musikbibliothek der Stadt Leipzig: Figures —=.2 (PM 5696); 15.1 (Becker III. 6.12); 15.3,

15.4 (Becker III. 6.13); 15.15, 15.6 (Becker III. 6.14); 15.7, 15.8 (PM 1403); 15.9, 15.10 (PM 1400); 18.5 (PM 5696)

Staatsbibliothek Preußischer Kulturbesitz, Berlin: Figure 8.2 (Mus. ms. 1169, fol. 84v); 11.2 (Mus. ms. Bach P 180); 20.2 (Mus. ms. Bach P 167)

Stadtarchiv Leipzig: Figure 17.5 (Riemer Chronik)

Stadtbibliothek Lübeck: Figures 5.1, 5.2 (Lub 133)

William H. Scheide Collection, Princeton, N.J.: Figures 13.3a, 14.1–14.4, cover illustration

Yale University, John Herrick Jackson Music Library, New Haven, Conn.: Figures 9.1, 9.2 (LM 4708); 9.3–9.5 (LM 4630); 9.6 (LM 4708)

Index of Works by
Johann Sebastian Bach

1. Individual Compositions

2. Collections

Index of Archival Sources

Dresden, Sächsische Landesbibliothek
Mus. 2405–D-21, Aut. 2 (BWV 232¹), 411;
Mus. 2405–R-1 (BWV 1023), 229; Mus.
2392–O-35a (Telemann) 299

Frankfurt/Main, Mozart-Stiftung
Ms. Schelble-Gleichauf (lost), 126, 408

Frankfurt/Main, Stadt- und Universitätsbibliothek
Mus. Hs. 1538 (Grigny), 299

Fulda, Hessische Landesbibliothek
K.W.F. 138/84 (BWV 1079), 247

The Hague, Gemeente Museum
Bach-Doos, Nr. III (BWV 1079), 247; Ms.
4.G.14 (J.G. Walther), 123–127

Hamburg, Staats- und Universitätsbibliothek
MS 202/2b (Fux), 93

Königsberg (Kaliningrad), Universitätsbibliothek
(see Winterthur)
Ms. Gotthold 15839 (lost), 118, 123–126, 407

Kraków, Biblioteka Jagiellońska
Mus. ms. Bach St 127 (BWV 1055), 230–233;
St 148 (BWV 1043), 234–237
Mus. ms. 40035 (Eckelt tablature book), 60f.,
403

Leipzig, Bach-Archiv
Gorke Collection: Go.S. 25 (Hohlstein), 123

Leipzig, Musikbibliothek, 402
PM 1403 (Clavier-Übung III), 181, 415, 418;
PM 5696 (BWV 1079), 247
Becker Collection: III.6.12 (BWV 826), 418;
III.6.17 (BWV 1079), 247; III.8.3 (Andreas
Bach Book), 407
Mempell-Preller Collection, 107; Ms. 7 (Organ
Works), 124
Poelitz Collection: Mus. ms. 39 (J. N. Geb-
hardi), 123
Rudorff Collection: R 18 (Four-Part Chorales),
389, 435; R 24, 406

Leipzig, Stadtarchiv
Gorke Collection: Go.S. 301 (Albinoni), 299

Leningrad, Saltykov Shchedrin Library
BWV 80b (Ms. without shelfmark), 153, 155,
413

London, British Library
K.8.g.7 (Clavier-Übung II), 163, 414, 416,
418; K.10.b.28 (BWV 1079), 247
Hirsch Collection: III.37 (Clavier-Übung I),
215, 218, 220, 414f., 418

Munich, Bayerische Staatsbibliothek
Mus. pr. 2°, 777 (BWV 1079), 247

New Haven, Connecticut, Yale University, Music
Library
Lowell Mason Collection: LM 4630 (Sorge), 407;
LM 4693 (J. M. Bach), 408; LM 4708 (Neumeister Collection), 107–127, 300, 301–304,
403, 406–408, 426; LM 4803, 406; LM
4839b, 107; LM 4843, 107; LM 4982, 107;
LM 4983 (J. G. Bach Book), 107, 124; LM
5056 (Codex E. B. 1688), 107

New York, New York, Private Collection
BWV 131, 299

Paris, Bibliothèque Nationale
Ms. 17669 (BWV 988), 163, 166, 209, 414,
417f.

Paris, Musée Adam Mickiewicz
Album Musical de M. Szymanowska (BWV 80b;
without shelfmark), 153, 155, 413

Princeton, New Jersey, Scheide Library
BWV 80b (Ms. without shelfmark), 153, 413;
Schübler Chorales (without shelfmark), 163,
178–186

Rochester, New York, Eastman School of Music,
Sibley Music Library
M3.3.B 118 (BWV 1079), 247

Tokyo, Nanki Library
Catalogue of Zelter Collection (no shelfmark),
424

Urbana, Illinois, University of Illinois, Library
xq.786.41/B 12cu (Clavier-Übung I), 215,
217f., 221

Vienna, Österreichische Nationalbibliothek
Hoboken Collection: J. S. Bach 56 (Clavier-
Übung I), 217, 221; J. S. Bach 100–102
(BWV 1079) [Copies A-C], 247, 418

Washington, D.C., Library of Congress
LM 3.3 B2 Case (Clavier-Übung I) [G 25],
215f., 218–221; M 3.3.B 2 (BWV 1079),
246f., 419; ML 30.8b.B2M4 (BWV 10),
184f.; ML 96.B 186.case (BWV 80), 413

Winterthur, Stadtbibliothek
Microfilm copies of lost or inacessible manu-
scripts (see Berlin, Hochschule für Musik, and
Königsberg)

General Index

Denner, Johann Balthasar, 20, 400f.
Deutsch, Otto Erich, 6, 410
Deyling, Salomon, 39
Diefenbach, Johann Philipp, 407
Diehl, Wilhelm, 407
Diener, Hermann, 419
Dieskau, Carl Heinrich von, 36f.
Dietel, Johann Ludwig, 389
Dietrich, Fritz, 407
Dieupart, François, 10
Donat, Friedrich-Wilhelm, 406
Dörffel, Alfred, 240
Dorfmüller, Kurt, 408
Douglass, Fenner, 417
Dresden, 12, 15, 21, 23, 28, 31, 35–37, 88, 94,
    141–143, 191, 197, 201, 207, 212f., 227,
    231, 359f., 362, 373, 400, 412, 414, 434;
    Frauenkirche, 207f., 417; St. Sophia, 94, 360
Drese, Johann Samuel, 29
Dreyfus, Laurence, 234, 410, 413, 428
Dröbs, Johann Andreas. *See* Copyists
Dropa, Matthias, 62
Droysen, Johann Gustav, 4
Düben Collection, 42
Düben family, 401
Du Mage, Pierre, 393
    Livre d'orgue (1708), 207, 380
Dürer, Albrecht, 384
Dürr, Alfred, 128f., 132f., 137, 334, 404, 406,
    408–411, 413, 425f., 430, 432

Ebersdorf (Vogtland), 108, 110, 407f.
Eckelt, Johann Valentin, 60, 403, 405
Edler, Arnfried, 402, 404
Eggebrecht, Hans Heinrich, 330, 429f.
Ehmann, Wilhelm, 431
Ehricht, Karl, 431
Eichberg, Hartwig, 298, 402f., 426
Eilmar, Georg Christian, 37f.
Einstein, Alfred, 411
Eisenach, 14f., 17–19, 25, 64, 115, 399; Latin
    School, 26; St. George, 25, 112
Eisler, Rudolf, 435
Eleanore d'Olbreuse, Duchesse of Braunschweig-
    Lüneburg and Celle, 62
Eleonore Wilhelmine, Princess of Anhalt-Cöthen,
    34
Eller, Rudolf, 72, 75, 405, 432
Emanuel Ludwig, Prince of Anhalt-Cöthen, 35
Emery, Walter, 406, 413f., 418, 431
Eppstein, Hans, 418
Erdmann, Georg, 7, 19, 26, 35, 231
Erfurt, 14, 17, 25, 59f., 110, 115; St. Thomas,
    59

Erich, Daniel, 115f., 122, 124, 407
Erlebach, Philipp Heinrich, 60
Ernesti, Johann August, 39, 361
Ernesti, Johann Heinrich, 39
Ernst August, Duke of Saxe-Weimar, 34
Eskew, Harry, 407
Ewert, Aleksander, 415

Fabian, B., 435
Fall, Henry C., 108, 406f.
Fasch, Johann Friedrich, 6
Fellerer, Karl Gustav, 411
Finscher, Ludwig, 435f.
Fischer, Albert F. W., 425
Fischer, Gabriel, 197, 373
Fischer, Johann Caspar Ferdinand, 93
Fischer, Michael Gotthard, 110. *See also* Copyists
Floros, Constantin, 427
Flotzinger, Rudolf, 414
Fock, Gustav, 59, 402f.
Forchert, Arno, 423
Forkel, Johann Nicolaus, 4f., 21, 73f., 83, 94,
    163f., 181, 212f., 274, 283f., 325, 383,
    399, 402, 405, 412, 414f., 419f., 424f.,
    428, 434f.
Franck, Salomo, 34, 410
Frankfurt/Main, 108f., 252, 407, 420
Franklin, Don O., 435
Franz Anton, Count von Sporck, 36
Frederick II, King of Prussia, 36, 231, 239f.,
    246–248, 250, 258, 266, 324–326, 328,
    331, 352, 421f., 428
    Sonata for Flute and Continuo in c, 325, 326
Frescobaldi, Girolamo, 46, 52, 73, 249, 306, 329,
    331
    Fiori Musicali (Venice, 1635), 87, 88, 94, 365
    Il primo libro di Capricci (Venice, 1626), 343
    Il secondo libro di Toccate (Rome, 1627), 404
Friderica Henrietta, Princess of Anhalt-Bernburg,
    7, 29, 35
Friedberg (Hesse), 109, 110, 112, 300, 407; Burg-
    kirche, 110; Latin School, 109, 112; Stadt-
    kirche, 109f.
Friedländer, Max, 424
Friedrich August I, Elector of Saxony [August II,
    King of Poland], 35, 411
Friedrich August II, Elector of Saxony [August III,
    King of Poland], 31, 35f., 40, 231, 379, 412
Friesen (Vogtland), 109
Froberger, Johann Jacob, 44, 52, 58, 60, 73, 329,
    428f.
    Canzonas (DTÖ 13: no. 6; DTÖ 21: no. 4), 60
    Capriccio, Prelude, and Fugue (DTÖ 21: Doubt-
    ful Works, pp. 125–126), 61

Hoffmeister & Kühnel, 372
Hohenberg, Bodo von, 425
Hohlstein, Gustav, 123
Hoke, Hans Gunter, 266, 432
Holschneider, Andreas, 412
Homburg vor der Höhe, 108–110
Hunold, Christian Friedrich, 410
Husmann, Heinrich, 409, 432

Jahn, Otto, 4
Jena, 19, 435
Joachim, Joseph, 178–180, 415
Joelson-Strohbach, Harry, 122
Johann Ernst, Duke of Saxe-Weimar (1664–1707), 25, 33
Johann Ernst, Prince of Saxe-Weimar (1696–1715), 34, 411
Jones, Richard D., 215, 218f., 414, 418
Joseph I, Emperor, 47, 402

Karstädt, Georg, 401, 402, 403
Kassel, 23; St. Martin, 360
Kast, Paul, 404, 410, 433
Kauffmann, Georg Friedrich, 130
    Harmonische Seelen Lust (Leipzig, 1733), 199, 206
Kee, Piet, 428
Keiser, Reinhard, 46, 94, 410
Keller, Hermann, 65, 306, 325, 404, 427f.
Kellner, Johann Peter. See Copyists
Kelly, Clark, 425
Kerll, Johann Caspar, 60, 73, 93, 307
    Missa Superba, 93
Keyserlingk, Hermann Carl Count von, 36, 212f.
Kilian, Dietrich, 399, 403, 427
Kinsky, Georg, 181, 214, 240, 246, 249, 413, 415, 417, 419f., 430–433
Kirkendale, Ursula, 421f., 424
Kirnberger, Johann Philipp, 11, 157, 167, 360, 414, 417, 419, 434
Kittel, Johann Christian, 110, 424. See also Copyists
Klein-Zschocher, 36
Klotz, Hans, 122, 285, 425, 431
Kobayashi, Yoshitake, 406, 410, 414, 419, 424–427, 430, 432
Koch, Heinrich Christoph, 330, 429
Koch, Johann Wilhelm, 205, 433
Kollmann, August Friedrich Christoph, 383f., 419
Kolneder, Walter, 72, 405
Körner, Gotthilf Wilhelm, 110
Kranemann, Detlev, 426
Krause, Peter, 415, 433

Krebs, Johann Ludwig
    Andere Piece (1741), 209
    Dritte Piece (1741), 209
Krebs, Johann Tobias, 27. See also Copyists
Krieger, Johann, 307, 330, 429
    Anmuthige Clavier-Übung (Nuremberg, 1690), 190
Krieger, Johann Philipp, 60
Kropffganss, Johann, 362
Krüger, Elke, 298, 402, 426
Krügner, Johann Gottfried, 194, 198f., 201, 205f., 375, 417, 420
Krumbach, Wilhelm, 406
Krummacher, Friedhelm, 402
Kuhnau, Johann, 6, 30, 44, 130, 189f., 318, 367
    Neue Clavier-Übung I (Leipzig, 1689), II (Leipzig, 1692), 189f., 193, 433
Kuhnau, Johann Andreas. See Copyists

Lämmerhirt family, 15, 17
Lämmerhirt, Elisabeth. See Bach, Elisabeth
Lämmerhirt, Tobias, 297, 404, 426
Landshoff, Ludwig, 240, 329, 419f., 429, 431
Lang, Johann Gottfried, 108, 110,
Lang, Paul Henry, 406
Lasso, Orlando di, 23, 84, 87
Leaver, Robin A., 407, 426
Lebègue, Nicolas Antoine, 10, 62,
Legrenzi, Giovanni, 46, 66, 71, 143, 225, 404, 411
    Trio Sonata "La Mont' Albana" op. 2, no. 11 (Venice, 1655), 66
Leipzig, 5–12, 18–22, 29–31, 34–40, 43–45, 50, 57, 69, 93f., 115, 128–131, 134f., 141f., 154f., 157, 168, 189, 194, 196, 200f., 205f., 213, 223–238, 240, 252, 255, 258, 260, 268, 282, 288, 299, 318, 320, 359f., 363f., 366f., 372–376, 378–380, 386, 389, 400, 404, 409, 411f., 415–418, 420f., 423–425, 429, 433f.; Academy of Art, 18; Collegium Musicum, 7, 11f., 19, 30f., 40, 103, 191, 224, 226f., 230f., 237f., 279, 359, 361, 363, 379, 409, 418; Gewandhaus, 226; Grosses Concert, 238, 361; Neues Concert, 226; Neukirche, 226, 361, 409; Societät der musicalischen Wissenschaften, 3f., 110, 168, 170, 258, 266, 290, 349, 373, 382, 430; St. Nicholas, 30, 130, 136, 317, 410; St. Thomas, 8, 10, 30f., 38, 40, 93, 128, 130f., 136, 143, 189, 194, 223f., 279, 317f., 326, 359, 379, 386, 389, 408, 412; Thomas-Schule, 21, 30, 38f., 93, 361; Zimmermann Coffee House, 30, 226f.

Ohrdruf, 15, 25f., 44, 58f., 61, 64, 116, 118, 298, 403; Lyceum, 26, 59
Oley, Johann Christoph, 204
Orel, Alfred, 420
Osthoff, Helmuth, 428
Osthoff, Wolfgang, 421

Pachelbel, Johann, 25, 44, 58–61, 73, 107, 112, 115–118, 122, 124f., 200, 307, 403, 407, 428, 434
    Chorale Preludes (DTB IV/1, Part 2: nos. 5, 11, 26, 60), 60
    Suites (DTB II/1: nos. 16, 33b), 60
    Toccatas, Preludes, Fugues, and Ciacona (DTB IV/1, Part 1: nos. 1, 4, 5, 7–9, 11, 20, 23, 25, 26, 31, 41, 42), 60
    Was mein Gott will, das g'scheh allzeit, 408
Palestrina, Giovanni Perluigi da, 11, 84–95, 99, 101, 141, 207, 329, 367, 371, 380, 385f., 393, 405
    Missa sine Nomine, 85, 94, 95, 364, 409
    Missa Papae Marcelli, 91, 92
Parsons, William, 418
Penna, Lorenzo, 330, 429
Penzel, Christian Friedrich, 418
Peranda, Marco Gioseffo, 299
Pergolesi, Giovanni Battista
    Stabat Mater, 94, 364, 409
Peters, C. F., 178, 315
Petersen, Peter, 427
Petzold, Christian, 197, 373
Pfannkuch, Wilhelm, 240, 412, 419, 426, 434
Pierozynski, Jan, 403
Pirro, André, 42, 401, 427
Pisendel, Georg, 142
Pitschel, Theodor Leberecht, 395
Platen, Emil, 434
Plato, 87
Plotinus, 397
Poelchau, Georg, 142, 181, 411
Poglietti, Alessandro, 404
Porpora, Nicola, 227
Postel, Christian Heinrich, 410
Potsdam, 36, 239, 252f., 266, 324, 326, 328, 331, 353
Praetorius, Michael, 45, 330, 371, 426
Prelinger, Fritz, 435
Preller, Johann Gottlieb. See Copyists
Prinz, Ulrich, 433
Proske, Carl, 91
Purcell, Henry, 307

Quantz, Johann Joachim, 44, 58, 383, 403
Quintilian, 401, 421f., 424

Raison, André
    Livre d'Orgue (Paris, 1688), 307, 313, 427
Raphael, 384
Reger, Max, 91, 306
    Patriotic Overture, op. 140, 154
Rehm, Wolfgang, 406, 433
Reichardt, Johann Friedrich, 372, 385, 390, 434
Reichert, Georg, 412
Reidemeister, Peter, 422
Reinemann, Johann Christoph, 112
Reinhold, Ferdinand, 403
Reinken, Johann Adam, 26, 44–46, 56–71, 74, 225, 298, 402–405
    Hortus Musicus (Hamburg, 1687), 57, 65, 66, 404
    An Wasserflüssen Babylon, 63
    Was kann uns kommen an für Not, 63
Rembt, Johann Ernst. See Copyists
Rempp, Frieder, 413
Riccio, Teodoro, 360
Richter, Bernhard Friedrich, 408f.
Riedel, Friedrich W., 404
Riemann, Hugo, 42????
Rietsch, Hermann 431
Rinck, Christian Heinrich, 107f., 110f., 407. See also Copyists
Ritter, August Gottfried, 110, 122–127, 407
Ritter, Joachim, 435
Robinson, Ray, 417
Rochlitz, Friedrich, 152, 412
Roitzsch, Ferdinand August, 413, 419
Rollberg, Fritz, 399
Rolle, Christian Friedrich, 8
Ronneburg, 205
Rosenthal, Albi, 415
Rossi, D. A., 403
Roth, Hermann, 427
Roth, Johann Michael, 197, 373
Rousseau, Jean-Jacques, 377, 429
Rubinstein, Anton, 180
Ruhnke, Martin, 405, 432f.
Rust, Wilhelm, 94, 178, 180–182, 184, 284f., 294, 298, 409f., 412, 415, 423–425
Ryom, Peter, 72, 405

Sachs, Klaus-Jürgen, 405, 432
Sackmann, Dominik, 122
Samuel, Harold E., 406
Sangerhausen, 59

Wolff, Christian, 389
Wolff, Christoph, 107, 122, 399, 401–407, 410, 412–415, 417–420, 424, 426, 431–433

Zachow, Friedrich Wilhelm, 28, 108, 112, 115f., 121–123, 126, 378f., 406f., 409
Zander, Ferdinand, 409
Zarlino, Gioseffo, 45, 404
Zedler, Johann Heinrich, 418
Zehnder, Jean-Claude, 122

Zelenka, Jan Dismas, 88, 94, 142
Zella, 21, 240, 252, 375f.
Zelter, Carl Friedrich, 424
Zenck, Martin, 435
Zeraschi, Helmut, 425
Ziegler, Johann Gotthilf, 197, 373
Ziesecke, Matz, 17
Zietz, Hermann, 298, 406, 408, 425f.
Zimmermann, Gottfried, 226
Zinzendorf, Count, 407
Zucchi, Lorenzo, 194